Securing HP NonStop™ Servers in an Open Systems World

Computer Security and Computer Forensic Related Book Titles:

Rittinghouse & Hancock, *Cybersecurity Operations Handbook*,
ISBN 1-55558-306-7, 1336pp, 2003.

Rittinghouse & Ransome, *Instant Messaging Security*, ISBN 1-55558-338-5, 432pp, 2005.

Rittinghouse, *Wireless Operational Security*, ISBN 1-55558-317-2, 496pp, 2004.

Ransome & Rittinghouse, *VoIP Security*, ISBN 1-55558-332-6, 450pp, 2005.

De Clercq, *Windows Server 2003 Security Infrastructures: Core Security Features*,
ISBN 1-55558-283-4, 752pp, 2004.

Erbschloe, *Implementing Homeland Security for Enterprise IT*,
ISBN 1-55558-312-1, 320pp, 2003.

Erbschloe, *Physical Security for IT*, ISBN 1-55558-327-X, 320pp, 2005.

Speed & Ellis, *Internet Security*, ISBN 1-55558-298-2, 398pp, 2003.

XYPRO, *HP NonStop Server Security*, ISBN 1-55558-314-8, 618pp, 2003.

Casey, *Handbook of Computer Crime Investigation*, ISBN 0-12-163103-6, 448pp, 2002.

Kovacich, *The Information Systems Security Officer's Guide*,
ISBN 0-7506-7656-6, 361pp, 2003.

Boyce & Jennings, *Information Assurance*, ISBN 0-7506-7327-3, 261pp, 2002.

Stefanek, *Information Security Best Practices: 205 Basic Rules*,
ISBN 0-878707-96-5, 194pp, 2002.

Securing HP NonStop™ Servers in an Open Systems World

TCP/IP, OSS, & SQL

XYPRO® Technology

ELSEVIER
DIGITAL
PRESS

AMSTERDAM • BOSTON • HEIDELBERG • LONDON
NEW YORK • OXFORD • PARIS • SAN DIEGO
SAN FRANCISCO • SINGAPORE • SYDNEY • TOKYO

Elsevier Digital Press
30 Corporate Drive, Suite 400, Burlington, MA 01803, USA
Linacre House, Jordan Hill, Oxford OX2 8DP, UK

∞ Recognizing the importance of preserving what has been written, Elsevier prints its books on acid-free paper whenever possible.

Library of Congress Cataloging-in-Publication Data
Application Submitted.

ISBN13:   978-1-55558-344-6

ISBN10:   1-55558-344-X

British Library Cataloguing-in-Publication Data
A catalogue record for this book is available from the British Library.

Neither XYPRO Technology Corporation, nor the Hewlett-Packard Company, or any third party shall be liable for any technical errors, editorial errors or omissions that may be contained in this book. No representations or warranties of any kind are made that procedures, practices, recommendations, standards and guidelines described, referenced or recommended in the book will work on any particular computer, computer system or computer network, as each computer environment and its configuration is unique to its particular industry, corporate culture and business objectives.

XYPRO is a registered trademark of XYPRO Technology Corporation. All other brand or product names, trademarks or registered trademarks are acknowledged as the property of their respective owners.

Please send your comments to book@xypro.com

For information on all Elsevier Digital Press publications
visit our Web site at www.books.elsevier.com

To our customers, for the strength of their partnership and
the influence of their thinking on this book.

Contents

Foreword

I am in the risk business.

I coach soccer, I play golf, I drive a sports car. These activities involve a lot of risk assessment. Then for fun I manage a mission critical computer network. Quantum physics and detective stories keep the grey matter ticking over and stress relief is provided by my drum kit.

I recently discovered an amazing pictorial account of NASA's Apollo lunar missions. It rekindled fantastical boyhood memories and prompted overwhelming feelings of awe and humility. Inevitable consideration of the technology brought back further juvenile wonderment but then, like a storm cloud, came adult realisation of the risks, practices and procedures.

Computing power in the 1960's was a little lacking by today's standards and an average calculator is now much more powerful than the on-board system used for a moon landing. Sadly, NonStop Servers weren't available so reliability and resilience topped the list for those considering what might go wrong.

Also near the top of the risk register was a major section on security where the threats of international competition, espionage, press intrusion, system malfunction, accidents, sabotage, malicious activity, miscalculation and countless more were defined, assessed and mitigated. NASA successfully landed a dozen men on the moon. Achieving that on time and ahead of the competition took a thorough understanding of those risks and how to address them. I would love to read NASA's equivalent of XYPRO's books on securing the NonStop server.

I do not know what you are using your NonStop Server for and I doubt you are sending it to Mars but I suspect you or your administrators need to understand the risks that today's world poses your system and its environment. XYPRO's first book. *HP NonStop Server Security: A Practical Handbook* has already helped many professionals to both understand and mitigate many of the risks faced and this subsequent book, *Securing HP NonStop Servers in an Open Systems World* is an important expansion worthy of its own place in the auditor's as well as the administrator's library.

Risks are there to spoil things just when you are having fun, feeling content and off your guard. NASA got a few nasty shocks like Apollo 13 which only just made it home, but of course NASA is at the forefront of exploration, breaking new ground.

The authors of this book have explored the HP NonStop universe of risk and laid out their findings for us all to benefit. Here you will find guiding practices and principles essential for the protection of your organisation's assets and to help you keep things running securely.

And if your system *should* end up on Mars I would like some pictures.

Mark Norman
BT Global Services, UK
6th May 2006

Preface

This second handbook represents the efforts of many individuals at XYPRO, who collectively have over 250 years of experience with the HP NonStop platform. In addition, we've been privileged to work with a group of contributors and expert reviewers from the HP NonStop Server user community. Their cooperation and experience added dimension to this publication and we believe the reader will greatly benefit from their contributions.

As a vendor of third party security software for the HP NonStop server platform, we were very careful to ensure that this handbook was useful for security administrators, system resource personnel, auditors and the general HP NonStop server community whether or not they chose to use our suite of software tools.

The lack of reference material for the Guardian Operating system prompted us to author our previous book in the hopes that it would facilitate securing the HP NonStop server. *HP NonStop Server Security, A Practical Handbook* was such a success that we received many requests to tackle more subject matter in a second book. We at XYPRO believe in this platform and have dedicated over 23 years to developing software to take advantage of its unmatched functionality, reliability and scalability. So clearly we also felt a second volume was well worth the effort.

Plenty of other companies believe in the NonStop server too. According to a June 2005 *Illuminata Inc.* article by Gordon Haff, NonStop servers run many of the world's banking systems and HP estimates that it powers 75% of the 100 largest electronic funds transfer networks. NonStop servers also handle the majority of ATM and credit card transactions at major international banks. 95% of the world's securities transactions take place on Non-Stop servers at over 100 stock exchanges, including the New York Stock Exchange, the London Stock Exchange, and the Hong Kong Stock Exchange. NonStop servers are also used in healthcare, telecommunications, manufacturing, retain, and government. They handle about half of the 911 emergency calls in the United States.

This volume again seeks to familiarize auditors and those responsible for security configuration and monitoring with information that allows identification of security risks and the best ways to mitigate these risks. It extends the knowledge presented in the previous book in several ways. It updates the discussion of some products, such as Safeguard, which have had significant changes since the publication of the previous book in 2003. Additionally, we've introduced new topics such as Open System Services, TCP/IP, and SQL database security. To avoid repeating large amounts of information, in some instances the reader is referred to a particular section in the previous book for additional Risks and Best Practice recommendations.

Please remember that the needs of the corporation, computer center, applications and customers must always take precedence over our recommended Best Practices in the environment. Use this handbook as a guideline, not a rule.

Readers of the previous book will find the presentation familiar. This time there are two Gazettes:

> The Guardian Gazette includes the Guardian components of the subsystems discussed in this book.

> The OSS Gazette includes the OSS files found in the subdirectories created when OSS is installed as well as those that are installed by File Sharing Protocols such as NFS and Samba.

We have endeavored to provide the information needed to remove some of the mystery with OSS (and UNIX). Appendix A explains OSS file and directory security, including **umasks** and the calculation of both the binary and octal versions of the security string. Appendix B is a Table of File and Directory Permissions that includes all the possible security strings in text, octal and binary formats and the equivalent **umasks**.

If the material in this book supports easier and more informed decisions, then we've accomplished our goal.

Distinguished Contributors

Contributor: Thomas Anderson; Open Database Connectivity (ODBC/MP)

Mr. Anderson has over 16 years in NonStop systems experience in a career of over 32 years of application and system development. He was a contributing editor to the SQL Access Interoperability specification published as the *X/Open CAE, Structured Query Language (SQL)* and its companion, *X/Open CAE Data Management: SQL Call Level Interface*. He participated on the original panel which developed the DoD Trusted Computer System Evaluation Criteria for Database Security. He is recognized as a NonStop Expert in for SQL Connectivity Solutions.

NonStop Connectivity Architect
Technologies Solutions: NonStop Enterprise
Hewlett-Packard Company

Author: Kevin Christian for NonStop SQL and Database Security

Mr. Christian is Chief Technology Officer and CEO of Enterprise IT Today, LLC. He coaches and guides companies and employees to build Information Technology solutions on strong database foundations. His

20-plus years working with NonStop systems includes several years as HP's NonStop SQL Product Manager and numerous speaking engagements about database throughout the world. He may be contacted by email at *kevin.christian@eit-today.com.*

CTO & CEO
Enterprise IT Today, LLC

Contributor: Charlie Martenis for OSS Personality & OSS Gazette

Mr. Martenis has 20 years of experience working with the Nonstop Server. Bringing with him previous experience in the Telco industry, he has spent the last 5 years in server administration for a business intelligence project.

Senior Analyst
Global IT
Hewlett-Packard Company

Contributor: John Morris for FIPS 140-2 and Common Criteria topics

Mr. Morris has over 15 years of experience in the security technology and validation industries. He is the co-founder of Corsec Security, Inc., which has over 9 years of validation experience and specializes in helping companies navigate through the complex process of receiving FIPS 140 and Common Criteria (CC) validations. *www.corsec.com*

President
Corsec Security, Inc.

Contributor: Mark Norman for TCP/IP and the Foreword

Mr. Norman has been working with data communications networks since 1976. Over the last 12 years he has been the primary TCP/IP network architect for British Telecom's SettleNET project, which provides secure resilient access for electronic settlement of securities in the UK and Ireland.

More recently he has been focusing on Quantum Cryptography and advanced change control mechanisms.

Network Architect
British Telecom

Contributor: Larry Ruch for OSS Personality & OSS Gazette

Mr. Ruch has over 21 years in NonStop systems and applications experience. In 2005, he won the **Top Ten Winter Corp Award** for the *World's Largest and Most Heavily Used Event Store, Largest Normalized Size and Workload.* He is recognized as a NonStop Expert in the BI/DW, Retail, and Credit Authorization industries.

NonStop Platform Architect
NonStop Lead DBA and SysAdmin
Global IT
Hewlett-Packard Company

XYPRO Technology

Author: Bob Alvarado for Pathway Security

Bob Alvarado has worked in the NonStop industry since 1980. He worked as a field analyst for Tandem and as a consultant for Tandem to their Alliance partners. He owned a third party software company that provided a NonStop database administration tool for the SQL/MP environment. Bob applies his NonStop expertise to help develop security and compliance software solutions for XYPRO.

Author: Ellen Alvarado for Pathway Security

Ellen Alvarado has worked in the NonStop industry since 1980. She has been a customer, an analyst, a 3rd party vendor and a consultant. Ellen brings her practical experience and depth of knowledge about exercising the advantages of NonStop server technology to XYPRO as a designer and developer of security and compliance software solutions.

Chief Author & Editor: Terri Hill

Terri Hill has over 17 years of computer systems experience with expertise in systems security, quality assurance, user documentation and education. As a Security Analyst, she provides Security Review and Implementation Services to HP NonStop Server customers. Terri is also a valuable link between customers' business requirements and XYPRO's software development.

Author: Harriet Hood for ODBC/MP & Diagrams

Harriet Hood has over 25 years of computer systems experience; the last 19 yrs have been spent in the NonStop industry. Her experience as a developer includes applications in a variety of industries such as banking, insurance, manufacturing and securities. Currently she applies her technical and industry background to XYPRO's customer support and quality assurance processes.

Assistant Editor: Sheila Johnson

Sheila was one of the founders of XYPRO in 1983. As CEO, she has the privilege of working closely with XYPRO's sales, marketing, product development, quality assurance and administration groups, plus more than a few customers. Under her leadership the company, product line and customer base have experienced continuous growth.

Author: Jack Peters for Systems Management Tools & Compliance Concepts

Jack's career in IT began in the 1970's as an IBM COBOL and BAL programmer working in the retail and insurance industries. He migrated into the aerospace industry and became an IMS/DBII DBA. During that time, he was assigned to support a project that purchased what was then a Tandem Computer system. He has worked as a system manager and security administrator on NonStop systems ever since for companies in the Securities trading and credit card processing industries.

Author: Greg Swedosh for TCP/IP

Greg has worked on the NonStop platform since 1985 in both Australia and the United Kingdom. For 9 years he was an employee of Tandem Australia before working as a consultant in system management, business continuity and security to NonStop customers through his company Knightcraft Technology. Greg has presented on NonStop security in the USA, UK, India, Netherlands and Australia. Knightcraft Technology is XYPRO's distributor for the Asia Pacific Region.

Author: Lauren Uroff for the Introduction and general copy editing

Ms. Uroff has over 27 years in NonStop systems applications and security. For the first 13 of those 27 years Lauren worked in the healthcare and banking industries. Since 1992, she has worked for XYPRO Technology in the area of security software design, documentation and education.

Contributor: Scott Uroff for technical review

Scott Uroff installed Tandem system #278 and has more than 22 years of experience with the NonStop platform. During this time, his focus has been on systems management, performance tuning and security. At XYPRO since 1992, Scott helped launch and is now product manager for XYPRO's suite of security and encryption software.

Reviewers

Pamela H. Brooks, Systems Engineer

Mark A. Chapman, HPCP NonStop System—AIS, CSE, ASE & Integrity NonStop Migration Specialist Manager & Consultant; NonStop Systems Engineering Group, LLC.

James Hamilton, EDS Information Security

Rob Lesan, Principle Database Analyst; HP Certified NonStop ASE AOL LLC, Login Systems

David N. Smith, CareCast Services (HP NonStop Support) | London LSP Infrastructure Team | BT Global Services

Geoff Woodcock, Head of Systems Management, International Capital Market Association.

We also want to recognize those NonStop professionals who gave generously of their time and knowledge and then declined our offer to acknowledge their contributions in the book.

Introduction

"Q: . . . What is meant by 'defense-in-depth'?

A: Unlike a simple "perimeter" approach, security professionals have been talking for years about layering defenses. The basic concept is a bit like wearing lots of layers of clothes in cold weather; it works better than a single thick layer (the perimeter approach). The layered approach is more flexible and if you lose a layer you still have several more layers to rely on.

In security, if one layer fails, you want to have another layer behind it. This makes it harder to penetrate a network and even harder to do so while remaining undetected. For most companies, however, a layered approach to security was cost-prohibitive, so they simplified it to a single layer, the perimeter firewall. As threats have increased, layering defenses make more and more sense from a cost/benefit (for cost/risk avoidance) perspective. In practical terms, this could be something like anti-virus in a gateway, on the mail server, on the desktop, and on the mobile phone/PDA.

Q: This suggests that enterprises are moving away from perimeter-based security—what is the reason for this? Is perimeter-based security failing us?

A: Yes, the perimeter makes less and less sense. Where is the perimeter? In the past, it was 'around the edges of the network.' Today the network extends applications to partners, suppliers, and customers. It's harder to find an "edge" to it. So as companies become more wired, more distributed, and more mobile, the perimeter becomes more and more porous. Eventually it shrinks back to surround just the data center. But beyond these problems, the perimeter was always a somewhat flawed concept, because, it did not provide any depth to your defenses. If someone is able to breach that single layer, they are free to roam anywhere in the internal network. Add to that the fact that most attacks come from the inside, and you can see why this is not a good risk management approach.

Excerpt from an interview with Nemertes Research analyst Andreas Antonopoulos by Linda Leung, *Network World*, 02/08/06

Open systems and standard protocols have increased the ability of divergent computer platforms to interconnect. This increased flexibility has blurred the perimeters between computer platforms and expanded the boundaries of computer usage. Simultaneously, it has increased both the scope of damages possible from security breaches and the challenges faced by security professionals to implement defenses appropriate to the information assets managed in multi-platform computer environments.

This interconnectivity of computer systems was not possible until a few years ago without custom software. Now such connectivity is routinely performed by standard products available to any computer that supports the Open Systems standards.

In the general sense, standards provide a common set of agreed-upon practices that will be used to perform some action. In the specific sense, the HP NonStop Server's Open Systems Services (OSS) complies with the POSIX standard, which mandates a set of security measures. Some of these measures directly contradict what already existed in the original Guardian personality of the NonStop Server.

For security administrators, system managers, and information system auditors, it can be confusing and frustrating to switch between OSS and Guardian environments, each with its own security system. Our previous book, *HP NonStop Server Security: A Practical Handbook* (hereafter referred to as the previous book) focused on security the Guardian environment. This book seeks to familiarize auditors and those responsible for security configurations and monitoring with the aspects of the HP NonStop Server operating system that make the platform unique in the Open Systems world, the security risks these aspects create and the best ways to mitigate these risks. Specifically, it endeavors to explain the special security needs of the OSS personality, as well as dealing with updates to Safeguard, database security, various file sharing protocols and other relevant software systems.

A Wider Perspective

In our earlier book, we used the analogy of the castle to characterize the role of security:

> If a company's applications are the castle, then access control is the moat or first level of defense. Logon controls are the outer gate, dial up and FTP access are the postern gates, and CMON and Safeguard are the gatekeepers, lookouts, and tattletales. Safeguard Protection Records and Guardian Security vectors are the bricks in the castle wall encircling all the application objects files, source files, and data files. Other subsystems, such as TMF and SCF, and the operating system in general are the underpinnings or foundation that support the applications and also "live" within the walls. Application databases and reports, proprietary corporate data, and personal employee data are the treasures that must be protected.

> Application users are the tenants of the castle. The security, operations, and technical support groups are the staff that assist the tenants and keep the castle's systems functioning.

> The security group's mission is to protect the castle, its tenants and its contents. Their job is fourfold. First, they must minimize the likelihood of damaging mistakes by the tenants or staff. Second, they must prevent plots, intrigues, and pilfering by the castle's tenants and staff. Third, they must prevent invasion by outsiders. Fourth, they must mitigate the damage possible in the event of mistakes or breaches.

The castle, initially built in a hidden valley, secure in its obscurity, is now right on the highway. In the Open Systems world, the castle moat is gone, the gates are gone, and some of the walls are only shoulder height. Furthermore, the tenants can suspend baskets out the windows or over the walls to trade goods and information.

Security's goals are the same, but the challenges are clearly more numerous.

Some New Terms

Since the previous book was published, new products have been introduced to the NonStop Server environment, including:

SQL/MP

SQL/MP is the new name for the standard SQL product on the NonStop Server. The new name reflects the addition of SQL/MX to the NonStop Server.

SQL/MX

SQL/MX is a new SQL product that complies with the ANSI SQL 92 standard. It is different from SQL/MP, which used to be the only SQL available on the NonStop Server.

ODBC

ODBC is Open Data Base Connectivity. It allows host- or PC-based applications to use SQL/MP databases on the NonStop Server.

JDBC/MX

JDBC is Java Data Base Connectivity. It allows Java host- or PC-based applications to use SQL/MX databases on the NonStop Server.

Integrity NonStop

This new operating system is equal to the Guardian operating system, except that it runs on the Intel Itanium processor. There are many programs that are common to the two operating systems, such as EDIT, FUP, and DDL, but there are also some that differ, such as the set of programmer development tools.

File Code 800

A new file code has been added in order to support the Integrity NonStop. File code 800 is the file code for executables that have been compiled using the Integrity NonStop compilers. As always, file code 100 files, which are the original object files supported by all older NonStop systems, remain supported. File code 700 object files, which have been optimized for execution on the S-series hardware, are not supported on the Integrity NonStop.

About This Handbook

This book extends the knowledge presented in the previous book by:

> Updating the discussion of some products, such as Safeguard, which have had significant changes

> Introducing new topics such as Open System Services, TCP/IP, and SQL database security

To avoid repeating large amounts of information, in some instances the reader is referred to a particular section in the previous book for additional Risks and Best Practice recommendations.

As in the first book, this volume seeks to familiarize auditors and those responsible for security configuration and monitoring with information that allows identification of security risks and the best ways to mitigate these risks.

Disclaimer

This handbook represents the efforts of many individuals who collectively have more than 225 years of experience in the field of NonStop Server security. While the most painstaking efforts have been made to ensure correctness and completeness, errors and omissions may be found.

Please remember that the needs of the corporation, computer center, application and customer may take precedence over our recommended Best Practices when specific corporate needs must be met and no other way is feasible. Use this handbook as a guideline, not a rule.

Compliance

In the last few years, many new security-related standards and legislative regulations have been enacted. These regulations have shifted management's thinking about the importance of protecting information and are now driving forces in the world of security. The sheer number of regulations and their often hazy requirements makes compliance a daunting endeavor.

The regulations have a worthy goal, even if they add a level of stress and complexity to already overburdened audit, security, and system support staffs. In an effort to simplify the task, we've included a chapter that both boils down the requirements of several representative regulations and provides direction on securing the NonStop Server to meet the requirements.

Nonstop servers secured according to the Best Practice recommendations in this and our previous book, your HP NonStop Server will be in compliance with the majority of the standards and regulations.

How this Book is Organized

As the title suggests, this book focuses on the NonStop Server's increased exposure in the open systems world and all the ways that information housed on the NonStop Server is accessed remotely. There are chapters on OSS, File Sharing Protocols, ODBC, and TCP/IP. Because the only way to prevent unauthorized access to that information is to secure the files where the information resides, we have included chapters on SQL/MP, SQL/MX, database, and Pathway security.

Readers of the previous book, will find the presentation familiar. This time there are two Gazettes:

> The Guardian Gazette includes the Guardian components of the subsystems discussed in this book.

> The OSS Gazette includes the OSS files found in the subdirectories created when OSS is installed, as well as those that are installed by file sharing protocols such as NFS and Samba.

Because many long-time Guardian users are unfamiliar with OSS (and UNIX), we've endeavored to provide the information needed to remove at least some of the mystery. Appendix A explains OSS file and directory security, including **umasks** and the calculation of both the binary and octal versions of the security string. Appendix B is a Table of File and Directory Permissions that includes all the possible security strings in text, octal, and binary formats and the equivalent **umasks**.

OSS filenames, commands, and options are always printed in **boldtext** with the full pathname so that they readily stand out in the text.

Appendix C contains instructions for gathering audit information.

Parts of the Handbook

In addition to explanations about a particular topic, each chapter or section includes Discovery, Best Practices, Advice, and Policy Suggestions.

Discovery

Each Discovery subsection includes a list of questions that, when answered, provides the information necessary for evaluating the risk posed by the particular subsystem, file, or program.

In the Discovery tables, each question has a reference to the kind of method used to gather the data needed to respond to the question. The data-collection methods are detailed in Appendix C: Gathering the Information.

Best Practice

Each Best Practice identified discusses the recommended method of minimizing or mitigating each risk present in the particular subsystem. Each Best Practice item is numbered; the numbers correspond with those in the Discovery tables.

About the Best Practice Numbering Convention

The Best Practice (BP) numbering convention is designed to uniquely identify each Best Practice item.

To provide a shorthand means of referring to a practice and to support a checklist for security review summaries, there is an identifier associated with each item in every Best Practice subsection throughout the handbook. The identifiers are based on the Best Practice points for each subsystem or subsystem component. The Best Practice numbers correspond with the stipulated risks and the discovery questions.

The BP identifiers are made up of four parts:

Part 1	BP (Best Practice). This prefix is dropped in the Discovery tables.
Part 2	The subsystem identifier. Each section has a subsystem identifier. For example, the Safeguard subsystem uses an identifier of **SAFEGARD**.
Part 3	The category identifier within each subsystem. In general, each subsection has a category identifier. For example, CONFIG is the category for items that discuss configuration options.
Part 4	A number identifying each particular issue in question. Within each subsystem (section), the primary numbers begin with 01.

Guardian Examples:

BP-FILE-MXAUDSRV-01   MXAUDSRV should be secured "UUUU".

BP-OPSYS-LICENSE-02   MXAUDSRV must be LICENSED.

BP-OPSYS-OWNER-02   MXAUDSRV should be owned by SUPER.
SUPER.

BP-OPSYS-FILELOC-02   MXAUDSRV resides in $SYSTEM.SYSTEM.

BP-ODBC-CONNECT-01 ODBC tracing should be configured to capture logons.

<u>**OSS Examples:**</u>

BP-BIN-CHMOD-01   **chmod** should be secured 711 (rwx --x --x)

BP-BIN-OSSOWN-01   **chmod** should be owned by SUPER.SUPER

BP-BIN-OSSLOC-01   **chmod** resides in **/bin**

BP-CRON-PROCESS-03   To ensure that only one process runs, always start **cron** as a named process. Set the CRON_NAMED environment variable before starting any copy of **cron**.

Refer to the beginning of the OSS and Guardian Gazettes for a more complete explanation of the numbering conventions for each environment.

Advice and Policy Recommendations

Advice and policy recommendations are noted throughout this handbook. These are ideas or suggestions that may or may not be important to a specific company.

Some advice topics may recommend the use of third-party products to enhance the "native" security provided by the HP Guardian, OSS, and Safeguard security mechanisms.

About the Advice Numbering Convention

Each policy and advice recommendation is uniquely identified.

The identifiers are made up of four parts:

Part 1   AP for advice or recommendation; 3P for a recommendation best supported by a third party

	tool. This part is dropped in the Discovery listing.
Part 2	The subsystem identifier or "ADVICE".
Part 3	The category identifier within each subsystem. In general, each subsection has a category identifier. For example, ALIAS is the category for user alias related items in Safeguard. For example, AP-ADVICE-ALIAS.
Part 4	A number identifying each particular issue in question. Within each subsystem (section), the primary numbers begin with 01. For example, AP-ADVICE-ALIAS-01.

Examples:

3P-ADVICE-ALIAS-01   Third-party software should be used to grant and manage privileges for users and aliases in a granular way. This provides the ability to limit access and privileges to just those users who need it to perform their job. For example, help desk personnel can be restricted to just password change functions.

AP-ADVICE-INETD-02   Create **/etc/hosts.equiv** file as a zero-length file. This enables it to be monitored for modification. If it does not exist or is empty, it cannot cause any problems.

AP-POLICY-PROFILE-01   The corporate security policy should determine whether or not users are allowed to modify their own **$HOME/.profile** file.

RISK Identification

Risks are addressed throughout the handbook in a format intended to bring these to the reader's attention.

Examples:

RISK   Due to the absence of an authorization list, alternate owners have full access to each User or Alias Record where they appear. This means that there is no way to limit the functions that an alternate owner can perform.

RISK   OSS shell programs, such as **/bin/chmod**, that perform recursive actions, make no distinction between Guardian and OSS files or between local and remote files. The **/G** and **/E** directories both appear in users' local **root** directory, which puts both remote files and Guardian files at risk.

Applying the Security

Throughout this handbook, specific security values and configuration settings are suggested. Each HP NonStop Server may have unique security requirements. In researching those requirements, three distinct security levels were identified:

Highly secure system
Commercially secure system
Moderately secure system

Highly Secure

A highly secure system contains both strict user authorization and enforced user-operation-object restrictions, which are called Access Control Lists.

When corporate needs require this level of security, only the most complete implementation of Safeguard software or a third-party product will suffice. Each user's identity must be positively verified, often with an additional identification mechanism such as a cryptographic token. There must be explicit permission for each user to access each object necessary for the user's job function and no implicit security measures are acceptable.

Authorized system activity and audit reports must be reviewed often and violations must be aggressively and rapidly pursued to a resolution.

Commercially Secure

A commercially secure system has strict user authorization and user-operation-object restrictions, ensuring that the system is functionally secure.

When a corporation uses this level of security, the amount of time spent on security implementation is balanced against likelihood and potential magnitude of loss. Each user must be positively identified, though an additional identification mechanism such as a cryptographic token is unusual. Both implicit and explicit user-operation-object controls are acceptable. All user access attempts that are not explicitly permitted are denied, but some userids have implicit privileges that may override restrictions; therefore, users are generally not assigned personal userids in the SUPER Group or as the 255 member of any group.

System activity that has been authorized is reviewed as necessary. Failed activity reports are reviewed often and violations must be pursued to a resolution.

Moderately Secure

A moderately secure system is one that does not handle confidential information and has all resources generally available to all users on the system. The user is positively identified when logging on to the system, but there are generally few or no user-operation-object controls. Many general users have access to system tools, configuration files, and applications. While these systems are secured from external entry, the internal security is very open to the users of the system.

With this level of security, the system must be available only to internal personnel; external access to the system must be restricted. If external access to such a system is permitted, the system must be considered insecure and cut off from accessing more highly secured systems.

Failed activity reports are reviewed on this system on a regular basis and any External access violations must be pursued, but internal violations are often handled by direct contact.

Determining a System's Security Level

The Corporate Security Policy and/or Security Standards should specify how the HP NonStop Server should be secured in the environment. The following questions can help determine a general security level:

Is this system connected via an interactive network to other systems?
Does this system supply data to another system?
Will users from networked systems have access to this system?
What is the primary use of the system?

- Production

- Development

- Backup

- Testing

- Communications

- Other

What is the level of sensitivity of the data contained on the system?
What is the level of confidentiality of the data contained on the system?
What methods are used to physically secure the system?
What methods are used to secure user access to the system?

- Guardian system

- Safeguard subsystem

- OSS file permissions

- Third-party tools

- Other tools

Are there outside security requirements that must be met, such as governmental or industry-specific regulations?

Assumptions

For the purpose of reading this handbook, the security standards that are discussed are those for the "commercially secure" system.

This book primarily addresses the security of HP NonStop Servers, especially in the OSS environment.

Please note that although this book discusses the higher level issues surrounding the security requirements for individual applications, it cannot address specific application security needs, because each application has unique requirements. In addition, although tough methods of physical security are very important to the overall security of any computer system, they are not within the scope of this book.

Expectations

> . . . [Security professionals have] recognized all along that perfect security isn't possible, nor would it be practical if it were possible. Our fundamental purpose as professionals is to help our employers manage the frequency and magnitude of loss.

> Excerpt from: *An Introduction to Factor Analysis of Information Risk (FAIR), a framework for understanding, analyzing, and measuring information risk*, 2005, by Jack A. Jones, CISSP, CISM, CISA

It would be inappropriate to expect an automobile security system to thwart one hundred percent of theft or vandalism attempts. From a realistic point of view, the value of the car should be balanced with the cost of the security system and (per Jack A. Jones) with the likely frequency and magnitude of loss.

Realistic expectations about system and information security, too, are very important. The goal of security is not perfection, but effective, efficient risk management. The goal of this book is to supply information and advice to help the HP NonStop Server user community meet security and risk management goals appropriate and realistic to an Open Systems world.

Compliance Concepts

Many new standards and legislative regulations impacting IT departments have been enacted in the last few years. These regulations put a new onus on IT personnel responsible for implementing security. At an overview level, these regulations are aimed at twin goals:

The first goal is to affix responsibility for protecting the privacy of customers' personal data firmly on those who direct and "police" the companies that hold such data. New regulations require that CEOs, CFOs, and external auditors personally certify that financial and IT controls are in place and are effective.

The second goal is to ensure that customers (both consumers and companies) are notified in the event their private data has been compromised. New regulations require service providers that hold or process private data to explicitly state any known deficiencies in security and provide timely, written notification to all customers whose private data has been or might have been compromised. To date, literally millions of consumers have received such notices from service providers whose electronic data systems have been breached.

This section does not attempt to comprehensively study all relevant security compliance standards and regulations. Rather, it discusses six samples representing a variety of regulatory organizations. Examining compliance standards and regulations as defined in these samples reveals that they have some basic requirements in common. Further, the common requirements can be logically grouped into one of four categories:

Authentication

Authorization

Auditing

Integrity & Confidentiality

Each of these categories has implications particular to HP NonStop Servers.

Representative Regulations

Figure 1.1
Representative compliance regulations.

Name of Regulation	Attributes
Common Criteria	Internationally recognized set of information security standards
FIPS 140-2	National-level standards applicable to cryptographic products, for use by government agencies as well as commercial market
HIPAA	National-level legislation specific to one industry, healthcare
PCI	Set of standards and penalties set by leaders in one industry to govern companies who handle private financial data
SOX	National-level legislation applicable across industries with international implication
SB1386	Local-level legislation forcing disclosure by companies whose information systems have been breached

Common Criteria for Information Technology Security Evaluation

The Common Criteria for Information Technology Security Evaluation, abbreviated as "Common Criteria" or "CC," is an internationally recognized set of information security standards. It is also internationally known as ISO 15408. The CC standards codify a language for defining and evaluating information technology security systems and products. The CC objectives are intended to:

> Provide a consistent, international standard against which security functionality is tested

> Improve product security by uncovering vulnerabilities before a product (or a new version) is released

> Provide customers with third-party assurance, confirming that the product will function and perform per the vendor's specifications

The framework provided by the Common Criteria allows government agencies and other groups to define sets of specific Functional and Assurance requirements, called Protection Profiles. The standard also provides accredited evaluation laboratories, which are certified by their local governmental entity, with procedures for evaluating the products or systems against the specified requirements.

Common Criteria evaluations are measured by evaluation assurance level (EAL), ranging from the lowest, EAL 1, to the highest, EAL 7. Currently, 22 countries participate in a reciprocal recognition agreement that allows a product validated in any participating country to be accepted by any other participating country, up to EAL 4. The current version of the standard, v2.2, is in the process of being updated to v3.1, which greatly simplifies and clarifies the overall structure of the standard. Clarifications will include reorganization of the requirements to eliminate duplicated areas and create consistency within the documents that make up the Common Criteria standard.

Common Criteria can be applied to hardware, software, or firmware products individually or as part of a larger system. The evaluation does not necessarily focus on the product alone, but rather on its security components as outlined by the vendor in a Security Target (ST) document. Vendors use a Target of Evaluation (TOE) to define a boundary around the portions of the product that will be included in the evaluation. Accredited, independent laboratories then test against vendor-specified claims and send results to the appropriate evaluating body.

Common Criteria evaluations are costly and time consuming. They typically take significantly longer and cost significantly more than validations of the same products under FIPS 140-2 as described below. This is partially due to the scope of Common Criteria evaluation efforts and partially due to the complexity of the CC language and evaluation methodologies. Expertise in Common Criteria terminology and methodologies becomes a pre-requisite for efficient or even successful CC evaluation efforts.

Federal Information Processing Standard 140-2

Federal Information Processing Standard (FIPS) 140-2: "Security Requirements for Cryptographic Modules" was released in 1994. The objectives of this standard are to:

Provide a consistent standard against which cryptographic modules are tested

Provide third-party assurance of the cryptographic security of a product

Ensure that security products purchased by the government meet government-specified requirements

The FIPS 140-2 standard describes requirements that hardware and software products must meet for Sensitive but Unclassified (SBU) use within the USA's federal government. This standard was published by the National Institute of Standards and Technology (NIST) in the USA, in partnership with the Canadian government's Communications Security Establishment (CSE), and is being adopted by the financial community through the American National Standards Institute (ANSI).

FIPS 140-2 is the third and current version of the standard, with a fourth version, FIPS 140-3, under draft. The standard is internationally recognized and is gaining worldwide recognition as an important benchmark for third-party validations of encryption products of all kinds. Currently, products purchased by the U.S. or Canadian governments are required to be FIPS 140-2 validated if they contain cryptography. Vendors who have FIPS 140-2 validated products use this achievement as a discriminator when competing for government sales, since both the U.S. and Canadian governments mandate the purchase of a validated product over one that is not.

The current FIPS 140-2 standard covers 11 areas of cryptographic security analysis (e.g. Physical Security, Key Management, Self-tests), and defines four levels of security, each one building upon the requirements of the previous level. Any vendor choosing to validate their product must produce extensive documentation and submit both the required documents and the product to an accredited testing laboratory. The lab then submits successful test results to NIST and CSE for government approval.

The validation process can be long and costly. However, independent consulting companies are available to facilitate navigation through the process. Competent consultants who have completed many validations over the years also have the knowledge and experience needed to produce documentation and manage the process effectively so that the product vendors can focus on their core business.

Health Insurance Portability & Accountability Act

The Health Insurance Portability and Accountability Act (HIPAA) was passed in the USA in 1996. HIPAA is specific to a single country and to a specific industry, healthcare. The deadline for compliance by large business entities was April 2005. For smaller companies the deadline was April 2006. When a company fails to comply, the individuals responsible face substantial civil and criminal penalties, including imprisonment.

HIPAA outlines several general objectives. Those that pertain to information security are:

Protect the health information of individuals against unauthorized access

Specific requirements under this general objective put IT departments under pressure to:

Implement procedures for creating, changing, and safeguarding passwords

Implement unique names and/or numbers to individually identify and track user identities

Implement procedures to verify that persons or entities seeking access to protected health information are who they claim to be

Implement technical policies and procedures that allow access only to those persons or software programs that have "a need to know"

Implement automatic procedures that terminate an electronic session after a predetermined time of inactivity

Implement procedures for monitoring log-in attempts and reporting discrepancies

Implement regular reviews of system activity via audit logs, access reports, and security incident tracking reports

Implement hardware, software, and/or procedural mechanisms that record and review activity of systems that store or use protected health information

Implement a mechanism to encrypt and decrypt protected health information

Implement policies and procedures to protect protected health information from improper alteration or destruction

Implement electronic mechanisms to corroborate that protected health information has not been altered or destroyed in an unauthorized manner

Implement technical security measures to guard against unauthorized access to protected health information transmitted over an electronic communications network

Implement security measures to ensure that electronically transmitted protected health information is not improperly modified without detection until such time as it is properly destroyed

Payment Card Industry (PCI) Data Security Standard

VISA began a program in 2001 called the Cardholder Information Security Program (CISP). This program was designed to protect the privacy of consumer information by merchant and service providers who handle VISA payments or card data. All of the major credit card issuers have formulated detailed security programs. Among them are:

American Express Data Security and Compliance Program

Discover Information Security and Compliance Program

MasterCard Site Data Protection Program

VISA, MasterCard, American Express, Diner's Club, Discover, and JCB joined forces to create a new data security standard based on CISP and other standards. The deadline for compliance with the new standard, Payment Card Industry (PCI) Data Security Standard was June 30, 2005.

PCI is not a law. However, it is enforceable. The participating companies can impose contractual penalties and sanctions, including revoking a company's right to accept or process credit card transactions. Under PCI, companies can also incur monetary penalties of up $500,000 per incident for non-compliance and $100,000 per incident for failure to immediately notify issuers of known or suspected compromise of customer data. PCI contains six categories with twelve requirements as shown in Figure 1.2.

Figure 1.2
Table of PCI categories and requirements.

Categories	Requirements
Build and maintain a secure network	Install and maintain a firewall
	Do not use vendor-supplied defaults for system passwords and other security parameters
Protect cardholder data	Protect stored data
	Encrypt transmission of cardholder data and sensitive information across public networks

(Continued)

Figure 1.2 (*Continued*)

Categories	Requirements
Maintain a vulnerability management program	Use and regularly update anti-virus software
	Develop and maintain secure systems and applications
Implement strong access control measures	Restrict access to data on a "need to know" basis
	Assign a unique ID to each person with computer access
	Restrict physical access to cardholder data
Regularly monitor and test networks	Track and monitor access to network resources and cardholder data
	Regularly test security systems and processes
Maintain an information security policy	Maintain a policy that addresses information security

For companies doing fewer than 6 million transactions per year, PCI compliance validation is based on self-assessment questionnaires with 75 "yes or no" answers. Those processing more than 6 million MasterCard or Visa transactions a year are required to submit to formal PCI compliance audits involving formally trained security specialists.

Sarbanes-Oxley Act

Sarbanes-Oxley regulations apply to any publicly traded company in the USA, including any and all divisions and wholly owned subsidiaries. It also applies to any company based outside of the USA but publicly traded and/or doing business in the USA. This act is a national-level law that affects businesses across many industries and in many countries. The United States Congress passed the Sarbanes-Oxley Act of 2002 (SOX) in response to stock market losses and fraud. Although it mainly targets internal controls over accounting procedures and financial reporting, it brings pressure on IT groups to move their companies toward compliance by providing greater physical and electronic security for IT resources.

The deadline for SOX compliance has already passed. However, the U.S. Securities and Exchange Commission recently granted small companies another extension for compliance related to one section of the SOX requirements. Companies with market capitalization of up to US$75 million qualify as small companies. They have up to July of 2007 to meet Section 404 regulations, which require company executives and their auditors to sign off on corporate adherence to internal controls. The Commission is also receiving requests to revise its definition of small businesses to include companies with a market float of up to US$1 billion.

One tool used by many auditing firms for guiding a company toward SOX compliance is the Control Objectives for Information and related Technology (COBIT). COBIT consists of 34 high-level control objectives and more than 300 detailed objectives. Some of the key requirements as stated in the COBIT objectives are:

Users should systematically control the activity of their proper account(s). Also, information mechanisms should be in place to allow them to oversee normal activity as well as to be alerted to unusual activity in a timely manor.

In an online IT environment, IT management should implement procedures in line with the security policy that provides access security control based on the individual's demonstrated need to view, add, change, or delete data.

The logical access to and use of IT computing resources should be restricted by the implementation of adequate identification, authentication, and authorization mechanisms, linking users and resources with access rules. Such mechanisms should prevent unauthorized personnel, dial-up connections, and other system (network) entry ports from accessing computer resources and minimize the need for authorized users to use multiple logins. Procedures should also be in place to keep authentication and access mechanisms effective (e.g., regular password changes).

Policies and techniques should be implemented for using, monitoring, and evaluating the use of systems utilities. Responsibilities for using sensitive software utilities should be clearly defined and understood by personnel, and the use of the utilities should be monitored and logged.

IT security administration should ensure that security activity is logged and any indication of imminent security violation is reported immediately to all who may be concerned, internally and externally, and is acted upon in a timely manner.

IT security administration should ensure that violation and security activity is logged, reported, reviewed, and appropriately escalated on a regular basis to identify and resolve incidents involving unauthorized activity. The logical access to the computer resources accountability information (security and other logs) should be granted based upon the principle of least privilege, or need-to-know.

Management should define and implement procedures and protocols to be used for generation, change, revocation, destruction, distribution, certification, storage, entry, use, and archiving of cryptographic keys to ensure the protection of keys against modification and unauthorized disclosure. If a key is compromised, management should ensure this information is propagated to any interested party through the use of Certificate Revocation Lists or similar mechanisms.

Excerpt from the COBIT objects as quoted www.isaca.org

Senate Bill 1386

In April 2002, a break-in to a database at a California State data center compromised the personal information of virtually all state employees, including legislators and the governor. Following this incident, a state senator introduced SB1386, which was subsequently signed into law by the governor. It became effective in July of 2003.

This bill requires every business or state agency that maintains computerized personal information to disclose any security breach to every

California resident whose unencrypted personal information was, or was reasonably believed to have been, compromised. An important aspect of this bill is that it links the breach of personal information with civil penalties.

The key objectives of SB1386 are:

Prevent unauthorized acquisition of computerized data that compromises the security, confidentiality, or integrity of personal information

Encrypt data to avoid the negative consequences of the disclosure requirement

SB1386 is an example of local governmental legislation that has far-reaching effects. Companies operating outside of California have been forced to make disclosures because they maintained personal information about California residents. Other states have since enacted similar legislation and effort is being made to pass equivalent regulations at the national level in the United States. While SB1386 seems simple, it implies as much responsibility and liability as all of the other regulations.

Analysis of Requirements in Common

Examining the sample compliance standards and regulations reveals they have some basic requirements in common. As the cross-reference table in Figure 1.3 depicts, these requirements can be logically grouped into four security categories:

Authentication

Authorization

Auditing

Integrity and Confidentiality

Figure 1.3 *Cross-reference of compliance requirements.*

Requirements common to the sample standards and regulations	Requirement Category	Common Criteria	FIPS 140-2	HIPAA	PCI	SOX	SB1386
Base user management schema on separation of duties and least privilege	Authentication	X	X	X	X	X	X
Eliminate shared userids and multiple userids	Authentication	X	X			X	
Enforce password rules with frequent, regular password changes	Authentication	X	X	X	X	X	Implied
Control access to the system	Authorization	X	X	X	X	X	Implied
Control access to files	Authorization	X	X	X	X	X	Implied
Control access to utilities	Authorization	X	X	X	X	X	Implied
Audit security events	Auditing	X		X	X	X	Implied
Monitor security reports	Auditing	X		X	X	X	Implied
Produce alerts for critical security events	Auditing	X			X	X	Implied
Encrypt data in transit	Integrity and Confidentiality	X	X	X	X	Implied	Implied
Encrypt data at rest	Integrity and Confidentiality	X	X	Implied	Implied	Implied	Implied

These requirements apply to all platforms. Following is a discussion particular to the NonStop environment.

Authentication Requirements

Native HP NonStop Guardian security provides a foundation for userids and passwords. There are, however, limitations within this foundation. As configured in TACL, users can completely remove any password from their account. No minimum length is enforced. Unless disallowed by customizing the TACL object file, users can input the password as part of the logon line, allowing it to be viewed in the clear on the screen or to be embedded in obey files or TACL macros.

Safeguard provides the following enhancements to Guardian security:

Required password on user accounts

Password history

Encryption of passwords in the userid data bases

Minimum length of passwords

Password expiration

Use of aliases

Industry standards and best practices all require that each user be given a unique userid to logon to the system. Assigning multiple aliases to one underlying userid as a substitute for shared userids does not meet compliance standards. While providing identification for logon, this practice grants all the privileges of the underlying userid, even though alias users typically need only a subset of privileges to perform their job. Also, aliases may not appear in all audits, so tracking true user identification and individual accountability are impossible.

Safeguard will be included with the shipment of all new Itanium systems. This is a valuable move forward that emphasizes HP's commitment to help its customers secure the NonStop platform.

Third-party security products provide complementary security enhancements, such as multi-factor authentication and granular quality control for passwords and alias management.

Authorization Requirements

In native Guardian mode and OSS, security strings protect files. Access to files is authorized via one setting for each of four operations: READ, WRITE, EXECUTE, and PURGE. Each operation may be granted to one of three classes of users: owner, Guardian group or anybody. Each of these three classes can be limited to local only or remote access. When someone is authorized for network wide access, it is commonly referred to as "the World." Access to the World is a surprisingly common and very risky practice, especially for READ and EXECUTE.

Used in conjunction with Guardian, Safeguard provides more granularity and selectivity in granting access. Safeguard Protection Records allow security administrators to grant or restrict access to objects such as files, subvolumes, and disks to multiple groups and/or users.

The practice of using Safeguard to secure an executable file so that it will launch a process as the owner of the file rather than the person who executed the file is called PROGID. This practice is an inadequate substitute for true access control and can lead to more problems than it solves, because PROGID'd programs can easily be used for malicious purposes.

Third party products can enable system managers and security administrators to fine-tune access to files and programs. They make it possible to:

Permit system utilities to be executed as a privileged userid (removing the need to PROGID), but restrict commands within the utility to those required for the user's job function.

Permit operators to manipulate reports in the SPOOLER, but prevent them from viewing report contents.

Permit operators to bring up a Pathway as the correct application owner without having to logon as the application owner.

Auditing Requirements

Without audits, it is impossible to determine what actions were performed on your system, when and by whom. Auditing and effective tools for

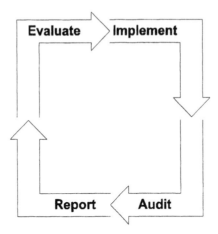

Figure 1.4
The security monitoring process.

monitoring, reporting, and alerting are essential to properly securing an HP NonStop Server system. A continuous cycle of auditing security events as shown in Figure 1.4 is crucial to achieving and sustaining compliance.

The Safeguard audit service provides the ability to record and retrieve information about a wide range of audited events recorded in the Safeguard audit files. Some entities are automatically recorded; for others, auditing is configurable.

HP's Event Management Service (EMS) messaging environment provides auditing of system events. Applications can be programmed to output messages to the EMS system. This provides operations groups with the ability to monitor system activity and react to any abnormal condition in a timely manner.

Third-party products are available to supply enhanced auditing capabilities. More comprehensive auditing, greater granularity, and convenient reporting tools are some of the benefits of third-party products.

Although Event Management Service Analyzer (EMSA) can be used to view EMS logs and SAFEART can be used for Safeguard audits, third-party products are essential for comprehensive audit reporting and alerting. In addition, third-party products that combine Safeguard and EMS audits with their own product audits make audit reporting simpler with flexibility to customize reporting based on specific business and security goals.

Audit reports can be classified as three different types:

Scheduled reports

Research or ad hoc reports

Alerts-related critical security events

Scheduled reports usually document only exception events. This approach avoids the time and errors associated with reviewing pages and pages of common and expected activities. Scheduled exception reports are intended to run automatically and be reviewed in a timely manner. Even the best, most informative reports are useless if no one looks at them and takes action based on the content.

Just as important as regularly scheduled reports are ad hoc reports. Promptly finding answers to questions as they arise is a prerequisite to making intelligent security decisions. Another use of ad hoc reporting is investigating suspected security breaches. Reporting tools must be quick, flexible, and easy to use for these important security administration activities.

Automatic real-time or near-real-time alerting is absolutely essential to maintaining proper security and reliable systems. Messages just rolling off a printer or terminal in the operations area are not an effective alerting system. E-mail, pager, phone, and/or text messaging are crucial to protecting the system. If someone is repeatedly attempting to logon as SUPER.SUPER, it is not acceptable to wait until tomorrow's report to address the threat. The same urgency applies to software or hardware failures.

Integrity and Confidentiality Requirements

Encryption is the most effective way to protect the privacy and integrity of sensitive data. It solves many problems, including those resulting from lost or stolen backup tapes, disks or hard copies of files. NonStop Server processing power efficiently supports encryption activities. While native Non-Stop security and Safeguard provide no provisions for encrypting data other than passwords, HP offers the Atalla line of encryption devices that can be used for hardware-based encryption. Third-party products provide mechanisms to implement both hardware and software encryption in applications, databases, files and network communications.

Figure 1.5 illustrates how sensitive fields of data records can be encrypted by applications as the data is being saved to disk. This protects data at rest, accessed either while on the local disk or residing on backup medium. When encryption is built into application databases, only the sensitive data fields need to be encrypted. The non-sensitive data fields remain readable for processing or reporting purposes.

Figure 1.5
Protecting data
at rest.

Non-Compliant

SSN	Name	Address	Account No.
123-12-1234	John Smith	1 Penny Lane	13711131719

Compliant

SSN	Name	Address	Account No.
&H&]\!#n74%	John Smith	1 Penny Lane	&iw@]{oi^8*

A related area is that of protecting communications between systems. This is important because at every logon via telnet session to the NonStop Server, passwords and data are transmitted in clear text from the user's desktop PC across the network to the NonStop Server. Network ports are almost as numerous in offices as electrical outlets. This makes it easy to attack a system with a rogue sniffer connected to an internal or external network. Sniffing is transparent to applications, which reduces the chances of catching intruders before userids and sensitive data are harvested. Capturing authorized userids enables intruders to gain further access to company systems and data. Intruders masquerading as authorized users can be very difficult to detect.

Other types of communications between systems have the same or similar vulnerabilities as telnet sessions. File transfers, FTP, EXPAND, and products that provide connectivity from one system to another are used at increasing risk unless passwords and other sensitive information are encrypted.

Third-party products, using a variety of crypto mechanisms, are available to encrypt data as it is transported. Compared to the increasing frequency and costs of breaches, encryption products are very cost effective. The following diagram illustrates the potential for exposure related to data in transit across a network.

Figure 1.6
Protecting Data in Transit.

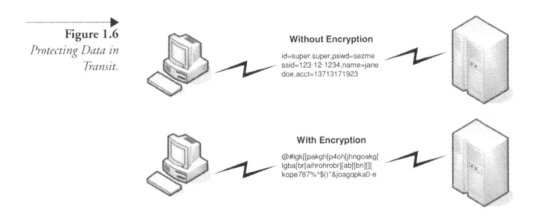

Conclusions

According to *Fortune* magazine (May 16, 2005), compliance systems in place today are enabling companies to review budgets and performance more frequently. This increased visibility into security and business activities allows managers to shift marketing dollars, productive capacity, and investment much more quickly, in addition to protecting information assets and protecting against security breach liabilities.

> "If you have a more dynamic, more continuous cycle of business review and scrutiny, you're actually going to uncover opportunities for growth as well as risk."

Although the various standards and regulations seem complicated and many do contain unique requirements, the bulk of the mandates are familiar best practices. This chapter provides a high-level framework to organize compliance requirements. The following chapters drill down to the detailed components fundamental to efficiently securing data and systems in real-world NonStop Server environments. All of the advice and best practices in this book, as well as our previous book, are aimed at implementing security measures to meet not only compliance regulations, but industry standards, corporate policies, and common sense.

While our previous book concentrated on securing the NonStop Server Guardian environment, this book concentrates on protecting Open Systems Services, databases, and connections to "The World."

2

Changes to Safeguard Since G06.21

There have been a number of changes to Safeguard since the previous book, *HP NonStop Server Security,* was published. This section will discuss the changes for releases G06.21 through G06.28.

Safeguard Changes Included in Release G06.21

Prior to release G06.21, a Diskfile Object Protection record could only be created for an existing diskfile. In addition, a Diskfile Object Protection record could only be designated persistent after the Protection record was created.

New:

Global parameter: ALLOW-DISKFILE-PERSISTENT

Global Parameter: ALLOW-DISKFILE-PERSISTENT

With the addition of the global parameter ALLOW-DISKFILE-PERSISTENT, Diskfile Object Protection Records can be created prior to the existence of the desired diskfile. When the Object Protection Record is created, an OWNER and the parameter PERSISTENT ON must be specified.

The values are:

IF ALLOW-DISKFILE-PERSISTENT is set to NORMAL, Safeguard will *not* allow Object Protection Records to be created until the object exists.

IF ALLOW-DISKFILE-PERSISTENT is set to ALWAYS, Safeguard will allow Object Protection Records ACLs to be created for nonexistent objects.

BP-SAFEGUARD-GLOBAL-65   ALLOW-DISKFILE-PERSISTENT should be set to ALWAYS

Safeguard Changes Included in Release G06.22

There were no user interface changes to Safeguard in release G06.22 of the NonStop operating system.

Safeguard Changes Included in Release G06.23

The changes in release G06.23 of the HP NonStop Server operating system are enhancements to Safeguard's Warning Mode behavior.

New:

Global parameter:	SYSTEM-WARNING-MODE
Global parameter:	OBJECT-WARNING-MODE
Protection Record attribute:	WARNING-MODE

Global Parameter: SYSTEM-WARNING-MODE

Prior to release G06.23, when the global parameter WARNING-MODE was set to ON, it applied to all Object Protection Records.

The new Global parameter SYSTEM-WARNING-MODE was added to represent systemwide Warning Mode. It is a synonym for the old WARNING-MODE parameter, which puts the Safeguard subsystem into Warning Mode. Either parameter name is accepted in SAFECOM commands.

The values are:

If SYSTEM-WARNING-MODE is ON, system Warning Mode is enabled.

If SYSTEM-WARNING-MODE is OFF, system Warning Mode is disabled.

The default value is OFF.

When either SYSTEM-WARNING-MODE or WARNING-MODE is set to ON, Safeguard bases its access ruling on the global parameter WARNING-FALLBACK-SECURITY. It will either GRANT all accesses or use the Guardian file security string. Please refer to the previous book, for more information.

BP-SAFEGUARD-GLOBAL-10   SYSTEM-WARNING-MODE should be set to OFF.

Global Parameter: OBJECT-WARNING-MODE

The addition of the new global parameter OBJECT-WARNING-MODE makes it possible to test individual Object Protection Records without having to undertake the risk of putting the entire node into Warning Mode. The OBJECT-WARNING-MODE value determines whether or not Safeguard will evaluate the WARNING-MODE attribute in individual Object Protection Records.

RISK   OBJECT-WARNING-MODE is only examined when SYSTEM-WARNING-MODE is set to OFF and OBJECT-WARNING-MODE is set to ON.

The values are:

> If OBJECT-WARNING-MODE is ON, Safeguard will evaluate the individual Protection Record WARNING-MODE value.

> If OBJECT-WARNING-MODE is OFF, Safeguard will *not* evaluate the individual Protection Record WARNING-MODE value.

The default value is OFF.

BP-SAFEGUARD-GLOBAL-62   OBJECT-WARNING-MODE should be ON if you intend to test individual Protection Records.

Protection Record Attribute: WARNING-MODE

The addition of the new Protection Record WARNING-MODE attribute makes it possible to put individual Object Protection Records into Warning Mode without having to undertake the risk of putting the entire node into Warning Mode.

The new WARNING-MODE attribute applies to the Protection Records for the following objects:

> VOLUME
> SUBVOLUME
> DISKFILE
> DISKFILE-PATTERN (as of G06.25)
> DEVICE
> SUBDEVICE
> PROCESS
> SUBPROCESS

The values are:

> If WARNING-MODE is ON, Warning Mode is enabled.
> If WARNING-MODE is OFF, Warning Mode is disabled.

The default value is OFF.

RISK If WARNING-MODE is ON, the Object Protection Record is not enforced.

RISK If the global parameter OBJECT-WARNING-MODE is set to OFF, Safeguard does not prevent the Protection Record WARNING MODE attribute being set to ON, but the record will *not* be in Warning Mode. This could lead to unexpected results.

BP-SAFEGUARD-OBJECTS-01 WARNING-MODE should be OFF.

There is no individual object level equivalent to the global WARNING-FALLBACK-SECURITY parameter. When individual Protection Records are in Warning Mode, Safeguard bases its access ruling on the global WARNING-FALLBACK-SECURITY parameter. It will either GRANT all accesses to the objects protected by the Protection Record or use the Guardian file security string. Please refer to the previous book, for more information.

Safeguard Changes Included in Release G06.24

Prior to release G06.24 the only option for granting access from remote nodes in an ACL was all nodes (*) or local access only.

As of release G06.24 of the HP NonStop Server operating system, remote access has been enhanced. Now actual node names may be specified (\NODE1) for userids within Protection Record ACLs.

New:

   Global parameter: ALLOW-NODE-ID-ACL

Global Parameter: ALLOW-NODE-ID-ACL

The addition of the new global ALLOW NODE ID ACL parameter allows specific node names to be used in object Protection Record ACLs. This makes it possible to control access to objects based on the node where the user was authenticated.

The ALLOW NODE ID ACL value determines whether or not Safeguard will accept specific node names in Protection Record ACLs.

The values are:

If ALLOW-NODE-ID-ACL is ON, Safeguard will accept specific node names in Protection Record ACLs.

IF ALLOW-NODE-ID-ACL is OFF, Safeguard will *not* accept specificnode names in Protection Record ACLs.

The default value is OFF.

BP-SAFEGUARD-GLOBAL-63   ALLOW-NODE-ID-ACL should be set to OFF.

RISK Even when ALLOW-NODE-ID-ACL is set to OFF, Safeguard does not prevent the specific node names being added to a Protection Record ACL.

RISK If the global parameter ALLOW-NODE-ID-ACL is set to OFF, any ACLs in a Protection Record that contains specific node names in the ACL will be ignored. Safeguard will behave as if the Protection Record did not exist.

Unless DISPLAY USER AS NAME is specified in SAFECOM INFO commands, the system number for the node, rather than the node name, will be displayed.

Explicit Nodes Example

Explicit nodes can be used to selectively prevent access to an object from a subset of nodes in an environment.

The diagram in Figure 2.1 describes a group of HP NonStop Servers connected via expand. The environment contains both production and development nodes. The requirement is that only the users authenticated on one of the production nodes (\PROD1, \PROD2) are permitted to access the file $APP1.APPMAN.CONFIG on \PROD1.

Figure 2.1
*Node-Specific
ACLs.*

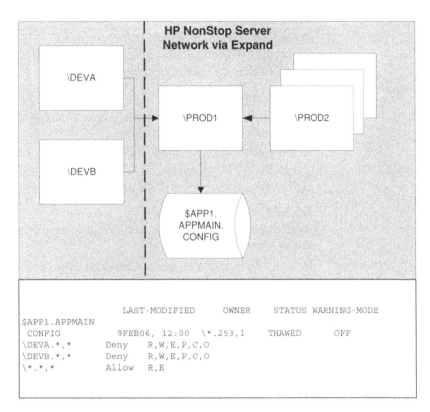

The ACL list translates to:

Allow remote access to the file $APP1.APPMAN.CONFIG by users logged onto any nodes except \DEVA and \DEVB

It is important to understand that Node-specific ACL entries specify the access allowed or denied to a user "last authenticated" on the particular node, not access from that node for a particular user.

Example 1:

User logs on to node \A and runs a program on \B.

In Example 1, node-specific ACL entries present in the Protection Records of \B will view the user as "coming from" \A.

Example 2:

User logs on to node \A and runs a program on \B which opens a file on \C.

In Example 2, access is from node \B, but the user was authenticated on system \A. So, Node-specific ACL entries present in the Protection Records of \C will view the user as if "coming from" \A.

Example 3:

User logs on to node \A and runs a progided program on \B which opens a file on \C.

In Example 3, the user was authenticated on node \A, but PROGID'ed programs implicitly authenticate the user on the node where the PROGID'ed object file resides. So, Node-specific ACL entries present in the Protection Records of \C view the user as if "coming from" \B.

Safeguard Changes Included in Release G06.25

Prior to the release of G06.25, it was not possible to specify a wildcarded object names in Object Protection Records. Release G06.25 made it possible to use wildcards in object names.

New:

Files:	$*.SAFE.PATGUARD (one per disk)
Global parameter:	CHECK-DISKFILE-PATTERN
Protection Record Type:	DISKFILE-PATTERN
INFO command modifier:	ALL
DETAIL information enhanced	Create date and userid that made the change

Global Parameter: CHECK-DISKFILE-PATTERN

The new CHECK-DISKFILE-PATTERN global parameter has been added to control the use of DISKFILE PATTERN Protection Records. The value assigned to this parameter determines when the DISKFILE PATTERN Protection Records are evaluated in relationship to the non-pattern (VOLUME, SUBVOLUME, and DISKFILE) Protection Records. The values are:

If CHECK-DISKFILE-PATTERN is set to OFF, pattern checking is disabled. Any existing DISKFILE-PATTERN Protection Records will be ignored.

If CHECK-DISKFILE-PATTERN is set to ONLY, only DISKFILE-PATTERN Protection Records will be checked. Any exisiting non-pattern Protection Records will be ignored.

If CHECK-DISKFILE-PATTERN is LAST, pattern checking will be done after non-pattern Protection Records are evaluated

IF CHECK-DISKFILE-PATTERN is FIRST, pattern checking will be done before non-pattern Protection Records are evaluated.

The default value is OFF.

The SMON processes consult the PATGUARD files on the disk where the file being accessed resides if the new CHECK-DISKFILE-PATTERN global parameter in set to ONLY, LAST, or FIRST. If the CHECK-DISK-FILE-PATTERN global parameter is set to OFF, the SMONs do not check the PATGUARD files.

RISK If CHECK-DISKFILE-PATTERN is set to LAST or FIRST, a DISKFILE-PATTERN Protection Record can contradict a SUBVOLUME Protection Record or DISKFILE Protection Record, yielding unexpected results.

RISK If CHECK-DISKFILE-PATTERN is set to ONLY, existing non-pattern Protection Records are ignored.

RISK If CHECK-DISKFILE-PATTERN is set to ONLY, it may result in too many denials due to wildcards being too narrow.

RISK If CHECK-DISKFILE-PATTERN is set to ONLY, it may result in allowing too much access due to the wildcards being too broad.

BP-SAFEGUARD-GLOBAL-64 CHECK-DISKFILE-PATTERN should be set to OFF

PATGUARD Configuration Files

The new DISKFILE-PATTERN Object Protection Records are stored in PATGUARD files. PATGUARD files are the equivalent of the GUARD files and just like the GUARD files, a PATGUARD file resides in the SAFE subvolume on every disk (volume).

The PATGUARD files should be secured like the GUARD files. Please refer to the Guardian Gazette for more information.

New INFO, DETAIL Information

Additional information fields have been added to the DISKFILE-PATTERN Protection Records. The fields store Creation and Modification timestamps and information about the user who made the most recent change to the record.

```
                CREATION                LAST-MODIFIED
    USER NAME   SUPER.SUPER             SUPER.SUPER
    USER TYPE   USER  (ID 255,255)      USER (ID 255,255)
    USER NODE   LOCAL                   LOCAL
    TIMESTAMP   11JUL2005, 16:56:32.927  03MAR2006, 17:16:53.065
```

If the user making the change had been logged on as an alias, the USER TYPE would have been ALIAS with its underlying userid displayed in the parentheses.

DISKFILE-PATTERN Protection Records

The new DISKFILE-PATTERN Object Protection Record type allows wildcarded diskfile and/or subvolume names.

DISKFILE-PATTERN Examples

The valid wildcard characters are:

?: Each occurrence of a question mark signifies one character

*: An asterisk signifies zero or more characters

The rules governing valid wildcarded filenames are:

Each DISKFILE PATTERN Protection Record must contain a wildcard character in either the SUBVOLUME or FILENAME portion of the Protection Record Name.

Wildcards are *not permitted* in the VOLUME portion of the pattern.

Sample valid patterns:

```
$XFR1.CUST???.D*
$XFR1.MONTHLY.FL*
```

Sample invalid patterns:

`$XFR*.MONEY.TRN????`	This pattern would be rejected due to the wildcard character in the volume name.
`$XFR1.SEPT.FILEONE`	This pattern would be rejected because there are no wildcards in either the subvolume or filename portions of the pattern.

RISK Locating all pattern records in an environment can be difficult because the INFO command will, by default, find only exact matches to the pattern queried.

The new modifier for the INFO command, ALL, will find all patterns that match the wildcard, regardless of how the PATTERN itself was wildcarded.

Example:

Using the SAFECOM INFO command to locate DISKFILE-PATTERNs.

The following patterns were added:

```
$VXYZ.XYZ*.*                          $DATAF.XYZ???.*
     222,077   R,W,E,P,C,O                 222,077   R,W,E,P,C,O
     222,078   R, E                        222,078   R, E
     \*.*,*    R                           \*.*,*    R,W,E,P

 $VXYZ.XYZ*.T                          $DATAE.XYZ???.T*
     222,077   R,W,E,P,C,O                 222,077   R,W,E,P,C,O
     222,078   R, E                        222,078   R, E
     \*.*,*    R                           \*.*,*    R

$VXYZ.XYZ???.*                        $DATAH.XYZ???.*
     222,077   R,W,E,P,C,O                 222,077   R,W,E,P,C,O
     222,078   R, E                        222,078   R, E
     \*.*,*    R                           \*.*,*    R,W,E,P

$VXYZ.XYZ???.T*                       $DATAG.XYZ???.*
     222,077   R,W,E,P,C,O                 222,077   R,W,E,P,C,O
     222,078   R, E                        222,078   R, E
     \*.*,*    R                           \*.*,*    R,W,E,P
```

The following queries were run against the above DISKFILE-PATTERN Protection Records:

Query	Patterns Found
info diskfile-pattern $*.xyz*.*	$VXYZ.XYZ*.*
info diskfile-pattern $*.xyz???.*	$VXYZ.XYZ???.* $DATAF.XYZ??? * $DATAH.XYZ???.* $DATAG.XYZ??? *
info diskfile-pattern $*.xyz*.* all	$VXYZ.XYZ*.* $VXYZ.XYZ*.T* $VXYZ.XYZ???.* $VXYZ.XYZ???.T* $DATAF.XYZ???.* $DATAE.XYZ???.T* $DATAH.XYZ???.* $DATAG.XYZ???.*

(Continued)

Query	Patterns Found
info diskfile-pattern $data*.xyz???.*	$DATAF.XYZ???.* $DATAH.XYZ???.* $DATAG.XYZ???.*
info diskfile-pattern $data*.xyz???.* all	$DATAF.XYZ???.* $DATAE.XYZ???.T* $DATAH.XYZ???.* $DATAG.XYZ???.*
info diskfile-pattern $data*.xyz???.t*	$DATAE.XYZ???.T*
info diskfile-pattern $data*.xyz*.t*	Nothing
info diskfile-pattern $data*.xyz*.t* all	$DATAE.XYZ???.T*
info diskfile-pattern $vxyz.xyz*.t*	$VXYZ.XYZ*.T*
info diskfile-pattern $vxyz.xyz*.t* all	$VXYZ.XYZ*.T*
info diskfile-pattern $vxyz*.xyz*.*	$VXYZ.XYZ*.*
info diskfile-pattern $vxyz*.xyz*.* all	$VXYZ.XYZ*.* $VXYZ.XYZ*.T* $VXYZ.XYZ???.* $VXYZ.XYZ???.T*

AP-SAFEGUARD-PATTERN-01   Always use the ALL modifier on the SAFECOM INFO command when you are researching DISKFILE-PATTERN records.

Safeguard Changes Included in Release G06.26

Prior to the release of G06.26, Safeguard was consulted to see if a volume rule existed when an OSS file was being created. This check was removed in release G06.26.

RISK Safeguard ignores any activities in the OSS workspace. OSS files can be created anywhere on any disks that are part of OSS fileset storage pools.

Safeguard Changes Included in Release G06.27

The changes to Safeguard in release G06.27 are all related to Users and Aliases.

New:

Files:	$SYSTEM.SAFE.LUSERAX
	$SYSTEM.SYSTEM.USERAX
User Record fields	OWNER-LIST
	TEXT-DESCRIPTION
	BINARY-DESCRIPTION

OWNER-LIST for Users and Aliases

Prior to the release of G06.27, User and Alias records had only a Primary Owner.

The addition of the new OWNER-LIST attribute allows User and Alias records to have multiple owners.

Adding and deleting alternate owners is much like adding entries to an ACL for other Safeguard Protection Records. The difference between the alternate owner list and other ACLs is the absence of an authorization string.

Up to 50 alternate owners may be specified per user/alias.

RISK Because there is no authorization list, alternate owners have full access to each User or Alias Record where they appear. This means that there is no way to limit the functions that an alternate owner can perform.

3P-ADVICE-USERS-01 Third-party products should be used to grant granular management of users. This allows privileges to be limited to just those tasks, such as password resets, that users require to perform their job.

3P-ADVICE-ALIAS-01   Third-party products should be used to grant granular management of aliases. This allows privileges to be limited to just those tasks, such as password resets, that users require to perform their job.

BP-SAFE-USERS-01   Additional owners should not be added to user records.

TEXT-DESCRIPTION Field for Users and Aliases

Prior to the release of G06.27, there was no place to enter free text comments in User or Alias records.

The addition of the new TEXT-DESCRIPTION attribute provides a field for text comments for each User and Alias record. This field can contain up to 2047 characters. It is updated by specifying TEXT-DESCRIPTION in the ALTER command.

Records are only written to the appropriate file (LUSERAX or USERAX) if the TEXT-DESCRIPTION parameter is updated.

The TEXT-DESCRIPTION can be set or reset. Unfortunately, text cannot be appended to the existing text; the entire comment must be reentered each time a change is desired.

Any action that causes a change to a User or Alias Record, such as a LOGON (because Safeguard updates the LAST-LOGON field), causes Safeguard to write a before and after image of the User/Alias Record into the audit trail. Both the before and after images include all 2047 characters of the TEXT-DESCRIPTION even if there is no data in the field.

RISK The TEXT-DESCRIPTION field is 2047 characters in length regardless of the actual number of characters entered. This can significantly increase disk space usage on the $SYSTEM volume.

RISK Using the text description field will increase the rate at which the Safeguard Audit files fill up.

AP-ADVICE-SAFEGARD-10 The system must have sufficient disk space to accommodate the increased size of the Safeguard audit trail(s)

AP-ADVICE-SAFEGARD-11 The system must have adequate system resources such as CPUs and memory to handle the increased amount of audit activity.

BINARY-DESCRIPTION Field for Users and Aliases

Prior to the release of G06.27, there was no place to enter customized text comments in User or Alias records.

The addition of the new BINARY-DESCRIPTION field provides a field where information can be inserted in each User and Alias record. The field can only be added or altered programmatically via the SPI interface. However, the contents of the field can be deleted via Safecom using the RESET-BINARY-DESCRIPTION command.

The size of the BINARY-DESCRIPTION field reflects the actual binary size of the information it contains.

The contents of the field cannot be viewed via Safecom, only its length is displayed.

RISK The information contained in the BINARY-DESCRIPTION field will only be written to the Safeguard audit trail if the field length changes. There is no way to know if a change is made that does not alter the length of the field.

New Safeguard Configuration Files

Two new files were created. They contain the new TEXT-DESCRIPTION and BINARY-DESCRIPTION fields.

Name	Filecode	Contents
LUSERAX	540	Alias Text Description and Binary Description
USERAX	540	User Text Description and Binary Description

The LUSERAX and USERAX files should be secured like the USERID* and LUSERID* files. Please refer to the Guardian Gazette for more information.

Records are only written to the appropriate file, LUSERAX or USERAX, if the TEXT-DESCRIPTION parameter is updated.

The following is the excerpt from the Guardian Gazette:

Safeguard Changes Included in Release G06.28

There were no changes to Safeguard in Release G06.28.

Safeguard Changes Included in Release G06.29

The changes to Safeguard in Release G06.29 are related to increased password security and to the addition of OSS ACLs for file and directory security in the OSS environment. Though OSS ACLs are still in development and, therefore, are not covered in this book, the required changes to Safeguard Global values are presented here.

New:

Global parameters:	AUDIT-CLIENT-OSS
	AUDIT-CLIENT-GUARDIAN
	AUDIT-CLIENT-OSS
	PASSWORD-ALGORITHM
	PASSWORD-LENGTH default changed from 0 to 6
OSS Objecttype:	OSSPROCESS
Security Group:	SECURITY-OSS-ADMINISTRATOR
New configuration file	CONFIGP
New utility	PWCONFIG

Global Parameter: AUDIT-CLIENT-GUARDIAN

AUDIT-CLIENT-GUARDIAN is a synonym for the previous AUDIT-CLIENT-SERVICE parameter except that it no longer controls the acceptance of CLIENT audit records from the following OSS objects:

> OSS diskfiles
> OSS filesets
> OSS processes

The AUDIT-CLIENT-GUARDIAN parameter does continue to control the acceptance of CLIENT audit records for OSS devices.

The values are:

> If AUDIT-CLIENT-GUARDIAN is set to ON, Safeguard will accept audit records from Guardian CLIENTs and OSS devices.

> If AUDIT-CLIENT-GUARDIAN is set to OFF, Safeguard will *not* accept audit records from Guardian CLIENTs and OSS devices.

The default value is ON.

BP-SAFEGARD-GLOBAL-66   If the corporate security policy requires that Safeguard accept audit records from Guardian CLIENTs or OSS devices, the AUDIT-CLIENT-GUARDIAN parameter must be ON.

Global Parameter: AUDIT-CLIENT-OSS

HP privileged subsystems such as FUP, SCF, and the OSS subsystem, are known as Clients. The original AUDIT-CLIENT-SERVICE parameter determined whether or not Safeguard would accept information for these CLIENTs and write the event records into its audit trail on their behalf.

Prior to Release G06.29, there was no way to select only OSS subsystem events. The addition of the AUDIT-CLIENT-OSS Global parameter makes this possible.

The values are:

> If AUDIT-CLIENT-OSS is set to ON, Safeguard will accept audit records from the OSS subsystem.

If AUDIT-CLIENT-OSS is set to OFF, Safeguard will not accept audit records from the OSS subsystem.

The default value is ON.

BP-SAFEGARD-GLOBAL-65   AUDIT-CLIENT-OSS should be OFF if OSS is *not* in use on the system.

BP-SAFEGARD-GLOBAL-65   AUDIT-CLIENT-OSS should be ON if OSS is in use on the system.

The following OSS events generate audit records in the Safeguard audit trail:

Guardian FILE_OPEN_ of an OSS file
OSS opens and creates of OSS files
OSS pathname resolution
Access authorization
chmod authorization
chown authorization
link authorization
rename authorization
delete authorization
purge authorization
utime authorization
setacl authorization

In order to obtain any auditing within the OSS environment, however, the following parameters must be configured correctly:

Fileset AUDITENABLED

Safeguard Global AUDIT-PROCESS-ACCESS-[PASS|FAIL]

G06.28 and earlier releases: Safeguard global AUDIT-CLIENT-SERVICE

G06.29 and later releases: Safeguard global AUDIT-CLIENT-OSS

Please refer to the chapter on the OSS Personality for more information on the AUDITENABLED and AUDIT-PROCESS-ACCESS-[PASS|FAIL] parameters.

Some General notes on CLIENT auditing

RISK Turning AUDIT-CLIENT-GUARDIAN and/or AUDIT-CLIENT-OSS ON will generate a greatly increased number of auditable events and require more system resources to write the audit records.

AP-ADVICE-SAFEGARD-11 The system must have sufficient disk space to accommodate the increased size of the Safeguard audit trail(s)

AP-ADVICE-SAFEGARD-12 The system must have adequate system resources such as CPUs and memory to handle the increased amount of audit activity.

The new CLIENT auditing possibilities are:

If both AUDIT-CLIENT-OSS and AUDIT-CLIENT-GUARDIAN are ON, Safeguard will accept audit records from both the OSS subsystem and Guardian CLIENTS. This is the equivalent of the now outdated AUDIT-CLIENT-SERVICE parameter.

If AUDIT-CLIENT-OSS is ON and AUDIT-CLIENT-GUARDIAN is OFF, Safeguard will accept audit records from the OSS subsystem only. This is ideal for systems with applications running in the OSS environment.

If AUDIT-CLIENT-OSS is OFF and AUDIT-CLIENT-GUARDIAN is ON, Safeguard will accept audit records from Guardian CLIENTs only.

If both AUDIT-CLIENT-OSS and AUDIT-CLIENT-GUARDIAN are OFF, Safeguard will not accept audit records from Guardian CLIENTs or the OSS subsystem. This is ideal for systems that do not have any OSS applications.

RISK Safeguard only checks to see if CLIENT auditing is enabled at the time a process starts. This means that if long-running processes such as TELNET or disk processes are being audited, changing AUDIT-CLIENT-SERVICE, AUDIT-CLIENT-OSS, or AUDIT-CLIENT-GUARDIAN from ON to OFF, will *not* signal Safeguard to stop accepting audit records from these processes.

Bouncing Safeguard will *not* cause it to stop accepting audit records from any processes that are already running.

The only way to force Safeguard to stop accepting audit records from CLIENTs that were started during the time that Safeguard was configured to accept CLIENT audits, is to stop and restart the processes themselves.

RISK Because the default value for both AUDIT-CLIENT-OSS and AUDIT-CLIENT-GUARDIAN is ON, if these values are not changed before any long-running system processes are brought up after upgrading to release G06.29, Guardian CLIENTs and the OSS subsystem will be audited.

When upgrading to release G06.29, determine the CLIENT auditing requirements from the corporate security policy:

Is OSS auditing required?
Is OSS device auditing required?
Is Guardian CLIENT auditing required?

Once the requirements are established, take the following steps:

AP-ADVICE-GLOBAL-14   Start Safeguard early during start up. Alter either or both of the AUDIT-CLIENT-OSS and AUDIT-CLIENT-GUARDIAN parameters to OFF and then stop the system and start it again.

Once the Global configuration is set as required, Safeguard will "remember" the values during subsequent SYSGENs to new OS releases.

Global Parameter: PASSWORD-ALGORITHM

Prior to release G06.29 there was a single encryption algorithm used to encrypt passwords, DES. The new PASSWORD-ALGORITHM adds a second algorithm, HMAC256. This parameter only takes effect if PASSWORD-ENCRYPT is ON.

The default value is DES.

If HMAC256 is selected, user passwords will be stored in the USERAX and LUSERAX files.

OSS OBJECTTYPES: OSSPROCESS

To accommodate the enhanced OSS auditing and facilitate generating useful Safeguard audit reports on OSS activity, G06.29 adds the OSSPROCESS Safeguard OBJECTTYPE.

Security Group: SECURITY-OSS-ADMINISTRATOR

Safeguard SECURITY GROUPS make it possible to delegate to specific users the authority to execute certain restricted commands. Previously, there were two SECURITY GROUPs:

SECURITY-ADMINISTRATOR GROUP
SYSTEM-OPERATOR GROUP

The introduction of the SECURITY-OSS-ADMINISTRATOR in release G06.29 makes it possible to delegate the ability to change the ownership and permissions of OSS directories and files without operating as SUPER.SUPER.

BP-SAFEGARD-OSSADMIN-01 The SECURITY-OSS-ADMINISTRATOR Group should be defined if OSS is in use on the system.

Userids added to the SECURITY-OSS-ADMINISTRATOR Group are granted additional OSS security management privileges for the operations:

get acl
set acl
chmod
chown
chdir
opendir

Membership in the SECURITY-OSS-ADMINISTRATOR Group is determined at LOGON. At that time a flag is set in the user's environment.

RISK If a user is already logged on when his userid is added to the SECURITY-OSS-ADMINISTRATOR Group, he will not gain the OSS-ADMINISTRATOR privileges until he next logs on.

RISK If a user is already logged on when his userid is removed from the SECURITY-OSS-ADMINISTRATOR Group, he will retain the OSS-ADMINISTRATOR privileges until he ends his session.

Creation of the SECURITY-OSS-ADMINISTRATOR Group generates a Safeguard audit event.

The SECURITY-OSS-ADMINISTRATOR Group cannot alter the Safeguard Globals, including the AUDIT-CLIENT-OSS parameter.

Some General Notes on SECURITY GROUPs

The following are some general notes on SECURITY GROUPS, including the new SECURITY-OSS-ADMINISTRATOR Group:

SECURITY GROUPS do not exist until they are added.

Only a member of the local SUPER group can ADD Security-Group Definition Records. Once the groups have been created, each group definition record determines who is allowed to ALTER or PURGE it.

The following access authorities can be granted to users and user groups in a SECURITY-GROUP:

EXECUTE   EXECUTE the appropriate restricted commands

OWNER   ALTER or DELETE the Security-Group Record
itself

In addition to the Primary Owner, the Primary Owner's group manager, and local SUPER.SUPER, any userid with OWNER authority in the SECURITY-GROUP Definition Record can modify the Record.

SECURITY GROUPS can have a maximum of 50 user entries.

The STATUS is either FROZEN or THAWED. If a SECURITY-GROUP Record is FROZEN, only the primary owner, the primary owner's group manager, and local SUPER.SUPER can execute the commands restricted to that SECURITY-GROUP.

BP-SAFEGARD-OSSADMIN-02 STATUS should be THAWED

SECURITY-GROUP audit attributes follow the same standards as other Protection Record Audit Attributes. The SECURITY-GROUP Audit Attributes are:

AUDIT-ACCESS-PASS

AUDIT-ACCESS-FAIL

AUDIT-MANAGE-PASS

AUDIT-MANAGE-FAIL

BP-SAFEGARD-OSSADMIN-03 AUDIT-ACCESS-PASS should be ALL

BP-SAFEGARD-OSSADMIN-04 AUDIT-ACCESS-FAIL should be ALL

BP-SAFEGARD-OSSADMIN-05 AUDIT-MANAGE-PASS should be ALL

BP-SAFEGARD-OSSADMIN-06 AUDIT-MANAGE-FAIL should be ALL

BP-SAFEGARD-OSSADMIN-07 AUDIT-ACCESS-PASS should be ALL

BP-SAFEGARD-OSSADMIN-08 AUDIT-ACCESS-FAIL should be ALL

BP-SAFEGARD-OSSADMIN-09 AUDIT-MANAGE-PASS should be ALL

BP-SAFEGARD-OSSADMIN-10 AUDIT-MANAGE-FAIL should be ALL

Configuration File: CONFIGP

One new file was created. $SYSTEM.SAFE.CONFIGP contains the password related Global parameters:

BLINDPASSWORD

ENCRYPTPASSWORD

PASSWORD-ALGORITHM

PASWORD-MINIMUM-LENGTH

PROMPTPASSWORD

This file is created by $ZSMP as soon it starts following an upgrade to G06.29. If Safeguard is not installed on the system, the first time the new PWCONFIG utility is run, the file will be created.

Utility: PWCONFIG

Though PWCONFIG is not part of the Safeguard subsystem, it is covered here for the sake of completeness.

Prior to release G06.29, password configuration parameters had to be bound into the $SYSTEM.SYSnn.PASSWORD program using BIND. The PWCONFIG utility replaces this method of configuration. It is used to set the following PASSWORD program parameters when Safeguard is not installed:

PWCONFIG ALGORITHM*

PWCONFIG ENCRYPTPASSWORD*

PWCONFIG PROMPTPASSWORD

PWCONFIG MINPASSWORDLEN*

If Safeguard is installed, PWCONFIG will display the following message when the commands marked with an asterisk are attempted:

    SAFEGUARD IS RUNNING; USE SAFECOM TO CONFIGURE PASSWORDS

BIND will no longer be supported to set the options for the PASSWORD program.

Safeguard Subsystem Component Updates

This section contains Best Practice recommendations for the new files added to the Safeguard subsystem in releases G06.21 through G06.29. Please refer to the Safeguard Subsystem section of the previous book, for Best Practice recommendations for the entire subsystem.

CONFIGP Configuration File

The new CONFIGP file contains Password-related Globals.

> BLINDPASSWORD
>
> ENCRYPTPASSWORD
>
> PASSWORD-ALGORITHM
>
> PASWORD-MINIMUM-LENGTH
>
> PROMPTPASSWORD

The CONFIGP file should be secured like the CONFIG and CONFIGA files.

BP-FILE-SAFEGUARD-12 CONFIGP should be secured "- - - -"

BP-OPSYS-OWNER-03 CONFIGP should be owned by SUPER. SUPER.

BP-OPSYS-FILELOC-03 CONFIGP should reside in $SYSTEM.SAFE

	Discovery Questions:	Look here:
File-Policy	Is release G06.29 or greater installed on the system?	Policy
OPSYS-OWNER-03	Who owns CONFIGP?	Fileinfo
FILE-SAFEGUARD-12	Is CONFIGP correctly secured via Guardian or Safeguard?	Fileinfo

LUSERAX and USERAX Configuration Files

Two new files were created. They contain the new TEXT-DESCRIPTION and BINARY-DESCRIPTION fields.

HMAC256 passwords and user HMAC256 password history are stored in the LUSERAX and USERAX files. DES algorithm passwords and the user DES password history continue to be stored in the USERID and LUSERID files.

Name	Filecode	Contents
LUSERAX	540	Alias Text Description and Binary Description
USERAX	540	User Text Description and Binary Description

Records are only written to the appropriate file, LUSERAX or USERAX, if the TEXT-DESCRIPTION parameter is updated or HMAC256 encryption is selected.

BP-FILE-SAFEGUARD-13 LUSERAX should be secured "- - - -".

BP-OPSYS-OWNER-03   LUSERAX should be owned by SUPER. SUPER.

BP-OPSYS-FILELOC-03   LUSERAX should reside in $SYSTEM.SAFE.

BP-FILE-SAFEGUARD-14 USERAX should be secured "- - - -".

BP-OPSYS-OWNER-02   USERAX should be owned by SUPER. SUPER.

BP-OPSYS-FILELOC-02   USERAX should reside in $SYSTEM. SYSTEM.

	Discovery Questions	Look here:
File-Policy	Is release G06.27 or greater installed on the system?	Policy
OPSYS-OWNER-03	Who owns LUSERAX?	Fileinfo
OPSYS-OWNER-03	Who owns USERAX?	Fileinfo
FILE-SAFEGUARD-13	Is LUSERAX correctly secured via Guardian or Safeguard?	Fileinfo
FILE-SAFEGUARD-14	Is LUSERAX file correctly secured via Guardian or Safeguard?	Fileinfo

PATGUARD Configuration Files

The new DISKFILE-PATTERN Object Protection Records are contained in PATGUARD files. The PATGUARD files are the equivalent of the

GUARD files. A PATGUARD file resides in the SAFE subvolume on every disk (volume). The SMON processes consult the PATGUARD files on the disk where the file being accessed resides if the new CHECK-DISKFILE-PATTERN global parameter in set to ONLY, LAST, or FIRST.

If CHECK-DISKFILE-PATTERN is set to ONLY, only DISKFILE-PATTERN Protection Records will be checked; any exisiting non-pattern Protection Records will be ignored.

If CHECK-DISKFILE-PATTERN is LAST, pattern checking will be done after non-pattern Protection Records are evaluated.

IF CHECK-DISKFILE-PATTERN is FIRST, pattern checking will be done before non-pattern Protection Records are evaluated.

If CHECK-DISKFILE-PATTERN is set to OFF, pattern checking is disabled; any existing DISKFILE-PATTERN Protection Records will be ignored.

The PATGUARD files should be secured like the GUARD files. Please refer to the Safeguard Subsystem section of the Gazette in the previous book, for more information.

BP-FILE-SAFEGUARD-15 PATGUARD files should be secured "- - - -".

BP-OPSYS-OWNER-03 PATGUARD files should be owned by SUPER. SUPER.

BP-OPSYS-FILELOC-03 PATGUARD files should reside in each SAFE subvolume.

	Discovery Questions	Look here:
File-Policy	Is release G06.27 or greater installed on the system?	Policy
OPSYS-OWNER-03	Who owns the PATGUARD files?	Fileinfo
FILE-SAFEGUARD-15	Is the PATGUARD files correctly secured via Guardian or Safeguard?	Fileinfo

PWCONFIG Utility

The $SYSTEM.SYSnn.PWCONFIG utility replaces the use of BIND to set the PASSWORD program parameters on non-Safeguard systems.

Only SUPER Group members can execute PWCONFIG.

Corporate policy should determine if system managers or the security staff set the PASSWORD program parameters.

BP-FILE-SAFEGUARD-12 PWCONFIG should be secured "- - - -"

BP-OPSYS-OWNER-01 PWCONFIG should be owned by SUPER. SUPER.

BP-OPSYS-FILELOC-01 PWCONFIG should reside in $SYSTEM. SYSnn

	Discovery Questions:	Look here:
File-Policy	Is release G06.29 or greater installed on the system?	Policy
OPSYS-OWNER-01	Who owns PWCONFIG?	Fileinfo
FILE-SAFEGUARD-12	Is PWCONFIG correctly secured via Guardian or Safeguard?	Fileinfo

3

Securing Pathway Applications

Pathway applications, like most enterprise computer applications, include software for end-user input devices, for database manipulation, and for communication: directing the transaction between the end-user and the database programs.

Pathway provides an application platform that includes a multithreaded terminal control process (TCP) for communicating with terminals, including fault tolerance and transaction protection. This Pathway TCP relieves developers from having to develop complex communication code.

Pathway applications consist of two types of programs: requester programs and server programs:

> Requester programs are the data entry presentation functions that drive end-user input devices or workstations.

> Server programs accept requests from requester programs through the Pathway communications layer to manipulate databases or perform other functions.

A Pathway run-time environment is a set of system software that manages transactions, provides the communications layer, manages multiple user throughput, and manages load balancing. This system software makes up an Online Transaction Processing (OLTP) environment: PATHMON.

PATHMON, via the PATHCOM interactive interface, provides a management tool to configure and manage an application's requesters and servers. PATHMON manages and distributes functions over physical nodes from a single Pathway application. The Pathway run-time configuration and requester and server configurations are defined according to a specific scheme required by PATHMON.

A Pathway application has numerous parts and features. This chapter will only address the features that present security compliance issues within a Pathway application.

Pathway Development

The following components are part of the Pathway development platform.

Pathway Application Source Code

Pathway is a requester/server application model. The Pathway monitor (PATHMON) provides the interface for the communication layer and the management layer between the requester (client) and server. A Pathway application has two major components:

Requesters are screen programs or GUI client components that interact directly with the terminal. The screen part of the application is written in SCOBOLX (SCREEN COBOL) or in a GUI language. Components that comprise the requester code may include libraries or code modules that are bound into the requester as a run-time or compiled unit.

Servers are user programs running on the host system that interact with the databases and perform user calculations, database manipulation, etc. The server part of the application can be written in any language supported by the NonStop Server. It may include libraries or code modules that are bound into the server as a run-time or compiled unit.

RISK If source code isn't managed properly, two developers can unknowingly make alterations to the same code. Whichever one load their changes last would "win," and the other person's alterations would be lost, possibly irretrievably.

RISK If application source code isn't stored in a secure manner, developers can move inappropriate or untested software into production, putting the enterprise application at risk.

AP-PATHWAY-SOURCE-01 An appropriate source code repository and management application should be used to store Pathway application source code.

RISK If Pathway development and production environments share components, the availability and stability of the production environment can be jeopardized.

AP-PATHWAY-SOURCE-02 Pathway development and production environments should be kept separate and should not share components. Ideally, no application development work at all will ever be done on a secure system.

Pathway Configuration Source Code

A Pathway application requires configuration commands, which are defined within a text file. This file can be part of a system startup procedure to start or restart Pathway applications.

Pathway configuration commands define the run-time application required by a specific enterprise application. The commands are written in a Pathway-specific syntax.

RISK If Pathway configuration scripts are not managed properly, two developers can unknowingly make alterations to the same scripts and important alterations could be lost. The application Pathway could be started with an incorrect configuration.

RISK   If Pathway configuration scripts are not stored in a secure manner, developers can move inappropriate or untested software into production, putting the enterprise application at risk.

AP-PATHWAY-SOURCE-03   An appropriate source code repository and management application should be used to store Pathway configuration source code.

RISK   Pathway configurations can also be started and stopped from any terminal or within a running process, if the security allows a user this capability.

AP-PATHWAY-SOURCE-04   Pathways should be secured so that only appropriate users can alter the configuration of the Pathways.

Pathway Run-Time Components

The following components are part of the run-time Pathway processing application:

PATHCOM

PATHTCP2 (TCP)

Application Requesters

Application Servers

Terminal Objects

Pathway Configurations

Databases

Programs

LINKMON

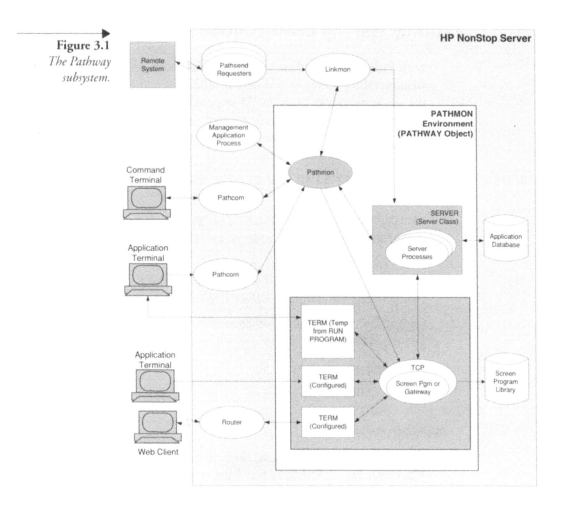

Figure 3.1
The Pathway subsystem.

PATHMON Process

PATHMON is the supervising process that manages a specific run-time Pathway application. Each Pathway application has a named PATHMON process pair. When PATHMON processes are started, they read the startup configuration file.

Pathway Startup Configuration File

Each Pathway is started via a startup configuration text file. The file is read whenever the Pathway is cold started. This startup file should be owned by the application's job function ID responsible for starting, modifying and stopping the Pathway, generally referred to as the Executing ID. It should be secured so that only those users responsible for managing the application's Pathway can alter the file.

AP-PATHWAY-STARTUP-01 The Pathway configuration text file should be owned by the application's executing ID.

AP-PATHWAY-STARTUP-02 The Pathway configuration text file should be secured so that only personnel responsible for managing the Pathway can alter the file.

Before any Pathway application is deployed, the Security Administrator should review the security-related statements in the startup file.

General Pathway configuration commands that should be addressed by the Security Administrator are:

OWNER

SECURITY

Pathway OWNER

The Pathway owner should be defined in the Startup Configuration file. The owner has the following privileges and attributes:

The ability to perform commands via PATHCOM or programmatically to affect the application

Ownership to which other user ids will be relative. For example, if the Pathway security is set to "G", all members of the owner's user group will be able to alter the pathway configuration.

RISK All executables started by PATHMON are run using the PAID of the PATHMON process unless otherwise configured, not the OWNER setting.

AP-PATHWAY-CONFIG-01   Application Pathways should be owned by a privileged job function userid, known as the application execution ID, designated specifically for ownership of Pathway.

RISK   Regardless of the user who initiates the startup file, the OWNER keyword identifies the OWNER of the Pathway application.

RISK   If the Pathway owner is not explicitly set, the Pathway ownership will default to the userid that starts the Pathway configuration.

AP-PATHWAY-CONFIG-02   Always explicitly set the Pathway owner.

RISK   Running a Pathway application as SUPER.SUPER can potentially allow access to the NonStop Server as SUPER.SUPER without the need for a password.

AP-PATHWAY-CONFIG-03   No PATHMON should run as SUPER. SUPER unless specifically required, documented, and signed off by a person of authority and secured correctly.

3P-ACCESS-PATHWAY-01   A third party access control product that can secure at the command level and provide an audit of user activity should be deployed to grant only appropriate users access to the Pathway configuration files as the application owner.

Pathway Security

The security attribute specifies the users who can issue PATHCOM commands that directly alter the state of a running Pathway application. Security attributes are the same as the Guardian security attributes. The possible settings are:

"A" Any local user

"G" Any local group member or owner

"O" Local owner only

"–" Local SUPER.SUPER

"N" Any local or remote user

"C" Any local or remote member of owner's community

"U" Local or remote owner only

RISK The default security value is "N," which allows any user to modify ASSIGNS, DEFINES, server names, and other objects that are integral to the integrity of the Pathway.

AP-PATHWAY-CONFIG-04 Pathway security should not allow general access of "N" or "A".

Configured terminals are defined and started via the PATHCOM interface.

RISK If users are responsible for starting and stopping their configured terminals they must be able to modify the Pathway via PATHCOM.

PATHCTL File

Each PATHMON process creates and maintains its own PATHCTL file, in which it stores the configuration information about the specific Pathway application. The configuration information defines requester and server locations, database locations, and execution parameters.

The PATHCTL file is a binary file that is actively controlling the application configuration. Initially, the PATHCTL file is created from the configuration text file that is used when Pathway is cold-started.

The PATHCTL file is usually owned by the application's executing ID. The Pathway runs as the application owner, so only the application owner needs access.

If the System Administrator or System Operator is responsible for starting and stopping the application, he or she may also need to access the configuration file.

RISK Alterations to Pathway startup files can compromise the integrity of the enterprise applications.

RISK The Pathway configuration PATHCTL file defaults to the file creator's default security.

AP-PATHWAY-CONFIG-05 The security of each PATHCTL file limits access to only those responsible for managing the application Pathway.

3P-ACCESS-PATHWAY-01   A third-party access control product that can secure at the command level and provide an audit of the user's activity should be deployed to grant only appropriate users access to the Pathway configuration files as the application owner.

RISK   Modifications performed via PATHCOM or programmatically are not stored in the PATHCTL file. Modifications are transient; they are maintained during a warm start of Pathway but lost upon a cold start.

AP-PATHWAY-CONFIG-06   Modifications to a running Pathway that are intended to be permanent should be made in the Pathway's startup file to ensure that they aren't lost when the Pathway is cold started.

Pathway Log Files

The log files are assigned during the startup of a Pathway application to capture errors and configuration events. Two logs are available: LOG1 and LOG2. The output can be directed to a device, to a file, or to an EMS log.

RISK   If the LOG parameter is omitted, output is directed to the home-term. The Pathway logs should always be directed to a device or file where these events can be monitored.

	Discovery Questions	Look here:
FILE-POLICY	Who is allowed to start, stop and modify this Pathway?	Policy
OPSYS-OWNER-03	Who owns the Pathway environment?	Policy
FILE-POLICY	Who owns the Pathway configuration files?	Fileinfo
OPSYS-OWNER-03	Who owns the PATHCTL file?	Fileinfo
FILE-POLICY	What is the internal Pathway security vector?	Pathway info
FILE-POLICY	Is the Pathway owner explicitly set?	Configuration file
FILE-POLICY	Is the internal owner the same as the running owner?	Pathway info
SAFE-PATHWAY-01	Is there a Safeguard Protection Record to control access to the Pathway application?	Safecom

PATHCOM Process

PATHCOM is the user interface to manage a specific Pathway application. PATHCOM is an interactive utility that accepts commands from an input file. These commands are used to create and manage Pathway objects. Users that often need PATHCOM access to a Pathway application are:

Job Functions	Need to access PATHCOM
Pathway Owner	To make changes to the running Pathway application
System Administrator/System Operator	To start or stop terminals, freeze, thaw or abort terminals, start or stop Pathway
Users starting terminals in Pathway	To run commands to start terminals

PATHCOM Commands with Security Implications

The following PATHCOM commands have security implications. If a third-party access control product is used to grant selected users access to PATHCOM running as SUPER.SUPER, the sensitive commands listed in the table below should be denied to all users other than system management or other appropriate groups.

PATHCOM allows users to change the active Pathway application configuration. The following commands have security implications.

ADD
ALTER
DELETE
CONTROL
FREEZE
RUN
START
STOP
THAW
SHUTDOWN/SHUTDOWN2

3P-ACCESS-PATHWAY-02   A third-party access control product that can secure at the command level and provide an audit of the user's activity should be used to grant only appropriate users access to PATHCOM as the Pathway owner or as another privileged ID, such as the database owner.

System Administrators and authorized operations staff should have access to PATHCOM to enable them to stop and start servers, terminals, and the application.

RISK   Allowing less restrictive security to the Pathway configuration may allow unauthorized users to affect the running Pathway application.

Please refer to the *Gazette* section on the Pathway Subsystem in the previous book for more information.

	Discovery Questions	Look here:
OPSYS-OWNER-02	Who owns the PATHCOM object file?	Fileinfo
FILE-PATHWAY-02 SAFE-PATHWAY-02	Is the PATHCOM object file correctly secured with Guardian or Safeguard?	Fileinfo Safecom

Requester Objects

Two basic types of requesters can utilize the Pathway environment. Traditional applications may use screen interface programs written in SCOBOLX. These programs are managed by a PATHTCP2 process. Other screen interfaces, such as GUI applications, can utilize the Pathway model, using Pathsend commands via LINKMON. From this point forward in this document, specific notations to requesters (TCP) and requesters (PATHSEND) will represent this variation.

PATHTCP2 Process for Requesters (TCP)

A Terminal Control Processes (TCP) manages requesters written in SCOBOLX. The program that provides this functionality is the

PATHTCP2 program. A PATHTCP2 process concurrently manages one or more terminals and transactions using the requester programs. The TCP interprets SCOBOLX requesters on individual end-user terminals and handles message routing and preliminary editing of user input. The primary function of a TCP is to handle the complexities associated with multi-terminal applications.

General Pathway configuration commands that should be addressed by the security administrator are

```
TCP-1
PROGRAM
TCLPROG
```

RISK There are no interactive functions that control the PATHTCP2 program. It is automatically managed by the PATHMON process. **$SYSTEM.SYSTEM.PATHTCP2** is the HP NonStop Server supported program.

Individual SCOBOLX programs are collectively stored in a set of program object files, usually named POBJCOD and POBJDIR. SCOBOLX code is interpreted by the PATHTCP2 program. The TCLPROG definition points to the location of these two files.

RISK The POBJCOD and POBJDIR files should be restricted from unauthorized access.

AP-PATHWAY-CONFIG-07 The program owner should be the same as the Pathway owner.

AP-PATHWAY-CONFIG-08 The program entity should be set the same as the Pathway security.

Please refer to the *Gazette* section on the Pathway Subsystem in the previous book for more information.

	Discovery Questions	Look here:
FILE-POLICY	Is the Pathway using PATHTCP2 to manage screen interface?	Policy

(Continued)

	Discovery Questions	Look here:
OPSYS-OWNER-03	Who owns the POBJCOD/POBJDIR files?	Fileinfo
FILE-PATHWAY-02 SAFE-PATHWAY-02	Are the POBJCOD/POBJDIR files correctly secured with Guardian or Safeguard?	Fileinfo Safecom

PATHSEND Process for Requesters (PATHSEND)

PATHSEND processes are user-written programs that contain PATH-SEND procedure calls to make requests to Pathway server classes. Two levels of security should be considered for PATHSEND processes: network level and server class level.

If the PATHSEND process accesses a Pathway server class on another node, the userid of the PATHMON process controlling the server class has to have the corresponding userids and remote passwords that allow the requesting PATHSEND to access any remotely referenced system.

LINKMON processes perform authorization checks for each server class request operation to verify that the userid of the PATHSEND process conforms to the Server class's owner and security attributes.

AP-PATHWAY-PATHSEND-01   Determine if any Pathway applications are using the PATHSEND procedures and if any applications are sending to remote Pathways.

Terminal Objects

TERM objects manage the tasks that use requester (TCP) programs to control input-output devices, such as terminals and workstations, and input-output processes that enable users to communicate with a Pathway application. Each task runs as a thread in the TCP. The TCP can manage many threads concurrently. There are two types of TERM objects: configured TERM objects and temporary TERM objects. Configured TERM objects are user defined and added to the PATHMON configuration file.

Temporary TERM objects are created and deleted automatically by the PATHMON process when the RUN PROGRAM is invoked interactively from the PATHCOM interface.

RISK An active Pathway terminal provides directly connected access to the enterprise application and databases. Physical controls should be placed on access to terminals that are connected and logged on.

RISK The Pathway application runs as the Pathway owner without password protection unless otherwise programmatically managed.

AP-PATHWAY-LOGON-01 It is best to use the HP NonStop Server userid and password for the logon. The logon user can then be authenticated by the HP NonStop Server operating system.

AP-PATHWAY-LOGON-02 Only use temporary TERM objects when necessary, as this allows a user to access the PATHCOM program and start a terminal without access authority.

RISK Pathway applications are vulnerable to unauthorized usage if not controlled by physical restrictions and password controls.

AP-PATHWAY-LOGON-03 Userids and passwords should be secured and the passwords should be encrypted.

3P-ACCESS-PATHCOM-03 If a third-party access control product is used to grant selected users access to PATHCOM, the RUN PROGRAM command to start a terminal can be controlled.

	Discovery Questions	Look here:
FILE-POLICY	Is the Pathway using PATHTCP2 to manage the screen interface?	Policy
FILE-POLICY	Are terminals configured or temporary?	Configuration file
FILE-POLICY	Is there physical security on terminals?	Policy

PROGRAM Objects

PROGRAM objects are used by PATHMON to initiate requesters (TCP). To start a terminal, the RUN PROGRAM command is used to initiate a program on that terminal object.

<u>Example 1:</u>

```
RUN PROGRAM PROG-1, TCP TCP-1, TYPE T16-6530
```

3P-ACCESS-PATHCOM-03 If a third-party access control product is used to grant selected users access to PATHCOM, the RUN PROGRAM command to start a terminal can be controlled.

SERVER Objects

SERVER objects are defined as server classes. Server classes are added to PATHMON via PATHCOM ADD SERVER statements. Pathway will start many server processes for a single server class based upon the number of requests for that server class. We refer to the server class as the definition of the server, and to the server process as a specific running instance.

Server classes contain pointers to the required server process's program object. Server classes also contain pointers to the application database files, via DEFINE or ASSIGN statements. Since the server class is the window into the enterprise application's databases and functionality, many aspects of the server definition are crucial to security compliance of the application. Server classes can access both Guardian and OSS files. These will be addressed separately.

The following are configuration commands for the general Pathway application for both Guardian and OSS server classes. The items below should be addressed by the Security Administrator:

HOMETERM
OWNER
SECURITY

Server Class HOMETERM

The server class hometerm defines where a server's messages, inspect prompts, and errors are sent.

RISK If this parameter is not explicitly set, this output is directed to the hometerm of the PATHMON.

BP-PATHWAY-HOMETERM-01 The hometerm should always be directed to a device or file where these events can be monitored.

Server Class Owner

The server class owner is only applicable to requester (PATHSEND) applications. Requester (TCP) applications default to the Pathway owner. For the use of these attributes, please refer to the appropriate sections below.

Requester (TCP)—The owner attribute specifies users who can issue PATHCOM commands that directly alter the state of a running server class. Please refer to the owner attribute of PATHMON.

Requester (LINKMON)—The owner attribute specifies users who can access a specific server class. Please refer to the owner attribute of the LINKMON command.

Server Class Security

The server class security is only applicable to requester (PATHSEND) applications. Requester (TCP) applications default to the Pathway security. For the use of these attributes please refer to the appropriate sections below.

Requester (TCP)—The security attribute controls the users (relative to the server class owner) who can issue PATHCOM commands that alter the state of a running server class. Please refer to the security attribute of PATHMON.

Requester (LINKMON)—The security attribute controls users relative to the server owner who can access the server class. Please refer to the security attribute of the LINKMON command.

RISK If the application does not authenticate users entering a request into a GUI application, the server will provide the information to the GUI without user security checking.

AP-PATHWAY-LOGON-04 Ensure that the application has user authentication methods.

GUARDIAN Server Classes

Guardian server class objects are defined with the PROCESSTYPE of GUARDIAN.

The following configuration commands are specific to Guardian servers. They should be addressed by the Security Administrator.

> ASSIGN LOG
> DEFINE
> PARAM
> PROGRAM
> VOLUME

ASSIGN and DEFINE commands are ways to allow different physical components to be assigned to Pathway server classes without code changes. By using logical names to identify files, the server class definition supplies the physical components.

RISK If a server class is redirected to improper physical locations, the application could be reading and writing to unauthorized file locations.

AP-PATHWAY-SERVERS-01 ASSIGN and DEFINE locations must be monitored to a ensure that they are pointing to the correct database file locations.

Server Class ASSIGNs

The ASSIGN command within a Pathway server class is used to associate the name of a physical file to a logical file name used in a server program, and, optionally, to specify the attributes of such files. The program uses the logical name, thus allowing the physical file name associated with the logical name to vary from node to node or application to application.

Example 2 shows an ASSIGN.

Example 2:

```
SET SERVER ASSIGN MASTERFILE, $DATA1.CUSTMR.MSTFILE
```

Example 3 shows an ASSIGN with Create File characteristics.

Example 3:

```
SET SERVER ASSIGN OUTFILE, $DATA2.CUSTMR.NEWMST, EXT 32,
CODE 123
```

RISK ASSIGNs allow programs to be attached to the assigned file logically. If the physical name is changed to a file that is not expected or authorized, output or input could be misdirected.

Please refer to the section on ASSIGNs in Part 7 of the previous book, for more information.

	Discovery Questions	Look here:
FILE-POLICY	Is the Pathway using ASSIGNs to manage logical paths?	Policy
FILE-POLICY	Are the ASSIGNs pointing to the appropriate file?	Pathway info

Server Class DEFINEs

DEFINEs are named sets of attributes and associated values. They specify information meant to be communicated to a server program that will associate the logical name to a physical file or location.

A DEFINE has the following components:

NAME is a unique descriptor starting with "=" and up to 23 characters

CLASS is a designation of usage class

ATTRIBUTE is a defined attribute of the class

VALUE is the value associated with the attribute, filename, tape name, etc.

Example 4:

```
SET SERVER DEFINE = EMPLOYEE, CLASS MAP,
FILE \NODE.$VOL.APPDB.EMPLOYEE
```

Example 4 shows a DEFINE.

RISK DEFINEs allow programs to access the defined file logically. If the physical name is changed to a file that is not expected or authorized, output or input could be misdirected.

Please refer to the section on DEFINEs in Part 7 of the previous book, for more information.

	Discovery Questions	Look here:
FILE-POLICY	Is the Pathway using DEFINEs to manage logical paths?	Policy
FILE-POLICY	Are the DEFINEs pointing to the appropriate file?	Pathway info

Server Class PARAMs

A PARAM assigns a string value to a parameter name, which is sent to the server program upon startup. Use of this value within the code is internal to the server program.

Example 5:

```
SET SERVER PARAM SWITCH-1 "ON"
```

Example 5 shows a PARAM for a string value.

RISK PARAMs send a value to the server. If the string is changed, it could cause the server to perform incorrect actions.

	Discovery Questions	Look here:
FILE-POLICY	Is the Pathway using PARAMs to send values to the server?	Policy
FILE-POLICY	Are the PARAMs correct?	Pathway info

Server Class Programs

The program attribute identifies the program name that is run when this server class is initiated by the Pathway application. Each server class uses a program that is either a Guardian or an OSS executable. Multiple copies of the same object used in different server classes will be automatically managed by Pathway to load balance requests. Each copy will be passed the same startup parameters as assigned in the server class definition.

The server program is run as the PAID of the Pathway application, unless one of the following occurs:

> The program is PROGID'd to an alternate userid.

> The internal software requires users to logon with an individual logon and the internal program performs a user authenticate and logon after the server is started by Pathway.

AP-PATHWAY-LOGON-05   Pathway applications should authenticate the username and password of any user attempting to use the application.

The server program is the running program that allows the Pathway access to the enterprise data.

RISK   Running unauthorized programs or allowing changes to the startup parameters of the program can allow unauthorized access or erroneous access to the enterprise data.

RISK   A Guardian server program name can refer to a remote node. Remote servers must maintain the appropriate security to allow remote access controls.

AP-PATHWAY-SERVER-02   Do not PROGID Pathway server programs, especially if the server object is owned by a SUPER group member.

AP-PATHWAY-SERVER-03   Generally, Pathway server programs are not LICENSED, because licensing allows SUPER capabilities.

AP-PATHWAY-SERVER-04   Pathway applications should generate an audit trail or logging method of tracking users that log into the application and, if necessary, a more detailed audit of functions performed by each user.

A server class can be designed as an associative server, which is a process. This process can be started outside the Pathway environment. Associative servers can also be used to simulate a terminal or communications device.

Example 6:

```
SET SERVER PROCESS $<process name> (ASSOCIATIVE ON)
```

RISK The program used to create the associative server must be given the same level of security as any other program used by the Pathway.

	Discovery Questions	Look here:
FILE-POLICY	Are the startup parameters for the server classes monitored appropriately?	Policy
FILE-POLICY	Are any server classes PROGID'd?	Pathway info Fileinfo
FILE-POLICY	Are any server classes LICENSED?	Pathway info Fileinfo
FILE-POLICY	Are there any associative servers?	Configuration file

Server Class Volume

Server class volume is used to default partially qualified names to fully qualified file locations of Guardian names. The server Volume command sets the an _DEFAULTS DEFINE for this Pathway explicitly.

RISK If the server class volume is not explicitly set, it will default to the _DEFAULTS DEFINE for this Pathway.

AP-PATHWAY-CONFIG-09 Always explicitly set the server class volume.

OSS Server Classes

OSS server objects are defined as server classes with the PROCESSTYPE of OSS.

The following configuration commands are specific to OSS server classes. Items below should be addressed by the Security Administrator.

> CWD
> ARGLIST
> ENV DEBUGLOGFORMAT
> PROGRAM
> STDERR
> STDIN
> STDOUT

Server Class CWD

A server class CWD is used to default partially qualified names to fully qualified file locations of OSS names. The CWD is an absolute path to a directory.

RISK If the server class CWD is not explicitly set, it will default to the current working directory for the Pathway.

AP-PATHWAY-OSS-01 Always explicitly set the absolute path.

Server Class ARGLIST

The ARGLIST is the startup command that is sent to an OSS program. The ARGLIST can contain values, filenames, and locations.

Example 7 shows an ARGLIST for an OSS program.

Example 7:

```
SET SERVER ARGLIST -1, -t:process/log, -u:debug
```

RISK The ARGLIST sends values to the server process. If the string is changed, it could cause the server to perform incorrect actions.

	Discovery Questions	Look here:
FILE-POLICY	Is the Pathway using an ARGLIST to send values to the server?	Policy

(Continued)

	Discovery Questions	Look here:
FILE-POLICY	Is the ARGLIST correct?	Pathway info

Server Class ENVs

An ENV is a parameter name, which is sent to the server process upon startup and associated with a value. Use of this value within the code is internal to the server program.

Example 8 shows an ENV for a string value.

Example 8:

```
SET SERVER ENV DEBUGLOGFORMAT TRUE
```

RISK ENVs send values to the server process. If the string is changed, it could cause the server program to perform incorrect actions.

	Discovery Questions	Look here:
FILE-POLICY	Is the Pathway using ENVs to send values to the server?	Policy
FILE-POLICY	Are the ENVs correct?	Pathway info

Server Class Programs

The program attribute identifies the program name that is run when this server class is initiated by the Pathway application. Each server class uses a program that is an OSS executable. Multiple copies of the program will be automatically managed by Pathway to load-balance requests. Each copy will be passed the same startup parameters as assigned in the server class definition.

The server program is run as the PAID of the Pathway application, unless one of the following occurs:

The program has the SETUID or SETGID set to an alternate userid.

The internal software requires users to logon with an individual logon, and the program performs a user authenticate and logon after the server is started by Pathway.

The running server program allows the Pathway access to the enterprise data.

RISK Running unauthorized programs or allowing changes to the startup parameters of the program can allow unauthorized access or erroneous access to the enterprise data.

AP-PATHWAY-OSS-02 Do not use SETUID or SETGID for OSS Pathway server programs, especially if the server object is owned by a SUPER group member.

	Discovery Questions	Look here:
FILE-POLICY	Are the startup parameters for the server classes monitored appropriately?	Policy
FILE-POLICY	Is the program name fully qualified or using the CWD qualification?	Configuration file
FILE-POLICY	Do any server classes have SETUID set?	Pathway info ls
FILE-POLICY	Are any server classes have SETGID set?	Pathway info ls

Server Class STDERR

STDERR is the location name for the server program's error file. It is also possible to direct output to an OSSTTY process.

RISK The STDERR can be the server's error file location. If the string is changed, it could cause the server to write to an unauthorized location.

Server Class STDIN

STDIN is the file from which input is received. This parameter is optional depending upon any usage by a server program.

RISK STDIN can be the server's input file location. If the string is changed, it could cause the server program to read from an unauthorized location.

Server Class STDOUT

STDOUT is the file where output can be sent. This parameter is optional depending upon any usage by a server program.

RISK STDOUT can be the server's output file location. If the string is changed, it could cause the server program to write to an unauthorized location.

Databases

Most Pathway server classes use the logical name approach, with the Pathway configuration defining the physical location of the file. The logical versus physical mapping is managed by the Pathway configuration.

The database may be any valid format file on a NonStop Server system.

Server programs can be "hard-coded" to access files. This is not recommended. If files are "hard-coded" within the server program, the only method to determine exactly which files are being accessed by a server class is to use a tool such as Measure or a third-party tool.

AP-PATHWAY-DATABASE-01 Always use ASSIGNs or DEFINEs to manage database locations. Hard-coded file names are not recommended.

When assigning security vectors and ownership to a database that is accessed by a Pathway, you should separate the ownership of the Pathway from the ownership of the database.

RISK If the ownership is not separated, any user that can run Pathway has ownership to the database and could potentially access the database outside of Pathway.

AP-PATHWAY-DATABASE-02 The Pathway object owner must not be the same as the owner of the application database owner.

The Pathway owner must have access to READ and WRITE to the database. The owner of the database will have access to READ, WRITE, and PURGE access.

RISK   Program objects and application database files should be located in a separate subvolumes to allow a separation of security at the subvolume level.

AP-PATHWAY-DATABASE-03   Name subvolumes with a recognized suffix or prefix such as OBJ or DAT to readily determine if they contain unauthorized Program objects and/or database files.

AP-PATHWAY-DATABASE-04   Separate application log files into separate subvolumes with a recognized suffix or prefix such as LOG.

These steps make it easier to locate the program objects, database files, and logs. It also makes it easier to administer their security.

LINKMON Process

The LINKMON process is supplied as part of the Pathway environment. Together with PATHMON, LINKMON controls communication between requesters (PATHSEND) and server classes.

LINKMON cannot be directly controlled from the PATHCOM interface, and there are no other security implications that relate to LINKMON processes for Pathway that are not covered directly by other parts of the environment. However, for Pathway applications that use PATHSEND there are two levels of security to consider:

> Network-level security
> Server-class security

Network-Level Security

Security at the network level is a complex problem not addressed in this section. Physical and network security of GUI client software must be controlled through a variety of methods. Pathway does not provide network security features.

Encryption of data transmission, firewalls, and other network security methods should be employed between the GUI requesters and the Pathway application.

RISK   Unprotected networks allow unauthorized access to a system and businessed.

AP-ADVICE-PATHWAY-09   Use industry-recognized network security methods to protect the application, application data, and communications.

Server-Class Security

Server class security attributes determines the userid that controls access to the server class from a PATHSEND process. The security required to access the Pathway server class is described earlier in this chapter.

Users making a Pathway application server request must be authenticated by the application software.

RISK   If the application does not authenticate users entering a request into a GUI application, the server will send data to the GUI without confirming user identity or access privileges.

AP-PATHWAY-LOGON-04   Ensure that the application has user authentication methods.

4

TCP/IP

TCP/IP is a set of protocols used for communication and file transfer.

TCP (Transmission Control Protocol) enables two hosts to establish a connection and exchange streams of data. TCP guarantees not only that the data will be delivered but that the packets will be delivered in the same order that they were sent.

IP (Internet Protocol) specifies the format of the packets (also called datagrams) of information that are sent across the network. IP also specifies the addressing scheme.

Wikipedia says "IP by itself is something like the postal system. It allows you to address a package and drop it in the system, but there's no direct link between you and the recipient. TCP, on the other hand, establishes a connection between two hosts so that they can send messages back and forth for a period of time."

TCP/IP Security

The only real requirement for Network security (from an end user point of view) is that the data sent across the network be ENCRYPTED. There are all the administrative security issues as with any functional application: authenticating who is logging on to control the network and making changes to configurations, routing, encryption key management, etc. Everything else must be handled by the platform (the HP NonStop server) and application in question. If each node took good care of its own security, then the risk from all the intrusions would be mitigated. About the only things that are legitimate "network security issues" for HP NonStop server networks are:

1. Network administration and configuration security

2. Communication path encryption and key management (a shared concern between the network and production nodes)

3. Denial of service detection and prevention

AP-ADVICE-TCPIP-01   All the firewall issues should be handled by securing production nodes appropriately REGARDLESS of whether or not the node is part of a network.

TCP/IP Architecture

The TCP/IP protocols are a family of data communications protocols that allows communication between heterogeneous systems in a multi-network environment. This allows for communication between HP NonStop servers and other systems.

The HP NonStop TCP/IP subsystem actually consists of a variety of products in the TCP/IP protocol family and provides services at the Network through Application Layers of the OSI Reference Model. The TCP/IP subsystem is the base subsystem for all the other components of the TCP/IP software. It provides a file-system interface to the TCP, UDP (User Datagram Protocol), and IP protocols. The TCP/IP subsystem runs as a single or NonStop process on the NonStop server.

TCP/IP Functional Layers

The functional layers of TCP/IP are defined by either the Department of Defense (DoD) or OSI data communications models. The OSI model is made up of seven layers. The DoD model (also known as the TCP/IP Model or DARPA Model) is made up of four layers (five in some implementations of TCP/IP). The table below shows the functional layers and the TCP/IP protocols that occur in each layer.

DoD Model	OSI Model	Protocols
Application Layer	Application Layer Presentation Layer Session Layer	DNS, NFS, BOOTP SNMP FTP, TFTP Telnet SMTP Kerberos RPC
Host to Host Layer	Transport Layer	TCP UDP
Internet Layer	Network Layer	IP ICMP, IPSec RIP, OSPF ARP, RARP
Network Interface Layer	Data Link Layer Physical Layer	PPP SLIP

The **Application Layer** is the layer containing user applications such as Telnet and FTP as well as administrative protocols such as DNS or SNMP. It encompasses layers five through seven of the OSI model.

The **Host to Host Layer** is the layer responsible for enabling end to end communication between devices on the network. It is responsible for managing connections and for data delivery which can be either reliable (TCP) or unreliable (UDP). See the definitions of these protocols below for further detail.

The **Internet-Layer** (Inter-Network Layer) is responsible for such activities as logical device addressing, basic datagram communication and data routing. The Internet Protocol (IP) runs as part of this layer.

The **Network Interface Layer** is the layer is responsible for interfacing the TCP/IP protocol suite to the physical hardware on which it runs.

TCP/IP Related Protocols

TCP/IP is a collection of protocols. Some of the more common protocols:

ARP

DNS

ICMP

IP

RARP

SMTP

TCP

UDP

ARP (Address Resolution Protocol)

ARP is a protocol responsible for providing dynamic address resolution within an IP network. Its function is to resolve IP addresses of Network Interface Cards (Ethernet ports on the NonStop system) to their specific MAC address. Lower level protocols use the MAC address rather than IP address to communicate with each other.

DNS (Domain Name Service)

The Domain Name Service maps IP addresses to names of devices on the network. Its function is to provide a simplified mechanism for addressing network devices. If the network structure or IP addresses change, applications using the name won't need to be modified. By modifying the particular device's entry in the DNS tables, all applications using the device name will automatically point to the new IP address of the device.

ICMP (Internet Control Message Protocol)

ICMP is a protocol that provides message control and informational messages from remote systems or gateways on an IP network. The program PING, for example, uses ICMP packets to determine if a remote host at a particular IP address is available (or can be "seen") from the local host.

IP (Internet Protocol)

IP is the basis of the World Wide Web and gives the Internet its name. IP is a connectionless protocol at the inter-network or network layer responsible for addressing and routing of data.

The IP Address is the unique address of a device on any given network.

RARP (Reverse Address Resolution Protocol)

RARP acts in a manner similar to ARP but in reverse. That is it resolves a network device's MAC addresses to its corresponding IP address.

SMTP (Simple Mail Transport Protocol)

SMTP is the standard host-to-host mail protocol used over a TCP/IP network and, more widely, across the World Wide Web. It is a simple text based protocol that provides the ability to establish communication between machines as easily as communication between humans, making it possible to control devices via this mechanism. SMTP uses well-known port 25.

The SMTP gateway on NonStop servers is a mechanism used for providing an interface between TRANSFER mail systems (Guardian based mail system) and external network mail systems via TCP/IP.

RISK The SMTP interface to a Network can be vulnerable to attacks such as denial of service.

AP-ADVICE-TCPIP-02 If a NonStop server has an SMTP service configured, external firewalls should be used to restrict access to the IP Address and port (usually port 25) on the NonStop server on which it is running. Firewall configuration should restrict access to the service to authorized devices (IP Addresses).

RPC Protocol

The RPC protocol enables process-to-process communication over an IP network. This enables a client program to invoke a service application running on a remote machine.

In the NonStop environment, the TSM (system console) uses RPC to provide the low-level link communication to the service processors used for rebooting the system.

TCP (Transmission Control Protocol)

TCP is the most commonly known protocol from the host to host (transport) layer providing the "TCP" in TCP/IP. It is a reliable protocol meaning that it provides end-to-end error checking and correction. If a transmission error occurs, the data will be retransmitted.

TCP is a connection based protocol, meaning that it provides a "handshake" mechanism to establish connection before any data is transmitted.

Applications that require confirmation that all packets sent are actually received at the other end use TCP as the transport mechanism.

In the NonStop system, the TCP protocol is a component of the TCPIP process.

UDP (User Datagram Protocol)

UDP is an unreliable connectionless protocol at the transport layer. This means that delivery of data is not guaranteed, so all connection handling and data delivery confirmation is handled by the application layer above. For this reason, there is less overhead associated with UDP than TCP.

UDP is often used by applications where it is easier to just resend packets if required. For example on the NonStop system, Expand-over-IP uses UDP as the transport layer because error checking and delivery confirmation is provided within the Expand protocol.

TCP/IP Subsystem Definitions

Connection States

The connection STATE is the current state of a specific TCP based socket. Some of the more common states are:

LISTEN   When waiting for a connection request to come in to the IP address on the specified port.

ESTAB   When a connection has been established from a remote application running on the machine with the specified remote IP address (Faddr) and the specifed port (Fport), to the local host (Laddr) on the specified port (Lport).

CLOSE-WAIT   When waiting for a terminate request from the local user.

CLOSING   When waiting for a terminate request acknowledgement from the remote site.

Default Gateway

A GATEWAY is a device (usually a router) on the network used by a SUBNET to communicate to other devices on a different network.

The Default Gateway is the IP Address of a device (router) on a network through which a SUBNET will communicate with other devices across the network. Any traffic that is not addressed to a device within the local subnet will be forwarded through the default gateway.

On the HP NonStop server, all subnets are configured with a default gateway as part of their definition.

The path that traffic takes through the network can be overridden by adding a STATIC ROUTE so that the Default Gateway is not used for a specified range of IP Addresses.

Host IP Address

A host can have one or more Internet addresses on each network to which it is attached. The address is known as the IP address. Applications on an IP network establish communication with each other by addressing intended packets of data to the remote application's IP address. For example, the class A address 38.3.9.24 identifies the network address as 38 and the local host address as 3.9.24.

Host Name

A host name is the official name by which the host system is known on an IP network. On an HP NonStop server, the host name can be associated with the system's internet address in the TCP/IP HOSTS configuration file, or it can be mapped to an address through a domain name server (DNS).

Please refer to the *Guardian Gazette* section for information on securing the HOSTS file.

If a host name has been configured, applications may address the host using this DNS name rather than the IP Address. This simplifies management because if the IP Address changes for some reason, only the IP address for the host DNS name needs to be changed. Applications using the name will not require any change.

LISTNER Process

The LISTNER process listens to configured TCP/IP ports, waiting for incoming connection requests from clients. LISTNER starts a configured program when a request is made via TCP/IP to a specified port.

BP-TCPIP-LISTNER-01   The LISTNER process must have a static or continuously available input file, output file and home terminal. $ZHOME or $VHS is recommended.

The TCP/IP process will notify the configured LISTNER process when a request is received on the port for which it is configured. A port is configured in a <portconf> file along with the server process that will be started when a request is received for the port and any optional startup message. When the LISTNER process receives the notification, it starts the target server process. The target server creates a socket using the hostname and source-port information, then accepts the pending connection request on the newly created socket. Every connection to a single port will generate a unique instantiation of the defined server process for use by each individual remote user.

BP-TCPIP-LISTNER-02   LISTNER is also responsible for starting the ECHO, FINGER, and FTP servers when a client request is received for those processes. These processes are included by default in the provided

PORTCONF file and should be removed if they are not specifically required for a particular network.

LISTNER is used only for TCP/IP processing requests. LISTNER is a TCP-oriented program and listens only to TCP ports; not UDP ports.

Once the connection has been made to the target server process, the LISTNER process is no longer involved in the communication and continues to process new incoming requests.

Multiple LISTNER processes may be running on the system. Each LISTNER has a defined <portconf> file.

RISK The LISTNER process requires privileged access to some TCP/IP ports, so it may need to be started by a SUPER Group member. LISTNERs not started by a member of the SUPER Group cannot use port numbers less than 1024.

RISK Programs started by the LISTNER inherit the CAID and PAID of the LISTNER and may, therefore, grant SUPER access privileges.

AP-ADVICE-LISTNER-01   Any program started by a LISTNER should always authenticate users by processing a logon and password sequence.

Note that stopping and restarting the LISTNER process will not affect any currently running sessions, including those running unauthorized services. It will only stop any new connections/sessions being created to ports where listens are posted via that LISTNER process.

AP-ADVICE-LISTNER-02   To terminate an unauthorized session/connection, it is best to terminate the host process that is doing the work for that relevant session. For example, to terminate an unauthorized FTP session, the specific process in question that is running the FTPSERV program should be terminated.

	Discovery Questions	Look here:
TCPIP-POLICY	Does each LISTNER startup script specify the appropriate PORTCONF file?	SCF
TCPIP-POLICY	Are all LISTNER/PORTCONF pairs documented?	SCF

(Continued)

	Discovery Questions	Look here:
TCPIP- POLICY	What LISTNERSs are currently configured on a specified IP Address?	SCF
TCPIP- POLICY	What connections are currently established to the system on a specified TCP/IP process?	SCF
TCPIP- POLICY	Which process name is associated with established sessions or LISTNER for a specific TCP/IP process?	SCF LISTOPENS
TCPIP- POLICY	Which program is being run for a specific process?	status

The LISTNER uses the PORTCONF and SERVICES files.

Logical Interface (LIF)

The Logical Interface (LIF) is the interface by which an application communicates with a physical network device (physical interface).

MAC

A MAC (Media Access Control) is a hard coded, manufacturer-generated serial number that is embedded within each Network Interface Card (or Ethernet Adapter, in the case of HP NonStop Servers). It should be tamper proof. It is the real address of the system on the network and must be unique on any given network. The MAC is made up of a 12 digit hex manufacturer's code and a unique serial number assigned by the manufacturer.

On a NonStop system, the MAC address is associated with a Logical Interface (LIF).

A network can be made more secure by associating the MAC address of a specific Ethernet port with the IP Address. This is performed by adding an ENTRY for the TCP/IP Process directly into the ARP table. This means however that if an Ethernet adapter is replaced, the ENTRY will need to be updated to reflect the new MAC address.

The ARP table for a TCP/IP process exists on the NonStop system as an ENTRY type object associated with the relevant TCP/IP process. To find the contents of the ARP table for a specific TCP/IP process, use the SCF INFO ENTRY command.

An entry to the ARP table (ENTRY) can only be modified by a SUPER Group member.

	Discovery Questions	Look here:
TCPIP-MAC-01	What is the ARP address associated with each TCP/IP process?	SCF
TCPIP-MAC-02	What is the MAC address associated with each Ethernet adapter?	SCF

Physical Interface (PIF)

The Physical Interface (PIF) is the actual hardware (for example, Ethernet adapter) that connects a system to a network.

Port

Ports are used by both TCP and UDP to map data to a specific application running on a given IP address. This is performed by using port numbers as part of the address in the communication sequence. Basically, this is a mechanism used for ensuring that the incoming data ends up with the correct application.

The Port type will be either TCP or UDP depending on which transport layer is being used by the application.

Some common applications are typically associated with specific ports:

Figure 4.2
Lis2t of well known ports.

Port	Application
7	Echo
20,21	FTP
22	SSH
23	Telnet
25	SMTP
53	DNS
69	TFTP
79	Finger
80	HTTP
88	Kerberos
161,162	SNMP

Many of these well-known ports are configured in the SERVICES file. If a LISTNER has been configured to listen on one of these ports for a particular application, it will be listed in the relevant PORTCONF file for that LISTNER.

RISK   If well-known ports are configured for services on your system, a hacker will likely know which services are available on which port. If the hacker can gain access to these ports, he may potentially gain access to the system.

AP-ADVICE-PORT-01   Restrict access to well-known ports by using routers and firewalls to permit access only from authorized users or IP addresses.

AP-ADVICE-PORT-02   Consider using different ports for services running on the system. For example, rather than running Telnet on the well-known port of 23, consider using a different port number.

Remote IP Address

The Remote IP Address is the IP address of the remote system running an application that is in communication with an application on the local system.

To address a remote host, specify either a host internet address or a host name.

ROUTE Objects

A route establishes the first hop that data is to take when transmitted to another IP Address on the network. A default route, pointing to the default GATEWAY of the subnet is added whenever a SUBNET is created. Often an extra route will be added that points to a network device such as a router or hub that contains a more complete routing table for the network.

Socket

Sockets route data between application processes. Each socket is identified by the combination of IP Address and Port. For example, 10.2.21.3:9951, is one end of a communication link between two applications running on an IP network.

SUBNET Objects

On an HP NonStop server, a SUBNET associates an IP Address with a specific Logical Interface (LIF) which in turn points to a specific Ethernet adapter (Physical Interface or PIF). It is possible to have multiple subnets per adapter.

On each adapter a Loop Back subnet named #LOOP1 is automatically added with an IP Address of 127.0.0.1. This is to provide a method of testing the TCP/IP process.

Each SUBNET is associated with a SUBNET MASK depending on the class of the network.

TCP/IP-Related Files

The following files are used by the TCP/IP Subsystem:

    HOSTS
    PORTCONF
    NETWORKS
    SERVICES

Please refer to the *Guardian Gazette* section for more information on securing these files.

The OSS equivalent of the LISTNER is the **inetd**. The OSS equivalents of the configuration files are:

    /etc/hosts
    /etc/networks
    /etc/inetd.conf
    /etc/services

Please refer to the *OSS Gazette* section for more information on the **inetd** Subsystem and the configuration files.

HOSTS File

The HOSTS file maps host names to IP addresses so that systems can be addressed by name for simplicity purposes. By default, the HOSTS file is located in $SYSTEM.ZTCPIP.

The HOSTS file provides the benefit that if IP addresses or network structures change, applications that address the host name need not be changed. Only the HOSTS file needs to be modified to reflect the new IP address for the host.

Please refer to the Gazette section of the previous book for more information on the **inetd** Subsystem.

NETWORKS File

The NETWORKS file contains a list of the networks known to the current host. Each network's name, number and aliases are listed. When a program calls the functions GETNETBYADDR or GETNETBYNAME, the NETWORKS file is used to resolve the Internet network address to a symbolic name.

The NETWORKS file is created by making a copy of the SMPLNETW file which resides in the same $SYSTEM.ZTCPIP directory. The file is provided by HP as a sample. It contains examples of common networks.

Do not make any changes to the sample file since they will be overwritten when a new operating system version is installed. Copy the file and name the copy NETWORKS.

RISK The SMPLNETW file will be overwritten with each operating system upgrade.

AP-ADVICE-NETWORKS-01 Do not change the sample file to customize it to your environment. Make changes in the NETWORKS file created by copying the sample file.

PORTCONF

The PORTCONF file is used to designate the usage of specific ports. The primary PORTCONF file is normally located in the $SYSTEM.ZTCPIP subvolume, but can be located elsewhere as defined to TCP/IP.

Different portconf files can be used for different listener processes. This is good practice if different LISTNER processes have different functions/ requirements. The default <PORTCONF> should never be used for a LISTNER process without evaluating which functions are specifically required for the TCP/IP process in question.

For example, if a particular network connection (TCP/IP Process) requires FTP access as part of its functionality, the LISTNER for that TCP/IP process should use a PORTCONF file that has FTP configured. If however, no FTP access should be available for a particular network connection (TCP/IP process), the FTP entry should be removed from the PORT-CONF file used by the relevant LISTNER process.

RISK FINGER, ECHO and FTP are configured by default in the standard PORTCONF file. These may provide information or access to unauthorized users and should be removed if not specifically required for a network connection (TCP/IP Process).

AP-ADVICE-LISTNER-03   Different PORTCONF files should be used for LISTNERs with different network service requirements.

RISK If no specific location for the PORTCONF file is provided when a LISTNER process is started, the process will load the default PORTCONF in the $SYSTEM.ZTCPIP subvolume, which might not be expected, if alternative locations for the PORTCONF are used.

AP-ADVICE-LISTNER-04   The command to start a LISTNER should explicitly specify the location of the PORTCONF file.

RISK Discerning which LISTNER is using which <PORTCONF> file is not easily done. This cannot be easily monitored for unauthorized changes.

RISK Once the LISTNER has read the <PORTCONF> file, the file is closed. If the <PORTCONF> file is modified, the LISTNER will not accept the changes without stopping and restarting the LISTNER.

AP-ADVICE-LISTNER-05   If multiple PORTCONF files are used, document the LISTNER/PORTCONF pairs.

RISK If two LISTNER processes are started pointing to the same <PORTCONF> using the same TCP/IP process, collisions will occur. Whenever this happens, whichever process is second won't listen at the port. It will issue EMS messages.

If you must have multiple PORTCONF files, they must be carefully created and maintained. Take the following precautions:

AP-ADVICE-PORTCONF-01 The PORTCONF file is so important from a security perspective that many companies choose to track changes to it via a source control program.

AP-ADVICE-PORTCONF-02 Any allowed PORTCONF files should be justified and documented.

AP-ADVICE-PORTCONF-03 Use a batch job to periodically:

Check for the existence of any unexpected PORTCONF files

Report the contents of all PORTCONF files

Remove any unauthorized ports before restarting the relevant LISTNER process.

	Discovery Questions	Look here:
TCP/IP-POLICY	Does each LISTNER startup script specify the appropriate PORTCONF file?	SCF
TCP/IP-POLICY	Are all LISTNER/PORTCONF pairs documented?	SCF
TCP/IP- POLICY	Which ports have LISTNERs specified for a specific TCP/IP process?	SCF STATUS
TCP/IP- POLICY	Which ports have sessions established for a specific TCP/IP process?	SCF STATUS
TCP/IP- POLICY	Which process name is associated with established sessions or LISTNER for a specific TCP/IP process?	SCF LISTOPENS
TCP/IP- POLICY	Which program is being run for a specific process?	status

Preventing Port Collisions

In the OSS environment, the **/usr/ucb/inetd** daemon provides the equivalent function as LISTNER.

RISK   Collisions between the services provided by the LISTNER and the **inetd** daemon can occur if both processes are assigned to the same TCP/IP process using the same port. When this happens, the second process issues an EMS message and stops listening for a specific service.

To prevent this condition, modify one or both of the configuration files (PORTCONF or **/etc/inetd.conf**):

> In the **/etc/inetd.conf** file specify a TCP/IP process (Transport Provider) that doesn't have a LISTNER running on it.

> In the PORTCONF file, take advantage of the fact that LISTNER supports only TCP ports. Comment out the TCP port for the service in the *inetd.conf* file. This will allow the LISTNER process to provide the service (on the TCP port) from the Guardian environment while the **inetd** daemon will provide the service (on the UDP port) from the OSS environment.

SERVICES File

The SERVICES file contains the Internet port level services that are available with NonStop TCP/IP. Applications refer to the file to get the service port numbers and service names. Each entry specifies a service name, the port number through which that service is accessed, and the corresponding protocol, such as TELNET or FTP, which supports that service. Aliases can be used to identify the service. The SERVICES file is maintained by HP, but can be customized for your environment. By default this is located in $SYSTEM.ZTCPIP.

Please refer to the *Gazette* section of the previous book for more information the LISTNER program.

HP NonStop Server Implementation of TCP/IP

There are currently three flavors of TCP/IP implementation on the HP NonStop Server. These are:

> Conventional TCP/IP
> Parallel Library TCP/IP
> IPv6 TCP/IP

Each of these allows for applications on the HP NonStop Server to communicate with applications running on other devices on a TCP/IP network. The mechanism by which this occurs within the system differentiates the different flavors. Each implementation has a completely different set of object programs that it runs and different sets of associated attributes. This means that determining which implementations are running on the system is not difficult. To an external device on the network, however, there is not necessarily any way to differentiate.

More than one flavor of TCP/IP may exist within the same system; however, Parallel Library TCP/IP and IPv6 may not run on the same system.

Different Flavors of HP NonStop TCP/IP

Conventional TCP/IP

Conventional TCP/IP on the NonStop system is based on the Department of Defense model. It uses IP addresses made up of four octets (for example, 10.1.21.3) to route data to other computers or devices on the network.

Conventional TCP/IP consists of a single process running the TCP/IP program, which is the Conventional TCP/IP object program that provides the functionality of the TCP, UDP, IP, ICMP, and ARP protocols. When one application wants to communicate with another application on the network, it must first communicate with the TCP/IP process which then passes the data to the network device.

TCP/IP runs as a NonStop process pair.

Parallel Library TCP/IP

Like conventional TCP/IP, Parallel Library TCP/IP uses standard four-octet IP addresses. Due to its architecture, it provides significant performance improvements over conventional TCP/IP.

In Parallel Library TCP/IP, each CPU has a TCP/IP library that is shared by all applications running in that CPU. This allows for a process to communicate directly with a device rather than having to communicate via a TCP/IP process as in conventional TCP/IP.

RISK Parallel Library TCP/IP provides no ability for Logical Network Partitioning (LNP). This means that if the system has TCP/IP connections to multiple networks, all configured with Parallel TCP/IP, there is no way of restricting which of these network connections has access to which application.

For example, if two completely different applications are running on the system, each with different sets of users connecting in from different networks, via different ethernet adapters, it is possible for either set of users to access either application.

Figure 4.3
Parallel TCP/IP.

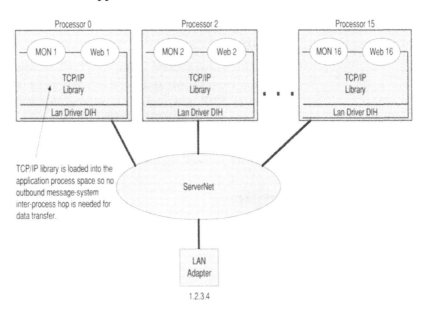

AP-TCPIP-CONFIG-AP-TCPIP-CONFIG-01 Ensure that multiple applications on the same system, that need to be isolated to different sets of users on different networks, are not accessed by Ethernet adapters configured with Parallel Library TCP/IP.

AP-TCPIP-CONFIG-02 Because HP considers Parallel Library TCP/IP HP to be a mature product and is no longer making enhancements, all customers should consider migrating to IPv6 rather than implementing Parallel Library TCP/IP if they are looking for the features provided by this version of TCP/IP.

Parallel Library TCP/IP Components

Parallel Library TCP/IP consists of a group of processes running the following programs:

TCPMAN

TCPMON

TCPSAM

ZTCPSRL

TCPMAN

TCPMAN is the Parallel Library TCP/IP Manager process. It runs as a NonStop process pair and is the management interface to the Parallel Library TCP/IP subsystem. It is responsible for starting the TCPMON processes.

The TCPMAN process is always named $ZZTCP and only one TCPMAN process pair can exist in each system.

TCPMON

TCPMON is the Parallel Library TCP/IP Monitor process. One TCPMON process runs in each CPU.

The names of the TCPMON processes follow the convention $ZZTCP.#ZPTMn where n is the corresponding processor number in hexadecimal.

TCPSAM

TCPSAM is a process pair provided only for backward compatibility with socket-based applications.

ZTCPSRL

ZTCPSRL is the shared runtime library that contains the majority of the TCP/IP stack for Parallel Library TCP/IP, unlike conventional TCP/IP where the stack resides in the TCP/IP process. This runtime library is loaded into an application's process space as soon as it issues a TCP/IP socket request.

NFS (Network File System)

NFS is not supported by Parallel Library TCP/IP.

Please refer to the *OSS Gazette* section on the **inetd** subsystem, for more information.

IPv6

IPv6, also known as IPng (next generation) came about due to the expectancy that at some time not too far away, the world will run out of IP addresses due to the rapid growth of the Internet. The addressing for IPv6 is 128-bit addressing, written generally as eight-hex octets (for example, 10:1:1:10:23:145:7:FF00). This provides 2^{128} unique IP addresses to be used by computers and devices connecting into a network.

The HP NonStop Server implementation of IPv6 incorporates all features of Parallel Library TCP/IP such as performance improvements, single IP and failover IP.

It also provides the ability to run in several modes:

IP4 mode (operates with four-octet addresses only)

Mixed Mode (operates with both four-octet and six-octet addresses)

IP6 mode (six-octet addresses only)

The different operating modes allow for an easier conversion path from conventional TCP/IP to IPv6.

IPv6 also provides the capability of setting up Logical Network Partitioning so that applications can be isolated to specific networks.

RISK   While logical network partitioning is a feature of IPv6, if it is not configured correctly it is possible to inadvertently provide access to an application from all IPv6 networks connected to the system.

AP-TCPIP-CONFIG-03   Use Logical Network Partitioning to ensure that applications are isolated to specific authorized networks.

IPv6 Components

IPv6 consists of a group of processes running the following programs:

TCP6MAN

TCP6MON

TCP6SAM

ZTCP6REL/ZTCP6SRL

TCP6MAN

TCP6MAN is the IPv6 Manager process. It runs as a NonStop process pair and is the management interface to the IPv6 subsystem. It is responsible for starting the TCP6MON processes.

The TCP6MAN process is always named $ZZTCP and only one TCP6MAN process pair can exist in each system.

TCP6MON

TCP6MON is the IPv6 Monitor process. One TCP6MON process runs in each CPU.

The names of the TCP6MON processes follow the convention $ZPTMnn, where nn is the processor number in hexadecimal.

TCP6SAM

TCP6SAM is a process pair provided only for backward compatibility with socket-based applications.

ZTCP6REL/ZTCP6SRL

ZTCPLREL and ZTCP6SRL are the shared runtime libraries that contains the majority of the TCP/IP stack for IPv6. This runtime library is loaded into an application's process space as soon as it issues a TCP/IP socket request.

Common TCP/IP Objects

The TCP/IP subsystem is configured and managed via SCF. Objects common to all HP NonStop implementation flavors of TCP/IP are as follows:

Processes

Subnets

Routes

	Discovery Questions	Look here:
PROCESS-TCPIP-01	Which conventional TCP/IP processes are running on the system (the TCP/IP object)?	Status
PROCESS-TCPIP-01	Is Parallel Library TCP/IP running on the system (the TCPMON process)?	Status
PROCESS-TCPIP-01	Is IPv6 TCP/IP running on the system (the TCP6MON process)?	Status
TCP/IP-NETWORK-02	What subnets (IP Addresses) are configured for a particular TCP/IP process?	SCF
TCP/IP-NETWORK-02	What routes are configured for a particular TCP/IP process?	SCF

TCP/IP Applications

This section describes the applications supported by TCP/IP.

ECHO

ECHO is used to test the connection to a remote system by sending data to the ECHO server on that system. If the connection is successful, the server returns the data transmitted in the sequence that the data was entered.

RISK   ECHO is configured by default in the PORTCONF file as port 7. This entry allows connection to be established to the system by any computer on the network that can reach the system. Potentially it could be used to clog up a network and provide potential for denial of service.

BP-ADVICE-ECHO-01   To eliminate this risk, ECHO should be removed from the TCP/IP PORTCONF file.

Unless it is specifically required by a site it should be removed.

HP NonStop TCP/IP ECHO does not service UDP ports.

The components of ECHO are:

    ECHO
    ECHOSERV

Please refer to the *Gazette* section of the previous book for more information on the ECHO program.

FINGER

FINGER is a program that allows for a connection to be established to the system by any computer on the network that can reach the system. It provides information about users currently logged on to the system and the terminal on which they are logged on. As such, FINGER potentially provides information to external computers about the system that may give hackers information that will help them hack into the system.

FINGER is configured by default in the PORTCONF file. This entry should be removed unless specifically required.

RISK Someone familiar with FINGER could use it from a remote machine to get IP addresses and other connection information about a system.

RISK FINGER could be used to obtain a list of user names from a system without logging on to the system, thus giving an attacker a starting point to try to logon.

AP-ADVICE-FINGER-01 To eliminate this risk, FINGER should be removed from the TCP/IP PORTCONF file.

The components of FINGER are:

FINGER

FINGSERV

Please refer to the *Gazette* section of the previous book for more information on the FINGER program.

PING

The PING (Packet Internet Grouper) program is used to test whether another host is reachable. PING sends an Internet Control Message Protocol (ICMP) echo request message to a host, expecting an ICMP echo reply to be returned. PING measures the round-trip time of the message exchange and monitors any packet loss across network paths.

RISK Although PING is a reporting program only, it poses a potential security risk if a virus or Trojan horse creates a "PING of death" by sending so many PING requests that the NonStop server cannot process them in a timely manner or keep up with other, non-PING requests. An external PING (that is, a PING coming from another device on the network) can also potentially provide information to external devices that a system (device) exists at the particular IP address. On determining that a device exists at that address, a hacker may potentially then start attempting to identify particular vulnerabilities to enable a way into the system.

AP-ADVICE-PING-01   To eliminate these risks, external firewalls should allow ICMP packets from authorized devices on the network only, thus stopping unwanted PINGs from reaching the system.

Please refer to the *Gazette* section of the previous book for more information on the PING program.

TRACER

TRACER is used to display the path taken by IP packets to a network host. It displays the details of the IP route taken by packets to a remote system on the network detailing each "hop" or accessed network device along the way to the final destination.

Please refer to the *Gazette* section of the previous book for more information on the TRACER program.

FTP (File Transfer Protocol)

FTP is widely used for exchanging files between different platforms. For example, Guardian files can be transferred to PC workstations. Bi-directional binary and text transfers are done by copying exact images of a file.

FTP supports transfer of the following types of files:

ASCII

Unstructured

Structured (key-sequenced, relative, and entry-sequenced)

FTP does not support the transfer of SQL files.

RISK   HP's implementation of FTP has no encryption capabilities. Sensitive data, userids, and passwords are transferred between remote nodes in the clear and unprotected, vulnerable to capture with a network sniffer.

3P-FTP-FTP-01   Some third-party products provide encryption for both the command channel (port) and the data transmission channel (port) between the client FTP software and the server FTP software on the NonStop Server.

RISK FTP server has no built-in security; it relies entirely on the security native to the resident operating system. If the system hosting the FTP server is not properly secured, users can explore the system at will, copy any files that they have read access to, and place unauthorized files anywhere on the system. It is possible for FTP users to damage applications and databases and steal business data.

3P-FTP-FTP-02 Some third-party FTP products can prevent users from exploring the system by restricting the use of the LIST command to selected subvolumes.

RISK The HP FTP server does not produce audits of its activity.

Safeguard will audit file accesses by FTP users if configured to do so.

AP-ADVICE-FTP-01 Files on the NonStop Server should be secured to prevent users from copying sensitive information from the system.

3P-FTP-FTP-03 Some third-party FTP products provide comprehensive auditing of FTP activity on the NonStop Server as well as encryption and restriction of the FTP commands available to users.

RISK FTP provides a way to copy sensitive data from an HP NonStop Server to a remote, perhaps less secure, system.

AP-ADVICE-FTP-02 FTP activity must be strictly controlled.

RISK FTP is configured by default in the PORTCONF file as port 21. This entry allows connection to be established to the system by any computer on the network that can reach the system.

AP-ADVICE-FTP-03 FTP should be removed from the TCP/IP PORTCONF file for subnets that do not expressly require the FTP service or assigned to another port.

AP-ADVICE-FTP-04 If FTP is required, assign it to different port.

Please refer to the *Gazette* section of the previous book for more information on securing the following FTP components:

FTP
FTPEXTH
FTPSERV
FTPCSTM (FTP Custom Files)

FTP

FTP is the HP NonStop Server FTP client. It is used to interactively transfer or manage files on a remote system. The remote system need not be another NonStop Server.

FTPSERV

FTP servers respond to file transfer requests from the client FTP. The FTPSERV server is initiated from the LISTNER on the FTP port. The typical port for FTP is 21.

FTP CUSTOM Files

FTP reads the FTPCSTM file before it issues its first prompt. This allows the creation of a customized FTP environment before entering any commands.

Please refer to the Gazette section of the previous book, for more information on securing the *CSTM customization files.

FTP Systems

Both local and remote systems can place restrictions on which files can be transferred and where the files can be placed.

FTP Userids

BP-FTP-USERIDS-01   NonStop Server users should login to FTP with their own userids to ensure that they only have access to the appropriate files.

BP-FTP-USERIDS-02   NonStop Server users who are restricted from FTP access should be added to the FTPUSERS file in $SYSTEM.ZTCPIP.

Securing the Anonymous FTP Userid and Environment

Anonymous FTP is primarily intended for and supported in the OSS environment, but can be used in the Guardian environment.

The Anonymous FTP userid by convention is named NULL.FTP.

RISK Only implement Anonymous FTP if it is absolutely necessary. Anonymous FTP opens the system for general access. To mitigate the risks, implement the following precautions:

BP-FTP-USERIDS-03 Create an alias to the NULL.FTP userid, called "anonymous" or "ftp". This alias will be used to log into the FTP subsystem.

BP-FTP-USERIDS-04 Expire NULL.FTP's password. No password is necessary within the FTP subsystem.

BP-FTP-USERIDS-05 Freeze NULL.FTP to prevent users from logging onto the Anonymous userid outside of the FTP subsystem.

RISK If Safeguard is down for any reason, the frozen userids (though still frozen) behave as if they are thawed.

Assign NULL.FTP and any of its aliases an appropriate "home" where any users logging into FTP as anonymous will begin their session:

> In the OSS environment, assign an INITIAL DIRECTORY, such as / guest/FTP.
>
> In a Guardian environment, assign a default subvolume, for example FTPGUEST.

BP-ADVICE-FTP-02 In the OSS environment, the NULL.FTP user should not own any directories, especially the initial root directory. Directory owners can alter the security of the directory. Directories should be owned by SUPER.SUPER or another appropriate userid.

RISK Any references (symbolic links) to directories or files that are outside of the anonymous FTP subtree should be avoided.

A *symbolic link* is a file that refers to another file. If a system operates on symbolic links, a user can be directed to the file that the symbolic link points to. When the user displays a file that has a symbolic link, the user can see the original file as well as its link, which, depending on the contents of the file, could pose a security risk.

RISK Any absolute symbolic links that start in root should be avoided within a subtree. Absolute symbolic links will be understood by the system as referring to the Initial-Directory, rather than to the root directory of the OSS fileset.

BP-FTP-USERIDS-06 Do not grant NULL.FTP write access to any files.

RISK Files that NULL.FTP or its alias must drop onto the system should be limited to a single "WRITE only" location. NULL.FTP should not be granted READ access to the "WRITE only" location. This requires a lot of user (administrator's) intervention.

3P-FTP-ADVICE-01 Third-party FTP products that restrict access by user and FTP command can control where FTP users drop files.

The following three steps provide a safe area that the Anonymous FTP users can't get out of, while trusted users can easily get at the anonymous mount point's files and drag them wherever they need to without lots of security headaches. The key is to contain anonymous users strictly to this OSS mount point.

AP-FTP-USERIDS-07 Set up an OSS partition on one isolated disk pair and make it a separate mount point.

AP-FTP-USERIDS-08 Secure the parent directory of this mount point so that anonymous FTP users can't navigate out of this directory tree.

AP-FTP-USERIDS-09 If this directory tree is intended to be NFS-mountable from other anonymous nodes, use SCF to set up an NFS alias for guests.

AP-FTP-USERIDS-10 Make sure the NULL.FTP user account is configured the same as the anonymous alias's account, so that neither can get at anything except the anonymous OSS file space. The Safeguard initial directory and Guardian default subvolume should both point to this file space.

With CMON

Some CMONs can restrict FTP logon access by PORT and by IP address to limit the IP addresses from which authorized users can logon to a system and access the FTP subsystem.

Please refer to the *Gazette* section of the previous book for more information on the CMON program.

BP-PROCESS-CMON-01   Using a third party CMON product or a modified CMON, restrict the IP addresses that can use the FTP ports.

Without Safeguard

To try to minimize the risks of FTP, grant READ access only those files that FTP users are allowed to GET. This can be difficult because of the large number of files on a system. On a more restricted system, secure the FTP programs or eliminate FTP access through TCP/IP to mitigate the risks.

RISK   In the Guardian environment, there is no way to restrict where FTP users PUT files.

RISK   The HP FTP server does not produce audits of its activity.

With Safeguard

Safeguard provides some support for securing FTP. Use Safeguard VOLUME and SUBVOLUME rules to restrict where FTP users PUT files. To try to minimize the risks of FTP, grant READ access only to those files that FTP users are allowed to GET. This can be difficult because of the large number of files on a system. On a more restricted system, secure the FTP program, or eliminate FTP access through TCP/IP to mitigate the risks.

Safeguard will audit file accesses by FTP users if configured to do so.

AP-SAFE-FTP-01   Add Safeguard VOLUME and SUBVOLUME rules to restrict where FTP users PUT files.

AP-SAFE-FTP-02   Add a Safeguard Protection Record to grant appropriate access to the FTP program.

With Third-party Products

3P-FTP-USERIDS-01   Third-party FTP products provide granular access to FTP commands and can provide the following security functions:

Authenticate and authorize users as they logon to the FTP subsystem.

Limit the IP addresses from which authorized users can logon to the FTP subsystem

Limit what FTP users can explore by restricting the use of the FTP DIR and LIST commands

Limit what files FTP users can retrieve from the system by restricting the use of the FTP GET command

Limit where FTP users write files by restricting the use of the FTP PUT command

Provide auditing of FTP activity

The NonStop Server FTP server provides no control over what users can see once logged in.

RISK   They can view the files in any subvolume or directory with the LIST or DIR command.

RISK   They can GET (copy) any file that isn't secured against READ access.

RISK   HP's implementation of FTP has no encryption capabilities. Sensitive data, userids, and passwords are transferred between remote nodes, in the clear and unprotected; they are vulnerable to capture with a network sniffer.

3P-FTP-FTP-01   Some third-party products provide encryption for both the command channel (port) and the data transmission channel (port) between the client FTP software and the server FTP software on the NonStop Server.

NFS and FTP

NFS files have a format compatible with DOS or UNIX systems. They are are "special case files". NFS security differs from the security of standard files. Please refer to part 5, *File Sharing Protocols*, for more information about NFS.

RISK   FTP does not have a mechanism to distinquish NFS mounted files from regular files.

AP-ADVICE-FTP-06   Take extreme caution securing NFS files if they will be accessed by the anonymous FTP userid.

AP-ADVICE-FTP-07   An anonymous user should never be allowed to own NFS files, since it will give the user extended access privileges.

TFTP (Trivial File Transfer Protocol)

The Trivial File Transfer Protocol (TFTP) is an Internet-standard protocol for file transfer that uses minimal capability and minimal overhead. TFTP depends only on the unreliable, connectionless datagram delivery service (UDP), so it can be used on machines like diskless workstations that keep such software in ROM and use it to bootstrap themselves.

Remote TFTP clients are used to transfer public files to and from an HP Nonstop Server host system's TFTP server (TFTPSRV).

The HP TFTP client is used to transfer public files to and from a remote system.

Files can be transferred to or from any system on a network that has a TFTP server that accepts requests from the TFTP client.

RISK   TFTP does not provide any mechanism for users to logon to the remote system with a userid and password and verify which files they can access. The files remote users are allowed to retrieve from a remote system are typically secured for public access; that is, anyone on the network can read the files. The TFTP server on the remote system sets the restrictions on which files users can retrieve, as well as restrictions on storing files.

Users can GET (retrieve) only files that grant *all users* remote READ access. That is, the files must be secured "Nxxx". TFTP ignores the rest of the security string.

Users can only PUT (drop) files where they have remote WRITE access.

To overwrite a file, the existing file security must grant *all users* remote WRITE access. That is, the files must be secured "xNxx". TFTP ignores the rest of the security string.

Remote users can only create new files in a subvolume specified when the TFTP server was started. If no subvolumes were specified, users can create new files only in $DATA.PUBLIC and only if $DATA.PUBLIC is present on the system.

RISK   TFTP assigns new files dropped onto the system a security string of "NUNU", which allows network access.

AP-ADVICE-TFTP-01   Use Safeguard SUBVOLUME Protection Records to control access to files that can be transferred with TFTP and where remote files can be placed via TFTP.

TFTP Components

Starting with G06.12, the TFTP server consists of two distinct process types that use the following programs:

TFTP
TFTPSRV
TFTPCHLD

TFTP

TFTP is the HP NonStop Server TFTP client. It is used to interactively transfer or manage files on a remote system. The remote system need not be another NonStop Server.

TFTPSRV

The TFTPSRV process validates requests and starts the TFTPCHLD processes. For every 16 TFTP requests, TFTPSRV generates a new TFTPCHLD process.

TFTPCHLD

The TFTPCHLD processes handle data transfers. The individual TFTPCHLD processes terminate when they've handled 16 requests and no further request is pending or when they have been idle for 10 minutes.

TELNET/Telserv

The TELNET protocol is a general, bidirectional, eight-bit byte-oriented protocol in the TCP/IP protocol suite that provides a standard method of interfacing terminal devices and terminal-oriented processes to each other. A TELNET connection is a TCP connection that contains TELNET control information.

On HP Nonstop Servers, the TELNET application allows users to emulate a virtual terminal connected to a remote host. Users can connect to any remote host on the network that has a TELNET server.

The TELNET subsystem is a server and uses the sockets library routines of the TCP/IP subsystem for TCP access to accommodate the incoming TELNET applications.

TELNET does not use the LISTNER process. It requires a TELSERV process to be running against the port at the relevant IP address. It is typically configured on well known port 23.

	Discovery Questions	Look here:
TELNET-NETWORK-01	Is TELSERV configured on the node?	SCF
TELNET-NETWORK-02	Is TELNET run on the system to support terminals?	SCF
PROCESS-TELSERV-01	Is the TELSERV object file running on the system?	Status

SNMP (Simple Network Management Protocol)

SNMP is the protocol used to monitor and control devices on a network. Each device contains certain information about its configuration and its status. The information is stored in the device's Management Information Database (MIB), which describes the collection of objects on the device that can be managed.

The application used to manage network resources is known as a MANAGER. A MANAGER monitors and controls resources on the network by sending messages to applications known as AGENTS, which have access to resources manageable using SNMP.

Messages exchanged between managers and agents are called packets. Packets identify specific resources described in the MIB.

SNMP agents run on the device and are responsible for its SNMP management.

SNMP managers that run as Tandem NonStop Kernel processes can run in either the Guardian or OSS environments. Managers running in either environment can communicate with NonStop SNMP entities running in the other environment. Currently, the NonStop agent and subagents run in the Guardian environment, but are accessible using either the IPC or the TCP/IP protocol by managers that run in the OSS environment.

Managers can interact with AGENTS running on any network device, using any transport protocol by which the agents can be addressed.

RISK There is only very rudimentary SNMP support on the HP Non-Stop Server. It provides information on a variety of components, but does not allow control. It still could however provide hackers with useful information about the system or devices on the system.

SNMP Components

SNMP components are installed in two subvolumes. The subvolumes may be placed on any appropriate disk:

The ZSNMPMGR subvolumes contains the MIB compiler and Manager Services library files.

The ZSNMPMEX subvolume contains sample files.

The components of SNMP are:

SNMPAGT

SNMP TRAP

SNMP TRAPDEST
SNMP PROFILE

SNMPAGT

SNMPAGT is the object file for the HP NonStop Server SNMP Agent. It is used to interactively transfer or manage files on a remote system. The remote system need not be another NonStop Server.

	Discovery Questions	Look here:
SNMP-NETWORK-01	Is SNMP configured for communications on this node?	SCF
SNMP-NETWORK-02	Are SNMP ports blocked from the internet and external networks?	SCF
SNMP-NETWORK-03	Are devices configured with READ/WRITE security correctly set?	SCF

SNMP TRAP

SNMP Traps are notification events sent by a network device. The Traps are defined usually by the manufacturer of the device and are often associated with a change of status of a device (for example, device goes down).

The SNMP agent can be configured to send traps to one or more specific SNMP managers or to suppress traps altogether.

SNMP TRAPDEST

A SNMP TRAPDEST is a location on the network where SNMP Traps are to be sent. Often this will be to a central network monitoring host running an application, such as HP OpenView.

	Discovery Question	Look here:
SNMP-NETWORK-04	Are SNMP Traps being sent where they are supposed to?	SCF

SNMP PROFILE

The SNMP PROFILE is an entry in the authentication table for a particular SNMP Agent. It sets the name of the community, the IP address of a SNMP manager station, and the authorized access (READONLY or READWRITE). When a SNMP request is received by the SNMP Agent, the components of the request are matched with a PROFILE defininition to decide if access is to be provided. If there is no PROFILE that matches, the SNMP request is rejected.

	Discovery Questions	Look here:
SNMP-NETWORK-05	Is the correct access configured for a PROFILE?	SCF
SNMP-NETWORK-06	What is the COMMUNITY name configured?	SCF

TSM SNMP Agent

The process $ZTSMS is an SNMP agent process that was formerly used when $ZTSM communicated with the TSM Service Application using SNMP. As in version 7.0 of the TSM, $ZTSM uses HTTP to talk to its client, so the $ZTSMS process is no longer used. As such, if the TSM is running version 7.0 or later, this process can be safely stopped and deleted from the customer configuration. All of the associated TRAPDEST, PRO-FILE, and endpoint objects are no longer required for the TSM console.

Firewalls and Routers

While measures need to be taken to ensure that all TCP/IP components on a system are adequately secured, unauthorized access to the system should be controlled by network firewalls and routers as well. These devices stop external network traffic from reaching the NonStop Server unless specifically allowed.

As well as denying unauthorized access to the system, many firewalls or routers have intrusion detection capabilities that can also help prevent denial, of service attacks, for example, by blocking attacks such as smurfing (a continuous stream of PINGS sent to the broadcast IP address of a device).

VPN

A VPN is a Virtual Private Network. This is a common mechanism used to provide remote access for a user to a corporate system over the Internet. It involves establishing an encrypted tunnel between the client and a device on the corporate network that authenticates the user and encrypts all traffic that flows in the session between the client and the network. This ensures that the connection is secure and session data cannot be intercepted and used by any third party, even though access is from a public network such as the Internet.

AP-ADVICE-NETWORK-13   If remote users need to connect into the system, they should only do so via an encrypted session. A VPN provides a sound mechanism for providing authorized users access to the system from an Internet connection.

SSH Subsystem

SSH (Secure SHell) is a protocol for encrypted remote logins, file copying and TCP connection tunneling (port forwarding).

SSH is a client server system. **/usr/local/bin/ssh** is the HP client. It is used by local users to connect to remote systems. **/usr/local/bin/sshd** is the local server process. It responds to connection requests from remote systems.

There are two versions of SSH:

Version 1 (SSH1) relies on RSA public key encryption algorithm for authentication and initial key exchange.

Version 2 (SSH2) allows both RSA and DSA (Digital Signature Algorithm) public key encryption algorithms for authentication and initial key exchange.

AP-ADVICE-SSH-01   Version 2 is recommended because of its extended functionality and because it includes fixes for flaws in Version 1.

Tunneling

SSH can be used in two ways: to LOGON directly to a remote host or to tunnel to a remote host.

Tunneling is a network protocol that encapsulates one protocol or session inside another. For example, protocol A is encapsulated within protocol B, so that A treats B as though it were a data link layer. Tunneling may be used to transport a network protocol through a network that would not otherwise support it. Tunneling may also be used to provide various types of VPN functionality such as private addressing.

On the HP NonStop Server, if the full functionality of **vi** is desired, tunneling is required.

SSH Authentication Options

In conventional password authentication, a user proves he is who he claims is by telling the server what he thinks the password is. If the server has been hacked or *spoofed*, an attacker can learn that password.

SSH seeks to eliminate this risk. All SSH sessions are encrypted, and three authentication options are provided. Listed from least secure to most secure, they are:

> Host-based
>
> Password
>
> Public/private keypairs

The mode of authentication required on your system depends on settings configured in:

The SSH client's configuration file, **/usr/local/bin/ssh_config**, which determines what information your local client will present to a remote SSH server

The SSH server's configuration file, **/usr/local/bin/sshd_config**, which determines what it will demand from a remote SSH client attempting to connect to your system

Host-based Authentication

Host-based authentication is noninteractive. Rather than authenticating the user requesting SSH access, it authenticates the requesting host.

If, on the target machine, a) the SSH user has the same userid as he has on the local system, and b) the local system is listed in either the **/etc/hosts.equiv** or the userid's personal **shosts.equiv** file, the target machine will accept the user as authenticated.

Disadvantages:

The individual user is not authenticated.

The use of **hosts.equiv** or **shosts.equiv** files and the **rsh** protocol in general is inherently insecure. Please refer to the *OSS Gazette* sections on **rsh/rshd** and the **hosts.equiv** file for more information.

Any noninteractive login is inherently insecure. Whenever authentication without user challenge is permitted, some level of risk must be assumed.

Host-based Authentication authentication is implemented by setting the **ssh.conf HostbasedAuthentication** parameter to YES.

BP-SSH-SSHCONF-06   Set the **HostbasedAuthemtication** value to NO in the **ssh.conf** file.

Host-based Authentication with RSA Authentication

This is a noninteractive form of authentication that uses the public host key of the client (requesting) machine to authenticate a user to the remote SSH server.

If on the target machine, a) the SSH user has the same userid as he has on his local (requesting) system and b) the local system is listed in either the **/etc/hosts.equiv** or the userid's personal **shosts.equiv** file and can decrypt information that is encrypted with that public key, the target machine will accept the user as authenticated

Advantages:

The user's local host is authenticated.

Disadvantages:

The individual user is not authenticated.

The use of **hosts.equiv** or **shosts.equiv** files and the **rsh** protocol in general is inherently insecure.

Any noninteractive login is inherently insecure. Whenever authentication without user challenge is permitted, some level of risk must be assumed.

Host-based Authentication authentication is implemented by setting the **ssh.conf** file **RhostsRSAAuthentication** parameters to YES.

BP-SSH-SSHCONF-14   Set the **RhostsRSAAuthemtication** value to NO in the **ssh.conf** file.

Public Key/Private Key Authentication

Public key authentication is a means of identifying an individual user to a remote SSH server without sending the password across the network.

The user generates a *key pair*, consisting of a public key (which everybody is allowed to know) and a private key (which he keeps secret and does not share with anyone). The private key is used to generate *signatures*. A signature created using a private key cannot be forged by anyone who does not have that key; however, anybody who has the user's public key can verify that a particular signature is genuine.

The user generates a key pair on his own computer, and copies the public key to the server. Then, when the server asks him to prove who he is, a signature is generated using his private key. The server can verify that signature (since it has his public key) and allow him to log in. If the server is hacked or spoofed, the attacker does not gain the private key or password; he only gains one signature. And signatures cannot be reused, so they are useless to him.

RISK   The stored private key must be protected because anybody who gains access to *it* will be able to generate signatures as if they were the user and they would be able to log into the remote server under his account.

BP-SSH-KEYS-01   Private keys should *encrypted* when they are stored, using a passpharse of the user's choice.

In order to generate a signature, the key must be decrypted, so the user must type his passphrase so the key can be read. This can make public-key authentication less convenient than password authentication: every time the user logs in to the server, instead of typing a short password, he has to type a longer passphrase. One solution to this is to use an *authentication agent;* a separate program that holds decrypted private keys and generates signatures on request. The NonStop Server's authentication agent is called **ssh-agent**. When a user begins an SSH session, he types his passphrase once. The agent is started and loads the private key into memory. For the rest of his session, the agent automatically generates signatures without the user having to do anything. When the session closes, the agent shuts down, without ever having stored the decrypted private key on disk.

BP-SSH-KEYS-01   Use an **ssh-agent** so that users do not continually need to re-enter their passphrase and so that decrypted private keys are never stored on disk.

The HP NonStop Server supports both RSA and DSA public key cryptography. In addition, users can be authenticated using a system-defined challenge/response protocol like Kerberos or S/Key.

Advantages:

> The individual user is authenticated.
> The user's local host is authenticated.
> The remote host is validated.
> The password is encrypted and is authenticated locally; it never crosses the network.
> The password is never saved to disk.

Disadvantages:

The Safeguard global value PASSWORD-REQUIRED must be OFF

3P-AUTHSEC-SSH-01   A third-party product that allows the PASS-WORD-REQUIRED value to be set on a user-by-user basis and/or on a program-by-program basis should be used. Thus a rule could exempt only the SSH server (**sshd**) from being required to enter a password when logging down to start the requested SSH session as the requesting user's ID.

Public/private key authentication, especially when used with an agent, is a good compromise between security and convenience.

Public/private key authentication is implemented by settings in the **ssh.conf** file **PubkeyAuthentication** parameters to YES.

BP-SSH-SSHCONF-10   Set the **PubkeyAuthemtication** value to YES in the **ssh.conf** file.

Summary of the Authentication Requirements of the 3 SSH Options		
Host-based	**Host-based with Password**	**Public Key/Private Key**
The SSH user has the same userid on both the local system and the target system.	The SSH user has the same userid on both the local system and the target system.	
The user's local system is listed in the target system's/ etc/hosts.equiv or the $HOME.shosts.equiv file.	The user's local system is listed in the target system's /etc/hosts.equiv or the $HOME.shosts.equiv file.	
	The local client presents a key contained in the target system's file and can decrypt information that is encrypted with that public key.	The local client presents a key contained in the target system's **authorized_keys** file and can decrypt information that is encrypted with that public key.
		The user must enter his personal passphrase /password.

Figure 4.4
Summary of SSH authentication options.

SSH Subsystem Components

The SSH subsystem consists of the following components:

SSH Client Program (**ssh**)
SSH Server Program (**sshd**)
SSH configuration files
SSH libraries
prngd
Key generation programs
Private key files
Public key files
SSH-related programs

ssh

The object file for the SSH client is **/usr/local/bin/ssh**. The client is used to logon to a remote machine and to execute commands on a remote machine. It is intended as a more secure replacement for **/bin/rlogin** and **/bin/rsh** by providing encrypted communications between two hosts over an insecure network without specifying each other as trusted hosts.

BP-SSH-SSH-01   **/usr/local/bin/ssh** should not be **setuid** to SUPER. SUPER.

The SSH client connects and logs into the specified host. The user must prove his/her identity to the remote machine using one of several methods depending on the protocol version used and the configuration of the remote host's SSH server:

SHH clients can prove their identity using public key cryptography if the client presents a key contained in the **authorized_keys** file and can decrypt information that is encrypted with that public key.
SHH clients can provide a valid password for an account on the remote machine.

Clients on a host that is listed in the remote user's **known_hosts** file and in either the **$HOME/.rhosts** or **$HOME/.shosts** file can also provide a user name.

The hosts can be authenticated solely on the basis of DNS, which is the equivalent of **rsh**, **rcp**, and **rlogin** and, therefore, is not secure.

RISK   The trusted host mechanism relies on the security of any trusted host; anyone with unauthorized access to a trusted host could misuse that trust to logon to a trusting system. If that system is, in turn, a trusted host for other systems, those systems are now vulnerable as well.

A host can be authenticated using its SSH host key if the public key is stored in the **known_hosts** file on the remote server's computer.

SSH's public key authentication is the preferred authentication method. SSH authentication modes are controlled via parameters in the **sshd_ config** file.

BP-OSS-INETD-07   Do not rely on the trusted host mechanism. Do not use **rsh/rshd**; use SSH public key methodology instead.

AP-ADVICE-SSHCONF-06   The   HostbasedAuthentication   value should be NO.

AP-ADVICE-SSHCONF-10   The PubkeyAuthentication value should be YES.

sshd

The object file for the SSH server (daemon) is **/usr/local/sbin/sshd**. The server listens for connections from remote clients. For each connection made, the server forks a new process. These forked processes handle key exchange, encryption, authentication, command execution, and data exchange.

When an SSH client connects to the server, the server provides its public key, which is then added to the remote server's **$HOME/.ssh/ known_hosts** file. This key serves two purposes:

First, the client uses this key to encrypt information that is sent back to the remote server during the authentication phase.

Second, the remote client, use this key to verify that it is communicating with the same server it connected to before.

If SSH is used on the system, the server should be started by SUPER.SUPER and should always be running, waiting for incoming connections.

The SSH server runs as SUPER.SUPER. When a remote client connects, it provides the user name of the account that it wishes to use. It then provides suitable authentication. If the server is satisfied by the client's credentials, it changes its UID to the user's UID, starts a copy of the user's shell, and logs the user in.

SSH Configuration Files

The SSH client is configured by settings in the **/usr/local/bin/ssh_config** file or the individual **$HOME/.ssh/config** files. The client configuration determines how it will respond to requests for authentication from remote SSH servers that it contacts.

The SSH server configured by settings in the **/usr/local/bin/sshd_config** file. The server configuration determines the security on your system because it controls how the server will respond to connection requests from remote SSH clients.

ssh_config (Client) Configuration File

Parameters established in this file determine how your local SSH client will interact with the remote SSH servers that it contacts. The values determine, among other things, the method of authentication that will be used when connecting to each remote host.

The SSH client can be set up to create a unique SSH environment for each remote host or use the same parameters for all remote hosts.

The **/usr/local/bin/ssh_config** file applies to all local users and will be read whenever any user invokes **/bin/ssh**.

BP-SSH-SSHCONF-01 Because of the security ramifications of the SSH configuration files, there should be a single (global) copy of the **ssh_config** file on a system. This ensures that important security-related changes are made to the correct file and cannot be overridden.

AP-ADVICE-SSHCONF-01   The **/usr/local/bin/ssh_config** file is so important from a security perspective that many companies choose to track changes to it via a source control program.

When a user initiates an SSH session, he supplies the remote host name on the command line. The client then obtains the host configuration data from the **/usr/local/bin/ssh_config** file. It searches the file, from the top, for rules specific to the specified host. If there are no rules for that host, the general rules will be applied.

AP-ADVICE-SSHCONF-02   Because the first obtained value for each configuration parameter is used, declarations for specific hosts should be at the top of the file with general defaults at the end.

ssh_config Keywords with Security Implications

The parameters in the SSH client configuration file of importance to security are:

BatchMode	ChallengeResponseAuthentication
EnableSSHKeysign	GlobalKnownHostsFile
HostbasedAuthentication	IdentityFile
KeepAlive	NoHostAuthenticationForLocalHost
PubkeyAuthentication	StrictHostKeyChecking
UsePrivilegedPort	UserKnownHostsFile
RhostsRSAAuthentication	RSAauthentication

Keyword	Description	Default	Recommended
BatchMode	Determines whether or not passphrase/password querying will be disabled.	No	No

Disabling **BatchMode** is useful in scripts and other batch jobs where no user is present to supply the password.

BP-SSH-SSHCONF-02   The **BatchMode** value should be NO unless you must run scripts on a remote host.

Keyword	Description	Default	Recommended
Challenge Response Authentication	Determines whether or not users can be authenticated using a system-defined challenge/response protocol like Kerberos or S/Key.	Yes	Yes

The **ChallengeResponseAuthentication** feature requires operating system support.

BP-SSH-SSHCONF-03   If you have Kerberos, S/Key, or a similar system in place, the **ChallengeResponseAuthentication** value should be YES.

Keyword	Description	Default	Recommended
EnableSSH Keysign	Determines whether or not the helper program **ssh-keysign** can be used when doing host-based authentication.	No	No

BP-SSH-SSHCONF-04   The **EnableSSHKeysign** value should be NO unless the helper process is necessary on your system.

Keyword	Description	Default	Recommended
GlobalKnown-HostsFile	Indicates the location of a global host key database, if one is used.	**/user/local /bin/ ssh_known_hosts**	Policy

If you choose to maintain only a global **known_hosts** file and disable personal **known_hosts** files, the management of the hosts that users are allowed to connect to will be simplified.

BP-SSH-SSHCONF-05   The **GlobalKnownHostsFile** value should be determined by corporate policy.

Keyword	Description	Default	Recommended
HostbasedAuth-entication	Determines if the client should try **rhosts**-based authentication with public key authentication.	No	No

HostbasedAuthentication applies only to SSH2.

BP-SSH-SSHCONF-06 The **HostbasedAuthentication** value should be NO.

Keyword	Description	Default	Recommended
IdentityFile	Specifies the location of the file where users' RSA or DSA authentication identities are stored.	**$HOME/.ssh/id_rsa** and **$HOME/.ssh/id_dsa** files	Policy

It is possible to have multiple identity files. If multiple files exist, the client will try all of them in sequence during authentication.

BP-SSH-SSHCONF-07   Only the default **identity** files should be used.

Keyword	Description	Default	Recommended
KeepAlive	Determines whether or not the SSH client should send TCP "keep alive" messages to the remote host's SSH server.	Yes	Policy

If the client sends "keep alive" messages, it will notice when the connection goes away. This is important when running remote scripts; however, if a connection goes away temporarily, the session will die, which may be annoying to users.

RISK   TCP "I'm alive" messages are spoofable.

BP-SSH-SSHCONF-08 The **KeepAlive** value value should be determined by corporate policy.

Keyword	Description	Default	Recommended
NoHost AuthenticationForLocalHost	Determines whether or not the local host will check the user's home directory on a different host.	No	No

NoHostAuthenticationForLocalHost applies only to SSH2.

RISK If this value is set to YES, the local host's host key will not be checked, so authentication is disabled on the local host.

BP-SSH-SSHCONF-09 The **NoHostAuthenticationForLocalHost** value should be NO.

Keyword	Description	Default	Recommended
PubkeyAuthentication	Determines whether or not users can be authenticated using a personal RSA or DSA public key.	Yes	Yes

PubkeyAuthentication applies only to SSH2.

BP-SSH-SSHCONF-10 The PubkeyAuthentication value should be YES.

Keyword	Description	Default	Recommended
StrictHostKeyChecking	Determines whether or not users will be prompted when a host's host key doesn't match the existing host key in the **known_hosts** file.	Yes	Yes

BP-SSH-SSHCONF-11 The **StrictHostKeyChecking** value should be YES. To prevent Trojan Horse attacks, host keys should not be updated automatically.

Keyword	Description	Default	Recommended
UsePrivilegedPort	Determines whether or not the SSH client should use a privileged port for outgoing connections.	No	No

If **UsePrivilegedPort** is set to YES, **/bin/ssh** must be running (setuid) as SUPER.SUPER.

BP-SSH-SSH-01 **/usr/local/bin/ssh** should not be **setuid** to SUPER.SUPER.

BP-SSH-SSHCONF-12 The **UsePrivilegedPort** value should be NO.

Keyword	Description	Default	Recommended
UserKnown-HostsFile	Specifies an alternate file to use for the user host key database.	**$HOME/.ssh/ known_hosts**	Policy

If you choose to maintain only a global **known_hosts** file and disable personal ($HOME) **known_hosts** files, the management of the hosts that users are allowed to connect to will be simplified.

BP-SSH-SSHCONF-13 The **UserKnownHostsFile** value should be determined by corporate policy.

Keyword	Description	Default	Recommended
RhostsRSA-Authentication	Determines whether or not the trusted host mechanism for hosts in the **rhosts** file with keys in the **/usr/local/bin/ssh_known_hosts** is allowed for remote authentications.	No	No

RhostsRSAAuthentication applies only to SSH1.

The **RhostsRSAAuthentication** and **RSAAuthentication** keywords apply only to SSH1.

BP-SSH-SSH-01 **/usr/local/bin/ssh** should not be **setuid** to SUPER. SUPER.

BP-SSH-SSHCONF-14 The **RhostsRSAAuthentication** value should be NO.

Keyword	Description	Default	Recommended
RSA Authentication	Determines whether or not users can be authenticated using a personal RSA public key.	Yes	No

RSAAuthentication applies only to SSH1.

BP-SSH-SSH-01   **/usr/local/bin/ssh** should not be **setuid** to SUPER. SUPER.

BP-SSH-SSHCONF-15   The **RSAAuthentication** value should be NO.

	Discovery Questions	Look here:
SSH-SSHCONF-02	Is the **BatchMode** keyword set to NO?	cat
SSH-SSHCONF-03	Is the **ChallengeResponseAuthentication** keyword set to YES?	cat
SSH-SSHCONF-04	Is the **EnableSSHKeysign** keyword set to NO?	cat
SSH-SSHCONF-05	Is the **GlobalKnownHostsFile** keyword set according to the Corporate Security Policy?	cat
SSH-SSHCONF-06	Is the **HostbasedAuthentication** keyword set to NO?	cat
SSH-SSHCONF-07	Is the **IdentityFile** keyword set according to the Corporate Security Policy?	cat
SSH-SSHCONF-08	Is the **KeepAlive** keyword set according to the Corporate Security Policy?	cat
SSH-SSHCONF-09	Is the **NoHostAuthenticationForLocalHost** keyword set to NO?	cat
SSH-SSHCONF-10	Is the **PubkeyAuthentication** keyword set to YES?	cat
SSH-SSHCONF-11	Is the **StrictHostKeyChecking** keyword set to YES?	cat
SSH-SSHCONF-12	Is the **UserPrivilegedPort** keyword set to NO?	cat
SSH-SSHCONF-13	Is the **UserKnownHostsFile** keyword set to NO?	cat

(Continued)

Discovery Questions	Look here:
SSH-SSHCONF-14 Is the **RhostsRSAAuthentication** keyword set to NO?	cat
SSH-SSHCONF-15 Is the **RSAAuthentication** keyword set to NO?	cat

Personal SSH Configuration Files

When a user initiates an SSH session, he supplies the remote host name on the command line. The client then obtains the host configuration data from the following sources in the following order:

1. Command-line options
2. Individual user's configuration files
3. System-wide configuration file

If users have personal **$HOME/.ssh/config** files, their configuration values will take precedence over the global values set by the local system administrator in the **/usr/local/bin/ssh_config** file. There are few genuine needs for a personal SSH config files, and their use opens up security holes.

BP-SSH-SSHCONF-02   Do not allow personal copies of SSH config (**$HOME/.ssh/config**) files.

If you must use allow personal copies of the SSH config file in users' home directories, they must be carefully created and maintained. Take the following precautions:

AP-ADVICE-SSH-12   Any allowed "personal" **ssh/config** files should be justified and documented.

AP-ADVICE-SSH-13   Use a **/bin/cron** task to periodically:

Check for the existence of any unexpected **ssh/config** files

Report the contents of all **$HOME/ssh/config** files

Delete (or clear) any unapproved copies

sshd_config (Server) Configuration File

The behavior of the SSH server is determined by parameters in the **/usr/local/bin/sshd_config** file. The server configuration protects its local system.

BP-SSH-SSHDCONF-01   Because of the security ramifications of the file, there should be a single (global) copy of the **/usr/local/bin/sshd_config** file on a system. This ensures that important security-related changes are made to the correct file and tracked.

AP-ADVICE-SSHDCONF-01   The **/usr/local/bin/ssh_config** file is so important from a security perspective that many companies choose to track changes to it via a source control program.

sshd_config Keywords with Security Implications

The parameters in the SSH server configuration file of importance to security are:

AllowTcpForwarding	Banner
ChallengeResponseAuthentication	ClientAliveInterval
ClientAliveCountMax	HostbasedAuthentication
HostKey	HostDSAKey
IgnoreRhosts	IgnoreUserKnownRhosts
KeepAlive	PasswordAuthentication
PermitEmptyPasswords	PermitRootLogin
PermitUserEnvironment	PubkeyAuthentication
ServerKeyBits	StrictModes
Subsystem	UserPrivilegeSeparation
RhostsRSAAuthentication	RSAAuthentication

Parameter	Description	Default	Recommended
AllowTcpForwarding	Determines whether or not TCP forwarding (also called tunneling) is permitted.	Yes	Yes

Note that disabling TCP forwarding does not improve security unless users are also denied shell access, as they can always install their own forwarders. Many SSH applications rely on tunneling to carry out their task.

BP-SSH-SSHDCONF-02   The AllowTcpForwarding value should be YES.

Parameter	Description	Default	Recommended
Banner	Determines whether or not a banner will be displayed when a remote user connects via SSH.	Yes	Yes

BP-SSH-SSHDCONF-03   The **Banner** value should be YES. An appropriate message warning against unauthorized use should always be displayed when an SSH client attempts to connect. The text of the banner should be approved by the corporate legal department.

Parameter	Description	Default	Recommended
Challenge-Response-Authentication	Determines whether or not users can be authenticated using a system-defined challenge/response protocol like Kerberos or S/Key.	No	Yes[1]

A system-defined challenge/response protocol like Kerberos or S/Key requires operating system support.

BP-SSH-SSHDCONF-04   If you have Kerberos, S/Key or a similar system in place, the **ChallengeResponseAuthentication** value should be YES.

Parameter	Description	Default	Recommended
Client-AliveInterval	Determines the amount of time elapsed without any activity from the remote client that will trigger the host to send an "are you alive" query to remote client. The message is sent through the encrypted channel to the client.	0 sec	Policy

(Continued)

Parameter	Description	Default	Recommended
ClientAlive-CountMax	Determines the number of "are you alive" queries the server will send before disconnecting a nonresponsive client.	3	Policy

The **ClientAliveInterval** parameter applies only to SSH2. It must be used in conjunction with the **ClientAliveCountMax** parameter.

> If "are you alive" queries are sent, the death of a connection will be properly noticed. The disadvantage is that if a route goes down temporarily, sessions will be ended, which may be annoying for the users.

> If "are you alive" queries are not sent, sessions may hang indefinitely, consuming resources and leaving "ghost" users.

The **ClientAliveCountMax** value (number of repetitions) determines the number of "are you alive" queries the server will send before disconnecting a non-responsive client. This parameter applies only to SSH2. If, for example, the **ClientAliveInterval** is set to 15 seconds and the **ClientAliveCountMax** is set to 3, a nonresponsive client will be disconnected after about 45 seconds.

BP-SSH-SSHDCONF-05 Policy should determine whether "are you alive" messages should be sent and how soon a nonresponsive client should be disconnected.

Parameter	Description	Default	Recommended
Hostbased-Authentication	Determines whether or not the trusted host mechanism for hosts in the **rhosts** file with keys in the **/etc/ssh_known_hosts** is allowed for remote authentications.	No	No

HostbasedAuthentication applies only to SSH2.

BP-ADVICE-SSHDCONF-06   The **RhostsRSAAuthentication** value should be NO, which disables the trusted host mechanism.

BP-OSS-RHOSTS-07   Do not rely on the trusted host mechanism.

Parameter	Description	Default	Recommended
HostKey	Specifies the location of the host's RSA key.	none	none
HostDSAKey	The **HostDSAkey** filename specifies the location of the host's DSA key.	none	none
HostRSAKey	The **HostDSAkey** filename specifies the location of the host's RSA key.	none	none

It is possible to have host key files. If you are using SSH2, you may also have **HostDSAKey** files and **HostRSAKey** files on the system.

BP-OSS-RHOSTS-07   Do not rely on the trusted host mechanism.

BP-SSH-SSHDCONF-07   Do not use a **HostKey** file.

BP-SSH-SSHDCONF-08   Do not use a **HostDSAKey** file.

BP-SSH-SSHDCONF-09   Do not use a **HostRSAKey** file.

RISK   SSH will refuse to use a hostkey if it is group or world accessible.

AP-ADVICE-SSHDCONF-02   If a **HostKey** files exists, it must only be accessible by SUPER.SUPER.

AP-ADVICE-SSHDCONF-03   If a **HostDSAKey** files exists, it must only be accessible by SUPER.SUPER.

AP-ADVICE-SSHDCONF-02   If a **HostRSAKey** files exists, it must only be a accessible by SUPER.SUPER.

If you must use the trusted host mechanism, it is important that only the system manager be able to define trusted hosts in the global **/etc/rhosts** and **/etc/shosts** files. Disable personal **.rhosts** and **.shosts** file by setting the

IgnoreUserRhosts value to YES, so that that SSH server will not query personal **.rhosts** and **.shosts** files.

BP-SSH-SSHDCONF-10   The **IgnoreRhosts** value should be YES, which disables trusted hosts.

BP-OSS-RHOSTS-07   Do not rely on the trusted host mechanism.

Parameter	Description	Default	Recommended
IgnoreUser-Rhosts	Determines whether or not users can specify trusted hosts in personal **.rhosts** and **.shosts** files.	No	Yes

If you must use the trusted host mechanism, it is important that only the system manager be able to define trusted hosts in the global **/etc/rhosts** and **/etc/shosts** files.

BP-SSH-SSHDCONF-11   Disable personal **.rhosts** and **.shosts** file by setting the **IgnoreUserKnownRhosts** value to YES, so that that SSH server will not query personal **.rhosts** and **.shosts** files.

Parameter	Description	Default	Recommended
KeepAlive	Determines whether or not the system should send "keep alive" messages to the other host.	Yes	No

RISK   TCP "I'm alive" messages are spoofable.

BP-SSH-SSHDCONF-12   The **KeepAlive** value should be NO. Use the **ClientAlive** mechanism instead. See the **ClientAliveCountMax** and **Client AliveCountMax** parameters described in the section on the **ssh_config** file.

Parameter	Description	Default	Recommended
Password Authentication	Determines whether or not users can be authenticated using a password.	Yes	Policy

BP-SSH-SSHDCONF-13   The PasswordAuthentication value should be
NO. Public key authentication is more secure.

Parameter	Description	Default	Recommended
PermitEmpty-Passwords	Determines whether or not users must enter a password when prompted for one. If YES, no password is required.	No	No

BP-SSH-SSHDCONF-14   The **PermitEmptyPasswords** value should
be NO. If you must allow **PasswordAuthentication**, all users should be
required to enter a valid password.

Parameter	Description	Default	Recommended
PermitRootLogin	Determines whether or not SUPER.SUPER will be allowed to log into the system via SSH.	No	No

The options for **PermitRootLogin** are:

Yes	SUPER.SUPER is allowed to login via SSH.
No	SUPER.SUPER is not allowed to login via SSH.
Without-password	SUPER.SUPER is allowed to login without a password.
Forced commands only	SUPER.SUPER is allowed to login if authenticated via Public key authentication and a command is specified.

Setting **PermitRootLogin** to "forced-commands-only" would allow root to
connect and run a command that is specified for the key in question (configured in the options field of the authorized_keys file).

BP-SSH-SSHDCONF-15   Unless you require SUPER.SUPER to automatically run a script from a remote system, the **PermitRootLogin** value should be NO.

Parameter	Description	Default	Recommended
PermitUserEn-vironment	Determines whether or not users can override the default session environment created by the SSH server.	No	No

BP-SSH-SSHDCONF-16   The **PermitUserEnvironment** value should be NO, otherwise users may bypass restrictions using mechanisms such as LD_RELOAD.

Parameter	Description	Default	Recommended
Pubkey-Authentication	Determines whether or not users can be authenticated using a personal RSA or DSA public key.	No	Yes

PubkeyAuthentication applies only to SSH2.

BP-SSH-SSHDCONF-17   The PubkeyAuthentication value should be YES.

Parameter	Description	Default	Recommended
ServerKeyBits	Determines the number of bits in the server's RSA keyword. The longer the key, the better. The default is 768 bytes.	768 bytes	At least 1024 bytes

BP-SSH-SSHDCONF-18   The **ServerKeyBits** value should be at least 1024 bits.

Parameter	Description	Default	Recommended
StrictModes	Determines whether or not the SSH server should check security and owner-ship of the user's files and home directory before accepting the logon.	Yes	Yes

BP-SSH-SSHDCONF-19   The **StrictModes** value should be YES to protect the system from users from leaving their files or home directories world-writable.

Parameter	Description	Default	Recommended
Subsystem	Specifies a subsystem external SSH, such as SFTP, that should be executed by the SSH server.	None	sftp

BP-SSH-SSHDCONF-20   The **Subsystem** value should be **/usr/local/bin/sftp-server** to ensure that file transfers are encrypted.

Parameter	Description	Default	Recommended
UserPrivilege-Separation	Determines whether or not the SSH server will spawn an unprivileged child process to deal with incoming network traffic.	Yes	Yes

After authentication, another process will be created that has the privileges of the authenticated user.

BP-SSH-SSHDCONF-21   The **UserPrivilegeSeparation** value should be YES to prevent privilege escalation by containing any corruption within the unprivileged processes.

The following keywords apply only to SSH1. If you must use SSH1, use the following settings:

Parameter	Description	Default	Recommended
RhostsAu-thentication	The **RhostsAuthentication** value (yes/no) determines whether or not the trusted host mechanism is allowed for remote authentications.	No	No

RhostsAuthentication applies only to SSH1.

BP-SSH-SSHDCONF-22   The **RhostsAuthentication** value should be NO which disables the trusted host mechanism.

BP-OSS-RHOSTS-07   Do not rely on the trusted host mechanism.

Parameter	Description	Default	Recommended
RhostsRSA-Authentica-tion	Determines whether or not the trusted host mechanism for hosts in the **rhosts** file with keys in the /etc/ssh_known_hosts is allowed for remote authentications.	Yes	No

RhostsRSAAuthentication applies only to SSH1.

BP-SSH-SSHDCONF-23   The **RhostsRSAAuthentication** value should be NO. Because **rhosts**-based authentication is not secure, and the SSH client process should not run (**setuid**) as SUPER.SUPER.

BP-OSS-SSH-01   /etc/ssh should not be **setuid** to SUPER.SUPER.

Parameter	Description	Default	Recommended
RSAAuthentication	Determines whether or not users can be authenticated using a personal RSA public key.	Yes	No

This parameter applies only to SSH1.

BP-SSH-SSHDCONF-24   The RhostsRSAAuthentication value should be NO.

	Discovery Questions	Look here:
SSHD-SSHDCONF-02	Is the AllowTcpForwarding keyword set to YES?	cat
SSHD-SSHDCONF-03	Is the Banner keyword set to YES?	cat
SSHD-SSHDCONF-04	Is the CallengeResponseAuthentication keyword set to YES?	cat
SSHD-SSHDCONF-05	Is the ClientAliveInterval keyword set according to the Corporate Security Policy?	cat
SSHD-SSHDCONF-05	Is the ClientAliveCountMax keyword set according to the Corporate Security Policy?	cat
SSHD-SSHDCONF-06	Is the Hostbased Authentication keyword set to NO?	cat
SSHD-SSHDCONF-07	Is the HostKey keyword present?	cat
SSHD-SSHDCONF-08	Is the HostDsaKey keyword present?	cat
SSHD-SSHDCONF-09	Is the HostRsaKey keyword present?	cat
SSHD-SSHDCONF-10	Is the IgnoreRhosts keyword set to YES?	cat
SSHD-SSHDCONF-11	Is the IgnoreUserRhosts keyword set to YES?	cat
SSHD-SSHDCONF-12	Is the KeepAlive keyword set according to the Corporate Security Policy?	cat
SSHD-SSHDCONF-13	Is the PasswordAuthentication keyword set according to the Corporate Security Policy?	cat
SSHD-SSHDCONF-14	Is the PermitEmptyPasswords keyword set to NO?	cat
SSHD-SSHDCONF-15	Is the PermitRootLogin keyword set to NO?	cat
SSHD-SSHDCONF-16	Is the PermitUserEnvironment keyword set to NO?	cat
SSHD-SSHDCONF-17	Is the PubkeyAuthentication keyword set to YES?	cat
SSHD-SSHDCONF-18	Is the ServerKeyBits keyword set to ≥ 1024?	cat
SSHD-SSHDCONF-19	Is the StrictModes keyword set to YES?	cat
SSHD-SSHDCONF-20	Is the Subsystem keyword set to sftp?	cat

(Continued)

	Discovery Questions	Look here:
SSHD-SSHDCONF-21	Is the UserPrivilegeSeparation keyword set to YES?	cat
SSHD-SSHDCONF-22	Is the RhostsAuthentication keyword set to NO?	cat
SSHD-SSHDCONF-23	Is the RhostsRSAAuthentication keyword set to NO?	cat
SSHD-SSHDCONF-24	Is the RSAAuthentication keyword set to NO?	cat

Environment File

SSH **environment** files contain parameters that configure an SSH environment. They are read at login and their values override the global environment settings.

> The **/usr/local/bin/environment** file is global; it is read whenever any user logins via SSH.

> Individual users may have their own **environment** files. If so, they reside in each user's **$HOME/.ssh** directory. They are read at login, and their values override the global environment settings.

Personal Environment Files

SSH **environment** files contain parameters that configure an SSH environment. They are read at login and the values override the global environment settings.

Individual **environment** files reside in each user's **$HOME/.ssh** directory. They are read at login and their values override the global environment settings.

BP-SSH-ENVIRONM-01 Do not allow personal environment files, otherwise users may bypass restrictions using mechanisms such as LD_RELOAD.

By default, personal environments are disabled. If you must enable them, use the **PermitUserEnvironment** parameter in the SSH server's configuration file (**sshd_config**).

BP-SSH-SSHDCONF-16   The **PermitUserEnvironment** value should be NO to prevent users from bypassing restrictions set globally.

If you must allow personal copies of the SSH config file in users' home directories, they must be carefully created and maintained. Take the following precautions:

AP-SSH-ENVIRONM-02   Any allowed "personal" **$HOME/.ssh/environment** files should be justified and documented.

AP-SSH-ENVIRONM-03   Use a **/bin/cron** task to periodically:

- Check for the existence of any unexpected **$HOME/.ssh/environment** files
- Report the contents of all **$HOME/.ssh/environment** files
- Delete (or clear) any unapproved copies

moduli File

/usr/local/etc/moduli contains Diffie-Hellman groups used for Diffie-Hellman Group Exchange.

rc File

$HOME/.ssh/rc files are much like a shell startup file (a **.profile**, for example), but they execute only when a user's account is accessed by SSH. The files are run for both interactive logins and remote commands. Any commands can be placed in this script that the user would like executed when he uses SSH, rather than an ordinary login. For example, a user could run and load his ssh-agent in this file **$HOME/.ssh/rc** is used to run any initialization routines necessary before the user's home directory becomes usable.

AP-SSH-RC-07   Do not use individual **$HOME/.ssh/rc** files unless required in your environment.

If no **$HOME/.ssh/rc** file exists, the **/usr/local/bin/ssh/sshrc** file is used. If neither file exists, **xauth** must be used to add the cookie.

sshrc File

/usr/local/bin/ssh/sshrc is used to specify machine-specific login initializations for all users. It is the global equivalent of the individual **$HOME/.ssh/rc** files.

AP-SSH-SSHRC-07   Do not use the **/usr/local/bin/ssh/sshrc** file unless required in your environment.

shosts File

The **/usr/local/etc/shosts** file is processed exactly the same as the **/etc/hosts.equiv** file. It should not be present on your system unless you must run both **rsh/rlogin** and SSH.

SSH Libraries

The SSH libraries are located in:

/usr/local/Floss/
/usr/local/Floss/openssh/contrib./suse
/usr/local/Floss/openssh/regress

prngd

/usr/local/bin/prngd is the object file for the Random Number Generator process used by the cryptographic algorithms for SSH.

Encryption Key-Related Programs

There are several key-related programs:

ssh-add
ssh-agent
ssh-keygen
ssh-keyscan
ssh-keysign

ssh-add

The **/usr/local/bin/ssh-add** program inserts and removes keys from the agent's key cache. On the HP NonStop Server, it adds RSA or DSA identities. When run without arguments, the program creates the following files:

$HOME/ssh/identity
$HOME/ssh/id_dsa
$HOME/ssh/id_rsa

These files can be given different names and/or locations via command line parameters.

If any file requires a password or passphrase, **ssh-add** will attempt to read the passphrase from the user's **tty**. If no passphrase is found, **ssh-add** prompts the user for the passphrase. If the passphrase is needed to open more than one file, **ssh-add** will retry the passphrase on the others before prompting again.

Because it is so important that individual **identity** files be readable only by the user, **ssh-add** ignores any **identity** file that is secured so that anyone other than its owner can read it.

For **ssh-add** to work, the authentication agent (**ssh-agent**) must be running and must be an ancestor of the current process.

ssh-add can also be used to display the keys currently being held by the **ssh-agent**.

ssh-agent

SSH agents perform two tasks:

Store your private keys in memory

Answer questions (from SSH clients) about those keys

Once loaded, private keys remain within an agent, unseen by SSH clients. To access a key, a SSH client asks the agent for the key. The agent sends the results back to the client.

SSH agents are labor-saving devices, handling all key-related operations and eliminating the need for a user to retype his passphrase, to store authentication data on the user's PC, or to send passphrases across the network.

On the HP NonStop Server, the **/usr/local/bin/ssh-agent** holds the private keys used for public key authentication (RSA and DSA). It is started during the beginning of a session or a login session, and all other programs are started as clients to the agent program.

Initially, the **ssh-agent** doesn't have any private keys. The keys are added using **ssh-add**, which creates the personal identity, **id_rsa** and **id_dsa** files. If the **identity** file has a passphrase, **ssh-add** asks for it, then sends the identity to **ssh-agent**, which will store multiple identities.

ssh-keygen

/usr/local/bin/ssh-keygen generates authentication keys for SSH. It also manages and converts the keys. It will create RSA keys for use by SSH protocol and for Diffie-Hellman group exchange (DH-GEX).

The system administrator uses **/usr/local/bin/ssh-keygen** to generate host private keys. And, normally, each user permitted to use SSH with RSA or DSA authentication runs this program once to create their personal authentication key in $HOME/.ssh/identity, $HOME/.ssh/id_dsa or $HOME/.ssh/id_rsa file.

/usr/local/bin/ssh-keygen generates the key and prompts for the filename where the private key will be stored. The public key is stored in a file of the same name but with ".pub" appended. The program also asks for a passphrase.

The passphrase is a string of any length.

The passphrase may be empty to indicate no passphrase (host keys must have an empty passphrase).

A passphrase is similar to a password, except it can be a phrase with a series of words, punctuation, numbers, whitespace, or any string of characters you want. Good passphrases are 10 to 30 characters long, are not simple sentences or otherwise easily guessable (English prose has only 1 to 2 bits of entropy per character, and provides very bad passphrases), and contain a mix of upper and lowercase letters, numbers, and non-alphanumeric characters. The passphrase can be changed later by using the **-p** option.

RISK   There is no way to recover a lost passphrase. A new key must generated and copied to the corresponding public key on other machines.

Once generated, the keys have to be activated.

ssh-keyscan

/usr/local/libexec/ssh-keyscan is used to gather the public host keys of multiple hosts. It is used to build and verify **ssh_known_hosts** files. For efficiency's sake, **ssh-keyscan** contacts as many hosts as possible in parallel. For scanning, neither encryption nor login access is required.

ssh_known_hosts files built with **ssh-keyscan** should be reviewed and the keys reverified, or users may be vulnerable to man-in-the-middle attacks. However, **ssh-keyscan** can help detect tampered keyfiles or man-in-the-middle attacks started after the **ssh_known_hosts** file was created.

AP-ADVICE-SSH-14   Review **ssh_known_hosts** files built with **ssh-keyscan** and verify all the keys.

AP-ADVICE-SSH-14   Use **ssh-keyscan** to detect tampered keyfiles or man-in-the-middle attacks started after the **ssh_known_hosts** file was created.

RISK   If the remote host SSH server is older than version 2.9, **ssh-keyscan** will generate a "Connection closed by remote host" message on the console of the remote system and then drop the connection.

ssh-keysign

/usr/local/bin/ssh-keysign is a helper process used by SSH to access the local host keys and generate the digital signature required during host-based authentication with SSH protocol version 2.

ssh-keysign is not invoked by users directly, only via the SSH client (ssh) or the SSH server (sshd).

By default this program is not enabled. It is enabled by setting the EnableSSHKeySign value to YES in the SSH client's global configuration file (ssh_config).

Host Private Key Files

The individual private key files are:

/usr/local/bin/ssh_host_key
/usr/local/bin/ssh_host_dsa_key
/usr/local/bin/ssh_host_rsa_key

These file are updated by the **/usr/local/bin/ssh-keygen** program. It is possible to enter a passphrase when generating any of these keys. If entered, the passphrase will be used to encrypt the private part of the key using triple DES.

The contents of these files should be kept secret. They should not be readable by anyone but the user.

In addition, there are two related files of interest to security:

/usr/local/etc/authorized_keys
/usr/local/etc/known_hosts

ssh_host_key File

The **/usr/local/bin/ssh_host_key** file contains the protocol version 1 RSA authentication **ssh_host_key** of the local system. This file is not created automatically by **ssh-keygen**, but it is the default location used if no other filename is entered. The contents of this file should be kept secret.

The SSH client (**/usr/local/bin/ssh**) will read this file when a user attempts to logon to a remote system via SSH.

ssh_host_dsa_key File

The **/usr/local/bin/ssh_host_dsa_key** file contains the protocol version 2 RSA authentication id of the local system. This files are not created automatically by **ssh-keygen**, but it is the default location used if no other filename is entered. The contents of this file should be kept secret.

The SSH client (**/usr/local/bin/ssh**) will read this file when a user attempts to logon to a remote system via SSH.

ssh_host_rsa_key File

The **/usr/local/bin/ssh_host_rsa_key** file contains the protocol version 2 RSA authentication id of the local system. These files are not created automatically by **ssh-keygen**, but it is the default location used if no other filename is entered. The contents of this file should be kept secret.

The SSH client (**/usr/local/bin/ssh**) will read this file when a user attempts to logon to a remote system via SSH.

Known_hosts Files

The **/usr/local/bin/ssh_known_hosts** file contains host public keys for all known hosts. This global file should be maintained by the system administrator. It maps each remote host name and IP address with its public key.

Getting the public keys from **known_hosts** isn't particularly useful in itself; *public* keys are, after all, that keys. Much more dangerous is the exposure of the private key counterparts. Combine the two, and you may have a easy path to another machine.

Host Public Key Files

These file are updated by the **/usr/local/bin/ssh-keygen** program. The individual public key files are:

    usr/local/bin/ssh_host_key.pub
    usr/local/bin/ssh host dsa key.pub
    usr/local/bin/ssh host rsa key.pub

These files are updated by the **/usr/local/bin/ssh-keygen** program.

Though, in theory, there is no need to keep the contents of these files secret, there is no reason to secure them loosely either. Best practice states that they should be secured so that only the user to whom the public keys apply should have access to them.

ssh_host_key.pub File

The **/usr/local/bin/ssh_host_key.pub** file contains the protocol version 1 DSA public key for authentication the local system. The contents of the file should be added to the **/usr/local/etc/authorized_keys** file on each system, where a user will log in using public key authentication.

The SSH client (**/usr/local/bin/ssh**) will read this file when a user attempts to logon to a remote system via SSH.

ssh_host_dsa_key.pub File

The **/usr/local/bin/ssh_host_dsa_key.pub** file contains the protocol version 1 DSA public key for authentication of the local system. The contents of the file should be added to the **/usr/local/etc/authorized_keys** file on each system where the user will log in using public key authentication.

The SSH client (**/usr/local/bin/ssh**) will read this file when a user attempts to logon to a remote system via SSH.

ssh_host_rsa_key.pub File

The **/usr/local/bin/ssh_host_rsa_key.pub** file contains the protocol version 1 DSA public key for authentication of the local system. The contents of the file should be added to the **/usr/local/etc/authorized_keys** file on each system where a user will log in using public key authentication.

The SSH client (**/usr/local/bin/ssh**) will read this file when a user attempts to logon to a remote system via SSH.

Individual Private Key Files

The individual private key files are:

$HOME/.ssh/identity
$HOME/.ssh/id_dsa
$HOME/.ssh/id_rsa

These file are updated by the **/usr/local/bin/ssh-keygen** program. It is possible to enter a passphrase when generating any of these keys; if entered, the passphrase will be used to encrypt the private part of the key using triple DES.

The contents of these files should be kept secret. They should not be readable by anyone but the user.

identity Files

The individual **$HOME/.ssh /identity** files contain the protocol version 1 RSA authentication identity of each user. These files are not created automatically by **ssh-keygen**, but it is the default location used if no other filename is entered. The contents of these files should be kept secret.

The SSH client (**/usr/local/bin/ssh**) will read this file when the user attempts to logon to a remote system via SSH.

id_dsa Files

The individual **$HOME/.ssh /id_dsa** files contain the protocol version 2 RSA authentication id of each user. These files are not created automatically by **ssh-keygen**, but it is the default location used if no other filename is entered. The contents of this file should be kept secret.

The SSH client (**/usr/local/bin/ssh**) will read this file when the user attempts to logon to a remote system via SSH.

id_rsa Files

The individual **$HOME/.ssh /id_rsa** files contain the protocol version 2 RSA authentication id of each user. These files are not created automatically by **ssh-keygen**, but it is the default location used if no other filename is entered. The contents of this file should be kept secret.

The SSH client (**/usr/local/bin/ssh**) will read this file when the user attempts to logon to a remote system via SSH.

Individual Public Key Files

These file are updated by the **/usr/local/bin/ssh-keygen** program. The individual public key files are:

$HOME/.ssh/identity.pub
$HOME/.ssh/id_dsa.pub
$HOME/.ssh/id_rsa.pub

These files are updated by the **/usr/local/bin/ssh-keygen** program.

Though, in theory, there is no need to keep the contents of these files secret, there is no reason to secure them loosely either. Best practice states that they should be secured so that only the user to whom the public keys apply should have access to them.

In addition, there are two related files of interest to security:

$HOME/.ssh /authorized_keys
$HOME/.ssh /known_hosts

identity.pub Files

The individual **$HOME/.ssh /identity.pub** files contain the protocol version 1 RSA public key for authentication of each user. The contents of each of the files, if they exist, should be added to the **$HOME/.ssh/ authorized_keys** files on each system where the user will log in using RSA authentication.

id_dsa.pub Files

The individual **$HOME/.ssh /id_dsa.pub** files contain the protocol version 1 DSA public key for authentication of each user. The contents of each of the files, if they exist, should be added to the **$HOME/.ssh/ authorized_keys** files on each system where the user will log in using public key authentication.

id_rsa.pub Files

The individual **$HOME/.ssh /id_rsa.pub** files contain the protocol version 1 RSA public key for authentication of each user. The contents of each of the files, if they exist, should be added to the **$HOME/.ssh/ authorized_keys** files on each system where the user will log in using public key authentication.

Authorized_keys Files

The SSH client stores within each user's home directory a list that maps the host names and IP addresses of every remote host the user has connected to with each host's public key. This database is known as the **authorized_keys** file. It resides in **$HOME/.ssh/**.

Getting the public keys from **authorized_keys** isn't particularly useful in itself; public keys are, after all, "public" keys.

It is possible to specify an OSS command for a particular remote host. Use this if you configure the **PermitRootLogin** value to **forced-commands-only** value in the **sshd_config** file.

Known_hosts Files

The SSH client stores within each user's home directory a list that maps the host names and IP addresses of every remote host the user has connected to with each host's public key. This database is known as the **known_hosts** file. It resides in **$HOME/.ssh/**.

These per-user files are maintained automatically. Whenever the user connects from an unknown host, its key is added to his **$HOME/.ssh/ known_hosts** file.

RISK   If both the hosts' public keys and the user's private keys are known, the remote hosts are at risk.

Authorized_keys files should only be readable by the user.

SSH-Related Programs

The following programs are external to SSH but are used or started by SSH.

scp

/usr/local/bin/scp (Secure Copy Client) copies files between hosts on a network. It uses SSH for data transfer, and the same authentication and security as SSH. Unlike **rcp**, **scp** prompts for passwords or passphrases if they are required for authentication.

Any filename may contain a host name and user name to indicate that the file is to be copied to or from that host. Copies to two remote hosts are allowed.

SFTP Subsystem

SFTP (Secure File Transfer Program) is a client server system. **/etc/sftp** is its object File. It is used to connect to a remote system. **/usr/local/bin/sftp-server** is the local server process. It responds to connection requests from remote systems.

sftp

usr/local/bin/sftp is the SSH secure file transfer client program. It is similar to FTP, but moves the files via encrypted SSH. It may also use other features of SSH, such as public key authentication and compression.

If an interactive authentication method is used, **sftp** connects and logs into the specified host and then enters interactive command mode. It can also start an SFTP session on a remote host.

If a non-interactive authentication method is used, **sftp** can be used to automatically retrieve files from a remote host.

sftp-server

/usr/local/libexec/sftp-server is the SSH secure file transfer server. It is never accessed by users directly. It is started by the SSH server (**sshd**) when a file transfer request from a remote system arrives. The **sftp-server** must be entered as the argument for the **Subsystem** parameter in the **sshd_config** file.

5

File Sharing Programs

This section contains a discussion of the Samba and NFS file-sharing subsystems from a security standpoint. Please refer to the OSS Gazette chapters on NFS and Samba for recommendations on securing the subsystem components.

It should be emphasized that the best defense against inadvertent or malicious external attacks is a well secured file system. Files on the NonStop Server should be secured as if there was no firewall. Users should never be able to access a system using a file transfer protocol that does not authenticate the user before granting the connection. File transfer protocols that grant remote users SUPER.SUPER privileges should not be installed on your NonStop Server.

Network File System (NFS) Subsystem

The Network File System (NFS) is a widely used and primitive protocol that allows computers to share files over a network. The implementation on the HP NonStop Server is based on the one developed by Sun

Microsystems. It allows PCs or other network hosts to create or use files on the NonStop Server via TCP/IP over a LAN.

The NFS protocol is independent of the system, operating system, network architecture, and transport protocol. This independence is achieved by using Remote Procedure Call (RPC) primitives and an external data representation (XDR).

RISK NFS transactions are not encrypted. Data is transferred in the clear. Anyone can capture sensitive data.

AP-NFS-CONFIG-01 Encrypt the sensitive fields/columns or encrypt the entire file so that if an unauthorized person reads or acquires the file, the sensitive information is still protected.

RISK Hosts and users cannot be easily authenticated in NFS.

RISK There are many NFS clients available. Some do not require passwords.

RISK There are many NFS clients available. Some allow users to login with a user number rather than a user name.

AP-NFS-CONFIG-02 Verify that the NFS client used in your organization requires a valid password that cannot be blanks.

AP-NFS-CONFIG-03 Verify that the NFS client used in your organization requires users to enter a name rather than a user number to logon.

AP-NFS-CONFIG-04 The NFS subsystem should not be enabled on production systems or any other system where confidential or sensitive data resides until all the security implications of NFS have been evaluated.

The NFS subsystem is dependent on the following NonStop Server subsystems:

TCP/IP
QIO
PTrace
RPC port mapper

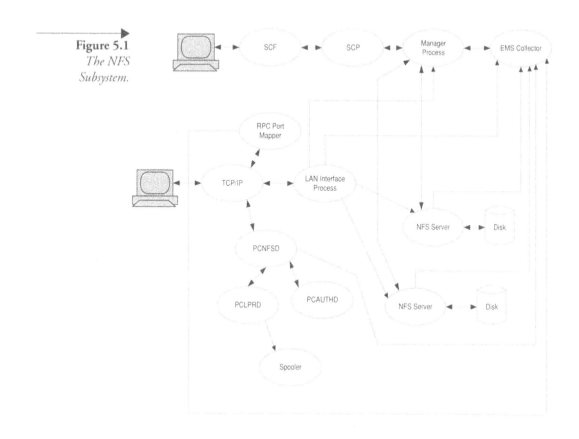

Figure 5.1
*The NFS
Subsystem.*

NFS Components

The NFS subsystem is made up of the following components:

Various NFS servers

NFS LAN server

NFS configuration files

NFS userid files

RPC portmap

NFSCONV

NFSCONV is the object file for the NFS Configuration Quickstart Utility, which is used to configure the NFS subsystem on the NonStop Server.

The program is used to generate a sample PCNFSD config file and create obey files that will stop and start the NFS subsystem.

NFSMGR

NFSMGR is the object file for the NFS manager program, $ZNFS, which accepts commands, reports errors, and generates event messages. The NFS server security is configured using SCF NFS server object commands.

$ZNFS starts the NFSSVRHP and NFSLAN processes.

NFSMGR2

NFSMGR2 is the object file for the helper process, which provides address resolution and other LAN-related services to the manager process. The process is started and stopped by NFSMGR as needed.

NFSLAN

NFSLAN is the object file for the LAN interface process, which acts as a front end for NFS requests received from the NonStop TCP/IP subsystem. It forwards mount protocol requests to the manager process and relays NFS protocol requests to the appropriate server processes. Configure the NFSLAN with SCF NFS LAN object commands.

NFSSVRHP

NFSSVRHP is the object file for the server headpin process, which manages the files in the hierarchy defined for each NFS server. There is one headpin process per fileset (EXPORT object). The one for the root fileset is typically called $ROOT. The server headpin processes start the NFSSVRWB processes.

SCF NFS server commands are used to configure the server headpin.

NFSSVRWB

NFSSVRWB is the object file for the worker bee processes, which are started by a server headpin (NFSSVRHP) process. Each headpin server may start multiple worker bee processes.

PCAUTHD

PCAUTHD is the object file for the authentication server process. It is started by the PCNFSD process, $PCDP2.

PCLPRD

PCLPRD is the object file for the NFS print spool server process, which communicates with the Guardian spooler subsystem. It is started by the PCNFSD ($PCDP2) process.

PCNFSD

PCNFSD is the object file for the $PCDP2 process, which is an extension to NFS that allows non-UNIX clients to interact in a secure manner with NFS servers. The PCNFSD process starts the PCLPRD and PCAUTHD processes.

PRNFSD uses the RPC service over UDP or TCP to transport information.

ZNFSPTR

ZNFSPTR is the object file for Ptrace's NFS module.

ZNFSSCF

ZNFSSCF is the object file for SCF's NFS module.

ZNFSTEXT

The ZNFSTEXT file contains SCF's help text for the NFS module.

ZNFSUSR and ZNFSUSRI Files

The ZNFSUSR file stores information used by the NFS server to translate NFS userids to Guardian userids, which are used to the determine NFS user's file access. NFS users are configured with SCF NFS user object commands. ZNFSUSR1 is the alternate key file.

ZZNFSnnn

The NFSMGR processes keep all their configuration information (other than userids) in files in the ZOSSNFS subvolume. The files are named ZZNFSnnn, where n represents a number. These files are updated programmatically, not by users directly.

BP-NFS-ZZNFSNNN-15 The ZZNFSnnn files must be owned by SUPER.SUPER and secured so that only SUPER.SUPER has access to them.

ZNFSTMPL

ZNFSTMPL is the EMS template for the NFS subsystem.

ZRPCTMPL

ZRPCTMPL is the EMS template for the RPC service.

Gaining Access to NFS Files

Access to NFS files is checked in three stages:

> Translation of the user's NFS userid to a Guardian userid
> User access to the Export object (fileset)
> Each NFS operation on a specific NFS file.

How Access to the NFS Subsystem is Evaluated

The steps an OSS NFS server uses to determine the actual Guardian userid from the supplied NFS client userid are:

1. The NFS client userid is looked up in the list of OSS NFS users:

    If found, go to step 4.
    If not found, then ...

2. Check the SERVER attribute NULL-ALIAS-OK value:

   If the value is FALSE, the request is *rejected.*
   If the value is TRUE, then …

3. Check the list of OSS NFS users for the **nobody** client userid:

   If the **nobody** userid is not found, the request is *rejected.*
   If the **nobody** userid is found, then …

4. Check to see if the NFS client userid (including **nobody**) is mapped to 65535 (SUPER.SUPER):

   If the userid is not mapped to SUPER.SUPER, the request is *granted.*
   If the userid is mapped to SUPER.SUPER, then …

Figure 5.2
How NFS evaluates access.

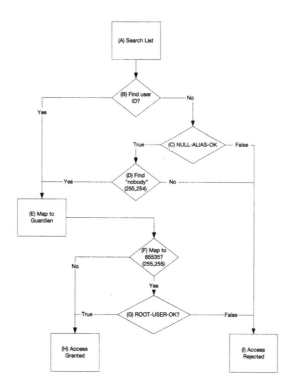

5. Check the SERVER attribute ROOT-USER-OK value:

    If the value is TRUE, the access to NFS is *granted*.

    If the value is FALSE, the request is *rejected*.

OSS NFS ignores group names supplied by NFS clients. It uses the mapped Guardian userid to determine the Guardian group name.

How Access to an Export Object is Evaluated

Once a user has successfully gained access to the NFS subsystem, access to the NFS fileset (EXPORT object) is evaluated:

1. When a remote mount request is received, the server responsible for the requested directory checks to see if the directory is a defined EXPORT object:

    If the EXPORT object is not defined, the request is *rejected*.
    If the EXPORT object is defined, then …

2. Check to see if the EXPORT object has an ACCESS list:

    If no ACCESS list is defined, the request is *granted*.
    If an ACCESS list is defined, then …

3. Check to see if the requesting client host is in the ACCESS list:

    If the client host is on the ACCESS list, the request is *granted*.
    If the client host is not on the ACCESS list, the request is *rejected*.

RISK If an NFS file is accessed via any method other than NFS, NFS file security is not enforced.

AP-NFS-CONFIG-03 NULL.FTP should never be allowed to own NFS files, since it will give the user extended access capabilities.

How NFS File Operations Are Evaluated

Once a user has successfully gained access to the NFS subsystem and to the requested fileset (EXPORT object), each NFS file operation attempted will be evaluated against the security settings of the target file and its containing directory.

The following table shows the file access privileges required for the various NFS file operation:

NFS Cmd	File	Containing Directory	Other	Server in READ-ONLY
CREATE		WRITE, EXECUTE	Pre G06.27 – CREATE on Safeguard Volume rule	Denied
GETATTR	none	none		
LINK		WRITE, EXECUTE		Denied
LOOKUP		EXECUTE		Denied
MKDIR		WRITE, EXECUTE		Denied
READ	READ or EXECUTE			
READDIR		READ		
READLINK		EXECUTE		Denied
REMOVE		WRITE, EXECUTE		Denied
RENAME		WRITE		Denied
RMDIR		WRITE		Denied
SETATTR			Depending on the attribute, WRITE, CHMOD, or CHOWN permission required	
STATFS	none	none		
SYMLINK		WRITE, EXECUTE		Denied
WRITE		WRITE		Denied

NFS Configuration

The NFS subsystem is managed via SCF, which treats the various NFS entities as OBJECTS. The NFS OBJECTS are:

SUBSYS

PROCESS

EXPORT

GROUP

LAN

NETGROUP

SERVER

USER

NFS EXPORT Objects

An EXPORT object allows a file system to be exported to specified NETGROUPS and host machines. The directory is exported when the EXPORT object is created. The EXPORT object definition consists of a server mount point.

The ACCESS keyword is used to define client systems that are allowed to request remote mounts of any EXPORT object. The argument to the ACCESS keyword is a list of host names and/or NETGROUP names. Unfortunately, the ACCESS keyword is optional.

When a remote mount request is received:

1. The server responsible for the requested directory checks to see if the directory is a defined EXPORT object:

    If the EXPORT object is not defined, the request is *rejected*.
    If the EXPORT object is defined, then ...

2. Check to see if the EXPORT object has an ACCESS list:

    If no ACCESS list is defined, the request is *granted*.
    If an ACCESS list is defined, then ...

3. Checks to see if the requesting client host is in the ACCESS list:

If the client host is on the ACCESS list, the request is *granted*.

If the client host is not on the ACCESS list, the request is *rejected*.

RISK If no ACCESS list is specified for an EXPORT object, then *any* client can perform a remote mount of the file system.

BP-NFS-CONFIG-01 Define an ACCESS list for every EXPORT object.

NFS GROUP Objects

NFS GROUPs identify a virtual set of users. GROUP objects consist of a list of NFS userids, which are called group members. Each member must already be defined as an NFS USER object. Each NFS GROUP has a name and a number. GROUP objects are used to:

Translate group numbers to group names

Define user "sets" in NETGROUP objects

NFS LAN Objects

A LAN object specifies the local area network (LAN) interface process that acts as a front end for NFS requests received from the NonStop TCP/IP communications process. The LAN OBJECT definition consists of its process name, its configuration, and information about the TCP/IP process it uses. One LAN configuration value, ADDR-CHECK, has security implications:

The ADDR-CHECK value determines whether or not the LAN server will check the requesting client host name against the expected IP address when a mount or unmount request is received.

If ON, a check is made to determine whether the host name corresponds with the Internet Protocol (IP) address of the request. If it does, then a helper process is started each time the LAN object is started to perform the NFS tasks or is stopped when the request is completed. The default value is ON.

If OFF, no check is made to determine whether the host name corresponds with the Internet Protocol (IP) address of the request.

RISK   Clients provide their host name and IP address when they establish communication with the NFS server. However, unless the LAN server verifies that the host name matches the expected IP address, the client can provide a false host name, mimicking a valid host name in the network.

BP-NFS-CONFIG-02   The NFS LAN object ADDR-CHECK value should be ON to ensure that the NFS server validates the host name against the expected IP address.

NFS NETGROUP Objects

A NETGROUP object defines a group of host systems with similar access requirements within specified network domains. NETGROUP objects are used in EXPORT object ACCESS lists to control access to EXPORT object's files.

A NETGROUP consists of a list of client hosts or other NETGROUPs (keyword netgroupx-name). Each NETGROUP has a one to sixty-four–character name.

NFS PROCESS Objects

The NFS process refers to the NFSMGR server process which, by default, is $ZNFS. If your NonStop Server has more than one NFS subsystem configured, the secondary subsystems will have different process names.

NFS SERVER Objects

An NFS SERVER object defines the server headpin (NFSSVRHP) process for a particular NFS subsystem. A SERVER object consists of values for a number of parameters that determine how the server will behave.

Each server headpin process provides access to a specific OSS fileset. Each server has an attribute that identifies a mount point within the file hierarchy on the local NonStop Server. A local mount occurs whenever a server is started.

Three SERVER parameters have security implications:

NULL-ALIAS-OK
ROOT-USER-OK
READ-ONLY

NULL-ALIAS-OK

The NULL-ALIAS-OK value determines whether or not a remote NFS userid not mapped to a local Guardian userid will be allowed access to files managed by the local NFS server.

> If the value is TRUE, undefined users are mapped to the **nobody** userid, if it exists and gain the access privileges granted to the **nobody** userid.

> If the value is FALSE, a user must have a mapped userid or the access attempt will be rejected.

The default value is FALSE.

BP-NFS-CONFIG-03   To protect against unauthorized access to NFS files, the NFS SERVER object NULL-ALIAS-OK value should be FALSE. Only specifically authorized users should have access to the NFS file system.

ROOT-USER-OK

The ROOT-USER-OK value determines whether or not remote NFS userids can be mapped to the SUPER.SUPER Guardian userid.

> If the value is TRUE, NFS userids can be mapped to SUPER.SUPER.

> If the value is FALSE, NFS userids cannot be mapped to SUPER. SUPER.

The default value is FALSE.

RISK SUPER.SUPER has access to all NFS files, regardless of file ownership and file security settings.

BP-NFS-CONFIG-04 The NFS SERVER object ROOT-USER-OK value should be FALSE. Users should access NFS files as themselves, with their own limited privileges, not as SUPER.SUPER or any other privileged userid.

RISK If the **nobody** userid is not present or is not mapped to Guardian userid 65534 (255,254), NFS will not evaluate the server ROOT-USER-OK value.

BP-NFS-NFSUSRID-03 The **nobody** userid must be present and must be mapped to Guardian user 65534 (255,254).

READ-ONLY

READ-ONLY specifies whether or not access to the file system serviced by the server is on a read-only or read/write basis.

> If the value is TRUE, NFS users can not alter any NFS files managed by this server.

> If the value is FALSE, NFS users can alter any NFS files managed by this server.

The default value is FALSE; the file system allows read/write access.

> If TRUE, the file system must be initialized before you create this server by a server that is not configured as read-only.

AP-NFS-CONFIG-05 The NFS SERVER object READ-ONLY value should be set appropriately for each NFS fileset (EXPORT object).

	Discovery Questions	Look here:
NFS-CONFIG-01	Does every EXPORT object have an access control list?	scf
NFS-CONFIG-02	Does every LAN object have the ADDR-CHECK keyword set to ON?	scf
NFS-CONFIG-03	Is the NULL-ALIAS-OK keyword set to FALSE?	scf
NFS-CONFIG-04	Is the ROOT-USER-OK keyword set to FALSE?	scf

NFS SUBSYSTEM Objects

The SUBSYSTEM refers to NFS as a whole. Each of the other objects can only apply to one subsystem, though there can be multiple NFS subsystems on the host.

SCF commands related to the SUBSYSTEM let you manage it as a whole, thus you can STOP all subordinate OBJECTs with a single command.

NFS User Objects

A USER object registers a user with the NFS subsystem and maps the user's Guardian name to an NFS userid. Each user is assigned a USER NAME, GROUP number, a USER number, and an ALIAS, which is actually the user's existing Guardian user name.

The NFS user name can be up to 64 characters long and include numbers, letters, and underscores, but no spaces.

The GROUP number is an NFS GROUP number (between 0 and 4294967295). It should be an existing NFS GROUP, but a user can be assigned to a non-existent group.

The USER number is between 0 and 4294967295.

There are two reserved user numbers in the NFS subsystem:

    0 = SUPER.SUPER (root)
    65534 **nobody**

ALIAS OSS is the Guardian user name that the NFS userid will map to determine access to NFS files. The Guardian user name must already be defined in the $SYSTEM.SYSTEM.USERID file. The ALIAS OSS can be entered as the Guardian user name or the scalar form of the Guardian userid.

Scalar form of a Guardian userid is calculated as follows:

    (Group-number × 256) + member-number.

Examples of the scalar forms of some NonStop Kernel userids:

```
10,10 is (10 x 256) + 10 = 2570
SUPER.SUPER  is (255 x 255) + 255 = 65535
nobody is  255,254 = (255 x 254) + 254 = 65534
```

RISK   The file's owner can do anything to it in NFS.

RISK   SUPER.SUPER has access to all NFS files, regardless of file owner-ship and file security settings.

AP-NFS-NFSUSRID-01   Each NFS user should be assigned a unique NFS userid, which is mapped to an appropriate Guardian userid so that they are only granted access to the files they require.

AP-NFS-NFSUSRID-02   NFS userids should never be mapped to privi-leged Guardian userids such as SUPER Group members, database owners or application owners.

RISK   Users without NFS userids will be assigned the **nobody** NFS userid, if it exists and if the server NULL-ALIAS-OK value is TRUE. The user will then gain the access privileges granted to the **nobody** userid, which is required to be in the SUPER Group.

BP-NFS-CONFIG-03   To protect against unauthorized access to NFS files, the NULL-ALIAS-OK server value should be FALSE. Only specifi-cally authorized users should have access to the NFS file system.

BP-NFS-CONFIG-04   The ROOT-USER-OK value should be FALSE. Users should access NFS files as themselves, with their own limited privi-leges, not as a member of the SUPER Group or any other privileged userid.

RISK   If the **nobody** userid is not present and mapped to Guardian userid 65534 (255,254), NFS will not evaluate the server ROOT-USER-OK value.

BP-NFS-NFSUSRID-03   The **nobody** userid must be present and must be mapped to Guardian user 65534 (255,254).

RISK   If NFS users are mapped to Guardian user names that have different underlying userids on different nodes, the users may gain unexpected privi-leges because NFS does not validate the Guardian user name and userid.

AP-NFS-NFSUSRID-04 Ensure that all NFS users have unique Guardian userids on all nodes where their access privileges differ.

	Discovery Questions	Look here:
NFS-NFSUSERS-01	Does every NFS user have a unique NFS userid?	scf
NFS-NFSUSERS-02	Are any NFS userids mapped to a privileged userid?	scf
NFS-NFSUSERS-03	Is the nobody userid present and mapped to user 65534 (255,254)?	scf
NFS-NFSUSERS-04	Does every NFS user have a unique Guardian userid?	scf

SCF NFS Commands with Security Implications

The following NFS-related SCF commands are considered sensitive; they can only be executed by a userid in the SUPER Group:

ABORT

ADD

ALLOWOPENS

ALTER

DELETE

PRIMARY

START

STATS, with RESET option

STOP

STOPOPENS

TRACE

The following NFS-related SCF commands are considered very sensitive; they can only be executed by SUPER.SUPER:

ADD EXPORT

ADD NETGROUP

ADD USER

ALTER EXPORT

ALTER NETGROUP

ALTER USER

DELETE EXPORT

DELETE NETGROUP

DELETE USER

RISK   Unauthorized use or misuse of SCF NFS subsystem commands could result in exposure of information and mismanagement of resources that are vital to the system's performance.

If a third-party access control product is used to grant selected users access to SCF running as a SUPER Group member, or a member of a subsystem owners' groups, the sensitive commands listed above should only be granted to users whose responsibilities include configuring NFS and denied to all others.

3P-ACCESS-SCF-01   Use a third-party access control product to allow the users responsible for configuring the NFS subsystem access only to NFS SCF commands as SUPER.SUPER.

Samba

Samba provides file and print services for Microsoft Windows clients. The services can be hosted on any TCP/IP-enabled platform. It enables users to access NonStop files from their PC or print NonStop files on a PC printer.

This chapter discusses the HP NonStop Server implementation of Samba, which is freeware; HP neither supports nor endorses this application, however, its popularity within the NonStop community justifies including its host components in this book.

The only way to protect a system from misuse of its resource by Samba users is to secure every file so that only the appropriate users can access it.

AP-ADVICE-SAMBA-01 All files and directories should be appropriately secured whether they are Samba shares or not.

AP-ADVICE-SAMBA-02 Only appropriate subdirectories should be available via Samba.

AP-ADVICE-SAMBA-03 Each Samba user should only be granted access to appropriate files.

Directories and any underlying subdirectories that are made available to Samba are called shares or services.

How Access to the Samba Subsystem is Evaluated

When a connection request is made:

1. The Samba server and the Samba client negotiate the protocol (Samba version) level.

2. The user or requesting system is authenticated.

3. A connection to a resource (share/service) is established.

4. File access requests are evaluated based on the OSS file and directory security strings.

How the Samba server performs the authentication depends on settings in the **smb.conf** file.

Whether or not both a username and a password are required depends on the **security** keyword in the **smb.conf** file. Please refer to the section on "Controlling What Samba Users Can Access" for more information.

Whether or not the Samba server validates the password itself or sends it to a secondary server depends on the **password server** keyword in the **smb.conf** file. Please refer to the "smb.conf Keywords with Security Implications" section for more information.

Regardless of how the user is authenticated, the Samba server performs the following steps to determine whether it will allow a connection to a service.

If all the steps fail, the connection request is refused. If any of the steps pass, then the following steps are omitted.

1. If the client passes a username/password pair test that the server can validate via the host's password file, the connection is made with that username.

2. If the client has previously registered a username and password with the system and now supplies a correct password for that username, the connection is allowed.

3. If the supplied password is correct for the client's netbios name *or any previously used usernames*, the connection is allowed as the corresponding user.

4. If the client previously validated a username/password pair with the server and the client now passes the correct validation token, then the connection is allowed as that *previously validated* username. This step will be skipped if the keyword **revalidate** = **yes** in the **smb.conf** file.

5. If the service specifies a **user** = list in the **smb.conf** file and the client supplies a password that matches any one of the usernames on the list, the connection is allowed. Note that if the username is specified as a group name (**@<name>**), any user in the group will be able to connect.

RISK   If the service specifies a **user** = list in the **smb.conf** file and the username is specified as a group name (**@<name>**), any user in the group will be able to connect.

6. If the service is a guest service, then a connection is made as the username specified by the **guest account** keyword in the **smb.conf** file, regardless of the password supplied.

7. If the requested name is found, the user's home directory is determined.

8. If a matching username is not located, Samba denies the connection and returns an error message to the client.

Once the connection request is made, the Samba server (**smbd**) scans the **smb.conf** file looking for a service (stanza) that matches the one requested.

On the HP NonStop implementation of Samba, the **/etc/passwd** file is not used. No Safeguard authentication is performed.

The **smbd** process for a connection runs as SUPER.SUPER until it is necessary to perform some operation on behalf of the connected user. At that time, the process **uid** becomes the user's userid. Once the task it complete, the process switches back to SUPER.SUPER.

RISK Because the **smbd** server runs as SUPER.SUPER, it is difficult to determine which **smbd** process belongs to which user. Use the **smbstatus** program to display the list of connected users.

How to Control What Samba Users Can Access

The resources (shares) available to each user depends on the host system's OSS file security and, internal to Samba, on settings in the **smb.conf** file.

Different levels of control within Samba are available:

Remote host (client) authentication
Share-based authentication
User-based authentication
User level
Domain level
Server level

Remote Host Authentication

You can limit connections to your system via Samba based on the requesting client's IP address. The following keywords tell the Samba server to validate the clients requesting access rather than the user attempting the access. Please refer to the "smb.conf Keywords with Security Implications" section for more information about these keywords:

allow hosts
deny hosts
hosts equiv

Share-Level Controls

Samba's authentication method is determined by the **security** keyword in the **smb.conf** file. When **security = share** a password is associated with each share *independent of the user*. The client (PC) authenticates itself separately for each share, sending the password to the server with the share mount (tree connection) request. It does not send the username with this operation.

RISK The Samba server has to figure out what username the client probably wants to use, since the server is not explicitly sent the username.

RISK The password is sent from client to host in the clear.

Some Samba clients also send a session setup request, which does contain the username. In this case, the server will add the username to the list it is checking against the password provided.

BP-POLICY-SMBCONF-01 Do not use share-based authentication.

AP-ADVICE-SMBCONF-01 If you must use share-based security, be sure to choose a Samba client that sends session setup requests so each session can be associated with a specific username. Not all Samba clients will support share-level security.

User-Based Controls

The authentication method is determined by the **security** keyword in the **smb.conf** file. The user-related values are:

> user level
>
> domain level
>
> server level

All three of these levels authenticate based on a username and password pair that are transmitted by the client. In each case, the Samba server accepts the username/password pair and attempts to validate them against its account database.

Whether or not the Samba server validates the password itself or sends it to a secondary server depends on the **password server** keyword in the

smb.conf file. The process is the same regardless of the user account backend, even though the proof of identity might be some derived value (such as an encrypted password hash) rather than the actual password itself. Samba doesn't care what the backend is, as long as it provides the required user information. The client requests a connection and the Samba server will contact the account database through the defined interface.

RISK Clients would need to run the smbpasswd program and users would have to keep their PC passwords synchronized.

Please note that authentication levels are also affected by password considerations. Refer to the "smb.conf Keywords with Security Implications" section for more information about the password-related keywords:

encrypt passwords

null passwords

password level

password program

password server

User Level

When **security** = **user**, the client sends a session setup request after the protocol negotiation is complete. The request includes the username and password, which the server can either accept or reject. If accepted, the client expects to be able to mount shares without further specifying a password unless the keyword **revalid** = **yes** is set in the **smb.conf** file.

RISK Security is primarily dependent on the client.

RISK The password is sent from client to host in the clear.

Domain Level

When **security** = **domain**, authentication is based on the same concept as user-level security, except that the Samba server becomes a member of the Windows domain, which means that it can participate in trust relationships.

Domain-level security provides a mechanism for storing all user and group accounts in a central, shared account repository. Servers that act as domain controllers provide authentication and validation services to all machines that participate in the security context for the domain.

With domain-level security, you must also define a password server that will validate authentication requests, much as you would in server-level mode. You should also use encrypted passwords (**encrypt passwords** = **yes**).

RISK   Unless Samba is configured for encrypted passwords, the password is sent from client to host in the clear.

Each server process only needs to connect to the password server long enough to perform the validation.

Domain-level security has been superseded in favor of active directory security (ADS), which is Microsoft's implementation of LDAP directory services. It is a hierarchical framework of objects like printers and user information that controls access and sets security. Samba can join a domain using NT4-style RPC-based security if the domain is run in active mode (ADS).

Samba can participate in Kerberos authentication. The term *realm* is used to describe a Kerberos-based security architecture (used by Microsoft ADS). If Samba cannot correctly identify the appropriate ADS server using the realm name, use the **password server** keyword in **smb.conf**.

RISK   Domain-level authentication is the superior method. However, at the time of writing this book, the domain-level authentication does not appear to function properly on the HP NonStop.

Server Level

When **security** = **server**, the Samba server reports to the client that it is in user-level security mode. The client then does a session setup as described in user-level security. The Samba server then uses the username and password it receives from the client and attempts to login to the password server using the same username and password. The password server is defined by the **password server** keyword in the **smb.conf** file.

RISK You can use any password server to validate the password, but then the local Samba server is only as secure as the system hosting the password server.

Once the Samba server has granted the session setup, it must have some means of obtaining a userid for the user in order to control access to files. This means that although local accounts are not used to authenticate the user, the user still must have a userid on the local system. You must either create local accounts for all PC Samba usernames or create a file to map PC usernames to NonStop usernames and add the file's location to the **smb.conf** file (**username map = **).

RISK Each server process must keep an open connection to the authentication server, which drains Windows resources.

RISK The Samba server cannot participate in domain trust relationships.

BP-SAMBA-SMBCONF-41 Domain-level authentication does not work properly on the HP NonStop, therefore, the value should be **security = server** and **password server = <Windows PDC>**.

smb.conf Configuration File

The location of the **smb.conf** file is determined at compile-time. If you install the precompiled ITUG version of Samba, the file will be placed in the **/usr/local/lib** directory. This is the location assumed in this book.

The **/usr/local/lib/smb.conf** is used to configure the Samba environment.

The **smb.conf** file is constantly checked by the **smbd** and every process that it spawns, **nmbd**. This makes it desirable to keep this file as small as possible, but it is good practice to thoroughly document your configuration settings. One solution to this problem is to do all documentation and configuration in a file that has another name, such as **smb.conf.master**. The **testparm** utility can be used to generate a fully optimized **smb.conf** file from this master configuration and documentation file, as shown below:

```
root# testparm -s smb.conf.master > smb.conf
```

This makes it possible to maintain detailed configuration change records while at the same time keeping the working **smb.conf** file size small.

BP-USR-SAMBA-08   The **/usr/local/lib/smb.conf** file should be secured so that only SUPER.SUPER can WRITE to it or delete it.

BP-SAMBA-SMBCONF-01   The settings in the **/usr/local/lib/smb.conf** file should be reviewed on a periodic basis.

AP-ADVICE-SMBCONF-02   Use a **/bin/cron** task to periodically report the contents of **/usr/local/lib/smb.conf** file.

AP-ADVICE-SMBCONF-03   The **/usr/local/samba/lib/smb.conf** file is so important from a security perspective that many companies choose to track changes to it via a source control program.

smb.conf File Layout

The **smb.conf** file is styled after a Windows .ini file. It is divided into logical sections called **stanzas**. A stanza can be either a service (share) or a meta-service on the server's host system. Each stanza is defined by its name, which is placed within brackets. Each stanza contains keywords that define its characteristics.

The **smb.conf** file accepts variables in the arguments to its keywords. The variables are denoted by the % (percent) character. Variables are replaced when the **smb.conf** file is parsed at runtime. For example, **%u** refers to the username of the connecting user. So, for example, if DBA.JOE connects to Samba, when the file is parsed, every occurrence of **%u** will be changed to DBA.JOE. **%H** represents the user's home directory. So, at runtime every occurrence of **%H** will be changed to DBA.JOE's home directory.

Please refer to your Samba documentation for a complete list of variables. Those relevant to security for a specific keyword are mentioned in the discussion of the keyword.

Services

Services are either file-space services (shares) or print services.

File-space services (shares) are used by a Samba client as an extension of its native file system. So, for example, the dba-access service shown in Example 1 would appear in the Explorer tree on a dba's PC as **/apps/dba/b24/tools**.

Example 1: A file space (share) service
```
[dba-access]
path = /apps/dba/b24/tools
writable = true
public = false
```

Print services are used by a Samba client to access printers on the host via the Samba server. So DBA.JOE could send jobs to a printer connected to the NonStop Server from his PC if a print service is configured.

Meta-services

Meta-services have specific, predefined uses. The Samba meta-services are:

[global]

[homes]

[printers]

[global] Meta-service

The [global] meta-service stanza contains settings that apply to the whole server and provide the default values for services that don't have the various parameters defined.

If a parameter is set in both an individual service and the [global] meta-service, the value in the individual service wins.

AP-ADVICE-SMBCONF-04 Individual services for which the global values are incorrect must be configured to override the global value.

[homes] Meta-service

The [homes] meta-service stanza causes Samba to provide a personal home share for each user. It allows the server to create home directories for connecting clients on the fly.

When the connection request is made, the server (**smbd**) scans the **/usr/local/lib/smb.conf** file looking for a service (stanza) that matches the requesting client.

If the matching service is found, it is used.

If the matching service isn't found, the service name is treated as a user name and looked up in the local password file. If the name exists and the password matches, a service is created (a new stanza is added to the **/usr/ local/lib/smb.conf** file) by cloning the [homes] stanza. The service name of the newly created section is changed from [homes] to the remote user's username. If no path was defined in the [homes] meta-service, the new service's path is set to the user's home directory.

RISK   If guest access is specified in the [homes] section, all home directories will be accessible to all clients *without a password.*

BP-SAMBA-SMBCONF-02 Do not configure guest access to your system in the [homes] meta-service.

The browseable flag for home directories created (auto home directories) by Samba (see the section on "How Access to the Samba Subsystem is Evaluated") will be inherited from the [global] browseable value, not the [homes] browseable value. This means that setting **browseable = no** in the [homes] meta-service will hide the [homes] service but make any auto home directories visible to the user they belong to.

BP-SAMBA-SMBCONF-03 Set **browseable = no** in the [homes] meta-service to hide the [homes] service but make any auto home directories visible to their owners.

A sample [homes] meta-service:

```
[homes]
comment = OSS home directory
browseable = no
path = %H
writeable = yes
valid users = %S
create mode = 600
directory mode = 700
```

In the example above, **valid users** = %S restricts access to the user whose username is the same as the name of the service (share). The **path** = %H, causes a share to be created using the parameters from the [homes] meta-service, but is renamed to the matched username. Therefore, the only user allowed to connect is the owner of the home directory. The **browseable** = **no** hides the new home directory from everyone else. The next time the user logs on, he will be able to go directly to his home directory, which will appear in his tree.

All the keywords available in a [service] (share) stanza are available in the [homes] meta-service stanza.

[printers] Meta-service

The [printers] meta-service stanza establishes which print jobs are received from Windows clients prior to being dispatched to the print spooler. This meta-service will cause every printer that is either specified in a **printcap** file, via **lpstat**, or via the CUPS API, to be published as a shared print queue.

It works like the [homes] meta-service, but for printers. If a [printers] stanza is present in the **smb.conf** file, users are able to connect to any printer specified in the local host's printcap file.

When the connection request is made, the server (smbd) scans the **/usr/ local/lib/smb.conf** file looking for a service (stanza) that matches the requesting client.

If the matching service is found, it is used.

If the matching service isn't found, but the [homes] meta-service is defined, it is used as described above.

If the matching service is found and no [homes] meta-service is defined, the requested service name is treated as a printer name and the appropriate printcap is scanned to see if the requested service name is a valid printer name. If a match is found, a new service is created (a new stanza is added to the **/etc/samba/smb.conf**.conf file) by cloning the [printers] stanza. The name of newly created section is then changed to the requested printer name. If no printer name is given, the printer name is set to the located printer.

If the service does not permit guest access and no user name is given, the username is set to the located printer name.

The [printers] meta-service must be printable. If it is not configured as printable, the host will not scan the **/usr/local/lib/smb.conf** file.

Example 2: A printable service

```
[lp1]
path = /usr/spool/public
printable = true
public = true
```

You can name the meta-service anything you like, but Samba assumes that the meta-name, in this case [lp1], is a printer name. If it isn't, use the **printer =** keyword to define the actual printer:

```
[printer]
path = /usr/spool/public
printable = true
printer = lp1
public = true
```

The path defines the location where the client will drop the file during printing. Typically, the path specified in the service is that of a world-writable spool directory with the sticky bit set on it.

BP-SAMBA-SMBCONF-04   Set the sticky bit on any world-writable Samba spool directory.

smb.conf Keywords with Security Implications

The keywords define the specific attributes of services. Each of these keywords can be applied to individual services (stanzas or shares) or placed in the [global], [printers], or [homes] meta-services, as appropriate for your environment.

The following keywords have security implications:

Parameter	Description	Default	Recommended
admin users	A list of users granted administrative privileges on the share.	Absent	Absent

RISK File permissions do not apply to **admin users**; they can create, alter and remove any file, regardless of the file permissions.

BP-SAMBA-SMBCONF-05 Do not use the **admin users** keyword in any service or meta-service in the **smb.conf** file.

Parameter	Description	Default	Recommended
allow hosts hosts allow	A list of client hosts that are permitted to access the service.	Absent	Policy

Allow hosts and **hosts allow** keywords are synonyms and can be used interchangeably.

RISK If the **allow hosts** keyword is used in the [global] meta-service, matching hosts will be allowed access to any service that doesn't explicitly exclude them.

BP-SAMBA-SMBCONF-06 Do not use the **allow hosts** or **hosts allow** keywords in the [global] meta-service stanza.

If you must use the **allow hosts** keyword in the [global] meta-service stanza, take the following precaution.

AP-ADVICE-SMBCONF-05 Place **allow hosts** or **hosts allow** lists in appropriate individual services to override the **allow hosts** list in the [global] meta-service.

Parameter	Description	Default	Recommended
browseable	Determines whether or not the service will appear in list of available files in a net view or browse list.	Yes	Policy

BP-SAMBA-SMBCONF-07   If there are subdirectories within a share that contain sensitive information, they may need to be set as **browseable = no**.

Parameter	Description	Default	Recommended
config file	The file name and location of a secondary **smb.conf** file for a particular share. Because the "master" **smb.conf** file must be read to find this secondary file, any parameters loaded from the "master" file will be reloaded from the secondary file.	Absent	Absent

BP-SAMBA-SMBCONF-08   Don't use secondary **smb.conf** files unless absolutely necessary.

AP-ADVICE-SMBCONF-06   Use a **/bin/cron** task to periodically to:

Check for the existence of any unexpected **smb.conf** files
Report the contents of all **smb.conf** files
Delete (or clear) any unapproved copies

Parameter	Description	Default	Recommended
create mask/ create mode	Determines the security string that will be applied to any new OSS files created from DOS files. The creator must have have READ, WRITE and EXECUTE. If the keyword is not present, all such files will be created with the default security string.	744 (rwx r--r--)	700 (rwx --- ---)

The **create mask** and **create mode** keywords are identical and can be used interchangeably.

BP-SAMBA-SMBCONF-09 Unless there is a need to share such files, set create mask = 700.

Parameter	Description	Default	Recommended
dead time	The number of minutes of inactivity before the Samba server will consider a connection dead and disconnect. A value of zero means that the Samba server will never disconnect an inactive session.	0 mins	5-20

BP-SAMBA-SMBCONF-10 The **dead time** value should be between five and twenty minutes, as appropriate for your system. Because most clients have an autoreconnect feature, the disconnect will be invisible to the user if the connection is actually still in use.

Parameter	Description	Default	Recommended
debug level log level	Determines the level of auditing that the Samba server will write to its log.	0	1

The range is 0 to 10. Level 0 logs only the most important messages. Level 1 is recommended. Level 3 and above are primarily for debugging and slow the server down considerably.

BP-SAMBA-SMBCONF-11 The **debug level** value should be 1.

Parameter	Description	Default	Recommended
default service	Defines the service that should be accessed if the requested service isn't defined.	Absent	Policy

If no **default service** is defined, a connection request for a nonexistent service will be denied.

BP-SAMBA-SMBCONF-12 Do not allow connections when the client requests a invalid service. Do not use the **default service** keyword.

Parameter	Description	Default	Recommended
deny hosts hosts deny	A list of client hosts that should be denied access to a service (or the system, if placed in the [global] meta-service.)	Absent	Policy

The **deny hosts** and **hosts deny** keywords are synonyms and can be used interchangeably.

BP-SAMBA-SMBCONF-13 Policy should determine the use of the deny hosts keyword. If, for example you must use the **allow hosts** keyword in the [global] meta-service stanza, you might choose to place **deny hosts** lists in appropriate individual services to override the **allow hosts** list in the [global] meta-service.

Parameter	Description	Default	Recommended
don't descend	Subdirectories in the **don't descend** list will always be shown as empty, preventing a user from exploring them. This is intended to block infinitely deep (recursive) directories.	Absent.	/E, /G

BP-SAMBA-SMBCONF-14 The /E and /G directories should always be included in the **don't descend** list to prevent Samba users from accessing files on a remote NonStop Server or in the Guardian file space.

Parameter	Description	Default	Recommended
encrypt passwords	Determines whether or not encrypted passwords will be negotiated with the host.	No	Yes

Setting **encrypt passwords** = **yes** has no effect unless the necessary DES libraries and encryption code have been put in place and compiled.

Samba password encryption is irreversible; the passwords entered by users are encrypted and then compared against the hash of the password stored in the file. The same password always produces the same hashed result.

If the NonStop Samba server isn't configured **security = user**, a connection will not be established.

RISK   Because of the way the server and client generate and compare the hashed password, if someone knows the encrypted version of the password, he can participate in the authentication without knowing the unencrypted password.

The encrypted passwords are stored in the **/usr/local/private/smbpsswd** file. If you wish to create this file in another location, use the **smb password file** keyword and the absolute path to the file.

BP-SAMBA-SMBCONF-15   Compile the necessary DES libraries and encryption code and set **Encrypt password = yes**.

If **Encrypt Passwords = yes** and **security = user**, the client's password is checked against the smbpasswd file and no native authentication is performed.

Parameter	Description	Default	Recommended
force group	Specifies a group name that should be used to make all connections to the particular service.	Absent	Absent

BP-SAMBA-SMBCONF-16   Do not use the **force group** keyword. Each user should access files with an individual userid in the appropriate administrative group.

Parameter	Description	Default	Recommended
force user	Specifies a user name that should be used to make all connections to the particular service.	Absent	Absent

BP-SAMBA-SMBCONF-17   Do not use the **force user** keyword. Each user should access files with an individual userid in the appropriate administrative group.

Parameter	Description	Default	Recommended
guest account	Specifies the user name that will be used to access services which are specified as "guest ok". All users connecting to the guest service will gain the access privileges of the userid specified as the guest account.	Absent	Absent

Guest file access will be determined by the **guest account** userid's permissions.

BP-SAMBA-SMBCONF-18   Unless you have a public service available, don't use the **guest account** keyword. Each user should access files with an individual userid in the appropriate administrative group.

Parameter	Description	Default	Recommended
guest ok / public	A guest-only service will grant users without a local userid access.	Absent	Absent

The **guest ok** and **public** keywords are will have no effect if the **guest ok** or **public** keyword is not also present in the same service's stanza.

The guest's file access privileges will be determined by the the **guest account** userid.

BP-SAMBA-SMBCONF-19   Unless a public service is available, don't use the **guest only** or **public** keywords. Each user should access files with an individual userid in the appropriate administrative group.

Parameter	Description	Default	Recommended
guest only	A guest only service will grant users without a local userid access.	Absent	Absent

A **guest only** value will have no effect if the **guest ok** or **public** keyword is not also present in the same service's stanza.

The guest's file access privileges will be determined by the **guest account** userid.

BP-SAMBA-SMBCONF-20   Unless a public service is available, don't use the **guest only** keyword. Each user should access files with an individual userid in the appropriate administrative group.

Refer to the user/password validation for more information about this option.

Parameter	Description	Default	Recommended
hide dot files	Determines whether or not OSS. (**dot**) (hidden) files will show in directory listings.	Yes	Yes

BP-SAMBA-SMBCONF-21   Hidden files should be hidden; **hide dot files = yes**.

Parameter	Description	Default	Recommended
host equiv	Specifies Samba clients that can access the service without a password. This is the Samba equivalent of the **hosts.equiv** file.	Absent	Absent

BP-SAMBA-SMBCONF-22   Don't rely on the trusted host mechanism. Do not use the **host equiv** keyword.

Parameter	Description	Default	Recommended
invalid users	A list of userids that should not be allowed to logon to the service. This provides a way to ensure that an improper setting does not breach security.	Absent	Absent

BP-SAMBA-SMBCONF-23   The **invalid user** list specifies userids that should not be allowed to logon to the service. This provides a way to ensure that an improper setting does not breach security.

Parameter	Description	Default	Recommended
include	Specifies a second **smb.conf** file to be included (literally, as if the contents were typed into the current file) in the "master" **smb.conf**.	Absent	Absent

BP-SAMBA-SMBCONF-24   Don't use secondary **smb.conf** files unless absolutely necessary.

Parameter	Description	Default	Recommended
log file	The log file keyword determines the location of the samba log file (also known as the debug file). The value can contain substitutions, so it is possible to configure separate logs for each user or each client.	/usr/local/samba	Policy

The log Samba to which writes its audit is dependent on the order of events during connection:

1. If a file is specified using the -l switch at startup, the server writes the initial connection entries to the filename on the command line.

2. If no logname is specified, then the server writes the initial connection entries to the file specified when it (the server) was initially started.

3. Once the **smb.conf** is parsed, if a log file is specified, the rest of the session will be written to the file specified.

RISK   If a log file is specified for a share, it is not possible to log an entire session in a single file.

BP-SAMBA-SMBCONF-25   The Samba log file provides a means of monitoring Samba users' activities. If the default isn't appropriate in your

environment, specify a directory that is appropriate when the server is
started initially.

AP-ADVICE-SMBCONF-07   If you choose to specify log files for different services or for specific users, be aware that the audits pertaining to their
actual connection to the server will be logged in the location specified
when the server was initially started, as long as the user doesn't specify a
location on the command line upon connection.

Parameter	Description	Default	Recommended
magic script	Specifies a file which, if opened, will be executed by the server after it reads and closes the file. This is intended to execute a script on behalf of the connected user. The scripts are deleted once executed.	Absent	Absent

Samba Magic scripts provide a way to run a host program and send the
output back to the client.

RISK   HP's documentation states that magic scripts are "experimental"
and users should not rely on them.

BP-SAMBA-SMBCONF-26   Do not use magic scripts. Do not include
the **magic script** keyword.

Parameter	Description	Default	Recommended
map hidden	Determines whether or not hidden DOS files will be mapped to the OSS **executable by other** bit.	No	No

BP-SAMBA-SMBCONF-27   Hidden files should be hidden, **map hidden = no**.

Parameter	Description	Default	Recommended
map to guest	Determines what Samba will do if a connection request comes from an invalid username or password.	Never	Never

The choices are **Never, Bad User** or **Bad Password.**

If the value is set to **Never,** Samba rejects the connection request.

If the value is **Bad User,** the connection request is only rejected if the username is invalid.

If the value is **Bad Password,** the request is accepted and the user mapped to the guest userid. There is no message to the user stating that he is logged on as a guest.

BP-SAMBA-SMBCONF-28   Do not allow connections for invalid users; set **map to guest = never.**

Parameter	Description	Default	Recommended
Netbios aliases	A list of netbios names by which the Samba server will advertise itself.	Absent	Absent

BP-SAMBA-SMBCONF-29   Unless required, do not define any **netbios aliases.**

Parameter	Description	Default	Recommended
null passwords	Determines whether or not accounts without passwords will be allowed access to the service.	No	No

BP-SAMBA-SMBCONF-30   Do not allow access without passwords; set **null passwords = no.**

Parameter	Description	Default	Recommended
only user	If set to true, then only users on the **user / username** list will be allowed access to the service.	False	True

RISK   If **only user = true,** clients will be unable to supply a username to be used by the server.

RISK   If **only user** = **true**, Samba will not try to deduce usernames from the service name, which interferes with implementing the [homes] meta-service unless the %S is used.

The %S variable represents the current service name. If **user** = %S, then essentially the only username in the list is the current user's, which is also the name of that user's home directory share.

BP-SAMBA-SMBCONF-31   Do not set **only user** = **true** without also setting **user** = %S, which means the "user" list will be just the service name, which is, therefore, the current user's username.

Parameter	Description	Default	Recommended
password level	The maximum number of upper- and lower-case combinations that Samba will try when attempting to validate a password.	0	0

If **password level** = **0**, the server will try to validate the password twice: once as entered and once as all lower case.

If **password level** = **2**, for example, the server would make multiple attempts to validate the password: once as entered, once all lower case, and once for each combination of two upper-case characters. So if the password entered was "Marvel", Samba would try Marvel, marvel, MArvel, MaRvel, MarVel, MarvEl, ,mARvel, mArVel, and so on when authenticating a user.

The larger the number, the longer it can take to authenticate, but the better chance a match will be found.

RISK   The higher the **password level**, the more security is reduced because someone need only enter a password once and Samba would try all the upper and lower case combinations. The more tries it makes, the more likely that it will find a match.

RISK   The higher the **password level**, the more time the server takes to process a new connection.

BP-SAMBA-SMBCONF-32   Set **password level** = **0**.

Parameter	Description	Default	Recommended
password server	Specifies the name of another server, such as a PC, that will do all the username/password validation.	Absent	PDC

PDC stands for Primary Domain Controller.

The keyword **security** = **server** must be present in order to use a **password server**.

RISK   Using a **password server** adds to security concerns because access to your NonStop Server is now dependent on another machine and is therefore vulnerable to any security failures on that machine.

RISK   Pointing a Samba server to itself for password serving will cause a loop and lock up the server.

BP-SAMBA-SMBCONF-33   Do not configure a remote authentication server. Do not include the **password server** keyword.

AP-ADVICE-SMBCONF-08   If a **password server** is used, don't use the **%m** variable, which tells the Samba server to use the incoming client as the password server.

AP-ADVICE-SMBCONF-09   If a **password server** is used and the **%m** variable set, you must restrict the clients allowed to connect to the system via the **hosts allow** keyword.

Parameter	Description	Default	Recommended
postexec	Specifies a command that will be run each time the service is disconnected.	Absent	Absent

RISK   The command may run as root on some systems.

BP-SAMBA-SMBCONF-34   Do not use the **postexec** keyword. It does not work on HP NonStop Servers.

Parameter	Description	Default	Recommended
preexec	Specifies a command to run whenever the service is connected to. It can be used to send the user a welcome message, for example.	Absent	Absent

RISK   As of the publish date, a bug on the HP NonStop causes **preexec** commands to run as SUPER.SUPER server.

BP-SAMBA-SMBCONF-35   Do not use the **preexec** keyword.

Parameter	Description	Default	Recommended
printable / print ok	Determines whether or not clients may open, write to and submit spool files on the directory specified for the service.	Absent	Policy

The **printable** and **print ok** keywords are identical and can be used interchangeably.

The **read only** parameter controls only nonprinting access to the resource. A printable service will always allow writing to the service path (user privileges permitting) to spool print data.

BP-SAMBA-SMBCONF-36   The tasks of users with access to the service will determine whether or not it should be printable.

Parameter	Description	Default	Recommended
read list	The userids on the **read list** will only be allowed read access to the service, regardless of the **read only** keyword value.	Absent	Absent

BP-SAMBA-SMBCONF-37   The tasks of users with access to the service will determine whether or not a **read list** is necessary.

Parameter	Description	Default	Recommended
read only	Determines whether or not users will be able to write to service.	Absent	Policy

Read only is really the equivalent of **writable = false**.

BP-SAMBA-SMBCONF-38   The tasks of users with access to the service will determine whether or not it should be **read only**.

Parameter	Description	Default	Recommended
revalidate	Determines whether or not the Samba server will allow a previously authenticated user to access a another service without re-entering the password.	Absent	True

BP-SAMBA-SMBCONF-39   Users should be reauthenticated for each service they wish to access. Set **revalidate = true**.

Parameter	Description	Default	Recommended
root directory	Specifies a top-level directory that the server will chroot to on startup.	/ (root)	Absent

Specifying a top-level directory is a way to deny access to file trees, but even without specifying a **root directory**, the server will deny access to files not included in the service's path.

RISK   Adding a **root directory** other than / (root) could deny access to symbolic links to parts of the file system not included in the service's file tree.

RISK   Adding a **root directory** other than / (root) could deny access to some programs needed for complete operation of the server.

AP-ADVICE-SMBCONF-10 If a **root directory** other than / (**root**) is specified, it may be necessary to put copies of some system files, such as utilities or printer configuration files, into the specified tree.

Parameter	Description	Default	Recommended
root preexec	Specifies a command to run when a connection made to the service. It can be used to send the user a welcome message, for example.	Absent	Absent

BP-SAMBA-SMBCONF-40 Do not use the root **preexec** keyword unless absolutely necceasary.

RISK   The commands run as SUPER.SUPER on HP NonStop systems.

Parameter	Description	Default	Recommended
security	Based on this value, clients decide whether or not (and how) to transfer user and password information to the Samba server.	server	server

The valid entries are share, user, domain, or server.

Please refer to the *Controlling Samba Access* section of this chapter for more information on the implications and recommendations for this keyword.

BP-SAMBA-SMBCONF-41 Use domain-level security, **security** = *ʹ* **server** and **password server** = **<PDC>**.

Parameter	Description	Default	Recommended
status	Determines whether or not the service will log to the status file used by the **smbstatus** program.	Yes	Yes

RISK   If **status** = **no**, the **smbstatus** program won't be able to show which connections are active.

BP-SAMBA-SMBCONF-42 Logging should be enabled, set **status = on.**

Parameter	Description	Default	Recommended
username level	Specifies the maximum number of upper- and lower-case combinations that Samba will try when attempting to validate a username.	0	0

If **username level = 0**, the server will try to validate the username twice: once as entered and once as all lower case.

If **username level = 2**, for example, the server would make multiple attempts to validate the username: once as entered, once all lower case, and once for each combination of two upper-case characters.

The larger the number, the more time will be needed to authenticate, but the chance a match will be found will be increased.

If **username level = 2**, for example, the server would make multiple attempts to validate the username: once as entered, once all lower case, and once for each combination of two upper-case characters.

RISK The higher the **username level**, the more security is reduced because someone need only enter a username once and Samba would try all the upper- and lower-case combinations. The more tries it makes, the more likely that it will find a match.

RISK The higher the **username level**, the more time it takes to process a new connection.

BP-SAMBA-SMBCONF-43 Set **username level = 0.**

Parameter	Description	Default	Recommended
username / user	A list of userids that the Samba server will test against the supplied password for authentication with share-level security.	null	Absent

The **username** and **user** keywords are synonyms and can be used interchangeably.

RISK If a user list is supplied, Samba will try to validate the password against each of the userids on the list. This does not restrict who can login, it just offers hints to the Samba server on what userids might correspond to the supplied password. Users can login as whoever they want. The amount of damage that could be done while when logged on as another user would only be limited by file security.

RISK If the username is specified as group name (@<name>), any user in the group will be able to connect. This negates any accountability for individual users.

The %S variable represents the current service name. If you set **user** = %S, then essentially the only username in the list is the current user's, which is also the name of that user's home directory.

BP-SAMBA-SMBCONF-44 Accept the default and omit the **user/username** keyword.

BP-SAMBA-SMBCONF-45 If you choose to supply a user list, do not specify group names in the list.

AP-ADVICE-SMBCONF-11 If a user list is required, use the **valid users** keyword to restrict the users who can access a service.

Parameter	Description	Default	Recommended
username map	Specifies a file that contains a map of userids from a client to the those on the server.	Absent	Absent

Each line in the file maps a single username to a single userid. The server processes the file line-by-line, looking for a match. If a match is found, the mapped userid will be used for the connection.

RISK The password supplied will be validated against the mapped userid, not the originally supplied userid, so passwords are shared. This is true unless you have a password server configured (refer to the **password server** keyword).

RISK There is no backward mapping, which means that users who have been mapped may have trouble deleting print jobs because they won't own them.

There are two common uses for this configuration:

To map PC userids to the Samba server's host userids

To map multiple users to a single user name so they can share files

BP-SAMBA-SMBCONF-46 Do not map userids unless absolutely necessary.

BP-SAMBA-SMBCONF-47 If mapping userids is required, consider using a password server.

Parameter	Description	Default	Recommended
valid user	A list of the userids authorized to login to the service.	Absent	Policy

If the **valid user** list is empty, any user can login. A name starting with @ is interpreted as a group name.

The %S variable represents the current service name. If **valid user** = %S, then the only username in the list is the current user's which is also the name of that user's home directory.

BP-SAMBA-SMBCONF-48 Use %S to substitute the current service name so you can assign each user to his own home directory. Refer to the [homes] meta-service.

BP-SAMBA-SMBCONF-49 Restrict access to services via valid user lists.

Parameter	Description	Default	Recommended
wide links	Determines whether or not links beyond the service's file system are followed.	Yes	Policy

Links within the service's file system are always allowed.

RISK Setting wide **links** = **no** could deny access to symbolic links to parts of the file system not included in the service's file tree.

BP-SAMBA-SMBCONF-50 When **wide links** = **yes**, steps must be taken to guarantee that only the appropriate links are available to Samba users.

BP-SAMBA-SMBCONF-50 If **wide links** = **no**, copies of programs must be created within the share.

Parameter	Description	Default	Recommended
work group	Determines the Windows work group that the server will appear in when queried by clients.	Value in the Samba makefile	Policy

BP-SAMBA-SMBCONF-51 This value will be determined the network environment.

Parameter	Description	Default	Recommended
write ok/ writable	Determines whether or not users can create or alter files in the service's directory.	No	Policy

Writable and **write ok** keywords are synonyms and can be used interchangeably.

Writable is really the equivalent of **Read only** = **false**.

A printable service (**printable** = **yes**) will always allow writing to the directory (user privileges permitting), but only via spooling operations.

BP-SAMBA-SMBCONF-52 The tasks of users with access to the service will determine whether or not it should be writable.

Parameter	Description	Default	Recommended
write list	A list of the userids authorized to create or alter files in the service's directory even if **read only** = **yes**.	Absent	Policy

Users on both a read list and a write list will be given write access.

BP-SAMBA-SMBCONF-53   The tasks of users with access to the service will determine whether or not a **write list** is necessary.

	Discovery Questions	Look here:
SAMBA-SMBCONF-05	Is the **admin users** keyword present in any service?	testparm
SAMBA-SMBCONF-06	Is the **allow hosts/hosts allow** keyword present in any service?	testparm
SAMBA-SMBCONF-07	Is the **browseable** keyword present in any service?	testparm
SAMBA-SMBCONF-08	Is the **config file** keyword present in any service?	testparm
SAMBA-SMBCONF-09	Is the **create mask/create mode** keyword security string correct?	testparm
SAMBA-SMBCONF-10	Is the **dead time** keyword present in any service?	testparm
SAMBA-SMBCONF-11	Is the **debug level/log level** keyword present in any service?	testparm
SAMBA-SMBCONF-12	Is the **default service** keyword present in any service?	testparm
SAMBA-SMBCONF-13	Is the **deny hosts/hosts deny** keyword present in any service?	testparm
SAMBA-SMBCONF-14	Is the **don't descent** keyword set to /E, /G?	testparm
SAMBA-SMBCONF-15	Is the **encrypt passwords** keyword set to **yes**?	testparm
SAMBA-SMBCONF-16	Is the **force group** keyword present in any service?	testparm
SAMBA-SMBCONF-17	Is the **force user** keyword present in any service?	testparm
SAMBA-SMBCONF-18	Is the **guest account** keyword present in any service?	testparm

(Continued)

	Discovery Questions	Look here:
SAMBA-SMBCONF-19	Is the **guest ok/public** keyword present in any service?	testparm
SAMBA-SMBCONF-20	Is the **guest only** keyword present in any service?	testparm
SAMBA-SMBCONF-21	Is the **hide dot files** keyword set to **yes**?	testparm
SAMBA-SMBCONF-22	Is the **hosts equiv** keyword present in any service?	testparm
SAMBA-SMBCONF-23	Is the **invalid users** keyword present in any service?	testparm
SAMBA-SMBCONF-24	Is the **include** keyword present in any service?	testparm
SAMBA-SMBCONF-25	Is the **log file** keyword present and set to an appropriate location for every service?	testparm
SAMBA-SMBCONF-26	Is the **magic script** keyword present in any service?	testparm
SAMBA-SMBCONF-27	Is the **map hidden** keyword set to **no** in every service?	testparm
SAMBA-SMBCONF-28	Is the **map to guest** keyword set to **never** in every service?	testparm
SAMBA-SMBCONF-29	Is the **netbios aliases** keyword present in any service?	testparm
SAMBA-SMBCONF-30	Is **null passwords** keyword set to **no** in every service?	testparm
SAMBA-SMBCONF-31	Is the **only user** keyword set to **true** in every service?	testparm
SAMBA-SMBCONF-32	Is the **password level** keyword set to **0** (zero)?	testparm
SAMBA-SMBCONF-33	Is the **password server** keyword set appropriately?	testparm
SAMBA-SMBCONF-34	Is the **postexec** keyword present in any service?	testparm
SAMBA-SMBCONF-35	Is the **preexec** keyword present in any service?	testparm
SAMBA-SMBCONF-36	Is the **printable/print ok** keyword set appropriately?	testparm

(Continued)

	Discovery Questions	Look here:
SAMBA-SMBCONF-37	Is the **read list** keyword present?	testparm
SAMBA-SMBCONF-38	Is the **read only** keyword set appropriately?	testparm
SAMBA-SMBCONF-39	Is the **revalidate** keyword set to true?	testparm
SAMBA-SMBCONF-40	Is the **root preexec** keyword present in any service?	testparm
SAMBA-SMBCONF-41	Is the **security** keyword set to server?	testparm
SAMBA-SMBCONF-42	Is the **status** keyword present in any service?	testparm
SAMBA-SMBCONF-43	Is the **username level** keyword set to 0 (zero)?	testparm
SAMBA-SMBCONF-44	Is the **username/user** keyword present in any service?	testparm
SAMBA-SMBCONF-45	If the **username/user** keyword is present, are any group names used in the user-list in any service?	testparm
SAMBA-SMBCONF-46	Is the **username map** keyword present in any service?	testparm
SAMBA-SMBCONF-48	Is the **valid user** keyword present in any appropriate services?	testparm
SAMBA-SMBCONF-49	If the **valid user** keyword is present is the value set to %S?	testparm
SAMBA-SMBCONF-50	Is the **wide links** keyword set appropriately for every service?	testparm
SAMBA-SMBCONF-51	Is the **work group** keyword present in any service?	testparm
SAMBA-SMBCONF-52	Is the **write ok/writable** keyword set appropriately for every service?	testparm
SAMBA-SMBCONF-53	Is the **write list** keyword present in any service?	testparm

Samba Subsystem Components

Samba includes the following components:

nmbd program

nmblookup program

nmb.pid file

passdb configuration file

secrets configuration file

share_info file

smbclient

smbcontrol

smbd

smbpasswd program

smbpasswd file

smbrun

smbstatus

smbspool

smbtar

nmbd

The **/usr/local/samba/bin/nmbd** (NetBIOS name server) is used to provide NetBIOS over IP naming service to Samba clients.

The server listens for IP address requests from Samba clients that broadcast the DNS name of the host the client user wishes to contact. When its own NetBIOS name is specified, the nmbd server responds with the IP address of the host on which it is running.

The server's name is, by default, the primary DNS name of the host on which it is running, but this can be overridden. It always listens for its own name. Additional names for nmbd to respond on can be set via parameters in the **smb.conf** file. Refer to the **netbios aliases** and **netbios name** keywords in the section on the **smb.conf** file for more information.

/usr/local/samba/bin/nmbd also can be configured to:

Respond to different DNS names (**netbios aliases** =)

Act as a WINS database server, creating a database from name registration requests that it receives and replying to queries from clients for these names

Act as a WINS proxy, relaying broadcast queries from clients that do not understand how to talk the WINS protocol to a WIN server

nmblookup

The **/usr/local/bin/nmblookup** program is the **nmb** client used to lookup NetBIOS names. It can be used to query NetBIOS names and map them to IP addresses in a network using NetBIOS over TCP/IP queries. Queries can be directed at a particular IP broadcast area or to a particular machine. All queries are done over UDP.

nmbd.pid

The **/usr/local/var/locks/nmbd.pid** contains the process ID of the **nmbd** process.

passdb Configuration File

The **passdb** file will exist only if the **tdbsam** passwd backend is used on your system. It stores the SambaSAMAccount information. This file requires that user POSIX account information is available from an alternative system source.

This file contains very sensitive information that must be tightly secured.

secrets Configuration File

The **/usr/local/private/secrets** file, if present, contains users' encrypted Samba passwords.

This file is only used if the Samba server is configured for encrypted passwords. Please refer to the "smb.conf Keywords with Security Implications" section for more information.

This file contains very sensitive information that must be tightly secured.

smbclient

The **/usr/local/bin/smbclient** program is used by NonStop Samba users to connect to a remote Samba server. It presents an interface similar to FTP. If the host to which the user wishes to connect requires a password, the user must supply a password.

Once the client is running, the user is presented with a prompt, "**smb: \>**". The backslash ("\") indicates the current working directory on the server, and will change if the current working directory is changed. The prompt indicates that the client is ready to carry out a user command.

Note that all commands operating on the server are actually performed by issuing a request to the target server so the behavior may differ from server to server, depending on how the target server was implemented.

smbcontrol

/usr/local/bin/smbcontrol is the object file for the Samba command interpreter. It communicates with the **smbd** and **nmbd** servers. Any item that can be configured in the **smb.conf** file can be submitted to the running **smbd** or **nmbd** servers.

If the **smbd** type is selected, but no process name, the message is broadcast to all **smbd** server daemons.

If the **nmbd** destination is selected, the message is sent to the **nmbd** daemon specified in the **nmbd.pid** file.

If a process ID is provided, the message is sent to only that process.

Only users responsible for managing the Samba subsystem should have execute access to this program.

3P-ACCESS-SAMBA-01 Use a third-party access control product to allow the users responsible for managing the Samba subsystem the ability to run **smbcontrol** as SUPER.SUPER.

smbd

/usr/local/bin/smbd is the object file for the Samba server daemon. It provides filespace and printer services to clients using the SMB protocol or LanManager clients.

A session is created whenever a client requests one. Each client gets a copy of the server for each session. This copy then services all connections made by the client during that session. When all connections from its client are closed, the copy of the server for that client terminates.

The smb.conf configuration file is automatically reloaded if it changes. Users can force a reload.

smbpasswd Program

The /usr/local/private/smbpasswd program allows users to change their encrypted Samba password, which is stored in the smbpasswd file. It handles the encryption of the stored password.

The program can be run without options, in which case the user is prompted once for their old password and twice for their new password.

Users should not have access to this program if Samba is not configured security = user.

smbpasswd File

The /usr/local/private/smbpasswd file contains users' encrypted Samba passwords.

This file is only used if the Samba server is configured for encrypted passwords. Please refer to the "smb.conf Keywords with Security Implications" section for more information.

smbrun

The /usr/local/bin/smbrun program is an interface program that runs shell commands for the Samba server (smbd). The program can only be started by the Samba server (smbd).

It first changes to the highest level userid that it can, then runs the command line provided.

This program is necessary to allow some operating systems to run external programs as nonroot.

If **smbrun** is executed without a fully qualified path, the path variable set for the environment will be used.

smbstatus

The **/usr/local/bin/smbstatus** program returns a list of current Samba connections and locks and their statuses.

If **status = no** in the smb.conf file, the **smbstatus** program won't be able to show what connections are active. Please refer to the "smb.conf Keywords with Security Implications" for more information.

smbspool

The **/usr/local/bin/smbspool** is a print-spooling program that sends a print file to an SMB printer. The **smbspool** program can be used with any printing system or from a program or script.

smbtar

The **/usr/local/bin/smbtar** program is used to backup and restore files on remote shares to tape via the smbclient utility.

RISK /usr/local/bin/smbtar only requires READ access to perform the file read function. If the **/usr/local/bin/smbtar** program is accessible to general users, files containing sensitive data could be backed up and restored under their userid.

SWAT

/usr/local/bin/swat is a Web-based graphical interface used to edit the **smb.conf** file. It is part of the freeware Samba package. The program should only be moved to the PCs used by the people authorized to configure the **smb.conf** file.

Samba man pages

The **/usr/share/man** directory and all the subdirectories under it contain the Samba **man** pages.

RISK   The **man pages** for freeware packages are in **nroff/troff** format, which is not supported by the **man** utility supplied with OSS.

AP-ADVICE-FLOSS-01   Install **groff** so you can view the **Floss man pages**. A package called **man.db** can be also be installed, which simplifies queries on the **Floss man pages**.

Refer to the OSS Gazette chapters on the **man** program and the **/usr/local/floss** directory for more information.

Temporary Samba Files

The following temporary files are created when Samba is running. They all reside in the **/usr/local/var/locks** directory. These files are created and maintained by Samba and should only be accessable by Samba. They should not be backed up.

Temporary Files Created and Maintained by Samba

Name	Description
Brlock.tdb	Byte-range locking information
Connections.tdb	Cached current connection information used to enforce max connections
login_cache	Cached login information, especially bad password attempts
messages.tdb	Temporary storage of messages being processed by smbd
nonetsamlogon_cache	Cached user net_info_3 structure data from net_samlogon requests (as a domain member)
perfmon/*.tdb	Cached performance information
printing.tdb	Caches output from lpq command created on a per-print-service basis

(Continued)

Name	Description
schannel_store	A confidential file, stored in the PRIVATE_DIR, containing cryptographic connection information so that clients who have temporarily disconnected can reconnect without needing to renegotiate the connection setup process
sessionid	Temporary cache for miscellaneous session information and for utmp handling
share_info.tdb	Stores per-share access information for Samba services (shares)
unexpected.tdb	Stores packets received for which no process is actively listening

testparm program

The /user/local/bin/testparm program is used to syntax check and display the correct parameters set in the smb.conf file. It only guarantees that the file will load it does not validate that the configuration makes sense and will operate as expected.

NonStop SQL and Database Security

A database is a collection of interrelated data with a given structure for storing and providing data, on demand. It is an electronic filing cabinet or data repository. This data repository is a collection of programs called a database management system (DBMS) that enables users to enter, manage, and retrieve data from the database. Today, the term "database" usually refers to *both* the data repository *and* the DBMS.

The enterprise database has evolved into the vital central repository for all customer, partner, marketing, sales, and operational data and intelligence. It is the hub for creating brand identity, strategic and tactical planning, management, and decision-making. Many companies also seek to expand customer and partner relationships by offering new trusted Web services to these customers and partners. The enterprise database is now the uniquely permanent competitive asset—the crown jewel—of today's corporation.

Enterprise database security should focus on preventing accidental damage, mistakes, premeditated fraud, theft, and sabotage. Security policies must control and monitor access by user, specialist, program, and server maintainers as well as general consumers. These policies must consider each user's access from local, remote, and offline access points. They might even consider restricting access to standard data that could potentially infer private or unauthorized information. Finally, security policies should provide sufficient audit, backup, and recovery methods.

At the same time, customers, partners, auditors, and regulatory agencies are demanding accountability for enterprise data. The Health Insurance Portability and Accountability Act (HIPAA) sets standards to protect the privacy of citizens' health information. The Sarbanes-Oxley Act of 2002 requires better internal controls over accounting procedures and financial reporting by companies that trade publically in the U.S. The Payment Card Industry (PCI) data security standard requires all companies that accept credit cards to encrypt transmissions, to provide logical and physical access controls, and to demonstrate monitoring and logging of access to cardholder data.

What is Database Security?

Security Administrators, Auditors, and Database Administrators (or DBAs) each view database security issues differently. This chapter, intended for all three audiences, attempts to summarize SQL concepts and use SQL database terms that relate to securing SQL databases on the HP NonStop Server.

So what does database security include? Minimally, it ensures uninterrupted and flexible database access to appropriate users in proper locations while limiting or denying access from unauthorized users or improper locations. Regulatory requirements like HIPAA and Sarbanes-Oxley may also demand documented and demonstrable auditability and accountability policies and procedures. Each organization's database security ultimately includes whatever access, confidentiality, control, auditability, and accountability components are pertinent to its situation.

Introduction to ANSI SQL and NonStop SQL Security

The relational database management system model is the most popular approach to building and querying corporate databases. The Enscribe database, available with every NonStop system ever shipped, is based on the relational DBMS model but does not contain the active data dictionary found in the ANSI SQL DBMS. As a result, Enscribe is not covered in this chapter. The relational model deals with relationships between database objects.

In a relational DBMS, database objects typically include tables, views, indexes, SQL-invoked routines, and user-defined types. (Note: Some SQL objects, including assertions and user-defined types, are not supported by SQL/MP or SQL/MX). Some objects are built from other objects. For example a table or a view is defined by a set of logically related columns. Columns are database objects.

The Structured Query Language (SQL) is the most common language and is the international standard used to structure, create, load, access, and manage relational databases. The American National Standards Institute (ANSI) ratified the SQL-86 standard and improved it with the SQL-89 standard. SQL/MP is based on ANSI SQL-86 and SQL-89.

ANSI SQL standards generally deal with three entities: objects, actions, and users. SQL objects are defined within the database schema using SQL's Data Definition Language (DDL). Actions are operations performed on SQL objects. Actions include: SELECT, INSERT, DELETE, and UPDATE. Users granted these privileges may invoke one or more of these actions on SQL objects.

NonStop SQL/MX is based on ANSI SQL-92 DML compliance, which developed new object naming rules and introduced stronger security access control standards based on the GRANT/REVOKE model. It was significantly enhanced in 2004 to include full or partial conformance to ANSI's Core SQL:1999.

SQL only focuses on user authentication and controlling user access to SQL objects and some SQL system-wide resources. It does *not*:

Standardize auditing of who did what to which object when.

Encrypt data or manage cross-node, multi-node, or federated (heterogeneous) database security.

Each DBMS vendor may add proprietary extensions beyond the ANSI SQL standards.

AP-ADVICE-SQL-01   Do not rely on SQL security standards to address all database security concerns. SQL only focuses on user authentication and controlling user access to SQL objects and some SQL system-wide resources.

Choosing Between SQL/MP and SQL/MX

DBAs designing a a new application can choose to use SQL/MP, SQL/MX or a combination of both. This section discusses the advantages and disadvantages of each choice.

SQL/MP and SQL/MX are different SQL engines based on different ANSI SQL standards. Each engine supports different SQL directory structures, metadata, and table structures. Each engine uses different approaches to securing the database. Each NonStop customer must decide when and whether to use SQL/MP, SQL/MX or both.

The choice is often automatic. If an existing application was created to use an SQL/MP database, it is unlikely that it will be revised to use the SQL/MX engine or to use the newer SQL/MX metadata and table structures. New applications that need features found only in SQL/MX (such as Publish/Subscribe, rowsets, referential integrity, grant/revoke security, triggers, and more) will be written to use the SQL/MX engine and metadata. Likewise, upgrades of old applications that need the new SQL/MX-unique features will be rewritten to take advantage of the SQL/MX engine. Such upgrades may also require converting data to the new SQL/MX structures.

AP-POLICY-SQLMX-01   If portability of databases and database applications to/from other SQL database server platforms is a requirement, it is recommended that SQL/MX engine be used to create and manage new NonStop SQL table structures.

Both SQL/MX and SQL/MP engines can be run on the same server at the same time.

AP-POLICY-SQLMX-02   SQL/MX is the recommended engine for all future NonStop SQL applications because it supports both SQL/MP tables and the newer ANSI SQL-compliant table-types. Existing SQL/MP applications in production need not be changed because both engines can be run on the same server at the same time.

SQL/MP Architecture and Security

The SQL/MP engine is tightly coupled with Guardian. Its engine executes in the Guardian space and adopts the underlying Guardian security model for its SQL security. It does not use the ANSI SQL standard for GRANT/REVOKE security (outlined later is this chapter). SQL/MP catalogs and tables rely on Guardian file naming for SQL object names.

Guardian security creates and maintains user authorizations using the Guardian security concepts of group access authorizations and user access authorizations. It also distinguishes between local and network access authorization. Safeguard manages userids.

The Guardian security vectors (RWEP) are copied by the SQL/MP engine into the SQL/MP catalog when the tables, indexes, views, collations, and SQL programs are first created. Later, the stored security vectors are checked when the SQL/MP engine operates on those SQL/MP tables, indexes, views, collations, and SQL programs that execute in the Guardian environment.

READ access is required at both the catalog and table or view level. WRITE access is required to the table or view to make INSERTS, UPDATES or DELETES to the data.

SQL/MX Architecture and Security

SQL/MX was designed to conform with ANSI SQL-92, ANSI SQL:1999, and SQL:2003 standards.

SQL/MX uses the ANSI SQL GRANT/REVOKE security paradigm. ANSI SQL requires a valid authorization ID (user name) to allow actions to be performed on objects. SQL/MX uses the Guardian user name validated during LOGON as the session's authorization ID.

RISK The SQL/MX engine performs all access control. It bypasses Safeguard and Guardian security checking on SQL objects.

SQL/MX remains loosely coupled with Guardian in at least two ways:

Although the SQL/MX engine executes in the OSS space. SQL/MX relies on Guardian file structures underneath its SQL naming veneer for its SQL objects. In other words, every SQL object name is mapped (at execution time) to underlying Guardian physical files.

Because the ANSI SQL standard doesn't dictate an exact structure of user names, SQL/MX takes the Guardian userid authenticated at LOGON as the SQL authorization id (userid) to compare against the table of userids that have been GRANTED access to each SQL/MX object and operation.

SQL/MX's database catalogs use expanded metadata to implement GRANT/REVOKE security, ANSI name mapping, and additional constraints.

SQL/MX's engine can also work with SQL/MP tables by mapping ANSI names to SQL/MP tables, then invoking the SQL/MP engine to properly deal with opening and managing the tables. This means the SQL/MX engine can effectively work with SQL/MX and SQL/MP tables in the same queries.

	Discovery Questions	**Look here:**
FILE-POLICY	Is SQL/MP installed on the system?	FILEINFO
FILE-POLICY	Is SQL/MX installed on the system?	FILEINFO
FILE-POLICY	Do applications use: a. SQL/MP engine and tables b. SQL/MX engine with SQL/MP tables c. SQL/MX engine with SQL/MX tables d. SQL/MX engine with mix of MP & MX tables	Policy

Understanding Levels of the SQL Database

Think of each SQL database as an electronic filing cabinet containing:

The database's collection of interrelated tables (or files) of data that may reside both on the current server or may be partitioned across other servers

Additional indexes for some SQL tables, used to improve performance

One or more catalogs of metadata describing database tables (and other DB objects) and how they relate to each other

At the highest level of an SQL environment, every server node (or system) with an SQL database must first have installed the SQL DBMS engine programs to control and permit access to data within the SQL database. Each server must also contain a single SQL system catalog of descriptors (called metadata) to define the structure and locations of the user catalogs and track the usage of SQL objects on the server.

BP-OPSYS-SQLCAT-01   The SQL system catalog should be not be placed on $SYSTEM because if it is and disk ever needs to be replaced, all the system metadata information stored in the catalog will be lost. It should be on a mirrored drive.

BP-OPSYS-SQLCAT-02   The NonStop SQL subsystems (SQL/MP and SQL/MX) should be installed by SUPER.SUPER.

RISK   ANSI did not formalize the SQL system catalog until the SQL-92 standard, so SQL/MP and other DBMS products were forced to define their own, proprietary system catalog structures. Once defined, the SQL/MP catalog structure could not be modified for the ANSI SQL-92 definition without critical impact to SQL/MP customers.

SQL/MP databases have two levels:

A system catalog, which maintains definitions for one or more user catalogs.

One or more user catalogs, which maintain definitions for objects within the user catalog.

SQL/MX databases have 3 levels:

A system catalog, which maintains definitions for one or more user catalogs.

Each user catalog can logically consist of one or more named schemas.

Each schema contains objects for that schema. The schema level is somewhat equivalent to the SQL/MP user catalog level.

The SQL system catalog is, itself, simply a master set of SQL tables containing the metadata describing that database and pointing to all other database catalogs and schemas created on that server. This makes it simple for properly authorized SQL users to routinely discover all components of all database objects stored on the server (and with some SQL DBMS products, on related remote nodes).

AP-ADVICE-USERCAT-01   The DBA should consider a multiple-catalog approach to simplify security considerations if different user groups or applications have different security requirements.

BP-SQL-USERCAT-01   SQL user catalogs should only be installed by the enterprise DBA.

DBAs should design the access matrix for database objects, considering what classes of internal and external users will require access to which objects of subsets of the user databases and what type of actions will be allowed.

	Discovery Questions	Look here:
SQLMP-SYSCAT	Where is the SQL/MP System Catalog located?	SQLCI
SQLMP-SYSCAT	Who owns the SQL/MP System Catalog?	SQLCI
SQLMP-SYSCAT	Is the SQL/MP System Catalog secured correctly?	SQLCI
SQLMP-SYSCAT	What version is the SQL/MP System Catalog?	SQLCI
SQLMP-USERCAT	Are there SQL/MP user catalogs defined/	SQLCI
SQLMP-USERCAT	What is the location and version of each SQL/MP User Catalog?	SQLCI, dba/m
SQLMX-SYSCAT	Where is the SQL/MX System Catalog located?	mxci
SQLMX-SYSCAT	Who owns the SQL/MX System Catalog?	mxci
SQLMX-SYSCAT	Is the SQL/MX System Catalog secured correctly?	mxci
SQLMX-SYSCAT	What version is the SQL/MX System Catalog?	mxci

(Continued)

	Discovery Questions	Look here:
SQLMX-USERCAT	Are there SQL/MX user catalogs defined/	mxci
SQLMX-USERCAT	What is the location and version of each SQL/MX User Catalog?	mxci, NSM/web

SQL Security Features

The SQL DBMS software is the "gate keeper," guarding every access to the database—checking every package before it enters the database and checking every program or user before allowing access into the database. The SQL standard offers built-in database integrity features and well-defined access control structures to help guard against fraud, accidental or premeditated damage to database integrity, or other unauthorized actions. These SQL features include:

Constraints
Referential Integrity
SQL Users and Privileges
Views

Constraints

Constraints can be applied to SQL columns and/or base tables to set conditions that data must meet in order to be entered into the database.

Constraints help assure appropriateness of data in an SQL table and may guard against some forms of fraudulent insider activities. Add a constraint by specifying a condition or conditions that all values in a column within a table (or for table constraints, all columns in that table) must first meet before the values can be stored in the table.

RISK   Constraints may be added or dropped by authorized users.

BP-SQL-SECURITY-01   Only DBAs should have the ability to add or drop contraints.

Referential Integrity

Referential integrity enforces a greater degree of validity checking and will reinforce stability between related SQL tables.

SQL/MX introduced the ability to use referential integrity with the SQL database. Referential integrity is a set of columns in a table that may only contain values matching those in a set of columns in a referenced table.

SQL Users and Privileges

SQL Users and Privileges (including GRANT/REVOKE Security available in SQL/MX tables) further limit information and actions available to specific users inside an organization as well as general users outside the organization.

Actions are operations performed on SQL objects: SELECT, INSERT, DELETE, and UPDATE. Users with the right privileges may invoke one or more of these actions on SQL objects.

A privilege is normally an authorization for a user to perform an operation on an object. Each privilege is stored in the database's SQL catalog.

SQL/MP stores the object owner's userid and the Guardian security string (RWEP) for each object in the catalog.

SQL/MX stores a row in the catalog for each object. The row contains the following:

Grantor
Grantee
Object
Action
Grantable

A grantor, usually the owner of the table, is authorized to GRANT authorization to other users to perform an action on the specific object. The grantee is the user who receives the authorization to perform an action on an object from the grantor.

When an object is first created, a user is assigned ownership of that object. At that point, only the owner may perform any action on the object unless the owner or another privileged userid GRANTED the action. But the owner may also make other users grantors of privileges for a particular object.

The following table shows the SQL/MX GRANT privileges, the security protection used for each privilege, and the SQL object that the privilege applies to.

Figure 6.1
Grantable privileges

Type of Protection	Privilege	Applicable Object(s)
Viewing	SELECT	Tables and columns
Creating	INSERT	Tables and columns
Modifying	UPDATE	Tables and columns
Deleting	DELETE	Tables
Referencing	REFERENCES	Tables and columns
Using	USAGE	Domains, characters sets
Activating	TRIGGER	Tables
Executing	EXECUTE	SQL-invoked routines (SQL/MX stored procedures in JAVA).

Access to SQL databases may be REVOKED by the owner.

BP-SQL-SECURITY-02   SQL databases should be owned by a privileged Job Function ID, not an individual user.

BP-SQL-SECURITY-03   Only users who require access to the database in order to perform their jobs should be given access to any data tables.

3P-ACCESS-SQLCI-01   A third party access control product that can secure at the command level and provide an audit of the user's activity should be used to grant only appropriate users access to SQLCI or **mxci** as the database owner.

AP-ADVICE-SQL-02   When using SQL/MX, the DBA should consider restricting access to certain base tables (or combinations of tables) for *any* class of users.

AP-ADVICE-SQL-03   When using SQL/MX, the DBA should base access to specific columns and rows on each user's tasks.

The SQL/MX engine uses ANSI SQL Authorization IDs to identify users during the processing of SQL statements. An SQL/MX authorization ID is a valid Guardian user name. Additionally, ANSI SQL adds two special Authorization IDs:

PUBLIC ID
SYSTEM ID

The PUBLIC ID represents all authorization IDs known to the network at all times, present and future, and can be used in the GRANT and REVOKE statements.

The SYSTEM ID is the implicit grantor of privileges to the creators of objects.

The SYSTEM ID cannot be specified in any DDL statement. This is an internal mechanism, mentioned here only because it is visible from a query of the metadata.

The SYSTEM ID cannot be specified in GRANT and REVOKE statements.

NonStop SQL/MX recognizes Safeguard or Guardian userids and records them in the SQL/MX metadata and file labels. However, NonStop SQL/MX does not grant access to, recognize or consider the Guardian user group. It does not allow aliases or wildcarded userids to be used in GRANT and REVOKE statements. SQL/MX does not currently support SQL ROLES.

SQL and SUPER.SUPER

The SQL creator of an object is the owner of the object. This userid is the one who can grant access to that object. Normally, the DBA creates database catalogs, base tables, constraints, and stored procedures, and then GRANTS the appropriate actions for the SQL/MX database objects to appropriate users. These users may then create views and GRANT appropriate access to the views to their list of appropriate users.

NonStop SQL enables SUPER.SUPER to act in the place of the owner of any object on a given node. However, whenever SUPER.SUPER creates an object in a schema owned by some other user, the actual ownership of that object is assigned to that user, not to SUPER.SUPER.

AP-ADVICE-SQL-04   The application's DBA Job Function ID should be the owner of the application's SQL database.

AP-ADVICE-SQL-05   The security administrator should have the right to GRANT and REVOKE privileges.

AP-ADVICE-SQL-06   Do not design SQL databases so that every-day actions require the use of SUPER.SUPER.

Views and Privileges

A view is an SQL object that acts like a regular table to its authorized user, though, in fact, it is simply a logical table resulting from a SELECT statement on one or more base tables or other views to create what the user sees.

AP-ADVICE-SQL-07   Views are a good way to restrict a user's access to sensitive data.

SQL views provide the tightest granular level of security for data within a database. They make it possible to secure down to a single row and a single column within that row.

BP-SQL-VIEW-01   For certain base tables (or combinations of tables) access to the base table should only be granted via views to ANY class of users.

Security with Dynamic, Static, & Embedded SQL

SQL is flexible and may be less than predictable. This raises concerns on the best ways to secure SQL queries.

Embedded SQL Queries

Embedded SQL, as the term implies, offers the ability to directly include SQL declarations and statements within another, more traditional programming language like COBOL, or C/C++. Since the program and SQL statements are written and compiled in advance, they generally are more reliable, predictable, and may perform better.

Security should apply the same restrictions as to what SQL objects users may access within embedded SQL queries.

AP-ADVICE-SQL-08   Make use of embedded SQL to control each query more tightly in advance and to restrict access to a smaller subset of the users authorized to use the application.

Dynamic SQL Queries

Dynamic SQL allows an SQL user to execute SQL statements that are structured and compiled at run-time. Dynamic SQL queries may include a user typing ad hoc SQL statements into an SQL command line interface (SQLCI or **mxci**) or a different user picking options from a windows-based application that constructs, compiles, and executes an SQL query on behalf of the user.

The dynamic SQL query offers great flexibility, but it is more difficult to assure safe, predictable statements will be generated.

3P-ACCESS-SQLCI-01   A third party access control product that can secure at the command level and provide an audit of the user's activity should be used to grant only appropriate users access to SQLCI or **mxci** as the database owner.

Static SQL Queries

Static SQL simply means that the source text of the SQL statements are part of application programs. The enterprise application should have control over users given access to run these programs.

Securing dynamic or static SQL queries requires the same thought as to what users may access and to which database objects they need access.

Encrypting Database Data

Accidental or premeditated access to, damage of, or theft from an enterprise database may come from many different sources. A remote attack might occur from a public network like the Internet. An internal user might attempt unauthorized access or "short-cuts" across a local area network or from a locally-attached terminal. Simple precautions and thoughtful design of database access control will stop most unwanted activity. However, determined attackers often use different software tools to persistently attempt multiple password schemes, to search for "back door" entry points, and to "sniff" and monitor sessions containing authorized users' userids and passwords to gain access to an enterprise database.

Encryption, or translation of data into a secret code, may be one of the most effective ways to achieve data security. To make sense of encrypted data, a user must have access to both the original encryption algorithm and the secret key that enables him to decrypt it.

RISK   ANSI SQL does not have standards for encrypting database data. Neither SQL/MP nor SQL/MX has database encryption extensions.

Data can be encrypted data in either or both of the following states:

Data at rest
Data in transit

Data at Rest

Data at rest includes:

Data stored in an online database
Data stored on disk
Data stored online or offline database extracts
Backups transferred to disk, tape, or optical (CD/DVD) media
Print media

The only system that is safe from network intrusion is one that has no network capability. Sensitive data should never be stored as plain text without a solid business reason and adequate access controls. Many companies have suffered from the theft of sensitive data by employees.

BP-POLICY-ENCRYPT-01   Sensitive data at rest should never be stored as plain text in the clear when accessible from the Internet or other public network or access points.

RISK Disks, tapes, and optical disks can contain sensitive data. Therefore, access to such media must be controlled physically to ensure security.

AP-ADVICE-SQLDATA-01 Physical and procedural protection of data at rest is vital. Offline copies of sensitive data must be carefully handled and tracked to avoid theft or loss.

AP-ADVICE-SQLDATA-02 Copies of sensitive data should only be made by authorized personnel.

AP-POLICY-BACKUP-04 The Corporate Security Policy should detail procedures for validating requests for backup disks, tapes, and optical disks and for securing such media in an appropriate manner.

3P-ENCRYPT-SQLDATA-01 Use a third party encryption product to secure data at rest.

Data in Transit

Data in transit is data on the move by any means, including:

Data traveling over any voice or data networks

Data gathered through publicly accessible programs, database query tools, search engines, dial-ups, and other wired or wireless access points.

BP-POLICY-ENCRYPT-02 Sensitive data-in-transit should be encrypted using appropriate hardware or software technologies.

3P-ENCRYPT-SQLDATA-02 Use a third party encryption product to secure the transmission of data across public transit.

Auditing Database Operations

It is important to go beyond active access control and provide after-the-fact tracing of actions by all users. To help reconstruct details of financial and business transactions, audit trails contain logs of who accessed or changed what information, when, and possibly why. Some database products offer options to even rollback or undo changes.

In the context of SQL DBMS products, auditing functions should log:

DML operations (INSERT, UPDATE, DELETE, SELECT)
DDL operations (CREATE xxx, ALTER xxx, DROP xxx, etc.)
Certain utility operations (GRANT, REVOKE LOAD, MODIFY, PURGE, SECURE)
Compiles and RUN statements

AP-POLICY-AUDITING-01 Develop an end-to-end logging and auditing strategy.

RISK SQL databases are often used as general database servers. This means the DBMS, itself, often can log only the operations requested by a session from a communications subsystem (ODBC, JDBC, etc.). Such logs may not show the true identity of the original requester.

RISK Enterprise database transactions often span more than one server, and auditing requires locating logs on multiple database server nodes.

RISK Completely legitimate replication software often copies data to unaudited nodes.

To effectively audit database operations, you must identify all components (end-to-end and to replicates) and assure logs can be coordinated to identify the true identity of all users.

BP-SQL-AUDITING-01 SQL databases should utilize TMF transaction auditing to ensure transaction consistency. All SQL/MP catalogs are automatically audited by TMF.

3P-ACCESS-SQLCI-01 A third party access control product that can secure at the command level and provide an audit of users activity should be used to grant only appropriate users access to SQLCI or **mxci** as the database owner.

Safeguard & NonStop SQL

Safeguard provides provides ways to centralize NonStop server platform security and Enscribe data security, but it has limited control over SQL objects.

SQL/MP

The NonStop SQL/MP engine operates in the Guardian space and relies on Guardian security vectors (RWEP). SQL users are authorized to operate on SQL/MP objects running in the Guardian environment based on their Guardian userid and the object's assigned security vector stored in the SQL/MP catalog.

SQL/MP programs stored in the OSS environment are secured via OSS file security.

RISK   Safeguard can only control access to SQL/MP tables at the VOLUME and SUBVOLUME level. SQL/MP objects cannot be secured at the file level, therefore individual SQL tables, views, indexes, etc, cannot be protected by Safeguard.

3P-ADVICE-OBJSEC -01   To adequately secure SQL/MP databases, a third party object security module that can secure the objects at the file level is required.

With SQL/MP, Safeguard is used for:

Process startups, though not very helpful
To limit CREATE actions
User administration
User authentication.

SQL/MX

The SQL/MX engine continues to use the SQL/MP engine to check the Guardian-based security vectors to control access to SQL/MP tables and views.

The NonStop SQL/MX Release 1 engine operates in the OSS space. It supports ANSI SQL-92 compliant actions (DML) to be used with traditional SQL/MP objects that still reside in the Guardian space and use Guardian-based security vectors for its DB objects. It does *not* support ANSI SQL-92 compliant objects (DDL).

The NonStop SQL/MX Release 2 engine operates in the OSS space. It adds support for ANSI SQL-92 compliant objects (DDL). Security authorization to operate on the SQL/MX tables, views, and stored procedures in Java (SPJs) is maintained by ANSI SQL's GRANT and REVOKE security statements and completely *ignores* any Safeguard rules that might have been associated with these SQL/MX objects. SQL/MX source programs and related files stored in the OSS space are subject to the same OSS security rules as any other files stored in OSS.

RISK Safeguard is never involved in accesses to SQL/MX objects at all, not even at the VOLUME or SUBVOLUME level. Therefore, SQL/MX files can be created on any disk, regardless of any existing Safeguard VOLUME Protection Records that would deny a user such access in the Guardian environment.

With SQL/MX, Safeguard is used for:

Process startups, though not very helpful
User administration
User authentication.

Security Choices: Hardware or Software

Whether the approach includes aggressive encryption, auditing, and access control to specific types or instances of data or a more basic access control to a site's database, consider costs and trade-offs associated with securing your database using hardware, application software, or the database engine itself.

SQL DBMS Engine

The database engine is generally the best control point for database security. The DBA group begins by identifying all internal and external user communities and mapping out their individual database access needs. Next, the DBA group should implement comprehensive security policies where the SQL engine becomes the primary enforcer of these security policies.

Application Software

Application software with embedded SQL is generally the most flexible control point for database security. The application can control user access to the databases via logon scripts, checks and balances, passwords, etc. Security is controlled if the application is secure and the only method of accessing the database is through the application. Applications should also audit all user activity.

Hardware

Hardware is sometimes the most economical point for simple point-to-point database encryption and some access control. Encrypting modems or security processors might be a much more cost-efficient method to minimize impact on NonStop server performance than encrypting with software libraries.

Software

Software is the most economical because only the confidential fields within the database need to be encrypted. The data is encrypted on the disk and in transit. This method is easy to update, is replicable, and can ease the processing load.

How SQL/MX Maps ANSI SQL Objects to Guardian File Structures

NonStop SQL/MX introduced several major architectural changes from SQL/MP. Two of the more dramatic changes pertain to how the SQL/MX engine creates and manages SQL objects and how it maps logical SQL object names to Guardian physical files that contain both metadata and actual data for those objects.

SQL/MP keeps structural descriptions of its tables and views within:

Metadata tables
DP2 volume labels

DP2 volume labels are a rather limited resource. SQL/MX overcomes the limitations by keeping all its runtime metadata information in a new SQL/MX-generated file called a resource fork. Resource forks are created for *every* persistent SQL/MX object.

The resource fork is one of two physical files instantiated whenever the SQL/MX object is created. The second file, the data fork (where user data resides), is similar to an SQL/MP format object.

Since SQL/MX instantiates new pairs of physical Guardian files for each new SQL/MX object, the act of creating a simple database may easily result in hundreds of Guardian files being created.

RISK The SQL/MX engine completely controls access security for these new files, so they pose no additional security concerns.

The SQL/MX engine can use any of three different naming options when working with SQL/MP tables and views:

1. The physical Guardian name for an SQL/MP table or view. If the NAMETYPE attribute for an object is set to NSK, the SQL/MX engine, unless explicitly specified, automatically qualifies a physical table or view name with the current default node, volume, and sub-volume names.

2. A DEFINE name created within **mxci** or inherited from the TACL process or the OSS shell can be used as a logical name for an SQL/MP table, view, or partition to provide location independence or more understandable names. For example, the name =CUSTOMERS is simpler to understand than \S1.$DATA.WEST. CSTMERS. When SQL/MX compiles a statement, it replaces the DEFINE name in the statement with the associated Guardian physical name.

    NOTE: DEFINE names cannot be used to refer to SQL/MX tables, views, partitions, or stored procedures.

3. An ANSI name for an SQL/MP table or view. The NAMETYPE attribute defaults to ANSI, allowing you to use logical names of SQL/MP aliases for SQL/MP objects. To use ANSI names for SQL/MP tables and views, create mappings from logical to physical names by issuing a command in the form:

```
CREATE   SQLMP   ALIAS   catalog-name.schema-name
table-name [\node.]$volume.subvol.filename
```

This command inserts a row in the SQL/MX catalog's OBJECTS table for the SQL/MP alias to simulate the ANSI name that represents the underlying Guardian physical name of the SQL/MP object. True ANSI names do not exist for SQL/MP objects. The OBJECTS table, created at SQL/MX installation time, is used to store mappings from logical object names to physical Guardian locations.

When a new SQL/MX object is created, the ANSI object name is mapped to a system-generated Guardian file name, and two physical Guardian files are instantiated:

The data fork, which contains the user data

The resource fork, which contains structural information such as the partition map

The new object includes a logical file label to store the object's file attributes and information about its dependent objects. The resource fork is a new file that contains structural descriptions of a table.

Within an **mxci** session, the SHOWLABEL command (and its DETAIL option) shows the object version, physical (Guardian) location, security and other characteristics of the SQL/MX tables, triggers temporary tables, views, or indexes. SHOWLABEL does not support stored procedures, SQL/MP objects, or SQL/MP aliases. It requires that TMF be available and running on the system.

The Guardian files representing SQL/MX objects can reside on any node from which the object's catalog is visible. The volume must be an audited, non-virtual volume on the specified node. The subvolume is the designated SUBVOLUME for the schema in which the object is being created. Subvolume names all begin with the letters ZSD, followed by a letter (for example, ZSDF) and must be exactly eight characters. The file name is a Guardian file name that is exactly eight characters in length and ends with the digits 00.

Whenever a Guardian file name for an SQL/MX object is explicitly specified, it must match the designated schema SUBVOLUME name for the schema in which the object exists. Otherwise, SQL/MX returns an error.

PARTITION-NAME is an SQL identifier for a partition.

SQL Large Objects (BLOBs/CLOBs)

ANSI SQL:1999 introduced the Binary Large Object (BLOB) standard data type to enable SQL to store, manage, and deliver audio, photo, and video content. The Character Large Object (CLOB) was also introduced to include XML and other large character requirements.

RISK Neither SQL/MP nor SQL/MX Release 2.0 directly supports BLOB or CLOB data types within the database engine.

HP introduced *Large Objects for NonStop SQL* to satisfy a growing demand for high-performance management of BLOBs and CLOBs on the NonStop server. This product provides a C API (which can also be called from COBOL) and a separate set of utility functions that manage a combination of NonStop SQL/MP and Enscribe files to store and manage large binary and character objects. This product only manages a LOB database on a single NonStop node—its data structures do not partition across EXPAND. Since it writes LOBs to Enscribe files and SQL/MP tables, that node may use TMF and RDF to audit and replicate new and changed large objects to other nodes.

Guardian security vectors (RWEP) control access to these SQL/MP large objects.

SQL/MX Release 2.1 supports BLOB/CLOB data type support in JDBC/MX. This feature maps the LOB data type used with JDBC/MX into VARCHAR columns in one or more rows of a SQL/MX ANSI-compliant table. On the SQL/MX database side (transparent to the Java application), the physical implementation employs two tables—one for the standard data types and another for the large objects—referred to as the base table and LOB table, respectively. Both tables can be treated as any other SQL/MX table.

GRANT/REVOKE security controls access to the SQL/MX base tables and LOB tables.

Compiling and Executing NonStop SQL Programs

An SQL program is an SQL query embedded within a host language program such as COBOL or C/C++.

At a basic level, an SQL compiler processes an SQL query and produces a query execution plan. Then, the SQL executor uses the execution plan to produce the query result. The execution plan may be used for the SQL session and discarded, cached for reuse, or even stored for later reuse. Each SQL engine may handle this differently.

SQL/MP queries may be embedded within COBOL, TAL, or C programs. SQL/MX queries may be embedded within COBOL, C, or C++ programs. (SQL/MX Release 1.8 supported SQL in Java [SQLJ]; however, Java programmers use JDBC to interface to SQL databases, and HP discontinued support for SQL within Java.)

Embedding SQL statements and directives in host language programs (COBOL, C/C++) and precompiling these programs, has significant advantages. This practice:

> Combine the flexibility and access control of SQL databases with the power of a procedural language to process and manipulate stored data
>
> Abstract the data layer from the program; for example: Adding a column to a table does not affect the logic of the program
>
> Generate efficient execution plan once, before runtime, since the SQL database access request is compiled and optimized in advance
>
> Prepare Static SQL statements to specifications under controlled conditions, making them less susceptible to accidental or deliberate alterations

Compiling and Running NonStop SQL programs under OSS and GUARDIAN

SQL/MP queries may be entered directly into the Guardian *SQLCI* program in conversational mode or via an INFILE. SQL/MX queries may be directly entered into the OSS **mxci** program, either as batch input files or in conversational mode. These queries will be compiled and immediately executed.

SQL/MP and SQL/MX use different approaches to manage SQL statements and directives embedded in host language programs. Both products separate embedded SQL statements and directives from the host language source statements, but how this is achieved and how resulting modules are stored and processed are quite different. Both SQL/MP and SQL/MX offer compiling options under Guardian and under OSS. Each has different options to carefully consider. Please consult the following manuals for specific details:

> For SQL/MP, refer to the *SQL/MP Programming Manual for C*, the *SQL/MP Programming Manual for COBOL*, and the *SQL Programming Manual for TAL*.
>
> For SQL/MX, refer to the *SQL/MX Programming Manual for C and COBOL*.

SQL/MP

After adding any required DEFINEs, a host language program with embedded SQL/MP statements and directives is input directly into the appropriate host language compiler (C, COBOL, etc.) for processing. The compiler separates the SQL and compiles the host language code, creating an object code file that is bound together with the original SQL source statements.

Next, the SQL/MP compiler is invoked to produce the query execution plan and to register the program and dependencies in the SQL/MP catalog. This approach requires customized HP host language compilers to recognize and deal with embedded SQL/MP statements and directives.

BP-SQL/MP-SQLCOMP-01   Use SQLCOMP to register compiled SQL/MP program files in SQL/MP catalogs. Then, use the SQLCI utility command DISPLAY USE OF to display a list of SQL objects and registered SQL/MP object programs that directly or indirectly depend on the specified object.

DISPLAY USE OF only lists registered SQL programs, since neither unregistered SQL programs nor their dependencies are described in catalogs.

When SQLCOMP is used to register compiled SQL/MP program files in SQL/MP catalogs, the SQL/MP programs files take on the Guardian security vectors from the SQL program files.

RISK   Because the compiled and registered SQL/MP programs files take on the Guardian security vectors from the SQL program files, in some cases Safeguard Protection Records are lost during compilation.

BP-SQL/MP-SQLCOMP-02   Any Safeguard Protection Records must be explicitly restored after SQL compilation.

3P-ADVICE-OBJSEC-01   Use a third party object security product to secure both the source code and the compiled objects.

SQL/MX

SQL/MX Release 2 uses special PC-based or NonStop Server–based preprocessors to split the host language code (with annotated SQL statements) and the embedded SQL. It can direct the host language code to crosscompilers located on a PC or to standard-language compilers on the NonStop Server to generate a compiled object containing definitions of the CLI procedure calls for the translated SQL statements. The preprocessor creates separate SQL/MX module definitions with the SQL source statements. The SQL module definitions may either be packaged back into the compiled object (embedded) or be stored as a standalone file that may be called from more than one compiled object. With either option, the SQL/MX compiler is invoked next to produce the query execution plan. The SQL/MX compiler (**mxcmp**) does not register the program or dependencies within the SQL/MX catalog. This is a major change from SQL/MP.

The NonStop SQL/MX subsystem, including the compiler and executor, operates within the OSS space. HP provides the following two optional capabilities. SQL/MX users may use one, both, or neither of these options:

Compile source programs containing embedded SQL/MX code using a Guardian-based compiler. This approach offers some features in the Guardian-based COBOL or C compilers that are not offered under the same OSS-based compilers.

Execute an object program under Guardian that uses SQL/MX-based objects. This approach offers the ability to use Guardian-based runtime options not available under OSS.

At runtime, the SQL/MX-compiled object is still executed by the SQL Executor running in the OSS space. The *SQL/MX Programming Manual for C and COBOL* further discusses how to use these options.

AP-ADVICE-POLICY-01   Let corporate policies determine whether to secure and manage your host language source code and embedded SQL/MX statements in the Guardian space, using Guardian/Safeguard-based security, or in the OSS space, using OSS file security strings. It is simple to pull source code into the SQL/MX preprocessor from either location.

BP-SQL/MX-MXCMP-01   Information about dependencies between object types is derived from the Explain section of a compiled module. Use the DISPLAY USE OF command before an SQL/MX DDL change to determine program dependencies and to identify modules that need to be recompiled.

Since SQL/MX focuses on ANSI's Catalog.Schema.Object naming, issues with SQL/MX program module management include:

Keeping track of executables and their SQL/MX modules

Identifying which module files go with which application and grouping of module files belonging to the same application

Securing modules against accidental overwrites or module tampering, because:

– An application accessing different sets of tables requires multiple compiled copies

– Multiple development and production versions of the same application may exist

– Several developers often work on copies of the same application

Moving an application into production, often requires that supporting files be moved along with the executables.

BP-SQL/MX-MXCMP-02   Co-locate all modules for a specific application in a single directory, even when they support both test and production environments on the NonStop system. Name the module in the source file and include the application name in the module name. Use preprocessor command line options to group modules by application naming conventions, targeting a set of tables, and/or for versioning of modules. For instance, Application.exe could be named:

```
Catalog.Schema.<group>^ApplicationModuleM^
<tableset>^<version>
```

BP-SQL/MX-MXCMP-03   When moving an SQL/MX program with compiled modules, compile the program on the development system and move the executable and its modules to the production system. This way, no SQL recompilation is required on the secure system. The SQL statements in the program must use Late Name Resolution. They can use MAP DEFINEs for SQL/MP objects or PROTOTYPE statements for MP or MX objects, which specify a host variable name in place of a table. On the production system, specify which table to access by changing the table name in the DEFINE before running the program or by passing the table name in the value of the host variable for the PROTOTYPE statement. Similarity checking must be enabled for MP and MX objects.

Policy should determine if SQL programs may be compiled on production systems. There may be instances where this is required.

BP-SQL/MX-MXCMP-04   Disable automatic recompilation by using:

```
CONTROL QUERY DEFAULT AUTOMATIC_RECOMPILATION 'OFF';
```

The executor uses similarity checking to determine whether the statement's query execution plans are valid. If similarity check fails (or is not enabled) the executor (by default) automatically recompiles the statement. Since automatically recompiled plans are not stored, each time the application is re-executed, plans will be recompiled.

BP-SQL/MX-MXCMP-05   Since compiled objects are not registered in SQL/MX catalogs, they can not use GRANT/REVOKE security. Secure OSS-based SQL modules by setting the sticky bit of the /usr/tandem/sqlmx/ USERMODULES directory.

	Discovery Questions	Look here:
SQL-POLICY	Is compiling allowed on the system?	Policy
SQL-POLICY	Is the language source code secured in the OSS file space or the Guardian file space?	Policy
SQL-POLICY	Are all SQL modules, both development and production, for each application located in the same directory?	Policy
SQL-POLICY	Is auto-compiling allowed on the system?	Policy
SQL-POLICY	Are procedures in place to ensure that any Safeguard Protection Records are restored after SQL compiles?	Policy
SQL-POLICY	Are procedures in place to locate all dependencies when modules are recompiled ?	Policy

Securing Client Queries from ODBC/MX and JDBC/MX

ODBC/MX and JDBC/MX are database access transport programs that provide a method for using DBMS independent of the programming language or operating system on the host.

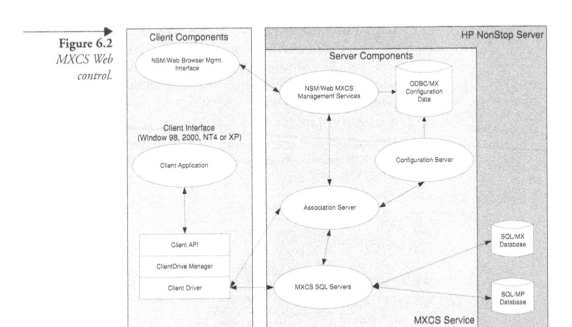

Figure 6.2
MXCS Web control.

MXCS Access authorization

Authorization to access NonStop SQL databases begins with an authenticated Guardian user name. The MXCS SQL server program (MXOSRVR) follows SQL/MX rules for accessing SQL/MX objects (and SQL/MP rules for SQL/MP objects), and as such, the SQL objects are subject to the normal SQL rules that govern access to those objects. For example, to read from an MX table, the user must have the SELECT privilege.

Each MXCS SQL process runs under a Guardian user name that is used to authorize access to SQL objects.

User Authentication

MXCS uses a model in which users request a connection to a named service, known as the data source. To complete the connection, the user provides a user name and a password, which are passed in a secure, private packet to the MXCS server.

The username can be either a Guardian userid or a Safeguard alias.

Since Safeguard supports multiple alias and password pairs for a single Guardian username, it may be better to use the Safeguard alias name format. In effect, this maps to a default schema and can improve performance because reusing the underlying username leads to object caching.

Passwords

Safeguard supports multiple alias and password pairs for a single Guardian username. This can improve performance because object caching reuses the underlying username.

AP-ADVICE-SQLODBC-01 ODBC clients should manage expired passwords to allow for continuous availability.

To enable notification of password expiration, set the SQL_ATTR_ WARNING environment variable in the SET tab to 1. (The default value of SQL_ATTR_WARNING is 0 (disabled).) The expired password can be detected and managed or the access refused.

MXCS Object Access Controls

AP-ADVICE-SQLODBC-02   To prevent users from seeing or updating NonStop SQL/MX object metadata, control access to either the NonStop SQL MP_PARTITIONS table or the catalog tables.

AP-ADVICE-SQLODBC-03   To allow users to access the SQL/MX object metadata but not the data itself, control access to the individual SQL/MX object.

RISK   Initiating changes to access privileges causes all existing opens to fail. This can disrupt service to the database.

MXCS Access Control:

Use SUPER.SUPER. when installing MXCS. Starting the association server requires that you are logged on with a userid that has Guardian access to run the MXOAS file. Thereafter, a userid with MXCS OPERA-TOR permission can enable and disable the MXCS service and manage MXCS from NSM/web or **mxci**.

All operations in MXCS, require the correct access privileges to:

> NonStop SQL catalogs
> MXCS catalogs
> Individual NonStop SQL objects.

A userid with OPERATOR permission is the only userid that can manage MXCS.

MXCS users have access permissions based on the security values for their Guardian userid. PUBLIC has USER permission and the SUPER.SUPER has OPERATOR permission by default.

Permissions can be assigned and changed using NSM/Web only by SUPER.SUPER. All other users can view permissions but not assign or change them.

There are two permissions:

MXCS Permission	Access
USER	View status and configuration of MXCS services, data sources, and server.
	View permissions.
OPERATOR	Enable, disable, manage, and configure MXCS.
	View permissions.

Use and Limitations of SQL/MX Engine Features

The SQL/MX Release 2.0 engine first introduced several ANSI SQL-92–and SQL:1999-compliant security features, such as Referential Integrity and GRANT/REVOKE security. These features are not available in the SQL/MP engine or the SQL/MX Release 1.x engines.

The SQL/MX engine executes SQL queries with simultaneous and secure access to both SQL objects defined in SQL/MP catalogs and SQL objects defined in SQL/MX catalogs. It is important to understand, though, that Referential Integrity constraints and GRANT/REVOKE security will not be used with SQL objects defined in SQL/MP catalogs. The SQL/MX engine simply calls on the SQL/MP engine to check the Guardian-based security vectors for access control. In order to actually use GRANT/REVOKE security with these objects (tables, views, etc.), they would first require conversion into ANSI SQL-compliant objects—typically a major conversion.

Securing Dynamic SQL Queries

Dynamic SQL queries could pose one of the greater threats for accidental or intentional impact to the contents of an SQL database and to the performance of a NonStop Server. Dynamic SQL offers automatic generation, compilation, and execution of SQL statements at runtime. Dynamic SQL makes it simple to write SQL code that can adjust to varying databases, conditions, or servers. It also could make it easier to bypass security vectors that were carefully pre-assigned to precompiled, stored applications.

Unlike static SQL statements, dynamic SQL is not typically embedded and precompiled in a source program and can change from one execution to the next. Potential problems might include reduced online system performance (usually due to SQL statement compile time at every execution), possible selection or modification of the wrong data source, or deliberate data fraud, damage, or theft from unauthorized users.

Dynamic SQL queries are routinely issued from legitimate database access points, such as SQL query tools or traditional PC client programs using the

ODBC API, Web browsers or Java applets using JDBC queries, and by IMPORT and other utilities. From Guardian, users issue dynamic SQL queries to the SQL/MP engine from the SQL Conversational Interface (SQLCI). From OSS, they issue dynamic SQL queries to the SQL/MX engine from the SQL/MX Conversational Interface (**mxci**).

AP-ADVICE-SQL-10   Although every access (static or dynamic) to SQL tables or views is controlled by the SQL engine via predetermined security vectors, the security staff should:

Carefully identify every possible access point into your database

Make certain that dynamic SQL queries cannot inherit security vectors from a running process's own authorization ID

Consider automated policies (e.g., CMON, stored procedure, etc.) that can limit database access points capable of generating dynamic SQL to operate only during low-activity windows

Using Triggers to Manage Dynamic SQL/MX queries

Triggers are a mechanism that resides in the database and specifies that when a particular action—an INSERT, DELETE, or UPDATE—occurs on a particular table, SQL/MX should automatically perform one or more additional actions.

Triggers can be used to stop, detect, and alarm on ANSI SQL standard security features. They may have an impact on performance. In that case, an asynchronous technique like the use of the SQL/MX Publish-Subscribe feature may offer a better alternative.

RISK   In a change-intensive environment, triggers may dramatically reduce throughput.

An asynchronous technique, such as the use of the SQL/MX Publish-Subscribe feature, may offer a better alternative in a change-intensive environment.

AP-ADVICE-SQL-11   In data warehouse environments, there would be little performance impact in adding triggers, since the triggers would *only*

occur during unauthorized changes to these environments. Data in data marts and data warehouse applications is static except during batch update times, so these applications would rarely use triggers. Data corrections are already done before the data is batch-loaded into the data warehouse, so triggers are turned off to improve performance during the batch loads.

For OLTP, ODS, or other real-time applications, triggers are traditionally very important. They are used as an alarm mechanism to start actions when the data has significantly changed. A common action is to call a stored procedure in this situation. Typically, the stored procedures are kept small (for performance reasons again). Some situations where this might apply are:

Fraud detection, meaning data entered that is completely incompatible with an expected data norm, such as an outrageous account number for a bank or a strange are a code/country code for a telecom company

Data has dropped below a threshold, meaning that the customer is now in trouble (e.g., bank balance gone negative)

Major database security violations might trigger messages to the security administrator's pocket PC or mobile phone

AP-ADVICE-SQL-12   If using the SQL/MX engine, consider using database triggers (with ANSI-compliant tables) and/or stored procedures written in Java (SPJs) as effective methods to trap and manage unauthorized database changes. However, carefully consider the likely performance impact before using these tools.

Four NonStop SQL Security Paradigms

Each NonStop SQL installation can choose from four ways to install and operate NonStop SQL.

Option 1: Install/Operate only the SQL/MP Engine

This approach allows the continued use of SQL/MP-based applications with existing SQL/MP tables without any code modifications and without any database conversions.

Security focus:

> Guardian security vectors govern SQL/MP subsystem components, authorization to operate on SQL/MP objects, and SQL programs that are developed and run in the Guardian environment.

> Safeguard security management may be used for additional security protection. Only authorization for SQL/MP programs stored in the OSS environment will involve OSS file system security.

Option 2: Install/Operate both SQL/MP and SQL/MX Engines

This approach allows the continued use of MP-based applications with existing MP tables without any code modifications and without any database conversions.

This option also enables SQL users to use ANSI-compliant SQL actions (DML) against SQL/MP tables and/or to build or port ANSI-compliant SQL applications requiring features of the MX tables, without disrupting any MP based applications and without any SQL/MP database conversions.

This is the most popular approach for existing SQL/MP customers moving toward use of SQL/MX, however, it requires the greatest amount of security planning:

Security focus:

> Guardian security vectors continue to govern MP subsystem components, authorization to operate on MP objects, and SQL programs that are developed and run in the Guardian environment.

> Safeguard security management may be used for additional security protection of MP objects, but it is not available for MX objects.

> Authorization for MP and MX programs stored in the OSS environment will involve OSS file system security.

> Only MX tables (and other MX objects) will use the GRANT/ REVOKE security.

Option 3: Install/Operate SQL/MX Engine with MP & MX Tables

This approach requires converting existing SQL/MP-based application code to use the ANSI-compliant syntax. The conversion enables SQL users—within the same program—to use ANSI-compliant SQL actions (DML) against both SQL/MP tables and the SQL/MX tables, without any SQL/MP database conversions.

Security focus:

SQL/MX tables (and other MX objects) will use GRANT/REVOKE security.

Guardian security vectors continue to govern authorization to operate on MP objects and SQL programs that are developed and run in the Guardian environment.

Safeguard security management may be used for additional security protection of some MP objects.

Only authorization for MP and MX programs stored in the OSS environment will involve OSS file system security.

Option 4: Install / Operate SQL/MX Engine with ONLY MX Tables

This option is most useful for new NonStop customers who do not require SQL/MP databases or applications and want to use ANSI-compliant SQL actions (DML) with the benefits of the ANSI-compliant SQL/MX tables. This option is least desirable for customers or partners with existing SQLMP-based applications, as it would require converting existing SQL/MP-based application code to use the ANSI-compliant syntax and migrating any SQL/MP databases to the SQL/MX database structures.

Security focus:

SQL users first receive security authorization to operate on SQL/MX objects based on their session's Guardian logon userid, which is created and maintained via safeguard.

The SQL/MX engine checks the object's assigned security vector stored in the SQL/MX catalog to confirm that this user has been granted security authorization to operate on the requested SQL/MX objects.

ANSI SQL's GRANT and REVOKE security completely ignores any Safeguard rules that might have been physically associated with these SQL/MX objects.

Only authorization for MP and MX programs stored in the OSS environment will involve OSS file system security.

NonStop SQL Interactions with other Utilities

SQL affects and is affected by common utilities, such as RDF, TMF, and FUP.

NonStop SQL, RDF, and Security

HP's Remote Database Facility (RDF) subsystem monitors changes made to selected NonStop databases (Enscribe, SQL/MP, and SQL/MX) on a local (primary) system and continuously updates replicated copies of these selected databases on one or more preconfigured remote (backup) systems. This means operations may be switched from the primary to the backup system with minimal interruption and loss of data in the event of planned or unplanned system outages.

It is critical to understand that RDF does not replicate SQL structural changes or unaudited database changes. In other words, any catalog structure change, any DDL operation (including creating, dropping, or altering tables, indexes, and views), any partition key change, and any table purge must be performed manually and identically by the DBA on both the primary and backup systems for any SQL table or catalog residing on volumes protected by RDF.

RISK If the primary and backup nodes are not kept synchronized for catalog and definition changes, data replication could fail.

3P-ADVICE-SQL-01 Use a third-party tool that helps to identify discrepancies in SQL definitions or helps replicate DDL changes.

SQL/MX adds a few more considerations for RDF users. As of the publication date, RDF, TMF, and Measure do not understand ANSI SQL object names. Since each SQL/MX object has an underlying Guardian name, RDF only knows about the object's underlying Guardian name. This poses challenges when trying to REGISTER CATALOG or limit SQL/MX object replication or when looking at RDF event messages generated against an SQL/MX object (i.e., with a Guardian subvolume name starting with ZSD).

By default, RDF provides volume-level protection, wherein changes to all audited Enscribe files and SQL tables on each protected primary system data volume are replicated to an associated backup system data volume. RDF also offers the ability to limit replication by using INCLUDE and EXCLUDE clauses when configuring RDF updaters to identify specific database objects that should or should not be replicated.

AP-SQL-RDF-01 The RDF INCLUDE and EXCLUDE clauses require the use of Guardian names. If you have an SQL/MX object with an ANSI SQL compliant name that you want to INCLUDE or EXCLUDE, then first get the underlying Guardian name by using the MXGNAMES utility or the MXCI SHOWDLL command for the SQL/MX object.

SQL/MX and BACKUP/RESTORE Issues

BACKUP and RESTORE are used to backup and restore OSS files and SQL/MX databases and their objects. Using BACKUP or RESTORE, you may directly specify one or more catalog, schema, table, and table partition objects. You cannot explicitly list indexes, index partitions, or constraints. Underlying objects are automatically backed up as a unit with their base object.

Restoring a catalog includes restoring all its subordinate objects in its object hierarchy, such as schemas, tables, and the subordinate objects of the tables.

Restoring a schema includes restoring all the subordinate tables.

Restoring a table includes restoring constraints (except Referential Integrity constraints), table data, table partitions, indexes, and index partitions. The CONSTRAINTS EXCLUDED or INDEXES EXCLUDED options may be used to exclude either or both of these subordinate objects.

RISK   Pieces of an SQL object cannot be independently restored. Indexes cannot be restored separately from the base table.

RISK   If pieces of an SQL object are not backed up as a unit, it will be impossible to restore that unit. Volume backups are not compatible with the SQL hierarchy.

A user can attempt to back up or restore an SQL/MX catalog using any valid userid. However, the SUPER.SUPER (255,255) or the owner ID for all schemas subordinate to the catalog should be used. Otherwise, only the catalog and schemas owned by the userid are backed up or restored.

It is possible to replace a current SQL/MX table with a previous backup copy, as long as the current table has no referential integrity constraints, no views, no stored procedures, and no triggers. In those cases, the existing table is not dropped and the backup is not restored. Use the **mxci** SHOWDDL command to determine if a table has subordinate objects. For more information on the **mxci** SHOWDDL command, see the *SQL/MX Reference Manual.*

When replacing an existing SQL/MX table with a previous backup copy, the existing object and its subordinate objects are first dropped and then the backup copy is restored. Only the original subordinate objects that were backed up will be present after the restore operation. Any subordinate objects that were added after the original backup are lost.

At the time this is written, the following SQL/MX objects cannot be directly restored:

> Referential Integrity constraints—constraints that specify that a column or set of columns in the table can only contain values matching those in a column or set of columns in the referenced table

Stored procedures—a type of SQL user-defined routine (UDR) in Java (SPJ) that operates within a database server. A stored procedure does not return a value to the caller

Triggers—a mechanism that resides in the database and specifies that when a particular action—an insert, delete, or update—occurs on a particular table, SQL/MX should automatically perform one or more additional actions

Views—a table that has a logical definition and a file label but contains no data.

BACKUP and RESTORE do not capture the data definition language (DDL) for the four object types listed above. You can use the DDL information to manually recreate these objects.

FUP

Ordinarily all NonStop SQL utility functions must be executed via SQLCI or **mxci**. Enscribe's File Utility Program (FUP) can only be used on SQL/MP objects for a few informational functions that list file label information, aggregate statistics like record counts, and for LISTLOCKs.

7

Open Database Connectivity (ODBC) SQL/MP

The NonStop ODBC (Open Database Connectivity) server allows access to HP NonStop SQL/MP tables from PC and UNIX client applications that use Microsoft's ODBC or an SQL server product such as Microsoft Access. The NonStop ODBC Server runs on HP Nonstop systems, allowing it to act as a server.

Please refer to the chapter on SQL and Database Security for information about JDBC and SQL/MX.

Figure 7.1 shows a generalized overview of the ODBC architecture. PC clients send ODBC messages to the NonStop host ODBC process. ODBC interprets the SQL statements and routes the request to the appropriate SQL/MP database or a Pathway server for further processing.

ODBC can logically be divided into a number of subsystems:

Connectivity

Users

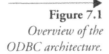

Figure 7.1
Overview of the
ODBC architecture.

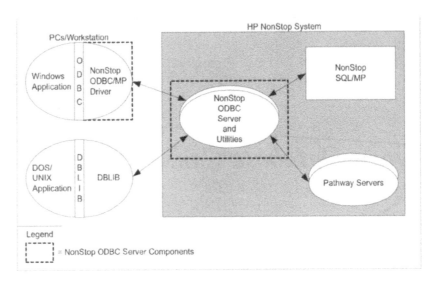

Security Configuration

Auditing

Programs and Utilities

Connectivity

ODBC provides an entry point into the HP NonStop Server via a TCP/IP address and PORT (Figure 7.2). The association of a PORT with an ODBC SCS process is made using the SERVER CLASS Name.

The SQL Communications Subsystem (SCS) handles all communication with the client workstation. It is also responsible for managing the NonStop ODBC server classes. Parameters for each SCS are configured within ODBC. Each SCS that is configured within ODBC is associated with one or more ODBC server classes. The SCS process starts a copy of the program NOSUTIL. The NOSUTIL program is called by the SCS process to collect information from the ODBC configuration tables.

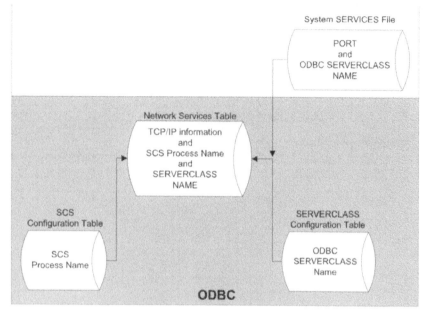

Figure 7.2
ODBC port configuration.

To avoid the overhead associated with process startup, SCS maintains a group of running ODBC servers. Each connection creates an association between the Alias-name used to sign on and an available NonStop ODBC server. SCS passes the authentication message to the ODBC server. After the client is authenticated, the SCS process passes messages in both directions.

ODBC logons are audited by Safeguard if Safeguard is configured to audit user authentications.

ODBC logoffs are not audited by Safeguard.

RISK ODBC does not issue a LOGOFF message when a session ends. The server class continues to run as the last authenticated user after a PC client disconnects. When the next PC client connects with a different Guardian username, the Safeguard audit event looks as if the previous user has logged down to the new userid. This makes it very difficult to monitor ODBC logons.

Figure 7.3
*SCS and ODBC
server class
relationships.*

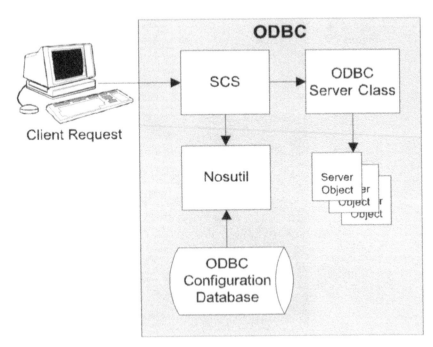

RISK When a PC client connects to the port configured for ODBC, there is no logging outside the ODBC environment.

RISK If tracing is not configured for the Alias-name connecting to the ODBC port, there is no record of connections to ODBC.

BP-ODBC-CONNECT-01 ODBC tracing should be configured to capture logons.

	Discovery Questions	**Look here:**
ODBC-POLICY	Is ODBC used on the system?	Policy
ODBC-POLICY	Does policy require auditing of user activity within ODBC?	Policy
ODBC-PORTS	What ports are used by ODBC?	Noscom

Users

Any valid Guardian username or alias can be used to connect to the HP NonStop Server via ODBC. However, ODBC also maintains a set of tables containing user information and session parameters.

Users can connect to the HP NonStop Server from a PC client using a username, commonly referred to as an Alias-name. The Alias-name information is stored in the ODBC tables.

An Alias-name is linked to a Logical-username. This Logical-username may be shared by more than one Alias-name.

A Logical-username is linked to a Guardian-username. There is a one-to-one correspondence between a Logical-username and a Guardian-username. This mapping information is stored in an ODBC table. When the client connects to the NonStop, the Guardian-username and password are used for authentication.

Each Alias-name is associated with a named profile. The profile contains parameters and default values that will be used during a session. If a profile is not specified when an Alias-name is added, the Default profile is used. The profile connects the Alias-name with the proper database and specifies tracing (auditing).

Default Profile

The Default profile is added to the profile table when ODBC is installed. The purpose of the Default profile is to supply default values that are not specified when a profile is added.

If a user logs on from a PC client using a Guardian userid or alias rather than an ODBC Alias-name, the Default profile will be used.

RISK When multiple Alias-names share a Logical-username within ODBC, many people are sharing a Guardian username and password, which decreases individual accountability.

RISK Because the Default profile is used if a Guardian username or alias is used to connect to ODBC, if the Default profile is not configured

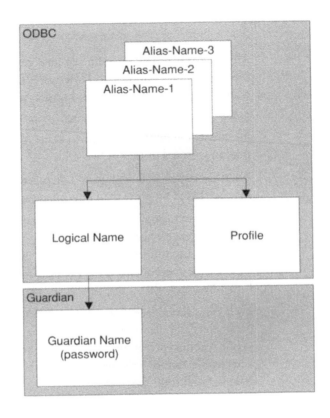

Figure 7.4
Relationship between ODBC Alias-names and Guardian userids.

correctly, a user may have more access to the NonStop environment than they need to perform their job.

BP-ODBC-PROFILE-01 Secure the Default profile so that only the ODBC administrator can alter it.

	Discovery Questions	**Look here:**
ODBC-POLICY	Does policy require ODBC users to alter their passwords on a regular basis?	Policy
ODBC-POLICY	Are Logical-usernames shared by multiple ODBC Alias-names?	Policy

(Continued)

	Discovery Questions	**Look here:**
ODBC-POLICY	Are Guardian userids shared by multiple Logical-user-names?	Policy
ODBC-POLICY	Do ODBC users use ODBC Alias-names to logon?	Policy
ODBC-POLICY	Do ODBC users use ODBC Logical-usernames to logon?	Policy
ODBC-POLICY	Do ODBC users use Guardian usernames to logon?	Policy
ODBC-PROFILE	Are all profiles secured so that only the ODBC administrator can alter them?	Policy
ODBC-PROFILE	Is the default profile configured to prevent unauthorized access?	Policy
ODBC-USERS	What ports are used by ODBC?	Noscom
ODBC-TRACE	Is TRA_MODE_ON in all ODBC profiles?	Noscom
ODBC-SAFEGARD	Is Safeguard configured to audit user authentications?	Safecom

Authentication

When a request to connect to the NonStop is initiated, either a Guardian username or alias or an ODBC Alias-name can be entered. The password that is entered always belongs to a Guardian username or alias.

The ODBC server first tries to find the username in the ODBC Alias-name table. If the username submitted by the client does not correspond to an Alias-name, the server checks to see if it is a valid Guardian username or alias. If the input username is found to be a valid Guardian name, then the authentication process continues.

RISK Any valid Guardian userid or alias can connect to the NonStop via ODBC.

If authentication is successful, the ODBC server will run as the Guardian userid of the connected client.

RISK   If an Alias-name is used to connect to ODBC, the PC client inherits all the access privileges of the associated Guardian userid. If the Guardian userid is the database owner, anyone logging on with this userid will have full READ/WRITE access to the SQL/MP tables.

BP-ODBC-USER-01 The Guardian userids associated with ODBC users should only be given permission to perform the operations you wish the user at the PC client to have.

BP-ODBC-USER-02   Since any valid Guardian userid or alias can connect to the NonStop via ODBC, all SQL/MP tables should be secured to allow only appropriate access.

Password Administration

ODBC users connect to the HP NonStop Server using their Alias-name and the password that belongs to the associated Guardian userid. The values of the CHANGE_PASSWORD_OPTION within ODBC and PASSWORD-EXPIRY-GRACE within Safeguard determine the user's option when the password is about to expire or has already expired.

Value	Level of Notification
0	The client will not be allowed to logon even if password-expiry-grace has been set for the Guardian username in Safeguard.
1	The client is notified that the password is expired, but if it is still within the PASSWORD-EXPIRY-GRACE period, the user will be permitted to change the password and logon.
2	The client will be warned that the password is about to expire and told that he has the option of changing the password. If the password has expired but it is still within the grace period, he will be prompted to immediately change this password and then he will be permitted to logon.

The default value for CHANGE_PASSWORD_OPTION is 0.

RISK If Logical-names are shared, it makes it difficult to require that the Guardian-username have a password that will expire unless someone within the organization is willing to take on the responsibility of resetting the Guardian password and notifying all the appropriate individuals.

RISK If the PC client application does not support the Guardian password change dialog, the Guardian username cannot have a password that expires unless the security administrators are willing to take on the responsibility of resetting the password and notifying the appropriate individuals.

BP-ODBC-USER-03 Each individual accessing the HP NonStop Server via ODBC should have a unique Alias-name.

BP-ODBC-USER-04 If the client software can handle the password change dialog, each Alias-name should have a password that expires.

	Discovery Questions	**Look here:**
ODBC-POLICY	Does policy require ODBC users to alter their passwords on a regular basis?	Policy
ODBC-POLICY	Are procedures in place to manage passwords for ODBC users?	Policy
ODBC-POLICY	Does the ODBC client support the Guardian password change dialog?	Policy

Security Configuration

ODBC security consists of configuring the security-related parameters and configuring the audit environment.

Changes to the ODBC configuration should be only be made by the ODBC owner privileged userid. The HP NonStop ODBC manual suggests that the NOSUTIL program be PROGID'ed to allow non-privileged users to perform various ODBC maintenance functions, but this increases the risk that the ODBC environment could be compromised by accident or intentionally.

BP-ODBC-NOSUTIL-01   Do not PROGID the NOSUTIL program.

AP-ADVICE-ODBC-01 If you must PROGID the NOSUTIL program, use Safeguard to limit access to only the ODBC Privileged Owner ID.

3P-ACCESS-ODBC-01   Third-party access control software should be used to grant granular management of processes running as any Privileged ID for users who require these privileges in order to perform their jobs. These products generally also provide comprehensive auditing of the activities they secure.

NOSCOM

NOSCOM is the client interface used to execute NOSUTIL. NOSCOM is used to add, modify, or remove items from the ODBC catalog.

NOSUTIL

The NOSUTIL utility is a server process that is used to manage the ODBC environment. It is executed directly by the SCS and NonStop ODBC server processes.

The SCS process calls NOSUTIL to retrieve initial server class definitions. When a connection request is received by the SCS process, NOSUTIL is called to retrieve information regarding which ODBC server class to use.

The NonStop ODBC server calls NOSUTIL to assist in executing requests such as create or drop tables.

The Security-Related Parameters

The System Configuration table, ZNSSCFG, is part of the ODBC catalog. It contains ODBC system configuration information.

The values in this table are only used to provide the defaults when the pertinent value is not specified when an ODBC entity is added. Once an entity is added, the information in the System Configuration table is not accessed again.

RISK Care should be taken in specifying the default values within the System Configuration table, or various entities that are added with ODBC will be assigned default parameters that may not be desirable.

BP-ODBC-CONFIG-01 Always specify all the parameters when entering a particular ODBC entity, or verify that the System Configuration default value is appropriate.

If a value in the System Configuration table is changed, it only affects entities added after the change. The values in existing entities will not be changed.

RISK If the System Configuration table is not secured correctly, system defaults can be modified in inappropriate ways.

BP-ODBC-CONFIG-02 All ODBC catalog tables should be secured so that only the ODBC Privileged Owner ID can alter them.

The following ODBC parameters have security implications.

> DEFAULT_DATABASE
>
> DEFAULT_LOCATION
>
> DEFAULT_SECURITY
>
> SQL_ACCESS_MODE
>
> SQL_CURSOR_MODE

These attributes are found in the Profile table and the ODBC System Configuration table.

DEFAULT_DATABASE

The DEFAULT_DATABASE parameter specifies the catalog for the tables that will be accessed during an ODBC session. The name entered for this parameter points to an entry in the ODBC Database table. Entries in the Database table point to an SQL/MP catalog.

RISK If a DEFAULT_DATABASE is not specified when a profile is added, the value assigned to the DEFAULT_DATABASE record in the System Configuration table will be used.

BP-ODBC-PROFILE-02 Wherever possible, a default catalog other than the Master ODBC catalog should be specified.

DEFAULT_LOCATION

The DEFAULT_LOCATION specifies the default location for files created using this profile.

The default value for this attribute is the subvolume that contains the catalog belonging to the DEFAULT_DATABASE.

BP-ODBC-PROFILE-03 Wherever possible a default location should be specified.

DEFAULT_SECURITY

The DEFAULT_SECURITY parameter specifies the Guardian security vector (RWEP) that will be assigned to objects created via the CREATE DATABASE, CREATE TABLE, CREATE VIEW, and CREATE INDEX statements issued by users associated with the profile.

By default, tables will be created with the creating user's Safeguard User Record GUARDIAN DEFAULT SECURITY value.

BP-ODBC-PROFILE-04 The string that is specified in DEFAULT_ SECURITY should match the Guardian security vector associated with the application owner. This will help avoid unnecessary access denials.

SQL_ACCESS_MODE

The SQL_ACCESS_MODE specifies the default locking mode if the information is not specified by the command issued from the PC client. The values are:

RO (read-only)
RW (read and write)

With read-only access, INSERT, UPDATE, or DELETE statements return errors.

The default value is READ and WRITE access (RW).

BP-ODBC-PROFILE-05   The value assigned to this parameter depends on the tasks the user must perform.

SQL_CURSOR_MODE

The SQL_CURSOR_MODE specifies the default mode for an SQL cursor if the information is not specified by the command issued by the PC client. The values are:

RO (read-only)
RW (read and write)

The default value is READ and WRITE access (RW).

BP-ODBC-PROFILE-06   The value assigned to this parameter depends on the tasks the user must perform.

RISK   All of the above attributes can be overridden if pass-through commands can be entered from the PC client.

	Discovery Questions	**Look here:**
ODBC-PROFILE	Are all profiles secured so that only the ODBC administrator can alter them?	Policy
ODBC-PROFILE	Is the Default profile configured to prevent unauthorized access?	Policy
ODBC-PROFILE	Is the DEFAULT_DATABASE correct for each profile	Noscom
ODBC-PROFILE	Is the DEFAULT_LOCATION correct for each profile?	Noscom
ODBC-PROFILE	Is the DEFAULT_SECURITY correct for each profile?	Noscom
ODBC-PROFILE	Is the SQL_ACCESS_MODE correct for each profile?	Noscom
ODBC-PROFILE	Is the SQL_CURSOR_MODE correct for each profile?	Noscom

Auditing in ODBC

There are two ways to obtain some auditing of ODBC user activity:

Resource accounting
Tracing

Resource accounting is intended to gather ODBC usage statistics, but it does record logons and, optionally, the actual SQL statements passed to the ODBC server.

Tracing is more resource intensive but is more granular. It was intended more as a debugging tool, but does provide some useful audit information.

Each Alias-name is assigned a Profile. Each Profile has its own audit configuration.

If ACC_MODE_ON is Y(es), resource accounting will be performed and the audits will be written to the table specified by the ACC_LOGTABLE_NAME.

If TRA_MODE_ON is (Y)es, tracing will be performed. The TRA_NAME parameter points to a record in the Trace Configuration

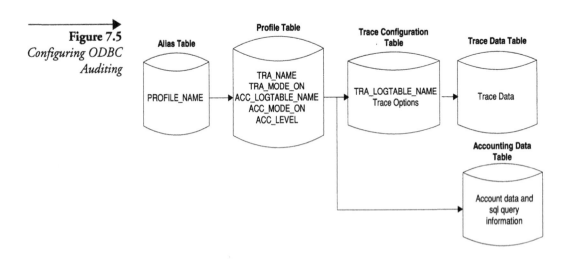

Figure 7.5
Configuring ODBC Auditing

Table. The Trace Configuration Table record determines what activity will be audited and where the audits will be sent.

Resource Accounting

Resource accounting is configured for each profile. The following list shows just some of the information that will automatically be captured when resource accounting is activated.

Logon username
The start and end times of a session
The profile used for the session
The number of inbound and outbound messages

In addition, if desired, the first 3000 bytes of each prepared SQL statement can be captured.

The Profile parameters that activate and configure resource accounting are:

ACC_LEVEL
ACC_LOGTABLE_NAME
ACC_MODE_ON

RISK Care should be taken when configuring resource accounting. There is no granularity. Once activitated, all the information (other than SQL statements) will always be written to the Accounting Log. If, in addition, all SQL statements are audited, the logs could be very large.

ACC_LEVEL

The value in ACC_LEVEL specifies the amount of detail for accounting log table entries.

If set to SESSION, one record will be written to the log table at the end of the session that summarizes all the activity for that session.

If set to SQL_STATEMENT, each SQL statement issued will be written to the log table.

The system default for this parameter is SESSION.

BP-ODBC-PROFILE-07   If you allow pass-thru mode you many wish to set ACC_LEVEL to SQL_STATEMENT.

ACC_LOGTABLE_NAME

The parameter ACC_LOGTABLE_NAME specifies the name of the existing accounting log table to use for this profile.

RISK   The ACC_LOGTABLE_NAME must contain a valid value or resource accounting will not be performed even if ACC_MODE_ON is set to Y(es).

BP-ODBC-PROFILE-08   If you intend to gather resource accounting information, always provide an ACC_LOGTABLE_NAME.

ACC_MODE_ON

The ACC_MODE_ON parameter specifies whether to include query accounting in this profile:

If set to Y(es), query accounting will be performed using the table specified in ACC_LOGTABLE_NAME

If set to N(o), query accounting will not be performed

BP-ODBC-PROFILE-09   If Account Resource auditing is required, set ACC_MODE_ON.

RISK   The ACC_LOGTABLE_NAME must contain a valid value or resource accounting will not be performed even if ACC_MODE_ON is set to Y(es).

Tracing

Tracing is configured for each profile. The ODBC server provides a trace feature that can record the following information:

All input requests received from the client by the NonStop ODBC Server

All output returned from the NonStop ODBC Server to the client

All SQL/MP statements generated by the NonStop ODBC Server

All error and informational messages generated by the NonStop ODBC Server

The statistics related to statement caching
Stored procedure messages sent between the ODBC Server and the Pathway server

The output from the trace can be written to either a NonStop SQL/MP table or to a terminal, or both destinations. Many of the above mentioned events can be optionally specified when the trace log is configured.

RISK Care should be used regarding which options are turned on in the trace log. For example, if you choose to log the results of all query requests, the trace logs could be very large.

Tracing parameters

The parameters within the Profile used to control Tracing are:

TRA_NAME
TRA_MODE_ON

TRA_NAME:

The TRA_NAME parameter points to a record within the Trace configuration table. Each TRA_NAME record in the Trace configuration table contains the parameters that control what information will be written to the Trace Log table and the name of the trace log file.

There is no default assigned for this parameter.

RISK The TRA_NAME parameter must be present in the Profile or tracing will not be performed even if TRA_MODE_ ON is set to Y(es).

BP-ODBC-PROFILE-10 If you intend to trace user activity, always provide a TRA_NAME.

TRA_MODE_ON

The TRA_MODE_ ON parameter determines whether or not tracing will be performed for all Alias-names using the associated Profile.

If set to Y(es), tracing will be performed using the trace entity specified in TRA_NAME.

If set to N(o), tracing will not be performed

The default value for this parameter is N.

BP-ODBC-PROFILE-11   Set TRA_MODE_ON to Y(es).

RISK   The TRA_NAME parameter must be present in the Profile or tracing will not be performed even if TRA_MODE_ON is set to Y(es).

TRACE CONFIGURATION TABLE

The Trace configuration table controls what will be traced and where the audits will be written. The parameters defined within this table are:

CACHE_STATISTICS
INPUT_STREAM
LOG_TO_HOMETERM
NSSQL
OUTPUT_STREAM
SP_READ
SP_WRITE
TRA_ERROR
TRA_TABLE_NAME

CACHE_STATISTICS

The CACHE_STATISTICS keyword determines whether or not statement cache SUCCESS/MISS statistics will be traced. If auditing is not required, this parameter will still gather some statistics such as the number of connections.

If CACHE_STATISTICS is set to Y(es), statement cache SUCCESS/ MISS statistics will be traced.

If CACHE_STATISTICS is set to N(o), statement cache SUCCESS/ MISS statistics will not be traced.

BP-ODBC-TRACE-01   If policy requires that usage statistics be traced, CACHE_STATISTICS should be set to Y.

INPUT_STREAM

The INPUT_STREAM keyword determines whether or not messages read by the NSODBC server will be traced.

If INPUT_STREAM is set to Y(es), each message read by the NSODBC server will be traced.

If INPUT_STREAM is set to N(o), messages read by the NSODBC server will not be traced.

BP-ODBC-TRACE-02   If policy requires that commands sent to ODBC be traced, INPUT_STREAM should be set to Y.

LOG_TO_HOMETERM

The LOG_TO_HOMETERM keyword determines whether or not trace records will be copied to the NSODBC process's HOMETERM.

If LOG_TO_HOMETERM is set to Y(es), TRACE records are copied to the HOMETERM of the NSODBC server process.

If CACHE_STATISTICS is set to N(o), TRACE records are not copied to the HOMETERM.

BP-ODBC-TRACE-03   Unless procedures are in place to monitor the output, LOG_TO_HOMETERM should be set to N.

NSSQL

The NSSQL keyword determines whether or not SQL/MP statements generated by the NonStop ODBC Server will be traced.

If NSSQL is set to Y(es), SQL statements prepared or executed by the NonStop ODBC Server will be traced.

If NSSQL is set to N(o), statements prepared or executed by the Non-Stop ODBC Server will be not traced.

BP-ODBC-TRACE-04   If policy requires that SQL commands issued to the ODBC server be traced, NSSQL should be set to Y.

OUTPUT_STREAM

The OUTPUT_STREAM keyword determines whether or not output returned from the NonStop ODBC Server to the client will be traced.

If OUTPUT_STREAM is set to Y(es), all output returned from the NonStop ODBC Server to the client will be traced.

If OUTPUT_STREAM is set to N(o), all output returned from the NonStop ODBC Server to the client will be not traced.

BP-ODBC-TRACE-05   If policy requires that output sent to the client be traced, OUTPUT_STREAM should be set to Y.

SP_READ

The SP_READ keyword determines whether or not READ messages sent between the NonStop ODBC Server and the Pathway server using a stored procedure will be traced.

If SP_READ is set to Y(es), READ messages sent between the NonStop ODBC Server and the Pathway server using a stored procedure will be traced.

If SP_READ is set to N(o), READ messages sent between the NonStop ODBC Server and the Pathway server using a stored procedure will be not traced.

BP-ODBC-TRACE-06   If policy requires that Stored Procedure READ commands be traced, SP_READ should be set to Y.

SP_WRITE

The SP_WRITE keyword determines whether or not WRITE messages sent between the NonStop ODBC Server and the Pathway server using a stored procedure

> If SP_WRITE is set to Y(es), WRITE messages sent between the Non-Stop ODBC Server and the Pathway server using a stored procedure will be traced.

> If SP_WRITE is set to N(o), WRITE messages sent between the Non-Stop ODBC Server and the Pathway server using a stored procedure will be not traced.

> **BP-ODBC-TRACE-07** If policy requires that Stored Procedure WRITE commands be traced, SP_WRITE should be set to Y.

TRA_ERROR

The TRA_ERROR keyword determines whether or not ODBC errors such as security violations, connection and command syntax problems will be traced.

> If TRA_ERROR is set to Y(es), trace errors will be traced.

> If TRA_ERROR is set to N(o), trace errors will be not traced.

BP-ODBC-TRACE-08 If policy requires that ODBC errors be traced, TRA_ERROR should be set to Y.

TRA_LOGTABLE_NAME

The TRA_LOGTABLE_NAME specifies the table where the audits will be written.

BP-ODBC-TRACE-09 Always provide a TRA_LOGTABLE_NAME in the Trace configuration table.

	Discovery Questions	**Look here:**
ODBC-POLICY	Does the Security Policy require that ODBC activity be traced?	Noscom
ODBC-POLICY	Does the Security Policy mandate resource accounting?	Noscom
ODBC-POLICY	Does the Security Policy mandate Tracing?	Noscom
ODBC-PROFILE-07	Is the ACC_LEVEL parameter appropriate for all ODBC profiles?	Noscom
ODBC-PROFILE-08	Is ACC_LOGTABLE_NAME set according to policy?	Noscom
ODBC-PROFILE-09	Is ACC_MODE_ON set to Y(es) in all appropriate ODBC profiles?	Noscom
ODBC-PROFILE-10	Is the TRA_NAME parameter present in all appropriate ODBC profiles?	Noscom
ODBC-PROFILE-11	Is TRA_MODE_ON set to Y(es) in all appropriate ODBC profiles?	Noscom
ODBC-TRACE-01	Is CACHE_STATISTICS set according to policy?	Noscom
ODBC-TRACE-02	Is INPUT_STREAM set according to policy?	Noscom
ODBC-TRACE-03	Is LOG_TO_HOMETERM set to N?	Noscom
ODBC-TRACE-04	Is NSSQL set according to policy?	Noscom
ODBC-TRACE-05	Is OUTPUT_STREAM set according to policy?	Noscom
ODBC-TRACE-06	Is SP_READ set according to policy?	Noscom
ODBC-TRACE-07	Is SP_WRITE set according to policy?	Noscom
ODBC-TRACE-08	Is TRA_ERROR set according to policy?	Noscom
ODBC-TRACE-09	Is TRA_NAME_TABLE set according to policy?	Noscom

Other ODBC Programs and Utilities

The ODBC subsystem also includes the following components:

ODBC Server
ODBC System Catalog
SPELIB

ODBC Server

An SCS process starts an ODBC server. The relationship between the SCS process and the ODBC server class is specified within the ODBC configuration tables. A copy of the ODBC server object from the appropriate server class runs for each client connection.

A profile is specified for each ODBC server class. The parameters within the profile are used during the startup process for the server class.

When a client connection is made, the ODBC server is responsible for performing the authentication sequence. Once the authentication process is successfully completed, the parameters with the profile associated with the Alias-name are used. The ODBC server then executes as the Guardian userid associated with the Alias-name.

The NonStop ODBC server executes two types of commands:

pass-through commands
stored procedures.

Pass-through Commands

Pass-through commands allow a user to execute HP NonStop SQL/MP statements, catalog utility statements, and trace statements from the PC client. Additionally, various ODBC options and configuration parameters can be modified.

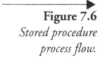

Figure 7.6
Stored procedure
process flow.

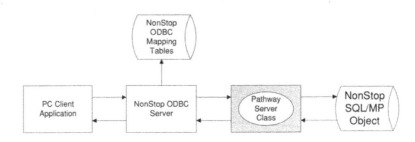

RISK If SQL/MP tables and catalogs are not secured correctly, commands can be issued from the PC client in pass-through mode. This could result in unintended modifications to ODBC databases.

BP-ODBC-CONFIG-02 All ODBC catalog tables should be secured so that only the ODBC Privileged Owner ID can alter them.

BP-ODBC-CONFIG-03 Application-specific ODBC tables and the application database tables should be secured appropriately to limit who can modify them.

Stored Procedures

A Stored Procedure is a program that has been written to perform a specific operation. The program that contains the stored procedure must be a server class within a pathway.

When the ODBC server receives a request to call a stored procedure, the server sends a message, via the LINKMON process, to the appropriate server class within the specified pathway. The stored procedure request is sent to the pathway server as the same Guardian user that owns the ODBC server process.

An advantage of using stored procedures is that the server class containing the stored procedure will perform all of its processing, including any actions involving the SQL database, as the owner of the server class, the

Guardian userid used to connect to ODBC does not have to have direct permission to access the SQL tables.

AP-ADVICE-ODBC-03 Use stored procedures.

ODBC System Catalog

The following are the tables that reside only in a NonStop ODBC Server system catalog:

Table	Description
ZNSALT	Contains the mapping of Alias-names to Logical-names and a profile
ZNSCON	Describes the NonStop SQL/MO CONTROL statements that must be executed at initialization or re-initialization time
ZNSDB	Maps ODBC of SQL server database names to NonStop SQL/MP catalog names
ZNSDEF	Defines settings for process entities
ZNSGOV	Contains accounting profile settings
ZNSMSG	Contains all error messages that could be generated by the NonStop ODBC server
ZNSNET	Contains network service attributes
ZNSPROF	Contains the profile
ZNSPROT	Contains user protection information for compatibility purposes with the SQL Server system table SYSPROTECTS. However, the HP NonStop ODBC server does not support this function, so users are granted authority to use all statements
ZNSSCFG	Contains global configuration and default values for ODBC
ZNSSCS	Contains the SCS configurations
ZNSSER	Contains the ODBC server configurations
ZNSSMAP	Contains the SCS to ODBC server mapping information
ZNSTRA	Contains trace information

(*Continued*)

Table	Description
ZNSUMAP	Contains records that link a login username and an SCS to an ODBC Server class.
ZNSUS	Contains the records mapping logical usernames to Guardian usernames
ZNSUDT	Used for data type translation to and from NonStop SQL
ZNSDUMMY	Static table used for DLIB API
ZNSVALUE	Helps support SYSVALUES for TSQL

SPELIB

SPELIB is the ODBC program library. It contains the subroutines necessary for inclusion in Pathway Server Classes that will execute stored procedures.

8

System Management Tools

HP has provided tools to facilitate the management of the NonStop Server:

TSM replaced the D-series Tandem Maintenance and Diagnostic Subsystem (TMDS) and the Remote Maintenance Interface (RMI) subsystems.

OSM replaced TSM in version G06.02. OSM is required for Integrity NonStop systems.

The DMS/SCM subsystem is used to install new software releases into a running system.

Tandem Service Management (TSM) Subsystem

The TSM subsystem is used to manage HP G06.21 and earlier S-series NonStop systems. It is a client/server application with a PC GUI client communicating with the NonStop server via TCP/IP.

TSM replaces the Tandem Maintenance and Diagnostic Subsystem (TMDS), and the Remote Maintenance Interface (RMI).

TSM is used to:

> Start and stop the system
>
> Check the hardware configuration
>
> Verify status of system resources

AP-ADVICE-TSM-01   TSM consoles should be connected to the Non-Stop server via a dedicated and isolated TCP/IP network.

AP-ADVICE-TSM-02   Do not connect TSM consoles to more than one NonStop server unless it is absolutely necessary. If one TSM console must be used to manage multiple servers, precautions should be used to ensure that any actions are applied only to the intended system.

TSM Client Components

The TSM client components are:

TSM EMS Event Viewer	Used to view the TSM event logs
TSM Low-Level Link	Used for system installation, system startup, some initial configuration tasks, and certain recovery operations. This program communicates with the server when the NonStop server operating system is not running.
TSM Notification Director	Used to display TSM incident reports
TSM Service Application	Used to perform most service management tasks and view service and maintenance status when the NonStop server operating system is up and running.

Users and Roles

Users are managed differently in the Low-Level Link and in the Service Application.

Low-Level Link Users

The Low-Level Link application uses its own userids and passwords. The application comes with one userid defined (root) and the password is blank. The root user can add other userids and set passwords for them. These other userids cannot add userids, but can change their own password.

RISK Low-Level Link userids with no passwords puts system integrity at risk.

RISK Authorizing too many users Low-Level Link userids puts system integrity at risk.

AP-ADVICE-TSM-03 Assign a password to the root userid as soon as the Low-Level Link application is installed. This password should only be distributed to those authorized to COLDLOAD the system.

Service Application Users

Service Application users logon to the application with Guardian userids and passwords. SUPER Group members have full privileges, while members of other groups have read-only access and cannot initiate any actions other then discovery and display.

RISK Allowing unauthorized users access to a workstation running the TSM application could compromise system files and processes.

AP-ADVICE-TSM-04 Access to TSM consoles should be limited by physical protection to employees who are authorized to use TSM. Even members of the SUPER group such as SUPER.OPER, should be prevented from performing unauthorized actions on a workstation configured with TSM.

TSM Host Components

Software and hardware components on the NonStop S-series server enable communication between the HP NonStop Server and the TSM client software on the workstation. These components include the TSM server software, the Master Service Processors (MSPs) and related software, and the TSM EMS Event Viewer Server Manager and related processes.

NonStop Himalaya S-series servers are shipped with four preconfigured TCP/IP addresses and the corresponding subnet masks and gateway IP addresses. The IP addresses correspond to two connections on the primary MSP (MSP0) and two connections on the backup MSP (MSP1).

TSM applications use one pair of connections to communicate with the MSPs. They use the other pair of connections to communicate with the NonStop operating system using the TCP/IP processes $ZTCP0 and $ZTCP1. The MSP1 is used as a backup path to access MSP1 when MSP0 is down. All servers are shipped with the same preconfigured IP addresses for $ZTCP0 and $ZTCP1.

AP-ADVICE-SCF-01   The ability to ADD, DELETE, ALTER, START, and STOP the TSM processes should be limited to the personnel who perform system management.

3P-ACCESS-SCF-01   Third-party products may be required to restrict access within SCF for groups other than the system administrators, such as system operators who may need limited access to SCF functionality.

ADDTCPIP Script

The $SYSTEM.ZTSM.ADDTCPIP script starts two processes named $TSMM0 and $TSMM1, which start the $ZTCP0 and $ZTCP1 TCP/IP processes. Once the TCP/IP processes are started, $TSMM0 and $TSMM1 stop themselves.

ADDTCPIP creates a log file of its activity called LOGTCPIP.

The INIT0 and INIT1 scripts are used by the ADDTCPIP script to configure and start the $ZTCP0 and $ZTCP1 processes:

INIT0 configures the $ZTCP0 TCP/IP process. INIT0 creates a log file of its activity called LOGTCP0.

INIT1 configures the $ZTCP1 TCP/IP process. INIT1 creates a log file of its activity called LOGTCP1.

$SYSTEM.ZTSM.ALTERIP is the script used to restart $ZTCP0 and $ZTCP1 when necessary.

BP-TSM-TCPIP-01 $ZTCP0 should be reserved for TSM use.

BP-TSM-TCPIP-02 $ZTCP1 should be reserved for TSM use.

ADDTOSCF

ADDTOSCF is the script to add TSM persistent processes into SCF. The processes it adds and starts are:

Process	Object File	SCF Object
$ZCVP0	$SYSTEM.SYSTEM.CEVSMX	$ZZKRN.#CEV-SERVER-MANAGER-P0
$ZCVP1	$SYSTEM.SYSTEM.CEVSMX	$ZZKRN.#CEV-SERVER-MANAGER-P1
$ZLOG	$SYSTEM.SYSnn EMSACOLL	$ZZKRN.#TSM-ZLOG
$ZRD9	$SYSTEM.SYSnn.EMSDIST	$ZZKRN.#ROUTING-DIST
$ZSPE	$SYSTEM.SYSTEM.ZSPE	$ZZKRN.TSM-SP-EVENT
$ZTSM	$SYSTEM.SYSTEM.SRM	$ZZKRN.#TSM-SRM
$ZTSMS	$SYSTEM.SYSTEM.SNMPPAGT	$ZZKRN.#TSM-SNMP

ADDTOSCF creates a log of its activities called $SYSTEM.ZTSM.LOGSCF.

$ZCVP0 and $ZCVP1

$SYSTEM.SYSTEM.CEVSMX is the object file for the TSM event servers:

$ZCVP0 is the process name for the $ZZKRN.#CEV-SERVER-MANAGER-P0 SCF object. It is the primary TSM event server.

$ZCVP1 is the process name for the $ZZKRN.#CEV-SERVER-MANAGER-P1 SCF object. It is the secondary TSM event server.

$ZLOG

$ZLOG is the process name of the $ZZKRN.#TSM-ZLOG SCF object. It is an instance of the EMS collector program, $SYSTEM.SYSTEM.EMSA-COLL. It logs events to the following files:

The primary log files are named $SYSTEM.ZSERVICE. ZZSVnnnn files, where nnnn is a incrementing number.

The alternate key files are named $SYSTEM.ZSERVICE. ZZSKnnnn, where nnnn is an incrementing number.

Use EMS event viewers, such as EMSA, EMSDIST, OSM, the TSM Event Viewer, or ViewPoint, to review messages in $ZLOG.

RISK   Some events might lack printing templates or contain data not visible in the template-printed form when printing from a $ZLOG file.

AP-ADVICE-TSM-05   Use EMSDIST to print from $ZLOG. It will accept an (undocumented) option, DUMP ON, that will list all the tokens in an event.

$ZRD9

$ZRD9 is the process name for the $ZZKRN.#ROUTING-DIST SCF object, which is the TSM Routing Distributor. It is an instance of the EMSDIST program, started by a TACL process with the $SYSTEM. ZTSM.INITRD file as input.

$ZSPE

$SYSTEM.SYSTEM.ZSPE is the object file for the $ZSPE process, which is the $ZZKRN.#TSM-SP-EVENT SCF object. It is the Service Processor (SP) Event Distributor process, which writes SP events to $ZLOG.

$ZTSM

$SYSTEM.SYSTEM.SRM is the object file for the $ZTSM process, which is the $ZZKRN.#TSM-SRM SCF object. It is the main TSM process.

$ZTSMS

$SYSTEM.SYSTEM.SNMPPAGT is the object file for the $ZTSMS process, which is the $ZZKRN.#TSM-SNMP SCF object. $ZTSMS is the SNMP agent process. It was used formerly when $ZTSM communicated with the TSM Service Application using SNMP. The process is started by the ADDTOSCF script.

AP-ADVICE-TSM-06 As of version 7.0 of the TSM, $ZTSM uses HTTP to talk to its client, so the $ZTSMS process is no longer used. As such, if the TSM is running version 7.0 or later, this process can be safely stopped and deleted from the customer configuration. All of the associated trapdest, profile, and endpoint objects are no longer required for the TSM console.

Master Service Processors (MSPs)

The NonStop operating system communicates with the workstation running the TSM software through the connection service processors (MSPs), "UNIX-on-a-chip" processors that are not part of the NonStop operating system and are dedicated to the TSM/OSM connectivity and low-level tasks.

The workstation can communicate with the MSPs on the server whether the NonStop operating system is running or not. MSPs provide these basic functions as well as the Ethernet ports that connect the TSM workstations to the Nonstop server.

TSMERROR Log

TSMERROR is the log file for the TSM System Resource Model (SRM). The file is opened when the SRM starts. If it doesn't already exist, it is created.

TSMERROR is used by the GCSC and Development for debugging purposes.

TSMINI Configuration File

$SYSTEM.ZSERVICE.TSMINI is the default configuration file. Parameters set in this file can override default values for the TSM startup.

TSM Tables

TSM uses the following tables:

$SYSTEM.ZSERVICE.PERSIST is the TSM current alarm objects database.

$SYSTEM.ZSERVICE.PERSSUPP is the current configuration database file.

$SYSTEM.ZSERVICE.ZCT08153 is a table used by the TSM client for converting alarm and incident report (IR) binary values into text strings.

The $SYSTEM.ZSERVICE.ZCT08458 is a table used by TSM to convert binary values into text strings for use in reporting errors.

TSM Alarm, Snapshot and Scan Files

TSM creates the following files as required. Depending on the current state of the system, these files may or may not be present:

Server Alarm files are named ZZALnnnn, where nnnn is an incrementing number.

Inventory Snapshot files are named ZZDCnnnn, where nnnn is an incrementing number.

Processor Scan Strings are named ZZSSnnnn, where nnnn is an incrementing number.

ZZUSERS and ZZUSERS2 Files

The ZZUSERS and ZZUSERS2 files contain TSM service application connection audit information. ZZUSERS is always the active audit file. When the maximum number of records for the ZZUSERS file is reached, the ZZUSERS file is copied to the ZZUSERS2 file, a new ZZUSERS file is opened, and logging activity is resumed.

These files are used for support and development and contain such fields as user name, IP address, date and time, action name, action object, object ID, and object type.

The ZZUSERS files may be viewed by using the SHARE option of the FUP COPY command.

Open System Management (OSM)

OSM has been the recommended system management tool since version G06.22. OSM is required for Integrity NonStop systems.

OSM provides the same functionality as TSM, with the following enhancements:

Improved scalability and performance

SSL Encryption

Online upgrades for client and providers

Better persistence, because OSM runs as a process pair and is faster

More accurate status and alarm updates for resource objects

Secure Sockets Layer

OSM can be configured to utilize Secure Sockets Layer (SSL) to encrypt sessions between the OSM host and the OSM client. While this feature is disabled by default, it can be enabled in the OSMCONF file.

BP-OSM-CONFIG-01 Enable SSL encryption by setting the USESSL parameter to ON.

OSM Persistent Processes

The NonStop Server and the OSM console communicate through two TCP/IP processes, named $ZTCP0 and $ZTCP1 by default. These processes are added to SCF by the file $SYSTEM.ZOSM.ADDTCPIP.

Once OSM is installed, the file $SYSTEM.ZOSM.ADDTOSCF is run to invoke the OSM configuration script and start the OSM persistent processes. Once the persistent OSM processes are started, they in turn start and stop other processes with dynamically assigned names.

AP-ADVICE-OSMSCF-01   The ability to ADD, DELETE, ALTER, START, and STOP OSM processes in SCF should be limited to the personnel who perform system management.

3P-ACCESS-SCF-01   Use a third-party access control product to restrict access within SCF to groups other than the system administrators; system operators, for example, may need only limited access to SCF functionality.

OSM Client Components

The client components of OSM are:	
OSM Guided Procedures	Guided procedures are activated from within the OSM Service Connection, not from separate start menu entries.
OSM EMS Event Viewer	A browser based application used to view the OSM various event logs. It also provides event details such as cause, effect, and recovery information.
OSM Low-Level Link	Used for system installation, system startup, some initial configuration tasks, and certain recovery operations. This program communicates with the server when the Non-Stop Server operating system is not running.
OSM Notification Director	Used to display OSM incident reports. It can be configured to start whenever Windows starts and run without a user logon.
OSM Service	Java-based client and server application used to perform most service management tasks and view service and maintenance status when the NonStop Server operating system is up and running. Once installed, it is accessed from a PC using Microsoft Internet Explorer.

AP-ADVICE-OSM-02   OSM consoles should be connected to the Non-Stop Server via a dedicated and isolated TCP/IP network.

OSM Host Components

The startup and configuration files for OSM generally reside in the $SYSTEM.ZOSM subvolume. Some program files reside in $SYSTEM. SYSTEM and $SYSTEM.SYSnn. Data files and event files are found in the $SYSTEM.ZSERVICE subvolume which OSM shares with TSM.

OSM and TSM both use the $SYSTEM.ZSERVICE subvolume in order to take advantage of the same event logs. Files that serve the same purpose in these two subsystems are named differently and noted in the section for each subsystem.

ADDTCPIP Script

The $SYSTEM.ZOSM.ADDTCPIP script starts processes named $OSMM0 and $OSMM1, which start the $ZTCP0 and $ZTCP1 TCP/IP processes. Once the TCP/IP processes are started, $OSMM0 and $OSMM1 stop themselves.

ADDTCPIP creates a log file of its activity called LOGTCPIP.

$SYSTEM.ZOSM.ALTERIP is the script used to restart $ZTCP0 and $ZTCP1 when necessary.

CTCPIP0 and CTCPIP1

CTCPIP0 and CTCPIP1 are the scripts that configure the $ZTCP0 and $ZTCP1 TCP/IP processes that communicate with the OSM client.

CTCPIP0 configures the $ZTCP0 TCP/IP process. CTCPIP0 creates a log file of its activity called LOGTCP0.

CTCPIP1 configures the $ZTCP1 TCP/IP process. CTCPIP1 creates a log file of its activity called LOGTCP1.

INIT0 and INIT1 Scripts

The INIT0 and INIT1 scripts are used by the ADDTCPIP script to configure and start the $ZTCP0 and $ZTCP1 processes.

INIT0 starts the $ZTCP0 TCP/IP process. INIT0 creates a log file of its activity called LOGTCP0.

INIT1 starts the $ZTCP1 TCP/IP process. INIT1 creates a log file of its activity called LOGTCP1.

ADDTOSCF

ADDTOSCF is the script to add TSM persistent processes into SCF. The processes it adds and starts are:

Process	Object File	SCF Object
$ZCMOM	$SYSTEM.SYSnn.CIMON	$ZZKRN.#OSM-CIMON
$ZLOG	$SYSTEM.SYSnn EMSACOLL	$ZZKRN.#TSM-ZLOG
$ZOEV	$SYSTEM.SYSnn.EVTMGR	$ZZKRN.#OSM-OEV
$ZOLHD	$SYSTEM.SYSnn.EMSDIST	$ZZKRN.#OSMCONFLH-RD
$ZOSM	$SYSTEM.SYSnn.APPSRVR	$ZZKRN.#OSM-APPSRVR
$ZSPE	$SYSTEM.SYSTEM.ZSPE	$ZZKRN.TSM-SP-EVENT

ADDTOSCF creates a log of its activities called $SYSTEM.ZOSM.LOGSCF.

$ZCMOM

$SYSTEM.SYSnn.CIMON is the object file for the $ZCMOM process, which is the $ZZKRN.#OSM-CIMON SCF object. It is the main OSM server process.

$ZLOG

$ZLOG is the process name of the $ZZKRN.#OSM-ZLOG SCF object. It is an instance of the EMSA collector program, $SYSTEM.SYSTEM. EMSACOLL. It is started by the ADDTOSCF script and logs events to the following files:

The primary log files are named $SYSTEM.ZSERVICE.ZZSVnnnn files, where nnnn is a incrementing number.

The alternate key files are named $SYSTEM.ZSERVICE. ZZSKnnnn, where nnnn is an incrementing number.

Use EMS event viewers such as EMSA, EMSDIST, OSM, the OSM Event Viewer, or ViewPoint to review messages in $ZLOG.

RISK   Some events might lack printing templates or contain data not visible in the template-printed form when printing from a $ZLOG file.

AP-ADVICE-OSM-02   Use EMSDIST to print from the $ZLOG. It accepts an (undocumented) option, DUMP ON, that will list all the tokens in an event.

$ZOEV

$SYSTEM.SYSnn.EVTMGR is the object file for the $ZOEV process, which is the $ZZKRN.#OSM-OEV SCF object. It is the server for Event Viewer requests.

$ZOEV launches the Open Event Viewer Providers. $SYSTEM. SYSnn.OEVPRVD is the object file for Open Event Viewer Providers, which are responsible for retrieving EMS events.

$ZOLHD

$ZOLHD is the process name for the $ZZKRN.#OSMCONFLH-RD SCF object, which is the the EMS Routing Distributor. It is an instance of the EMSDIST program, started by a TACL process named $ZOLHI with the $SYSTEM.ZOSM.INITRD file as input.

$ZOSM

$SYSTEM.SYSnn.APPSRVR is the object file for the $ZOSM process, which is the $ZZKRN.#OSM-APPSRVR SCF object. It is the Applet Server process that uploads client files via the server connection.

$ZOSM launches the Applet Providers, which are responsible for serving client files. $SYSTEM.SYSnn.APPPRVD is the object file for the Applet Providers.

$ZSPE

$SYSTEM.SYSTEM.ZSPE is the object name for the $ZSPE process, which is the $ZZKRN.#SP-EVENT SCF object. It is the Service Processor (SP) Event Distributor process that writes SP events to $ZLOG.

EVNTPRVD

$SYSTEM.SYSnn.EVNTPRVD is the Event Listener Provider.

FDIST

$SYSTEM.SYSnn.FDIST is the Fast EMS Event Distributor process. Launched by the EVNTPRVD process, the Fast EMS Event Distributor process is responsible for retrieving EMS events from $ZLOG and $0.

IAPRVD

$SYSTEM.SYSnn.IAPRVD is the object file for the Incident Analysis Provider, which is responsible for state propagation and generation of incident reports (IRs). The Incident Analysis Provider is started by the $ZCMOM process.

IAREPO

$SYSTEM.ZSERVICE.IAREPO is the Enscribe file of alarm history created by IAPRVD.

OSMCONF Configuration File

The OSMCONF file is used to customize the OSM Environment. The file is created by making a copy of the OSMINI file. Once created, $OSMM0 and $OSMM1 use the file to configure the OSM environment.

AP-ADVICE-OSM-03   All changes to the OSM configuration should be made in the OSMCONF file rather than the OSMINI file, which is overwritten when upgrades are installed

AP-ADVICE-OSM-04   HP recommends that there be no blank lines in the OSMCONF file.

OSMINI Configuration File

The OSMINI file is provided by HP as a template for entries in the OSMCONF file.

RISK   The OSMINI file is overwritten each time OSM is upgraded; any customized entries will be overwritten during a product update.

AP-ADVICE-OSM-05   Name a copy of the OSMINI file OSMCONF and make any necessary changes in the OSMCONF file.

Resource Access Layer Providers

$ZCMOM launches the Resource Access Layer Providers. They perform the following tasks:

> Interact with the SP and subsystems, such as Storage, SLSA, etc., to gather attributes and states for system resources
>
> Execute all actions on OSM objects
>
> Triggering Incident Analysis to generate and clear alarms

The two Resource Access Layer Providers are:

RALPRVD

RALPRVNP

RALPRVD

RALPRVD is the object file for the OSM Resource Layer Provider process, which is used for initial discovery, initial incident analysis, event processing, and all operations that require SUPER Group access.

The program creates the Processor Scan Strings files depending on the current state of the system; these files may or may not be present. The naming convention for the Processor Scan Strings files is ZZPSnnnn, where nnnn is an incrementing number.

RALPRVNP

RALPRVNP is the object file for the OSM Resource Layer Provider process, which is used for operations that do not require SUPER Group access.

SECPRVD

SECPRVD is the object file for the OSM Security Provider processes, which perform OSM user authentications. There may be up to eight Security Provider processes running at one time. They are started by $ZCMOM as required.

SPDIST2

SPDIST2 is the SP Event Distributor process. Launched by the EVNTPRVD process, the SP Event Distributor process is responsible for retrieving SP events from $YMIOP.

SUPPREPO

SUPPREPO is the Enscribe file containing dial-out configuration information.

TACLPRVD

TACLPRVD is the object file for the TACL Provider process, which is responsible for performing embedded TACL actions such as RELOAD PROCESSOR. There may be up to eight TACLPRVD processes running at one time. They are started by $ZCMOM as required.

ZTRC

The ZTRC file contains the pointer to the current user trace log.

The user trace logs are created and maintained by CIMON. The naming convention for the trace files is ZTRCn, where n is an incrementing number.

OSM Alarm, Snapshot and Scan Files

OSM creates the following files as required. Depending on the current state of the system, these files may or may not be present.

The naming convention for the Server Alarm files is ZZAAnnnn, where nnnn is an incrementing number. Alarms are generated by the IAPRVD program.

The naming convention for the Inventory Snapshot files is ZZSNnnnn, where nnnn is an incrementing number.

Processor scan strings are named ZZPSnnnn, where nnnn is an incrementing number. Processor scans are created by RALPRVD.

Distributed Systems Management/Software Configuration Manager

HP periodically releases new operating systems or revised software product upgrades. The Distributed Systems Management/Software Configuration Manager (DMS/SCM) subsystem is used to install these releases into a running system.

DSM/SCM is the replacement product for INSTALL. While initially it may seem more complicated than INSTALL, DSM/SCM offers many new features. Some of which are:

PATHWAY and a graphical interface for ease of use. Eliminates difficult syntax and command line interfaces.

System profiles can be defined to help assigning roles and responsibilities to various support groups or individuals. This allows some task to be accomplished without the use of the SUPER.SUPER password.

Batch scheduling is available to allow running resource consuming jobs during off hours.

Software can be managed and prepared for installation on a central machine and the prepared software package moved and installed onto target machines.

Host System

The host system controls the software upgrades for its target systems. The host system includes itself as a target, because the host activates and manages the system software on itself. Environments with multiple systems can be configured so that every system is its own host and target. However, in environments with many machines, where performance of production servers may be an issue, using one host to provide control of the configuration of many targets is a common practice. The host system maintains the DSC/SCM archives, the host database, and its own target database. Host systems connect to target systems via Expand or network connections using file transfer tools. If no connection exists between a host and target, magnetic tapes can be used to transfer the files.

Target System(s)

The target system is where new software is to be placed and implemented. Basically any system that is not a host system is a target system. Each target system consists of a physical target and one or more logical targets.

Physical Targets

Any system managed by DSM/SCM that is not the host system is a physical target system. Much of the time, these systems are simply referred to as target systems. A physical target system contains at least one logical target.

Logical Targets

A logical target is a specific software configuration on a target system. Every system, including the host system, contains at least one logical target. To manage different software configurations independently on the same physical target, DSC/SCM can manage multiple logical targets. This can be useful in environments where products must be tested against several versions of the operating system. Each logical target on the physical system requires its own separate $SYSTEM volume. The same host system must manage all the logical targets on a system.

Host and Target Databases

Each NonStop Server managed by DSM/SCM has one or more SQL databases containing configuration information. These databases must be located on a volume that is audited by TMF. The volumes should also have sufficient free space for DSM/SCM to use. The volume name, including the dollar sign, cannot exceed seven characters. To ensure the volume name does not change, do not place the host or target database on an alternate system disk. DSM/SCM files can be classified as Host database, Target database, and Archive.

Host Database

Host databases contains information about requests, software, snapshots, configurations, and profiles. They must reside on the host system.

Target Database

Each target database contains information about the files managed by DSM/SCM for a logical target. Some of this information includes file names, attributes, and fingerprints. Fingerprints are checksum-type file identifiers. It is typical for the target database for a host system to reside on the same volume as the host database on the host system. Target databases usually are created and maintained on their respective target systems. However, the target databases can also be maintained on a different system if an Expand connection exists to the target system.

Archive

The DSM/SCM archive on the host system provides storage for software received into DSM/SCM. The DSM/SCM archive stores all the software input into DSM/SCM from release version updates (RVUs), software product revisions (SPRs), and third-party products. The archive files are the source used by the configuration revisions when the new software is configured. The system generation output for configurations, including the OSIMAGE file, are also kept in the archive. The archive is located on one or more volumes of the host system. The most common volume is

$DSMSCM. The archive volumes are specified when configuring DSM
/SCM. The volume list can be changed using the Host Maintenance Interface (ZPHIHMI). Please refer to the Gazette section on DSC/SCM in the
previous book for more information.

Figure 8.1
DSM/SCM
environment.

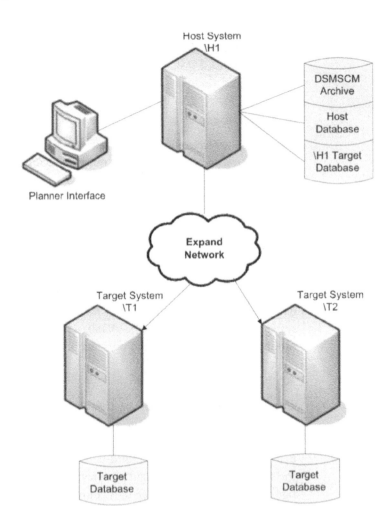

DSM/SCM Uses

DSM/SCM activities include:

1. Restore or UNPAK the software

2. Receive new software into archive

3. Create a software revision

4. Build the new revision

5. Apply the new revision

6. Activate the new software on the target system

7. Perform the rename function

The DSM/SCM Planner GUI Interface is used to perform steps 1–4. The DSM/SCM Pathway application ($YPHI) is used to perform step 5. Once the system is restarted, step 7 is performed via the TACL interface.

Steps 1 and 2—Receive New Software into Archive

When a software update (SUT) is received, the first step restores the SUT's contents to a target subvolume (TSV). The TSVs are named T<product number><suffix>.

HP software updates can be downloaded off the web in a pack-type form. The downloaded files must be uncompressed and placed in the TSV subvolume.

The TSV can be located anywhere on the system, but is usually on $DSMSCM.

AP-ADVICE-DSMSCM-01 HP recommends that the TSV be placed on $DSMSCM.

Next, the new files must be received into DSM/SCM. This should be done as soon as possible. Once received into DSM/SCM, the new files are transitioned into a compressed format that can only be used by the DSM/SCM subsystem.

RISK If the software has been downloaded or restored from tape, but not received into DSM/SCM, the files are not compressed and are, therefore, vulnerable.

AP-ADVICE-DSMSCM-02 Files should be received into DSM/SCM immediately to compress the files and mitigate any risk that the new files could be altered.

AP-ADVICE-DSMSCM-03 The SUT should be also stored in a secured place for both disaster recovery purposes and to prevent unauthorized access and modification.

Step 3—Create a Software Revision

As each new software revision is archived, it is up to the system administrator to determine when a new operating system upgrade is required. Not all products apply to all systems, and multiple revisions can be applied at one time to minimize impact to the running system.

When the system administrator decides to upgrade the operating system, the inclusion of software for this revision is created in DSM/SCM and defined in DSM/SCM's database.

Steps 4 and 5—Build and Apply New Configuration Revision

The software revision is then built for the target system. The target system can be the host system or a remote system. DSM/SCM can create and build software revisions for multiple systems and multiple software revision levels, as defined by the system administrator.

The software revision is built into a temporary location on the $SYSTEM disk.

RISK In some cases, the BUILD step is done some period of time prior to the system coldload that brings the new revision online. These temporary staging areas must be secured from tampering during the staging period.

AP-ADVICE-DSMSCM-04 Secure these temporary staging areas with Safeguard or a third party object security product during the staging period.

Step 6—Activate the New Software on the Target System

Finally, the software revision is activated on the server. In many cases, the revision may require a full coldload. In other cases the revision may require the stopping and restarting of subsystems. The resulting subvolumes are:

A new SYSnn subvolume will be created or updated.

A new CSSnn subvolume will be created or updated.

Step 7—Rename Function

Following the activation of new software, the rename function moves software components into their final location. Rename is performed from a TACL running the ZPHIRNM program.

The appropriate files in $SYSTEM.SYSTEM will be replaced.

The appropriate files in TSV subvolumes will be replaced.

RISK File security is propagated to the new operating system files. For instance, if the EDIT object file is owned by 255,255 and secured "UUNU", this security will be propagated into the next operating system.

AP-ADVICE-DSMSCM-05 Within DSM/SCM, set the default security for new files to "CUCU".

Securing the Old and New Program Version Files

DSM/SCM can be configured to require that Safeguard must be running whenever DSM/SCM places files on the target system by updating the System Profile Information in the Planner Interface, the Host maintenance interface (ZPHIHMI), or the Target Maintenance Interface (ZPHITMI).

AP-ADVICE-DSMSCM-05 Safeguard or a third party object security product should be used to protect the DSM/SCM environment.

DSM/SCM renames the old object files out of the way when it loads the new version. The naming convention for the old files is ZFB00xxxx, where xxxx represents an alphanumeric string.

Old Version Files

During a SYSGEN, DSM/SCM renames any operating system program that has an update out of the way before a new version is copied into place and renamed.

The naming convention for these renamed obsolete files is ZFB00xxxx where xxxx represents an alphanumeric string.

RISK   The copies of obsolete programs are left in the same subvolume as the new working version resides and retain the Guardian security string, so anyone who can execute the new version, can also execute its obsolete counterpart.

RISK   If there is a Safeguard subvolume Protection Record, anyone who can execute the new version of program can also execute its obsolete counterpart.

RISK   If the old object file was LICENSED, the copy of the obsolete program remains LICENSED.

3P-ADVICE-OBJSEC-01   Use a third-party object security product to secure the DSM/SCM copies of obsolete programs.

Every subvolume that contains copies of old versions of object files also has several files that serve as a catalog for the ZFB files residing in that subvolume. The HP DSM/SCM documentation states that the files should not be deleted; they will be removed by DSM/SCM when appropriate, which generally is when the next SYSGEN is being built. The naming conventions for the DSM/SCM catalog and configuration files are:

The map files are all in that TSV are named ZMPnnnnn in Guardian and dsmscm.ZMPnnnnn is OSS.

The presence of the ZPHI6030 file in a subvolume indicates that the subvolume is managed by DSM/SCM. In OSS sub-directories this file is named zzDSMSCM.Managed.

The DSM/SCM archives are named $<volume>.ZPHIcncc. ZPHIcncc contain. These files should not be altered or purged.

The $SYSTEM.SYSnn.ZSSLIST file contains. The $SYSTEM.SYSnn.ZOSSLIST file has the same function for OSS file system.

RISK The 'catalog' displays the real names of obsolete programs in the clear. Users could look up the names of the copies and execute them instead of the current versions if the copies are not secured to prevent it.

3P-ADVICE-OBJSEC-02 Use a third-party object security product to secure the DSM/SCM catalogs.

New Version Files

By default, any Safeguard DISKFILE Protection Records that apply to upgraded program files are carried over to the new system configuration, even if the PERSISTENT attribute is not set. It is possible, however, to turn off this feature with the IGNORE-SAFEGUARD-PROTECTION parameter.

IGNORE-SAFEGUARD-PROTECTION

The IGNORE-SAFEGUARD-PROTECTION parameter causes DSM/SCM to ignore any Protection Records and, instead, replicate the file's Guardian security string.

Note that if the Protection Record has the PERSISTENT attribute set, DSM/SCM will replicate the Protection Record even if the IGNORE-SAFEGUARD-PROTECTION parameter is present.

RISK If the IGNORE-SAFEGUARD-PROTECTION parameter is set, Safeguard protection records without the PERSISTENT attribute will be lost.

BP-DSM/SCM-SECURE-01 Do not use the IGNORE-SAFE-GUARD-PROTECTION parameter.

When starting the Build/Apply Request, specify on the OUTPUT screen who the owner is and what security string to use for new files placed on the target system. This will only set the ownership/security for new files. It cannot be used to change the security of existing files.

BP-OPSYS-OWNER-01   Explicitly specify ownership for new DSC /SCM files.

AP-DSMSCM-SECURE-01   Explicitly specify the security for new DSC/SCM files.

Figure 8.2

Setting the owner and Guardian security string for new files.

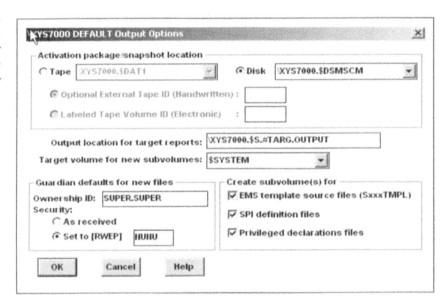

	Discovery Questions	Look here:
SAFE-DSMSCM-02	Is the IGNORE-SAFEGUARD-PROTEC-TION parameter present?	Pathcom
SAFE-DSMSCM-03	Are DSM/SCM host and target systems configured to require that Safeguard be running?	Planner Interface. YPHIHMI, or YPHITMI

Roles and Responsibilities within DSM/SCM

DSM/SCM provides for the definition of three major roles for DSM/SCM users:

Planners

Operators

Database Administrators (DBAs)

The actual number and titles of people assuming these responsibilities depend on environment. For example, a larger site with multiple systems might have several operators and DBAs, whereas a single-system environment might have one person assuming all three roles. Regardless of the number of people assigned, each role should have at least one backup person capable of performing the duties in case the assigned personnel are unavailable.

AP-ADVICE-DSMSCM-05   Users of DSM/SCM must have a working knowledge of HP NonStop server subsystems including, but not restricted to, NonStop SQL/MP and the Transaction Management Facility (TMF).

AP-ADVICE-DSMSCM-06   The roles for all three type of users of DSM/SCM can be defined within the host maintenance interface, ZPHI-HMI, and the roles of operators and database administrators can be defined within the target maintenance interface, ZPHITMI.

AP-ADVICE-DSMSCM-07   The procedures and examples in the HP documentation and guides often indicate the use of SUPER.SUPER (255, 255) for certain tasks. Of course, if the security policy requires, the system can be configured so other users can perform these tasks.

Planners

Planners' duties include receiving SUT tapes or other software inputs, building, and applying software configurations and the installation of software using DSM/SCM. The planner must have a working knowledge of the NonStop server environment and a complete understanding of installation procedures and DSM/SCM operations.

Operator

Operators are defined in DSM/SCM to perform the activities on target systems that implement new software and activate the system to use the new software. These activities are specified in the operator instructions created by the BUILD AND APPLY phase. Since this activity often includes a COLDLOAD of the target system, it is not something operator should perform.

Database Administrator

The DSM/SCM subsystem requires the role of a database administrator to manage the SQL databases and the software archives. This role may also include maintaining and upgrading DSM/SCM software versions on host and target systems. In addition, security requirements must be maintained to restrict access to DSM/SCM functions. The database administrator role requires a thorough understanding of DSM/SCM concepts, SQL database administration, and NonStop server security concepts and procedures.

The following table summarizes the typical duties for each of the three roles involved in DSM/SCM:

Figure 8.3
Roles and responsibilities in DSM/SCM.

	Planner	Operator	DBA
Build	X		
Build/Apply	X		
Maintain Reports	X		
Enable/Disable Tool Assign	X		
Prepare Reports	X		
Enable Trace	X	X	X
Prepare Release Documents	X		
Create New Software Revision	X		
Prepare Softdocs	X		
Maintain Targets	X		

(*Continued*)

Figure 8.3 (*Continued*)

	Planner	Operator	DBA
Receive Snapshots	X		
Export Files	X		
Receive Software	X		
Maintain Groups	X		
Apply an Activation Package		X	
Backout a Configuration		X	
Request a Snapshot		X	
Request an Audit		X	
Request a System Report		X	
Verify the Database		X	
Maintenance for Systems			X
Maintenance for Volumes			X
Maintenance for CM Profile			X
Check-out Cancellation			X
Security Maintenance			X
Archive Maintenance			X
Register System			X
Request Deletion			X
Archive Relocation			X
Database Relocation			X

9

The Guardian Gazette A–Z

The Gazette consists of a chapter per program, process, or subsystem, each containing a discussion of the object, the security concerns and best practice recommendations.

The naming conventions are:

User Program	Object files that users can execute
System Program	Object files that other programs, not users, execute
System Utility	Object files that are generally used by system administrators or operators for system-oriented functions
Configuration File	Library, DLL, or *CSTM files used by System and User Programs
Subsystem	A set of System Programs, User Programs and Configuration files such as Safeguard, Measure or SQL
Application	A subsystem installed and run as an application

ADDTOSCF Script

The ADDTOSCF script adds TSM or OSM persistent processes into SCF. Please refer to the Guardian Gazette sections on the TSM Subsystem or the OSM Subsystem.

TSM was superseded by OSM in version G06.22. OSM is required for Integrity NonStop systems.

ADDTCPIP Script

The $SYSTEM.ZTSM.ADDTCPIP script starts the two TCP/IP processes used by the TSM subsystem.

The $SYSTEM.ZOSM.ADDTCPIP script starts the two TCP/IP processes used by the OSM subsystem.

TSM was superseded by OSM in version G06.22. OSM is required for Integrity NonStop systems.

ALTERIP Script

The $SYSTEM.ZTSM.ALTERIP script is used to restart the TSM or OSM subsystem $ZTCP0 and $ZTCP1 TCP/IP processes when necessary.

TSM was superseded by OSM in version G06.22. OSM is required for Integrity NonStop systems.

APPPRVD System Program

APPPRVD is the object file for the OSM Applet Providers. Please refer to the Guardian Gazette section on the OSM Subsystem for more information.

APPSRVR System Program

APPSRVR is the object file for the $ZOSM process, which is the OSM Applet Server process. Please refer to the Guardian Gazette section on the OSM Subsystem for more information.

CIMON System Program

CIMON is the object file for the $ZCMOM process, which is the main OSM server process. Please refer to the Guardian Gazette section on the OSM Subsystem for more information.

CONFIG System Configuration File

The CONFIG file is referred to as the system configuration database. The initial file is created by HP and contains basic configuration information for such objects as disk drives, tape drives, ServerNet adapters, the TSM server process, etc. This file is used to load the system.

A second copy of the CONFIG file called CONF0000 is also saved in the same subvolume. All subsequent changes to the system configuration are made using SCF and saved on an ongoing basis in the ZSYSCONF.CONFIG and optional CONFnnnn files.

BP-OPSYS-CONFIG-01 Do not allow WRITE access to the CONFIG file by any user other than SUPER.SUPER.

BP-FILE-CONFIG-01 CONFIG should be secured "NUUU".

BP-OPSYS-OWNER-03 CONFIG should be owned by SUPER. SUPER.

BP-OPSYS-FILELOC-03 CONFIG resides in $SYSTEM. ZSYSCONF.

	Discovery Questions	**Look here:**
OPSYS-OWNER-03	Who owns CONFIG?	Fileinfo
FILE-CONFIG-01 SAFE-CONFIG-01	Is CONFIG secured correctly?	Fileinfo Safecom

Related Topics

SCF

ZPM

$ZCNF

CTCPIP0 and CTCPIP1 Scripts

CTCPIP0 and CTCPIP1 scripts configure the $ZTCP0 and $ZTCP1 TCP/IP processes that communicate with the OSM client.

CEVSMX System Program

CEVSMX is the object file for the TSM event servers $ZCVP0 and $ZCVP1. Please refer to the Guardian Gazette section on the TSM Subsystem for more information.

Distributed Systems Management/Software Configuration Manager (DSM/SCM)

HP periodically releases new operating systems or revised software product releases. The Distributed Systems Management/Software Configuration Manager (DMS/SCM) subsystem is used to install these releases into a running system.

Please refer to Part 8, System Management Tools, for a more complete discussion of the DSM/SCM Subsystem.

DSM/SCM's Obsolete Files

During a SYSGEN, DSM/SCM renames any operating system program that has an update out of the way before placing the new version of the program into place. The naming convention for these renamed obsolete files is ZFB00xxxx, where xxxx represents an alphanumeric string.

RISK   The copies of obsolete programs remain in the same subvolume with the new working version.

RISK   If the old object file was LICENSED, the copy of the obsolete program remains LICENSED.

RISK   The copies of obsolete programs retain their original Guardian security string; anyone who can execute the new version can also execute its obsolete counterpart.

RISK   If there is a Safeguard subvolume Protection Record, anyone who can execute the new version of the program can also execute its obsolete counterpart.

Though the files have been renamed, it is not hard for users to deduce which copy matches the current program.

3P-ADVICE-OBJSEC-01   Use a third-party object security product to secure the DSM/SCM copies of obsolete programs.

Every subvolume that contains copies of old versions of object files also has several files that serve as a catalog for the ZFB* files residing in that subvolume. The HP DSM/SCM documentation states that the files should not be deleted; they will be removed by DSM/SCM when appropriate, which is, generally, when the next SYSGEN is being built. The naming conventions for the DSM/SCM catalog and configuration files are:

ZMPnnnnn files are the map files of all files in that TSV. In OSS, they are named dsmscm.ZMPnnnnn.

The presence of the ZPHI6030 file in a subvolume indicates that the subvolume is managed by DSM/SCM. In OSS subdirectories, this file is named zzDSMSCM.Managed.

$<volume>.ZPHIxxxx.ZPHIxxxx files contain DSM/SCM archives. These files should not be altered or purged.

$SYSTEM.SYSnn.ZSSLIST contains the directory list and name of the current ZMPnnnnn file for the current revision. Also in the $SYSTEM.SYSnn subvol is the ZOSSLIST file, which has the same function for OSS file systems.

RISK   The 'catalog' displays the real names of obsolete programs in the clear. So users could look up the names of the copies and execute them instead of the current version if the copies are not secured to prevent it.

3P-ADVICE-OBJSEC-02   Use a third-party object security product to secure the DSM/SCM catalogs.

Securing DSM/SCM Components

BP-PROCESS-DSMSCM-01 The $YPHI Pathway application should be running.

BP-FILE-DSMSCM-01	DSM/SCM* object programs should be secured "UUCU".
BP-OPSYS-OWNER-03	DSM/SCM* object programs should be owned by SUPER.SUPER.
BP-OPSYS-FILELOC-03	DSM/SCM* object programs reside in $<dsmscm-vol>.ZDSMSCM.
BP-FILE-DSMSCM-02	DSMSCM* non-object files should be secured "CCCU".
BP-OPSYS-OWNER-03	DSMSCM* non-object files should be owned by SUPER.SUPER.
BP-OPSYS-FILELOC-03	DSMSCM* non-object files reside in $<dsm-scm-vol>.ZDSMSCM.
BP-LICENSE-OPSYS-03	CBEXE is LICENSED.
BP-PROGID-OPSYS-03	CBEXE is PROGID'd.

BP-LICENSE-OPSYS-03   TAEXE is LICENSED.

BP-PROGID-OPSYS-03   TAEXE is PROGID'd.

BP-FILE-DSMSCM-03   DSM/SCM SQL catalogs should be secured "CCCU".

BP-OPSYS-OWNER-03   DSM/SCM SQL catalogs should be owned by SUPER.SUPER.

BP-OPSYS-FILELOC-03   DSM/SCM SQL catalogs reside in various sub-volumes.

BP-FILE-DSMSCM-04   The DSM/SCM SQL Database should be secured "CCCU".

BP-OPSYS-OWNER-03   The DSM/SCM SQL Database should be owned by SUPER.SUPER.

BP-OPSYS-FILELOC-03   The DSM/SCM SQL Database resides in various subvolumes.

BP-FILE-DSMSCM-05   ZFB00* files should be secured "UUUU".

BP-OPSYS-OWNER-03   ZFB00* files should be owned by SUPER.SUPER.

BP-OPSYS-FILELOC-03   ZFB00* files reside in various subvolumes.

BP-FILE-DSMSCM-06   ZMP* files should be secured "UUUU".

BP-OPSYS-OWNER-03   ZMP* files should be owned by SUPER.SUPER.

BP-OPSYS-FILELOC-03   ZMP* files reside in various subvolumes.

BP-FILE-DSMSCM-07   ZPHI* files should be secured "UUUU".

BP-OPSYS-OWNER-03   ZPHI* files should be owned by SUPER.SUPER.

BP-OPSYS-FILELOC-03   ZPHI* files reside in $DSMSCM. ZDSMSCM.

If available, use Safeguard or a third-party object security product to grant access to DSM/SCM object files and Pathway environment only to users who require access in order to perform their jobs.

BP-SAFE-DSMSCM-01 Add a Safeguard Protection Record to control access to the DSM/SCM Pathway environment and DSMSCM files equivalent to the Guardian file security listed above.

BP-SAFE-DSMSCM-03 Configure DSM/SCM Host and Target systems to require that Safeguard be running.

	Discovery Questions	**Look here**
FILE-POLICY	Who are the users who should have access to the DSM/SCM application?	Policy
PROCESS-DSMCM-01	Is the $YPHI process running?	Status
OPSYS-OWNER-03	Who owns the DSM/SCM Pathway objects in $<dsmscm-vol>.ZDSM-SCM.?	Fileinfo
OPSYS-OWNER-03	Who owns the DSM/SCM files in $<dsmscm-vol>.ZDSMSCM.?	Fileinfo
OPSYS-OWNER-03	Who owns the DSM/SCM subsystem files in $<dsmscm-vol>.ZDSMSCM.?	Fileinfo
OPSYS-OWNER-03	Who owns the DSM/SCM catlog and database?	SQLCI
OPSYS-OWNER-03	Who owns the ZFB00* files?	Fileinfo
OPSYS-OWNER-03	Who owns the ZMP* files?	Fileinfo
OPSYS-OWNER-03	Who owns the ZPHIcncc files?	Fileinfo
LICENCE-OPSYS-03	Is the CBEXE object file licenced?	Fileinfo
LICENCE-OPSYS-03	Is the TAEXE object file liecenced?	Fileinfo
PROGID-OPSYS-03	Is the CBEXE object file PROGID'd	Fileinfo
PROGID-OPSYS-03	Is the TAEXE object file PROGID'd	Fileinfo
SAFE-DSMSCM-01	Is the $YPHI Pathway correctly secured with safegaurd	Safecom

(Continued)

	Discovery Questions	**Look here:**
FILE-DSMSCM-01 SAFE-DSMSCM-01	Are the $<dsmscm-vol>.ZDSMSCM.* object files correctly secured with Guardian or Safeguard?	Fileinfo Safecom
FILE-DSMSCM-02 SAFE-DSMSCM-02	Are the $<dsmscm-vol>.ZDSMSCM.* nonobject files correctly secured with Guardian or Safeguard?	Fileinfo Safecom
FILE-DSMSCM-03	Is the DSM/SCM SQL catalog secured correctly?	SQLCI
FILE-DSMSCM-04	Are the DSM/SCM SQL database objects secured correctly?	SQLCI
FILE-DSMSCM-05	Are the ZFB00* files secured correctly?	Fileinfo
FILE-DSMSCM-06	Are the ZMP* files secured correctly?	Fileinfo
FILE-DSMSCM-07	Are the ZPHI* files secured correctly?	Fileinfo
SAFE-DSMSCM-02	Is the IGNORE-SAFEGUARD-PROTECTION parameter being used?	Pathcom
SAFE-DSMSCM-03	Are DSM/SCM Host and Target systems configured to require that Safeguard be running?	Planner Interface, YPHIHMI, or YPHITMI

ELD User Program

The TNS/E Link Editor (ELD) is the Integrity NonStop equivalent of the S-series NLD program, which resolves references to the Shared Runtime Libraries that are specified when building an executable program in native languages:

    Native C

    Native C++

    Native Cobol

    PTAL

The ELD utility links one or more TNS/R object files to produce an executable or nonexecutable native object file (file code 800). An executable native object file cannot be input to the ELD utility at a later time, but a nonexecutable native object file can.

Link one or more TNS/E native object files to produce a loadfile or linkfile

Modify existing loadfiles

Securing ELD

BP-FILE-ELD-01	ELD should be secured "UUNU".
BP-OPSYS-OWNER-02	ELD should be owned by SUPER.SUPER.
BP-OPSYS-FILELOC-02	ELD resides in $SYSTEM.SYSTEM.

If available, use Safeguard or a third-party object security product to grant access to ELD only to users who require access in order to perform their jobs.

BP-SAFE-ELD-01   Add a Safeguard Protection Record to grant appropriate access to the ELD object file.

	Discovery Questions	Look here:
OPSYS-OWNER-02	Who owns ELD?	Fileinfo
FILE-POLICY	Who is allowed to execute ELD on the system?	Policy
FILE-ELD-01 SAFE-ELD-01	Is ELD secured correctly?	Fileinfo Safecom

Related Topics

Compilers

Securing Applications

Libraries, SRLs & Common Routines

NLD

ENOFT User Program

The TNS/E Native Object File Tool (ENOFT) is the Integrity NonStop version of the S-series NOFT program, which reads and displays information from native object files. It is the native equivalent of BIND for native code programs written in Native C, Native C++, Native COBOL and PTAL.

ENOFT can be run interactively from a TACL prompt in the Guardian environment, or an OSS shell prompt, or as a batch process issuing commands from a terminal or an obey file. ENOFT can be used to:

Determine the optimization level of procedures in a file

Display object code with corresponding source code

List shared runtime library (SRL) references in an object file

List unresolved references in an object file

List object file attributes

RISK ENOFT commands are not destructive, but can be used to view native program code.

AP-FILE-ENOFT-01 Object files should be secured against unauthorized access to prevent the misuse of ENOFT.

Securing ENOFT

BP-FILE-ENOFT-01 ENOFT should be secured "UUNU".

BP-OPSYS-OWNER-02 ENOFT should be owned by SUPER.SUPER.

BP-OPSYS-FILELOC-02 ENOFT resides in $SYSTEM.SYSTEM.

If available, use Safeguard or a third-party object security product to grant access to ENOFT only to users who require access in order to perform their jobs.

BP-SAFE-ENOFT-01 Add a Safeguard Protection Record to grant appropriate access to the ENOFT object file.

	Discovery Questions	Look here:
OPSYS-OWNER-02	Who owns ENOFT?	Fileinfo
FILE-POLICY	Who is allowed to execute ENOFT on the system?	Policy
FILE-ENOFT-01 SAFE-ENOFT-01	Is ENOFT secured correctly?	Fileinfo Safecom

Related Topics

BIND

Compilers

Securing Applications

Libraries, SRLs & Common Routines

NLD

NOFT

EVNTPRVD System Program

EVNTPRVD is the object file for the OSM Event Listener Provider. Please refer to the Guardian Gazette section on the OSM subsystem for more Information.

EVTMGR Program

EVTMGR is the object file for the $ZOEV process, which is the server for the TSM Event Viewer requests. Please refer to the Guardian Gazette section on the OSM subsystem for more information.

FDIST System Program

FDIST is the object file for the Fast EMS Event Distributor process. Please refer to the Guardian Gazette section on the OSM subsystem for more information.

FSCK System Utility

The Guardian FSCK utility looks at every regular OSS file to verify that it has both a directory entry and data. FSCK makes sure that the superblock, inodes, and catalog files are consistent. It can also make repairs to the integrity of an OSS fileset.

FSCK is run via the SCF DIAGNOSE FILESET command. Only a member of the SUPER Group can use the DIAGNOSE FILESET command.

AP-ADVICE-FSCK-01 HP recommends that you have a fast-create fileset named TEMP mounted on **/tmp**. Secure the file set so that only SUPER.SUPER can delete directories or files from the fileset, but all users have read, write, and execute.

AP-ADVICE-FSCK-02 HP recommends that you spread fileset recovery after a system load across many processors so that filesets can be repaired in parallel. That practice allows for faster recovery and improves the availability of the OSS file system.

AP-ADVICE-FSCK-03 HP recommends that you specify processors for the FSCK utility that are not used by the OSS Monitor or any name servers.

Securing FSCK

BP-FILE-FSCK-01 FSCK should be secured "UUCU".

BP-OPSYS-OWNER-01 FSCK should be owned by SUPER.SUPER.

BP-OPSYS-FILELOC-01 FSCK resides in $SYSTEM.SYSnn.

If available, use Safeguard or a third-party object security product to grant access to FSCK only to users who require access in order to perform their jobs.

BP-SAFE-FSCK-01 Add a Safeguard Protection Record to grant appropriate access to the FSCK object file equivalent to the Guardian file security string listed above.

	Discovery Questions	Look here:
OPSYS-OWNER-01	Who owns FSCK?	Fileinfo
FILE-FSCK-01 SAFE-FSCK-01	Is FSCK secured correctly?	Fileinfo Safecom

Related Topics

OSS Subsystem

OSSMON

SCF

IAPRVD System Program

$SYSTEM.SYSnn.IAPRVD is the object file for the OSM Incident Analysis Provider. Please refer to the Guardian Gazette section on the OSM Subsystem.

IAREPO File

IAREPO is the Enscribe file of the OSM alarm history created by the IAPRVD program. Please refer to the Guardian Gazette section on the OSM Subsystem.

IMPORT System Program

The IMPORT utility is used to load data from an ASCII or UCS2 format file to a SQL/MX table. Please refer to the Guardian Gazette section on SQL/MX for more information.

INIT0 and INIT1 Scripts

The INIT0 and INIT1 scripts are used by the ADDTCPIP script to configure and start the $ZTCP0 and $ZTCP1 processes for either the TSM Subsystem or the OSM Subsystem.

INITRD File

INITRD is the input file for the $ZOLHI TACL process that starts the TSM and OSM EMS Routing Distributor. Please refer to the Guardian Gazette section on the TSM subsystem or the OSM Subsystem for more information. TSM was superseded by OSM in version G06.22. OSM is required for Integrity NonStop systems.

Integrity NonStop Compilers

The Integrity NonStop development tools (compilers and related files) are equivalent to the S-series development tools and should be secured identically. Please refer to the previous book, *HP NonStop Server Security*, for the discussion of Compiler security on secure (production) systems.

S-series	Integrity NonStop
C89	C89
NMC	CCOMP
NMCPLUS	CPPCOMP
NMCOBOL	ECOBOL
PTAL	EPTAL

CCOMP/CPPCOMP

Access to the native mode C/C++ language components is required for compilation. Securing the compiler object file controls the use of the language.

BP-FILE-CCOMP-01   CCOMP should be secured "UUNU".

BP-OPSYS-OWNER-02   CCOMP should be owned by SUPER.
SUPER.

BP-OPSYS-FILELOC-02   CCOMP resides in $SYSTEM.SYSTEM.

BP-FILE-CCOMP-02   CPPCOMP should be secured "UUNU".

BP-OPSYS-OWNER-02   CPPCOMP should be owned by SUPER.
SUPER.

BP-OPSYS-FILELOC-02   CPPCOMP resides in $SYSTEM.SYSTEM.

BP-FILE-CCOMP-03   CCOMP/CPPCOMP libraries should be
secured "NUNU".

If available, use Safeguard or a third-party object security product to grant access to CCOMP/CPPCOMP only to users who require access in order to perform their jobs.

BP-SAFE-CCOMP-01   Add a Safeguard Protection Record to grant appropriate access to the CCOMP object files.

BP-SAFE-CCOMP-02   Add a Safeguard Protection Record to grant appropriate access to the CPPCOMP object files.

	Discovery Questions	Look here:
OPSYS-OWNER-02	Who owns CCOMP?	Fileinfo
OPSYS-OWNER-02	Who owns CPPCOMP?	Fileinfo
FILE-POLICY	Who is allowed to use the CCOMP compiler on the secure system?	Policy
FILE-POLICY	Who is allowed to use the CPPCOMP compiler on the system?	Policy
	Discovery Questions	Look here:

(Continued)

FILE-CCOMP-01 SAFE-CCOMP-01	Is CCOMP secured correctly?	Fileinfo Safecom
FILE-CCOMP-02 SAFE-CCOMP-02	Is CPPCOMP secured correctly?	Fileinfo Safecom
FILE-CCOMP-03	Are the CCOMP libraries secured correctly?	Fileinfo

ECOBOL

Access to the native mode COBOL language components is required for compilation. Securing the compiler object file controls the use of the language.

ECOBOL Compiler Components:

> ECOBOL
>
> COBEX0
>
> COBEX1
>
> NMCOBEXT (libraries)

BP-FILE-ECOBOL-01 ECOBOL should be secured "UUNU".

BP-OPSYS-OWNER-02 ECOBOL should be owned by SUPER. SUPER.

BP-OPSYS-FILELOC-02 ECOBOL resides in $SYSTEM.SYSTEM.

BP-FILE-ECOBOL-02 ECOBOL libraries should be secured "NUNU".

BP-OPSYS-OWNER-02 ECOBOL libraries should be owned by SUPER.SUPER.

BP-OPSYS-FILELOC-02 ECOBOL libraries resides in $SYSTEM. SYSTEM.

If available, use Safeguard or a third-party object security product to grant access to ECOBOL only to users who require access in order to perform their jobs.

BP-SAFE-ECOBOL-01   Add a Safeguard Protection Record to grant appropriate access to the ECOBOL object file.

	Discovery Questions	**Look here:**
FILE-POLICY	Who is allowed to use the ECOBOL compiler on the system?	Policy
OPSYS-OWNER-01	Who owns ECOBOL?	Fileinfo
OPSYS-OWNER-02	Who owns the ECOBOL libraries ?	Fileinfo
FILE-ECOBOL-01 SAFE-ECOBOL-01	Is ECOBOL secured correctly?	Fileinfo Safecom
FILE-ECOBOL-02	Are the ECOBOL libraries secured correctly?	Fileinfo

EPTAL

Access to the TAL language components is required for compilation. Securing the compiler object file controls the use of the language.

EPTAL Compiler Components:

EPTAL

EPTALCOM

BP-FILE-EPTAL-01   EPTAL should be secured "UUNU".

BP-OPSYS-OWNER-02   EPTAL should be owned by SUPER.SUPER.

BP-OPSYS-FILELOC-02   EPTAL resides in $SYSTEM.SYSTEM.

BP-FILE-EPTAL-02   EPTALCOM should be secured "UUNU".

BP-OPSYS-OWNER-02 SUPER.SUPER.   EPTALCOM should be owned by SUPER.SUPER.

BP-OPSYS-FILELOC-02   EPTALCOM resides in $SYSTEM. SYSTEM.

If available, use Safeguard or a third-party object security product to grant access to EPTAL only to users who require access in order to perform their jobs.

BP-SAFE-EPTAL-01   Add a Safeguard Protection Record to grant appropriate access to the EPTAL object file.

	Discovery Questions	Look here:
FILE-POLICY	Who is allowed to use the EPTAL compiler on the system?	Policy
OPSYS-OWNER-02	Who owns EPTAL?	Fileinfo
OPSYS-OWNER-02	Who owns EPTALCOM?	Fileinfo
FILE-EPTAL-01 SAFE-EPTAL-01	Is EPTAL secured correctly?	Fileinfo Safecom
FILE-EPTAL-02	Is EPTALCOM secured correctly?	Fileinfo

SQL

SQL compilation is discussed in the Part 6, NonStop SQL and Database Security.

LISTNER System Utility

The LISTNER process listens to configured TCP/IP ports, waiting for incoming connection requests from clients. LISTNER starts a configured program when a request is made via TCP/IP to a specified port. Please refer to Part 4, *TCP/IP,* for more information.

BP-FILE-LISTNER-01   LISTNER should be secured "UUCU".

BP-OPSYS-OWNER-01   LISTNER should be owned by SUPER.
SUPER.

BP-FILE-FILELOC-01   LISTNER must reside in $SYSTEM.SYSnn.

	Discovery Questions	**Look here:**
FILE-POLICY	Who is allowed to start and stop LISTNERs on the system?	Policy
OPSYS-OWNER-01	Who owns LISTNER?	Fileinfo
FILE- LISTNER-01 SAFE-LISTNER-01	Is LISTNER correctly secured with Guardian or Safeguard?	Fileinfo Safecom

LOGTCPIP Log File

The ADDTCPIP script creates a log file of its activity called LOGTCPIP. Please refer to the Guardian Gazette section on the TSM Subsystem or the OSM Subsystem.

TSM was superseded by OSM in version G06.22. OSM is required for Integrity NonStop systems.

LOGSCF Log Fil l 8e

The ADDTOSCF script creates a log of its activities called LOGSCF. Please refer to the Guardian Gazette section on the TSM Subsystem or the OSM Subsystem.

TSM was superseded by OSM in version G06.22. OSM is required for Integrity NonStop systems.

LOGTCP0 and LOGTCP1 Log File

The INIT0 and INIT1 scripts each create a log file of their activity called LOGTCP0 or LOGTCP1. Please refer to the Guardian Gazette section on the TSM Subsystem or the OSM Subsystem.

TSM was superseded by OSM in version G06.22. OSM is required for Integrity NonStop systems.

LOGTCPIP Log File

The ADDTCPIP script creates a log file of its activity called LOGTCPIP. Please refer to the Guardian Gazette section on the TSM Subsystem or the OSM Subsystem.

TSM was superseded by OSM in version G06.22. OSM is required for Integrity NonStop systems.

MXANCHOR File Configuration File

When first installing SQL/MX on a system, the installer creates a simple Guardian text file named $SYSTEM.ZSQLMX.MXANCHOR, an anchor file, that containts the volume location of the SQL/MX system metadata tables.

MXAUDSRV System Program

The MXAUDSRV program is the SQL/MX version of AUDSERV, which makes it possible for applications to share the use of a table or index during DDL reorganization. MXAUDSRV is only used in the SQL/MX environment. It is not an interactive program; it is invoked by the TMF subsystem.

MXCMP User Program

MXCMP is the object file for the SQL/MX compiler. It compiles SQL statements in host language programs for execution by the SQL/MX executor processes and handles catalog updates. It must be available on any host where SQL/MX programs and databases reside.

MXESP System Program

MXESP is the object file for the SQL/MX executor server process. This subprogram is called when parallel operations are performed.

MXGNAMES System Program

The MXGNAMES program resolves SQL/MX OSS pathnames to Guardian file names.

MXOAS System Program

The MX Connectivity Service Association server (MXOAS) starts and manages the MXCS configuration server (MXCOCFG) and MXCS SQL server (MXOSRVR). Please refer to the Guardian Gazette section on SQL/MX for more information.

MXOCFG System Program

The MXOCFG is the configuration server that manages the MXCS configuration data. Please refer to the Guardian Gazette section on SQL/MX for more information.

MXODSN Configuration File

The MXODSN file is a template file that contains data source options for MXCS connectivity using SequeLink for NonStop SQL/MX.

MXOMSG File

The MXOMSG file contains the error text for messages generated by MXCS, which is the SQL/MX Connectivity Services process.

MXOSRVR System Program

The MXOSRVR server provides access to a NonStop SQL database. Please refer to the Guardian Gazette section on SQL/MX for more information.

MXRTDSRV System Program

MXRTDSRV is the bridge process between SQL/MX and SQL/MP. The SQL/MX compiler, MXCMP, communicates with this process to access SQL/MP tables.

MXUDR System Program

MXUDR is the SQL/MX User Defined Routine (UDR) server, which is the interface between the SQL/MX executor process and the Java Virtual Machine that executes the UDR. The only UDRs supported under SQL/MX are stored procedures in Java.

MXUTP System Program

A materialized view is a static view of data from a single point in time. MXUTP is the SQL/MX materialized view server. It manages and populates materialized views under SQL/MX.

Network File System (NFS) Subsystem

The Network File System (NFS) is a widely used and primitive protocol that allows computers to share files over a network. The implementation on the HP NonStop Server is based on that developed by Sun Microsystems. It allows PCs or other network hosts to create or use files on the NonStop Server via TCP/IP over a LAN.

This section focuses on securing the components of the NFS Subsystem. Please refer to the NFS section in Part 5 for a complete discussion of NFS and its configuration.

BP-NFS-CONFIG-01   Verify that the NFS client used in your organization requires a valid password that cannot be blanks.

BP-POLICY-NFS-02   The NFS subsystem should not be enabled on production systems or any other system where confidential or sensitive data resides until all the security implications of NFS have been evaluated.

	Discovery Questions	**Look here:**
FILE-POLICY	Does policy allow the use of NFS on the system?	Policy
PROCESS-POLICY	Who is authorized to start and stop the $ZNFS processes?	Policy

Securing the NFS Subsystem Components

The NFS subsystem is made up of the following components:

> Various NFS servers
>
> NFS LAN server
>
> NFS configuration files
>
> NFS userid files
>
> RPC subsystem components

NFSCONV

NFSCONV is the object file for the NFS Configuration Quickstart Utility, which is used to configure the NFS subsystem on the NonStop Server.

The program is used to generate a sample PCNFSD config file and create obey files that will stop and start the NFS subsystem.

BP-FILE-NFS-01   NFSCONV should be secured "UUNU".

BP-OPSYS-OWNER-03   NFSCONV should be owned by SUPER. SUPER.

BP-OPSYS-FILELOC-03   NFSCONV resides in $SYSTEM.ZOSSNFS.

	Discovery Questions	Look here:
FILE-POLICY	Does policy allow the use of NFS on the system?	Policy
OPSYS-OWNER-03	Who owns NFSCONV?	Fileinfo
FILE-NFS-01	Is NFSCONV secured correctly?	Fileinfo Safecom

NFSLAN

NFSLAN is the object file for the LAN interface process, which acts as a front end for NFS requests received from the NonStop TCP/IP subsystem. It forwards mount protocol requests to the manager process and relays NFS protocol requests to the appropriate server processes. Configure the NFS server security with SCF NFS LAN object commands.

The default name for the NFSLAN process is $LANP2.

BP-PROCESS-NFS-02   The $LANP2 process should not be running.

BP-FILE-NFS-02   NFSLAN should be secured "UUNU".

BP-OPSYS-OWNER-03   NFSLAN should be owned by SUPER. SUPER.

BP-OPSYS-FILELOC-03   NFSLAN resides in $SYSTEM.ZOSSNFS.

	Discovery Questions	Look here:
FILE-POLICY	Does policy allow the use of NFS on the system?	Policy
PROCESS-NFS-02	Is $LANP2 process running?	Status
OPSYS-OWNER-03	Who owns NFSLAN?	Fileinfo
FILE-NFS-02	Is NFSLAN secured correctly?	Fileinfo Safecom

NFSMGR

NFSMGR is the object file for the NFS manager program, $ZNFS, which accepts commands, reports errors, and generates event messages. Configure the NFS server security using SCF NFS server object commands.

$ZNFS starts the NFSSVRHP and NFSLAN processes.

BP-PROCESS-NFS-03   The $ZNFS process should not be running.

BP-FILE-NFS-03   NFSMGR should be secured "UUNU".

BP-OPSYS-OWNER-03 NFSMGR should be owned by SUPER.SUPER.

BP-OPSYS-FILELOC-03 NFSMGR resides in $SYSTEM.ZOSSNFS.

	Discovery Questions	Look here:
FILE-POLICY	Does policy allow the use of NFS on the system?	Policy
PROCESS-POLICY	Who is authorized to start and stop the $ZNFS processes?	Policy
OPSYS-OWNER-03	Who owns NFSMGR?	Fileinfo
FILE-NFS-03 SAFE-NFS-03	Is NFSMGR secured correctly?	Fileinfo Safecom

NFSMGR2

NFSMGR2 is the object file for the helper process, which provides address resolution and other LAN-related services to the manager process. The process is started and stopped by NFSMGR as needed.

BP-FILE-NFS-04 NFSMGR2 should be secured "UUNU".

BP-OPSYS-OWNER-03 NFSMGR2 should be owned by SUPER. SUPER.

BP-OPSYS-FILELOC-03 NFSMGR2 resides in $SYSTEM.ZOSSNFS.

	Discovery Questions	Look here:
FILE-POLICY	Does policy allow the use of NFS on the system?	Policy
OPSYS-OWNER-03	Who owns NFSMGR2?	Fileinfo
FILE-NFS-04	Is NFSMGR2 secured correctly?	Fileinfo Safecom

NFSSVRHP

NFSSVRHP is the object file for the server headpin process, which manages the files in the hierarchy defined for each NFS server. There is one headpin process per fileset (EXPORT object). The one for the root fileset is typically called $ROOT. The server headpin processes start the NFSSVRWB processes.

Configure the server headpin with SCF NFS server commands.

BP-FILE-NFS-05 NFSSVRHP should be secured "UUNU".

BP-OPSYS-OWNER-03 NFSSVRHP should be owned by SUPER. SUPER.

BP-OPSYS-FILELOC-03 NFSSVRHP resides in $SYSTEM. ZOSSNFS.

	Discovery Questions	Look here:
FILE-POLICY	Does policy allow the use of NFS on the system?	Policy
OPSYS-OWNER-03	Who owns NFSSVRHP?	Fileinfo
FILE-NFS-05	Is NFSSVRHP secured correctly?	Fileinfo Safecom

NFSSVRWB

NFSSVRWB is the object file for the worker bee processes, which are started by a server headpin (NFSSVRHP) process. Each headpin server may start multiple worker bee processes.

BP-FILE-NFS-06   NFSSVRWB should be secured "UUNU".

BP-OPSYS-OWNER-03   NFSSVRWB should be owned by SUPER.
                                        SUPER.

BP-OPSYS-FILELOC-03 NFSSVRWB resides in $SYSTEM.ZOSSNFS.

	Discovery Questions	Look here:
FILE-POLICY	Does policy allow the use of NFS on the system?	Policy
OPSYS-OWNER-03	Who owns NFSSVRWB?	Fileinfo
FILE-NFS-06	Is NFSSVRWB secured correctly?	Fileinfo Safecom

PCAUTHD

PCAUTHD is the object file for the authentication server process. It is started by the PCNFSD process, $PCDP2.

BP-FILE-NFS-07   PCAUTHD should be secured "UUNU".

BP-OPSYS-OWNER-03   PCAUTHD should be owned by SUPER.
                                        SUPER.

BP-OPSYS-FILELOC-03   PCAUTHD resides in $SYSTEM. ZOSSNFS.

	Discovery Questions	Look here:
FILE-POLICY	Does policy allow the use of NFS on the system?	Policy
OPSYS-OWNER-03	Who owns PCAUTHD?	Fileinfo
FILE-NFS-07	Is PCAUTHD secured correctly?	Fileinfo Safecom

PCLPRD

PCLPRD is the object file for the NFS print spool server process, which communicates with the Guardian spooler subsystem. It is started by the PCNFSD ($PCDP2) process.

BP-FILE-NFS-08   PCLPRD should be secured "UUNU".

BP-OPSYS-OWNER-03   PCLPRD should be owned by SUPER.SUPER.

BP-OPSYS-FILELOC-03 PCLPRD resides in $SYSTEM.ZOSSNFS.

	Discovery Questions	Look here:
FILE-POLICY	Does policy allow the use of NFS on the system?	Policy
OPSYS-OWNER-03	Who owns PCLPRD?	Fileinfo
FILE-NFS-08	Is PCLPRD secured correctly?	Fileinfo Safecom

PCNFSD

PCNFSD is the object file for the PC NFS process, which is an extension to NFS that allows non-UNIX clients to interact in a secure manner with NFS servers. The PCNFSD process starts the PCLPRD and PCAUTHD processes.

The default name for the PC NFS process is $PCDP2.

PRNFSD uses the RPC service over UDP or TCP to transport information.

BP-FILE-NFS-09   PCNFSD should be secured "UUUU".

BP-OPSYS-OWNER-03   PCNFSD should be owned by SUPER.SUPER.

BP-OPSYS-FILELOC-03 PCNFSD resides in $SYSTEM.ZOSSNFS.

	Discovery Questions	Look here:
FILE-POLICY	Does policy allow the use of NFS on the system?	Policy
OPSYS-OWNER-03	Who owns PCNFSD?	Fileinfo
FILE-NFS-09	Is PCNFSD secured correctly?	Fileinfo Safecom

PORTMAP

PORTMAP is the object file for the portmapper process, which converts host port numbers to Remote Procedure Call (RPC) program numbers. It corresponds to the **/etc/portmap** program found on many UNIX systems. The portmapper process is required by the NFS subsystem. Please refer to the Guardian Gazette section on the Remote Procedure Call Subsystem for more information.

RPC

The RPC file is an EDIT file containing program definitions. The definitions include the program name, program number and possible aliases for the program name. The file is used by the portmapper and RPCINFO processes. Please refer to the Guardian Gazette section on the Remote Procedure Call Subsystem for more information.

RPCINFO

RPCINFO is the object file for the RPCINFO process, which displays RPC program numbers. It can be used to alter running RPC servers or to monitor and change PORTMAP behavior. Please refer to the Guardian Gazette section on the Remote Procedure Call Subsystem for more information.

ZNFSPTR

ZNFSPTR is the object file for PTrace's NFS module. Please refer to HP's *PTrace Manual* for more information.

BP-FILE-NFS-10   ZNFSPTR should be secured "UUCU".

BP-OPSYS-OWNER-02   ZNFSPTR should be owned by SUPER.SUPER.

BP-OPSYS-FILELOC-02 ZNFSPTR resides in $SYSTEM.SYSTEM.

	Discovery Questions	Look here:
FILE-POLICY	Does policy allow the use of NFS on the system?	Policy
OPSYS-OWNER-02	Who owns ZNFSPTR?	Fileinfo
FILE-NFS-10	Is ZNFSPTR secured correctly?	Fileinfo Safecom

ZNFSSCF

ZNFSSCF is the object file for SCF's NFS module. Please refer to HP's *Open System Services NFS Management and Operations Manual* for more information on configuring NFS via SCF.

BP-FILE-NFS-11   ZNFSSCF should be secured "UUCU".

BP-OPSYS-OWNER-02 ZNFSSCF should be owned by SUPER.SUPER.

BP-OPSYS-FILELOC-02 ZNFSSCF resides in $SYSTEM.SYSTEM.

	Discovery Questions	**Look here:**
FILE-POLICY	Does policy allow the use of NFS on the system?	Policy
OPSYS-OWNER-02	Who owns ZNFSSCF?	Fileinfo
FILE-NFS-11	Is ZNFSSCF secured correctly?	Fileinfo Safecom

ZNFSTEXT

The ZNFSTEXT file contains SCF's help text for the NFS module.

BP-FILE-NFS-12   ZNFSTEXT should be secured "NUUU".

BP-OPSYS-OWNER-02 ZNFSTEXT should be owned be SUPER. SUPER.

BP-OPSYS-FILELOC-02 ZNFSTEXT resides in $SYSTEM.SYSTEM.

	Discovery Questions	**Look here:**
FILE-POLICY	Does policy allow the use of NFS on the system?	Policy
OPSYS-OWNER-02	Who owns ZNFSTEXT?	Fileinfo
FILE-NFS-12	Is ZNFSTEXT secured correctly?	Fileinfo Safecom

ZNFSUSR and ZNFSUSRI Files

The ZNFSUSR file stores information used by the NFS server to translate NFS userids to Guardian userids, which are used to the determine NFS user's file access. Configure NFS users with SCF NFS user object commands. ZNFSUSR1 is the alternate key file.

BP-FILE-NFS-13   ZNFSUSR should be secured "----".

BP-OPSYS-OWNER-03   ZNFSUSR should be owned by SUPER. SUPER.

BP-OPSYS-FILELOC-03 ZNFSUSR resides in $SYSTEM.ZOSSNFS.

BP-FILE-NFS-14   ZNFSUSR1 should be secured "----".

BP-OPSYS-OWNER-03   ZNFSUSR1 should be owned by SUPER. SUPER.

BP-OPSYS-FILELOC-03 ZNFSUSR1 resides in $SYSTEM. ZOSSNFS.

	Discovery Questions	**Look here:**
FILE-POLICY	Does policy allow the use of NFS on the system?	Policy
OPSYS-OWNER-03	Who owns ZNFSUSR?	Fileinfo
OPSYS-OWNER-03	Who owns ZNFSUSR1?	Fileinfo
FILE-NFS-13	Is ZNFSUSR secured correctly?	Fileinfo Safecom
FILE-NFS-14	Is ZNFSUSR1 secured correctly?	Fileinfo Safecom

ZNFSTMPL

ZNFSTMPL is the EMS template for the NFS subsystem.

BP-FILE-NFS-15   ZNFSTMPL should be secured "NUUU".

BP-OPSYS-OWNER-03   ZNFSTMPL should be owned by SUPER. SUPER.

BP-OPSYS-FILELOC-03 ZNFSTMPL resides in $SYSTEM.ZTEMPL.

	Discovery Questions	**Look here:**
FILE-POLICY	Does policy allow the use of NFS on the system?	Policy
OPSYS-OWNER-03	Who owns ZNFSTMPL?	Fileinfo
FILE-NFS-15	Is ZNFSTMPL secured correctly?	Fileinfo Safecom

ZRPCTMPL

ZRPCTMPL is the EMS template for the RPC service.

BP-FILE-NFS-16   ZRPCTMPL should be secured "NUUU".

BP-OPSYS-OWNER-03   ZRPCTMPL should be owned by SUPER.
SUPER.

BP-OPSYS-FILELOC-03   ZRPCTMPL resides in $SYSTEM.ZTEMPL.

	Discovery Questions	Look here:
FILE-POLICY	Does policy allow the use of NFS on the system?	Policy
OPSYS-OWNER-03	Who owns ZRPCTMPL?	Fileinfo
FILE-NFS-16	Is ZRPCTMPL secured correctly?	Fileinfo Safecom

ZZNFSnnn

The NFSMGR processes keep all their configuration information (other than userids) in files in the ZOSSNFS subvolume. The files are named ZZNF-Snnn, where n represents a number. These files are updated programmatically, not by users directly.

BP-NFS-ZZNFSNNN-15   The ZZNFSnnn files should be owned by SUPER.SUPER and secured so that only SUPER.SUPER has access to them.

BP-FILE-NFS-17   ZZNFSnnn files should be secured "----".

BP-OPSYS-OWNER-03   ZZNFSnnn files should be owned by SUPER.
SUPER.

BP-OPSYS-FILELOC-03   ZZNFSnnn   files   resides   in $SYSTEM.
ZOSSNFS

	Discovery Questions	Look here:
FILE-POLICY	Does policy allow the use of NFS on the system?	Policy
OPSYS-OWNER-03	Who owns the ZZNFSnnn files?	Fileinfo
FILE-NFS-17	Are the ZZNFSnnn files secured correctly?	Fileinfo Safecom

NFS

The Network File System (NFS) is a widely used and primitive protocol that allows computers to share files over a network.

Please refer to Part 5, *File Sharing Programs*, for a complete discussion of the Network File System (NFS) Subsystem, or to the Guardian Gazette section on the NFS Subsystem for Best Practice recommendations.

NOS System Program

NOS is the object file name of the ODBC server. Please refer to the Guardian Gazette section on ODBC.

NOSCOM User Program

NOSCOM is the command interpreter for NOSUTIL. NOSCOM is used to add, modify, or remove items from the ODBC catalog. Please refer to the Guardian Gazette section on ODBC.

NOSUTIL System Program

The NOSUTIL utility is a server process used to manage the ODBC environment. It is executed directly by the SCS and NonStop ODBC server processes. Please refer to the Guardian Gazette section on ODBC.

NS System Program

NS is the object file for the OSS name server process, which is managed by the OSS monitor. Please refer to the Guardian Gazette chapter on the *OSS Monitor Process* for more information.

OSMINI Configuration File

$SYSTEM.ZSERVICE.OSMIN is the default configuration file for the OSM subsystem.

OSSFM System Program

OSSFM is the object file for the OSS file manager process. Please refer to the Guardian Gazette chapter on the *OSS Monitor Process* for more information.

Object Code Accelerator (OCA) User Program

The Object Code Accelerator (OCA) is the Integrity NonStop (EPIC) version of the AXCEL program, which transforms HP NonStop Server compiled language object code to produce accelerated object code, which may run faster on the Integrity Nonstop.

OCA takes a code 100 (CISC) object file and appends a code 800 (EPIC) object file onto it so the code runs natively on the Integrity Nonstop.

OCA is used with TNS compilers and not with native compilers. Native languages are already accelerated for performance. Programs consisting mainly of calls on system code do not get much additional performance gain by acceleration, because system code has already been native-compiled. Programs consisting of large amount of user code may gain significant performance by the acceleration compilation.

RISK OCA is resource intensive and could potentially affect application processing. Code need not be accelerated on the system where the accelerated object file will be executed.

Securing OCA

BP-FILE-OCA-01   OCA should be secured "UUNU".

BP-OPSYS-OWNER-02 OCA should be owned by SUPER.SUPER.

BP-OPSYS-FILELOC-02   OCA resides in $SYSTEM.SYSTEM.

AP-ADVICE-OCA-01 To avoid impacting applications, programs should be accelerated on a development or test system, and the accelerated program should then be moved to the secure system.

If available, use Safeguard or a third-party object security product to grant access to OCA only to users who require access in order to perform their jobs.

BP-SAFE-OCA-01   Add a Safeguard Protection Record to grant appropriate access to the OCA object file.

	Discovery Questions	Look here:
FILE-POLICY	Are accelerations performed on the system?	Policy
OPSYS-OWNER-02	Who owns OCA?	Fileinfo
FILE-POLICY	Who is allowed to execute OCA on the system?	Policy
FILE-OCA-01 SAFE-OCA-01	Is OCA secured correctly?	Fileinfo Safecom

Related Topics

AXCEL

Compilers

Securing Applications

ODBC Subsystem

The NonStop ODBC server allows access to HP NonStop SQL/MP tables from PC and UNIX client applications that utilize Microsoft's ODBC or an SQL server product, such as Microsoft Access. The NonStop ODBC Server runs on HP NonStop systems, allowing it to act as a server.

ODBC Subsystem Components

The host portion of ODBC is composed of the following components:

ODBC Catalogs

NOSUTIL

NOSCOM

SCS and ODBC Server Processes

Please refer to Part 7, *ODBC*, for more information about the ODBC subsystem.

ODBC Catalogs

There are two types of ODBC catalogs:

System catalog

User catalogs

System Catalog

There is a single "Master" ODBC catalog that contains the configuration information used to control the overall ODBC environment.

As of Release 2 of NSODBC, the system catalog is no longer required to reside in the same subvolume as the SQL/MP system catalog. During the installation process, a Guardian subvolume can be specified to contain the ODBC system catalog. If a Guardian subvolume name is not is provided, the default location is the system catalog subvolume.

The following are the tables that reside only in a NonStop ODBC Server system catalog:

Table	Description
ZNSALT	Contains the mapping of Alias-names to Logical-names and a Profile
ZNSCON	Describes the NonStop SQL/MP CONTROL statements that must be executed at initialization or re-initialization time

(Continued)

Table	Description
ZNSDB	Maps ODBC or SQL Server database names to NonStop SQL/MP catalog names
ZNSDEF	Defines settings for process entities
ZNSGOV	Contains accounting profile settings
ZNSMSG	Contains all error messages that could be generated by the NonStop ODBC server
ZNSNET	Contains network service attributes
ZNSPROF	Contains the profile
ZNSPROT	Contains user protection information for compatibility purposes with the SQL Server system table SYSPROTECTS. However, the HP Non-Stop ODBC server does not support this function, so users are granted authority to use all statements
ZNSSCFG	Contains global configuration and default values for ODBC
ZNSSCS	Contains the SCS configurations
ZNSSER	Contains the ODBC server configurations
ZNSSMAP	Contains the SCS to ODBC server mapping information
ZNSTRA	Contains Trace information
ZNSUMAP	Contains records that link a login username and an SCS to an ODBC Server class.
ZNSUS	Contains the records mapping logical usernames to Guardian usernames
ZNSUDT	Used for data type translation to and from NonStop SQL
ZNSDUMMY	Static table used for DLIB API
ZNSVALUE	Helps support SYSVALUES for TSQL

All of the NonStop ODBC Server system catalog tables are secured "NNNO", with the exception of ZNSUDT, ZNSDUMMY, ZNSPROT, and ZNSVALUE, which are secured "NONO".

With Release 2, the ODBC system catalog tables do not have to reside in the same subvolume as the SQL system catalog.

BP-FILE-ODBC-01 The ZNSDUMMY catalog table should be secured "NONO".

BP-FILE-ODBC-02 The ZNSPROT catalog table should be secured "NONO".

BP-FILE-ODBC-03 The ZNSUPD catalog table should be secured "NONO".

BP-FILE-ODBC-04 The ZNSVALUE catalog table should be secured "NONO".

BP-FILE-ODBC-05 All other ZNS* catalog tables should be secured "NNNO".

BP-OPSYS-OWNER-03 All ZNS* catalog tables must be owned by the SUPER Group ODBC owner ID.

BP-OPSYS-FILELOC-03 All ZNS* catalog tables should reside in the appropriate location.

	Discovery Questions	**Look here:**
FILE-POLICY	Does policy allow the use of ODBC on the system?	Policy
OPSYS-OWNER-03	Who owns the ODBC system catalog?	Fileinfo
FILE-ODBC-01	Is each ODBC system catalog table secured correctly?	Fileinfo Safecom

User Catalogs

ODBC adds the following tables to each application's database:

Table	Description
ZNUDT	Maps ODBC or SQL Server data types to NonStop SQL/MP data types
ZNUIX	Maps logical index names to Guardian file names
ZNUMTRX	Used as the log for resource accounting

(*Continued*)

Table	Description
ZNUOBJ	This table Maps ODBC or SQL Server table and view names to NonStop SQL/MP table and view names
ZNUPROC	Maps stored procedure names to Pathway and Server Class names
ZNUQST	Contains resource accounting information
ZNUTRA	Contains the log of trace events

BP-FILE-ODBC-06   The ZNU* user catalog tables should be secured "NNNO".

BP-OPSYS-OWNER-03   The ZNU* user catalog tables must be owned by the SUPER Group ODBC owner ID.

BP-OPSYS-FILELOC-03   The ODBC user catalog tables must reside in the application's SQL/MP catalog.

	Discovery Questions	Look here:
FILE-POLICY	Does policy allow the use of ODBC on the system?	Policy
FILE-POLICY	Which SQL/MP application databases may be accessed via ODBC?	Policy
OPSYS-OWNER-03	Who owns the application SQL/MP database?	Fileinfo
FILE-ODBC-06	Is SQL/MP application database secured correctly?	Fileinfo Safecom

NonStop ODBC Server

NOS is the object file name of the ODBC server. An SCS process starts an ODBC server. The relationship between the SCS process and the ODBC Server Class is specified within the ODBC configuration tables. A copy of the ODBC server object from the appropriate Server Class runs for each client connection.

A Profile is specified for each ODBC Server Class. The parameters within the Profile are used during the startup process for the Server Class.

When a client connection is made, the ODBC server performs the authentication sequence. Once the authentication process is successfully completed, ODBC uses the parameters for the Profile associated with the Alias-name. The ODBC server then executes as the Guardian userid associated with the Alias-name.

BP-FILE-ODBC-07   The NOS should be secured "NONO".

BP-OPSYS-OWNER-03 NOS should be owned by a user in the super-group.

BP-OPSYS-FILELOC-03 NOS should reside in the default subvolume created when ODBC is installed.

	Discovery Questions	Look here:
FILE-POLICY	Does policy allow the use of ODBC on the system?	Policy
OPSYS-OWNER-03	Who owns NOS?	Fileinfo
FILE-ODBC-07	Is NOS secured correctly?	Fileinfo Safecom

NOSCOM

NOSCOM is the command interpreter for NOSUTIL. NOSCOM is used to add, modify, or remove items from the ODBC catalog.

BP-FILE-ODBC-08   NOSCOM should be secured "OOOO".

BP-OPSYS-OWNER-03 NOSCOM must be owned by the SUPER Group ODBC owner ID.

BP-OPSYS-FILELOC-03 NOSCOM must reside in the same subvolume as NOSUTIL.

	Discovery Questions	Look here:
FILE-POLICY	Does policy allow the use of ODBC on the system?	Policy
OPSYS-OWNER-03	Who owns NOSCOM?	Fileinfo
FILE-ODBC-08	Is NOSCOM secured correctly?	Fileinfo Safecom

NOSUTIL

The NOSUTIL utility is a server process used to manage the ODBC environment. It is executed directly by the SCS and NonStop ODBC server processes.

Only a member of the SUPER Group can perform many of the configuration commands in NOSUTIL required to change the ODBC configuration. The HP *NonStop ODBC Manual* suggests PROGID'ing NOSUTIL.

RISK PROGID'ing NOSUTIL grants more privileges than the users require.

3P-ODBC-PRIVLEGE-01 Third-party access control software should be used to grant granular management of processes running as any Privileged ID only to users who require these privileges in order to perform their jobs. These products generally also provide comprehensive auditing of the activities they secure.

BP-FILE-ODBC-09   NOSUTIL should be secured "OOOO".

BP-OPSYS-PROGID-03   NOSUTIL should *not* be PROGID'ed.

BP-OPSYS-OWNER-03   NOSUTIL should be owned by the SUPER Group ODBC owner ID.

BP-OPSYS-FILELOC-03 NOSUTIL should reside in the subvolume created when ODBC was installed.

	Discovery Questions	**Look here:**
FILE-POLICY	Does policy allow the use of ODBC on the system?	Policy
OPSYS-OWNER-03	Who owns NOSUTIL?	Fileinfo
FILE-ODBC-09	Is NOSUTIL secured correctly?	Fileinfo Safecom

SQL Communication Subsystem (SCS)

The file SCSOBJ or SCS handles all communication with the client workstation. It is also responsible for managing the NonStop ODBC Server Classes. The SCS process starts a copy of the program NOSUTIL.

To avoid the overhead associated with process startup, the SCS maintains a group of running ODBC Servers. SCS assigns each new connection request to one of the pool of servers. The assigned server then changes to Guardian userid linked to the authenticated ODBC Alias-name. SCS passes the authentication message to the ODBC server and, thereafter, continues to pass messages in both directions.

BP-FILE-ODBC-10   SCSOBJ should be secured "NUNU".

BP-OPSYS-LICENSE-03 SCSOBJ should be LICENSE'd.

BP-OPSYS-OWNER-03 SCSOBJ should be owned by the SUPER Group ODBC owner ID.

BP-OPSYS-FILELOC-03 SCSOBJ should reside in the subvolume created when ODBC is installed.

	Discovery Questions	Look here:
FILE-POLICY	Does policy allow the use of ODBC on the system?	Policy
FILE-POLICY	Are there multiple SCS processes running on the system?	Policy
OPSYS-LICENSE	Is the SCSOBJ object file licensed?	Policy
OPSYS-OWNER-03	Who owns the SCS process?	Fileinfo
FILE-ODBC-10	Is the SCS process secured correctly?	Fileinfo Safecom

SPELIB

This ODBC program library contains the subroutines necessary for inclusion in Pathway Server Classes that will execute stored procedures.

BP-FILE-ODBC-11   SPELIB should be secured "NONO".

BP-FILE-PROGID-03   SPELIB should not be PROGID'ed.

BP-OPSYS-OWNER-03   SPELIB should be owned by the SUPER Group
ODBC owner ID.

BP-OPSYS-FILELOC-03   SPELIB should reside in the subvolume created
when ODBC was installed.

	Discovery Questions	Look here:
FILE-POLICY	Does policy allow the use of ODBC on the system?	Policy
FILE-PROGID	Is SPELIB PROGID'ed?	Policy
OPSYS-OWNER-03	Who owns SPELIB?	Fileinfo
FILE-ODBC-11	Is SPELIB secured correctly?	Fileinfo Safecom

OEVPRVD System Program

OEVPRVD is the object file for the OSM Open Event Viewer Provider.
Please refer to the Guardian Gazette section on the OSM subsystem for more
information.

OSH User Program

OSH runs an OSS command from the Guardian environment. It is a Guardian process that spawns an OSS process on the local node only. Command options allow the user to:

> Set some characteristics of the environment

> Set the initial attributes of the child process

> Redirect the output from the initially open files of the child process

Users can access files in the local node's /E directory via the –prog <pathname>
option.

Securing OSH

BP-FILE-OSH-01   OSH should be secured "UUNU".

BP-OPSYS-OWNER-01   OSH should be owned by SUPER.SUPER.

BP-OPSYS-FILELOC-01 OSH resides in $SYSTEM.SYSnn.

If available, use Safeguard or a third-party object security product to grant access to OSH only to users who require access in order to perform their jobs.

BP-SAFE-OSH-01   Add a Safeguard Protection Record to grant appropriate access to the OSH object file.

	Discovery Questions	**Look here:**
FILE-POLICY	Is OSS being used on the system?	Policy
OPSYS-OWNER-02	Who owns OSH?	Fileinfo
FILE-POLICY	Who is allowed to execute OSH on the system?	Policy
FILE-OSH-01 SAFE-OSH-01	Is OSH secured correctly?	Fileinfo Safecom

Open System Management (OSM)

OSM has been the recommended system management tool since version G06.22. OSM is required for Integrity NonStop systems.

Please refer to Part 8, *System Management Tools*, for a more complete discussion of the OSM Subsystem.

OSM Host Components

The startup and configuration files for OSM generally reside in the $SYSTEM.ZOSM subvolume. Some program files reside in $SYSTEM.SYSTEM and $SYSTEM.SYSnn. Data files and event files are found in the $SYSTEM.ZSERVICE subvolume, which OSM shares with TSM.

OSM and TSM both use the $SYSTEM.ZSERVICE subvolume in order to take advantage of the same event logs. Files that serve the same purpose in these two subsystems are named differently and noted in the section for each subsystem.

ADDTCPIP Script

The $SYSTEM.ZOSM.ADDTCPIP script starts processes named $OSMM0 and $OSMM1, which start the $ZTCP0 and $ZTCP1 TCP/IP processes. Once the TCP/IP processes are started, $OSMM0 and $OSMM1 stop themselves.

CTCPIP0 and CTCPIP1 are the scripts that configure the $ZTCP0 and $ZTCP1 TCP/IP processes that communicate with the OSM client.

The INIT0 and INIT1 scripts are used by the ADDTCPIP script to configure and start the $ZTCP0 and $ZTCP1 processes. They log their activity to the LOGTCP0 and LOGTCP1 files, respectively.

$OSMM0 and $OSMM1 use the OSMCONF configuration file. Parameters set in this file can override default values for the OSM startup.

ADDTCPIP creates a log file of its activity called LOGTCPIP.

$SYSTEM.ZOSM.ALTERIP is the script used to restart $ZTCP0 and $ZTCP1 when necessary.

BP-FILE-OSM-01	ADDTCPIP should be secured "NUNU".
BP-OPSYS-OWNER-03	ADDTCPIP should be owned by SUPER. SUPER.
BP-OPSYS-FILELOC-03	ADDTCPIP must reside in $SYSTEM. ZOSM.
BP-FILE-OSM-02	ALTERIP should be secured "NUNU".
BP-OPSYS-OWNER-03	ALTERIP should be owned by SUPER. SUPER.
BP-OPSYS-FILELOC-03	ALTERIP must reside in $SYSTEM.ZOSM.
BP-FILE-OSM-03	CTCPIP0 should be secured "NUNU".
BP-OSM-OWNER-03	CTCPIP0 should be owned by SUPER. SUPER.
BP-OPSYS-FILELOC-03	CTCPIP0 must reside in $SYSTEM.ZOSM.

BP-FILE-OSM-04　　　　CTCPIP1 should be secured "NUNU".

BP-OPSYS-OWNER-03　　CTCPIP1 should be owned by SUPER. SUPER.

BP-OPSYS-FILELOC-03　CTCPIP1 must reside in $SYSTEM. ZOSM.

BP-FILE-OSM-05　　　　INIT0 should be secured "NUNU".

BP-OPSYS-OWNER-03　　INIT0 should be owned by SUPER.SUPER.

BP-OPSYS-FILELOC-03　INIT0 must reside in $SYSTEM.ZOSM.

BP-FILE-OSM-06　　　　INIT1 should be secured "NUNU".

BP-OPSYS-OWNER-03　　INIT1 should be owned by SUPER.SUPER.

BP-OPSYS-FILELOC-03　INIT1 must reside in $SYSTEM.ZOSM.

BP-FILE-OSM-07　　　　LOGTCP0 should be secured "NUNU".

BP-OPSYS-OWNER-03　　LOGTCP0 should be owned by SUPER. SUPER.

BP-OPSYS-FILELOC-03　LOGTCP0 must reside in $SYSTEM. ZOSM

BP-FILE-OSM-08　　　　LOGTCP1 should be secured "NUNU".

BP-OPSYS-OWNER-03　LOGTCP1 should be owned by SUPER. SUPER.

BP-OPSYS-FILELOC-03　LOGTCP1 must reside in $SYSTEM. ZOSM.

BP-FILE-OSM-09　　　　LOGTCPIP should be secured "NUNU".

BP-OPSYS-OWNER-03　　LOGTCPIP should be owned by SUPER. SUPER.

BP-OPSYS-FILELOC-03　LOGTCPIP must reside in $SYSTEM. ZOSM.

	Discovery Questions	**Look here:**
OPSYS-OWNER-03	Who owns ADDTCPIP?	Fileinfo
OPSYS-OWNER-03	Who owns ALTERIP?	Fileinfo
OPSYS-OWNER-03	Who owns CTCPIP0?	Fileinfo
OPSYS-OWNER-03	Who owns CTCPIP1?	Fileinfo
OPSYS-OWNER-03	Who owns INIT0?	Fileinfo
OPSYS-OWNER-03	Who owns INIT1?	Fileinfo
OPSYS-OWNER-03	Who owns LOGTCP0?	Fileinfo
OPSYS-OWNER-03	Who owns LOGTCP1?	Fileinfo
OPSYS-OWNER-03	Who owns LOGTCPIP?	Fileinfo
FILE-OSM-01	Is ADDTCPIP secured correctly?	Fileinfo
FILE-OSM-02	Is ALTERIP secured correctly?	Fileinfo
FILE-OSM-03	Is CTCPIP0 secured correctly?	Fileinfo
FILE-OSM-04	Is CTCPIP1 secured correctly?	Fileinfo
FILE-OSM-05	Is INIT0 secured correctly?	Fileinfo
FILE-OSM-06	Is INIT1 secured correctly?	Fileinfo
FILE-OSM-07	Is LOGTCP0 secured correctly?	Fileinfo
FILE-OSM-08	Is LOGTCP1 secured correctly?	Fileinfo
FILE-OSM-09	Is LOGTCPIP secured correctly?	Fileinfo

ADDTOSCF

ADDTOSCF is the script to add OSM persistent processes into SCF. The processes it adds and starts are:

Process	**Object File**	**SCF Object**
$ZCMOM	$SYSTEM.SYSnn.CIMON	$ZZKRN.#OSM-CIMON
$ZLOG	$SYSTEM.SYSnn.EMSACOLL	$ZZKRN.#SM-ZLOG

(*Continued*)

Process	Object File	SCF Object
$ZOEV	$SYSTEM.SYSnn.EVTMGR	$ZZKRN.#OSM-OEV
$ZOLHD	$SYSTEM.SYSnn.EMSDIST	$ZZKRN.#OSMCONFLH-RD
$ZOSM	$SYSTEM.SYSnn.APPSRVR	$ZZKRN.#OSM-APPSRVR
$ZSPE	$SYSTEM.SYSTEM.ZSPE	$ZZKRN.#TSM-SP-EVENT

ADDTOSCF creates a log file called $SYSTEM.ZOSM.LOGSCF.

BP-FILE-OSM-10   ADDTOSCF should be secured "NUNU".

BP-OPSYS-OWNER-03   ADDTOSCF should be owned by SUPER. SUPER.

BP-OPSYS-FILELOC-03   ADDTOSCF must reside in $SYSTEM.ZOSM.

BP-FILE-OSM-11   LOGSCF should be secured "NUNU".

BP-OPSYS-OWNER-03   LOGSCF should be owned by SUPER.SUPER.

BP-OPSYS-FILELOC-03   LOGSCF must reside in $SYSTEM.ZOSM.

	Discovery Questions	Look here:
OPSYS-OWNER-03	Who owns ADDTOSCF?	Fileinfo
OPSYS-OWNER-03	Who owns LOGSCF?	Fileinfo
FILE-TMS-10	Is ADDTOSCF secured correctly?	Fileinfo
FILE-OSM-11	Is LOGSCF secured correctly?	Fileinfo

$ZCMOM

CIMON is the object file for the $ZCMOM process, which is the $ZZKRN.#OSM-CIMON SCF object. It is the main OSM server process.

BP-PROCESS-OSM-01 $ZCMOM should be running.

BP-FILE-SRM-12   CIMON should be secured "NUNU".

BP-OPSYS-OWNER-01   CIMON should be owned by SUPER. SUPER.

BP-OPSYS-FILELOC-01   CIMON must reside in $SYSTEM.SYSnn

	Discovery Questions	Look here:
PROCESS-OSM-01	Is the $ZZKRN.#OSM-CIMON process defined correctly?	SCF info process
PROCESS-OSM-01	Is the $ZCMOM process running?	Status
OPSYS-OWNER-01	Who owns CIMON?	Fileinfo
FILE-OSM-12	Is CIMON secured correctly?	Fileinfo

$ZLOG

$ZLOG is the process name of the $ZZKRN.#OSM-ZLOG SCF object. It is an instance of the EMSA collector program, $SYSTEM.SYSTEM. EMSACOLL. It is started by the ADDTOSCF script and logs events to the following files:

> The primary log files are named $SYSTEM.ZSERVICE.SSSVnnnn files, where nnnn is a incrementing number.

> The alternate key files are named $SYSTEM.ZSERVICE.ZZSKnnnn, where nnnn is an incrementing number.

BP-OSM-ZLOG-01   The $ZZKRN.#OSM-ZLOG process should be defined as persistent.

BP-PROCESS-OSM-02   The $ZLOG process pair should be running.

BP-FILE-OSM-13   SSSV* should be secured "NUNU".

BP-OPSYS-OWNER-03 SSSV* should be owned by SUPER.SUPER.

BP-OPSYS-FILELOC-03 SSSV* must reside in $SYSTEM.ZSERVICE

BP-FILE-OSM-14   ZZSK* should be secured "NUNU".

BP-OPSYS-OWNER-03 ZZSK* should be owned by SUPER.SUPER.

BP-OPSYS-FILELOC-03 ZZSK* must reside in $SYSTEM.ZSERVICE.

	Discovery Questions	Look here:
PROCESS-OSM-02	Is $ZZKRN.#OSM-ZLOG defined properly?	SCF info process
PROCESS-OSM-02	Is $ZLOG running?	Status
OPSYS-OWNER-03	Who owns the SSSVnnnn files?	Fileinfo
OPSYS-OWNER-03	Who owns the ZZSKnnnn files?	Fileinfo
FILE-OSM-13	Are the SSSVnnnn secured correctly?	Fileinfo
FILE-OSM-14	Are the ZZSKnnnn files secured correctly?	Fileinfo

$ZOEV

EVTMGR is the object file for the $ZOEV process, which is the $ZZKRN.#OSM-OEV SCF object. It is the server for Event Viewer requests.

OEVPRVD is the object file for Open Event Viewer Provider processes, which are responsible for retrieving EMS events. These processes are started by $ZOEV.

BP-PROCESS-OSM-03	$ZOEV should be running.
BP-FILE-SRM-15	EVTMGR should be secured "NUNU".
BP-OPSYS-OWNER-01	EVTMGR should be owned by SUPER. SUPER.
BP-OPSYS-FILELOC-01	EVTMGR must reside in $SYSTEM.SYSnn.
BP-FILE-OEVPRVD-16	OEVPRVD should be secured "NUNU".
BP-OSM-OWNER-01	OEVPRVD should be owned by SUPER. SUPER.
BP-OSM-FILELOC-01	OEVPRVD must reside in $SYSTEM.SYSnn.

	Discovery Questions	Look here:
PROCESS-OSM-03	Is the $ZZKRN.#OSM-OEV process defined correctly?	SCF info process
PROCESS-OSM-03	Is the $ZOEV process running?	Status

(Continued)

	Discovery Questions	Look here:
OPSYS-OWNER-01	Who owns EVTMGR?	Fileinfo
OPSYS-OWNER-01	Who owns OEVPRVD?	Fileinfo
FILE-OSM-15	Is EVTMGR secured correctly?	Fileinfo
FILE-OSM-16	Is OEVPRVD secured correctly?	Fileinfo

$ZOLHD

$ZOLHD is the process name for the $ZZKRN.#OSM-CONFLH-RD SCF object, which is the EMS Routing Distributor. It is an instance of the EMSDIST program, started by a TACL process named $ZOLHI with the INITRD file as input.

BP-PROCESS-OSM-04 $ZOLHD should be running.

BP-FILE-OSM-17   INITRD should be secured "NUNU".

BP-OPSYS-OWNER-03   INITRD should be owned by SUPER.SUPER.

BP-OPSYS-FILELOC-03   INITRD must reside in $SYSTEM.ZOSM.

	Discovery Questions	Look here:
PROCESS-OSM-04	Is the $ZZKRN.#OSM-CONFLH-RD process defined correctly?	SCF info process
PROCESS-OSM-04	Is the $ZOLHD process running as EMSDIST?	Status
OPSYS-OWNER-03	Who owns INITRD?	Fileinfo
FILE-INITRD –17	Is INITRD secured correctly?	Fileinfo

$ZOSM

APPSRVR is the object file for the $ZOSM process, which is the $ZZKRN.#OSM-APPSRVR SCF object. The Applet Server process uploads client files via the Server Connection.

$ZOSM launches the Applet Providers, which are responsible for serving client files. APPPRVD is the object file for the Applet Providers.

BP-PROCESS-OSM-05 $ZOSM should be running.

BP-FILE-SRM-18   APPSRVR should be secured "NUNU".

BP-OPSYS-OWNER-01   APPSRVR should be owned by SUPER.
SUPER.

BP-OPSYS-FILELOC-01   APPSRVR must reside in $SYSTEM.SYSnn.

BP-FILE-APPPRVD-19   APPPRVD should be secured "NUNU".

BP-OSM-OWNER-01   APPPRVD should be owned by SUPER.
SUPER.

BP-OSM-FILELOC-01   APPPRVD must be reside in $SYSTEM.
SYSnn.

	Discovery Questions	Look here:
PROCESS-OSM-05	Is the $ZZKRN.#OSM-OEV process defined correctly?	SCF info process
PROCESS-OSM-05	Is the $ZOSM process running?	Status
OPSYS-OWNER-01	Who owns APPSRVR?	Fileinfo
OPSYS-OWNER-01	Who owns APPPRVD?	Fileinfo
FILE-OSM-18	Is APPSRVR secured correctly?	Fileinfo
FILE-OSM-19	Is APPPRVD secured correctly?	Fileinfo

$ZSPE

ZSPE is the object file for the $ZSPE process, which is the $ZZKRN.#SP-EVENT SCF object. The Service Processor (SP) Event Distributor process writes SP events to $ZLOG.

BP-OSM-PROCESS-06 The $ZZKRN.#SP-EVENT process should be defined as a persistent process.

BP-PROCESS-OSM-06 The $ZSPE process pair should be running.

BP-FILE-ZSPE-20   ZSPE should be secured "NUNU".

BP-OPSYS-OWNER-01   ZSPE should be owned by SUPER.SUPER.

BP-OPSYS-FILELOC-01 ZSPE must reside in $SYSTEM.SYSnn.

	Discovery Questions	**Look here:**
PROCESS-OSM-06	Is the $ZZKRN.#SP-EVENT process defined correctly?	SCF info process
PROCESS-OSM-06	Is the ZSPE process defined correctly?	Status
OPSYS-OWNER-01	Who owns ZSPE?	Fileinfo
FILE-OSM-20	Is ZSPE secured correctly?	Fileinfo

EVNTPRVD

EVNTPRVD is the object file for the OSM Event Listener Provider.

BP-FILE-OSM-21   EVNTPRVD should be secured "NUNU".

BP-OSM-OWNER-01   EVNTPRVD should be owned by SUPER.
SUPER.

BP-OSM-FILELOC-01   EVNTPRVD must be reside in $SYSTEM.
SYSnn.

	Discovery Questions	**Look here:**
OSM-OWNER-01	Who owns EVNTPRVD?	Fileinfo
FILE-OSM-21	Is EVNTPRVD secured correctly?	Fileinfo

FDIST

FDIST is the object file for the Fast EMS Event Distributor process. Launched by the EVNTPRVD process, the Fast EMS Event Distributor process is responsible for retrieving EMS events from $ZLOG and $0.

BP-FILE-OSM-22   FDIST should be secured "NUNU".

BP-OSM-OWNER-01   FDIST should be owned by SUPER.SUPER.

BP-OSM-FILELOC-01   FDIST must be reside in $SYSTEM.SYSnn.

	Discovery Questions	**Look here:**
OSM-OWNER-01	Who owns FDIST?	Fileinfo
FILE-OSM-22	Is FDIST secured correctly?	Fileinfo

IAPRVD

IAPRVD is the object file for the Incident Analysis Provider, which is responsible for state propagation and generation of incident reports (IRs). The Incident Analysis Provider is started by the $ZCMOM process.

BP-FILE-OSM-23   IAPRVD should be secured "NUNU".

BP-OSM-OWNER-01   IAPRVD should be owned by SUPER.SUPER.

BP-OSM-FILELOC-01   IAPRVD must reside in $SYSTEM.SYSnn.

	Discovery Questions	**Look here:**
OSM-OWNER-01	Who owns IAPRVD?	Fileinfo
FILE-OSM-23	Is IAPRVD secured correctly?	Fileinfo

OSMCONF Configuration File

The OSMCONF file is used to customize the OSM Environment. The file is created by making a copy of the OSMINI file. Once created, $OSMM0 and $OSMM1 use the file to configure the OSM environment.

AP-ADVICE-OSM-01   All changes to the OSM configuration should be made in the OSMCONF file rather than the OSMINI file, which is over-written when upgrades are installed.

BP-FILE-OSM-24   OSMCONF should be secured "NUUU".

BP-OSM-OWNER-01   OSMCONF should be owned by SUPER.
SUPER.

BP-OSM-FILELOC-01   OSMCONF must reside in $SYSTEM.SYSnn.

	Discovery Questions	Look here:
OSM-OWNER-01	Who owns OSMCONF?	Fileinfo
FILE-OSM-24	Is OSMCONF secured correctly?	Fileinfo

OSMINI Configuration File

The OSMINI file is provided by HP as a template for entries in the OSMCONF file.

RISK   The OSMINI file is overwritten each time OSM is upgraded, therefore any customized entries will be overwritten during a product update.

AP-ADVICE-OSM-01   Name a copy of OSMINI file OSMCONF and make any changes in the OSMCONF file.

BP-FILE-OSM-25   OSMINI should be secured "UUUU".

BP-OSM-OWNER-01   OSMINI should be owned by SUPER. SUPER.

BP-OSM-FILELOC-01   OSMINI must reside in $SYSTEM.SYSnn.

	Discovery Questions	Look here:
OSM-OWNER-01	Who owns OSMINI?	Fileinfo
FILE-OSM-25	Is OSMINI secured correctly?	Fileinfo

Resource Access Layer Providers

$ZCMOM launches the Resource Access Layer Providers:

RALPRVD is the object file for the OSM Resource Layer Provider process, which is used for the initial discovery, initial incident analysis, event processing, and all operations that require SUPER Group access.

RALPRVNP is the object file for the OSM Resource Layer Provider process, which is used for operations that do not require SUPER Group access.

BP-FILE-OSM-26   RALPRVD should be secured "NUNU".

BP-OSM-OWNER-01 RALPRVD should be owned by SUPER.SUPER.

BP-OSM-FILELOC-01 RALPRVD must reside in $SYSTEM.SYSnn.

BP-FILE-OSM-27   RALPRVNP should be secured "NUNU".

BP-OSM-OWNER-01 RALPRVNP should be owned by SUPER. SUPER.

BP-OSM-FILELOC-01 RALPRVNP must reside in $SYSTEM.SYSnn.

	Discovery Questions	**Look here:**
OSM-OWNER-01	Who owns RALPRVD?	Fileinfo
OSM-OWNER-01	Who owns RALPRVNP?	Fileinfo
FILE-OSM-26	Is RALPRVD secured correctly?	Fileinfo
FILE-OSM-27	Is RALPRVNP secured correctly?	Fileinfo

SECPRVD

SECPRVD is the object file for the OSM Security Provider processes, which perform OSM user authentications. There may be up to eight Security Provider processes running at one time. They are started by $ZCMOM as required.

BP-FILE-SECPRVD-28 SECPRVD should be secured "NUNU".

BP-OSM-OWNER-01 SECPRVD should be owned by SUPER. SUPER.

BP-OSM-FILELOC-01 SECPRVD must reside in $SYSTEM.SYSnn.

	Discovery Questions	Look here:
OSM-OWNER-01	Who owns SECPRVD?	Fileinfo
FILE-OSM-28	Is SECPRVD secured correctly?	Fileinfo

SPDIST2

SPDIST2 is the object file for the OSM Service Provider (SP) Event Distributor process. Launched by the EVNTPRVD process, the SP Event Distributor process is responsible for retrieving SP events from $YMIOP.

BP-FILE-OSM-29   SPDIST2 should be secured "NUNU".

BP-OSM-OWNER-01   SPDIST2 should be owned by SUPER.SUPER.

BP-OSM-FILELOC-01   SPDIST2 must reside in $SYSTEM.SYSnn.

	Discovery Questions	Look here:
OSM-OWNER-01	Who owns SPDIST2?	Fileinfo
FILE-OSM-29	Is SPDIST2 secured correctly?	Fileinfo

SUPPREPO

SUPPREPO is the Enscribe file containing dial-out configuration information.

BP-FILE-OSM-30   SUPPREPO should be secured "NUNU".

BP-OSM-OWNER-03   SUPPREPO should be owned by SUPER.SUPER.

BP-OSM-FILELOC-03 SUPPREPO must reside in $SYSTEM. ZSERVICE.

	Discovery Questions	Look here:
OSM-OWNER-03	Who owns SUPPREPO?	Fileinfo
FILE-OSM-30	Is SUPPREPO secured correctly?	Fileinfo

TACLPRVD

TACLPRVD is the TACL Provider process, which is responsible for performing embedded TACL actions such as RELOAD PROCESSOR. There may be up to eight TACLPRVD processes running at one time. They are started by $ZCMOM as required.

BP-FILE-OSM-31   TACLPRVD should be secured "NUNU".

BP-OSM-OWNER-01   TACLPRVD should be owned by SUPER. SUPER.

BP-OSM-FILELOC-01 TACLPRVD must reside in $SYSTEM.SYSnn.

	Discovery Questions	**Look here:**
OSM-OWNER-01	Who owns TACLPRVD?	Fileinfo
FILE-OSM-31	Is TACLPRVD secured correctly?	Fileinfo

ZTRC

The ZTRC file contains the pointer to the current user trace log.

The user trace logs are created and maintained by CIMON. The naming convention for the trace files is ZTRCn, where n is an incrementing number.

BP-FILE-OSM-32   ZTRC should be secured "NUNU".

BP-OSM-OWNER-03   ZTRC should be owned by SUPER.SUPER.

BP-OSM-FILELOC-03 ZTRC must reside in $SYSTEM.ZSERVICE.

BP-FILE-OSM-33   ZTRCn should be secured "NUNU".

BP-OSM-OWNER-03   ZTRCn should be owned by SUPER.SUPER.

BP-OSM-FILELOC-03 ZTRCn must reside in $SYSTEM.ZSERVICE.

	Discovery Questions	**Look here:**
OSM-OWNER-03	Who owns ZTRC?	Fileinfo
OSM-OWNER-03	Who owns ZTRCn files?	Fileinfo

(Continued)

	Discovery Questions	Look here:
FILE-OSM-32	Is ZTRC secured correctly?	Fileinfo
FILE-OSM-33	Are the ZTRCn files secured correctly?	Fileinfo

OSM Alarm, Snapshot and Scan Files

OSM creates the following files as required. Depending on the current state of the system, these files may or may not be present.

Server alarm files are named ZZAAnnnn, where nnnn is an incrementing number. Alarms are generated by IAPRVD.

Inventory snapshot files are named ZZSNnnnn, where nnnn is an incrementing number.

Processor scan strings are named ZZPSnnnn, where nnnn is an incrementing number. Processor scans are created by RALPRVD.

BP-FILE-OSM-34	ZZAA* should be secured "NUNU".
BP-OPSYS-OWNER-03	ZZAA* should be owned by SUPER.SUPER.
BP-OPSYS-FILELOC-03	ZZAA* if present, must reside in $SYSTEM. ZSERVICE.
BP-FILE-OSM-36	ZZPS* should be secured "NUNU".
BP-OPSYS-OWNER-03	ZZPS* should be owned by SUPER.SUPER.
BP-OPSYS-FILELOC-03	ZZPS* if present, must reside in $SYSTEM. ZSERVICE.
BP-FILE-OSM-35	ZZSN* should be secured "NUNU".
BP-OPSYS-OWNER-03	ZZSN* should be owned by SUPER. SUPER.
BP-OPSYS-FILELOC-03	ZZSN* if present, must reside in $SYSTEM. ZSERVICE.

	Discovery Questions	Look here:
OPSYS-OWNER-03	Who owns the ZZAA* files?	Fileinfo
OPSYS-OWNER-03	Who owns the ZZPS* files?	Fileinfo
OPSYS-OWNER-03	Who owns the ZZSN* files?	Fileinfo
FILE-OSM-34	Are the ZZAA* files secured correctly?	Fileinfo
FILE-OSM-35	Are the ZZPS* files secured correctly?	Fileinfo
FILE-OSM-36	Are the ZZSN* files secured correctly?	Fileinfo

OSMCONF Configuration File

The OSMCONF file is used to customize the OSM Environment. Please refer to the Guardian Gazette section on the OSM Subsystem for more information.

OSS File Manager (OSSFM)

The OSS file manager process manages the OSS file-system cache and satisfies OSS memory management requests from the NonStop Kernel memory manager.

There should be one file manager process per CPU. The process names are $ZFMnn, where nn represents the CPU number. Each process starts automatically when its processor starts.

RISK If an OSS file manager terminates abnormally, it takes down its processor.

AP-OSSMON-OSSFM-01 The file manager process can be stopped, but all applications with open OSS files should be stopped first.

OSSFM is the OSS File Manager object file.

Securing the OSS File Manager

BP-PROCESS-OSSFM-01	The $ZFMnn processes should be running.
BP-FILE-OSSFM-01	OSSFM should be secured "UUUU".
BP-OPSYS-OWNER-01	OSSFM should be owned by SUPER.SUPER.
BP-OPSYS-FILELOC-01	OSSFM resides in $SYSTEM.SYSnn.

If available, use Safeguard or a third-party object security product to grant access to OSSFM only to users who require access in order to perform their jobs.

BP-SAFE-OSSFM-01   Add a Safeguard Protection Record to grant appropriate access to the ZPOSSFM object file equivalent to the Guardian file security string listed above.

	Discovery Questions	Look here:
PROCESS-OSSFM-01	Are the $ZFMnn processes running?	Status
PROCESS-POLICY	Who is authorized to start and stop the $ZFMnn processes?	Policy
OPSYS-OWNER-01	Who owns OSSFM?	Fileinfo
FILE-OSSFM-01	Is OSSFM secured correctly?	Fileinfo Safecom

Related Topics

OSS Subsystem

OSSMON

SCF

OSS Monitor Process (OSSMON)

The OSS Monitor is a Guardian process that configures and administers the OSS environment. It is the gateway for all OSS activity on HP NonStop

Servers. The monitor manages the OSS Name Server and enables the OSS system to define OSS volumes.

BP-FILE-OSSMON-01   The OSS monitor process name must be $ZPMON.

RISK   The OSS Monitor terminates immediately if $ZPMON is already running or is given a different process name.

AP-ADVICE-OSSMON-01   Put procedures in place to ensure that the OSS Monitor is started with the correct process name and owner.

BP-FILE-OSSMON-01   The OSS monitor process name must be $ZPMON.

AP-ADVICE-OSSMON-01   Put procedures in place to ensure that the OSS Monitor is started with the correct process name and owner during system startup.

SCF communicates with OSSMON via the Subsystem Programmatic Interface (SPI). When OSS is installed, the OSS Product Module for SCF is also installed in $SYSTEM.SYSTEM. It provides a set of SPI error messages specific to the OSS environment that are returned to the OSS Monitor.

RISK   OSSMON contains privileged procedures.

BP-FILE-OSSMON-02   HP strongly recommends that OSSMON not be licensed because only SUPER.SUPER should start, manage, or stop the OSS monitor process.

AP-ADVICE-OSSMON-02   HP   recommends   that   you   specify processors for the OSS Monitor that are not used by the FSCK utility or any name servers.

BP-PROCESS-OSSMON-01 The $ZPMON process should be running.

BP-FILE-OSSMON-01   OSSMON should be secured "UUUU".

BP-OPSYS-LICENSE-01   OSSMON must NOT be LICENSED.

BP-OPSYS-OWNER-01   OSSMON should be owned by SUPER. SUPER.

BP-OPSYS-FILELOC-01	OSSMON resides in $SYSTEM.SYSnn.
BP-FILE-SCF-06	Z???SCF should be secured "UUNU".
BP-OPSYS-OWNER-02	Z???SCF should be owned by SUPER. SUPER.
BP-OPSYS-FILELOC-02	Z???SCF reside in $SYSTEM.SYSTEM.

	Discovery Questions	**Look here:**
PROCESS-OSSMON-01	Is a $ZPMON process running on the system?	Status
PROCESS-POLICY	Who is authorized to start and stop the $ZPMON process?	Policy
OPSYS-LICENSE-01	Is the OSSMON object file licensed?	Fileinfo
OPSYS-OWNER-01	Who owns OSSMON?	Fileinfo
FILE-OSSMON-01 SAFE-OSSMON-01	Is OSSMON secured correctly?	Fileinfo

OSSMON Configuration Files

The OSS Monitor uses the following configuration files to manage OSS name server operation and OSS file access. Please refer to the individual sections on these files for more information.

ZOSSFSET

ZOSSPARM

ZOSSSERV

RISK Some OSS Monitor commands require that the OSS Monitor access its configuration files. If the OSS Monitor cannot access these files or if they contain invalid data, an error is returned.

ZOSSFSET File

The ZOSSFSET file is an Enscribe alternate-key file. It contains information about filesets. It is updated via SCF OSS Monitor commands. Changes to the file take effect only when the name server assigned to the affected fileset is stopped and restarted.

The file contains two types of entries:

The names and catalog volumes of every fileset

The characteristics of the OSS sockets local server process, $ZPLS.

OSSMON creates the ZOSSFSET file, adding only the name server for the root fileset and the parameters for the sockets local server. Therefore, this file need to be configured before the root fileset is first mounted or before the first OSS sockets local server is started.

BP-ADVICE-ZOSSFSET-01 Restrict access to the ZOSSFSET file to prevent invalid or incorrect configuration data being introduced.

BP-ADVICE-ZOSSFSET-02 Secure the ZOSSFSET file so that OSS-MON can always access it.

BP-FILE-OSSMON-02 ZOSSFSET should be secured "NUUU".

BP-OPSYS-OWNER-03 ZOSSFSET should be owned by SUPER. SUPER.

BP-OPSYS-FILELOC-03 ZOSSFSET resides in $SYSTEM. ZXOSSMON.

	Discovery Questions	Look here:
OPSYS-OWNER-03	Who owns ZOSSFSET?	Fileinfo
FILE-OSSMON-02 SAFE-OSSMON-02	Is ZOSSFSET secured correctly?	Fileinfo Safecom

ZOSSPARM File

The ZOSSPARM file is an Enscribe data file. It contains the subsystem configuration database for the OSS Monitor. The default file is created by the OSS Monitor and contains the entry for the root fileset's name server process, $ZPNS.

The file must be present before the root fileset is first mounted and before the root name server ($ZPNS) is started.

The file is updated via SCF OSS Monitor commands. Changes take effect immediately.

AP-ADVICE-NS-02   HP recommends that the CPUs assigned as each name server's primary and backup processors be different from every other name server's CPU assignments, so that no single processor failure affects more than one name server process pair.

AP-ADVICE-ZOSSPARM-03   HP recommends that CPUs specified for name servers not be the same CPUs used by either the OSS Monitor or the FSCK utility.

BP-FILE-OSSMON-03   ZOSSPARM should be secured "NUUU".

BP-OPSYS-OWNER-03   ZOSSPARM should be owned by SUPER. SUPER.

BP-OPSYS-FILELOC-03 ZOSSPARM   resides   in $SYSTEM. ZXOSSMON.

	Discovery Questions	**Look here:**
OPSYS-OWNER-03	Who owns ZOSSPARM?	Fileinfo
FILE-OSSMON-03 SAFE-OSSMON-03	Is ZOSSPARM secured correctly?	Fileinfo Safecom

ZOSSSERV Configuration File

The ZOSSSERV file is an Enscribe data file. It stores the characteristics of all OSS name server processes. The default file is created by the OSS Monitor and initially contains the entry for the root fileset's name server process, $ZPNS.

The file must be present before the root fileset is first mounted and before the root name server ($ZPNS) is started.

The file is updated via SCF OSS Monitor commands. Changes take effect only when the affected name server is stopped and restarted.

BP-FILE-OSSMON-04 ZOSSSERV should be secured "NUUU".

BP-OPSYS-OWNER-03 ZOSSSERV should be owned by SUPER. SUPER.

BP-OPSYS-FILELOC-03 ZOSSSERV resides in $SYSTEM. ZXOSSMON.

	Discovery Questions	Look here:
OPSYS-OWNER-03	Who owns ZOSSSERV?	Fileinfo
FILE-OSSMON-04 SAFE-OSSMON-04	Is ZOSSSERV secured correctly?	Fileinfo Safecom

OSSMON-Managed Processes

The OSS Monitor controls the following processes:

OSS message queue server

OSS name server(s)

OSS sockets local server

OSS transport agent server

The OSS Monitor and the servers it manages are all configured and managed via SCF OSS Monitor commands.

The first time the OSS Monitor is run after the OSS subsystem is installed, it adds the default OSS name server for the root fileset and the other three servers. Thereafter, if any of these processes stop, the monitor will restart them.

All but the transport agent server can be run as fault-tolerant process pairs.

OSS Message Queue (ZMSGQ)

The OSS message queue process manages the OSS message queue. The default name of the message queue process is $ZMSGQ.

The message server configuration parameters are defined in the ZOSSSERV file. The message server object file is ZMSGQ.

BP-PROCESS-OSSMON-05   The $ZMSGQ process should be running.

BP-FILE-OSSMON-05   ZMSGQ should be secured "UUUU".

BP-OPSYS-OWNER-01   ZMSGQ should be owned by SUPER.
SUPER.

BP-OPSYS-FILELOC-01   ZMSGQ resides in $SYSTEM.SYSnn.

	Discovery Questions	Look here:
PROCESS-OSSMON-05	Are the $ZMSGQ processes running?	Status
PROCESS-POLICY	Who is authorized to start and stop the $ZMSGQ processes?	Policy
OPSYS-OWNER-01	Who owns ZMSGQ?	Fileinfo
FILE-OSSMON-05 SAFE-OSSMON-05	Is ZMSGQ secured correctly?	Fileinfo Safecom

OSS Name Server (NS)

Each OSS file and AF_UNIX socket has an underlying Guardian filename. Because the two names are different, the OSS environment must have a way to map (resolve) the OSS pathname to the Guardian name. This is the task of the OSS name servers. They translate the OSS file name to the ZYQ Guardian subvolume location where the file actually resides.

Configuration information for name servers is stored in the ZOSSSERV file. Every fileset must have a name server. The OSSMON creates the name server entry file for the root fileset, $ZPNS, in the ZOSSFSET automatically. More name servers should be added, as necessary, to share the work of locating OSS files.

The object file for name server processes is $SYSTEM.SYSnn.NS. The default process name for the root fileset is $ZPNS.

AP-ADVICE-NS-02   HP recommends that each name server must have both primary and backup processor numbers assigned, such that no single processor failure affects more than one name server process pair.

AP-ADVICE-NS-03   HP recommends that you specify processors for name servers that are not used by either the OSS Monitor or the FSCK utility.

BP-PROCESS-OSSMON-06 The $ZPNS process should be running.

BP-FILE-OSSMON-06   NS should be secured "UUUU".

BP-OPSYS-OWNER-01   NS should be owned by SUPER.SUPER.

BP-OPSYS-FILELOC-01   NS resides in $SYSTEM.SYSnn.

	Discovery Questions	**Look here:**
PROCESS-OSSMON-06	Are the $ZPNS processes running?	Status
PROCESS-POLICY	Who is authorized to start and stop the $ZPNS processes?	Policy
OPSYS-OWNER-01	Who owns NS?	Fileinfo
FILE-OSSMON-06 SAFE-OSSMON-06	Is NS secured correctly?	Fileinfo Safecom

OSS Sockets Local Server (OSSLS)

The OSS sockets local server process provides applications with access to OSS sockets. Sockets route data between application processes using a process called a transport agent. A transport agent routes data within a single processor.

The default name of the sockets local server is $ZPLS. It should run as a fault-tolerant process pair. The process can be stopped and started via the SCF OSS Monitor commands. Its configuration is stored in the ZOSSSERV file.

There must always be a #ZPLS entry for the OSS sockets local server process, $ZPLS, in the ZOSSSERV file. You cannot remove the OSS sockets local server, the OSS message-queue server, or an OSS transport agent server.

The sockets local server object file is OSSLS.

BP-PROCESS-OSSMON-07   The $ZPLS process should be running.

BP-FILE-OSSMON-07   OSSLS should be secured "UUUU".

BP-OPSYS-OWNER-01   OSSLS should be owned by SUPER. SUPER.

BP-OPSYS-FILELOC-01   OSSLS resides in $SYSTEM.SYSnn.

	Discovery Questions	Look here:
PROCESS-OSSLS-07	Is $ZPLS process running on the system?	Status
PROCESS-POLICY	Who is authorized to start and stop the $ZPLS process?	Policy
OPSYS-OWNER-01	Who owns OSSLS?	Fileinfo
FILE-OSSMON-07 SAFE-OSSMON-07	Is OSSLS secured correctly?	Fileinfo

OSS Transport Agent Server (OSSTA)

The OSS transport agent server is used for OSS sockets communication. There is one transport agent server per CPU. The process names are $ZTAnn, where nn is the CPU number.

Each OSS transport agent server is automatically started when the CPU it runs in is started. The processes can be started and stopped via the SCF OSS Monitor commands, but they cannot be added, altered, or removed.

The OSS transport agent object file is OSSTA.

BP-PROCESS-OSSMON-08   The $ZTAnn processes should be running.

BP-FILE-OSSMON-08   OSSTA should be secured "UUUU".

BP-OPSYS-OWNER-01 SUPER.   SSTA should be owned by SUPER.

BP-OPSYS-FILELOC-01   OSSTA resides in $SYSTEM.SYSnn.

	Discovery Questions	Look here:
PROCESS-OSSMON-08	Are the $ZTAnn processes running?	Status
PROCESS-POLICY	Who is authorized to start and stop the $ZTAnn processes?	Policy
OPSYS-OWNER-01	Who owns OSSTA ?	Fileinfo
FILE-OSSMON-08 SAFE-OSSMON-08	Is OSSTA secured correctly?	Fileinfo Safecom

OSS Pipe Server (OSSPS)

The OSS Pipe Server processes support the transfer of data between OSS processes that use pipes or FIFOs between processors. There should be one Pipe Server per CPU. The default process name is $ZPPnn, where nn is the CPU number.

Each OSS Pipe server is automatically started when the processor it runs on is started. The processes can be stopped and restarted via the SCF OSS Monitor commands.

The Pipe Server process object file is OSSPS.

Securing OSSPS

BP-PROCESS-OSSPS-01   The $ZPPnn processes should be running.

BP-FILE-OSSPS-01   OSSPS should be secured "UUUU".

BP-OPSYS-OWNER-01   OSSPS should be owned by SUPER.SUPER.

BP-OPSYS-FILELOC-01   OSSPS resides in $SYSTEM.SYSnn.

If available, use Safeguard or a third-party object security product to grant access to OSSPS only to users who require access in order to perform their jobs.

BP-SAFE-OSSPS-01   Add a Safeguard Protection Record to grant appropriate access to the OSSPS object file equivalent to the Guardian file security string listed above.

	Discovery Questions	Look here:
PROCESS-OSSPS-01	Is a $ZPPnn process running on the system?	Status
PROCESS-POLICY	Who is authorized to start and stop the $ZPPnn process?	Policy
OPSYS-OWNER-01	Who owns OSSPS?	Fileinfo
FILE-OSSPS-01	Is OSSPS secured correctly?	Fileinfo

Related Topics

OSS Subsystem

OSSMON

OSSLS System Program

OSSLS is the object file for the sockets local server, $ZPLS, which is managed by the OSS Monitor. Please refer to the Guardian Gazette section on the OSS Monitor Process for more information.

OSSMON System Program

OSSMON is the object file for the OSS monitor process, $ZPMON. Please refer to the Guardian Gazette section on the OSS Monitor Process for more information.

OSSPS System Program

OSSPS is the object file for the OSS Pipe Server processes, $ZPPnn, where nn refers to a CPU number. Please refer to the Guardian Gazette section on the OSS Pipe Server for more information.

OSSTA System Program

OSSTA is the object file for the OSS transport agent server, which is managed by the OSS Monitor. Please refer to the Guardian Gazette section on the OSS Monitor Process for more information.

OSSTTY System Utility

The OSSTTY facility enables OSS processes to interact with the Guardian environment. The program provides a way for OSS processes to redirect their standard input, output, and error files to Guardian processes. The standard output can also be directed to Guardian EDIT files.

A Guardian process has three standard files that normally possess the structure of an EDIT file: the STDIN, STDOUT, and STDERR files. When entered at a TACL prompt, they are usually referred to as the IN file, the OUT file, and the TERM file. By default, these files are associated with the user's home terminal. However, the command that runs a Guardian process can redirect those files to Guardian processes or files.

OSS processes use a similar set of default files, **stdin**, **stdout**, and **stderr**, but with a different file format: unstructured standard files. However, an OSS user normally launches an OSS shell by logging in through Telserv. That access method leaves the OSS standard files associated with the user's terminal but allows no way for those files to be redirected to Guardian processes or files. The OSSTTY utility makes the redirection possible.

The OSS **stdin**, **stdout**, and **stderr** are unstructured standard files, but otherwise are the equivalent of the Guardian STDIN, STDOUT and STDERR (EDIT type) files.

The OSSTTY object file is $SYSTEM.SYSnn.OSSTTY.

OSSTTY can be started via a TACL or OSH command. It can be started by an individual user in the Guardian environment, or through the OSH **osstty** command, or directly by an OSS administrator.

Telserv provides two kinds of windows: static and dynamic:

> A static window is created via SCF and opened with Telserv and with OSSTTY. It can exist independently of a connection to the OSS environment. (The OSSTTY windows #stdin, #stdout, and #stderr are considered to be static because they are preconfigured and cannot be changed while OSSTTY is running.)

> A dynamic window is opened by Telserv in response to a connection request. OSSTTY does not support dynamic windows.

Once started, OSSTTY becomes the standard input, standard output, and standard error of the OSS process, and redirects input, output, and error data to the Guardian targets specified as run options or through redirection operators.

Securing OSSTTY

BP-FILE-OSSTTY-01   OSSTTY should be secured "UUNU".

BP-OPSYS-OWNER-01 OSSTTY should be owned by SUPER. SUPER.

BP-OPSYS-FILELOC-01 OSSTTY resides in $SYSTEM.SYSnn.

If available, use Safeguard or a third-party object security product to grant access to OSSTTY only to users who require access in order to perform their jobs.

BP-SAFE-OSSTTY-01   Add a Safeguard Protection Record to grant appropriate access to the OSSTTY object file equivalent to the Guardian file security string listed above.

	Discovery Questions	Look here:
OPSYS-OWNER-01	Who owns OSSTTY?	Fileinfo
FILE-OSSTTY-01	Is OSSTTY secured correctly?	Fileinfo

PCAUTHD System Program

PCAUTHD is the object file for the NFS authentication server process. Please refer to Part 5, for a complete discussion of the Network File System (NFS) Subsystem or to the Guardian Gazette section on the NFS Subsystem for Best Practice recommendations.

PCLPRD System Program

PCLPRD is the object file for the NFS print spool server process, which communicates with the Guardian spooler subsystem. Please refer to Part 5, for a complete discussion of the Network File System (NFS) Subsystem or to the Guardian Gazette section on the NFS Subsystem for Best Practice recommendations.

PCNFSD System Program

PCNFSD is the object file for the $PCDP2 process, which is an extension to NFS that allows non-UNIX clients to interact in a secure manner with NFS servers. Please refer to Part 5, for a complete discussion of the Network File System (NFS) Subsystem or to the Guardian Gazette section on the NFS Subsystem for Best Practice recommendations.

PERSIST File

PERSIST is the TSM Current Alarm Objects database. Please refer to the Guardian Gazette section on the TSM Subsystem for more information.

Persistence Manager (ZPM) System Program

ZPM is the object file for the Persistence Manager process, $ZPM, which automatically restarts selected processes when they stop abnormally.

$ZPM is started by the $ZCNF process. Then, based on information in the CONFIG file, it starts all generic processes and optionally manages their persistence.

The Persistence Manager's IN, OUT, and TERM should be $YMIOP.#CLCI.

Securing ZPM

BP-FILE-ZPM-01   ZPM should be secured "UUCU".

BP-OPSYS-OWNER-01   ZPM should be owned by SUPER.SUPER.

BP-OPSYS-FILELOC-01   ZPM resides in $SYSTEM.SYSnn.

If available, use Safeguard or a third-party object security product to grant access to ZPM only to users who require access in order to perform their jobs.

BP-SAFE-ZPM-01   Add a Safeguard Protection Record to grant appropriate access to the ZPM object file equivalent to the Guardian file security string listed above.

	Discovery Questions	Look here:
OPSYS-OWNER-01	Who owns ZPM?	Fileinfo
FILE-ZPM-01	Is ZPM secured correctly?	Fileinfo

Related Topics

SCF

CONFIG file

$ZCNF

PERSSUPP Configuration File

PERSSUPP is the current configuration database file for the TSM subsystem.

QIO Subsystem

Client processes make use of QIO to transfer data from multiple, noncontiguous memory addresses without physically moving the data, which reduces processor overhead.

The QIO subsystem is configured via QIOMON SCF commands.

QIO Components

The QIO subsystem consists of the following major components.

QIO Monitor (QIOMON) Process

The QIOMON process creates the shared memory segment, manages it, and monitors the client processes that are using the segment.

QIOMON is the object file for the QIOMON processes.

There should be one QIOMON process per CPU with process names of $ZMnn, where nn is the CPU number.

QIOMON's IN, OUT, and TERM should be the same as the Persistence Manager's (ZPM), $YMIOP.#CLCI.

QIO Library

The library is a set of procedures for QIO functions used by client processes and the QIOMON process. Library procedures are used to manage the shared memory segment and the interface between the client processes. The QIO library interface is an internal interface and is not documented.

Securing QIOMON

BP-FILE-QIOMON-01   QIOMON should be secured "UUUU".

BP-OPSYS-OWNER-01   QIOMON should owned by SUPER.SUPER.

BP-OPSYS-FILELOC-01 QIOMON resides in $SYSTEM.SYSnn.

If available, use Safeguard or a third-party object security product to grant access to QIOMON only to users who require access in order to perform their jobs.

BP-SAFE-QIOMON-01   Add a Safeguard Protection Record to grant appropriate access to the QIOMON object file equivalent to the Guardian file security string listed above.

	Discovery Questions	**Look here:**
OPSYS-OWNER-01	Who owns QIOMON?	Fileinfo
FILE-QIOMON-01	Is QIOMON secured correctly?	Fileinfo

RALPRVD System Program

RALPRVD is the object file for the OSM Resource Layer Provider process. Please refer the Guardian Gazette section on the OSM subsystem for more information.

RALPRVNP System Program

RALPRVNP is the object file for the OSM Resource Layer Provider process. Please refer the Guardian Gazette section on the OSM subsystem for more information.

Remote Procedure Call (RPC) Subsystem

A Remote Procedure Call (RPC) provides a standard way to invoke services on remote servers that are linked by a network. Each server supplies a program, such as NFS, to respond to these calls. RPC does not depend on specific transport protocols, so it can be used with any underlying protocol.

The combination of host address, program number, and procedure number specifies one remote service procedure.

RPC Components

The RPC subsystem is made up of the following components.

PORTMAP

PORTMAP is the object file for the PORTMAPPER process, which converts host port numbers to Remote Procedure Call (RPC) program numbers. It corresponds to the /etc/portmap program found on many UNIX systems. The PORTMAPPER process is required by the NFS subsystem.

The PORTMAPPER program has one entry for each supported client protocol.

Each TCP/IP process has a PORTMAPPER process.

PORTMAP is started from a TACL prompt. It can be run as a persistent process. The naming convention is $ZPMPn or $ZPMn, where n represents a number that, by convention, matches that of its TCP/IP server process name.

When an RPC server process is started, it tells the PORTMAPPER process what host port number it is listening to and what RPC program numbers it is prepared to serve. When a client process wants to make an RPC call to a given program number, it contacts the PORTMAPPER process on the target system to determine the host port number to which RPC packets should be sent.

RPC

The RPC file contains program definitions. It is an EDIT file. The definitions include the program name, program number, and possible aliases for the program name. The file is used by the PORTMAPPER and RPCINFO processes.

RPCINFO

RPCINFO is the object file for the RPCINFO process, which displays RPC program numbers. It can be used to alter running RPC servers or to monitor and change PORTMAP behavior.

The RPCINFO process is started from a TACL prompt, not via **/bin/inetd**.

The PORTMAPPER process must be started before any RPC servers can be started.

Securing RPC

BP-FILE-RPC-01	PORTMAP should be secured "UUCU".
BP-OPSYS-OWNER-03	PORTMAP should be owned by SUPER. SUPER.
BP-OPSYS-FILELOC-03	PORTMAP resides in $SYSTEM.ZRPC.
BP-FILE-RPC-02	RPC should be secured "NUUU".
BP-OPSYS-OWNER-03	RPC should be owned by SUPER.SUPER.
BP-OPSYS-FILELOC-03	RPC resides in $SYSTEM.ZRPC.
BP-FILE-RPC-03	RPCINFO should be secured "UUNU".

BP-OPSYS-OWNER-03 RPCINFO should be owned by SUPER.
SUPER.

BP-OPSYS-FILELOC-03 RPCINFO resides in $SYSTEM.ZRPC.

If available, use Safeguard or a third-party object security product to grant access to RPC only to users who require access in order to perform their jobs.

BP-SAFE-RPC-01 Add a Safeguard Protection Record to grant appropriate access to the RPC object file equivalent to the Guardian file security string listed above.

	Discovery Questions	Look here:
OPSYS-OWNER-03	Who owns PORTMAP?	Fileinfo
OPSYS-OWNER-03	Who owns RPC?	Fileinfo
OPSYS-OWNER-03	Who owns RPCINFO?	Fileinfo
FILE-RPC-01	Is PORTMAP secured correctly?	Fileinfo
FILE-RPC-02	Is RPC secured correctly?	Fileinfo
FILE-RPC-03	Is RPCINFO secured correctly?	Fileinfo

Related Topics
SCF
CONFIG file
$ZCNF

RPC

Please refer to the Guardian Gazette section on the Remote Procedure Call (RPC) subsystem for more information.

(Continued)

Safeguard Subsystem

This section contains Best Practice recommendations for the new files added to the Safeguard subsystem in releases G06.21 through G06.28. Please refer to the *Safeguard Subsystem* section of the Gazette in the first volume, *Securing the HP NonStop Server*, Best Practice recommendations for the entire subsystem.

LUSERAX and USERAX Configuration Files

Two new files were created. They contain the new TEXT-DESCRIPTION and BINARY-DESCRIPTION fields.

Name	Filecode	Contents
LUSERAX	540	Alias Text Description and Binary Description
USERAX	540	User Text Description and Binary Description

Records are only written to the appropriate file, LUSERAX or USERAX, if the TEXT-DESCRIPTION parameter is updated.

BP-FILE-SAFEGUARD-12 LUSERAX should be secured "- - - -".

BP-OPSYS-OWNER-03 LUSERAX should be owned by SUPER.
SUPER.

BP-OPSYS-FILELOC-03 LUSERAX should reside in $SYSTEM.SAFE.

BP-FILE-SAFEGUARD-13 USERAX should be secured "- - - -".

BP-OPSYS-OWNER-02 USERAX should be owned by SUPER.
SUPER.

BP-OPSYS-FILELOC-02 USERAX should reside in $SYSTEM.
SYSTEM.

	Discovery Questions	Look here:
File-Policy	Is release G06.27 or greater installed on the system?	Policy
OPSYS-OWNER-03	Who owns LUSERAX?	Fileinfo

(Continued)

	Discovery Questions	Look here:
OPSYS-OWNER-03	Who owns USERAX?	Fileinfo
FILE-SAFEGUARD-12	Is LUSERAX secured correctly via Guardian or Safeguard?	Fileinfo
FILE-SAFEGUARD-13	Is USERAX secured correctly via Guardian or Safeguard?	Fileinfo

PATGUARD Configuration Files

The new DISKFILE-PATTERN Object Protection Records are contained in PATGUARD files. The PATGUARD files are the equivalent of the GUARD files. A PATGUARD file resides in the SAFE subvolume on every disk (volume). The SMON processes consult the PATGUARD files on the disk where the file being accessed resides if the new CHECK-DISKFILE-PATTERN global parameter in set to ONLY, LAST, or FIRST.

If CHECK-DISKFILE-PATTERN is set to ONLY, only DISKFILE-PATTERN Protection Records will be checked; any exisiting non-pattern Protection Records will be ignored.

If CHECK-DISKFILE-PATTERN is LAST, pattern checking will be done after nonpattern Protection Records are evaluated

IF CHECK-DISKFILE-PATTERN is FIRST, pattern checking will be done before nonpattern Protection Records are evaluated.

If CHECK-DISKFILE-PATTERN is set to OFF, pattern checking is disabled; any existing DISKFILE-PATTERN Protection Records will be ignored.

The PATGUARD files should be secured like the GUARD files. Please refer to the Safeguard Subsystem section of the Gazette in the first volume, *HP NonStop Server Security: A Practical Handbook*, for more information.

BP-FILE-SAFEGUARD-12 PATGUARD should be secured "- - - -".

BP-OPSYS-OWNER-03 PATGUARD should be owned by SUPER. SUPER.

BP-OPSYS-FILELOC-03   PATGUARD should reside in $.SAFE sub volumes.

	Discovery Questions	Look here:
File-Policy	Is release G06.27 or greater installed on the system?	Policy
OPSYS-OWNER-03	Who owns the PATGUARD files?	Fileinfo
FILE-SAFEGUARD-12	Is PATGUARD secured correctly via Guardian or Safeguard?	Fileinfo

SCS

SCS stands for the SQL Communication System. Please refer to the Guardian Gazette section on ODBC.

SCSOBJ

SCSOBJ is the object file for the SQL Communication System (SCS). Please refer to the Guardian Gazette section on ODBC.

SECPRVD

SECPRVD is the object file for the OSM Security Provider. Please refer to the Guardian Gazette section on the OSM subsystem for more information.

SNMP (Simple Network Management Protocol)

SNMP is the protocol used to monitor and control devices on a network. Each device contains certain information about its configuration and its status. SNMP compliant applications known as SNMP Agents run on the device and are responsible for its SNMP management.

A MIB is a database describing a collection of objects on the device that can be managed.

Network management tools, such as HP Openview, allow all devices on the network to be monitored centrally and controlled if required.

RISK There is only very rudimentary SNMP support on the HP Non-Stop Server. It provides information on a variety of components, but does not allow control. It still could however provide hackers with useful information about the system or devices on the system.

SNMP Components

The components of SNMP are:

SNMPAGT

SNMP TRAP

SNMP TRAPDEST

SNMP PROFILE

SNMPAGT

SNMPAGT is the HP NonStop Server SNMP Agent. It is used to interactively transfer or manage files on a remote system. The remote system need not be another NonStop Server.

AP-ADVICE-SNMP-01 SNMP's access to the system should be blocked either on the NonStop system or by network devices such as a firewall.

BP-FILE-SNMP-01 SNMPAGT should be secured "UUCU".

BP-OPSYS-OWNER-03 SNMPAGT should be owned by SUPER. SUPER.

BP-OPSYS-FILELOC-03 SNMPAGT resides in $SYSTEM.SYSTEM.

	Discovery Questions	**Look here:**
FILE-POLICY-01	Is SNMP configured on the node?	SCF
SNMP-POLICY-01	Are SNMP ports blocked from the Internet and external networks?	SCF
SNMP-POLICY-02	Are devices configured with READ/WRITE security correctly set?	SCF
OPSYS-OWNER-03	Who owns SNMPAGT?	Fileinfo
FILE-SNMP-01	Is SNMPAGT secured correctly?	Fileinfo

SNMP TRAP

SNMP Traps are notification events sent by a network device. The Traps are defined usually by the manufacturer of the device and are often associated with a change of status of a device (for example, when a device goes down).

SNMP PROFILE

The SNMP Profile is an entry in the authentication table for a particular SNMP Agent. It sets the name of the community, the IP address of a SNMP manager station, and the authorized access (READ ONLY or READ/WRITE). When an SNMP request is received by the SNMP Agent, the components of the request are matched with a PROFILE definition to decide whether access is to be provided. If there is no PROFILE that matches, the SNMP request is rejected.

BP-FILE-SNMP-03   PROFILE should be secured "UUCU".

BP-OPSYS-OWNER-03   PROFILE should be owned by SUPER. SUPER.

	Discovery Questions	Look here:
SNMP-POLICY-04	Is correct access configured for a PROFILE?	SCF
SNMP-POLICY-05	What is the COMMUNITY name configured?	SCF
OPSYS-OWNER-03	Who owns the PROFILE object file?	Fileinfo
FILE-SNMP-03	Is PROFILE secured correctly?	Fileinfo

TSM SNMP Agent

The process $ZTSMS is an SNMP agent process that was formerly used when $ZTSM communicated with the TSM Service Application using SNMP. As of version 7.0 of the TSM, $ZTSM uses HTTP to talk to its client, so the $ZTSMS process is no longer used. As such, if the TSM is running version 7.0 or later, this process can be safely stopped and deleted from the customer configuration. All of the associated trapdest, profile, and endpoint objects are no longer required for the TSM console.

SNMPPAGT

SNMPPAGT is the object file for the $ZTSMS process, which is the TSM SNMP agent process. Please refer to the Guardian Gazette section on the TSM subsystem for more information.

SPDIST2

SPDIST2 is the object file for the OSM SP Event Distributor process. Please refer to the Guardian Gazette section on the OSM subsystem for more information.

SQL Communication Subsystem (SCS)

SCSOBJ is the object file for the SQL Communication System (SCS). Please refer to the Guardian Gazette section on ODBC.

SQL/MX

SQL/MX is a relational database management system (RDBMS) used to define and manipulate data in an SQL/MX database.

To access data, users execute SQL statements interactively, by using the SQL/MX conversational interface (MXCI), or programmatically, by embedding SQL statements in a host program written in ANSI C/C++ or COBOL.

Please refer to Part 6, *SQL, NonStop SQL and Database Security*, for more information.

SQL/MX Guardian Components

The Guardian components of SQL/MX are:

IMPORT
MXANCHOR
MXAUDSRV
MXCMP
MXESP
MXGNAMES
MXOAS
MXOCFG
MXODSN
MXOMSG
MXOSRVR
MXRTDSRV

MXUDR
MXUTP
TDMNSM
TDMODBC
ZMXSTMPL

IMPORT System Program

The IMPORT utility is used to load data from an ASCII or UCS2 format file to a SQL/MX table. Import can only be executed from the shell prompt or from MXCI; it cannot be called from another program. Though the program resides in $SYSTEM.SYSTEM, it cannot be executed from a TACL prompt. To simplify execution from the OSS environment, a symbolic link is located at **/usr/tandem/sqlmx/bin/import**.

BP-FILE-IMPORT-01   IMPORT should be secured "UUNU".

BP-OPSYS-LICENSE-02   IMPORT must be LICENSED.

BP-OPSYS-OWNER-02   IMPORT should be owned by SUPER.
SUPER.

BP-OPSYS-FILELOC-02   IMPORT resides in $SYSTEM.SYSTEM.

If available, use Safeguard or a third-party object security product to grant access to IMPORT only to users who require access in order to perform their jobs.

BP-SAFE-IMPORT-01   Add a Safeguard Protection Record to grant appropriate access to the IMPORT object file equivalent to the Guardian file security string listed above.

	Discovery Questions	Look here:
OPSYS-OWNER-02	Who owns IMPORT?	Fileinfo
OPSYS-LICENSE-02	Is the IMPORT object file licensed?	Fileinfo
FILE-IMPORT-01 SAFE-IMPORT-01	Is IMPORT secured correctly with Guardian or Safeguard?	Fileinfo Safecom

MXANCHOR File

The /usr/tandem/sqlmx/bin/InstallSqlmx file is the SQL/MX install script. When first installing SQL/MX on a system, the installer runs this script from an OSS system prompt. It begins by verifying several prerequisites (such as required hardware support within CPUs), then creates a simple Guardian text file named $SYSTEM.ZSQLMX.MXANCHOR, an anchor file, that contains the volume location of the SQL/MX system metadata tables. The anchor file is assigned a security of "N---".

BP-FILE-SQLMX-01   MXANCHOR should be secured "N---".

BP-OPSYS-OWNER-03   MXANCHOR should be owned by SUPER.
SUPER.

BP-OPSYS-FILELOC-03   MXANCHOR   resides   in $SYSTEM.
ZSQLMX.

	Discovery Questions	Look here:
FILE-POLICY	Is SQL/MS installed on the system?	Policy
OPSYS-OWNER-03	Who owns MXANCHOR?	Fileinfo
FILE-NFS-01	Is MXANCHOR secured correctly?	Fileinfo Safecom

MXAUDSRV System Program

The MXAUDSRV program is the SQL/MX version of AUDSERV, which makes it possible for applications to share the use of a table or index during DDL reorganization. MXAUDSRV is only used in the SQL/MX environment. It is not an interactive program; it is invoked by the TMF subsystem.

MXAUDSRV is invoked when reorganization work is happening concurrently with normal data access. Splitting a partition is one situation where this can occur. When a partition is split, it takes some time for the rows in the table to be physically copied from one partition to another and then to be deleted from the first partition. During this time, the data access is suspended. If the partition is split while the application is running, MXAUDSRV interleaves the data access and reorganization functions, keeping track of all the "suspense" TMF audits generated by the data access and then applying them during the "commit" phase. This way, only a short table lock is needed to mark all the "suspensed" data changes being held in TMF as applied. If applications couldn't share operations, then all user access would be locked out for the duration of the data reorganization.

RISK   MXAUDSRV has no risk associated with user intervention.

BP-FILE-MXAUDSRV-01   MXAUDSRV should be secured "UUUU".

BP-OPSYS-LICENSE-02   MXAUDSRV must be LICENSED.

BP-OPSYS-OWNER-02   MXAUDSRV should be owned by SUPER. SUPER.

BP-OPSYS-FILELOC-02   MXAUDSRV   resides   in $SYSTEM. SYSTEM.

If available, use Safeguard or a third-party object security product to grant access to MXAUDSRV only to users who require access in order to perform their jobs.

BP-SAFE-MXAUDSRV-01   Add a Safeguard Protection Record to grant appropriate access to the MXAUDSRV object file equivalent to the Guardian file security string listed above.

	Discovery Questions	**Look here:**
OPSYS-OWNER-02	Who owns MXAUDSRV?	Fileinfo
OPSYS-LICENSE-02	Is the MXAUDSRV object file licensed?	Fileinfo
	Discovery Questions	**Look here:**
FILE-MXAUDSRV-01 SAFE-MXAUDSRV-01	Is MXAUDSRV secured correctly with Guardian or Safeguard?	Fileinfo Safecom

MXCMP

MXCMP is the object file for the SQL/MX compiler. It is used to verify and register SQL/MX programs.

A compiler prepares SQL statements to be executed by a host language program and registers the program to the SQL catalog. Only programs processed by SQLCOMP can access SQL objects.

MXCMP is invoked explicitly or implicitly by SQL. Unlike other compilers, MXCMP is normally available on secure systems, as it is an integral piece of the SQL subsystem. Automatic (implicit) recompilation is done whenever an invalid object is invoked. Explicit SQL compilation is used to initially register SQL application programs in the SQL catalogs.

AP-FILE-SQLCOMP-01   MXCMP should be available for execution by the SQL subsystem on any system to perform SQL recompilations.

BP-FILE-MXCMP-01   MXCMP should be secured "UUNU".

BP-OPSYS-LICENSE-02   MXCMP must be LICENSED.

BP-OPSYS-OWNER-02   MXCMP should be owned by SUPER. SUPER.

BP-OPSYS-FILELOC-02   MXCMP resides in $SYSTEM.SYSTEM.

If available, use Safeguard or a third-party object security product to grant access to MXCMP only to users who require access in order to perform their jobs.

BP-SAFE-MXCMP-01   Add a Safeguard Protection Record to grant appropriate access to the MXCMP object file equivalent to the Guardian file security string listed above.

	Discovery Questions	**Look here:**
OPSYS-OWNER-02	Who owns MXCMP?	Fileinfo
OPSYS-LICENSE-02	Is the MXCMP object file licensed?	Fileinfo
FILE-MXCMP-01 SAFE-MXCMP-01	Is MXCMP secured correctly with Guardian or Safeguard?	Fileinfo Safecom

MXESP System Program

MXESP is the object file for the SQL/MX executor server process. This sub-program is called when parallel operations are performed. Under SQL/MP, a parallel operation executes a single SQLESP for each physical partition of a table/index for a given parent query. SQL/MX executes no more than one MXESP per CPU/per query.

Each MXESP is an independent data gathering/aggregating process that is responsible for a subset of the database being queried. Once each MXESP completes gathering information, the data is returned to the parent process. Once all MXESPs have completed, the result is aggregated and returned to the calling process.

BP-FILE-MXESP-01   MXESP should be secured "UUNU".

BP-OPSYS-LICENSE-02   MXESP must be LICENSED.

BP-OPSYS-OWNER-02   MXESP should be owned by SUPER.SUPER.

BP-OPSYS-FILELOC-02   MXESP resides in $SYSTEM.SYSTEM.

If available, use Safeguard or a third-party object security product to grant access to MXESP only to users who require access in order to perform their jobs.

BP-SAFE-MXESP-01   Add a Safeguard Protection Record to grant appropriate access to the ZPMXESP object file equivalent to the Guardian file security string listed above.

	Discovery Questions	Look here:
OPSYS-OWNER-02	Who owns MXESP?	Fileinfo
OPSYS-LICENSE-02	Is the MXESP object file licensed?	Fileinfo
FILE-MXESP-01 SAFE-MXESP-01	Is MXESP secured correctly with Guardian or Safeguard?	Fileinfo Safecom

MXGNAMES System Program

The MXGNAMES program resolves SQL/MX internal names to Guardian file names. This is a necessary task because SQL/MX uses ANSI names, which need to be converted to Guardian file names for low-level access. SQL/MX database objects are protected in the same way OSS filesets are; they are located on subvolumes that are protected by the operating system.

BP-FILE-MXGNAMES-01   MXGNAMES should be secured "UUNU".

BP-OPSYS-OWNER-02   MXGNAMES should be owned by SUPER. SUPER.

BP-OPSYS-FILELOC-02   MXGNAMES   resides   in $SYSTEM. ZMXTOOLS.

If available, use Safeguard or a third-party object security product to grant access to MXGNAMES only to users who require access in order to perform their jobs.

BP-SAFE-MXGNAMES-01   Add a Safeguard Protection Record to grant appropriate access to the MXGNAMES object file equivalent to the Guardian file security string listed above.

	Discovery Questions	**Look here:**
OPSYS-OWNER-02	Who owns MXGNAMES?	Fileinfo
FILE-MXGNAMES-01	Is MXGNAMES secured correctly with	Fileinfo
SAFE-MXGNAMES-01	Guardian or Safeguard?	Safecom

MXOAS System Program

The MX Connectivity Service Association server (MXOAS) starts and manages the MXCS configuration server (MXOCFG) and MXCS SQL server (MXOSRVR). It also associates a client application with a specific MXCS SQL server. When the server components are started and available, the MXCS service is ready to accept incoming connections.

BP-FILE-MXOAS-01   MXOAS should be secured "UUUU".

BP-OPSYS-OWNER-02   MXOAS should be owned by SUPER.SUPER.

BP-OPSYS-FILELOC-02 MXOAS must reside in $SYSTEM.ZMX-ODBC.

If available, use Safeguard or a third-party object security product to grant access to MXOAS only to users who require access in order to perform their jobs.

BP-SAFE-MXOAS-01 Add a Safeguard Protection Record to grant appropriate access to the MXOAS object file equivalent to the Guardian file security string listed above.

	Discovery Questions	Look here:
OPSYS-OWNER-nn	Who owns MXOAS?	Fileinfo
FILE-MXAUDSRV-01 SAFE-MXAUDSRV-01	Is MXOAS secured correctly with Guardian or Safeguard?	Fileinfo Safecom

MXOCFG System Program

The MXOCFG is the configuration server that manages the MXCS configuration data.

BP-FILE-MXOCFG-02   MXOCFG should be secured "UUNU".

BP-OPSYS-OWNER-02   MXOCFG should be owned by SUPER. SUPER.

BP-OPSYS-FILELOC-02 MXOCFG must reside in $SYSTEM.ZMX-ODBC.

If available, use Safeguard or a third-party object security product to grant access to MXOCFG only to users who require access in order to perform their jobs.

BP-SAFE-MXOCFG-02 Add a Safeguard Protection Record to grant appropriate access to the MXOCFG object file equivalent to the Guardian file security string listed above.

	Discovery Questions	Look here:

OPSYS-OWNER-02	Who owns MXOCFG?	Fileinfo
FILE-MXOCFG-02 SAFE-MXOCFG-02	Is MXOCFG secured correctly with Guardian or Safeguard?	Fileinfo Safecom

MXODSN Configuration File

The MXODSN file is a template file that contains data source options for MXCS connectivity using SequeLink for NonStop SQL/MX.

BP-FILE-MXODSN-03   MXODSN should be secured "UUUU".

BP-OPSYS-OWNER-02   MXODSN should be owned by SUPER.
SUPER.

BP-OPSYS-FILELOC-02   MXODSN must reside in $SYSTEM.ZMX-ODBC.

If available, use Safeguard or a third-party object security product to grant access to MXODSN only to users who require access in order to perform their jobs.

BP-SAFE-MXOCFG-03   Add a Safeguard Protection Record to grant appropriate access to the MXODSN file equivalent to the Guardian file security string listed above.

	Discovery Questions	**Look here:**
OPSYS-OWNER-02	Who owns MXODSN?	Fileinfo
FILE-MXODSN-03 SAFE-MXODSN-03	Is MXODSN secured correctly with Guardian or Safeguard?	Fileinfo Safecom

MXOMSG Configuration File

The MXOMSG file contains the error messages for the MXCS connectivity service.

BP-FILE-MXOMSG-04   MXOMSG should be secured "NUUU".

BP-OPSYS-OWNER-02   MXOMSG should be owned by SUPER.
SUPER.

BP-OPSYS-FILELOC-02 MXOMSG must reside in $SYSTEM. SYSTEM.

BP-SAFE-MXOMSG-04 Add a Safeguard Protection Record to grant appropriate access to the MXOMSG file equivalent to the Guardian file security string listed above.

	Discovery Questions	Look here:
OPSYS-OWNER-02	Who owns MXOMSG?	Fileinfo
FILE-MXOMSG-04 SAFE-MXOMSG-04	Is MXOMSG secured correctly with Guardian or Safeguard?	Fileinfo Safecom

MXOSRVR System Program

The MXOSRVR server provides access to a NonStop SQL database.

BP-FILE-MXOSRVR-05 MXOSRVR should be secured "UUNU".

BP-OPSYS-OWNER-02 MXOSRVR should be owned by SUPER. SUPER.

BP-OPSYS-FILELOC-02 MXOSRVR must reside in $SYSTEM. ZMXODBC.

BP-SAFE-MXOSRVR-05 Add a Safeguard Protection Record to grant appropriate access to the MXOSRVR object file equivalent to the Guardian file security string listed above.

	Discovery Questions	**Look here:**
OPSYS-OWNER-02	Who owns MXOSRVR?	Fileinfo
FILE-MXOSRVR-05	Is MXOSRVR secured correctly with	Fileinfo
SAFE-MXOSRVR-05	Guardian or Safeguard?	Safecom

MXRTDSRV System Program

MXRTDSRV is the bridge process between SQL/MX and SQL/MP. The SQL/MX compiler, MXCMP, communicates with this process to access SQL/MP tables.

BP-FILE-MXRTDSRV-01   MXRTDSRV should be secured "UUNU".

BP-OPSYS-LICENSE-02   MXRTDSRV must be LICENSED.

BP-OPSYS-OWNER-02   MXRTDSRV should be owned by SUPER.SUPER.

BP-OPSYS-FILELOC-02   MXRTDSRV resides in $SYSTEM.SYSTEM.

If available, use Safeguard or a third-party object security product to grant access to MXRTDSRV only to users who require access in order to perform their jobs.

BP-SAFE-MXRTDSRV-01   Add a Safeguard Protection Record to grant appropriate access to the MXRTDSRV object file equivalent to the Guardian file security string listed above.

	Discovery Questions	**Look here:**
OPSYS-OWNER-02	Who owns MXRTDSRV?	Fileinfo
OPSYS-LICENSE-02	Is the MXRTDSRV object file licensed?	Fileinfo
FILE-MXRTDSRV-01	Is MXRTDSRV secured correctly with	Fileinfo
SAFE-MXRTDSRV-01	Guardian or Safeguard?	Safecom

MXUDR System Program

MXUDR is the SQL/MX User Defined Routine (UDR) server, which is the interface between the SQL/MX executor process and the Java Virtual Machine that executes the UDR. The only UDR's currently supported under SQL/MX are stored procedures in Java.

BP-FILE-MXUDR-01   MXUDR should be secured "UUNU".

BP-OPSYS-OWNER-02   MXUDR should be owned by SUPER. SUPER.

BP-OPSYS-FILELOC-02 MXUDR resides in $SYSTEM.SYSTEM.

If available, use Safeguard or a third-party object security product to grant access to MXUDR only to users who require access in order to perform their jobs.

BP-SAFE-MXUDR-01   Add a Safeguard Protection Record to grant appropriate access to the ZPMXUDR object file equivalent to the Guardian file security string listed above.

	Discovery Questions	Look here:
OPSYS-OWNER-02	Who owns MXUDR?	Fileinfo
FILE-MXUDR-01 SAFE-MXUDR-01	Is MXUDR secured correctly with Guardian or Safeguard?	Fileinfo Safecom

MXUTP System Program

A materialized view is a static view of data from a single point in time. MXUTP is the SQL/MX materialized view server. It manages and populates materialized views under SQL/MX.

BP-FILE-MXUTP-01   MXUTP should be secured "UUNU".

BP-OPSYS-LICENSE-02   MXUTP must be LICENSED.

BP-OPSYS-OWNER-02   MXUTP should be owned by SUPER. SUPER.

BP-OPSYS-FILELOC-02   MXUTP resides in $SYSTEM.SYSTEM.

If available, use Safeguard or a third-party object security product to grant access to MXUTP only to users who require access in order to perform their jobs.

BP-SAFE-MXUTP-01   Add a Safeguard Protection Record to grant appropriate access to the MXUTP object file equivalent to the Guardian file security string listed above.

	Discovery Questions	**Look here:**
OPSYS-OWNER-02	Who owns MXUTP?	Fileinfo
OPSYS-LICENSE-02	Is the MXUTP object file licensed?	Fileinfo
FILE-MXUTP-01 SAFE-MXUTP-01	Is MXUTP secured correctly with Guardian or Safeguard?	Fileinfo Safecom

TDMNSM Placeholder File

The TDMNSM Placeholder file is meant to be downloaded to PCs running the ODBC client. It is used to inform users that the NonStop Software Manager is not supported in the NonStop SQL/MX R2.0.

RISK   The NonStop Software Manager is unsupported.

AP-ADVICE-SQLMX-02   Use NSM/web to manage MXCS.

BP-FILE- TDMNSM-06   TDMNSM should be secured "NUUU".

BP-OPSYS-OWNER-02   TDMNSM should be owned by SUPER.
SUPER.

BP-OPSYS-FILELOC-02   TDMNSM must reside in $SYSTEM.
ZMXNSSM.

If available, use Safeguard or a third-party object security product to grant access to TDMNSM only to users who require access in order to perform their jobs.

BP-SAFE-TDMNSM-06   Add a Safeguard Protection Record to grant appropriate access to the TDMNSM file equivalent to the Guardian file security string listed above.

	Discovery Questions	Look here:
OPSYS-OWNER-02	Who owns TDMNSM?	Fileinfo
FILE-TDMNSM-06 SAFE-TDMNSM-06	Is TDMNSM secured correctly with Guardian or Safeguard?	Fileinfo Safecom

TDMODBC Configuration File

The TDMODBC file is meant to downloaded to a PC to install the ODBC client.

ZMXSTMPL Configuration File

When SYSGEN is run, the ZMXSTMPL EMS event messages are linked together into a general TEMPLATE file in the subvolume specified for SYSGEN.

BP-FILE-ZMXSTMPL-07   ZMXSTMPL should be secured "UUUU".

BP-OPSYS-OWNER-02   ZMXSTMPL should be owned by SUPER. SUPER.

BP-OPSYS-FILELOC-02   ZMXSTMPL must reside in $SYSTEM. ZTEMPL.

If available, use Safeguard or a third-party object security product to grant access to ZMXSTMPL only to users who require access in order to perform their jobs.

BP-SAFE-ZMXSTMPL-07   Add a Safeguard Protection Record to grant appropriate access to the ZMXSTMPL file equivalent to the Guardian file security string listed above.

	Discovery Questions	Look here:
OPSYS-OWNER-02	Who owns ZMXSTMPL?	Fileinfo
FILE- ZMXSTMPL-07 SAFE- ZMXSTMPL-07	Is ZMXSTMPL secured correctly with Guardian or Safeguard?	Fileinfo Safecom

SRM

SRM is the object file for the $ZTSM process, which is the main TSM process. Please refer to the Guardian Gazette section on the TSM Subsystem for more information.

Storage-Pool Files

A storage-pool file contains a list of disk volumes to be used by a fileset. As the assigned volumes are filled, more can be added via SCF. Additions or deletions of volumes take effect only after the fileset is restarted (remounted).

AP-ADVICE-STORPOOL-01 The initial or root pool must be defined before the OSS Monitor is started.

AP-ADVICE-STORPOOL-02 The root pool should have more than one disk volume, to allow for future growth.

AP-ADVICE-STORPOOL-03 No fileset should include the $SYSTEM or $DSMSCM disks in its storage pool.

AP-ADVICE-STORPOOL-04 The fewer the volumes in a storage pool, the better the performance.

AP-ADVICE-STORPOOL-05 Optical disks cannot be assigned to a storage pool.

AP-ADVICE-STORPOOL-06 Virtual disks cannot be assigned to a storage pool.

AP-ADVICE-STORPOOL-07 Disks should not be assigned to more than one storage pool. Sharing disks makes it more difficult to monitor and control free space within individual filesets.

Storage-Pool Names

HP recommends that the Guardian file identifier for an OSS storage-pool file should start with Z and/or have the form ZxxxPOOL, where xxx is a three-character fileset identifier. The example provided is the ROOT fileset, which would have a storage-pool file named either ZOSSPOOL or ROOTPOOL.

AP-ADVICE-ZOSSPOOL-01 Do not assign the name OSSPOOL to a storage-pool, because that is the name of the sample storage-pool installed with the OSS product set and it will be overwritten during each sysgen to a new OS version.

Securing Storage Pools

BP-FILE-ZOSSPOOL-01 ZOSSPOOL should be secured "UUUU".

BP-OPSYS-OWNER-03 ZOSSPOOL should be owned by SUPER. SUPER.

BP-OPSYS-FILELOC-03 ZOSSPOOL resides in $SYSTEM.ZXOSS-MON.

If available, use Safeguard or a third-party object security product to grant access to ZOSSPOOL only to users who require access in order to perform their jobs.

BP-SAFE-ZOSSPOOL-01 Add a Safeguard Protection Record to grant appropriate access to the ZOSSFSET object file equivalent to the Guardian file security string listed above.

	Discovery Questions	Look here:
OPSYS-OWNER-02	Who owns ZOSSPOOL?	Fileinfo
FILE-ZOSSPOOL-01 SAFE-ZOSSPOOL-01	Is ZOSSPOOL secured correctly?	Fileinfo Safecom

SUPPREPO

SUPPREPO is the Enscribe file containing OSM dial-out configuration information. Please refer to the Guardian Gazette section on the OSM Subsystem for more information.

TACLPRVD

TACLPRVD is the object file for the OSM TACL Provider process. Please refer to the Guardian Gazette section on the OSM Subsystem for more information.

TDMNSM Placeholder File

The TDMNSM Placeholder file is part of JDBC/MX. Please refer to the Guardian Gazette section on SQL/MX for more information.

TDMODBC Configuration File

The TDMODBC file is meant to downloaded to a PC to install the ODBC client.

Tandem Service Management (TSM) Subsystem

The TSM subsystem is used to manage HP S-series NonStop systems. It is a client/server application with a PC GUI client communicating with the NonStop Server via TCP/IP.

TSM replaced the Tandem Maintenance and Diagnostic Subsystem (TMDS) and the Remote Maintenance Interface (RMI).

TSM was superseded by OSM in version G06.22. OSM is required for Integrity NonStop systems.

Please refer to Part 8, *System Management* Tools, for a more complete discussion of the TSM Subsystem.

TSM Host Components

Software and hardware components on the NonStop S-series server enable communication between the HP NonStop Server and the TSM client software on the workstation. These components include the TSM server software, the Master Service Processors (MSPs) and related software, and the TSM EMS Event Viewer Server Manager and related processes.

ADDTCPIP Script

The $SYSTEM.ZTSM.ADDTCPIP script starts two processes named $TSMM0 and $TSMM1, which start the $ZTCP0 and $ZTCP1 TCP/IP processes. Once the TCP/IP processes are started, $TSMM0 and $TSMM1 stop themselves.

BP-TSM-TCPIP-01 $ZTCP0 should be reserved for OSM use.

BP-TSM-TCPIP-02 $ZTCP1 should be reserved for OSM use.

ADDTCPIP creates a log file of its activity called LOGTCPIP.

$SYSTEM.ZTSM.ALTERIP is the script used to restart $ZTCP0 and $ZTCP1 when necessary.

BP-FILE-TSM-01	ADDTCPIP should be secured "NUNU".
BP-OPSYS-OWNER-03 SUPER.	ADDTCPIP should be owned by SUPER.
BP-OPSYS-FILELOC-03 ZTSM.	ADDTCPIP must reside in $SYSTEM.
BP-FILE-TSM-02	ALTERIP should be secured "NUNU".
BP-OPSYS-OWNER-03 SUPER.	ALTERIP should be owned by SUPER.
BP-OPSYS-FILELOC-03 ZTSM.	ALTERIP must reside in $SYSTEM.

(Continued)

BP-FILE-TSM-03	INIT0 should be secured "NUNU".
BP-OPSYS-OWNER-03	INIT0 should be owned by SUPER.SUPER.
BP-OPSYS-FILELOC-03	INIT0 must reside in $SYSTEM.ZTSM.
BP-FILE-TSM-04	INIT1 should be secured "NUNU".
BP-OPSYS-OWNER-03 SUPER.	INIT1 should be owned by SUPER.
BP-OPSYS-FILELOC-03	INIT1 must reside in $SYSTEM.ZTSM.
BP-FILE-TSM-05	LOGTCP0 should be secured "NUNU".
BP-OPSYS-OWNER-03 SUPER.	LOGTCP0 should be owned by SUPER.
BP-OPSYS-FILELOC-03 ZTSM	LOGTCP0 must reside in $SYSTEM.
BP-FILE-TSM-06	LOGTCP1 should be secured "NUNU".
BP-OPSYS-OWNER-03 SUPER.	LOGTCP1 should be owned by SUPER.
BP-OPSYS-FILELOC-03 ZTSM.	LOGTCP1 must reside in $SYSTEM.
BP-FILE-TSM-07	LOGTCPIP should be secured "NUNU".
BP-OPSYS-OWNER-03 SUPER.	LOGTCPIP should be owned by SUPER.
BP-OPSYS-FILELOC-03 ZTSM.	LOGTCPIP must reside in $SYSTEM.

	Discovery Questions	**Look here:**
OPSYS-OWNER-03	Who owns ADDTCPIP?	Fileinfo
OPSYS-OWNER-03	Who owns ALTERIP?	Fileinfo
OPSYS-OWNER-03	Who owns INIT0?	Fileinfo
OPSYS-OWNER-03	Who owns INIT1?	Fileinfo

(Continued)

	Discovery Questions	Look here:
OPSYS-OWNER-03	Who owns LOGTCP0?	Fileinfo
OPSYS-OWNER-03	Who owns LOGTCP1?	Fileinfo
OPSYS-OWNER-03	Who owns LOGTCPIP?	Fileinfo
FILE-TSM-01	Is ADDTCPIP secured correctly?	Fileinfo
FILE-TSM-02	Is ALTERIP secured correctly?	Fileinfo
FILE-TSM-03	Is INIT0 secured correctly?	Fileinfo
FILE-TSM-04	Is INIT1 secured correctly?	Fileinfo
FILE-TSM-05	Is LOGTCP0 secured correctly?	Fileinfo
	Discovery Questions	Look here:
FILE-TSM-06	Is LOGTCP1 secured correctly?	Fileinfo
FILE-TSM-07	Is LOGTCPIP secured correctly?	Fileinfo

ADDTOSCF

ADDTOSCF is the script to add TSM persistent processes into SCF. The processes it adds and starts are:

Process	Object File	SCF Object
$ZCVP0	$SYSTEM.SYSTEM.CEVSMX	$ZZKRN.#CEV-SERVER-MANAGER-P0
$ZCVP1	$SYSTEM.SYSTEM.CEVSMX	$ZZKRN.#CEV-SERVER-MANAGER-P1
$ZLOG	$SYSTEM.SYSnn EMSACOLL	$ZZKRN.#TSM-ZLOG
$ZRD9	$SYSTEM.SYSnn.EMSDIST	$ZZKRN.#ROUTING-DIST
$ZSPE	$SYSTEM.SYSnn.ZSPE	$ZZKRN.#TSM-SP-EVENT
$ZTSM	$SYSTEM.SYSnn.SRM	$ZZKRN.#TSM-SRM
$ZTSMS	$SYSTEM.SYSTEM.SNMP-PAGT	$ZZKRN.#TSM-SNMP

ADDTOSCF creates a log file called $SYSTEM.ZTSM.LOGSCF.

BP-FILE-TSM-09   ADDTOSCF should be secured "NUNU".

BP-OPSYS-OWNER-03   ADDTOSCF should be owned by SUPER.
SUPER.

BP-OPSYS-FILELOC-03 ADDTOSCF must reside in $SYSTEM.
ZTSM.

BP-FILE-TSM-10   LOGSCF should be secured "NUNU".

BP-OPSYS-OWNER-03   LOGSCF should be owned by SUPER.
SUPER.

BP-OPSYS-FILELOC-03 LOGSCF must reside in $SYSTEM.ZTSM.

	Discovery Questions	Look here:
OPSYS-OWNER-03	Who owns ADDTOSCF?	Fileinfo
OPSYS-OWNER-03	Who owns LOGSCF?	Fileinfo
FILE-TMS-09	Is ADDTOSCF secured correctly?	Fileinfo
FILE-TSM-10	Is LOGSCF secured correctly?	Fileinfo

$ZCVP0 and $ZCVP1

CEVSMX is the object file for the TSM event servers:

> $ZCVP0 is the process name for the $ZZKRN.#CEV-SERVER-MANAGER-P0 SCF object. It is the primary TSM event server.

> $ZCVP1 is the process name for the $ZZKRN.#CEV-SERVER-MANAGER-P1 SCF object. It is the secondary TSM event server.

BP-PROCESS-TSM-01 $ZCVP0 should be running.

BP-PROCESS-TSM-02 $ZCVP1 should be running.

BP-FILE-TSM-11   CEVSMX should be secured "NUNU".

BP-OPSYS-OWNER-01 CEVSMX should be owned by SUPER.
SUPER.

BP-OPSYS-FILELOC-01 CEVSMX must reside in $SYSTEM.SYSnn.

	Discovery Questions	Look here:
PROCESS-TSM-01	Is the $ZZKRN.#CEV-SERVER-MANAGER-P0 process defined correctly?	SCF info process
PROCESS-TSM-01	Is the $ZCVP0 process running?	Status
PROCESS-TSM-02	Is the $ZZKRN.#CEV-SERVER-MANAGER-P1 process defined correctly?	SCF info process
PROCESS-TSM-02	Is the $ZCVP1 process running?	Status
OPSYS-OWNER-01	Who owns CEVSMX?	Fileinfo
FILE-TSM-11	Is CEVSMX secured correctly?	Fileinfo

$ZLOG

$ZLOG is the process name of the $ZZKRN.#ZLOG SCF object. It is an instance of the EMS collector program, $SYSTEM.SYSTEM.EMSACOLL. It logs events to the following primary and alternate key files:

The naming convention for the primary log files is ZZSVnnnn files, where nnnn is an incrementing number.

The naming convention for the alternate key files is ZZSKnnnn, where nnnn is an incrementing number.

BP-TSM-ZLOG-01 defined as persistent.

BP-PROCESS-TSM-03   The $ZLOG process pair should be running.

BP-FILE-TSM-12   ZZSK* should be secured "NUNU".

BP-OPSYS-OWNER-03   ZZSK* should be owned by SUPER.SUPER.

BP-OPSYS-FILELOC-03   ZZSK* must reside in $SYSTEM.ZSERVICE.

BP-FILE-TSM-13   ZZSV* should be secured "NUNU".

BP-OPSYS-OWNER-03   ZZSV* should be owned by SUPER.SUPER.

BP-OPSYS-FILELOC-03   ZZSV* must reside in $SYSTEM.ZSERVICE.

	Discovery Questions	Look here:
PROCESS-TSM-03	Is $ZZKRN.#ZLOG defined properly?	SCF info process
PROCESS-TSM-03	Is $ZLOG running?	Status
OPSYS-OWNER-03	Who owns the ZZSKnnnn files?	Fileinfo
OPSYS-OWNER-03	Who owns the ZZSVnnnn files?	Fileinfo
FILE-TSM-12	Are the ZZSKnnnn files secured correctly?	Fileinfo
FILE-TSM-13	Are the ZZSVnnnn secured correctly?	Fileinfo

$ZRD9

$ZRD9 is the process name for the $ZZKRN.#ROUTING-DIST SCF object, which is the TSM routing distributor. It is an instance of the EMSDIST program, started by a TACL process with INITRD file as input.

$TSMRD is not a persistent process.

BP-PROCESS-TSM-04   The $ZRD9 process pair should be running.

BP-FILE-TSM-14   INITRD should be secured "NUNU".

BP-OPSYS-OWNER-03 INITRD should be owned by SUPER.SUPER.

BP-OPSYS-FILELOC-03 INITRD must reside in $SYSTEM.ZTSM.

	Discovery Questions	Look here:
PROCESS-TSM-04	Is the $ZZKRN.#ROUTING-DIST process defined correctly?	SCF info process
PROCESS-TSM-04	Is the $ZRD9 process running as EMSDIST?	Status
OPSYS-OWNER-03	Who owns INITRD?	Fileinfo
FILE-INITRD –14	Is INITRD secured correctly?	Fileinfo

$ZSPE

ZSPE is the process name for the $ZSPE process, which is the $ZZKRN.#SP-EVENT SCF object. It is the Service Processor (SP) Event Distributor process, which writes SP events to $ZLOG.

BP-TSM-PROCESS-02   The $ZZKRN.#SP-EVENT process should be defined as a persistent process.

BP-PROCESS-TSM-05 $ZSPE process pair should be running.

BP-FILE-ZSPE-15   ZSPE should be secured "NUNU".

BP-OPSYS-OWNER-01   ZSPE should be owned by SUPER.SUPER.

BP-OPSYS-FILELOC-01   ZSPE must reside in $SYSTEM.SYSnn.

	Discovery Questions	**Look here:**
PROCESS-TSM-05	Is the $ZZKRN.#SP-EVENT process defined correctly?	SCF info process
PROCESS-TSM-05	Is the $ZSPE process running?	Status
OPSYS-OWNER-01	Who owns ZSPE?	Fileinfo
FILE-TSM-15	Is ZSPE secured correctly?	Fileinfo

$ZTSM

SRM is the object file for the $ZTSM process, which is the $ZZKRN.# TSM-SRM SCF object. It is the main TSM process.

BP-PROCESS-TSM-06 $ZTSM should be running.

BP-FILE-TSM-16   SRM should be secured "NUNU".

BP-OPSYS-OWNER-01   SRM should be owned by SUPER.SUPER.

BP-OPSYS-FILELOC-01   SRM must reside in $SYSTEM.SYSnn.

	Discovery Questions	Look here:
PROCESS-TSM-06	Is the $ZZKRN.#TSM-SRM process defined correctly?	SCF info process
PROCESS-TSM-06	Is the $ZTSM process running?	Status
OPSYS-OWNER-01	Who owns SRM?	Fileinfo
FILE-TSM-16	Is SRM secured correctly?	Fileinfo

$ZTSMS

SNMPPAGT is the object file for the $ZTSMS process, which is the $ZZKRN.#TSM-SNMP SCF object. $ZTSMS is the SNMP agent process. It was used formerly when $ZTSM communicated with the TSM Service Application using SNMP.

AP-ADVICE-TSM-02   As of version 7.0 of the TSM, $ZTSM uses HTTP to talk to its client, so the $ZTSMS process is no longer used. As such, if the TSM is running version 7.0 or later, this process can be safely stopped and deleted from the customer configuration. All of the associated trapdest, profile and endpoint objects are no longer required for the TSM console.

BP-PROCESS-TSM-07 TSM version 7.0 or greater. $ZTSMS should not be running if using

BP-FILE-TSM-17   SNMPAGT should be secured "NUNU".

BP-OPSYS-OWNER-02 SUPER.   SNMPAGT should be owned by SUPER.

BP-OPSYS-FILELOC-02 SYSTEM.   ZNMPAGT must reside in SYSTEM.

	Discovery Questions	**Look here:**
PROCESS-POLICY	Is the system running version 7.0 or greater of TSM?	Policy
PROCESS-TSM-07	Is the $ZZKRN.#TSM-SNMP process defined correctly?	SCF info process
PROCESS-TSM-07	Is the $ZTSMS process running?	Status
OPSYS-OWNER-02	Who owns SNMPAGT?	Fileinfo
FILE-TSM-17	Is SNMPAGT secured correctly?	Fileinfo

Master Service Processors (MSPs)

The NonStop operating system communicates with the workstation running the TSM software through the connection to the master service processors (MSPs). The workstation can communicate with the MSPs on the server whether the NonStop operating system is running or not. Service Processors (SPs) are the physical components of the S-series servers that control environmental and maintenance functions. MSPs provide these basic functions as well as the Ethernet ports that connect the TSM workstations to the NonStop Server. The group 01 enclosure (processors 0 and 1) contains the MSP pair.

TSMERROR Log

The TSMERROR file is the log file for the TSM System Resource Model (SRM) process.

BP-FILE-TSM-18   TSMERROR should be secured "NUNU".

BP-OPSYS-OWNER-03 TSMERROR should be owned by SUPER. SUPER.

BP-OPSYS-FILELOC-03 TSMERROR must reside in $SYSTEM. ZSERVICE.

	Discovery Questions	**Look here:**
OPSYS-OWNER-03	Who owns TSMERROR?	Fileinfo
FILE-TSM-18	Is TSMERROR secured correctly?	Fileinfo

TSM Tables

TSM uses the following tables:

PERSIST is the TSM current alarm objects database.

PERSSUPP is the current configuration database file.

ZCT08153 is a table used by the TSM client for converting alarm and incident report (IR) binary values into text strings.

ZCT08458 is a table used by TSM to convert binary values into text strings for use in reporting errors.

BP-FILE-TSM-19   PERSIST should be secured "NUNU".

BP-OPSYS-OWNER-03   PERSIST should be owned by SUPER.SUPER.

BP-OPSYS-FILELOC-03   PERSIST must reside in $SYSTEM.
ZSERVICE.

BP-FILE-TSM-20   PERSUPP should be secured "NUNU".

BP-OPSYS-OWNER-03   PERSUPP should be owned by SUPER.
SUPER.

BP-OPSYS-FILELOC-03   PERSUPP must reside in $SYSTEM.
ZSERVICE.

BP-FILE-TSM-21   ZCT08153 should be secured "NUNU".

BP-OPSYS-OWNER-03   ZCT08153 should be owned by SUPER.
SUPER.

BP-OPSYS-FILELOC-03   ZCT08153 must reside in $SYSTEM.
ZSERVICE.

BP-FILE-TSM-22   ZCT08458 should be secured "NUNU".

BP-OPSYS-OWNER-03   ZCT08458 should be owned by SUPER.
SUPER.

BP-OPSYS-FILELOC-03   ZCT08458 must reside in $SYSTEM.
ZSERVICE.

Discovery Questions	Look here:

OPSYS-OWNER-03	Who owns PERSIST?	Fileinfo
OPSYS-OWNER-03	Who owns PERSUPP?	Fileinfo
OPSYS-OWNER-03	Who owns ZCT08153?	Fileinfo
OPSYS-OWNER-03	Who owns ZCT08458?	Fileinfo
FILE-TSM-19	Is PERSIST secured correctly?	Fileinfo
FILE-TSM-20	Is PERSUPP secured correctly?	Fileinfo
FILE-TSM-21	Is ZCT08153 secured correctly?	Fileinfo
FILE-TSM-22	Is ZCT08458 secured correctly?	Fileinfo

TSM Alarm, Snapshot and Scan Files

TSM creates the following files as required. Depending on the current state of the system, these files may or may not be present.

Server alarm files are named ZZALnnnn, where nnnn is an incrementing number. They are created by the PERSIST program.

Inventory snapshot files are named ZZDCnnnn, where nnnn is an incrementing number.

Processor scan strings are named $SYSTEM.ZSERVICE.ZZSSnnnn, where nnnn is an incrementing number.

BP-FILE-TSM-23   ZZALnnnn should be secured "NUNU".

BP-OPSYS-OWNER-03 SUPER.   ZZALnnnn should be owned by SUPER.

BP-OPSYS-FILELOC-03 TEM. ZSERVICE.   ZZALnnnn, if present, must reside in $SYSTEM. ZSERVICE.

BP-FILE-TSM-24   ZZDCnnnn should be secured "NUNU".

BP-OPSYS-OWNER-03 SUPER.   ZZDCnnnn should be owned by SUPER.

BP-OPSYS-FILELOC-03 TEM.ZSERVICE.   ZZDCnnnn, if present, must reside in $SYSTEM.ZSERVICE.

BP-FILE-TSM-25   ZZSSnnnn should be secured "NUNU".

BP-OPSYS-OWNER-03   ZZSSnnnn should be owned by SUPER.
SUPER.

BP-OPSYS-FILELOC-03   ZZSSnnnn, if present, must reside in $SYS-
TEM.ZSERVICE.

	Discovery Questions	Look here:
OPSYS-OWNER-03	Who owns the ZZAL* files?	Fileinfo
OPSYS-OWNER-03	Who owns the ZZDC* files?	Fileinfo
OPSYS-OWNER-03	Who owns the ZZSS* files?	Fileinfo
FILE-TSM-23	Are the ZZAL* files secured correctly?	Fileinfo
FILE-TSM-24	Are the ZZDC* files secured correctly?	Fileinfo
FILE-TSM-25	Are the ZZSS* files secured correctly?	Fileinfo

ZZUSERS and ZZUSERS2 Files

The ZZUSERS and ZZUSERS2 files contain TSM service application connection audit information. ZZUSERS is always the active audit file. When
the maximum number of records for the ZZUSERS file is reached, the
ZZUSERS file is copied to the ZZUSERS2 file, a new ZZUSERS file is
opened, and logging activity is resumed.

BP-FILE-TSM-26   ZZUSERS should be secured "NUNU".

BP-OPSYS-OWNER-03   ZZUSERS should be owned by SUPER.
SUPER.

BP-OPSYS-FILELOC-03   ZZUSERS must reside in $SYSTEM.
ZSERVICE.

BP-FILE-TSM-27   ZZUSERS2 should be secured "NUNU".

BP-OPSYS-OWNER-03   ZZUSERS2 should be owned by SUPER.
SUPER.

BP-OPSYS-FILELOC-03   ZZUSERS2 must reside in $SYSTEM. ZSERVICE.

	Discovery Questions	Look here:
OPSYS-OWNER-03	Who owns ZZUSER?	Fileinfo
OPSYS-OWNER-03	Who owns ZZUSER2?	Fileinfo
FILE-TSM-26	Is ZZUSER secured correctly?	Fileinfo
FILE-TSM-27	Is ZZUSER2 secured correctly?	Fileinfo

TCP/IP Subsystem

TCP/IP is a set of protocols used for communication and file transfer. Please refer to Part 4, TCP/IP for more information.

TCP/IP uses the following components:

Configuration Files
Conventional TCP/IP components
Parallel TCP/IP components
IPv6 components

Configuration Files

The following files are used by the TCP/IP Subsystem:

HOSTS
PORTCONF
NETWORKS
SERVICES

HOSTS File

The HOSTS file maps host names to IP addresses so that systems can be addressed by name for simplicity purposes. By default, the HOSTS file is located in $SYSTEM.ZTCPIP. Please refer to Part 4, *TCP/IP*, for more information.

BP-FILE-TCPIP-01   HOSTS should be secured "NUUU".

BP-OPSYS-OWNER-03   HOSTS should be owned by SUPER.SUPER.

BP-OPSYS-FILELOC-03   HOSTS resides in $SYSTEM.ZTCPIP.

	Discovery Questions	**Look here:**
OPSYS-OWNER-03	Who owns HOSTS?	Fileinfo
FILE-HOSTS-01 SAFE-HOSTS-01	Is HOSTS secured correctly?	Fileinfo Safecom

NETWORKS File

The NETWORKS file contains a list of the networks known to the current host. Each network's name, number and aliases are listed. When a program calls the functions GETNETBYADDR or GETNETBYNAME, the NETWORKS file is used to resolve the Internet network address to a symbolic name. Please refer to Part 4, *TCP/IP*, for more information.

The NETWORKS file is created by making a copy of the SMPLNETW file which resides in the same $SYSTEM.ZTCPIP directory. The file is provided by HP as a sample. It contains examples of common networks.

Do not make any changes to the sample file since they will be overwritten when a new operating system version is installed. Copy the file and name the copy NETWORKS.

RISK The SMPLNETW file will be overwritten with each operating system upgrade.

AP-ADVICE-NETWORKS-01 Do not change the sample file to customize it to your environment. Make changes in the NETWORKS file created by copying the sample file.

BP-FILE-TCPIP-02 NETWORKS should be secured "NUUU".

BP-OPSYS-OWNER-03 NETWORKS should be owned by SUPER.
SUPER.

BP-OPSYS-FILELOC-03 NETWORKS resides in $SYSTEM. ZTCPIP.

BP-FILE-TCPIP-03 SMPLNETW should be secured "NUUU".

BP-OPSYS-OWNER-03 SMPLNETW should be owned by SUPER.
SUPER.

BP-OPSYS-FILELOC-03 SMPLNETW resides in $SYSTEM. ZTCPIP.

	Discovery Questions	**Look here:**
OPSYS-OWNER-03	Who owns NETWORKS?	Fileinfo
OPSYS-OWNER-03	Who owns SMPLNETW?	Fileinfo
FILE-NETWORKS-02 SAFE-NETWORKS-02	Is NETWORKS secured correctly?	Fileinfo Safecom
FILE-NETWORKS-03 SAFE-NETWORKS-03	Is SMPLNETW secured correctly?	Fileinfo Safecom

PORTCONF

The PORTCONF file is used to designate the usage of specific ports. The primary PORTCONF file is normally located in the $SYSTEM.ZTCPIP subvolume, but can be located elsewhere as defined to TCP/IP. Please refer to Part 4, *TCP/IP,* for more information.

BP-FILE-LISTNER-02 PORTCONF should be secured "NCUU".

BP-OPSYS-OWNER-03 PORTCONF should be owned by SUPER.
SUPER.

BP-OPSYS-FILELOC-03 PORTCONF resides in $SYSTEM.ZTCPIP.

	Discovery Questions	**Look here:**
OPSYS-OWNER-03	Who owns PORTCONF?	Fileinfo
FILE-LISTNER-02 SAFE-LISTNER-03	Is PORTCONF secured correctly?	Fileinfo Safecom

SERVICES File

The SERVICES file contains the Internet port level services that are available with NonStop TCP/IP. Applications refer to the file to get the service port numbers and service names. By default this is located in $SYSTEM.ZTCPIP. Please refer to Part 4, *TCP/IP,* for more information.

BP-FILE-TCPIP-04   SERVICES should be secured "NUUU".

BP-OPSYS-OWNER-03   SERVICES should be owned by SUPER.
SUPER.

BP-OPSYS-FILELOC-03   SERVICES resides in $SYSTEM.ZTCPIP.

	Discovery Questions	**Look here:**
OPSYS-OWNER-03	Who owns SERVICES?	Fileinfo
FILE-SERVICES-04 SAFE-SERVICES-04	Is SERVICES secured correctly?	Fileinfo Safecom

Conventional TCP/IP Components

Conventional TCP/IP consists of a single TCPIP program, $SYSTEM. SYSnn.TCPIP.

TCPIP

TCPIP is the object file for TCPIP processes.

BP-FILE-TCPIP-05   TCPIP should be secured "UUNU".

BP-OPSYS-OWNER-01   TCPIP should be owned by SUPER.SUPER.

BP-OPSYS-FILELOC-01   TCPIP resides in $SYSTEM.SYSnn.

	Discovery Questions	Look here:
OPSYS-OWNER-01	Who owns TCPIP?	Fileinfo
FILE-TCPIP-05 SAFE-TCPIP-05	Is TCPIP secured correctly?	Fileinfo Safecom

Parallel TCP/IP Components

Parallel TCP/IP includes the following components:

TCPMAN

TCPMON

TCPSAM

ZTCPSRL

TCPMAN

TCPMAN is the object file for the Parallel Library TCP/IP Manager process. It runs as a NonStop process pair and is the management interface to the Parallel Library TCP/IP subsystem. It is responsible for starting the TCPMON processes.

The TCPMAN process is always named $ZZTCP and only one TCPMAN process pair can exist in each system.

BP-TCPIP-06   TCPMAN should be secured "UUNU".

BP-OPSYS-OWNER-01 TCPMAN should be owned by SUPER.SUPER.

BP-OPSYS-FILELOC-01 TCPMAN resides in $SYSTEM.SYSnn.

	Discovery Questions	Look here:
OPSYS-OWNER-01	Who owns TCPMAN?	Fileinfo
FILE-TCPIP-06 SAFE-TCPIP-06	Is TCPMAN secured correctly?	Fileinfo Safecom

TCPMON

TCPMON is the object file for the Parallel Library TCP/IP Monitor process. One TCPMON process runs in each CPU.

The names of the TCPMON processes follow the convention $ZZTCP.#ZPTM*n* where *n* is the corresponding processor number in hexadecimal.

BP-FILE-TCPIP-07   TCPMON should be secured "UUNU".

BP-OPSYS-OWNER-01   TCPMON should be owned by SUPER. SUPER.

BP-OPSYS-FILELOC-01   TCPMON resides in $SYSTEM.SYSnn.

	Discovery Questions	Look here:
OPSYS-OWNER-01	Who owns TCPMON?	Fileinfo
FILE-TCPIP-07 SAFE-TCPIP-07	Is TCPMON secured correctly?	Fileinfo Safecom

TCPSAM

TCPSAM is the object file for a process pair that is provided only for backward compatibility with socket based applications.

BP-FILE-TCPIP-08   TCPSAM should be secured "UUNU".

BP-OPSYS-OWNER-01   TCPSAM should be owned by SUPER. SUPER.

BP-OPSYS-FILELOC-01   TCPSAM resides in $SYSTEM.SYSnn.

	Discovery Questions	Look here:
OPSYS-OWNER-01	Who owns TCPSAM?	Fileinfo
FILE-TCPIP-08 SAFE-TCPIP-08	Is TCPSAM secured correctly?	Fileinfo Safecom

ZTCPSRL

ZTCPSRL is the shared runtime library that contains the majority of the TCP/IP stack for Parallel Library TCP/IP, unlike conventional TCP/IP where the stack resides in the TCP/IP process. This runtime library is loaded into an application's process space as soon as it issues a TCP/IP socket request.

BP-FILE-TCPIP-09   ZTCPSRL should be secured "NUUU".

BP-OPSYS-OWNER-01 ZTCPSRL should be owned by SUPER. SUPER.

BP-OPSYS-FILELOC-01ZTCPSRL resides in $SYSTEM.SYSnn.

	Discovery Questions	Look here:
OPSYS-OWNER-01	Who owns ZTCPSRL?	Fileinfo
FILE-TCPIP-09 SAFE-TCPIP-09	Is ZTCPSRL secured correctly?	Fileinfo Safecom

IPv6 Components

IPv6 includes the following components:

TCP6MAN

TCP6MON

TCP6SAM

ZTCP6REL/ZTCP6SRL

TCP6MAN

TCP6MAN is the object file for the IPv6 Manager process. It runs as a Non-Stop process pair and is the management interface to the IPv6 subsystem. It is responsible for starting the TCP6MON processes.

The TCP6MAN process is always named $ZZTCP and only one TCP6MAN process pair can exist in each system.

BP-FILE-TCPIP-10   TCP6MAN should be secured "UUNU".

BP-OPSYS-OWNER-01 TCP6MAN should be owned by SUPER. SUPER.

BP-OPSYS-FILELOC-01TCP6MAN resides in $SYSTEM.SYSnn.

	Discovery Questions	Look here:
OPSYS-OWNER-01	Who owns TCP6MAN?	Fileinfo
FILE-TCPIP-10 SAFE-TCPIP-10	Is TCP6MAN secured correctly?	Fileinfo Safecom

TCP6MON

TCP6MON is the object file for the IPv6 Monitor process. One TCP6MON process runs in each CPU.

The names of the TCP6MON processes follow the convention $ZPTMnn where nn is the processor number in hexadecimal.

BP-FILE-TCPIP-11   TCP6MON should be secured "UUNU".

BP-OPSYS-OWNER-01 TCP6MON should be owned by SUPER. SUPER.

BP-OPSYS-FILELOC-01 TCP6MON resides in $SYSTEM.SYSnn.

	Discovery Questions	Look here:
OPSYS-OWNER-07	Who owns TCP6MON?	Fileinfo
FILE-TCPIP-11 SAFE-TCPIP-11	Is TCP6MON secured correctly?	Fileinfo Safecom

TCP6SAM

TCP6SAM is the object file for a process pair provided only for backward compatibility with socket based applications.

BP-FILE-TCPIP-12   TCP6SAM should be secured "UUNU".

BP-OPSYS-OWNER-01   TCP6SAM should be owned by SUPER. SUPER.

BP-OPSYS-FILELOC-01   TCP6SAM resides in $SYSTEM.SYSnn.

	Discovery Questions	Look here:
OPSYS-OWNER-01	Who owns TCP6SAM?	Fileinfo
FILE-TCPIP-12 SAFE-TCPIP-12	Is TCP6SAM secured correctly?	Fileinfo Safecom

ZTCP6REL/ZTCP6SRL

ZTCP6SRL is the shared runtime library that contains the majority of the TCP/IP stack for IPv6. This runtime library is loaded into an application's process space as soon as it issues a TCP/IP socket request.

BP-FILE-TCPIP-12   ZTCP6REL should be secured "NUUU".

BP-OPSYS-OWNER-01   ZTCP6REL should be owned by SUPER. SUPER.

BP-OPSYS-FILELOC-01   ZTCP6REL resides in $SYSTEM.SYSnn.

BP-FILE-TCPIP-13   ZTCP6SRL should be secured "NUUU".

BP-OPSYS-OWNER-01   ZTCP6SRL should be owned by SUPER. SUPER.

BP-OPSYS-FILELOC-01   ZTCP6SRL resides in $SYSTEM.SYSnn.

	Discovery Questions	Look here:
OPSYS-OWNER-01	Who owns ZTCP6REL?	Fileinfo
OPSYS-OWNER-01	Who owns ZTCP6SRL?	Fileinfo
FILE-TCPIP-12 SAFE-TCPIP-12	Is ZTCP6REL secured correctly?	Fileinfo Safecom
FILE-TCPIP-13 SAFE-TCPIP-13	Is ZTCP6SRL secured correctly?	Fileinfo Safecom

ZMXSTMPL Configuration File

The SQL/MX EMS template file. Please refer to the Guardian Gazette section on SQL/MX for more information.

TNS/E Link Editor (ELD) User Program

The TNS/E Link Editor (ELD) is the Integrity NonStop equivalent to the S-series NLD program. Please refer to the Guardian Gazette section on ELD for more information.

TNS/E Native Object File Tool (ENOFT) User Program

The TNS/E Native Object File Tool (ENOFT) is the Integrity NonStop equivalent of the S-series NOFT program. Please refer to the Guardian Gazette section on ENOFT.

TSMERROR Log

The TSMERROR file is the log file for TSM System Resource Model (SRM).

TSMINI Configuration File

TSMINI is the default configuration file for the TSM subsystem.

ZCT08153 File

ZCT08153 is a table used by the TSM client for converting alarm and incident report (IR) binary values into text strings.

ZCT08153 File

ZCT08458 is a table used by TSM to convert binary values into text strings for use in reporting errors.

ZFB* Files

ZFB00xxxx files are obsolete program files copied out of the way by DSM/SCM when new versions are installed. Please refer to the Guardian Gazette section on the DSM/SCM subsystem.

ZMPnnnnn Files

ZMP00xxxx files are DSM/SCM catalogs of obsolete program files copied out of the way by DSM/SCM when new versions are installed. Please refer to the Guardian Gazette section on the DSM/SCM subsystem.

ZMSGQ System Program

ZMSGQ is the object file for the OSS message queue process. Please refer to the Guardian Gazette section on the OSS Monitor for more information.

ZNFSPTR User Program

ZNFSPTR is the object file for PTrace's NFS module. Please refer to Part 5 for a complete discussion of the NFS Subsystem or to the Guardian Gazette section on the NFS Subsystem for Best Practice recommendations.

ZNFSSCF System Program

ZNFSSCF is the object file for SCF's NFS module. Please refer to Part 5 for a complete discussion of the NFS Subsystem or to the Guardian Gazette section on the NFS Subsystem for Best Practice recommendations.

ZNFSTEXT File

The ZNFSTEXT file contains SCF's help text for the NFS module. Please refer to Part 5 for a complete discussion of the NFS Subsystem or to the Guardian Gazette section on the NFS Subsystem for Best Practice recommendations.

ZNFSTMPL Template File

ZNFSTMPL is the EMS template for the NFS subsystem. Please refer to Part 5 for a complete discussion of the Network File System (NFS) Subsystem.

ZNFSUSR and ZNFSUSR I Files

The ZNFSUSR file stores information used by the NFS server to translate NFS userids to Guardian userids, which are used to the determine NFS user's file access.

Please refer to Part 5 for a complete discussion of the Network File System (NFS) Subsystem or to the Guardian Gazette section on the NFS Subsystem for Best Practice recommendations.

ZOSSFSET Configuration File

The ZOSSFSET file is one of the configuration files required by the OSS Monitor (OSSMON) process. Please refer to the Guardian Gazette section on the OSS Monitor Process for more information.

ZOSSPARM File Configuration File

The ZOSSPARM file is one of the configuration files required by the OSS Monitor (OSSMON) process. Please refer to the Guardian Gazette section on the OSS Monitor Process for more information.

ZOSSSERV Configuration File

The ZOSSSERV file is one of the configuration files required by the OSS Monitor (OSSMON) process. Please refer to the Guardian Gazette section on the OSS Monitor Process for more information.

ZPHIxxxx Files

ZPHIxxxx files contain DSM/SCM archives. Please refer to the Guardian Gazette section on the DSM/SCM subsystem.

ZPM System Program

ZPM is the object file for the persistence manager process, $ZPM. Please refer to the Guardian Gazette section on the persistence manager.

ZRPCTMPL Template File

ZRPCTMPL is the EMS template for the RPC service. Please refer to Part 5 for a complete discussion of the Network File System (NFS) Subsystem or to the Guardian Gazette section on the NFS Subsystem for Best Practice recommendations.

ZSPE System Program

ZSPE is the object name for the $ZSPE process, which is the OSM Service Processor (SP) Event Distributor process. Please refer to the Guardian Gazette section on the TSM subsystem or the OSM Subsystem for more information.

TSM was superseded by OSM in version G06.22. OSM is required for Integrity NonStop systems.

ZTRC File

ZTRC is the file containing the pointer to the current ZTRCn file. Please refer to the Guardian Gazette section on the OSM Subsystem for more information.

ZTRCn Files

ZTRCn files are the user trace logs created and maintained by the OSM $CIMON process. Please refer to the Guardian Gazette section on the OSM Subsystem for more information.

ZZAAnnnn Files

ZZAAnnnn files are the OSM Server alarm files. Please refer to the Guardian Gazette section on the OSM subsystem for more information.

ZZALnnnn Files

ZZALnnnn files are the TSM Server Alarm files. Please refer to the Guardian Gazette section on the TSM subsystem for more information.

ZZDCnnnn Files

ZZDCnnnn files are the TSM Inventory Snapshot files. Please refer to the Guardian Gazette section on the TSM subsystem for more information.

ZZNFSnnnn Files

The NFSMGR processes keep all their configuration information (other than userids) in files in the ZOSSNFS subvolume. The files are named ZZNFSnnnn, where n represents a number. These files are updated programmatically, not by users directly.

Please refer to Part 5 for a complete discussion of the Network File System (NFS) Subsystem or to the Guardian Gazette section on the NFS Subsystem for Best Practice recommendations.

ZZSNnnnn Files

ZZSNnnnn files are the OSM Inventory snapshot files. Please refer to the Guardian Gazette section on the OSM subsystem for more information.

ZZPSnnnnFiles

ZZPSnnnn files are the OSM Processor scan strings files. Please refer to the Guardian Gazette section on the OSM subsystem for more information.

ZZSKnnnn Log Files

ZZSKnnnn log files are the alternate key files for the EMS log created by the TSM $ZLOG. Please refer to the Guardian Gazette section on the TSM Subsystem or the OSM subsystem for more information.

TSM was superseded by OSM in version G06.22. OSM is required for Integrity NonStop systems.

ZZSSnnnn Files

ZZSSnnnn files are the TSM Processor Scan files. Please refer to the Guardian Gazette section on the TSM subsystem for more information.

ZZUSERS and ZZUSERS2 Files

The ZZUSERS and ZZUSERS2 files contain TSM service application connection audit information. Please refer to the Guardian Gazette section on the TSM subsystem for more information.

$ZCMOM Process

$ZCMOM is the main OSM server process. Please refer to the Guardian Gazette section on the OSM Subsystem for more information.

$ZLOG Process

$ZLOG is the process name of the OSM EMS collector process. Please refer to the Guardian Gazette section on the TSM Subsystem or the OSM Subsystem for more information.

TSM was superseded by OSM in version G06.22. OSM is required for Integrity NonStop systems.

$ZOEV Process

The $ZOEV process is the server for OSM Event Viewer requests. Please refer to the Guardian Gazette section on the OSM Subsystem for more information.

$ZOLHD Process

$ZOLHD is the OSM EMS Routing Distributor. Please refer to the Guardian Gazette section on the OSM Subsystem for more information.

$ZOSM Process

$ZOSM is the OSM Applet Server process, which uploads client files via the server connection. Please refer to the Guardian Gazette section on the OSM Subsystem for more information.

$ZOSM launches the Applet Providers, which are responsible for serving client files. $SYSTEM.SYSnn.APPPRVD is the object file for the Applet Providers. Please refer to the Guardian Gazette section on the OSM Subsystem for more information.

$ZFMnn Process

$ZFMnn is the OSS File Manager process. There should be one file manager process per CPU, with process names of $ZFMnn where nn is the CPU number. Please refer to the Guardian Gazette section on the OSS File Manager for more information.

$ZMSGQ Process

$ZMSGQ is the OSS message-queue server, which is managed by the OSS monitor. Please refer to the Guardian Gazette section on the OSS Monitor Process for more information.

$ZPLS Process

$ZPLS is the OSS sockets local server process, which is managed by the OSS monitor. Please refer to the Guardian Gazette section on the OSS Monitor Process for more information.

$ZPM Process

$ZPM is the Persistence Manager. Please refer to the Guardian Gazette section on the persistence manager for more information.

$ZPMON Process

$ZPMON is the OSS monitor process. Please refer to the Guardian Gazette section on the OSS File Manager for more information.

$ZPNS Process

$ZPNS is the OSS Name Server process for the root fileset. Please refer to the Guardian Gazette section on the OSS Monitor Process for more information.

$ZPPnn Process

$ZPPnn is the process name of the OSS Pipe Server process. There should be one Pipe Server per CPU, with process names of $ZPPnn where nn is the

CPU number. Please refer to the Guardian Gazette section on the OSS Pipe Server for more information.

$ZRD9 Process

$ZRD9 is the TSM Routing Distributor process. Please refer to the Guardian Gazette section on the TSM Subsystem for more information.

$ZSPE Process

$ZSPE is the TSM Service Processor (SP) Event Distributor process. Please refer to the Guardian Gazette section on the TSM Subsystem or the OSM Subsystem for more information.

TSM was superseded by OSM in version G06.22. OSM is required for Integrity NonStop systems.

$ZTAnn Process

$ZTAnn is the process name of the OSS Transport Agent Server. There should be one transport agent per CPU, with process names of $ZTAnn where nn is the CPU number. Please refer to the Guardian Gazette section on the OSS Transport Agent server for more information.

$ZTSM Process

$ZTSM is the main TSM process. Please refer to the Guardian Gazette section on the TSM Subsystem for more information.

$ZTSMS Process

$ZTSMS is the SNMP agent process formerly used by the TSM Service Application. Please refer to the Guardian Gazette section on the TSM Subsystem for more information.

10

The Open System Services Subsystem

The purpose of this chapter is to illustrate how to evaluate the security of the Open System Services (OSS) environment. It is an overview of the subsystem that concentrates on security. It is not a procedure manual. The commands necessary to gather the security information can be found in Appendix C.

The OSS Environment

Steve Bourne wrote the original UNIX shell, **sh**, known as the Bourne shell. In addition to **sh**, other common shells include the C shell (**csh**), the Korn shell (**ksh**), and PERL. Most of these shells are extensions or supersets of the Bourne shell and have many commands and features in common. The Korn shell is the default for OSS and the command **sh** is an alias for **ksh**. There is a great deal of information on the OSS environment in the **man** pages for the **sh** command.

OSS is based on the POSIX version of UNIX. It conforms to several industry standards, such as CAE, POSIX.1, POSIX.2, XPG4, and FIPS, that define requirements for computing systems and application portability. These standards include application program interfaces (APIs), run-time libraries, command interpreters, user commands, and utilities.

OSS is not an operating system. It interacts with Guardian and uses of many of Guardian's features. Several HP products, including Safeguard, must be running for OSS to operate.

Configuration and management of the OSS subsystem is done almost entirely through SCF in the Guardian space. Refer to the section on securing the OSS Monitor Process (OSSMON) in the Guardian Gazette for more information about securing the Guardian programs that manage the OSS environment.

The OSS subsystem is usually started when the NonStop Server is cold-loaded. It can be started later, but it is not recommended.

The OSS Monitor is a Guardian process that monitors and configures the OSS environment. It is the gateway for all OSS activity and coordinates all the objects and processes needed in the OSS environment.

Each OSS file and AF_UNIX socket has an underlying Guardian filename. Because the Guardian name and the OSS pathnames are different, there must be a way to map (resolve) the OSS pathname to the Guardian name. This is the task of the OSS name servers. They translate the OSS file name to the ZYQ Guardian subvolume where the file actually resides.

OSS files are stored under directories. Directories are grouped together, and each group is administered as an entity called a fileset. Each fileset has a name server and a fileset catalog. These are defined in the ZOSSFSET file.

An application running in the OSS environment gains access to OSS files via function calls in the OSS file system library. When the application opens an OSS file, an OSS Name Server locates the correct file within its fileset. The server provides the information to the system on behalf of the application program so that it can communicate with the disk process providing access to the file.

Sockets use Transport Agents and transport providers, called Sockets Local Servers, to route data between application processes.

OSS Pipe Server processes support the transfer of data between OSS processes that use pipes or FIFOs between processors.

Message queues are linked lists of messages used to pass data from one process to another. Messages are handled by the Message Queue Server.

Built-in Shell Commands

sh comes with built-in commands. Built-in commands are executed by the shell itself. They run entirely within the current shell process; they do not start a new shell process when they execute.

Several of these commands also have program versions with object files (primarily residing in **/bin**). The built-in command is always the default. To invoke the program rather than the built-in command, a user must use the full pathname to invoke the object file version.

RISK There is always the possibility that the object file version differs from the built-in version.

RISK Though it is possible to secure the object files, there is currently no way to prevent a user from executing a built-in shell command.

Figure 10.1
Built-in shell commands.

Built-in Command	Object File	Description
alias	/bin/alias	Lists or defines an alias
bg	/bin/bg	Puts jobs in the background
break		Exits from an enclosing loop
cd	/bin/cd	Changes the current working directory
continue		Resumes the next iteration of an enclosing loop
echo	/bin/echo	Writes its arguments to the standard output file
eval		Reads arguments and executes commands

(*Continued*)

Figure 10.1 (*Continued*)

Built-in Command	Object File	Description
exec	/bin/exec	Executes a command
exit		Exits the shell
export		Exports variables
fc	/bin/fc	Lists, edits, and re-executes commands previously entered in a shell
fg	/bin/fg	Brings specified jobs to the foreground
getopts	/bin/getopts	Parses command-line flags and arguments
hash		Affects the shell's memory of the location of the utilities
history		Displays a list of previously executed commands (the history list)
jobs	/bin/jobs	Lists information about jobs
kill	/bin/kill	Sends a signal to a running process
let		Evaluates arithmetic expressions
print		Provides shell output
pwd	/bin/pwd	Displays the current directory pathname
read	/bin/read	Reads one line from the standard input file
readonly		Marks specified names as read-only
return		Causes a shell function to return to the invoking script
set		Sets shell parameters
shift		Sets positional parameters
times		Times the execution of a command
trap		Specifies a command and signals for its execution by the shell

(*Continued*)

Figure 10.1 (*Continued*)

Built-in Command	Object File	Description
type		Writes a description of a file's type
typeset		Sets attributes and values for shell parameters
umask	/bin/umask	Sets a file mode creation mask
unalias	/bin/unalias	Removes names from the alias list
unexpand	/bin/unexpand	Replaces tabs or space characters
unset		Erases parameter values
wait	/bin/wait	Awaits process completion
whence		Tells how a name would be interpreted if used as a command
add_define		Creates one or more DEFINEs for the current OSS shell
del_define		Deletes one or more DEFINEs for the current OSS shell
info_define		Displays attributes and values of existing DEFINEs
reset_define		Restores a DEFINE's attributes to their initial settings
set_define		Sets values for DEFINE attributes in the working attribute
show_define		Displays values of attributes (a HP extension)

Command Aliases

OSS command aliases serve two purposes:

Aliases can be used to rename a command to something more meaningful for the user. For example, a user who is more familiar with the Guardian environment might prefer to type "vol" or "volume" rather than "cd" when he wishes to change directories.

Aliases can be also be abbreviations for long command lines. For example, if a user must frequently move to a subdirectory **/usr/robert/ sec/reports**, he could create an abbreviation such as "**srpts**" that would move him to that subdirectory without having to type out the complete pathname.

Aliases can be temporary or "permanent." If an alias is defined on the command line, it will apply only to the current shell. It won't work in any subshells the shell creates, and it will vanish when the session ends.

To make aliases "permanent," that is, to make them valid in future sessions, they must be defined in either the **/etc/profile** file or in the user's personal **$HOME/.profile** file. Aliases defined in the **/etc/profile** will apply to all users on the system. They can be replaced or supplemented by aliases defined in the individual **$HOME/.profile** files. Refer to the section on Profile Files for more information.

To make aliases valid in subshells or future sessions, they must be exported. Use the **-x** flag in **.profile** files:

alias -x aliasname = command

The **-x** flag **exports** the alias. See the **man** pages for the **alias** command for a fuller explanation of command aliases.

RISK Anyone who can change another user's **$HOME/.profile** can insert command aliases that may cause normally benign commands to perform unexpected and unauthorized activities.

BP-ETC-PROFILE-02 Only SUPER.SUPER should have WRITE or PURGE access to **/etc/profile.sample**.

AP-POLICY-PROFILE-01 The Corporate security policy should determine whether or not users are allowed to modify their own $HOME/.profile file.

The OSS File System

The OSS file system provides the same functionality as a UNIX file system, but internally it differs because it has to work with Guardian and the NonStop Kernel. The items unique to the NonStop Server are:

Disk management is done via the NonStop Kernel. The NonStop Kernel disk process performs READ, WRITE, and LOCK operations on disk volumes.

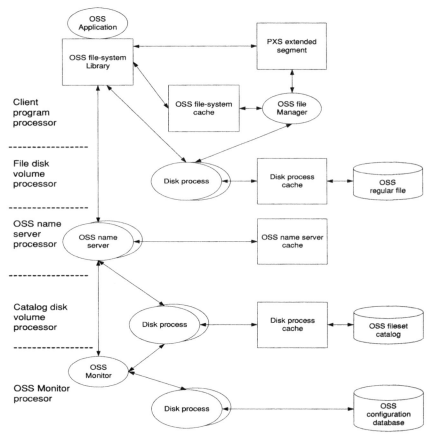

Figure 10.2
Components of the OSS file system.

OSS pathnames have underlying Guardian filenames. The mapping between OSS pathnames and Guardian filenames is known as filename resolution. Filename resolution is performed by an OSS name server.

The **/G** directory contains filesets for local files in the Guardian namespace.

The **/E** directory contains files on other nodes in the network.

The **/dev** directory is used in a special way because all devices reside in the Guardian environment.

The Structure of the OSS File System

OSS file system has an inverted tree structure, with the root directory at the top and all subdirectories in the hierarchy under it.

The root directory is represented by a slash (/).

There is a limit of 256 levels below it.

The maximum length of a file or directory name is 248 characters.

In reality, the number of levels under the root directory is limited because a fully qualified pathname has a maximum length of 1023 characters.

Filesets

Filesets reside on disk volumes that are grouped into storage pools. Each fileset has its own storage pool of one or more disk volumes. A fileset can span multiple disk volumes.

A single file must reside on a single disk. If space fills up, a file of the same name can be created in the same directory on a different disk, and as a storage pool's disk volumes are filled, more volumes can be added to accommodate the files in the fileset.

A fileset can contain up to 500,000 files as a practical limit.

Up to 20 disk volumes can be specified as current members of a storage pool.

A file cannot be renamed (**/bin/mv**) across filesets. A file can, however, be copied (**/bin/cp**) between filesets. This is similar to the behavior of RENAME in the Guardian space. A file cannot be RENAMEd to another disk drive, but it can be DUPed.

A fileset is a hierarchy of directories, subdirectories, and the files contained in them.

A fileset can have other filesets mounted on directories in it. In fact, the collection of directories and files under the root directory is part of one fileset.

Information about each fileset is stored in the ZOSSFSET file and in storage-pool files.

The **/G** directory is its own fileset in the OSS file system. Each disk volume within the Guardian file system and each terminal process also are separate filesets. However, these filesets are not managed via the SCF interface, and they do not appear in the fileset configuration database.

Fileset Catalogs

The OSS name servers use catalog files to maintain and manage fileset information. Each fileset's catalog contains:

Information about the hierarchical directory structure of the fileset.

Unique identifiers for the files, called **inode** numbers in OSS and UNIX terminology or file serial numbers in POSIX terminology. Each file in the OSS file system has such an identifier.

When a new fileset is added via SCF, its fileset catalog must be created in the volume and subvolume specified. The subvolume's name must begin with "ZX0". The catalog consists of three files which are created in this

ZX0 subvolume: PXINODE, PXLINK, and PXLOG. These files will be used by the fileset's Name Server.

The PXINODE contains one record for each directory, regular file, FIFO, and AF_UNIX socket. It is a key-sequenced file.

The PXLINK contains one record for each link name in the fileset. It is a key-sequenced file

The PXLOG is used to ensure catalog integrity after a failure. It is an unstructured file.

Fileset Storage Pool Files

Each fileset has a storage pool file. Storage-pool files are text files that contain the list of VOLUMES where the files in the fileset will reside.

The storage pool file must be in the same subvolume as the $SYSTEM. ZXOSSMON.ZOSSFSET file.

AP-ADVICE-STORPOOL-01   The initial or root pool must be defined before the OSS Monitor is started.

AP-ADVICE-STORPOOL-02   The root pool should have more than one disk volume, to allow for future growth.

AP-ADVICE-STORPOOL-03   No fileset should include the $SYSTEM or $DSMSCM disks in its storage pool.

AP-ADVICE-STORPOOL-04   The fewer the volumes in a storage pool, the better the performance.

AP-ADVICE-STORPOOL-05   Optical disks cannot be assigned to a storage pool.

AP-ADVICE-STORPOOL-06   Virtual disks cannot be assigned to a storage pool.

AP-ADVICE-STORPOOL-07   Disks should not be assigned to more than one storage pool. Sharing disks makes it more difficult to monitor and control free space within individual filesets.

FSCK Utility

FSCK is the fileset repair program. It is a Guardian utility that looks at every regular OSS file to verify that it has both a directory entry and data. FSCK makes sure that the superblock, inodes, and catalog files are consistent. It can also make repairs to the integrity of an OSS fileset.

FSCK is run via the SCF DIAGNOSE FILESET command. Only a member of the SUPER Group can use the DIAGNOSE FILESET command.

	Discovery Questions	Look here:
OSS-FILESET	How many filesets are defined on the system?	Policy
OSS-FILESET	How many disks are defined in each fileset's Storage Pool?	Policy
OSS-FILESET	Are any disks assigned to more than one Storage Pool?	Noscom
OSS-FILESET	Are $SYSTEM or $DSMSCM included in any Storage Pools?	Noscom
OSS-FILESET	Are all filesets configured?	Safecom

Regular Files

The POSIX standard mandates that regular files have the following attributes:

The file's length in bytes

The file owner's userid

The file's groupid

The **inode** number, which identifies the file with the filesystem

A permissions string (mode)

Timestamps recording:

The time the inode itself was last changed (ctime)

The time the contents of the file were last changed (mtime)

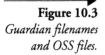

Figure 10.3
Guardian filenames
and OSS files.

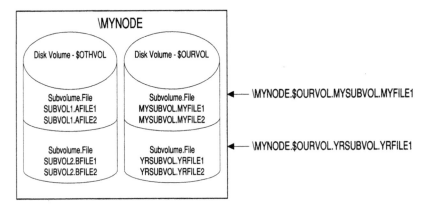

- The time the file was last accessed (atime)
- The number of hardlinks pointing to the inode

An **inode** is a number that uniquely identifies the file within the file system.

On the NonStop Server, the name of each file in the OSS file system is mapped to a Guardian filename. The file identifier is the Guardian representation of the inode for the actual OSS regular file.

OSS regular files:

> Are always stored in Guardian subvolumes whose names begin with the letters ZYQ
>
> Always have a Guardian file security string which displays as #### when a FILEINFO is done

Pathnames

An OSS pathname describes a path through the OSS directory.

OSS name servers resolve Guardian filenames and OSS pathnames and provide that information to the system on behalf of the application program so that it can communicate with the disk process providing access to the file. Each OSS filename points to an underlying Guardian file ID, such as Z0000DV3.

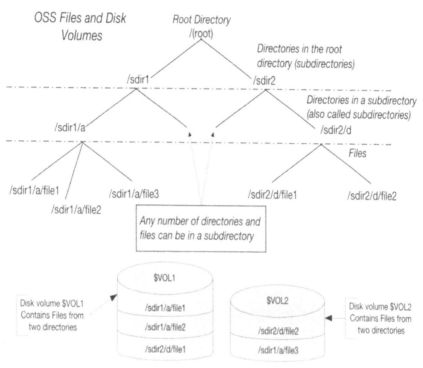

Figure 10.4
New OSS files and disks.

The OSS pathnames of Guardian files can have no more than four elements including the /G, and although they are technically OSS filenames, they are subject to the 8-character length restrictions for Guardian volume, subvolume, and file names.

Pathnames for Remote Files

Remote Guardian files appear in the /G directory of the remote node.

Remote OSS files appear in the root (/) directory of the remote node.

Files visible through a remote system's /E directory are not visible on the local system.

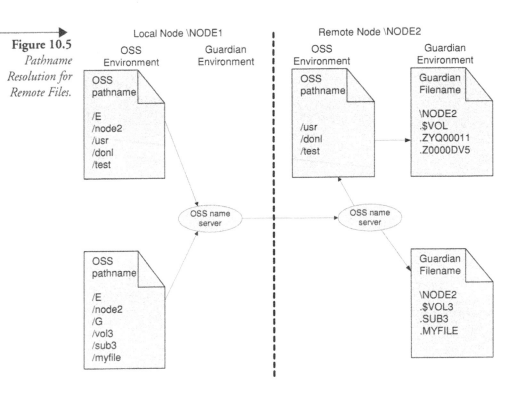

Figure 10.5
Pathname Resolution for Remote Files.

The local node also has an entry in its own /E directory. It is a symbolic link to its own root directory.

OSS Directories

In OSS, a directory is actually a special file containing link-to-inode pairs for the files and subdirectories located "under" it.

Making Directories

The **/bin/mkdir** program creates a new directory. It also creates the hard links to the "." (dot) and ".." (dot dot) directories for itself and its parent. The **-m** flag lets the user set the permissions for the new directory.

Creating a subdirectory implies updating the link-to-inode pairs in the parent directory file. The user must have WRITE permission in the new directory's parent directory in order to create it.

Removing Directories

The /**bin/rm** program removes files from a directory, or to be more exact, it unlinks or severs the connection between the filename in the directory and the inode number. If another link still exists to the inode number, the file continues to exist, just not in the directory from which the user removed it. When all links are severed and the file is closed, its space is reclaimed and it is no longer accessible.

To remove a file from a directory, a user doesn't have to have permissions to READ or WRITE the file, but he must have WRITE permission to its parent directory because the directory file is being modified to remove the name/**inode** connection.

Altering Directories

The /**bin/chown** program changes the owner of files and directories. When symbolic links are encountered, the ownership of the parent file or directory is changed, but the ownership of linked files and directories is not changed.

The /**bin/chmod** program changes access permissions and other file mode settings. Users can enter either permission strings or octal values to change the permission settings. Please refer to Appendix A, Understanding OSS Permission Strings and Octal Values, for a full discussion of permission strings and calculating their binary and octal equivalents.

Altering a directory requires WRITE access to the directory.

Searching Directories

Listing the contents of a directory requires READ access to the directory.

Links

A link is a special file that acts as a name pointer to another file.

In OSS, files are actually identified by their inode number. A link assigns an additional name to an inode number. Directories are actually files containing link-to-inode pairs. Every directory has at least two hard links:

.   points to itself
..   points to its parent directory

An OSS file can have up 128 links (pathnames pointing to the same file).

A Name Server can follow up to 20 symbolic links when resolving an OSS pathname.

Hard Links

Use the **/bin/link** program to create links.

By default, **/bin/ln** creates hard links. Hard links can only be created between files within the same fileset. With hard links, any changes in file characteristics affect any link to it, and all links are equal. However, if one name is deleted, the others will remain. To completely delete a hard-linked file, all of its links must be deleted first.

Symbolic Links

If the **/bin/ln -s** flag is used, a symbolic link is created. Symbolic links allow users to assign a file another name, but it doesn't link the file by inode number. There are some important differences between hard links and symbolic links as shown in the table below.

Hard Link	Symbolic Link
Linked file and target file must be in same fileset	Linked file and target file can be in different filesets
Underlying file must exist	Underlying file need not exist
Linked file and underlying file can have different security	Security to the linked file is based on the underlying file's permission string

Symbolic links are especially important to the shared library images in **/lib**.

Links to Guardian files must be symbolic links because Guardian files reside in their own fileset.

FIFO Files

Directory files, terminal device files, and FIFOs (named pipes) do not have underlying Guardian files or Guardian filenames. These OSS special files are managed entirely by OSS server processes. Such files do not require any configuration action by the system manager; their operation cannot be controlled through SCF FILESET commands.

The OSS Pipe Server processes support the transfer of data between OSS processes that use pipes or FIFOs between processors. Refer to the section on the Architecture of the OSS Subsystem for more information on the OSS Pipe Server process.

The /G Directory

The **/G** directory provides OSS access to Guardian files on the local system. Each Guardian filename has a corresponding OSS name and can be referenced using the OSS filenames in the local **/G** directory. The names are in the form **/G/volume/subvolume/file**. Case is ignored, so $SYSTEM.ZTCPIP.PORTCONF becomes **/G/system/ztcpip/portconf**.

The OSS pathnames of Guardian files can have no more than four elements including the /G, and although they are technically OSS filenames, they are subject to the 8-character length restrictions for Guardian volume, subvolume and file names.

Files residing on virtual disks are not visible in the /G directory.

RISK If files are added or deleted in the **/G/volume** level of this directory, only the amount of disk space used for volumes that contain the Guardian files increases or decreases. Free space for OSS files is not increased, and there is a risk that some files might be inadvertantly deleted.

AP-ADVICE-OSSGUARD-01   The /G directory itself is reserved for HP use. Users should not put anything in this directory.

RISK   Because OSS shell programs that perform recursive actions make no distinction between Guardian and OSS files or between local and remote files, users may inadvertently make changes to Guardian and remote OSS files. Because both the /G and /E directories appear in users' local root directory, both remote files and Guardian files at risk.

BP-GUARDIAN-FILESEC-01   Guardian files should be secured to prevent an OSS-only user from inadvertently altering their attributes.

OSS shell commands that perform recursive operations include:

```
chgrp
chmod
chown
cp
diff
find
ls
mv
pax
rm
rmdir
```

The following commands also have recursive behavior and should be used with great care in the / (root) directory because of the scope of the files involved:

```
cpio
egrep
fgrep
tar
```

AP-ADVICE-ROOT-02   Users working as SUPER.SUPER should be especially careful about specifying the / (root) directory or using the wildcard character * on any object in OSS shell commands, because it might have far-reaching consequences.

The /E Directory

The /E directory provides OSS access to OSS and Guardian files on remote NonStop systems running OSS. The Guardian names are in the form **/E/ volume/subvolume/file**. Case is ignored so the Guardian PORTCONF file on \NODEB (\NODEB/$SYSTEM.ZTCPIP.PORTCONF) becomes **/E/ nodeb/G/system/ztcpip/portconf**. A remote **.profile** file on \NODEB becomes **/E/node2/users/opjoe/.profile**.

RISK If files are added or deleted in the **/E/system** level of this directory, only the amount of disk space used for volumes that contain the Guardian files increases or decreases. Free space for OSS files is not increased, and there is a risk that some files might be inadvertantly deleted.

AP-ADVICE-OSSGUARD-02 The /E directory itself is reserved for HP use. Users should not put anything in this directory.

The /E directories on remote nodes are not visible on the local node. For example, from NODEA, the files on \NODEB are visible in NODEA's /E/ NODEB directory, but files in \NODEB's /E/NODEC directory are not visible from \NODEA.

BP-OSS-OSSGUARD-01 Use REMOTEPASSWORD definitions in SAFEGUARD to control users' access to the /E environment.

RISK Because OSS shell programs that perform recursive actions make no distinction between Guardian and OSS files or between local and remote files, users may inadvertently make changes to Guardian and remote OSS files. And /G and /E both appear in users' local root directory, which puts both remote files and Guardian files at risk.

OSS shell commands that perform recursive operations include:

chgrp
chmod
chown
cp
diff
find
ls

mv
pax
rm
rmdir

BP-GUARDIAN-FILESEC-01   Guardian files should be secured to prevent an OSS-only user from inadvertently altering their attributes.

The following commands also have recursive behavior and should be used with great care in the / (root) directory because of the scope of the files involved:

cpio
egrep
fgrep
tar

AP-ADVICE-ROOT-02   Users working as SUPER.SUPER should be especially careful about specifying the / (root) directory or using the wildcard character * on any object in OSS shell commands, because it might have the far-reaching consequences.

The /dev Directory

The **/dev** directory is the device directory. It exists for compatibility with existing UNIX software. Devices are added and configured in the Guardian environment; therefore, they do not appear in the **/dev** directory. Typically, only the two files shown below reside in the **/dev** directory:

tty the current controlling terminal for the application that is running.

null a data sink. Anything successfully sent to **/dev/null** disappears.

Securing Directories and Files

In the OSS file system, files are secured with a 10-place security string organized with a single character in front to indicate whether or not it is a directory, followed by three sets of three permissions (READ, WRITE, EXECUTE). The first set of three determines the access granted to the file's owner. The second set determines the access granted to the owner's group. The third set determines the access granted to everyone else. For each set of permissions, the values are either present, represented by a single character, or not present, represented by a dash.

The single character values are:

-	Not applicable
d	Directory
r	READ: allows users to view or print the file
w	WRITE: allows users to modify the file
x	EXECUTE: allows users to run the file or to search directories
s	**setgid** or **setuid** set for this directory or file
t	**sticky bit** set for this file

READ, WRITE, and EXECUTE are always listed left to right, as are owner, group, and world.

Unlike in Guardian, there is no PURGE permission in OSS file security strings. A user must have WRITE permission for a file to delete its contents and WRITE permission for the file's directory in order to remove (**rm**) the file.

Users are classified as:

Owner
Group Members
Others

The user/owner of a file or directory is generally the person who created it. The owner of a file and SUPER.SUPER can change the file permissions with the **/bin/chmod** command.

The group specifies the group to which the file belongs. The owner of a file and SUPER.SUPER can change the group ID of the file with the **/bin/chgrp** command.

"Others" or "the world" applies to all other users on the system.

Example 1—The permission string **-rw-rw-r--** is interpreted as:

-	Not a directory, so it must be a data file or executable file
rw-	The owner of the file can READ and WRITE to the file, but not EXECUTE it
rw-	Members of the group the file is assigned to can READ and WRITE to the file, but not EXECUTE it
r--	All other users on the system can READ the file, but not WRITE to the file or EXECUTE it.

Example 2—The permission string **drwxrwxr-x** is interpreted as:

d	A directory
rwx	The owner of the directory can READ, WRITE, and EXECUTE all files in the directory unless the file security of the file in the directory prohibits this access.
rwx	Members of the group the directory is assigned to can READ, WRITE, and EXECUTE all files in the directory, unless the file security of the file in the directory prohibits this access.
r-x	all other users can READ and EXECUTE files in the directory unless the file security of the file in the directory prohibits this access.

BP-OSS-FILESEC-01 All system programs should be owned by SUPER.SUPER and secured so that only SUPER.SUPER can alter them; such files should be secured rwx --x --x.

BP-OSS-FILESEC-01 All system configuration files should be owned by SUPER.SUPER and secured so that only SUPER.SUPER can alter them. Such files should be secured rw- r-- r--.

setuid

Set-user Identification (**setuid**) is the OSS equivalent of PROGID. When this permission is set on an executable file, any process started from the executable will run as the file owner rather than the person starting the process and thereby inherit the owner's access privileges.

The process's real user ID, effective user ID and saved-set-user ID are all set equal to the executable file's owner. The effective user ID determines the PAID (Process Access ID). All access to files and other resources is granted or denied based on the PAID, rather than the user who started the process.

setuid is only valid for executable files. The **setuid** permission is shown as an "s" in the fourth character of the file permissions.

> Example 3 -rws r-x --x 1 SUPER.SUPER SUPER 141616 Jun
> 28 2005 /bin/at

-       Not a directory

rws   The owner of the file can READ, WRITE and EXECUTE this file. The s in the fourth position is the **setuid** bit, which indicates that when this program is executed, the process uses the userid to which this file is assigned to access all resources needed by the program. Anyone allowed to execute the program will have the access privileges granted to the file owner. If, as in this example, the file is owned by SUPER.SUPER, the program will run as SUPER.SUPER and will have all of SUPER.SUPER's access privileges.

r-x   The group to which this file is assigned can READ and EXECUTE this file. Anyone allowed to execute the program will have the access privileges granted to the file owner. If, as in this example, the file is owned by SUPER.SUPER, the program will run as SUPER.SUPER and will have all of SUPER.SUPER's access privileges.

--x   All other users can EXECUTE this file. Anyone allowed to execute the program will have the access privileges granted to the file owner. If, as in this example, the file is owned by

SUPER.SUPER, the program will run as SUPER.SUPER
and have all of SUPER.SUPER's access privileges.

Only the file owner, SUPER.SUPER, and any aliases to SUPER.SUPER
are able to set **setuid** permission. The **/bin/chmod** command is used to set
setuid:

```
Chmod u+s <filename>
```

RISK   Because the program is executing as the owner's userid, often
SUPER.SUPER, the resources will be accessed as SUPER.SUPER. Without proper basic security, unexpected accesses could occur.

RISK   Because the program is executing as the owner's userid, any subordinate programs or slave shells started from this program will also start
using the owner's userid, allowing access to all of the resources available to
the program's owner.

BP-OSS-SETUID-01   Avoid using the **setuid** permission if possible.

3P-ACCESS-SETUID-01   Use a third-party access control product,
rather than the **setuid,** to enable users to run programs as SUPER.SUPER
or another privileged ID. Such third-party products should provide an audit
of the user's activities while working as the privileged ID.

BP-OSS-SETUID-02   If the **setuid** must be used, monitor the list of files
that have this permission set to ensure that no unauthorized programs have
the **setuid** permission.

BP-OSS-SETUID-03   Ensure that programs with the **setuid** permission do
not have the ability to start unauthorized subordinate programs or shells.

AP-ADVICE-SETUID-01   Create procedures to review and document
all requests to **setuid** programs.

The company's HP NonStop Server Security Procedures should include
the following instructions for managing **setuid** requests for in-house
programs:

1. The request for **setuid** should include a full explanation of the
    program's purpose and a justification of the use of privileged
    procedures.

2. The system manager or a trusted programmer must review the program's function.

3. Management must approve the **setuid** in writing with authorized signature(s).

4. To ensure that the source code matches the actual object program, the system manager, not the developer, should compile and bind the final program.

5. The program must be tested to ensure that it does not perform or allow any actions that would be considered security violations. This test is usually performed by the security staff.

6. The above document should be maintained in a file for future reference by auditors.

7. Requests for **setuid**ing user programs may be allowed if the following conditions are met:

    a. The function is legitimate and necessary.

    b. The function cannot be achieved using nonprivileged programming techniques.

Secure **setuid**'d programs so that only authorized users can execute them.

setgid

Set Group Identification (**setgid**) is similar to **setuid** and Guardian PROGID except that it sets the real group ID, effective group ID and saved-set-group ID. When this permission is set on an executable file, any process started from the executable will have access to files and other resources granted or denied based on the executable file's group rather than the group of the user who started the process.

Set-group identification (**setgid**) permission is only valid for executable files or directories.

The **setgid** permission is shown as an "s" in the seventh character of the file permissions.

Example 4 -r-x--s--x 1 SUPER.SUPER SUPER 141616 Jun 28 2005 /bin/blot

-	Not a directory
r-x	The owner of the file can READ and EXECUTE this program
--s	The group to which this file is assigned can EXECUTE this program. The **s** in the seventh position is the **setgid** bit, which indicates that when this program is executed, the process will run as the user. Anyone allowed to execute the program will have the access privileges granted to the owner.
--x	All other users can EXECUTE this program. Anyone allowed to execute the program will have the access privileges granted to the group.

Only the file owner, SUPER.SUPER, or an alias to SUPER.SUPER can set the **setgid** permission. The **/bin/chmod** command is used to **setgid**:

```
chmod g+s <filename>
```

RISK Because the program is executing as the owner's group, the resources will be accessed as the owner group. Without proper basic security, unexpected accesses could occur.

BP-OSS-SETGID-01 If **setgid** must be used, monitor the list of files that have this permission set to ensure that no unauthorized programs have the **setgid** permission.

BP-OSS-SETGID-02 Ensure that programs with the **setgid** permission do not have the ability to start unauthorized subordinate programs or shells.

3P-ACCESS-SETGID-01 Use a third-party access control product, rather than the **setgid**, to enable users to run programs as a SUPERGroup member or another privileged ID. Such third-party products should provide an audit of the user's activities while working as the privileged ID.

When the **setgid** permission is set for a directory, all new files created in the directory will belong to the group the directory belongs to, rather than the group of the owner of the process that creates the file. All of the other permissions are respected, so if a user is allowed to write to the directory, the user may create files there. All of the files created, however, will belong to the group of the directory.

RISK If a directory has the **setgid** permission set, files that are created will belong to the group that owns the directory. A user could create a file that he would then not be able to access.

BP-OSS-SETGID-03 Do not use the **setgid** permission on directories.

BP-OSS-SETGID-04 If **setgid** must be used on a directory, monitor the list of files for the directory so that files are not accumulating with creators who cannot access them.

Create procedures to review and document all requests to **setgid** programs.

The company's HP NonStop Server Security Procedures should include the following instructions for managing **setgid** requests for in-house programs:

1. The request for **setgid** should include a full explanation of the program's purpose and a justification of the use of privileged procedures.

2. The system manager or a trusted programmer must review program's function. The reviewer should look for security requirements of the program:

    The security requirements cannot be achieved without using **setgid**.

    The owner of the **setgid** can be verified.

3. Management must approve the **setgid** in writing with approved signature(s).

4. The above document should be maintained in a file for future reference by auditors.

5. To ensure that the source code matches the actual object program, the system manager, not the developer, should compile and bind the final program.

6. The program must be tested to ensure that it does not perform or allow any actions that would be considered security violations. This test is usually performed by the Security staff.

7. Requests for **setgid**ing user programs may be allowed if the following conditions are met:

    a.   The function is legitimate and necessary.

    b.   The function cannot be achieved using nonprivileged programming techniques.

Secure **setgid** programs so that only authorized users can execute them.

Sticky Bits

The **sticky bit** is set only for directories. When the **sticky bit** is set on a directory, files within the directory can only be deleted by their owners and only if the owner has WRITE permission to the directory. SUPER.SUPER can also delete files in directories with the **sticky bit** set.

The **sticky bit** is shown as a **t** in the tenth character of the file permissions.

```
Example 5  drwxrwxrwt 1 APPL01.HAILEY APPL01 4096 Mar 9
09:54 public
           ∧
```

d	A directory
rwx	The owner of the directory can READ, WRITE, and EXECUTE all files in the directory unless the file security of the file in the directory prohibits this access.
rwx	The group to which the directory is assigned can READ, WRITE, and EXECUTE all files in the directory unless the file security of the file in the directory prohibits this access.
rwt	All other users can READ, WRITE, and EXECUTE files in the directory unless the security of individual files prohibits this access. The **t** in the final position is the sticky bit, which indicates that the files in the directory can only be deleted by the owner of the directory, the owner of the file, or the SUPER.SUPER user.

Only the owner of the directory, SUPER.SUPER, or a Safeguard alias to SUPER.SUPER can set the **sticky bit**.

Type **chmod +t <filename>** to set the **sticky bit**.

When a directory has the **sticky bit** set, users can only delete files that they own from the directory.

RISK When a directory has the **sticky bit** set, a user can create a file that he may not be able delete.

BP-OSS-STICKY-01 Do not use **sticky bits** to secure nonpublic directories.

BP-OSS-STICKY-02 When creating directories meant to be available to more than one group of users, use the **sticky bit** to ensure that only authorized users can delete files from the directory.

Auditing OSS File Access

Two items must be configured in order to get any auditing of file access attempts within the OSS environment:

Filesets must be configured AUDITENABLED ON.

The Safeguard global parameter AUDIT-CLIENT-SERVICES must be set ON.

AUDITENABLED

The AUDITENABLED parameter is set via SCF.

BP-OSS-AUDIT-01 If applications are running in the OSS environment, AUDITENABLED must be ON for all filesets.

The following file-related operations generate audits:

access

kill

link / unlink / symlink

> **bind (af_unix)**
>
> **chown**
>
> **chmod**
>
> **mkdir**
>
> **mkfifo**
>
> **mknod**
>
> **open**
>
> **opendir**
>
> **rename**
>
> **rmdir**
>
> **untime**

The **DirsSearch** operation is performed by an OSS Name Server while resolving a pathname to ensure that the requesting user has search authority for the directory.

The **OssResolve** operation is performed by an OSS Name Server when mapping the target file's external name to its Guardian name

During pathname resolution, if directory search access is denied in a directory in an AUDITENABLED fileset, an audit record is generated, even if the operation being performed is not normally audited.

AUDIT-CLIENT-SERVICE

HP privileged subsystems such as FUP and SCF are known as clients. The AUDIT-CLIENT-SERVICE parameter determines whether or not Safeguard will accept event information from these clients and write the records into the Safeguard audit trail on their behalf.

Safeguard treats the entire OSS subsystem as a single "client." The only way to obtain any auditing at all of OSS activity is to configure Safeguard to accept audits via the AUDIT-CLIENT-SERVICES global parameter.

It is important to note the following facts about client auditing:

> Audit records from clients are not standardized. Each client's audit records have different content and a different format.

Clients might not create the same audit records with the same content from release to release.

Auditing HP clients will consume considerable system resources and add a large number of records to the Safeguard audit files.

Some of the Safeguard Global audit parameters also affect client auditing.

AP-ADVICE-SAFEGARD-11   The system must have sufficient disk space to accommodate the increased size of the Safeguard audit trail(s)

AP-ADVICE-SAFEGARD-12   The system must have adequate resources, such as CPUs and memory, to handle the increased amount of audit activity.

Processes in OSS

Just as in Guardian, OSS processes have a process ID and a process handle:

The OSS process ID is a nonnegative integer that uniquely identifies a process within a node.

The process handle is a data structure 10 words long that uniquely identifies a process within an HP NonStop network.

OSS processes have a full set of Guardian attributes, such as a process handle, that allow most Guardian process-management procedures to manipulate OSS processes, including changing the priority of a process, getting information about it, and terminating it.

As of release G06.25, once an OSS process is started, its priority cannot be altered via an OSS function. A Guardian procedure must be used to change process priority.

To adapt UNIX processes to the NonStop Server, HP added some extension functions that are used to set attributes when a process is created—attributes that cannot be set with the standard **fork()** and **exec()** set of functions. For example, the **tdm_fork()** function was added because the **fork()**

function does not allow the overwriting of the inherited values. These extended functions are:

tdm_fork()
tdm_execve()
tdm_execvep()
tdm_spawn()
tdm_spawnp()

There are many Guardian attributes that an OSS child process inherits from its parent. When a process is created using the OSS HP extension functions such as **tdm_fork()**, **tdm_execve()**, and **tdm_spawn()**, the inherited Guardian attributes can be overwritten by specifying values for the fields in the input structure that contains Guardian attributes:

Debug options, such as creating a saveabend file

Hometerm

Priority

Processor

DEFINES

Specifying a set of DEFINEs to be propagated to a new process allows information to be passed to the process. Guardian procedures, such as DEFINEADD and DEFINEDELETE, or OSS utilities such as **add_define** and **delete_define**, must be used to change the DEFINEs of a process once it is created.

Some OSS functions can alter Guardian process attributes such as the system-dependent system limits, times, and user ID of a Guardian process.

Guardian processes also have some OSS file system attributes that allow Guardian processes to access OSS objects and do OSS file system work:

Guardian processes include an extended security block of OSS attributes that allow them to access OSS and Guardian objects belonging to other groups.

Guardian processes have a process handle but not an OSS process ID, so OSS processes cannot send signals to a Guardian process, and a Guardian process cannot belong to an OSS process group or session.

Process Ownership

Several attributes control access to the process and what files the process can access.

Process Attribute	Description
Effective userid	The userid under which the process is currently running. It is always kept synchronized with the PAID.
	The effective userid is initialized to be the Real ID when the process is authenticated.
	The effective userid is changed if the process executes a program file that has the SETUID attribute.
Real ID	The userid that created the process (not always equal to the CAID).
Saved-Set-User-ID	A stored userid that allows a process to switch its effective userid between the value of the Saved-Set-User-ID and the Real ID.
	The Saved-Set-User-ID is initialized to the same value as the Real ID.
	The Saved-Set-User-ID is changed if the process executes a program file that has the SETUID attribute.
Group list	A list containing the file-sharing groups associated with the process.
Effective Group ID	The group ID under which the process is currently running.
	The Effective Group ID is initialized to the same group ID as the real group ID when the process is authenticated.
	The Effective Group ID is changed if the process executes a program file that has the SETGID attribute.
Real Group ID	The primary group of the userid that created the process.

(Continued)

Process Attribute	Description
Saved-Set-Group-ID	A stored group ID that allows a process to switch its effective group ID between the value of the Saved-Set-Group-ID and the real group ID.
	The Saved-Set-Group-ID is initialized to the same value as the real group ID.
	The Saved-Set-Group-ID is changed if the process executes a program file that has the SETGID attribute.

When a process is created, the Real User ID and Real Group ID are passed to the descendent process. The Effective IDs and Saved-Set-IDs of the new process can come from either of two sources:

The IDs of its creator (the usual case)

The owner of the program file, if the object file has the SETUID or SETGID attributes.

The Effective User ID, Effective Group ID, and Group List are used to determine whether file access is allowed. Other security attributes are also used to determine if an OSS process can **kill** another OSS process. A process can successfully send a **kill**() signal to another process if:

The sending process has the Effective User ID of SUPER.SUPER

The sending process has an Effective User ID equal to the Real User ID of the target process

The sending process has an Effective User ID equal to the Saved-Set-User-ID of the target process

The sending process has a Real User ID equal to the Real User ID of the target process

The sending process has a Real User ID equal to the Saved-Set-User-ID of the target process

Process Groups

All OSS processes are members of a process group. A process group is a set of processes that can signal associated processes. Each process group has a process group ID. A new process becomes a member of the process group of its creator.

TTY

The **tty** interface is the general interface for telserv terminals. It supplies all the functions needed for I/O. It consists of the special file **/dev/tty** and terminal drivers used for conversational computing.

Certain events, such as the delivery of keyboard-generated signals like **interrupt**, **quit**, and **suspend**, affect all the processes in the process group associated with the controlling terminal.

Open System Services supports the concept of a controlling terminal, the equivalent of the Guardian HOMETERM. Any process in the system can have a controlling terminal associated with it.

The controlling terminal also determines the physical device that is accessed when the indirect device **/dev/tty** is opened.

Auditing OSS Processes

Three items must be configured in order to get any auditing of OSS processes:

        AUDIT-CLIENT-SERVICES
        AUDIT-PROCESS-ACCESS-PASS
        AUDIT-PROCESS-ACCESS-FAIL

Please refer to the section on auditing OSS file access from more information about AUDIT-CLIENT-SERVICES.

The Global AUDIT-PROCESS-ACCESS-PASS or AUDIT-PROCESS-ACCESS-FAIL attribute values determine whether or not Safeguard will write audit records not only Safeguard-protected process objects but also for client operations that pertain to processes and subprocesses.

To capture OSS process-related audits, the Safeguard Global parameters AUDIT-PROCESS-ACCESS-PASS and AUDIT-PROCESS-ACCESS-FAIL must also be set ON. These attributes determine whether or not Safeguard will write audit records not only for Safeguard-protected process objects but also for client operations that pertain to processes and subprocesses.

BP-PROCESS-POLICY   The Security Policy should dictate whether all or just failed process access attempts should be audited.

BP-SAFEGARD-GLOBAL-43   If applications are running in the OSS environment, AUDIT-PROCESS-ACCESS-FAIL should be ALL.

BP-SAFEGARD-GLOBAL-44   If policy requires that *all* OSS process activity must be audited, AUDIT-PROCESS-ACCESS-PASS should be ALL.

The following process-related operations can be audited:

> **exec() family**
> **fork()**
> **setgid()**
> **setpgid()**
> **setsid()**
> **setuid()**
> **tdm_exec() family**
> **tdm_fork()**
> **tdm_spawn() family**
> **PROCESS_SPAWN_()**

Command interpreters are called shells in UNIX/OSS. Unlike the Non-Stop environment, where TACL is almost the only command interpreter, in UNIX (and therefore OSS) there are a variety of command interpreters. It is not uncommon for each user to use different shells or even to use more than one type of shell at the same time for different purposes.

Interactions With the Guardian Environment

OSS users can affect Guardian environment in a number of ways.

OSS Commands that Affect the Guardian Environment

The following OSS commands can interact with the Guardian Environment.

OSS command	Result
cancel	Deletes a SPOOLER print job
cp	Copies files
file	Reads files and classifies them by type
gtacl	Executes TACL from the OSS environment
kill	Sends signals to processes, used to stop processes
ls	Lists information about files
osh	Executes the OSS shell
pax	Extracts, writes, and lists archive files, copies files and directory
pintall	Extracts files from pax archive and copies them to the OSS file system
ps	Returns information on processes
run	Starts OSS processes with Guardian attributes
who	Lists users currently logged on to the OSS environment

RISK OSS programs listed above perform recursive actions and make no distinction between Guardian and OSS files or between local and remote files. The /G and /E directories both appear in users' local **root** directory, which puts both remote files and Guardian files at risk.

AP-ADVICE-ROOTDIR-01 Users should be careful using the se programs from the **root** directory, especially if they are working as SUPER.SUPER. If work must be done in the root directory, use the **–W NOG** and **–W NOE** flags

BP-GUARDIAN-FILESEC-01 Guardian files should be secured to prevent an OSS-only user from modifying them in any way.

3P-ADVICE-OBJSEC-01   If there are OSS users on the system who should not have access to Guardian files, consider a third-party obje security product that can prevent such users from accessing files in the Guardian file space.

gtacl

gtacl spawns a TACL session in the Guardian environment. The TACL can be used interactively or with a startup message that controls its execution.

RISK   gtacl relies on Guardian and Safeguard to control access to programs and resources. If the Guardian and Safeguard file securities are not properly set, **gtacl** will execute commands that could perform unexpected and unauthorized actions.

AP-GUARDIAN-FILESEC-01   Guardian files should be secured to prevent an OSS-only user from inadvertently altering their attributes.

osh

osh runs an OSS command from the Guardian environment. It is a Guardian process that spawns an OSS process on the local node only. Command options allow the user to:

Set some characteristics of the environment
Set the initial attributes of the child process
Redirect the output from the initially open files of the child process

Users can access files in the local node's /E directory via the **–prog <pathname>** option.

User Authentication in OSS

User authentication in OSS is performed by Safeguard. By default, users are assumed to be Guardian users. If the INITIAL-DIRECTORY field is left blank, the string is set to null (no pathname) and the Guardian default directory is assumed.

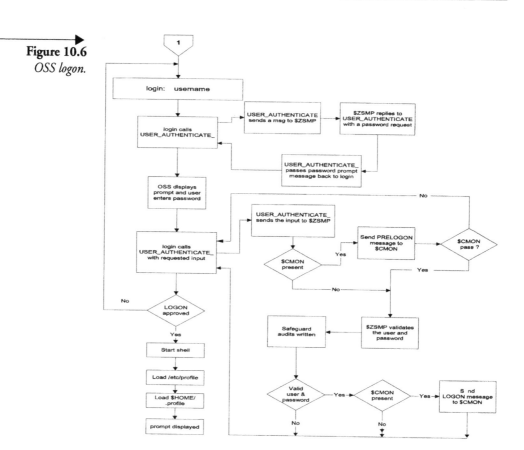

Figure 10.6
OSS logon.

OSS User Management

OSS user administration is done entirely through Safeguard in the Guardian space. Although OSS users are frequently assigned Safeguard aliases to make their experience more UNIX-like, Guardian usernames can be used to login to the OSS shell.

BP-ACCESS-ALIAS-01   Do not use Safeguard aliases unless required. Please refer to the previous book for more information.

3P-ACCESS-ALIAS-01   Aliases to privileged userids, such as SUPER. SUPER or the application owner IDs, should be used only as a last resort.

The most secure way to grant the necessary access to users who must act as a privileged userid in order to perform their job function is via a third-party access control product that can make access to resources much more granular and provide comprehensive auditing.

The Safeguard User Record

There are three OSS-related fields in Safeguard USER and ALIAS records:

INITIAL-DIRECTORY
INITIAL-PROGRAM
INITIAL-PROGTYPE

INITIAL-DIRECTORY [directory-path]

The INITIAL-DIRECTORY is the OSS equivalent of the GUARDIAN DEFAULT VOLUME. It determines the user's home directory within the OSS file system. The pathname is a case-sensitive text string of up to 256 characters. The entire path to the user's home directory must be entered and the final entry in the pathname is assumed to be a directory. So, if a new Base24 user's INIITIAL DIRECTORY is **/users/b24/joe**, enter **/users/b24/joe**, not **/users/b24/joe/personal**, because "personal" will be treated as b24joe's INITIAL-DIRECTORY.

By default, users are assumed to be Guardian users. If the INITIAL-DIRECTORY field is left blank, the string is set to null (no pathname) and the Guardian default directory is assumed.

RISK   The user's INITIAL-DIRECTORY must exist and be secured to allow him access, or the user will not be permitted to logon.

AP-ADVICE-OSSUSER-01   Procedures should be put in place to ensure that the assigned INITIAL-DIRECTORY is created and properly secured whenever a USER or ALIAS record is added for an OSS user.

3P-ADVICE-OSSUSER-01   There are third-party products capable of automatically starting a script to create and secure the appropriate subdirectory when a user or alias record is added with an entry in the INITIAL-DIRECTORY field.

In OSS, the user's home directory is usually referred to as either $HOME or with a tilde (~). In this book, we will use the $HOME convention.

Setting a user's INITIAL-DIRECTORY to an invalid OSS directory will prevent the user from accessing OSS.

BP-OSSUSER-CONFIG-01   A user's INITIAL-DIRECTORY should never be in directories such as **/root**, **/bin**, **/etc**, or any of the directories that are created when the OSS Subsystem is installed.

AP-ADVICE-CONFIG-01   Many companies either create a separate fileset for users' personal files or create a directory tree such as **/user** or **/home** where they place users' $HOME directories.

If a USER Record has an INITIAL-DIRECTORY specified, FTP will assume the user is an OSS user and begin the session in user's INITIAL-DIRECTORY ($HOME).

INITIAL-PROGRAM [prog-path]

The INITIAL-PROGRAM is the OSS equivalent of the Guardian CI PROG. It is used to assign the appropriate initial program, usually **/bin/sh**.

An initial program is automatically executed for a user as soon as they login to the OSS environment. An initial program is normally a command interpreter, but it can be any application that can read a standard input file.

If a user logs on and enters the OSS environment without specifying a program, OSS assumes that they are launching the initial program. This is similar to the concept of the default command interpreter (TACL) in the Guardian environment.

Assigning an Initial Program Using a TACLCSTM File

The initial program can be assigned in three ways:

The user can enter **RUN OSH -ls -prog <pathname>** at a TACL prompt

The user's INITIAL-PROGRAM parameter can assign the program.

For TELSERV indirect users only, it is possible to put the **RUN OSH -ls -prog <pathname>** command in their TACLCSTM file

The <pathname> must point to an existing OSS program file. The -**ls** specification forces execution behaviors appropriate for a UNIX shell program.

BP-OSS-USER-02   If it is necessary to start a particular program when a user logs in, HP recommends the INITIAL-PROGRAM in the Safeguard user record method.

RISK   When the user gains access to the OSS environment by logging in at a TACL prompt, the INITIAL PROGRAM assigned in the user record is ignored. Users can temporarily change their INITIAL PROGRAMs in this manner.

RISK   Assigning an initial program via a TACLCSTM file can cause unexpected behavior in OSS shell commands such as **newgrp**. HP does not recommend using this method.

AP-ADVICE-OSSUSER-03   If TACLCSTM files are used to manage the environment, a more stringent control over these files is suggested to mitigate the risks:

> TACLCSTMs should be owned by the System Administrator
>
> TACLCSTMs should be secured "NUUU".

INITIAL-PROGTYPE [prog-type]

Note that the INITIAL-PROGTYPE feature is not currently implemented on HP NonStop systems. It is reserved for future use. If implemented, it would determine the type of the initial program that would be started within the OSS environment. The valid <prog-types> are:

> PROGRAM
>
> SERVICE
>
> WINDOW

If <prog-type> is omitted, the initial program type is set to PROGRAM.

Scalar Userids

OSS displays userids in the familiar Guardian GROUP NUMBER, MEMBER NUMBER format, but userids are actually stored as scalar numbers. Some applications, such as NFS, rely on the scalar form of the userid.

The scalar form of a Guardian userid is calculated as follows:

```
(Group-number × 256) + member-number = scalar number
```

Some examples of the scalar forms of some userids:

```
10,10 = (10 × 256) + 10 = 2570
SUPER.SUPER = (255 × 256) + 255 = 65535
```

To convert a scalar userid to the Guardian form:

1. Divide the scalar value by 256. The number before the decimal is the group number.

2. Multiply this group number by 256.

3. Subtract the value calculated in step 2 from the original scalar value to get the member number.

```
Example 1:
Original value = 2570
Step 1: 2570/256 = 10.039 (So the group number is 10)
Step 2: 10 * 256 = 2560
Step 3: 2570
      -  2560
          10          (So the member number is 10)
Example 2:
Original value = 65535
Step 1: 65534/256 = 255.996 (So the group number is
        255)
Step 2: 255 * 256 = 65280
Step 3: 65535
      -  65280
         255          (So the member number is 255)
```

File-Sharing Groups

In the OSS file system, files are secured with a 10-place security string organized with a leading directory indicator, followed by three sets of three permissions (READ, WRITE, EXECUTE). The first set determines the access granted to the file's owner. The second set determines the access granted to the file's group. The third set determines the access granted to everyone else.

A group is a list of userids that qualify for the group set of a file permission string. The group may be the owner's primary group or a File-Sharing group.

The groups that Guardian users are accustomed to are referred to as Administrative Groups in the OSS environment. Administrative groups have group numbers between 0 and 255. Groups numbered above 255 exist solely for file-sharing purposes, but Administrative Groups can also function as File-Sharing groups.

Making a user a file-sharing member of the SUPER Group does not automatically allow that user to assume the privileges of a SUPER Group member. A user's Group List is only checked when an access decision is based on the evaluation of a Guardian security string, a Safeguard Protection Record, or an OSS file permission string. A file-sharing member of the SUPER Group is granted group privileges only in these instances, not when the privilege is based on a check of the specific userid.

How Groups are Processed when Logging On

LOGIN sets the group list of a process to contain the user's entire GROUP list, and also copies the user's PRIMARY GROUP to the Real Group ID, Effective Group ID, and Saved-Set-Group-ID of the process.

Because a user's primary group may differ from his ADMINISTRATIVE GROUP, a process's PAID may or may not be the user's ADMINISTRATIVE (PRIMARY) group.

$HOME

In OSS, the user's home directory is usually referred to as either $HOME or with a tilde (~). In this book, we use the $HOME convention.

Depending on which subsystems are installed on the system, a number of special files may be placed in each user's home directory:

.profile

.sh_history

SSH private encryption key files

.rhosts

.host.equiv

Refer to the chapter on SSH in Part 4, TCP/IP, for more information on the SSH private encryption key files and to the OSS and Guardian Gazettes for more information on the rhosts and host.equiv files.

.profile Files

Each time a user runs **osh** or logs in to OSS, the shell creates its working environment. The environment determines such characteristics as the sub-directory where the user begins a session, the commands to run, and the settings for various environment variables. The environment is created by variables defined in two files:

/etc/profile

$HOME/.profile

The following features are commonly set in the .**profile** files:

Terminal characteristics

Editor choice

Search path and other environment variables

Shell variables

Maximum permissions for new files with umask

Display of messages to the workstation

Trap command

Command aliases

History variables

BP-OSS-PROFILE-01 The **/etc/profile** file should be secured so that only SUPER.SUPER can update it and all others can READ it.

AP-ADVICE-PROFILE-01   Use a **/bin/cron** task to periodically:

Report the contents of all **.profile** files

Report the security of all **.profile** files

Repair any unauthorized settings

umask

The **/bin/umask** program sets the default permissions for files created by users. It is the OSS equivalent of the Safeguard User Record GUARDIAN DEFAULT SECURITY attribute.

When a user creates a file or directory, the system automatically supplies predetermined permissions. The default permissions are set by the system administrator in the **/etc/profile** file. The defaults relieve users of the task of specifying permissions every time they create a file or directory. However, if a user wants modify his defaults, he can change the permissions with the **/bin/umask** command.

There is no **umask** for **setuid**, **setgid**, or the **sticky bit**.

BP-OSS-UMASK-01 SUPER.SUPER's umask should be "022" or stricter, which maps to a default file protection of 755 (rwx r-x r-x).

BP-OSS-UMASK-02 The default umask for non privileged userids should be "027", which maps to a default file protection of 750 (rwx r-x ---).

/etc/profile File

The **/etc/profile** file is somewhat equivalent to the Guardian TACLOCL file. It is maintained by the system administrator and it creates the default environment for all users. The information in the **/etc/profile** file is executed when a user logs on.

BP-OSS-PROFILE-03 Any files that load aliases defined in the **.profile** file should be secured so that only SUPER.SUPER can READ or WRITE to it.

BP-GUARDIAN-FILESEC-01 Guardian files should be secured to prevent an OSS user from inadvertently altering their attributes.

Use the **/etc/profile** file to:

Set the default binary paths

Set the default library paths

Set the default prompt

Set the default umask

Set **–o** trackall

Some of the values can be overridden by entries in personal **.profile** files located in each user's home directory.

RISK If the security of the **/etc/profile** file permits users other than the owner WRITE or PURGE access, these users could modify the file or purge it and replace it with a new one.

RISK If a script is executed within a **.profile**, the script file must be also secured so that only authorized users can WRITE or PURGE it. Otherwise, someone could rename it and then install another file with the same name or simply insert commands that execute a Trojan Horse program by invoking the macro via the **.profile** file.

BP-ETC-PROFILE-01 Only SUPER.SUPER should have WRITE or PURGE access to **/etc/profile**.

The profile.sample File

HP provides a **profile.sample** file, which resides in the same directory. It provides examples of common settings. Do not make changes to the sample file, or they will be overwritten when a new operating system version is installed.

BP-ETC-PROFILE-02 Only the SUPER.SUPER should have WRITE or PURGE access to **/etc/profile.sample**.

$HOME/.profile Files

Individual **$HOME/.profile** files reside in each user's home directory. Variables in these files affect only the individual user's shell. The security policy will determine whether or not users are allowed to alter their personal **$HOME/.profile** file. Values in the individual files overrule settings in the **/etc/profile** file because they are executed after it.

$HOME/ .profile files are the OSS equivalent of the Guardian TACLCSTM files, but unlike TACLCSTM files, the **.profile** is not created automatically.

RISK   If the security of the **.profile** file permits users other than the owner WRITE or PURGE access, these users could modify the file or PURGE it and replace it with a new one.

RISK   The **.profile** commands will override similar commands in the **global /etc/profile**.

RISK   The **.profile** file is created using the user's default security. The default security may not be adequate.

RISK   The **.profile** file can contain PATH commands to alter the location that the shell uses to find a program file when a RUN command is issued without fully qualifying file name, which is the common practice.

RISK   SUPER Group members should not be able to alter their **.profile** files. They could put destructive commands in the file that will execute prior to the shell's first prompt.

BP-OSS-PROFILE-02   The individual **$HOME/.profile** files should be secured so that only the user and SUPER.SUPER can READ or WRITE to them.

RISK   If a script is executed within a **.profile**, the script file must be also secured so that only authorized users can WRITE or PURGE it. Otherwise someone could rename it and then install another file with the same name or simply insert commands that execute a Trojan Horse program by invoking the macro via the **.profile** file.

Environment Variables

The OSS environment has many variables that are used to define the characteristics of a shell session. These variables are most often defined in the **/etc/profile** and **$HOME/.profile** files. For a full list of the variables available and their function, consult the **man** pages for **sh** and **environ**. Fig. 10.7 includes some of the more commonly used environmental variables.

Figure 10.7
Environmental variables.

Variable	Description
EDITOR	Specifies the default editor.
ERRNO	Specifies the value of the error of the most recently failed system call. The value of ERRNO is system-dependent and is used for debugging.
FCEDIT	Specifies the default editor for the fc command. (The default value is **/bin/ed**.)
FPATH	Defines the search path for function definitions.
HISTFILE	Defines the pathname of the file used to store the command history.
HISTSIZE	Defines the maximum number of previously entered commands that can be held by the history file. (The default value is 128.)
HOME	Specifies the default value of the **cd** command.
LOGNAME	Returns the Guardian logon name of the current user.
OLDPWD	Returns the working directory set by the last execution of the **cd** command.
PATH	Specifies the directories and the order the system will search for execute commands. (The default value is **/bin**.)
PPID	Returns the process number of the parent of the current shell process.
PS1	Specifies the primary prompt string.
PWD	Specifies the current working directory.
UTILSGE	Determines the visibility of the Guardian /G and Expand /E filesets to the following commands: **chgrp**, **chmod**, **chown**, **cp**, **find**, **ls**, **mv**, **pax**, and **rm**.

AP-POLICY-PROFILE-01   The Corporate security policy should determine whether or not users are allowed to modify their own $HOME/.profile file.

Auditing User Activity

Auditing of OSS user logons is determined by the AUDIT-AUTHENTI-CATE-PASS and AUDIT-AUTHENTICATE-FAIL values in either the Safeguard Globals or the individual user records.

The Safeguard AUDIT-CLIENT-SERVICE Global attribute must be ON to audit any user activity within the OSS environment. The fileset must have AUDITENABLED set to ON.

BP-SAFEGARD-GLOBAL-21 Set AUDIT-CLIENT-SERVICE = ON if OSS is in use on the system.

BP-OSS-AUDIT-01   If applications are running in the OSS environment, AUDITENABLED must be ON for all filesets containing application data and program files.

If AUDIT-CLIENT-SERVICE is ON and the AUDITENABLED parameter is ON for the relevant fileset, the OSS name server submits audit records for certain OSS commands. Some of the commands that generate audit records are:

    mkdir
    chmod
    chown
    cp
    kill
    link
    rm
    rmdir
    su

The contents of each audit record depends on which operation is being performed and whether or not the command failed because of a security violation.

RISK   In cases where the operation is terminated because of an error and a security ruling has not yet been obtained, no auditing is performed.

	Discovery Questions	Look here:
USER-POLICY	Does policy determine whether or not OSS users are assigned Guardian userids or Safeguard aliases?	Policy
FILE-POLICY	Does policy require auditing in the OSS environment?	Policy
FILE-POLICY	Does policy require that successful attempts to access OSS processes be audited?	Policy
FILE-POLICY	Does policy require that failed attempts to access OSS processes be audited?	Policy
FILE-POLICY	Does policy require that successful attempts to logon be audited?	Policy
FILE-POLICY	Does policy require that failed attempts to logon be audited?	Policy
OSS-FILESET	Is AUDITENABLED set ON for all filesets?	Scf
SAFEGARD-GLOBAL-29	Is AUDIT-CLIENT-SERVICE set ON?	Safecom
SAFEGARD-GLOBAL-34	Is AUDIT-AUTHENTICATE-PASS set to the appropriate value?	Safecom
SAFEGARD-GLOBAL-35	Is AUDIT-AUTHENTICATE-FAIL set to the appropriate value?	Safecom
SAFEGARD-GLOBAL-42	Is AUDIT-PROCESS-ACCESS-PASS set to the appropriate value?	Safecom
SAFEGARD-GLOBAL-43	Is AUDIT-PROCESS-ACCESS-FAIL set to the appropriate value?	Safecom

OSS Subsystem Components

The OSS subsystem is made up of processes, configuration files, and tools.

The OSS Subsystem Processes

The OSS Monitor controls the following processes:

> OSS message queue server
> OSS name server(s)
> OSS sockets local server
> OSS transport agent server

The following servers must be started via SCF:

> OSS File Manager
> OSS Pipe Server

The OSS Monitor

$SYSTEM.SYSnn.OSMON is the object file for the OSS Monitor process. OSSMON is the heart of the OSS Subsystem. It runs in the Guardian space but is used to alter the characteristics of OSS objects and to make them available or unavailable for use. It manages the OSS subsystem processes.

When Open System Services is first installed, the OSS Monitor adds the default OSS name server for the root fileset the first time it is run. The OSS sockets local server, OSS message-queue server, and OSS transport agent servers are added, if needed, after the OSS Monitor process is started.

The OSS file system maps OSS files onto the physical Guardian disks.

The OSS monitor process manages most of the OSS processes and enables the OSS system to define OSS volumes.

RISK The OSS Monitor terminates immediately if $ZPMON is already running or is given a different process name.

BP-FILE-OSSMON-01 The OSS monitor process name must be $ZPMON.

AP-ADVICE-OSSMON-01 Put procedures in place to ensure that the OSS Monitor is started with the correct process name and owner during system startup.

RISK   OSSMON contains privileged procedures.

BP-FILE-OSSMON-01   HP strongly recommends that OSSMON not be licensed, because only SUPER.SUPER should start, manage, or stop the OSS monitor process.

AP-ADVICE-OSSMON-02   HP recommends specifying processors for the OSS Monitor that are not used by the FSCK utility or any name servers.

The OSS Monitor controls the following processes:

OSS message queue server (ZMSGQ; $ZMSGQ)

OSS name server(s) (NS; $ZPNS)

OSS sockets local server (OSSLS; $ZPLS)

OSS transport agent server (OSSTA; $ZTAnn)

The OSS Monitor and the servers it manages are all configured and managed via SCF OSS Monitor commands.

SCF communicates with OSSMON via the Subsystem Programmatic Interface (SPI). When OSS is installed, the OSS Product Module for SCF is also installed in $SYSTEM.SYSTEM. It implements a set of SPI messages specific to the OSS environment that are returned to the OSS Monitor.

The Subsystem and Process Attributes for the OSS Monitor are:

The subsystem ID is 143.

The device type is 24.

The device subtype is 0.

The first time the OSS Monitor is run after the OSS subsystem is installed, it adds the default OSS name server for the root fileset and the other three servers. Thereafter, if any of these processes stop, the monitor will restart them.

All but the transport agent server can be run as fault-tolerant process pairs.

Please refer to OSS Monitor Process section of the Guardian Gazette for more information on securing OSSMON and these servers.

OSS File Manager (OSSFM)

$SYSTEM.SYSnn.OSSFM is the object file for the OSS File Manager. The File Manager process manages the OSS file-system cache and satisfies OSS memory management requests from the NonStop Kernel memory manager.

There should be one file manager process per CPU. Each process starts automatically when its processor starts.

BP-FILE-NS-01   The process names are $ZFMnn, where nn represents the CPU number.

AP-OSSMON-OSSFM-01   The file manager processes can be stopped, but all applications with open OSS files should be stopped first.

OSS Message Queue (ZMSGQ)

The OSS Message Queue process manages the OSS message queue. The Message Queue server object file is $SYSTEM.SYSnn.ZMSGQ.

BP-FILE-ZMSGQ-01   The default name of the Message Queue process is $ZMSGQ.

Message queues are linked lists of messages used by programmers to pass data from one process to another.

The OSS Message Queue server must be added to the ZOSSSERV file after the OSS Monitor process is started. Use SCF to add the server and alter its configuration parameters.

OSS Name Server (NS)

$SYSTEM.SYSnn.NS is the object file for the Name Server.

Each OSS file and AF_UNIX socket has an underlying Guardian filename. Because the two names are different, the OSS environment must have a way to map (resolve) the OSS pathname to the Guardian name. This is the task of the OSS Name Servers. They translate the OSS file name to the ZYQ Guardian subvolume where the file actually resides.

Each fileset has a name server and a fileset catalog. These are defined in the ZOSSFSET file. When an application or user in the OSS environment opens an OSS file, the OSSMON reads the ZOSSFSET file to determine the fileset's name server. It then sends the Name Server the fileset's catalog location. The name server uses the catalog to locate (resolve) the file's actual Guardian subvolume (ZYQ) location.

Every fileset must have a name server. When OSSMON is first started, it creates the name server entry for the root fileset, $ZPNS, in the ZOSSFSET automatically. More name servers should be added, as necessary, to share the work of locating OSS files.

BP-FILE-ZMSGQ-01 The default process name for the Name Server for the root fileset is $ZPNS.

A fileset can only have one name server, but a single name server can manage multiple filesets.

AP-ADVICE-NS-02 HP recommends that each name server should have both primary and backup CPU numbers assigned, so that no single CPU failure will stop Name Server processing.

AP-ADVICE-NS-03 HP recommends specifying CPUs for Name Servers that are not used by either the OSS Monitor or the FSCK utility.

The OSS Sockets Local Server process provides applications with access to OSS sockets. Sockets route data between application processes via a transport agent. A transport agent routes data within a single processor.

Sockets

Sockets are end points for stream-oriented communication. Sockets route data between application processes using Transport Agents and Transport Providers:

> Transport Agent processes route data among sockets application processes for a single processor; each processor has its own copy of the Transport Agent Server.

> Transport Provider processes called Sockets Local Servers provide routing services for one socket address family.

Each socket has a file name.

There are two kinds of OSS sockets. They are named after the address families that use them to send and receive data:

AF_UNIX sockets, sometimes called local or UNIX domain sockets, allow an application program to use an OSS socket as if it were a named disk file or a named pipe.

AF_INET sockets, sometimes called Internet domain sockets, allow application programs to communicate with each other or with terminals using the underlying TCP/IP processes that also provide Telserv terminal access to the system.

OSS sockets facilities are separate from the sockets facilities provided within the Guardian environment.

OSS Pipe Server (OSSPS)

$SYSTEM.SYSnn.OSSPS is the object file for the OSS Pipe Server processes. These servers support the transfer of data between OSS processes that use pipes or FIFOs to transfer data between processors.

BP-PROCESS-OSSPS-01   There should be one Pipe Server per CPU.

BP-PROCESS-OSSPS-02   The default process name for pipe servers is $ZPPnn where nn is the CPU number.

Each OSS Transport Agent server is automatically started when the processor it runs on is started. The processes can be stopped and restarted via the SCF OSS Monitor commands.

OSS Sockets Local Server (OSSLS)

$SYSTEM.SYSnn.OSSLS is the OSS Sockets Local Server process. This server provides applications with access to AF_UNIX sockets, which route data between application processes using a process called a Transport Agent.
BP-PROCESS-OSSLS-01   The default process name for the OSS Sockets Local Server is $ZPLS.

BP-PROCESS-OSSLS-01   The Sockets Local Server should run as a fault-tolerant process pair.

The Sockets Local Server can be stopped and started via the SCF OSS Monitor commands. Its configuration is stored in the ZOSSSERV file.

The OSS Sockets Local Server must be added to the ZOSSSERV file after the OSS Monitor process is started. Use SCF to add the server and alter its configuration parameters.

OSS Transport Agent Server (OSSTA)

$SYSTEM.SYSnn.OSSTA is the object file for the OSS Transport Agent Server. The Transport Server is used for OSS sockets communication. The agents routes data between processes within a single CPU. There is one transport agent server per CPU.

BP-PROCESS-OSSTA-01   The default process names are $ZTAnn where nn is the CPU number.

Each OSS Transport Agent Server is automatically started when the CPU it runs in is started. The processes can be started and stopped via SCF OSS Monitor commands, but they cannot be added, altered, or removed.

OSSTTY System Utility

$SYSTEM.SYSnn.OSSTTY is the object file for the OSSTTY utility. This utility enables OSS processes to interact with the Guardian environment. It provides a way for OSS processes to redirect their standard **input**, **output**, and **error** files to Guardian processes. The standard output can also be directed to Guardian EDIT files.

BP-PROCESS-OSSTTY-01   HP recommends that the OSSTTY process be named $ZTTY.

BP-PROCESS-OSSTTY-02   The $ZTTY process should be running.

A Guardian process has three standard files that normally possess the structure of an EDIT file: the STDIN, STDOUT, and STDERR files. When entered at a TACL prompt, they are usually referred to as the IN file, the OUT file, and the TERM file. By default, these files are associated with the user's home terminal. However, the command that runs a Guardian process can redirect those files to Guardian processes or files.

OSS processes use a similar set of default files, **stdin**, **stdout**, and **stderr**, but with a different file format: unstructured standard files. However, an OSS user normally launches an OSS shell by logging in through Telserv. That access method leaves the OSS standard files associated with the user's terminal but allows no way for those files to be redirected to Guardian processes or files. The OSSTTY utility makes the redirection possible.

The OSS **stdin**, **stdout**, and **stderr** are unstructured standard files, but otherwise are the equivalent of the Guardian STDIN, STDOUT and STDERR (EDIT type) files.

OSSTTY can be started via a TACL or OSH command. It can be started by an individual user in the Guardian environment, or through the OSH **osstty** command, or directly by an OSS administrator.

Telserv provides two kinds of windows, static and dynamic:

A static window is created via SCF and opened with Telserv and with OSSTTY. It can exist independently of a connection to the OSS environment. (The OSSTTY windows #stdin, #stdout, and #stderr are considered to be static because they are preconfigured and cannot be changed while OSSTTY is running.)

A dynamic window is opened by Telserv in response to a connection request. OSSTTY does not support dynamic windows.

Once started, OSSTTY becomes the standard input, standard output, and standard error of the OSS process, and redirects input, output, and error data to the Guardian targets specified as run options or through redirection operators.

OSS Configuration Files

There are three primary configuration files to manage OSS:

ZOSSFSET
ZOSSPARM
ZOSSSERV

ZOSSFSET File

The $SYSTEM.ZXOSSMON.ZOSSFSET file is an Enscribe-key-sequenced file. It contains information about filesets. It is updated via SCF OSS Monitor commands. Changes to the file take effect only when the name server assigned to the affected fileset is stopped and restarted.

The file contains two types of entries:

The names and catalog volumes of every fileset

The characteristics of the OSS Sockets Local Server Process, $ZPLS

The file is created by OSSMON when it is started for the first time. OSSMON adds only the Name Server for the root fileset and the parameters for the Sockets Local Server. Therefore, this file needs to be configured before the root fileset is first mounted or before the first OSS process is started.

ZOSSPARM File

The $SYSTEM.ZXOSSMON.ZOSSPARM file is an Enscribe key-sequenced file. It contains the subsystem configuration database for the OSS Monitor. The default file is created by the OSS Monitor and contains the entry for the root fileset's Name Server process, $ZPNS.

The file must be present before the root fileset is first mounted and before the root Name Server ($ZPNS) is started.

The file is updated via SCF OSS Monitor commands. Changes take effect immediately.

ZOSSSERV Configuration File

The $SYSTEM.ZXOSSMON.ZOSSSERV file is an Enscribe key-sequenced file. It stores the characteristics of all OSS name server processes. The default file is created by the OSS Monitor and initially contains the entry for the root fileset's name server process, $ZPNS.

The file must be present before the root fileset is first mounted and before the root name server ($ZPNS) is started.

The file is updated via SCF OSS Monitor commands. Changes take effect only when the affected name server is stopped and restarted.

There must always be a $ZPLS entry for the OSS sockets local server process, $ZPLS, in the ZOSSSERV file. You cannot remove the OSS Sockets Local Server, the OSS Message-Queue Server, or an OSS Transport Agent server.

OSS Gazette a to z

The Gazette consists of a section per program, process or subsystem, containing a discussion of the object, security concerns, and best practice recommendations.

The naming conventions are:

User Program	Object files that users can execute
System Program	Object files that other programs, not users, execute
Shell Command	A built-in shell command that does not open a new shell session to execute
System Utility	Object files that are generally used by system administrators or operators for system-oriented functions
Configuration File	Text files, such as libraries, DLLs, or *CSTM files, which are used by system administrators
Subsystem	A set of System Programs and Configuration Files such as inetd, SSH, or Samba
Application	A subsystem installed and run as an application

BP numbering conventions make the OSSOWN and OSSLOC numeric suffixes always the same. The suffix is *based on the depth of the directory* where the file resides:

/etc	01
/usr/local/bin/ssh	04
/usr/local/man	03

So, if a file resides in **/etc** and should be owned by SUPER.SUPER, the OSSLOC and the OSSOWN numeric suffixes will both be 01:

BP-ETC-OSSOWN-01   **magic** should be owned by SUPER.SUPER.

BP-ETC-OSSLOC-01   **magic** resides in **/etc.**

If a file resides in **/usr/local/bin/ssh** and should be owned by SUPER.SUPER, the OSSLOC and the OSSOWN numeric suffixes will both be 04:

BP-ETC-OSSOWN-04   **ssh_config** should be owned by SUPER. SUPER.

BP-ETC-OSSLOC-04   **ssh_config** resides in **/usr/local/bin/ssh.**

If a file resides in **/usr/local/man** and should be owned by SUPER.SUPER, the OSSLOC and the OSSOWN numeric suffixes will both be 03:

BP-USR-OSSOWN-03   **cat5** should be owned by SUPER.SUPER.

BP-USR-OSSLOC-03   **cat5** resides in **/usr/local/man.**

When the text states that a user must have READ access to a particular file, it implies that the file's entire directory hierarchy grants the appropriate access.

Directory locations are designated as DIRLOC and DIROWN. The numeric identifier on directories will also reflect the depth of the directory:

BP-USR-DIROWN-01   **/usr** should be owned by SUPER.SUPER.

BP-USR-DIRLOC-01   **/usr** resides in the root directory (/).

BP-USR-DIROWN-02   /local should be owned by SUPER.SUPER.

BP-USR-DIRLOC-02   /local resides in /usr.

In OSS, the user's home directory is usually referred to as either $HOME or with a tilde (~). This book will use the $HOME convention. In BPs, it will appear as:

BP-HOME-PROFILE-01 Each user's .profile file should be owned by the user.

BP-HOME-OSSLOC-00   Each user's .profile file resides $HOME.

BP-HOME-OSSLOC-00   Each id_dsa file resides in $HOME/.ssh.

$HOME always has an OSSOWN and OSSLOC of 00:

BP-HOME-DIRSEC-00 $HOME should be secured 700 (rwx --- ---).

BP-HOME-DIROWN-00 $HOME should be owned by the individual user.

BP-HOME-DIRLOC-00 $HOME resides in the assigned file tree.

OSS Commands

Built-in Shell Commands

Built-in commands are executed by the shell itself. They run entirely within the current shell process; they do not start a new shell process when they execute.

Several of these commands also have program versions with object files (primarily residing in /bin). The built-in command is always the default. To invoke the program rather than the built-in command, a user must use the full pathname to invoke the object file version.

RISK There is always the possibility that the object file version differs from the built-in version.

RISK Though it is possible to secure the object files, there is currently no way to prevent a user from executing a built-in shell command.

Built-in Command	Object File?	Description
alias	Yes - **/bin/alias**	Lists or defines an alias.
bg	Yes - **/bin/bg**	Puts jobs in the background.
break		Exits from an enclosing loop.
cd	Yes - **/bin/cd**	Changes the current working directory.
continue		Resumes the next iteration of an enclosing loop.
echo	Yes* - **/bin/echo**	Writes its arguments to the standard output file.
eval		Reads arguments and executes commands.
exec	Yes - **/bin/exec**	Executes a command.
exit		Exits the shell.
export		Exports variables.
fc	Yes - **/bin/fc**	Lists, edits, and re-executes commands previously entered in a shell.
fg	Yes - **/bin/fg**	Brings specified jobs to the foreground.
getopts	Yes - **/bin/getopts**	Parses command-line flags and arguments.
hash		Affects the shell's memory of the location of the utilities.
history		Displays a list of previously executed commands (the history list).
jobs	Yes - **/bin/jobs**	Lists information about jobs.
kill	Yes* - **/bin/kill**	Sends a signal to a running process.
let		Evaluates arithmetic expressions.
print		Provides shell output.
pwd	Yes* - **/bin/pwd**	Displays the current directory pathname.

(Continued)

Built-in Command	Object File?	Description
read	Yes* - **/bin/read**	Reads one line from the standard input file.
readonly		Marks specified names as read-only.
return		Causes a shell function to return to the invoking script.
set		Sets shell parameters.
shift		Sets positional parameters.
times		Times the execution of a command.
trap		Specifies a command and signals for its execution by the shell.
type		Writes a description of a file's type.
typeset		Sets attributes and values for shell parameters.
umask	Yes - **/bin/umask**	Sets a file mode creation mask.
unalias	Yes - **/bin/unalias**	Removes names from the alias list.
unexpand	Yes - **/bin/unexpand**	Replaces tabs or space characters.
unset		Erases parameter values.
wait	Yes - **/bin/wait**	Awaits process completion.
whence		Tells how a name would be interpreted if used as a command.
add_define		Creates one or more DEFINEs for the current OSS shell.
del_define		Deletes one or more DEFINEs for the current OSS shell.
info_define		Displays attributes and values of existing DEFINEs.
reset_define		Restores a DEFINE's attributes to their initial settings.
set_define		Sets values for DEFINE attributes in the working attribute.
show_define		Displays values of attributes.

* = Documented by HP

Programs Grouped by Function

OSS programs can be grouped by function. Please refer to discussion of each command in the OSS Gazette for more information.

Archiving

The following commands are used for archiving:

ar	Creates and maintains archives and libraries
cpio	Copies files to and from archive storage
pax	Extracts, writes, and lists archive files
pinstall	Invokes a Guardian process that installs OSS files to an OSS file hierarchy (this is actually a TACL command)
tar	Manipulates tape archives

Comparing Files and Directories

The following commands are used for comparing files:

awk	Manipulates text and matches patterns in files
cmp	Compares two files
comm	Compares two sorted files
diff	Compares text files
dircmp	Compares two directories

Compressing and Uncompressing Files

The following commands are used for manipulating files and directories:

compress	Compresses data
expand	Replaces tabs or space characters
pack	Compresses files
uncompress	Expands data
unexpand	Replaces tabs or space characters in a file

| unpack | Expands files compressed by the pack command |
| zcat | Compresses and expands data |

Displaying Files and File Information

The following commands are used for displaying files.

cat	Concatenates or displays files
cut	Displays selected parts from each line of a file
gname	Displays the Guardian equivalent of an OSS filename
head	Displays the beginning of files
line displays it	Reads one line from the standard input file and
ls	Lists and generates statistics for files
more	Displays a file one screenful at a time
pname	Displays the OSS equivalent of a Guardian file-name
pr	Writes a file to the standard output file
printf	Writes formatted output

Editing and Text Manipulation

The following commands are used for text editing.

ed	Edits a file line by line
ex	Edits lines in a file interactively
sed	Edits selected lines within a file
vi	Edits files (screen editor)
awk	Manipulates text and matches patterns in files
strings	Finds printable strings in files
wc	Counts lines, words, characters, and bytes

File Security

The following commands are used for managing file owners and permissions:

chgrp	Changes group ownership of files and directories
chmod	Changes permission codes of files and directories
chown	Changes the owner and group owner of files and directories

Help

The following commands are used to view OSS documentation:

apropos	Lists commands by keyword
man	Displays reference pages
whatis	Describes a command's function

Printing and Formatting

The following commands are used for printing and formatting:

cancel	Removes job requests from the line printer spooling queue
jobs	Lists information about printing jobs
kill	Removes printing jobs from the spooling queue
lp	Sends files to a printer
· lpstat	Displays line printer and print job status information
print	Provides shell output

Searching

The following commands are used for searching, sorting, comparing, and listing operations:

find	Finds files matching an expression
grep	Search a file for a pattern
egrep	Search a file for a pattern

fgrep	Search a file for a pattern
strings	Finds printable strings in files
uniq	Removes or lists repeated lines in a file

Sorting

The following commands are used for sorting operations:

| sort | Sorts or merges files |

$HOME Directory

In OSS, the user's home directory is usually referred to as either $HOME or with a tilde (~). In this book, we will use the $HOME convention.

$HOME directories should be secured 700 (rwx --- ---) or 744 (rwx r-- r--) at the most lenient.

BP-HOME-OSSDIR-01   The system administrator should designate an appropriate directory tree where all users' home directories will be placed.

BP-HOME-OSSDIR-02   Just as in the Guardian environment, home directories should not be shared.

Your security policy should state whether or not users are allowed to share files in their home directory with other members of their group.

BP-HOME-OSSDIR-03   Even if files can be shared, they should only be writable by the owner: 740 (rwx r-- ---) or 744 (rwx r-- r--).

Securing $HOME

BP-HOME-DIRSEC-00   Individual $HOME directories should be secured 700 (rwx --- ---).

BP-HOME-DIROWN-00   Individual $HOME directories should be owned by the individual user.

BP-HOME-DIRLOC-00   Individual **$HOME** directories may reside any appropriate location.

	Discovery Questions	Look here:
HOME-DIROWN-00	Are all **$HOME** diretories owned by the appropriate user?	ls -al
HOME-DIRLOC-00	Are all **$HOME** diretories located in the appropriate directory tree?	ls -al
HOME-DIRSEC-00	Are all **$HOME** diretories secured correctly?	ls -al

Related Topics

sh

$HOME/.shh Directory

Files in the $HOME/.ssh directory contain SSH key files and other confidential information. This directory should be owned by the user and not be accessible to any other user.

BP-HOME-SSHDIR-01   All **$HOME/.ssh** directories should be owned and accessible only by the user. This directory contains SSH key files and other confidential information.

Securing $HOME/.ssh

BP-HOME-DIRSEC-00   Individual **$HOME/.ssh** directories should be secured 700 (rwx --- ---).

BP-HOME-DIROWN-00   Individual **$HOME/.ssh** directories should be owned by the individual user.

BP-HOME-DIRLOC-00   Individual **$HOME/.ssh** directories may reside any appropriate location.

	Discovery Questions	Look here:
HOME-DIROWN-00	Are all **$HOME/.ssh** directories owned by the appropriate user?	ls -al
HOME-DIRLOC-00	Are all **$HOME/.ssh** directories located in the appropriate directory tree?	ls -al
HOME-DIRSEC-00	Are all **$HOME/.ssh** directories secured correctly?	ls -al

Related Topics

$HOME

ssh

alias User Program

The **/bin/alias** program is used to define program aliases. It can also be used to list all the aliases in effect in the current session.

Users can create aliases on a session-by-session basis. Permanent aliases are defined in **.profile** files.

Aliases defined in the **/etc/profile** file are global.

Aliases defined in individual users' **$HOME/.profile** files are unique to the user.

For detailed information on creating and using aliases, please refer to the chapter on the **sh** program in HP's *OSS Shell and Utilities Reference Manual*.

There are two versions of the **alias** program that are identical except for the following:

The **/bin/alias** program starts a new shell process.

The built-in shell **alias** command doesn't start a new shell process.

The built-in shell **alias** command is the default. To invoke the program rather than the built-in command, you must use the full pathname to invoke **/bin/alias**.

unalias User Program

The **/bin/unalias** program removes command alias definitions. There is a single command line option which determines whether or not the definitions are permanently removed:

Entering the **unalias** without an argument removes aliases from the shell's alias list. The aliases are, therefore, permanently removed.

Entering **unalias** with the -a option removes all alias definitions from the current shell but not from the shell's alias list. The aliases are, therefore, not permanently removed.

There are two versions of the **unalias** command that are identical except for the following:

The **unalias** program starts a new shell process.

The built-in shell **unalias** command doesn't start a new shell process.

The built-in shell **unalias** command is the default. To invoke the program rather than the built-in command, you must use the full pathname to invoke **unalias**.

Securing /bin/alias and /bin/unalias

BP-BIN-ALIAS-01	alias should be secured 711 (rwx --x --x).
BP-BIN-OSSOWN-01	alias should be owned by SUPER.SUPER.
BP-BIN-OSSLOC-01	alias resides in /bin.
BP-BIN-ALIAS-02	unalias should be secured 711 (rwx --x --x).
BP-BIN-OSSOWN-01	unalias should be owned by SUPER.SUPER.
BP-BIN-OSSLOC-01	unalias resides in /bin.

	Discovery Questions	Look here:
BIN-OSSOWN-01	Is /bin/alias owned by SUPER.SUPER?	ls -al
BIN-OSSOWN-01	Is /bin/unalias owned by SUPER.SUPER?	ls -al

(Continued)

	Discovery Questions	Look here:
BIN-ALIAS-01	Is /bin/alias secured correctly?	ls -al
BIN-ALIAS-02	Is /bin/unalias secured correctly?	ls -al

Related Topics

sh

apropos User Program

The /bin/apropos program lists reference pages which contain a specified string. It works just like the man program with the -k flag.

AP-ADVICE-APROPOS-01   Users should be able to view man pages.

Securing /bin/apropos

BP-BIN-APROPOS-01   apropos should be secured 711 (rwx --x --x)

BP-BIN-OSSOWN-01   apropos should be owned by SUPER.
SUPER

BP-BIN-OSSLOC-01   apropos resides in /bin

	Discovery Questions	Look here:
BIN-OSSOWN-01	Is /bin/apropos owned by SUPER.SUPER?	ls -al
BIN-APROPOS-01	Is /bin/apropos secured correctly?	ls -al

Related Topics

man
whatis

ar User Program

The /bin/ar program creates and maintains archives made up of object files. It accepts OSS files, Guardian type 100 and 180 files, and TNS/R native object files.

RISK A single archive file should not include both OSS and Guardian objects, but /bin/ar will not prevent a user from creating such an archive.

RISK Archives that contain data from production files can be used to obtain sensitive information.

AP-ADVICE-AR-01 Archives should be at least as well secured as the files being archived.

RISK Archives files can be moved to a system with less security, leaving the information vulnerable to unauthorized access to the data.

RISK Archived files can be restored, overwriting existing files.

RISK Since archived files can contain sensitive data, protection of the utilities that can read or copy the data must be considered.

AP-ADVICE-AR-02 Only authorized personnel should be permitted to archive files.

Securing /bin/ar

BP-BIN-AR-01   ar should be secured 711 (rwx --x --x)

BP-BIN-OSSOWN-01   ar should be owned by SUPER.SUPER

BP-BIN-OSSLOC-01   ar resides in /bin

	Discovery Questions	Look here:
OSS-POLICY	Who is allowed to archive files?	Policy
BIN-OSSOWN-01	Is /bin/ar owned by SUPER.SUPER?	ls -al
BIN-AR-01	Is /bin/ar secured correctly?	ls -al

Related Topics

c89

make

nld

nm

strip

at Subsystem

There are three ways to control the scheduling of OSS programs and scripts. They are useful for running jobs that are especially time-consuming. The job scheduling programs are:

/bin/at   Runs a job at a time the user specifies. **/bin/at** jobs are once-only; the scheduled programs are executed at the specified time and not repeated.

/bin/batch   Runs a job at a time determined by the operating system. **/bin/batch** jobs are once-only; the program is executed and not repeated.

/bin/cron   Runs a job at a time the user specifies. The same job will then be run at the configured intervals until it is deleted from the relevant **crontab** file.

/bin/at runs a program or script at a later, user-specified, time. It reads from an input file or accepts as arguments the programs to be run at a later time.

If a file specified on the command line is an executable, **/bin/at** assumes that the job consists only of this program.

If a file specified on the program line is not executable, **/bin/at** assumes that the file contains the job instructions.

Variables in the shell environment, the current directory, any **umask** and **ulimit** settings are retained when the programs are run.

at Subsystem Components

The **at** subsystem is composed of the following components:

at.allow and at.deny files

atjobs directory and atjob files

logs

.proto file

queuedefs file

at.allow and at.deny Files

The **/usr/lib/cron/at.allow** and **/usr/lib/cron/at.deny** files determine which userids can submit jobs using the **/bin/at** program. When a user invokes the **/bin/at** program, it checks for the existence of these files:

The **at.allow** file is checked first. If it exists, only userids listed in it can use **/bin/at** to submit jobs.

Only if the **at.allow** file doesn't exist does **/bin/at** check for the existence of the **at.deny** file. If the **at.deny** file exists, userids listed in it cannot use **/bin/at** to submit jobs, but everyone else can.

If neither the **at.allow** or **at.deny** files exist, then only users with execute access for **/bin/at** can submit **at** jobs.

HP provides an **at.deny.sample** file, which resides in the same directory.

RISK   The **/usr/lib/cron/at.deny.sample** file will be overwritten with each operating system upgrade.

AP-AT-ADVICE-01   Do not change the sample file to customize it to your environment. Make changes in a **/usr/lib/cron/at.deny** file created by copying the sample file.

BP-BIN-AT-01   The **at.deny** file is the most common method of controlling the use of the at subsystem because the majority of users are allowed to submit jobs.

BP-BIN-AT-02   Unless required in your environment, the **at.allow** file should not exist.

BP-BIN-AT-03   If the **at.allow** file does exist, all userids intended to run **/bin/at** *must* be included in the file or they will be unable to submit jobs.

at job files

The job queue for the **/bin/at subsystem** is the **/var/spool/cron/atjobs** directory. When a user submits a job, a job file is placed in it. The job filename will be the user's uppercase user name (GROUPNAME.USER-NAME).nnnnnnnnn. where n is a number.

```
Example:
/var/spool/cron/atjobs/SUPER.SUPER.1132078800.a
```

In the example above, the job file is **SUPER.SUPER.1132078800.a**. It resides in SUPER.SUPER's subdirectory in the **/var/spool/cron/atjobs** directory.

The system automatically secures the files, granting the job creator READ access only.

BP-VAR-AT-02   **atjob** files to be executed should be owned by the submitter and should only be writable by the owner.

log

/bin/at logs its activities to the **/var/adm/cron/log** file. Please refer to the *OSS Gazette* section on the **cron** subsystem for more information.

.proto file

The **/var/adm/cron/.proto** file contains shell commands required to provide the correct **cron** shell environment for **at** and **batch** jobs. Please refer to the *OSS Gazette* section on the **cron** subsystem for more information.

queuedefs file

The **/var/adm/cron/queuedefs** file configures the task queues to be used for the **at**, **batch**, and **cron** programs. Please refer to the *OSS Gazette* section on the **cron** subsystem for more information.

Related Programs

The **/bin/atq** program prints the queue of **/bin/at** jobs scheduled to run at a later time. Please refer to the *OSS Gazette* section on **/bin/atq** for more information.

The **/bin/atrm** program removes jobs queued by the **/bin/at** program. Please refer to the *OSS Gazette* section on **/bin/atrm** for more information.

Securing /bin/at

BP-BIN-AT-01	**at** should be secured 4711 (rws --x --x).
BP-BIN-SETUID-01	**at** should have the **setuid** attribute.
BP-BIN-OSSOWN-01	**at** should be owned by SUPER.SUPER.
BP-BIN-OSSLOC-01	**at** resides in **/bin**.
BP-USR-AT-02	**at.allow** should be secured 600 (rw- --- ---).
BP-USR-OSSOWN-03	**at.allow** should be owned by SUPER.SUPER.
BP-USR-OSSLOC-03	**at.allow** resides in **/usr/lib/cron**.
BP-USR-AT-03	**at.deny** should be secured 600 (rw- --- ---).
BP-USR-OSSOWN-03	**at.deny** should be owned by SUPER.SUPER.
BP-USR-OSSLOC-03	**at.deny** resides in **/usr/lib/cron**.
BP-VAR-AT-04	Individual **atjob** files should be secured 400 (r-- --- ---).
BP-VAR-OSSOWN-04	Individual **atjob** files should be owned by each user.
BP-VAR-OSSLOC-04	Individual **atjob** files reside in **/var/spool/cron/atjobs**.
BP-VAR-DIRSEC-04	The **atjobs** directory should be secured 755 (rwx r-x r-x).

BP-VAR-DIROWN-03   The **atjobs** directory should be owned by SUPER.SUPER.

BP-VAR-DIRLOC-03   The **atjobs** directory resides in **/var/spool/cron**.

	Discovery Questions	Look here:
OSS-POLICY	Does the security policy mandate the use of the **/usr/lib/cron/at.allow** file?	Policy
OSS-POLICY	Does the security policy mandate the use of the **/usr/lib/cron/at.deny** file?	Policy
BIN-OSSOWN-01	Is **/bin/at** owned by SUPER.SUPER?	ls -al
USR-OSSOWN-03	Is **/usr/lib/cron/at.allow** owned by SUPER.SUPER?	ls -al
USR-OSSOWN-03	Is **/usr/lib/cron/at.deny** owned by SUPER.SUPER?	ls -al
VAR-DIROWN-03	Is the **/var/spool/cron/atjobs** directory owned by SUPER.SUPER?	ls -al
BIN-AT-01	Is **/bin/at** secured correctly?	ls -al
USR-AT-02	If **/usr/lib/cronat.allow** exists, is it secured correctly?	ls -al
USR-AT-03	If **/usr/lib/cronat.deny** exists, is it secured correctly?	ls -al
VAR-DIRSEC-04	Is the **/var/spool/cron/atjobs** directory secured correctly?	ls -al

Related Topics

atq

atrm

cron

at.allow and at.deny Files

The **/usr/lib/cron/at.allow** and **/usr/lib/cron/at.deny** files determine which userids can submit jobs using the **/bin/at** program.

atjobs Job Queue Directory

The **/var/spool/cron/atjobs** directory is the job queue for the **/bin/at** subsystem. It is also used by **/bin/batch**.

atq User Program

The **/bin/atq** program prints the user's queue of jobs in the **/var/spool/cron/atjobs** directory.

Users can only view their own **atjob** queue.

Securing /bin/atq

BP-BIN-ATQ-01	atq should be secured 4711 (rws --x --x).
BP-BIN-SETUID-01	atq should have the **setuid** attribute.
BP-BIN-OSSOWN-01	atq should be owned by SUPER.SUPER.
BP-BIN-OSSLOC-01	atq resides in **/bin**.

	Discovery Questions	Look here:
BIN-OSSOWN-01	Is **/bin/atq** owned by SUPER.SUPER?	ls -al
BIN-ATQ-01	Is **/bin/atq** secured correctly?	ls -al

Related Topics

at

at.allow

at.deny

atjobs

atrm

cron

atrm User Program

The /bin/atrm program removes jobs created via /bin/at from the user's atjob queue.

Users can only delete their own atjob files.

Securing /bin/atrm

BP-BIN-ATRM-01	atrm should be secured 711 (rwx --x --x).
BP-BIN-SETUID-01	atrm should have the setuid attribute.
BP-BIN-OSSOWN-01	atrm should be owned by SUPER.SUPER.
BP-BIN-OSSLOC-01	atrm resides in /bin.

	Discovery Questions	Look here:
BIN-OSSOWN-01	Is /bin/atrm owned by SUPER.SUPER?	ls -al
BIN-ATRM-01	Is /bin/atrm secured correctly?	ls -al

Related Topics
at
at.allow
at.deny
atjobs files
atq
cron

authorized_keys File

The SSH client stores an authorized_keys file in each user's home directory. It maps the host names and IP addresses of every remote host that the user has connected to with each host's public key. Please refer to the chapter on the **ssh** Subsystem in Part 4, *TCP/IP* for more information or to the *OSS Gazette* section on the **ssh** Subsystem for Best Practice recommendations.

awk User Program

The **/bin/awk** program is a pattern scanning and processing program. It provides a flexible text-manipulation language for reporting.

Users must have READ access to files used to generate the reports.

Securing /bin/awk

BP-BIN-AWK-01	awk should be secured 711 (rwx --x --x).
BP-BIN-OSSOWN-01	awk should be owned by SUPER.SUPER.
BP-BIN-OSSLOC-01	awk resides in /bin.

	Discovery Questions	Look here:
BIN-OSSOWN-01	Is /bin/awk owned by SUPER.SUPER?	ls -al
BIN-AWK-01	Is /bin/awk secured correctly?	ls -al

Related Topics

grep

locale

nawk

printf

sed

banner System Utility

The **/bin/banner** program displays the specified message in large letters on the screen.

Securing /bin/banner

BP-BIN-BANNER-01   **banner** should be secured 711 (rwx --x --x).

BP-BIN-OSSOWN-01   **banner** should be owned by SUPER.SUPER.

BP-BIN-OSSLOC-01   **banner** resides in **/bin**.

	Discovery Questions	Look here:
BIN-OSSOWN-01	Is **/bin/banner** owned by SUPER.SUPER?	ls -al
BIN-BANNER-01	Is **/bin/banner** secured correctly?	ls -al

basename User Program

The **/bin/basename** program returns specified parts of pathnames. It reads the string specified on the command line, deletes the portion from the beginning to the last / (slash), and returns the basefile name. **/bin/basename** is generally used in shell procedures to specify an output filename that is some variation of a specified input filename.

Securing /bin/basename

BP-BIN-BASENAME-01   **basename** should be secured 711 (rwx --x --x).

BP-BIN-OSSOWN-01   **basename** should be owned by SUPER.SUPER.

BP-BIN-OSSLOC-01   **basename** resides in **/bin**.

	Discovery Questions	Look here:
BIN-OSSOWN-01	Is **/bin/basename** owned by SUPER.SUPER?	ls -al
BIN-BASENAME-01	Is **/bin/basename** secured correctly?	ls -al

Related Topics

dirname

batch User Program

There are three ways to control the scheduling of OSS programs and scripts. They are useful for running jobs that are especially time consuming. The job scheduling programs are:

/bin/at	Runs programs at a time that you specify. The **/bin/at** program is a once-only program; the scheduled programs are executed at the specified time but is not repeated.
/bin/batch	Runs programs at a time determined by the operating system. The **/bin/batch** program is a once-only program; the program is executed and not repeated.
/bin/crontab	Submits a schedule of programs to the cron demon for execution at a specified time. The **/bin/cron** program will execute the same job at the configured intervals until the job is deleted from the relevant **/bin/crontab** file.

The **/bin/batch** program runs programs at a system-determined time. The program reads commands from an input file and executes them when the system load-level permits. It is the equivalent of the **/bin/at -q b now** command.

batch Components

The following files are used by **/bin/batch:**

   at.allow and at.deny files

   atjobs directory

   .proto file

   queuedefs file

at.allow and at.deny Files

The **/usr/lib/cron/at.allow** and **/usr/lib/cron/at.deny** files determine which userids can submit jobs using the **/bin/at** or **/bin/batch** programs.

atjobs

/bin/batch shares the **/var/spool/cron/atjobs** job queue file with the **/bin/at** subsystem.

.proto file

The **/var/adm/cron/.proto** file contains shell commands required to provide the correct **cron** shell environment for **at** and **batch** jobs. Please refer to the *OSS Gazette* section on the **cron** subsystem for more information.

queuedefs file

The **/var/adm/cron/queuedefs** file configures the task queues to be used for the **at**, **batch**, and **cron** programs. Please refer to the *OSS Gazette* section on the **cron** subsystem for more information.

Securing /bin/batch

BP-BIN-BATCH-01	**batch** should be secured 711 (rwx --x --x).
BP-BIN-OSSOWN-01	**batch** should be owned by SUPER.SUPER.
BP-BIN-OSSLOC-01	**batch** resides in **/bin.**

	Discovery Questions	Look here:
OSS-POLICY	Does policy retrict who can submit jobs to batch?	Policy
BIN-OSSOWN-01	Is /bin/batch owned by SUPER.SUPER?	ls -al
BIN-BATCH-01	Is /bin/batch secured correctly?	ls -al

Related Topics

at

atjobs

atq

atrm

cron

kill

bc User Program

The /bin/bc program provides unlimited precision arithmetic. It is a pre-processor for the /bin/dc program, which it invokes automatically unless the -c flag is used on the program line. It is the OSS equivalent of the TACL COMPUTE built-in command, which performs calculations and displays the results.

Securing /bin/bc

BP-BIN-BC-01	bc should be secured 711 (rwx --x --x).
BP-BIN-OSSOWN-01	bc should be owned by SUPER.SUPER.
BP-BIN-OSSLOC-01	bc resides in /bin.

	Discovery Questions	Look here:
BIN-OSSOWN-01	Is /bin/bc owned by SUPER.SUPER?	ls -al
BIN-BC-01	Is /bin/bc secured correctly?	ls -al

Related Topics

sh

Berkeley Internet Name Domain (BIND) Server

Systems using IP networks must know the IP address of a remote system in order to connect to it: however, most programs use domain names in their configuration files when referring to remote systems, because that allows IP addresses to be changed without making it necessary to modify the configuration files.

Programs called **nameservers** translate domain names to IP addresses and back again. A client application will request information from the **nameserver**, usually connecting to it on port 53. The name server will attempt to resolve the Fully Qualified Domain Name (FQDN) based on its database and make the necessary connection.

The service that facilitates this is called DNS, and it is normally implemented using centralized nameservers that are authoritative for some domains and refer to other DNS servers for information they do not already know.

BIND (Berkeley Internet Name Domain) is an implementation of the Domain Name System (DNS) protocols used on the vast majority of name-serving machines on the Internet. It includes a resolver library that provides the standard APIs for translation between domain names and Internet addresses and is intended to be linked with applications requiring name service. The major components of the Domain Name System are:

> A domain Name System server (named)
> A domain Name System resolver library
> Tools for verifying the proper operation of the DNS server

BIND DNS Components

The OSS BIND components are:

named

named.conf

nsupdate

resolv.conf

rndc

rndc.conf

/var/run/named/pid

named User Program

The **/etc/dns\<version\>/named** program is the HP implementation of BIND. It starts the doman name system (DNS) server that is part of the BIND distribution from the Internet Software Consortium (ISC). As of printing, the version was dns923, so the **named** program resides in the **/etc/dns923/** directory.

If the **named** program is invoked without any arguments, it reads the **/etc /named.conf** file and any initial data, then listens for queries.

AP-ADVICE-NAMED-01   Only users responsible for managing the DNS environment should have execute access to **/etc/dns\<version\>/named**

BP-ETC-NAMED-01	**named** should be secured 700 (rwx --- ---).
BP-ETC-OSSOWN-01	**named** should be owned by SUPER.SUPER.
BP-ETC-OSSLOC-01	**named** resides in **/etc/dns\<version\>**.

	Discovery Questions	Look here:
ETC-OSSOWN-01	Is **/etc/dns\<version\>/named** owned by SUPER.SUPER?	ls -al
ETC-NAMED-01	Is **/etc/dns\<version\>/named** secured correctly?	ls -al

named.conf Configuration File

The **/etc/named.conf** file is the main configuration file of the Name Server. It contains server parameters and references to other data files containing the host information.

The file is a collection of statements that define the options:

ACL (access control lists) statements define a list IP addresses for name servers that can or cannot be queried.

Control statements are security requirements necessary to use the **rndc** program to administer the **named** service.

Include statements specify a file where sensitive configuration information such as keys should be placed. This allows access to this data to be restricted even from users who are allowed to READ the **named.conf** file.

AP-ADVICE-NAMECONF-01   Any "include" files should be secured so that only SUPER.SUPER can READ, WRITE, or PURGE them

Key statements define keys by name. These keys are used to authenticate certain actions, such as secure updates or the use of the **rndc** command.

Logging statements define audit log configuration and file **names**. By default, named logs are written to the **syslog**.

Option statements define various parameters, such as which hosts a particular name server is allowed to query, whether or not recusive queries are allow, which network interfaces the name server should listen for requests, and the zone for which the name server is authoritative.

Zone statements specify the location and name of zone files. Zone files contain information about a particular namespace.

AP-ADVICE-NAMECONF-02   Any "zone" files should be secured so that only SUPER.SUPER can READ, WRITE, or PURGE them.

BP-ETC-NAMED-07   **named.conf** should be secured 744 (rwx r-- r--).

BP-ETC-OSSOWN-01   **named.conf** should be owned by SUPER. SUPER.

BP-ETC-OSSLOC-01   **named.conf** resides in **/etc.**

	Discovery Questions	Look here:
USR-OSSOWN-01	Is /etc/named.conf owned by SUPER.SUPER?	ls -al
USR-SAMBA-07	Is /etc/named.conf secured correctly?	ls -al

nsupdate User Program

The **/etc/dns<version>/nsupdate** is used to submit Dynamic DNS update requests to a BIND 9 domain name server. This allows resource records to be added or removed from a zone without manually editing the zone file.

RISK   Because manual edits could conflict with dynamic updates and cause data to be lost, resource records should not be edited by hand.

AP-ADVICE-NSUPDATE-01   Only users responsible for updating the DNS environment should have access to the **nsupdate** program.

BP-ETC-NSUPDATE-01   **nsupdate** should be secured 700 (rwx --- ---).

BP-ETC-OSSOWN-02   **nsupdate** should be owned by SUPER.SUPER.

BP-ETC-OSSLOC-02   **nsupdate** resides iqn **/etc/dns<version>**.

	Discovery Questions	Look here:
ETC-OSSOWN-01	Is /etc/dns<version>/nsupdate owned by SUPER.SUPER?	ls -al
ETC-NSUPDATE-01	Is /etc/dns<version>/nsupdate secured correctly?	ls -al

Remote Name Daemon Control (rndc) User Program

The **/etc/dns<version>/rndc** program controls the operation of a BIND 9 domain name server either locally or remotely. It uses the **/etc/dns<version>/rndc.conf** file for its configuration options, which can be overridden by using command-line options.

rndc communicates with the name server over a TCP connection, sending commands authenticated with digital signatures.

RISK **rndc** does not yet support all the commands of the BIND 8 **ndc** utility

RISK There is currently no way to provide the shared secret for a **key_id** without using the configuration file

BP-ETC-RNDC-01 **rndc** should be secured 700 (rwx --- ---).

BP-ETC-OSSOWN-02 **rndc** should be owned by SUPER.SUPER.

BP-ETC-OSSLOC-02 **rndc** resides in **/etc/dns<version>**.

	Discovery Questions	Look here:
ETC-OSSOWN-01	Is **/etc/dns<version>/rndc** owned by SUPER.SUPER?	ls -al
ETC-RNDC-01	Is **/etc/dns<version>/rndc** secured correctly?	ls -al

rndc.conf Configuration File

The **rndc.conf** is the configuration file for **rndc**, the BIND 9 name server control utility. This file has a similar structure and syntax to **named.conf**.

Statements in this file determine the name server and the port to connect. They also specify information about the keys to use to authenticate certain actions, such as secure updates.

BP-ETC-RNDC-07 **rndc.conf** should be secured 600 (rw- --- ---).

BP-ETC-OSSOWN-01 **rndc.conf** should be owned by SUPER.SUPER.

BP-ETC-OSSLOC-01 **rndc.conf** resides in **/etc**.

	Discovery Questions	Look here:
OSS-POLICY	Is a BIND 9 name server control utility in use on the system?	Policy
USR-OSSOWN-01	Is **/etc/rndc.conf** owned by SUPER.SUPER?	ls -al
USR-SAMBA-07	Is **/etc/rndc.conf** secured correctly?	ls -al

bg User Program

The **/bin/bg** program causes stopped job processes to restart in the background. If no process name is specified, then the most recently stopped process will be restarted.

There are two versions of the **bg** command that are identical except for the following:

> The **/bin/bg** program starts a new shell process.
>
> The built-in shell **bg** command doesn't start a new shell process.

The built-in shell **bg** command is the default. To invoke the program rather than the built-in command, you must use the full pathname to invoke **/bin/bg**.

Users other than SUPER.SUPER can only manipulate their own jobs.

Securing /bin/bg

BP-BIN-BG-01	**bg** should be secured 711 (rwx --x --x).
BP-BIN-OSSOWN-01	**bg** should be owned by SUPER.SUPER.
BP-BIN-OSSLOC-01	**bg** resides in **/bin**.

	Discovery Questions	Look here:
BIN-OSSOWN-01	Is **/bin/bg** owned by SUPER.SUPER?	ls -al
BIN-BG-01	Is **/bin/bg** secured correctly?	ls -al

Related Topics

dc

/bin Directory

The **/bin** directory is the OSS equivalent of $SYSTEM.SYSnn. It contains the current versions of OSS programs and utilities provided by HP.

Securing the **/bin** directory determines the accessibility to operating system files for all users. The users will need execute access to the majority of the programs in **/bin**. Only SUPER.SUPER should be able to create, alter, or copy any programs in **/bin**.

AP-ADVICE-BIN-01   All non-HP programs in **/bin** should be documented and moved to a separate location. The search list can be updated to include the new directory if these programs are of general interest, but only where there is a genuine need.

AP-ADVICE-BIN-02   No system files that are not placed there by DSM-SCM or other HP installation routines should ever reside in **/bin**, because they will not transfer to a new operating system image.

Operating system files located in **/bin** are created upon each revision of the operating system to a new SYSnn subvolume. This ensures that the Operating System set is cohesive and compatible.

AP-ADVICE-BIN-03   No personal or system obey files or any other type of file should reside in **/bin**. Only operating system files should reside in **/bin**.

AP-ADVICE-BIN-04   Only files for the current verion of the operating system should reside in **/bin**.

Securing /bin

BP-BIN-DIRSEC-01   **/bin** should be secured 711 (rwx --x --x).

BP-BIN-DIROWN-01   **/bin** should be owned by SUPER.SUPER.

BP-BIN-DIRLOC-01   **/bin** resides in / (**root**).

	Discovery Questions	Look here:
BIN-DIROWN-01	Is /bin owned by SUPER.SUPER?	ls -al
BIN-DIRSEC-01	Is /bin secured correctly?	ls -al

BIND

Please refer to the *OSS Gazette* section on the Berkeley Internet Name Domain (BIND) Server.

c89 User Program

The /bin/c89 program is the compiler for the TNS/R native C and C++ languages. Please refer to the *OSS Gazette* section on Compilers in the OSS Environment for more information about securing compilers on a secure system.

Guardian files can be accessed using OSS pathnames, but c89 requires that such files have a suffix. Guardian, however, does not allow suffixes in filenames; therefore, by default, the first letter of the OSS suffix becomes the last letter of the Guardian filename, and the dot between it and the Guardian name is dropped.

AP-ADVICE-COMPILER-01   To protect applications from inadvertent or malicious changes or outages, compilers and related utilities should be absent or very tightly locked down on secure systems.

Securing /bin/c89

BP-BIN-C89-01   c89 should be secured 711 (rwx --x --x).

BP-BIN-OSSOWN-01   c89 should be owned by SUPER.SUPER.

BP-BIN-OSSLOC-01   c89 resides in /bin.

	Discovery Questions	**Look here:**
OSS-POLICY	Does policy allow the use of compilers on the system?	Policy
BIN-OSSOWN-01	Is **/bin/c89** owned by SUPER.SUPER?	ls -al
BIN-C89-01	Is **/bin/c89** secured correctly?	ls -al

Related Topics

ar

nld

strip

locale

cal User Program

The **/bin/cal** program displays a calendar of the specified month or year, based on the Gregorian calendar.

Securing /bin/cal

BP-BIN-CAL-01   cal should be secured 711 (rwx --x --x).

BP-BIN-OSSOWN-01   cal should be owned by SUPER.SUPER.

BP-BIN-OSSLOC-01   cal resides in **/bin**.

	Discovery Questions	**Look here:**
BIN-OSSOWN-01	Is **/bin/cal** owned by SUPER.SUPER?	ls -al
BIN-CAL-01	Is **/bin/cal** secured correctly?	ls -al

Related Topics

locale

cancel User Program

The **/bin/cancel** program cancels print job requests and removes the jobs from the line printer spooling queue. It can only remove jobs that are in the READY or HOLD states.

Users can only cancel jobs that they initiated. SUPER Group members can cancel jobs initiated by other users.

The **/bin/cancel** program affects Guardian spooler jobs.

Securing /bin/cancel

BP-BIN-CANCEL-01   **cancel** should be secured 711 (rwx --x --x).

BP-BIN-OSSOWN-01   **cancel** should be owned by SUPER.SUPER.

BP-BIN-OSSLOC-01   **cancel** resides in /bin.

	Discovery Questions	Look here:
BIN-OSSOWN-01	Is **/bin/cancel** owned by SUPER.SUPER?	ls -al
BIN-CANCEL-01	Is **/bin/cancel** secured correctly?	ls -al

Related Topics

lp

lpstat

cat User Program

The **/bin/cat** program displays the contents of a file. It is frequently used to view a file, write a file to a new location, or to append one file to another.

RISK If critical text files, whether application or system configuration files, are not properly secured, **/bin/cat** can be used to display their contents.

Most systems contain many text files. Text files are used for configuration files, documents, and help files, among other things. They are resident in every directory. It is extremely hard to control the security of the numerous text files.

/bin/cat is often required by most users for everyday work. Securing such programs to restrict access is often not reasonable, but the risks remain.

AP-ADVICE-CAT-01   Rather than securing the **/bin/cat** object file, secure sensitive application data and scripts that are stored as text files so that they can only be viewed or copied by authorized personnel

AP-ADVICE-CAT-02   System text files, especially those in **/bin/etc**, **/usr/bin**, **/usr/include**, and **/usr/ucb**, should be secured properly to prevent changes by unauthorized personnel

Securing /bin/cat

BP-BIN-CAT-01	cat should be secured 711 (rwx --x --x).
BP-BIN-OSSOWN-01	cat should be owned by SUPER.SUPER.
BP-BIN-OSSLOC-01	cat resides in **/bin**.

	Discovery Questions	Look here:
BIN-OSSOWN-01	Is **/bin/cat** owned by SUPER.SUPER?	ls -al
BIN-CAT-01	Is **/bin/cat** secured correctly?	ls -al

Related Topics

more

pr

sh

cd User Program

The **/bin/cd** program changes the user's current directory to the directory specified. If no pathname is entered, the user is returned to his initial (home) directory.

RISK Because OSS shell programs that perform recursive actions make no distinction between Guardian and OSS files or between local and remote files, users may inadvertently make changes to Guardian and remote OSS files. **/G** and **/E** both appear in users' local root directory, which puts both remote files and Guardian files at risk.

There are two versions of the **cd** command that are identical except for the following:

The **/bin/cd** program starts a new shell process.

The built-in shell **cd** command doesn't start a new shell process.

The built-in shell **cd** command is the default. To invoke the program rather than the built-in command, you must use the full pathname to invoke **/bin/cd**.

Securing /bin/cd

BP-BIN-CD-01	cd should be secured 711 (rwx --x --x).
BP-BIN-OSSOWN-01	cd should be owned by SUPER.SUPER.
BP-BIN-OSSLOC-01	cd resides in **/bin**.

	Discovery Questions	Look here:
BIN-OSSOWN-01	Is **/bin/cd** owned by SUPER.SUPER?	ls -al
BIN-CD-01	Is **/bin/cd** secured correctly?	ls -al

Related Topics

jobs

sh

charmap Configuration Files

charmap files are the source files for supported character set descriptions. They are located in the **/usr/lib/nls/loc/charmap** directory. Please refer to the section on the Locale Subsytem for more information on how these files are used.

chgrp User Program

The **/bin/chgrp** program changes the group ownership of a file or directory. Users can only change the group owner of a file that they own and only to a file-sharing group that they belong to. Only SUPER.SUPER can change the group owner of a file that they don't own.

RISK Other users in the newly specified group will have access to the file or program by default. If the files contain sensitive data, the information could be put at risk.

Securing /bin/chgrp

BP-BIN-CHGRP-01	**chgrp** should be secured 711 (rwx --x --x).
BP-BIN-OSSOWN-01	**chgrp** should be owned by SUPER.SUPER.
BP-BIN-OSSLOC-01	**chgrp** resides in **/bin**.

	Discovery Questions	Look here:
BIN-OSSOWN-01	Is **/bin/chgrp** owned by SUPER.SUPER?	ls -al
BIN-CHGRP-01	Is **/bin/chgrp** secured correctly?	ls -al

Related Topics
chmod
chown
ls
sh

chmod User Program

The **/bin/chmod** program changes access permissions and other file mode settings. Users can enter either permission strings or octal values to change the permission settings. Please refer to Appendix A, Understanding OSS Permission Strings and Octal Values, for a full discussion of permission strings and calculating their binary and octal equivalents.

Users must have appropriate privileges in order to be able to change permissions on a file:

They must have EXECUTE authority for the directory containing the files they wish to modify.

They must have WRITE authority to the files they wish to modify.

The **/bin/chmod** program does not work on files in the **/G** directory or the **/G** directories on a remote node. Once a file is created in the **/G** directory, **/bin/chmod** cannot alter the permissions.

The **/bin/chmod** program is used to set the setuid and setgid attributes:

To setuid:

Chmod u+s <filename>

To setgid:

Chmod g+s <filename>

Securing /bin/chmod

BP-BIN-CHMOD-01	chmod should be secured 711 (rwx --x --x).
BP-BIN-OSSOWN-01	chmod should be owned by SUPER.SUPER.
BP-BIN-OSSLOC-01	chmod resides in **/bin**.

	Discovery Questions	Look here:
BIN-OSSOWN-01	Is **/bin/chmod** owned by SUPER.SUPER?	ls -al
BIN-CHMOD-01	Is **/bin/chmod** secured correctly?	ls -al

Related Topics

chgrp

chown

ls

sh

chown User Program

The **/bin/chown** program changes the owner of files and directories. When symbolic links are encountered, the ownership of the parent file or directory is changed, but the ownership of linked files and directories is not changed. Only SUPER.SUPER can change the owner of a file that he or she doesn't own.

Users must have EXECUTE authority for the directory containing the files they wish to modify.

RISK   OSS shell programs, such as **/bin/chown**, that perform recursive actions, make no distinction between Guardian and OSS files or between local and remote files. The **/G** and **/E** directories both appear in users' local **root** directory, which puts both remote files and Guardian files at risk.

AP-ADVICE-ROOTDIR-01   Users should be careful about running **/bin /chown** on the **root** directory, especially if they are working as SUPER. SUPER. If work must be done in the root directory, use the **–W NOG** and **–W NOE** flags.

BP-GUARDIAN-FILESEC-01   Guardian files should be secured to prevent an OSS-only user from modifying them in any way.

3P-ADVICE-OBJSEC-01   If there are OSS users on the system who should not have access to Guardian files, consider a third-party object security product that can prevent such users from accessing files in the Guardian file space.

Securing /bin/chown

BP-BIN-CHOWN-01	chown should be secured 711 (rwx --x --x).	
BP-BIN-OSSOWN-01	chown should be owned by SUPER.SUPER.	
BP-BIN-OSSLOC-01	chown resides in /bin.	

	Discovery Questions	Look here:
BIN-OSSOWN-01	Is /bin/chown owned by SUPER.SUPER?	ls -al
BIN-CHOWN-01	Is /bin/chown secured correctly?	ls -al

Related Topics

chgrp

chmod

ls

sh

cksum User Program

The /bin/cksum program displays the checksum and byte count of a file. It reads the files specified by the file argument and calculates a 32-bit Cyclic Redundancy Check (CRC) and the byte count for each file. Checksums are used to compare a suspect file copied or communicated over noisy transmission lines against an exact copy of a trusted file. The comparison made by the /bin/cksum program may not be cryptographically secure; however, it is unlikely that an accidentally damaged file will produce the same checksum as the original file.

RISK The checksum of a program can change. The first time a program is executed after the system is cold loaded, external references are resolved. This changes the contents of the program file and hence its checksum.

Users must have READ access in order to checksum a file.

Securing /bin/cksum

BP-BIN-CKSUM-01   cksum should be secured 711 (rwx --x --x).

BP-BIN-OSSOWN-01   cksum should be owned by SUPER.SUPER.

BP-BIN-OSSLOC-01   cksum resides in /bin.

	Discovery Questions	Look here:
BIN-OSSOWN-01	Is /bin/cksum owned by SUPER.SUPER?	ls -al
BIN-CKSUM-01	Is /bin/cksum secured correctly?	ls -al

Related Topics

wc

clear User Program

The /bin/clear program clears the terminal screen. It checks the ENV file for the terminal type and then uses the termcap database to determine how to perform the operation.

RISK   /bin/clear does not recognize 6530 terminals

Securing /bin/clear

BP-BIN-CLEAR-01   clear should be secured should be secured
711 (rwx --x --x).

BP-BIN-OSSOWN-01   clear should be owned by SUPER.SUPER.

BP-BIN-OSSLOC-01   clear resides in /bin.

	Discovery Questions	Look here:
BIN-OSSOWN-01	Is /bin/clear owned by SUPER.SUPER?	ls -al
BIN-CLEAR-01	Is /bin/clear secured correctly?	ls -al

Related Topics

termcap

cmp User Program

The **/bin/cmp** program compares two files. By default, it prints the byte and line number where any difference occurred and prints nothing if the files are the same. The **/bin/cmp** program is most often used to compare nontext files while the **/bin/diff** program is used to compare text files.

Users must have READ access to the files they wish to compare.

AP-ADVICE-DD-01 Rather than securing the **/bin/cmp** program, which may be required for legitimate activity, secure any sensitive files so that only authorized personnel have READ access to them.

Securing /bin/cmp

BP-BIN-CMP-01	cmp should be secured 711 (rwx --x --x).
BP-BIN-OSSOWN-01	cmp should be owned by SUPER.SUPER.
BP-BIN-OSSLOC-01	cmp resides in /bin.

	Discovery Questions	Look here:
BIN-OSSOWN-01	Is /bin/clear owned by SUPER.SUPER?	ls -al
BIN-CMP-01	Is /bin/clear secured correctly?	ls -al

Related Topics

comm

diff

cobol User Program

/**bin/cobol** is the driver of the COBOL85 language compiler. With the exception of /**bin/cobol** itself, all components are invoked as Guardian processes; however, OSS libraries are used.

COBOL85 Compiler Components:

> COBOL85
> COBOLEX0
> COBOLEX1
> COBOLEXT
> COBOLFE
> COBOLLIB
> CLULIB
> CBL85UTL
> CBLIBEXT

Safeguard and Guardian security control access to Cobol85.

When compiling, /**bin/cobol** looks for its libraries in the following default locations:

> /lib
> /nonnative/usr/lib
> /usr/lib
> /usr/local/lib

RISK   If the -L (upper case) flag is used when invoking /**bin/cobol**, and if library files named **libc.a, libm.a, libl.a** or **liby.a** exist in the specified directory, then the default locations *are not searched.*

/**bin/cobol** uses the following programs in /**G/system/system**.

> AXCEL
> BIND
> SQLCOMP

/bin/cobol and all its components are not affected by the settings in the locale file.

Please refer to the Gazette in the previous book, *HP NonStop Server Security: A Practical Handbook*, for more information.

AP-ADVICE-COMPILER-01   To protect applications from inadvertent or malicious changes or outages, compilers and related utilities should be absent or very tightly locked down on secure systems.

Securing /bin/cobol

Access to the **COBOL85** language components is required for compilation. Securing the compiler object file controls the use of the language and all of the compiler components. Because Safeguard and Guardian security control access to Cobol85, please refer to the Gazette chapter on compilers in the previous book, *HP NonStop Server Security: A Practical Handbook*, for more information.

BP-BIN-COBOL-01   cobol should be secured 711 (rwx --x --x).

BP-BIN-OSSOWN-01   cobol should be owned by SUPER.SUPER.

BP-BIN-OSSLOC-01   cobol resides in /bin.

BP-BIN-COBOL-02   cobol libraries should be secured 744
(rwx r-- r--).

	Discovery Questions	Look here:
OSS-POLICY	Does policy allow compilation on secure systems?	Policy
BIN-OSSOWN-01	Is /bin/cobol owned by SUPER.SUPER?	ls -al
BIN-COBOL-01	Is /bin/cobol secured correctly?	ls -al
BIN-COBOL-02	Are the COBOL libraries secured correctly?	ls -al

Related Topics

ar

strip

command User Program

The **/bin/command** program allows users to run command arguments as a command. It has two primary uses:

To run user-defined commands whose names correspond to built-in shell commands

To run system commands whose names correspond to built-in shell commands

Securing /bin/command

BP-BIN-COMMAND-01   **command** should be secured 711 (rwx --x --x).

BP-BIN-OSSOWN-01   **command** should be owned by SUPER. SUPER.

BP-BIN-OSSLOC-01   **command** resides in /**bin**.

	Discovery Questions	Look here:
BIN-OSSOWN-01	Is **/bin/command** owned by SUPER.SUPER?	ls -al
BIN-COMMAND-01	Is **/bin/command** secured correctly?	ls -al

Command Aliases

A program alias is a simple name or "shortcut" for a program or command string, such as "info = ls -al", that would allow the user to type "info" but execute **ls** with the -**al** options.

Aliases do not grant extra access. Security is determined by the underlying command referenced by an alias. Users can only execute programs that they have EXECUTE permission for, whether they attempt the access directly or via an alias.

RISK /bin/unalias and /bin/unalias pose minimal risk as long critical files such as the /etc/profile, are properly secured.

BP-BIN-.PROFILE-01 Secure the /etc/profile file so that only SUPER. SUPER can alter system-wide command aliases.

AP-ADVICE-.PROFILE-01 It may be desirable to secure the individual .profile files so that users can't alter them.

The /bin/alias program is used to create command aliases and list existing command aliases.

The /bin/unalias program is used to remove command aliases.

Compilers in the OSS Environment

Compilers generate object (executable) files from source code files. There are several utilities, libraries and objects used by compilers:

Compiler languages:

    C/C++

    COBOL85

    SQL

Objects:

    System libraries

    Common runtime libraries

    User libraries

Compilers and their related utilities are resources whose security varies depending on the Corporate Security Policy concerning compilation on secure systems. Many sites control compilations by enforcing the requirement that all compilation be performed on a development system. Application change control policy governs the method and security to update the secure application.

Some sites do not use certain languages, but all sites use at least one language compiler for the secure application. Language compilation controls are the fundamental method that a company has to control their application.

RISK Compilers can be destructive, because code can be inserted or deleted to circumvent previously implemented controls.

RISK Language compilers can be used to develop test or hacking programs to access sensitive data.

On secure systems, languages that are not in active use should be secured from use and other language compilers should be accessible only to necessary personnel.

On secure systems, only members of the group (if any) responsible for compiling programs on the secure system should have access to secure object files.

AP-ADVICE-COMPILER-01 To protect applications from inadvertent or malicious changes or outages, compilers and related utilities should be absent or very tightly secured on secure systems.

AP-ADVICE-COMPILER-02 On secure systems, compilers should not be accessible in order to prevent unauthorized access to secure data.

On development systems, members of the development group responsible for compiling programs should have access according to need.

AP-ADVICE-COMPILER-03 Compilers and their associated files should be accessible to the groups needing access.

/usr/include Directory

OSS functions are defined in library header files in the **/usr/include** directory. Developers require READ access to these files because compilers require READ access to these files.

Only SUPER.SUPER should have WRITE access to the files in the **/usr/include** directory.

BP-INCLUDE-DIRSEC-01   **/include** should be secured 744 (rwx r-- r--).

BP-INCLUDE-DIROWN-02 **/include** should be owned by SUPER.
SUPER.

BP-INCLUDE-DIRLOC-02 **/include** resides in **/usr**.

	Discovery Questions	**Look here:**
OSS-POLICY	Are compilers allowed on the secure system?	Policy
INCLUDE-DIROWN-02	Is the **/usr/include** directory owned by SUPER.SUPER?	ls -al
INCLUDE-DIRSEC-02	Is the **/usr/include** directory secured correctly?	ls -al

Securing Compiler Components

C Development Tools

Open System Services provides a variety of tools for developing applications in C in addition to the C compiler, **/bin/c89**. The following are some of the more useful C programming tools:

ar

c89

flex

lex

make

nm

strip

yacc

Cobol Development Tools

/bin/cobol is the driver of the COBOL85 language compiler.

Access to COBOL85 language components is required for compilation. Securing the compiler object file controls the use of the language:

/bin/cobol uses the following programs in **/G/system/system**:

AXCEL

BIND

NLD (ELD on Integrity NonStop Servers)

NOFT (ENOFT on Integrity NonStop Servers)

SQLCOMP

Please refer to the Gazette in the previous book, *HP NonStop Server Security: A Practical Handbook*, for more information.

comm User Program

The **/bin/comm** program compares two sorted files. It produces a three-column report showing lines that are common to both files and lines unique to each file.

Users must have READ access to the files being compared.

RISK   Comparing files exposes the contents of the files, therefore, files containing sensitive information must be secured so that only appropriate users have READ access.

Securing /bin/comm

BP-BIN-COMM-01	**comm** should be secured 711 (rwx -x -x).
BP-BIN-OSSOWN-01	**comm** should be owned by SUPER.SUPER.
BP-BIN-OSSLOC-01	**comm** resides in **/bin**.

	Discovery Questions	Look here:
BIN-OSSOWN-01	Is **/bin/comm** owned by SUPER.SUPER?	ls -al
BIN-COMM-01	Is **/bin/comm** secured correctly?	ls -al

Related Topics

cmp

diff

sort

unique

compress User Program

The **/bin/compress** program compresses and decompresses data. It reduces the size of the specified files, using adaptive Lempel-Ziv coding. Each compressed file is replaced by one with the filename extension of **.Z** (upper case) as opposed to the file extension used by the **/bin/pack** program, **.z** (lower case).

Compressed files can be restored using the -d option of **/bin/compress** or with the **/bin/uncompress** or **/bin/zcat** programs.

Users must have READ access to the files being compressed and WRITE access to the directory where the compressed files will be created.

RISK   Compression makes a file unusable. It must be decompressed first.

uncompress User Program

The **/bin/uncompress** program expands compressed data. The new file retains the compressed filename but removes the **.Z** suffix.

Users must have READ access to the compressed files and WRITE access to the directory where the new files will be created.

Securing /bin/compress and /bin/uncompress

BP-BIN-COMPRESS-01   compress should be secured 711 (rwx -x -x).

BP-BIN-OSSOWN-01   compress should be owned by SUPER.
SUPER.

BP-BIN-OSSLOC-01	compress resides in /bin.
BP-BIN-COMPRESS-02	uncompress should be secured 711 (rwx -x -x).
BP-BIN-OSSOWN-01 SUPER.	uncompress should be owned by SUPER.
BP-BIN-OSSLOC-01	uncompress resides in /bin.

	Discovery Questions	**Look here:**
BIN-OSSOWN-01	Is /bin/compress owned by SUPER.SUPER?	ls -al
BIN-OSSOWN-01	Is /bin/uncompress owned by SUPER.SUPER?	ls -al
BIN-COMPRESS-01	Is /bin/compress secured correctly?	ls -al
BIN-COMPRESS-02	Is /bin/uncompress secured correctly?	ls -al

Related Topics

uncompress

zcat

cp User Program

The /bin/cp program copies files or directories to new destinations. Users must have appropriate permission to READ (copy) the original files and CREATE and WRITE to the new ones.

/bin/cp can be used on unstructured Guardian files, but when a Guardian file is copied to the OSS file space, only its contents are preserved, not the file attributes.

/bin/cp will not move Guardian files residing on virtual disks; a 3503 error is generated.

RISK OSS shell programs, such as /bin/cp, that perform recursive actions, make no distinction between Guardian and OSS files or between local and remote files. The /G and /E directories both appear in users' local **root** directory, which puts both remote files and Guardian files at risk.

AP-ADVICE-ROOTDIR-01   Users should be careful about running **/bin/cp** on the **root** directory, especially if they are working as SUPER.SUPER. If work must be done in the root directory, use the –W NOG and –W NOE flags.

BP-GUARDIAN-FILESEC-01   Guardian files should be secured to prevent an OSS-only user from modifying them in any way.

3P-ADVICE-OBJSEC-01   If there are OSS users on the system who should not have access to Guardian files, consider a third-party object security product that can prevent such users from accessing files in the Guardian file space.

Securing /bin/cp

BP-BIN-CP-01   cp should be secured 711 (rwx -x -x).

BP-BIN-OSSOWN-01   cp should be owned by SUPER.SUPER.

BP-BIN-OSSLOC-01   cp resides in **/bin**.

	Discovery Questions	Look here:
BIN-OSSOWN-01	Is **/bin/cp** owned by SUPER.SUPER?	ls -al
BIN-CP-01	Is **/bin/cp** secured correctly?	ls -al

Related Topics

mv
UTILSGE

cpio User Program

The **/bin/cpio** program copies files to and from **cpio** archives.

AP-ADVICE-CPIO-01   Archives should be as well secured as the files being archived.

RISK   Archived files can be moved to a system with less security, leaving the information vulnerable to unauthorized access to the data.

RISK Archived files can be restored, overwriting existing files.

RISK Since archived files can contain sensitive data, protection of the utilities that can read or copy the data must be considered.

AP-ADVICE-CPIO-02 Archiving should be permitted for authorized personnel only.

Securing /bin/cpio

BP-BIN-CPIO-01	cpio should be secured 711 (rwx -x -x).
BP-BIN-OSSOWN-01	cpio should be owned by SUPER.SUPER.
BP-BIN-OSSLOC-01	cpio resides in /bin.

	Discovery Questions	Look here:
BIN-OSSOWN-01	Is /bin/cpio owned by SUPER.SUPER?	ls -al
BIN-CPIO-01	Is /bin/cpio secured correctly?	ls -al

Related Topics

ar
find
ls
pax
sh

cron Subsystem

The **/bin/cron** process runs commands at user-specified times. It runs programs (jobs) found in job queue files:

Jobs scheduled via **/bin/cron** are found in each user's **crontab** files. Please refer to the *OSS Gazette* section on **crontab** Job Queue Files for more information on securing these files.

Jobs scheduled via **/bin/at** or **/bin/batch** are found in the **/var/spool/cron/atjobs** directory.

When the **/bin/cron** process is initialized, it reads all the **crontab** files and the **/var/spool/cron/atjobs** files. Thereafter, when it detects a change to any of these directories, it rereads them.

/bin/cron invokes a new shell from the user's **$HOME** directory. It does not run the user's **.profile** file.

AP-ADVICE-CRON-01   If the user wants his **.profile** to be processed when his job executes, he must include the command to run it in the **crontab** file.

There should be a single **cron** process, and it should always be running.

BP-CRON-PROCESS-03   To ensure that only one process runs, always start **cron** as a named process: set the CRON_NAMED environment variable before starting any copy of **cron**.

The **/bin/cron** program creates a log of its activities.

The **/bin/cron** process starts each job with the following process attributes which are stored within each job (**crontab**) file:

    Effective and real userids
    Effective and real group IDs
    Supplementary groups

The cron process supports the following programs:

    atq
    atrm
    batch
    crontab

cron Components and Utilities

/bin/cron uses the following components:

    crontab
    cron.allow

cron.deny

crontab files

cron log

.proto file

queuedefs file

/**bin/cron** also processes **atjobs** files created by the /**bin/at** subsystem.

cron System Program

The /**bin/cron** process runs commands at user-specified times. It runs programs (jobs) found in job queue files.

BP-PROCESS-CRON-01	$cron process should always be running.
BP-BIN-CRON-01	**cron** should be secured 711 (rwx --x -x).
BP-BIN-OSSOWN-01	**cron** should be owned by SUPER.SUPER.
BP-BIN-OSSLOC-01	**cron** resides in /**bin**.

	Discovery Questions	**Look here:**
OSS-POLICY	Are all users allowed to submit scheduled jobs?	Policy
BIN-OSSOWN-01	Is /**bin/cron** owned by SUPER.SUPER?	ls -al
BIN-CRON-01	Is /**bin/cron** secured correctly?	ls -al

crontab User Program

The /**bin/crontab** program submits a schedule of jobs that are to be executed on a recurring basis to **cron**. Please refer to the *OSS Gazette* section on /**bin/crontab** for more information.

cron.allow and cron.deny Files

The /**var/adm/cron/cron.allow** and /**var/adm/cron/cron.deny** files determine which userids can submit jobs using the /**bin/crontab** program.

When a user invokes the **/bin/crontab** program, it checks for the existence of these files:

The **cron.allow** file is checked first. If it exists, only userids listed in it can use **/bin/cron** to submit jobs.

Only if the **cron.allow** file doesn't exist does **/bin/cron** check for the existence of the **cron.deny** file. If it exists, userids listed in it cannot use **/bin/cron** to submit jobs, but everyone else can.

If neither the **cron.allow** nor **cron.deny** files exist, then only users with execute access for **/bin/cron** can submit **cron** jobs.

HP provides a **cron.deny.sample** file that resides in the same directory.

Create the **/var/adm/cron/cron.deny** file by making a copy of the sample file in the same location and naming it **cron.deny.**

RISK   The **/var/adm/cron/cron.deny.sample** file will be overwritten with each operating system upgrade.

AP-ADVICE-CRON-01   Do   not   customize   the   **/var/adm/cron/ cron.deny.sample** file. Create the **/var/adm/cron/cron.deny** file and customize it.

BP-BIN-DENY-01   Use of **cron.deny** files is the most common method used to control the use of the **cron** subsystem. A "deny list" will usually be shorter than an "allow list," because the majority of users are allowed to submit jobs.

BP-BIN-ALLOW-01   Unless   required   in   your   environment,   the **cron.allow** file should not exist.

BP-BIN-ALLOW-02   If the **cron.allow** file does exist, all userids intended to run **/bin/cron** *must* be included in the file, or they will be unable to submit jobs.

BP-VAR-CRON-02   **cron.allow** should be secured 600 (rw- --- ---).

BP-VAR-OSSOWN-03 **cron.allow** should be owned by SUPER.SUPER.

BP-VAR-OSSLOC-03   **cron.allow** resides in **/var/adm/cron.**

BP-VAR-CRON-03   **cron.deny** should be secured 600 (rw- --- ---).

BP-VAR-OSSOWN-03 cron.deny should be owned by SUPER.SUPER.

BP-VAR-OSSLOC-03 **cron.deny** resides in **/var/adm/cron.**

	Discovery Questions	**Look here:**
OSS-POLICY	Are all users allowed to submit scheduled jobs?	Policy
OSS-POLICY	Does the security policy mandate the use of the **/var/adm/cron/cron.allow** file?	Policy
OSS-POLICY	Does the security policy mandate the use of the **/var/adm/cron/cron.deny** file?	Policy
VAR-OSSOWN-03	Is **/var/adm/cron/cron.allow** owned by SUPER.SUPER?	ls -al
VAR-OSSOWN-03	Is **/var/adm/cron/cron.deny** owned by SUPER.SUPER?	ls -al
BIN-ALLOW-01	Does the **/bin/cron.allow** file exist?	ls -al

crontab Files and the crontabs Directory

When a user submits a scheduled job by running **/bin/crontab**, the program copies the file into the "crontab" directory. The resulting crontab file name will be the user's user name (GROUPNAME.USERNAME). User **crontab** files are all contained in a single directory. The default location is **/var/spool/cron/crontabs.**

Each crontab file entry is a single line consisting of the following six fields:

1. The minute that the command sequence should start executing
2. The hour that the command sequence should start executing
3. The day of the month that the command sequence should start executing
4. The month of the year that the command sequence should start executing
5. The day of the week that the command sequence should start executing
6. The command string or script to be executed

RISK When entries are made to a **crontab** file, all previous entries are erased.

AP-ADVICE-CRONTAB-01 Users should maintain a file with all the jobs they wish to schedule. This file would then be included in field 6 of their **crontab** file.

The file is created with a permission string of (400) r-- --- ---. However, if the user has a **umask** entry in their **.profile** file, the **umask** value may override the default.

BP-VAR-CRONTAB-01 secured 400 (r-- --- ---).	Individual **crontab** files should be
BP-VAR-OSSOWN-04 owned by individual users.	Individual **crontab** files should be
BP-VAR-OSSLOC-04 **/spool/cron/crontabs.**	Individual **crontab** files reside in **/var**
BP-CRONTABS-DIRSEC-04 secured 777 (rwx rwx rwx).	The **crontabs** directory should be
BP-CRONTABS-DIROWN-04 owned by SUPER.SUPER.	The **crontabs** directory should be
BP-CRONTABS-DIRLOC-04 **spool/cron/.**	The **crontabs** directory resides in **/var/**

	Discovery Questions	Look here:
OSS-POLICY	Are all users allowed to submit scheduled jobs?	Policy
CRON-DIROWN-03	Is the **/var/spool/cron** directory owned by SUPER.SUPER?	ls -al
VAR-CRONTAB-01	Are the **/var/spool/cron/crontabs/*** files secured correctly?	ls -al
CRONTABS-DIRSEC-04	Is the **/var/spool/cron/crontabs** directory secured correctly?	ls -al

cron log

The **/bin/cron** program logs its activities to the **/var/adm/cron/log** file.

BP-VAR-CRONLOG-01   The cron **log** file should be secured 600 (rw- --- ---).

BP-VAR-OSSOWN-03   The cron **log** file should be owned by SUPER.SUPER.

BP-VAR-OSSLOC-03   The cron **log** file resides in **/var/adm/cron**.

	Discovery Questions	Look here:
VAR-OSSOWN-03	Is **/var/adm/cron/log** owned by SUPER.SUPER?	ls -al
VAR-CRONLOG-01	Is **/var/adm/cron/log** secured correctly?	ls -al

.proto and .proto.sample Files

The **/var/adm/cron/.proto** file contains shell commands required to provide the correct cron shell environment for **at** and **batch** jobs.

HP provides a **.proto.sample** file which resides in the same directory. The first time (only) that the **cron** subsystem is built, make of copy of this sample file, renaming it to **.proto** to create the production file.

RISK   The **/var/adm/cron/.proto.sample** file will be overwritten with each operating system upgrade.

AP-ADVICE-CRON-04   Do not change the sample file to customize it to your environment. Make your changes in the **.proto** file you created by copying the sample file.

RISK   Only system administrators should have write access to the **/var/adm/cron/.proto** file.

BP-VAR-PROTO-01   **.proto** should be secured 744 (rwx r-- r---).

BP-VAR-OSSOWN-03   **.proto** should be owned by SUPER.SUPER.

BP-VAR-OSSLOC-03   **.proto** resides in **/var/adm/cron**.

BP-VAR-SAMPLE-01   .proto.sample should be secured 600
(rw- --- ---).

BP-VAR-OSSOWN-03   .proto.sample should be owned by SUPER.
SUPER.

BP-VAR-OSSLOC-03   .proto.sample resides in /var/adm/cron.

	Discovery Questions	Look here:
VAR-OSSOWN-03	Is /var/adm/cron/.proto owned by SUPER.SUPER?	ls -al
VAR-OSSOWN-03	Is /var/adm/cron/.proto.sample owned by SUPER.SUPER?	ls -al
VAR-PROTO-01	Is /var/adm/cron/.proto secured correctly?	ls -al
VAR-SAMPLE-01	Is /var/adm/cron/.proto.sample secured correctly?	ls -al

queuedefs File

The /var/adm/cron/queuedefs file configures the task queues to be used
for the /bin/at, /bin/batch, and /bin/crontab commands. Each line in the
file describes the characteristics of one of the queues managed by the cron
process.

HP provides a queuedefs.sample file that resides in the same directory. The
first time that the cron subsystem is built, make of copy of this sample file,
naming it queuedefs to create the production file.

RISK   The /var/adm/cron/queuedefs.sample file will be overwritten with
each operating system upgrade.

AP-ADVICE-CRON-05   Do not change the sample file. Change the
queuedefs file created by copying the sample file to customize it for your
system.

AP-ADVICE-CRON-06   Only system administrators should have write
access to the /var/adm/cron/queuedefs file.

BP-VAR-QUEUEDEF-01   queuedefs should be secured 644 (rw- r-- r--).

| BP-VAR-OSSOWN-03 SUPER. | **queuedefs** should be owned by SUPER. |
| BP-VAR-OSSLOC-03 | **queuedefs** resides in **/var/adm/cron**. |

	Discovery Questions	**Look here:**
OSS-POLICY	Are all users allowed to submit scheduled jobs?	Policy
OSS-POLICY	Does the security policy mandate the use of the /var/adm/cron/cron.allow file?	Policy
VAR-OSSOWN-03	Is **/var/adm/cron/queuedefs** owned by SUPER.SUPER?	ls -al
VAR-QUEUEDEF-01	Is **/var/adm/cron/queuedefs** secured correctly?	ls -al

cron.allow and cron.deny Files

The **/var/adm/cron/cron.allow** and **/var/adm/cron/cron.deny** files determine which userids can submit jobs using the **/bin/crontab** program. Please refer to the *OSS Gazette* section on **/bin/cron** for more information.

cron log

The **/bin/cron** program logs its activities to the **/var/adm/cron/log** file.

crontab Job Queue Files

When a user submits a scheduled job by running **/bin/crontab**, the program copies the file into the "crontab" directory. The resulting crontab file name will be the user's user name (GROUPNAME.USERNAME). User **crontab** files are all contained in a single directory. The default location is **/var/spool/cron/crontabs**. Please refer to the *OSS Gazette* section on the **cron** Subsystem for more information.

crontab User Program

There are three ways to control the scheduling of OSS programs and scripts. They are useful for running jobs that are especially time consuming. The job scheduling programs are:

/bin/at	Runs a job at a time the user specifies. /bin/at jobs are once-only; the scheduled programs are executed at the specified time and not repeated.
/bin/batch	Runs a job at a time determined by the operating system. /bin/batch jobs are once-only; the program is executed and not repeated.
/bin/cron	Runs a job at a time the user specifies. The same job will then be run at the configured intervals until it is deleted from the relevant crontab file.

The **crontab** program submits a schedule of jobs that are to be executed on a recurring basis to **cron**. It copies a user's file into a directory that holds all users' **crontab** files. **cron** then runs the programs according to instructions in each **crontab** file.

The **/var/adm/cron/cron.allow** and **/var/adm/cron/cron.deny** files determine which userids can submit jobs using the **/bin/crontab** program. Please refer to the *OSS Gazette* section on **/bin/cron** for more information.

The **/bin/crontab** program stores the following attributes with the job:

Effective and real userid

Effective and real group ID

Supplementary groups

Typically, each user account has an associated **crontab** file that contains commands to be run at specified intervals. **Cron** processes the commands at the appropriate time, sending jobs to BATCH and generating logging messages.

Securing /bin/crontab Program

BP-BIN-CRONTAB-01   **crontab** should be secured 4711 (rws --x --x).

BP-BIN-SETUID-01   **crontab** should have the **setuid** attribute.

BP-BIN-OSSOWN-01   **crontab** should be owned by SUPER.SUPER.

BP-BIN-OSSLOC-01   **crontab** resides in **/bin**.

	Discovery Questions	Look here:
BIN-OSSOWN-01	Is **/bin/crontab** owned by SUPER.SUPER?	ls -al
BIN-CRONTAB-01	Is **/bin/crontab** secured correctly?	ls -al

Related Topics

at
batch
cron

csplit User Program

The **/bin/csplit** program reads a selected file and separates it into segments defined by the arguments specified. Arguments can be regular expressions. By default, **/bin/csplit** writes the file segments to files named xx00 ...xxn, where n is the number of arguments listed on the program line. It could be used, for example, to separate a text file into separate chapters or a source code file into separate sections.

The original file is not altered. Users must have READ access to the file being examined and must be able to create files in the target directory.

Securing /bin/csplit

BP-BIN-CSPLIT-01   **csplit** should be secured 711 (rwx --x --x).

BP-BIN-OSSOWN-01   **csplit** should be owned by SUPER.SUPER.

BP-BIN-OSSLOC-01   **csplit** resides in **/bin**.

	Discovery Questions	Look here:
BIN-OSSOWN-01	Is **/bin/csplit** owned by SUPER.SUPER?	ls -al
BIN-CSPLIT-01	Is **/bin/csplit** secured correctly?	ls -al

Related Topics

ed

grep

locale

sh

split

cut User Program

The **/bin/cut** program displays selected parts from each line of a file. It locates the specified parts in each line and displays the contained characters.

Users must have READ access to the file being examined.

RISK   Using **/bin/cut** on files exposes the contents of the files; therefore, files containing sensitive information must be secured so that only appropriate users have READ access.

Securing /bin/cut

BP-BIN-CUT-01	cut should be secured 711 (rwx --x --x).
BP-BIN-OSSOWN-01	cut should be owned by SUPER.SUPER.
BP-BIN-OSSLOC-01	cut resides in **/bin**.

	Discovery Questions	Look here:
BIN-OSSOWN-01	Is **/bin/cut** owned by SUPER.SUPER?	ls -al
BIN-CUT-01	Is **/bin/cut** secured correctly?	ls -al

Related Topics

grep

paste

date User Program

The **/bin/date** program displays the current date and time if called with no flags or with a flag list that begins with a + (plus sign). This program does not alter the system date.

Securing /bin/date

BP-BIN-DATE-01   **date** should be secured 711 (rwx --x --x).

BP-BIN-OSSOWN-01   **date** should be owned by SUPER.SUPER.

BP-BIN-OSSLOC-01   **date** resides in **/bin**.

	Discovery Questions	Look here:
BIN-OSSOWN-01	Is **/bin/date** owned by SUPER.SUPER?	ls -al
BIN-DATE-01	Is **/bin/date** secured correctly?	ls -al

Related Topics

locale

dc User Program

The **/bin/dc** program is an arbitrary-precision arithmetic calculator. It takes its input from a file or the command line until it reads an End-of-File character and then returns the result.

Securing /bin/dc

BP-BIN-DC-01	dc should be secured 711 (rwx --x --x).
BP-BIN-OSSOWN-01	dc should be owned by SUPER.SUPER.
BP-BIN-OSSLOC-01	dc resides in /bin.

	Discovery Questions	Look here:
BIN-OSSOWN-01	Is /bin/dc owned by SUPER.SUPER?	ls -al
BIN-DC-01	Is /bin/dc secured correctly?	ls -al

Related Topics

bc

locale

dd User Program

The /bin/dd program converts and copies a file. It reads the selected input file, does the selected conversion, and copies it to the output file specified. It might be used, for example, to convert an ASCII file to EBCDIC or IBM formats.

The user must have READ access to the input file and must be able to create files in the target directory.

RISK   Using /bin/dd, users could convert files containing sensitive data to a format that could be copied to another less secure system. Sensitive files should be secured so that only authorized personnel have READ access to them.

AP-ADVICE-DD-01   Rather than securing the /bin/dd program, which may be required for legitimate activity, secure any sensitive files so that only authorized personnel have READ access to them.

Securing /bin/dd

BP-BIN-DD-01	dd should be secured 711 (rwx --x --x).
BP-BIN-OSSOWN-01	dd should be owned by SUPER.SUPER.
BP-BIN-OSSLOC-01	dd resides in /bin.

	Discovery Questions	Look here:
BIN-OSSOWN-01	Is /bin/dd owned by SUPER.SUPER?	ls -al
BIN-DD-01	Is /bin/dd secured correctly?	ls -al

Related Topics

cp

pax

tar

tr

locale

df User Program

The /bin/df program displays statistics of filesets such as the amount of used and available disk space on the fileset, the status (started, stopped, or unknown), the total capacity of the fileset used, and the mount point of the fileset.

Refer to Part 9, Open Systems Services for information about filesets.

Securing /bin/df

BP-BIN-DF-01	df should be secured 711 (rwx --x --x).
BP-BIN-OSSOWN-01	df should be owned by SUPER.SUPER.
BP-BIN-OSSLOC-01	df resides in /bin.

	Discovery Questions	Look here:
BIN-OSSOWN-01	Is **/bin/df** owned by SUPER.SUPER?	ls -al
BIN-DF-01	Is **/bin/df** secured correctly?	ls -al

Related Topics

du

diff User Program

The **/bin/diff** program compares text files, while **/bin/cmp** is used to compare nontext files.

Users must have READ access to the files they wish to compare.

RISK /bin/diff poses minimal risk as long as critical or sensitive application and system files are properly secured.

Securing /bin/diff

BP-BIN-DIFF-01	diff should be secured 711 (rwx --x --x).
BP-BIN-OSSOWN-01	diff should be owned by SUPER.SUPER.
BP-BIN-OSSLOC-01	diff resides in **/bin**.

	Discovery Questions	Look here:
BIN-OSSOWN-01	Is **/bin/diff** owned by SUPER.SUPER?	ls -al
BIN-DIFF-01	Is **/bin/diff** secured correctly?	ls -al

Related Topics

cmp
comm
dircmp
ed
pr

dircmp User Program

The **/bin/dircmp** program compares two directories. It reads directory 1 and directory 2, compares their contents, and returns the results. When the same filename appears in both, dircmp compares the contents of the two files.

In the output, **dircmp** lists the files unique to each directory. It then lists the files with identical names but different contents. If entered without a flag, **dircmp** also lists files that have both identical names and identical contents.

Securing /bin/dircmp

BP-BIN-DIRCMP-01   **dircmp** should be secured 711 (rwx --x --x).

BP-BIN-OSSOWN-01   **dircmp** should be owned by SUPER.SUPER.

BP-BIN-OSSLOC-01   **dircmp** resides in **/bin**.

	Discovery Questions	Look here:
BIN-OSSOWN-01	Is **/bin/dircmp** owned by SUPER.SUPER?	ls -al
BIN-DIRCMP-01	Is **/bin/dircmp** secured correctly?	ls -al

Related Topics

cmp

diff

dirname User Program

The **/bin/dirname** program reads the string specified on the command line, deletes from the last / (slash) to the end of the line, and returns the remaining pathname. The program is generally used inside command substitutions within a shell procedure to specify an output filename that is some variation of a specified input filename.

/bin/dirname is the opposite of /bin/basename, which returns the filename but not the path.

Securing /bin/dirname

BP-BIN-DIRNAME-01   dirname should be secured 711 (rwx --x --x).

BP-BIN-OSSOWN-01   dirname should be owned by SUPER.SUPER.

BP-BIN-OSSLOC-01   dirname resides in /bin.

	Discovery Questions	Look here:
BIN-OSSOWN-01	Is /bin/dirname owned by SUPER.SUPER?	ls -al
BIN-DIRNAME-01	Is /bin/dirname secured correctly?	ls -al

Related Topics

basename

sh

dspcat User Program

The /bin/dspcat program displays all or part of a message catalog.

A message catalog is a file or storage area containing program messages, command prompts, and responses to prompts for a particular native language, territory, and code set. For example, C error messages are taken from the standard C library message catalog.

Users must have READ access to the message catalog(s) they wish to examine.

RISK   /bin/dspcat poses minimal risk as long as the message catalogs are secured appropriately.

Securing /bin/dspcat

BP-BIN-DSPCAT-01   **dspcat** should be secured 711 (rwx --x --x).

BP-BIN-OSSOWN-01   **dspcat** should be owned by SUPER.SUPER.

BP-BIN-OSSLOC-01   **dspcat** resides in **/bin**.

	Discovery Questions	Look here:
BIN-OSSOWN-01	Is **/bin/dspcat** owned by SUPER.SUPER?	ls -al
BIN-DSPCAT-01	Is **/bin/dspcat** secured correctly?	ls -al

Related Topics

dspmsg

gencat

mkcatdefs

dspmsg User Program

The **/bin/dspmsg** program returns the specified message from the specified message catalog. It returns a single message as opposed to the **/bin/dspcat** program that displays all or part of the catalog.

Users must have READ access to the message catalog(s) they wish to examine.

RISK   **/bin/dspmsg** poses minimal risk as long as the message catalogs are secured appropriately.

Securing /bin/dspmsg

BP-BIN-DSPMSG-01   **dspmsg** should be secured 711 (rwx --x --x).

BP-BIN-OSSOWN-01   **dspmsg** should be owned by SUPER.SUPER.

BP-BIN-OSSLOC-01   **dspmsg** resides in **/bin**.

	Discovery Questions	Look here:
BIN-OSSOWN-01	Is **/bin/dspmsg** owned by SUPER.SUPER?	ls -al
BIN-DSPMSG-01	Is **/bin/dspmsg** secured correctly?	ls -al

Related Topics

dspcat

gencat

mkcatdefs

du User Program

The **/bin/du** program displays a summary of disk usage. It displays the number of blocks in all directories (listed recursively) within each specified directory.

The size of the file space allocated to a directory is defined as the sum total of the space allocated to all files in the file hierarchy rooted in the directory, plus the space allocated to the directory itself.

The user requires READ access to the directories being queried.

Securing /bin/du

BP-BIN-DU-01	**du** should be secured 711 (rwx --x --x).
BP-BIN-OSSOWN-01	**du** should be owned by SUPER.SUPER.
BP-BIN-OSSLOC-01	**du** resides in **/bin**.

	Discovery Questions	Look here:
BIN-OSSOWN-01	Is **/bin/du** owned by SUPER.SUPER?	ls -al
BIN-DU-01	Is **/bin/du** secured correctly?	ls -al

Related Topics

df

ls

echo User Program

The **/bin/echo** program displays a specified string. It is frequently used to produce diagnostic messages in command files and to send data to a pipe.

There are two versions of the echo command that are identical except for the following:

The **/bin/echo** program starts a new shell process to display the information.

The built-in shell **echo** command doesn't start a new shell process to display the information.

The built-in shell **echo** command is the default. To invoke the program rather than the built-in command, you must use the full pathname to invoke **/bin/echo**.

Securing /bin/echo

BP-BIN-ECHO-01   echo should be secured 711 (rwx --x --x).

BP-BIN-OSSOWN-01   echo should be owned by SUPER.SUPER.

BP-BIN-OSSLOC-01   echo resides in **/bin.**

	Discovery Questions	Look here:
BIN-OSSOWN-01	Is **/bin/echo** owned by SUPER.SUPER?	ls -al
BIN-ECHO-01	Is **/bin/echo** secured correctly?	ls -al

Related Topics

sh

ed User Program

The **/bin/ed** program is a line-editor that works on one file at a time. The target file is copied into a temporary edit buffer and any changes are made to the copy. The original file is not altered until the write subcommand is issued.

Most systems contain many text files. Text files are used for configuration files, documents, and help files, among other things. They are resident on every volume and many subvolumes. It is extremely hard to control the security of the numerous text files.

Editors are often required by most users for everyday work. Securing editor programs to restrict access is often not reasonable, but the risks remain.

RISK   Editors can be used to alter data or modify text data files.

AP-ADVICE-ED-01   Sensitive application data stored in text files should be strictly secured to prevent changes by unauthorized personnel.

AP-ADVICE-ED-02   System text files, especially those in **/bin**, **/etc**, **/usr/bin** and **/usr/ucb** should be secured properly to prevent changes by unauthorized personnel.

Securing /bin/ed

BP-BIN-ED-01   **ed** should be secured 711 (rwx --x --x).

BP-BIN-OSSOWN-01   **ed** should be owned by SUPER.SUPER.

BP-BIN-OSSLOC-01   **ed** resides in **/bin**.

	Discovery Questions	Look here:
BIN-OSSOWN-01	Is **/bin/ed** owned by SUPER.SUPER?	ls -al
BIN-ED-01	Is **/bin/ed** secured correctly?	ls -al

Related Topics

chmod

edit

grep

sed

sh

stty

vi

egrep User Program

The **/bin/egrep** program is an obsolete version of the command **grep -E**, which searches for full regular expression patterns. It searches the specified files for lines containing characters that match the specified pattern and then returns matching lines.

Securing /bin/egrep

BP-BIN-EGREP- 01	**egrep** should be secured 711 (rwx --x --x).
BP-BIN-OSSOWN-01	**egrep** should be owned by SUPER.SUPER.
BP-BIN-OSSLOC-01	**egrep** resides in **/bin**.

	Discovery Questions	Look here:
BIN-OSSOWN-01	Is **/bin/egrep** owned by SUPER.SUPER?	ls -al
BIN-EGREP- 01	Is **/bin/egrep** secured correctly?	ls -al

Related Topics

ed

ex

grep

sed

sh

eld User Program

The **/bin/eld** program is the Integrity NonStop version of the NLD program.

enoft User Program

The **/bin/enoft** program is the Integrity NonStop version of the NOFT program.

env User Program

The **/bin/env** program displays or sets environmental variables. It lets users change their current environment and then run a program within the changed environment. Changes are only in effect while the specified program is running.

If no **env** option is entered, **/bin/env** displays information about the current environment.

RISK   **/bin/env** commands will override similar commands in both global and personal **.profile** files.

RISK   The **/bin/env** file can contain search path commands to alter the locations searched for a program file when a command is issued in which the filename is not fully qualified, as is the common practice. In this case, a user's program may not run.

Securing /bin/env

BP-BIN-ENV-01	env should be secured 711 (rwx --x --x).
BP-BIN-OSSOWN-01	env should be owned by SUPER.SUPER.
BP-BIN-OSSLOC-01	env resides in **/bin**.

	Discovery Questions	Look here:
BIN-OSSOWN-01	Is **/bin/env** owned by SUPER.SUPER?	ls -al
BIN-ENV-01	Is **/bin/env** secured correctly?	ls -al

Related Topics

sh

exec

environment Files

SSH **environment** files contain parameters that configure an SSH environment. The **environment** file is read at login and its values override the global environment settings.

There may also be environment files in individual user's $HOME directories.

Please refer to the chapter on the SSH Subsystem in Part 4, *TCP/IP* for more information or to the *OSS Gazette* section on SSH for Best Practice recommendations.

/etc Directory

The **/etc** directory contains system configuration files.

Please note that because OSS userids are managed via Safeguard, the following common user-and-password-related database files, even if present, are not used on the HP NonStop Server:

groups

passwd

security

shadow

Because these files are often the target of hackers on UNIX systems, the lack of these databases on NonStop Server adds a measure of security.

The information that would normally be pulled from these files by a program is provided via API calls to the Guardian operating system.

The following files are used by the **/bin/inetd** program and should be linked to their Guardian equivalents. Please refer to the *OSS Gazette* section on **/bin/inetd** for more information on these files.

OSS File	Symbolic Link	Guardian File
/etc/hosts	Link to:	$SYSTEM.ZTCPIP.HOSTS
/etc/inetd.conf	Link to:	$SYSTEM.ZTCPIP.PORTCONF
/etc/networks	Link to:	$SYSTEM.ZTCPIP.NETWORKS
/etc/protocol	Link to:	$SYSTEM.ZTCPIP.PROTOCOL
/etc/resolv.conf	Link to:	$SYSTEM.ZTCPIP.RESCONF
/etc/services	Link to:	$SYSTEM.ZTCPIP.SERVICES

RISK   Programs in **/etc** pose minimal risk as long as the directory and the files contained in it are properly secured.

AP-ADVICE-ETC-01   Only the users charged with creating and maintaining the system configuration files such as the **/etc/profile** or PORT-CONF (or **/etc/inetd.conf**) should have WRITE access to the system configuration files.

Securing /etc

BP-ETC-DIRSEC-01	**/etc** should be secured 744 (rwx r-x r-x).
BP-ETC-DIROWN-01	**/etc** should be owned by SUPER.SUPER.
BP-ETC-DIRLOC-01	**/etc** resides in / (**root**).

	Discovery Questions	Look here:
ETC-DIROWN-01	Is **/etc** owned by SUPER.SUPER?	ls -al
ETC-DIRSEC-01	Is **/etc** secured correctly?	ls -al

Related Topics

jobs

sh

ex User Program

The **/bin/ex** program edits lines in a file interactively. It is like **ed** but more powerful, providing multiline displays and access to a screen-editing mode.

Users may prefer to call **/bin/vi** directly to have environment variables set for screen editing. Also **edit**, a limited subset of **/bin/ex**, is available for novices or casual use.

Most systems contain many text files. Text files are used for configuration files, documents, and help files, among other things. They are resident on every volume and many subvolumes. It is extremely hard to control the security of the numerous text files.

Editors are often required by most users for everyday work. Securing editor programs to restrict access is often not reasonable, but the risks remain.

RISK   Editors can be used to alter data or modify text data files.

AP-ADVICE-EX-01   Sensitive application data stored in text files should be strictly secured to prevent changes by unauthorized personnel.

AP-ADVICE-EX-02   System text files, especially those in **/bin/etc**, **/usr/bin**, and **/usr/ucb** should be secured properly to prevent changes by unauthorized personnel.

Securing /bin/ex

BP-BIN-EX-01	**ex** should be secured 711 (rwx --x --x).
BP-BIN-OSSOWN-01	**ex** should be owned by SUPER.SUPER.
BP-BIN-OSSLOC-01	**ex** resides in **/bin**.

	Discovery Questions	Look here:
BIN-OSSOWN-01	Is **/bin/ex** owned by SUPER.SUPER?	ls -al
BIN-EX-01	Is **/bin/ex** secured correctly?	ls -al

Related Topics

ed

grep

vi

expand User Program

The **/bin/expand** program changes tab characters to spaces in specified files or in the display. Command flags control replacements.

Users must have WRITE access to the target file.

unexpand User Program

The **/bin/unexpand** program replaces tab characters that were previously removed via the **/bin/expand** program. Command flags control what will be replaced.

Users must have EXECUTE access to the directory where the new files will be created.

Securing /bin/expand and /bin/unexpand

BP-BIN-EXPAND-01   expand should be secured 711 (rwx --x --x).

BP-BIN-OSSOWN-01   expand should be owned by SUPER.SUPER.

BP-BIN-OSSLOC-01   expand resides in **/bin.**

BP-BIN-EXPAND-02   unexpand should be secured 711 (rwx --x --x).

BP-BIN-OSSOWN-01   unexpand should be owned by SUPER.SUPER.

BP-BIN-OSSLOC-01   unexpand resides in **/bin.**

	Discovery Questions	Look here:
BIN-OSSOWN-01	Is **/bin/expand** owned by SUPER.SUPER?	ls -al
BIN-OSSOWN-01	Is **/bin/unexpand** owned by SUPER.SUPER?	ls -al
BIN-EXPAND-01	Is **/bin/expand** secured correctly?	ls -al
BIN-EXPAND-02	Is **/bin/unexpand** secured correctly?	ls -al

expr User Program

The **/bin/expr** program evaluates arguments as expressions. The program reads an expression, evaluates it, and returns the result.

Securing /bin/expr

BP-BIN-EXPR-01	**expr** should be secured 711 (rwx --x --x).
BP-BIN-OSSOWN-01	**expr** should be owned by SUPER.SUPER.
BP-BIN-OSSLOC-01	**expr** resides in **/bin**.

	Discovery Questions	Look here:
BIN-OSSOWN-01	Is **/bin/expr** owned by SUPER.SUPER?	ls -al
BIN-EXPR-01	Is **/bin/expr** secured correctly?	ls -al

Related Topics

grep

sh

test

fc User Program

The **/bin/fc** (fix command) program lists, edits, or re-executes commands previously entered to an interactive shell.

There are two versions of the **fc** command that are identical except for the following:

The **/bin/fc** program starts a new shell process.

The built-in shell **fc** command doesn't start a new shell process.

The built-in shell **fc** command is the default. To invoke the program rather than the built-in command, you must use the full pathname to invoke **/bin/fc**.

RISK   The **/bin/fc** program does not behave like the Guardian FC command. It behaves like the **vi** editor. If the user is unfamiliar with **/bin/vi**, then usage can be very unpredictable.

Securing /bin/fc

BP-BIN-FC-01	fc should be secured 711 (rwx --x --x).
BP-BIN-OSSOWN-01	fc should be owned by SUPER.SUPER.
BP-BIN-OSSLOC-01	fc resides in **/bin**.

	Discovery Questions	Look here:
BIN-OSSOWN-01	Is **/bin/fc** owned by SUPER.SUPER?	ls -al
BIN-FC-01	Is **/bin/fc** secured correctly?	ls -al

Related Topics

grep

sh

test

fg User Program

The **/bin/fg** program brings background job processes to the foreground. It is the opposite of the **/bin/bg** program, which puts jobs into the background.

There are two versions of the **fg** command that are identical except for the following:

The **/bin/fg** program starts a new shell process.

The built-in shell **fg** command doesn't start a new shell process.

The built-in shell **fg** command is the default. To invoke the program rather than the built-in command, you must use the full pathname to invoke **/bin/fg**.

Users can only alter their own jobs. SUPER.SUPER can put anyone's jobs into the foreground.

Securing /bin/fg

BP-BIN-FG-01	**fg** should be secured 711 (rwx --x --x).
BP-BIN-OSSOWN-01	**fg** should be owned by SUPER.SUPER.
BP-BIN-OSSLOC-01	**fg** resides in **/bin**.

	Discovery Questions	**Look here:**
BIN-OSSOWN-01	Is **/bin/fg** owned by SUPER.SUPER?	ls -al
BIN-FG-01	Is **/bin/fg** secured correctly?	ls -al

Related Topics

bg
sh

fgrep User Program

The **/bin/fgrep** program searches a file for a fixed-string pattern. It searches the selected files for lines containing characters that match the specified pattern and then returns the matching lines. It is an obsolete version of the command **grep -F**, which searches for patterns that are fixed strings.

Users must have READ access to the files they wish to search.

Securing /bin/fgrep

BP-BIN-FGREP-01	**fgrep** should be secured 711 (rwx --x --x).
BP-BIN-OSSOWN-01	**fgrep** should be owned by SUPER.SUPER.
BP-BIN-OSSLOC-01	**fgrep** resides in **/bin**.

	Discovery Questions	Look here:
BIN-OSSOWN-01	Is **/bin/fgrep** owned by SUPER.SUPER?	ls -al
BIN-FGREP-01	Is **/bin/fgrep** secured correctly?	ls -al

Related Topics

ed

egrep

grep

sed

sh

file User Program

The **/bin/file** program reads input files, performs a series of tests on each one, and attempts to classify them by type. If file does not appear to be plain text, **/bin/file** attempts to distinguish a binary data file from a text file that contains extended characters.

For OSS text files, the program examines the file data and tries to determine what kind of text it contains. "string empty" is printed for any file type that has no data.

For regular files, the program checks the file format and returns its type. It can only detect object files created by HP compilers and tools. Object files generated by other sources are flagged as an unknown format.

If the file is not a regular OSS or Guardian file, its file type is identified as "directory", "fifo", "block", "special", and the message "character special" is displayed.

The program can be used on Guardian objects when specified with the /G pathname convention.

Guardian pathnames consisting of only G, volume names, or subvolume names are identified as directories.

For a Guardian regular nonobject file, the program invokes the Guardian procedure call FILE_GETINFO_ to retrieve the Guardian file type and file code attributes.

Guardian processes with subtype 30 are identified as character-special files.

Guardian nondisk devices and processes that are not of subtype 30 are identified as block special.

Users must have READ access to the files they are examining.

RISK   OSS shell programs such as **/bin/file** that perform recursive actions make no distinction between Guardian and OSS files or between local and remote files. The /G and /E directories both appear in users' local **root** directory, which puts both remote files and Guardian files at risk.

AP-ADVICE-ROOTDIR-01   Users should be careful about running **/bin/file** on the **root** directory, especially if they are working as SUPER.SUPER. If work must be done in the root directory, use the **–W NOG** and **–W NOE** flags.

3P-ADVICE-OBJSEC-01   If you have OSS users on the system who should not have access to Guardian files, consider a third-party object security product that can prevent such users from accessing files in the Guardian file space

Securing /bin/file

BP-BIN-FILE-01	file should be secured 711 (rwx --x --x).
BP-BIN-OSSOWN-01	file should be owned by SUPER.SUPER.
BP-BIN-OSSLOC-01	file resides in **/bin**.

	Discovery Questions	Look here:
BIN-OSSOWN-01	Is **/bin/owned** by SUPER.SUPER?	ls -al
BIN-FILE-01	Is **/bin/file** secured correctly?	ls -al

Related Topics

ls

locale

find User Program

The **/bin/find** program finds file names matching an expression. It recursively searches the directory tree for each specified pathname, seeking file names that match a Boolean expression written using terms given later. The output from **find** depends on the terms used in expression.

RISK OSS shell programs such as **/bin/find** that perform recursive actions make no distinction between Guardian and OSS files or between local and remote files. The **/G** and **/E** directories both appear in users' local **root** directory, which puts both remote files and Guardian files at risk.

AP-ADVICE-ROOTDIR-01 Users should be careful about running **/bin/find** on the **root** directory. If work must be done in the root directory, use the –W NOG and –W NOE flags.

3P-ADVICE-OBJSEC-01 If there are OSS users on the system who should not have access to Guardian files, consider a third-party object security product that can prevent such users from accessing files in the Guardian file space.

Securing /bin/find

BP-BIN-FIND-01	**find** should be secured 711 (rwx --x --x).
BP-BIN-OSSOWN-01	**find** should be owned by SUPER.SUPER.
BP-BIN-OSSLOC-01	**find** resides in **/bin**.

	Discovery Questions	Look here:
BIN-OSSOWN-01	Is **/bin/find** owned by SUPER.SUPER?	ls -al
BIN-FIND-01	Is **/bin/find** secured correctly?	ls -al

Related Topics

chmod

grep

ln

sh

test

flex User Program

The **/bin/flex** program is a tool for generating programs that recognize lexical patterns. It allows users to create structured input analyzers that generate a C language lexical analyzer from rules that provide tokens for an application. It has the same functionality as the **/bin/lex** program.

The user provides a file with a set of rules: paired regular expressions and C code. From this input file, **/bin/flex** generates a C source code file named lex.yy.c which can then be compiled and linked with the –ll library to produce an executable file. When the executable is run, it scans the specified input file and the rules. When it finds a match, it executes the associated C code.

AP-ADVICE-COMPILER-01   To protect applications from inadvertent or malicious changes or outages, compilers and related utilities should be absent or very tightly locked down on secure systems.

Related Files

flex.skel is the skeleton scanner.

lex.yy.c is the generated scanner C source.

lex.backtrack contains backtracking information generated when flex is run with the **-b** flag.

Securing /bin/flex

BP-BIN-FLEX-01   **flex** should be secured 711 (rwx --x --x).

BP-BIN-OSSOWN-01   **flex** should be owned by SUPER.SUPER.

BP-BIN-OSSLOC-01   **flex** resides in **/bin**.

	Discovery Questions	Look here:
BIN-OSSOWN-01	Is **/bin/flex** owned by SUPER.SUPER?	ls -al
BIN-FLEX-01	Is **/bin/flex** secured correctly?	ls -al

Related Topics
awk
lex
flex.skel
lex.yy.c
lex.backtrack
locale
sed
sh
yacc

flex.skel File

The **flex.skel** file is the skeleton scanner used by the **/bin/flex** program.

fold User Program

The **/bin/fold** program breaks (folds) lines in a file by inserting a new line character so that each output line is the maximum width possible but does not exceed the specified number of column positions (or bytes). The program is often used to send text files to line printers that truncate, rather than fold, lines wider than the printer is able to print (usually 80 or 132 column positions).

Users must have READ and WRITE access to the target file.

AP-ADVICE-DD-01 Rather than securing the **/bin/fold** program, which may be required for legitimate activity, secure any sensitive files so that only authorized personnel have READ access to them.

Reload the Gazette section of the previous book for more information on FTP.

Securing /bin/fold

BP-BIN-FOLD-01	**fold** should be secured 711 (rwx --x --x).
BP-BIN-OSSOWN-01	**fold** should be owned by SUPER.SUPER.
BP-BIN-OSSLOC-01	**fold** resides in **/bin**.

	Discovery Questions	Look here:
BIN-OSSOWN-01	Is **/bin/fold** owned by SUPER.SUPER?	ls -al
BIN-FOLD-01	Is **/bin/fold** secured correctly?	ls -al

Related Topics

expand

paste

unexpand

ftp in OSS

/usr/ucb/ftp is the OSS FTP client, which is invoked when users request an ftp connection to some other system.

The server is the Guardian FTPSERV process, which is invoked by the LISTNER each time a FTP connection request is made from either OSS or Guardian.

/usr/ucb/inetd does not initiate an FTP server (**ftpd**) as it would on other UNIX systems.

RISK   HP's implementation of FTP has no encryption capabilities. Sensitive data, userids, and passwords are transferred between remote nodes in the clear and unprotected, vulnerable to capture with a network sniffer.

AP-FTP-USERIDS-11   Some third-party products provide encryption for both the Command Channel (port) and the Data Channel (port) between the client FTP software and the FTP server software on the NonStop.

Refer to the Gazette section of the previous book for more information on FTP.

Securing /usr/ucb/ftp

BP-USR-FTP-01   **ftp** should be secured 711 (rwx --x --x).

BP-USR-OSSOWN-02   **ftp** should be owned by SUPER.SUPER.

BP-USR-OSSLOC-02   **ftp** resides in **/usr/ucb**.

	Discovery Questions	Look here:
USR-OSSOWN-02	Is **/usr/ucb/ftp** owned by SUPER.SUPER?	ls -al
USR-FTP-01	Is **/usr/ucb/ftp** secured correctly?	ls -al

Related Topics
expand
paste
sftp
unexpand

gencat User Program

The **/bin/gencat** program can be used to create a message catalog from a message text source file.

A message text source file is a text file created to hold messages meant to be printed by a program.

Message source files usually have the **.msg** suffix. They are created and altered with a text editor. Messages can be grouped into sets for functional subsets of a program. Each message must have a unique numeric identifier. The message text source file can also contain commands recognized by **gencat** for manipulating sets and individual messages.

RISK   The intent of the **/bin/gencat** program is to create message catalogs, not to alter existing catalogs; therefore, it deletes the old catalog before creating a new one.

AP-ADVICE-GENCAT-01   Only users responsible for creating and maintaining program messages should have WRITE and PURGE access to message text files.

Securing /bin/gencat

BP-BIN-GENCAT-01   **gencat** should be secured 711 (rwx --x --x).

BP-BIN-OSSOWN-01   **gencat** should be owned by SUPER.SUPER.

BP-BIN-OSSLOC-01   **gencat** resides in **/bin**.

	Discovery Questions	Look here:
BIN-OSSOWN-01	Is **/bin/gencat** owned by SUPER.SUPER?	ls -al
BIN-GENCAT-01	Is **/bin/gencat** secured correctly?	ls -al

Related Topics

dspcat

dspmsg

message text files

mkcatdefs

genxlt User Program

The **/bin/getxlt** program generates a code-set translation table. It reads a source code-set conversion table file from an input file and writes the compiled version to an output file.

Users must have READ access to the file being examined and be able to create files in the target directory.

AP-ADVICE-GENXLT-01 Rather than securing the **/bin/genxlt** program, which may be required for legitimate activity, secure any sensitive files so that only authorized personnel have READ access to them.

Securing /bin/genxlt

BP-BIN-GENXLT-01	**genxlt** should be secured 711 (rwx --x --x).
BP-BIN-OSSOWN-01	**genxlt** should be owned by SUPER.SUPER.
BP-BIN-OSSLOC-01	**genxlt** resides in **/bin**.

	Discovery Questions	Look here:
BIN-OSSOWN-01	Is **/bin/genxlt** owned by SUPER.SUPER?	ls -al
BIN-GENXLT-01	Is **/bin/genxlt** secured correctly?	ls -al

Related Topics

iconv

getconf User Program

The **/bin/getconf** program displays system configuration variable values and system path configuration variables.

The **/usr/include/limits.h file** defines maximum limits for certain system variables.

The **/usr/include/unistd.h file** defines system configuration variables.

Securing /bin/getconf

BP-BIN-GETCONF-01	**getconf** should be secured 711 (rwx --x --x).
BP-BIN-OSSOWN-01	**getconf** should be owned by SUPER.SUPER.
BP-BIN-OSSLOC-01	**getconf** resides in **/bin**.

	Discovery Questions	Look here:
BIN-OSSOWN-01	Is **/bin/getconf** owned by SUPER.SUPER?	ls -al
BIN-GETCONF-01	Is **/bin/getconf** secured correctly?	ls -al

Related Topics

env

SYSCONF

/usr/include/limits.h

/usr/include/unistd.h

getopts User Program

The **/bin/getopts** program parses command options for syntax errors and illegal options. It is a way to syntax check commands.

getopts is a built in shell program. It differs from regular programs because it does not open a new shell when it executes.

There are two versions of the **getops** command that are identical except for the following:

The **/bin/getops** program starts a new shell process.

The built-in shell **getops** command doesn't start a new shell process.

The built-in shell **getops** command is the default. To invoke the program rather than the built-in command, you must use the full pathname to invoke **/bin/getops**.

Securing /bin/getopts

BP-BIN-GETOPTS-01	**getopts** should be secured 711 (rwx --x --x).
BP-BIN-OSSOWN-01	**getopts** should be owned by SUPER.SUPER.
BP-BIN-OSSLOC-01	**getopts** resides in **/bin**.

	Discovery Questions	Look here:
BIN-OSSOWN-01	Is **/bin/getopts** owned by SUPER.SUPER?	ls -al
BIN-GETOPTS-01	Is **/bin/getopts** secured correctly?	ls -al

Related Topics

sh

gname User Program

The **/bin/gname** program displays the Guardian filename for an OSS file.

Securing /bin/gname

BP-BIN-GNAME-01	**gname** should be secured 711 (rwx --x --x).
BP-BIN-OSSOWN-01	**gname** should be owned by SUPER.SUPER.
BP-BIN-OSSLOC-01	**gname** resides in **/bin**.

	Discovery Questions	Look here:
BIN-OSSOWN-01	Is **/bin/gname** owned by SUPER.SUPER?	ls -al
BIN-GNAME-01	Is **/bin/gname** secured correctly?	ls -al

Related Topics

pname

grep User Program

The **/bin/grep** program searches a file for a string pattern.

Users must have READ access to the file being examined.

RISK   **/bin/grep** poses minimal risk as long as critical or sensitive application and system files are properly secured.

Securing /bin/grep

BP-BIN-GREP-01   **grep** should be secured 711 (rwx --x --x).

BP-BIN-OSSOWN-01   **grep** should be owned by SUPER.SUPER.

BP-BIN-OSSLOC-01   **grep** resides in **/bin.**

	Discovery Questions	Look here:
BIN-OSSOWN-01	Is **/bin/grep** owned by SUPER.SUPER?	ls -al
BIN-GREP-01	Is **/bin/grep** secured correctly?	ls -al

Related Topics
ed
locale
sed
shell
pname

group Configuration File

On systems other than the NonStop Server, the group file is used to assign userids to file-sharing groups. On the NonStop Server, Safeguard is used to create and manage file-sharing groups.

HP OSS processing does not use the **/etc/group, /etc/password**, or **/etc/ shadow** files. Some third-party software, such as Samba, NFS, Tuxedo, and OSI, may, however. Please refer to HP and the manufacturer's documentation on each of these products for information on the placement and use of these files as well as the risks involved.

gtacl User Program

The **/bin/gtacl** program runs a process in the Guardian environment from the OSS environment. It executes a Guardian program, TACL macro, TACL routine, TACL alias, or TACL command on the same node. The **gtacl** OSS process spawns a Guardian process.

The TACL object file is **/G/system/sysnn/tacl**.

If commands are entered via the OSS environment, the shell can process or expand operands on the command line before passing the line to gtacl to interpret.

All operands that the **gtacl** command does not interpret as OSS option arguments are passed in the Guardian environment startup message that is sent to the child process. **/bin/gtacl** does not expand operands or interpret special characters.

/bin/gtacl allows you to specify the environment and initial process attributes of the child process.

The **gtacl** program is commonly used to:

Start an interactive TACL process (**gtacl**)

Execute a single Guardian environment command **gtacl** with -c or -cv <command>

Run a Guardian environment program **gtacl -p** <program arguments>

The security of the Guardian object files determines the programs that OSS users can run via **/bin/gtacl**.

AP-ADVICE-GROUP-01   Secure Guardian object files appropriately.

RISK   Guardian security may not be configured to provide the OSS-based user with the proper access to appropriate utilities and data.

RISK   The **gtacl** inherits the Guardian userid. If **gtacl** is configured with a **setuid**, it will run as the owner of the program.

Securing /bin/gtacl

BP-BIN-GTACL-01	**gtacl** should be secured 711 (rwx --x --x).
BP-BIN-OSSOWN-01	**gtacl** should be owned by SUPER.SUPER.
BP-BIN-OSSLOC-01	**gtacl** resides in /**bin**.

	Discovery Questions	Look here:
BIN-OSSOWN-01	Is /**bin/gtacl** owned by SUPER.SUPER?	ls -al
BIN-GTACL-01	Is /**bin/gtacl** secured correctly?	ls -al

Related Topics

osh

sh

head User Program

The /**bin/head** program displays the first lines or bytes of each of the specified file(s).

Users must have READ access to the file being examined.

RISK   Displaying lines from files exposes the contents of the files.

AP-ADVICE-DD-01   Rather than securing the /**bin/head** program, which may be required for legitimate activity, secure any sensitive files so that only authorized personnel have READ access to them.

Securing /bin/head

BP-BIN-HEAD-01	**head** should be secured 711 (rwx --x --x).
BP-BIN-OSSOWN-01	**head** should be owned by SUPER.SUPER.
BP-BIN-OSSLOC-01	**head** resides in **/bin**.

	Discovery Questions	Look here:
BIN-OSSOWN-01	Is **/bin/head** owned by SUPER.SUPER?	ls -al
BIN-HEAD-01	Is **/bin/head** secured correctly?	ls -al

Related Topics

osh

sh

core

hosts Configuration File

The **/etc/hosts** file is used to resolve the common names of hosts into their corresponding **IP** addresses in the absence of a Domain Name Server. It is the OSS version of the Guardian HOSTS file. Please refer to the *OSS Gazette* section on the **inetd** Subsystem for more information.

hosts.equiv Configuration File

The **/bin/hosts.equiv** file specifies remote hosts from which users can execute programs on the local host (if these users have an account on the local host). Please refer to the *OSS Gazette* section on the **rsh/rshd** Subsystem for more information.

iconv User Program

The iconv program converts one code set to another. It looks for libraries as specified by LOCPATH. If none are specified, LOCPATH uses the default locations:

> The **/usr/lib/nls/loc/iconv/*** directory contains algorithmic converters.
> The **/usr/lib/nls/loc/iconvTable/*** directory contains table converters.
> The **/etc/nls/loc/*** directory contains table converters.

Users must have READ access to the files being converted and be able to create files in the target directory.

A character is any symbol used for the organization, control, or representation of data. A group of such symbols used to describe a particular language make up a character set. A code set contains the encoding values for a character set. It is the encoding values in a code set that provide the interface between the system and its input and output devices.

AP-ADVICE-DD-01   Rather than securing the **/bin/iconv** program, which may be required for legitimate activity, secure any sensitive files so that only authorized personnel have READ access to them.

Securing /bin/iconv

BP-BIN-ICONV-01   iconv should be secured 711 (rwx --x --x).

BP-BIN-OSSOWN-01 iconv should be owned by SUPER.SUPER.

BP-BIN-OSSLOC-01   iconv resides in **/bin**.

	Discovery Questions	Look here:
BIN-OSSOWN-01	Is **/bin/iconv** owned by SUPER.SUPER?	ls -al
BIN-ICONV-01	Is **/bin/iconv** secured correctly?	ls -al

Related Topics

genxlt

id User Program

The **/bin/id** program displays the userid and login (user) name of the invoking process or that of a specified user. When login names and userids do not match the real ones, the **/bin/id** command writes both.

If filesharing groups are supported:

> The group affiliations of the invoking process are also displayed.

> The group memberships of the specified user are displayed.

RISK   Unrestricted use of the **/bin/id** program can potentially make it easier for a hacker to launch a denial-of-service attack, because he can obtain a list of all userids on the system.

AP-ADVICE-ID-01   Restricting the use of the **/bin/id** program must be weighed against the inconvenience for users who cannot look up a user name when they only know the user number, and vice versa.

Securing /bin/id

BP-BIN-ID-01   id should be secured 711 (rwx --x --x).

BP-BIN-OSSOWN-01 id should be owned by SUPER.SUPER.

BP-BIN-OSSLOC-01   id resides in **/bin**.

	Discovery Questions	**Look here:**
BIN-OSSOWN-01	Is **/bin/id** owned by SUPER.SUPER?	ls -al
BIN-ID-01	Is **/bin/id** secured correctly?	ls -al

Related Topics

logname

id_dsa Files

$HOME/.ssh/id_dsa files contain the protocol version 1 DSA authentication RSA identity of each user.

There may also be equivalent public key files for each user named **$HOME/.ssh/id_dsa.pub.**

Please refer to the chapter on the SSH Subsystem in Part 4, *TCP/IP* for more information, or to the *OSS Gazette* section on SSH for Best Practice recommendations.

id_rsa Files

$HOME/.ssh/id_rsa files contain the protocol version 2 RSA authentication RSA identity of each user.

There may also be equivalent public key files for each user, named **$HOME/.ssh/id_rsa.pub.**

Please refer to the chapter on the SSH Subsystem in Part 4, *TCP/IP* for more information, or to the *OSS Gazette* section on SSH for Best Practice recommendations.

identity Files

$HOME/.ssh/identity files contain the protocol version 1 RSA authentication identity of each user. There might also be a global identity file.

There may also be equivalent public key files for each user named **$HOME/.ssh/id_identity.pub.**

Please refer to the chapter on the SSH Subsystem in Part 4, *TCP/IP* for more information, or to the *OSS Gazette* section on SSH for Best Practice recommendations.

import User Program

The **/usr/tandem/sqlmx/bin/import** file is a symbolic link to the $SYS-TEM.SYSTEM.IMPORT program provided to simplify execution of the Guardian program from OSS. Please refer to Guardian Gazette section on SQL/MX section for more information.

inetd Subsystem

The **/usr/ucb/inetd** process is the OSS equivalent of the Guardian environment's LISTNER. When inetd starts, it reads the **/etc/services** file to resolve the services configured in the **/etc/inetd.conf** (or Guardian PORTCONF, see below) file, and checks that the service name and corresponding port are valid. Once the accuracy of the **/etc/inetd.conf** file content is verified against the **services** file, the **inetd** process listens to the configured ports, waiting for incoming connection requests from remote clients. The **/etc/hosts** is also consulted for remote host address information.

/usr/ucb/inetd is required if OSS processes must be started via a LISTNER.

/usr/ucb/inetd is required if **rsh** (remote shell) is used.

The **/usr/ucb/inetd** program provides the following default services:

time	Displays the elapsed time, in machine-readable format, during the execution of a program, the time spent in the system, and the time spent in execution of the program on the diagnostic output system.
echo	Returns the string specified by the string argument.
discard	Discards characters or does nothing (for testing).
daytime	Displays the time in readable format.
chargen	Character generator.

Inetd is required for remote SQL/MX compiles. It is responsible for starting the **rexecd** process for the compiles.

AP-ADVICE-INETD-01   If the **inetd** subsystem is not required on the secure system, do not enable it.

BP-USR-INETD-01   **inetd** should be secured 711 (rwx --x --x).

BP-USR-OSSOWN-02   **inetd** should be owned by SUPER.SUPER.

BP-USR-OSSLOC-02   **inetd** resides in the **/usr/ucb** directory.

	Discovery Questions	Look here:
OSS-POLICY	Is the **inetd** subsystem required on the system?	Policy
USR-OSSOWN-02	Is **/usr/ucb/inetd** owned by SUPER.SUPER?	ls -al
USR-INETD-01	Is **/usr/ucb/inetd** secured correctly?	ls -al

inetd-Related Files

Installing **/usr/ucb/inetd** requires that its configuration files be copied from a Guardian subvolume to the OSS **/usr/ucb** directory. The configuration files are:

OSS File	Symbolic Link	Guardian File
/etc/hosts	Link to:	$SYSTEM.ZTCPIP.HOSTS
/etc/inetd.conf	Link to:	$SYSTEM.ZTCPIP.PORTCONF
/etc/networks	Link to:	$SYSTEM.ZTCPIP.NETWORKS
/etc/protocol	Link to:	$SYSTEM.ZTCPIP.PROTOCOL
/etc/resolv.conf	Link to:	$SYSTEM.ZTCPIP.RESCONF
/etc/services	Link to:	$SYSTEM.ZTCPIP.SERVICES

To use **rsh** (remote shell), each user must have an individual **.rhosts** file in his home directory.

To prevent confusion and conflicts between the LISTNER and **/etc/inetd** servers, HP recommends that the OSS versions of the files be symbolically linked to the Guardian files and that only the Guardian files be used to configure both servers.

hosts

TCP/IP hosts communicate with each other via IP addresses, but because IP addresses are difficult to remember, host (domain) names are usually assigned to the IP addresses and used to refer to them.

The **/etc/hosts** file is an edit file that contains an entry for each remote host known to a system. It is the OSS version of the Guardian HOSTS file and HP recommends that the OSS file be linked to the Guardian file so that the configuration can be maintained in a single place and used by both **inetd** and the LISTNER.

BP-LINK-INETD-01   Link **/etc/hosts** to the Guardian HOSTS file.

BP-FILE-HOSTS-01   The $SYSTEM.ZTCPIP.HOSTS file should be secured "NUUU".

A Domain Name Resolver (DNR) uses either a Domain Name Server (DNS) or a HOSTS file to match the domain name to an IP address. If there is no DNS server, the **/etc/hosts** is used to resolve the common names of hosts into their corresponding IP addresses.

HP provides a default version of the **/etc/hosts** file. It contains the same kind of information as the $SYSTEM.ZTCPIP.HOSTS file.

RISK   There may be more than one SERVICES and HOSTS file active for use with separate LISTNER processes. If more than one is used, it can become confusing, because it is sometimes difficult to determine which LISTNER is using which file.

BP-ETC-INETD-02	**hosts** should be secured 644 (rw- r-- r--).
BP-ETC-OSSOWN-01	**hosts** should be owned by SUPER.SUPER.
BP-ETC-OSSLOC-01	**hosts** resides in /etc.

	Discovery Questions	**Look here:**
OSS-POLICY	Does policy mandate that the **inetd** configuration files each be linked to their Guardian equivalents?	Policy
LINK-INETD-01	Is **/etc/hosts** file linked to the Guardian HOSTS file?	ls -al
ETC-OSSOWN-01	Is **/etc/hosts** owned by SUPER.SUPER?	ls -al
ETC-INETD-02	Is **/etc/hosts** secured correctly?	ls -al

hosts.equiv

The **/etc/hosts.equiv** file specifies trusted remote hosts. Any hostname listed in the file is completely trusted; a user connecting to the local system from a trusted system via **rsh/rshd** will be allowed to execute a command if he has the same userid on the local system.

This file can also specify a trusted user for each host; any user from a remote host will be allowed to access the local system with the identity of a local user and without a password.

RISK If a user is designated as trusted, then that user can access the local system without a password.

The remote authentication procedure determines whether a user from a remote host will be allowed to access the local system with the identity of a local user. This procedure first checks the **/etc/hosts.equiv** file and then checks the **$HOME/.rhosts** file in the home directory of the local user who is requesting access. The **/bin/rsh** program fails if the remote authentication procedure fails.

RISK If the local host trusts a remote host, any user who has the same userid on both systems can access the local system from the trusted host without a password.

RISK The trusted host mechanism relies on the security of the trusted host.

RISK Because trusted hosts are listed by hostname, an attacker who controls the DNS system could effectively log on to a system that relies on trusted hosts.

RISK Because the trusted host mechanism uses IP addresses for authentication, it is vulnerable to IP spoofing.

RISK Because the trusted host mechanism relies on the security of any trusted host, anyone with unauthorized access to a trusted host could misuse that trust to access another system that trusts it. If that system is, in turn, a trusted host for other systems, those systems are now vulnerable as well.

RISK DNS replication in a large network can be subject to long delays. Host names may resolve to more than one IP address.

If neither **/bin/rsh** nor **/bin/rcp** are not running, and no other systems are explicitly trusted, the **rhosts** file should either be removed or emptied and secured so that only SUPER.SUPER can WRITE to it.

BP-OSSFILE-INETD-01 Secure the **hosts.equiv** file to prevent its use.

AP-ADVICE-INETD-02 Create **/etc/hosts.equiv** file as a zero-length file. This enables it to be monitored for modification. If it does not exist or is empty, it cannot cause any problems.

AP-ADVICE-INETD-03 Use a **/bin/cron** task to periodically:

Check for the existence of any unexpected **hosts.equiv** files.

Report the contents of any **hosts.equiv** files.

Delete (or clear) any unapproved copies.

BP-ADVICE-INETD-04 Do not rely on the trusted host mechanism. Do not use any **hosts.equiv** files.

If you must use the **/etc/host.equiv** file, it must be carefully created and maintained. Take the following precautions:

AP-ADVICE-INETD-05   Keep only a small number of TRUSTED hosts in the **/etc/host.equiv** listed.

AP-ADVICE-INETD-06   Only trust systems within your domain or under your management.

AP-ADVICE-INETD-07   Ensure that the **/etc/host.conf** (or equivalent) is set to the order *host.equiv, bind*. Specify in the **/etc/host.equiv** file to allow "r" programs.

AP-ADVICE-INETD-08   Use only fully qualified hostnames such as hostname.domain.com in the **/etc/hosts.equiv file**.

AP-ADVICE-INETD-09   Only specific usernames should be included in **/etc/host.equiv** if access is truly required for specific users. Do not wildcard user names or groups.

AP-ADVICE-INETD-10   Do not have a + entry by itself anywhere in the **/etc/hosts.equiv** file, as this may allow any user access to the system.

AP-ADVICE-INETD-11   Validate the **/etc/hosts.equiv** file again after each patch or operating system installation.

BP-ETC-INETD-03   **hosts.equiv** should be secured 600 (rw- --- ---).

BP-ETC-OSSOWN-02   **hosts.equiv**   should   be   owned   by SUPER.SUPER.

BP-ETC-OSSLOC-02   **hosts.equiv** resides in **/etc**.

	Discovery Questions	**Look here:**
OSS-POLICY	Is the **hosts.equiv** file required on the system?	Policy
ETC-OSSOWN-02	Who owns **/etc/hosts.equiv**?	ls -al
ETC-INETD-03	Is **/etc/hosts.equiv** secured correctly?	ls -al

Personal hosts.equiv Files

There are few genuine needs for a **hosts.equiv** file in a user's home directory.

BP-OSSFILE-INETD-02   Do not allow copies of a **hosts.equiv** file in users' home directories.

If personal copies of a **hosts.equiv** file are required in users' home directories, they must be carefully created and maintained. Take the following precautions:

AP-ADVICE-INETD-12   Any allowed "personal" **hosts.equiv** files should be justified and documented.

AP-ADVICE-INETD-03   Use a **/bin/cron** task to periodically:

> Check for the existence of any unexpected **hosts.equiv** files
>
> Report the contents of all **hosts.equiv** files
>
> Delete (or clear) any unapproved copies, especially the **$HOME /.hosts.equiv** files.

BP-HOME-INETD-04   Each users's **hosts.equiv** files should be secured 600 (rw- --- ---).

BP-HOME-OSSOWN-00   Each user's **hosts.equiv** files should be owned by the user.

BP-HOME-OSSLOC-00   Each user's **hosts.equiv** files reside in $HOME.

	Discovery Questions	Look here:
OSS-POLICY	Are personal **hosts.equiv** files permitted on the system?	Policy
HOME-OSSOWN-00	Is each **$HOME/.hosts.equiv** file owned by the user?	ls -al
HOME-INETD-04	Is each **$HOME/. hosts.equiv** file secured correctly?	ls -al

inetd.conf

The inetd.conf file contains information on the services used for the Internet sockets on the system and is read by the **/usr/ucb/inetd** process as it starts. **inetd.conf** is the OSS equivalent of the Guardian PORTCONF file and, in fact, HP recommends that the OSS file be linked to the Guardian file so that the configuration can be maintained in a single place and used by both **inetd** and the LISTNER.

BP-LINK-INETD-02   Link **/etc/inetd.conf** to the Guardian PORT-CONF file.

BP-FILE-LISTNER-02   PORTCONF files should be secured "NUUU".

HP ships the **/etc/inetd.conf** file with the following default services:

time

echo

discard

daytime

chargen

RISK   Even seemingly innocuous services such as **echo** and **chargen** may be used in a denial-of-service attack.

AP-ADVICE-INETD-14   Comment out all unnecessary services, especially **echo** and **chargen**.

RISK   inetd can use any configuration file identified to it during its startup. The default is **/etc/inetd.conf**. If no specific configuration file is specified for **/etc/inetd**, the process will load the **/etc/inetd.conf** file, which might not be desired if alternative **inetd.conf** files are used.

AP-ADVICE-INETD-15   The program used to start the **/etc/inetd** process should explicitly specify the **inetd.conf** file.

RISK   Once the **/usr/ucb/inetd** process has read the **/etc/inetd.conf** file, the file is closed. If the **inetd.conf** file is modified, the changes will not be put into effect until **inetd** is told to do a reload.

RISK   If the **/etc/inetd.conf** file is used and the system does not have a **/etc/smplinetd.conf** file, your entries in **/etc/inetd.conf** can be overwritten during a product update.

AP-OSSFILE-INETD-16   Keep a tightly secured file called **/etc/ smplinetd.conf** to protect the customized **/etc/inetd.conf** file from being overwritten during product updates.

AP-ADVICE-INETD-17   Also make a copy of the **/etc/inetd.conf** configuration file whenever the file is changed in case the customized file is overwritten during product upgrades.

The **/etc/inetd.conf** file contains one line per service. Each line has at least six fields, separated by either spaces or tabs:

Service name	The name that appears in the **/etc/services** file
Socket type	Communicate via stream or datagram
Wait/Nowait	Multi-threaded or single threaded
User	The userid the process will run as
Command name	The program to start
Arguments	Any startup arguments

AP-ADVICE-INETD-18   If the **/etc/inetd.conf** file cannot be linked to the PORTCONF file, is a good idea to configure a service process to run as a userid other than SUPER.SUPER. It makes it possible to restrict access and therefore minimize the damage that can be done if a security hole in the server program should be exploited.

BP-ETC-INETD-05   inetd.conf should be secured 600 (rw- --- ---).

BP-ETC-OSSOWN-02   inetd.conf should be owned by SUPER. SUPER.

BP-ETC-OSSLOC-02   inetd.conf resides in /etc.

	Discovery Questions	**Look here:**
OSS-POLICY	Does policy mandate that the **inetd** configuration files each be linked to their Guardian equivalents?	Policy

(Continued)

	Discovery Questions	**Look here:**
LINK-INETD-02	Is the */etc/inetd.conf* file linked to the Guardian PORTCONF file?	ls -al
ETC-OSSOWN-02	Who owns */etc/inetd.conf*?	ls -al
ETC-INETD-05	Is */etc/inetd.conf* secured correctly?	ls -al

smplinetd File

The **/etc/smplinetd** file is provided by HP as a template for entries in the **/etc /inetd.conf** file.

RISK   If the **/etc/inetd.conf** file is used and the system does not have a **/etc/ smplinetd.conf** file, your customized entries in **/etc/inetd.conf** can be over-written during a product update.

BP-OSSFILE-INETD-16   Keep a tightly secured file called **/etc/ smplinetd.conf** to protect the customized **/etc/inetd.conf** file from being overwritten during product updates.

BP-ETC-INETD-06   **smplinetd** should be secured 600 (rw- --- ---).

BP-ETC-OSSOWN-01   **smplinetd** should be owned by SUPER.SUPER.

BP-ETC-OSSLOC-01   **smplinetd** resides in **/etc**.

	Discovery Questions	**Look here:**
OSS-POLICY	Does policy require that the exist?	ls -al
ETC-OSSOWN-01	Who owns */etc/smplinetd*?	ls -al
ETC-INETD-06	Is */etc/smplinetd* secured correctly?	ls -al

Networks File

The **/etc/networks** file contains information about the known networks that constitute the Internet. Each network is represented by a single line in the **networks** file, which defines the network name, number and any aliases (multiple names that map to the same IP address).

HP provides a default version of the **networks** file created from the official network database maintained at the Network Information Center (NIC). The file may need to be modified locally to include unofficial aliases or unknown networks.

/etc/networks is the equivalent of the Guardian NETWORKS file, and HP recommends that the OSS file be linked to the Guardian file, so that the configuration can be maintained in a single place and used by both **inetd** and the LISTNER

BP-LINK-INETD-03   Link **/etc/networks** to the Guardian NETWORKS file.

BP-FILE-NETWORKS-01   The $SYSTEM.ZTCPIP.NETWORKS file should be secured "NUUU".

BP-ETC-INETD-07   **networks** should be secured 644 (rw- r-- r--).

BP-ETC-OSSOWN-01   **networks** should be owned by SUPER.SUPER.

BP-ETC-OSSLOC-01   **networks** resides in **/etc**.

	Discovery Questions	**Look here:**
OSS-POLICY	Does policy mandate that the **inetd** configuration files each be linked to their Guardian equivalents?	Policy
LINK-INETD-03	Is the **/etc/networks** file linked to the Guardian NETWORKS file?	ls -al
ETC-OSSOWN-01	Who owns **/etc/networks**?	ls -al
ETC-INETD-07	Is **/etc/networks** secured correctly?	ls -al

Protocols File

The protocols file contains a list of protocols names supported by Non-Stop *TCP/IP.* Applications refer to the file to get protocol names and

Internet protocol numbers. This file is maintained by HP. It should not be changed.

AP-ADVICE-INETD-19   Do not alter the **protocols** file.

/etc/protocols is the equivalent of the Guardian PROTOCOLS file and HP recommends that the OSS file be linked to the Guardian file so that the configuration can be maintained in a single place and used by both **inetd** and the LISTNER.

BP-LINK-INETD-04   Link /etc/**protocols** to the Guardian PROTOCOLS file.

AP-ADVICE-INETD-20 If no Web services are used, the **protocols** file can be removed.

BP-ETC-INETD-08   **protocols** should be secured 644 (rw- r-- r--).

BP-ETC-OSSOWN-01   **protocols**   should   be   owned   by SUPER.SUPER.

BP-ETC-OSSLOC-01   **protocols** resides in /etc.

	Discovery Questions	Look here:
OSS-POLICY	Does policy mandate that the **inetd** configuration files each be linked to their Guardian equivalents?	Policy
LINK-INETD-04	Is the /etc/**protocols** file linked to the Guardian PROTOCOLS file?	ls -al
ETC-OSSOWN-01	Who owns /etc/**protocols**?	ls -al
ETC-INETD-08	Is /etc/**protocols** secured correctly?	ls -al

resolv.conf File

The Domain Name Resolver (DNR) resolves domain names to IP addresses using either a HOSTS file or a DNS server. If no TCPIP^HOST^FILE parameter is defined, then DNR assumes it must use a DNS. To determine which DNS to use, the DNR interrogates the **/etc/resolv.conf** file, which contains a list of valid Domain Name Servers and their IP addresses.

HP provides a default version of the **resolv.conf** file to use as a template.

/etc/resolv.conf is the equivalent of the Guardian RESCONF file, and HP recommends that the OSS file be linked to the Guardian file so that the configuration can be maintained in a single place and used by both **inetd** and the LISTNER.

AP-ADVICE-INETD-21   If you're using a DNS server, you must configure the **/etc/resolv.conf** and/or $SYSTEM.ZTCPIP.RESCONF files.

BP-LINK-INETD-05   Link **/etc/resolv.conf** to the Guardian RESCONF file.

BP-FILE-RESCONF-01   The $SYSTEM.ZTCPIP.RESCONF   file should be secured "NUUU".

BP-ETC-INETD-09   **resolv.conf** should be secured 644 (rw- r-- r--).

BP-ETC-OSSOWN-02   **resolv.conf** should be owned by SUPER.SUPER.

BP-ETC-OSSLOC-02   **resolv.conf** resides in **/etc**.

	Discovery Questions	**Look here:**
OSS-POLICY	Does policy mandate that the **inetd** configuration files each be linked to their Guardian equivalents?	Policy
LINK-INETD-05	Is the **resolv.conf** file linked to the Guardian RESCONF file?	ls -al
ETC-OSSOWN-01	Who owns **/etc/resolv.conf** ?	ls -al
ETC-INETD-09	Is **/etc/resolv.conf** secured correctly?	ls -al

Personal .rhosts Files

/bin/rsh queries the **$HOME/.rhosts** file, which specifies the remote hosts from which users can execute programs on the local host (if they have userids on the local host). This file can also specify a trusted user for each host. Please refer to the *OSS Gazette* section on the **rhosts** file for more information.

The **$HOME/.rhosts** files are required for **rsh/rshd** to authenticate the user.

Services File

The **/etc/services** file contains Internet port-level services that are available with NonStop *TCP/IP.*

Applications refer to this file to get the service port numbers and service names. Each entry specifies a service name, the port number through which that service is accessed, and the corresponding protocol, such as TCP or UDP, that supports that service. Aliases can be used to identify the service. This file is maintained by HP, but can be customized for your environment.

RISK There may be more than one Guardian SERVICES and HOSTS file active to separate LISTNER processes. If more than one is used, it can become confusing, because it is sometimes difficult to determine which LISTNER is using which file.

/etc/services is the equivalent of the Guardian SERVICES file, and HP recommends that the OSS file be linked to the Guardian file so that the configuration can be maintained in a single place and used by both **inetd** and the LISTNER.

BP-LINK-INETD-06 Link **/etc/services** to the Guardian SERVICES file.

BP-FILE-SERVICES-01 The $SYSTEM.ZTCPIP.SERVICES file should be secured "NUUU".

BP-ETC-SERVICES-10 **services** should be secured 644 (rw- r-- r--).

BP-ETC-OSSOWN-02 **services** should be owned by SUPER.SUPER.

BP-ETC-OSSLOC-02 **services** resides in **/etc.**

	Discovery Questions	Look here:
OSS-POLICY	Does policy mandate that the **inetd** configuration files each be linked to their Guardian equivalents?	Policy

(Continued)

	Discovery Questions	Look here:
LINK-INETD-06	Is the **services** file linked to the Guardian SERVICES file?	ls -al
ETC-OSSOWN-01	Who owns **/etc/services**?	ls -al
ETC-INETD-10	Is **/etc/services** secured correctly?	ls -al

Related Topics

rsh

rshd

DNS

DNR

LISTNER

NETWORKS

PORTCONF

PROTOCOL

RESCONF

SERVICES

InstallSqlmx

The **/usr/tandem/sqlmx/bin/InstallSqlmx** file is the SQL/MX install script.

ipcrm User Program

The **/bin/ipcrm** program removes message queues, semaphore identifiers, or shared memory identifiers and deallocates their data structures. The program can also be used to display the existing identifiers and keys, as can the **/bin/ipcs** program

Users must have WRITE access to the file being examined.

Securing /bin/ipcrm

BP-BIN-IPCRM-01   ipcrm should be secured 711 (rwx --x --x).

BP-BIN-OSSOWN-01 ipcrm should be owned by SUPER.SUPER.

BP-BIN-OSSLOC-01   ipcrm resides in /bin.

	Discovery Questions	Look here:
BIN-OSSOWN-01	Is /bin/ipcrm owned by SUPER.SUPER?	ls -al
BIN-IPCRM-01	Is /bin/ipcrm secured correctly?	ls -al

Related Topics

ipcs

ipcs User Program

The /bin/ipcs program reports interprocess communication (IPC) facilities status, including message queues, shared memory segments, semaphore sets, and local message queue headers.

Securing /bin/ipcs

BP-BIN-IPCS-01   ipcs should be secured 4711 (rws --x --x).

BP-BIN-SETUID-01   ipcs should have the **setuid** attribute.

BP-BIN-OSSOWN-01   ipcs should be owned by SUPER.SUPER.

BP-BIN-OSSLOC-01   ipcs resides in /bin.

	Discovery Questions	Look here:
BIN-OSSOWN-01	Is /bin/ipcs owned by SUPER.SUPER?	ls -al
BIN-IPCS-01	Is /bin/ipcs secured correctly?	ls -al

Related Topics

ipcrm

jobs User Program

The **/bin/jobs** program lists processes. If no job is specified, **/bin/jobs** displays information on all active processes.

There are two versions of the **jobs** command that are identical except for the following:

The **/bin/jobs** program starts a new shell process.

The built-in shell **jobs** command doesn't start a new shell process.

The built-in shell **jobs** command is the default. To invoke the program rather than the built-in command, you must use the full pathname to invoke **/bin/jobs**.

Securing /bin/jobs

BP-BIN-JOBS-01   **jobs** should be secured 711 (rwx --x --x).

BP-BIN-OSSOWN-01   **jobs** should be owned by SUPER.SUPER.

BP-BIN-OSSLOC-01   **jobs** resides in **/bin**.

	Discovery Questions	Look here:
BIN-OSSOWN-01	Is **/bin/jobs** owned by SUPER.SUPER?	ls -al
BIN-JOBS-01	Is **/bin/jobs** secured correctly?	ls -al

Related Topics

sh

join User Program

The **/bin/join** program joins the lines of two files. It reads both files, joins the lines that contain common fields, and displays the results.

Users must have READ access to both files and WRITE access to the target file and directory.

RISK If critical text files, whether application or system configuration files, are not properly secured, **/bin/join** can be used to display their contents.

AP-ADVICE-JOIN-01 Rather than securing the **/bin/join** object file, secure sensitive application data and scripts that are stored as text files so that they can only be viewed or copied by authorized personnel.

Securing /bin/join

BP-BIN-JOIN-01 **join** should be secured 711 (rwx --x --x).

BP-BIN-OSSOWN-01 **join** should be owned by SUPER.SUPER.

BP-BIN-OSSLOC-01 **join** resides in **/bin.**

	Discovery Questions	Look here:
BIN-OSSOWN-01	Is **/bin/join** owned by SUPER.SUPER?	ls -al
BIN-JOIN-01	Is **/bin/join** secured correctly?	ls -al

Related Topics

awk

cmp

comm

cut

diff

grep

paste

sort

uniq

locale

kill User Program

The **/bin/kill** program stops the specified process(es).

Users other than SUPER.SUPER can only stop processes they own.

/bin/kill can be used on Guardian processes if called with the process handle of the given process. The program issues a PROCESS_STOP_( ) against the named Guardian process.

There are two versions of the **kill** command that are identical except for the following:

The **/bin/kill** program starts a new shell process.

The built-in shell **kill** command doesn't start a new shell process.

The built-in shell **kill** command is the default. To invoke the program rather than the built-in command, you must use the full pathname to invoke **/bin/kill**.

Securing /bin/kill

BP-BIN-KILL-01   **kill** should be secured 711 (rwx --x --x).

BP-BIN-OSSOWN-01   **kill** should be owned by SUPER.SUPER.

BP-BIN-OSSLOC-01   **kill** resides in **/bin**.

	Discovery Questions	Look here:
BIN-OSSOWN-01	Is **/bin/kill** owned by SUPER.SUPER?	ls -al
BIN-KILL-01	Is **/bin/kill** secured correctly?	ls -al

Related Topics

ps

sh

known_hosts File

The SSH client stores a **known_hosts** file in each user's home directory. It maps the host names and IP addresses of every remote host that the user has connected to with the host's public key. Please refer to the section on the SSH Subsystem in Part 4, *TCP/IP* for more information or the *OSS Gazette* section on SSH for Best Practice recommendations.

ksh Command Interpreter

The **/bin/ksh** shell is an interactive command interpreter and a command programming language based on the UNIX Korn shell. **/bin/ksh** is actually an alias for **/bin/sh**.

/bin/ksh and **/bin/sh** are the OSS equivalents of TACL. All are command interpreters with scripting languages.

The OSS shell carries out commands either interactively from a terminal keyboard or from a file.

RISK   **/bin/ksh** poses minimal risk other than redirection.

Securing /bin/ksh

BP-BIN-KSH-01   ksh should be secured 711 (rwx --x --x).

BP-BIN-OSSOWN-01 ksh should be owned by SUPER.SUPER.

BP-BIN-OSSLOC-01   ksh resides in **/bin**.

	Discovery Questions	**Look here:**
BIN-OSSOWN-01	Is **/bin/ksh** owned by SUPER.SUPER?	ls -al
BIN-KSH-01	Is **/bin/ksh** secured correctly?	ls -al

Related Topics

sh

locale

lex User Program

The **/bin/lex** program generates scanners that recognize lexical patterns for the C language. It allows users to create structured input analyzers that generate a C language lexical analyzer from rules that provide tokens for an application.

The user provides a file with a set of rules: paired regular expressions and C code. From this input file, **/bin/flex** generates a C source code file named **lex.yy.c**, which can then be compiled and linked with the –ll library to produce an executable file. When the executable is run, it scans the specified input file and the rules. When it finds a match, it executes the associated C code.

The **/bin/lex** utility is often used in conjunction with **/bin/yacc**, which parses the stream of tokens that the lexical analyzer produces.

RISK **/bin/lex** poses minimal risk as long as critical files and process names, whether application or system utilities, are properly secured in both the OSS and Guardian environments.

AP-ADVICE-COMPILER-01 To protect applications from inadvertent or malicious changes or outages, compilers and related utilities should be absent or very tightly locked down on secure systems.

Securing /bin/lex

BP-BIN-LEX-01   lex should be secured 711 (rwx --x --x).

BP-BIN-OSSOWN-01 lex should be owned by SUPER.SUPER.

BP-BIN-OSSLOC-01 lex resides in **/bin**.

	Discovery Questions	**Look here:**
OSS-POLICY	Is **/bin/lex** utility allowed on the system	Policy
BIN-OSSOWN-01	Is **/bin/lex** owned by SUPER.SUPER?	ls -al
BIN-LEX-01	Is **/bin/lex** secured correctly?	ls -al

Related Topics

awk

flex

sed

yacc

locale

lex.backtrack File

The **lex.backtrack** file contains backtracking information generated when **/bin/flex** is run with the -b flag.

lex.yy.c File

The **lex.yy.c** file contains the scanner C source created by the **/bin/flex** program. It has the same functionality as the **/bin/lex** file.

Library Files

Libraries are sets of common utility routines that are called by other routines. A library is a set of procedures that the operating system can link to a program file at compile time. Libraries are used for the following reasons:

To reduce the storage space required for object code on disk and in main memory

To share a set of common procedures among applications

To extend a single application's code space

The majority of libraries are contained in the **/usr/lib** directory tree, but may be found under **/usr/tandem**. Open Source programs such as Samba, SSH, and SSL may place libraries in the **/usr/local** directory tree.

BP-BIN-LIBRARY-01   Only SUPER.SUPER should have WRITE and PURGE access to the library files or the directories where they reside.

BP-BIN-LIBRARY-02   The majority, if not all, users on the system should have READ access to libraries and to the directories where they reside.

Third-party applications often supply their own libraries. Refer to the product documentation for the location and security recommendation for these libraries.

Refer to HP's *Open Systems Services Library Calls Reference Manual* and *Open Systems Services System Calls Reference Manual* for detailed information about individual libraries.

Securing libraries

BP-OSSDIR-LIBRARY-01 Libraries should be secured 744 (rwx r-- r--).

BP-OSSDIR-OSSOWN-02 Libraries should be owned by SUPER.SUPER.

BP-OSSDIR-DIRLOC-02 Libraries reside in the **/usr/tandem** directory tree.

BP-OSSDIR-DIRLOC-02 Libraries reside in **/usr/local** directory tree.

BP-OSSDIR-DIRLOC-02 Libraries reside in **/usr/lib** directory tree.

	Discovery Questions	**Look here:**
OSS-POLICY	Does policy restrict access to libraries?	Policy
OSSDIR-OSSOWN-01	Are all library files owned by SUPER.SUPER?	ls -al
OSSDIR-LIBRARY-01	Are all library files secured correctly?	ls -al

Related Topics

nld

eld (Integrity servers)

ksh

sh

line User Program

The **/bin/line** program reads one line from the standard input file (stdin) and copies it to the standard output file (stdout). It is used within a shell to read from the user's terminal.

There are two versions of the **line** command that are identical except for the following:

The **/bin/line** program starts a new shell process.

The built-in shell **line** command doesn't start a new shell process.

The built-in shell **line** command is the default. To invoke the program rather than the built-in command, you must use the full pathname to invoke **/bin/line**.

Securing /bin/line

BP-BIN-LINE-01   **line** should be secured 711 (rwx --x --x).

BP-BIN-OSSOWN-01 **line** should be owned by SUPER.SUPER.

BP-BIN-OSSLOC-01   **line** resides in **/bin**.

	Discovery Questions	Look here:
BIN-OSSOWN-01	Is **/bin/line** owned by SUPER.SUPER?	ls -al
BIN-LINE-01	Is **/bin/line** secured correctly?	ls -al

Related Topics

echo

ksh

sh

In User Program

The **/bin/ln** program links a file to another file. It is a way to assign multiple names to a file.

In OSS, files are actually identified by their inode number. A link assigns an additional name to an inode number. Directories are actually files containing link-to-inode pairs. Every directory has at least two hard links:

    .   pointing to itself

    ..   pointing to its parent directory

By default, **/bin/ln** creates hard links. Hard links can only be created between files in the same fileset. With hard links, any changes in file characteristics affect any link to it, and all links are equal. However, if one name is deleted, the others will remain. To completely delete a hard-linked file, all of its links must be deleted.

If the **/bin/ln -s** flag is used, a symbolic link is created. Symbolic links allow users to assign a file another name, but it doesn't link the file by inode number. There are some important differences between hard links and symbolic links, as shown in the table below.

Hard Link	Symbolic Link
Linked file and target file must be in same fileset	Linked file and target file need not be in the same fileset
Target file must exist	Target file need not exist
Linked file and target file can have different security	Security to the linked file is based on the target file's permission string

Links to Guardian files must be symbolic links.

RISK Caution should be used when deleting files on a system that has hard links in place. The user must be sure whether it is the underlying file or the link that is being deleted.

AP-ADVICE-LN-01   Rather than securing the **/bin/ln** program, which may be required for legitimate activity, secure any sensitive files so that only authorized personnel have READ access to them.

Anyone who can see a file can create a link to it. Anyone who can search a directory can create a link to a file in it.

Securing /bin/ln

BP-BIN-LN-01   ln should be secured 711 (rwx --x --x).

BP-BIN-OSSOWN-01 ln should be owned by SUPER.SUPER.

BP-BIN-OSSLOC-01   ln resides in **/bin**.

	Discovery Questions	Look here:
BIN-OSSOWN-01	Is **/bin/ln** owned by SUPER.SUPER?	ls -al
BIN-LN-01	Is **/bin/ln** secured correctly?	ls -al

Related Topics

cp

mv

rm

locale Configuration File

The **/usr/include/locale** file contains system wide values that determine the display and print format for currency, numbers, and dates on a system. Please refer to the *OSS Gazette* section on **/bin/localedef** for more information.

locale Subsystem

The **locale** file contains systemwide values that determine the display and print format for currency, numbers, and dates on a system.

locale Subsystem Components

The following files are part of the **locale** processing:

locale program

localedef

locale file

source files for supported locales

source files for supported character sets

/bin/locale User Program

The **/bin/locale** program displays information from the **/usr/include/locale** file, which contains systemwide values that determine the display and print format for currency, numbers, and dates on a system.

The **locale** settings have implications for the **kill, ksh, lex, lp,** and **lpstat** programs, which refer to **locale** files for format and character set information.

BP-BIN-LOCALE-01   locale should be secured 711 (rwx --x --x).

BP-BIN-OSSOWN-01 locale should be owned by SUPER.SUPER.

BP-BIN-OSSLOC-01   locale resides in /bin.

	Discovery Questions	Look here:
BIN-OSSOWN-01	Is /bin/locale owned by SUPER.SUPER?	ls -al
BIN-LOCALE-01	Is /bin/locale secured correctly?	ls -al

localedef System Utility

The **/bin/localedef** program processes locale and character map files.

Locales can only be modified by creating a new **locale** source file with an editor and then using the **/bin/localedef** program to compile the new locale definition source file.

The locale settings have implications for the **kill, ksh, lex, lp,** and **lpstat** programs, which refer to locale files for format and character set information.

locale settings are intended to be systemwide and should only be configured by the system administrator.

BP-LOCALE-LOCALE-01 Only users responsible for configuring the display and print format for currency, numbers, and dates on a system should have access to the source files, which prevents unauthorized users from altering the settings via **/bin/localedef.**

BP-BIN-LOCALEDE-01 **localedef** should be secured 700 (rwx --- ---).

BP-BIN-OSSOWN-01 **localedef** should be owned by SUPER.SUPER.

BP-BIN-OSSLOC-01 **localedef** resides in **/bin.**

	Discovery Questions	**Look here:**
OSS-POLICY	Who are the users responsible for maintaining the system **locale** file?	Policy
BIN-OSSOWN-01	Is **/bin/localedef** owned by SUPER.SUPER?	ls -al
BIN-LOCALEDE-01	Is **/bin/localedef** secured correctly?	ls -al

usr/include/locale Configuration File

The **/usr/include/locale** file is comprised of three parts: language, territory, and code set. It is where the default display and print format for currency, numbers, and dates on a system is set.

The default locale is the C locale, which specifies the value English as the language, U.S. as the territory, and ASCII as code set.

The contents of the **/usr/include/locale** file can be displayed with the **/bin/locale** program.

RISK   The **/usr/include/locale** file settings are intended to be system-wide and should only be configured by the system administrator.

BP-LOCALE-LOCALE-02   Only SUPER.SUPER should have WRITE and PURGE access to the **/usr/include/locale** file.

BP-USR-LOCALE-01   **locale** configuration file should be secured 644 (rw- r-- r--).

BP-USR-OSSOWN-02 **locale** configuration file should be owned by SUPER.SUPER.

BP-USR-OSSLOC-02   **locale** configuration file resides in **/usr/include/**.

	Discovery Questions	**Look here:**
OSS-POLICY	Who are the users responsible for maintaining the system **locale** file?	Policy
USR-OSSOWN-02	Is **/usr/include/locale** owned by SUPER.SUPER?	ls -al
USR-LOCALE-01	Is **/usr/include/locale** secured correctly?	ls -al

Source Files for Supported Locales

The **/bin/localedef** program uses the source files for supported locales located in the **/usr/lib/nls/loc/src/*** directory.

BP-LOCALE-SOURCE-01   Only SUPER.SUPER should have WRITE and PURGE access to these files. Only users responsible for building new locale files require READ access to these files.

BP-USR-LOCALE-02   The locale source files should be secured 644 (rw- r-- r--).

BP-USR-OSSOWN-05 The locale source files should be owned by SUPER.SUPER.

BP-USR-OSSLOC-05   The locale source files reside in **/usr/lib/nls/loc/src.**

BP-LOC-DIRSEC-05   The **/usr/lib/nls/loc/src** directory should be secured 644 (rw- r-- r--).

BP-LOC-DIROWN-05 The **/usr/lib/nls/loc/src** directory should be owned by SUPER.SUPER.

BP-LOC-DIRLOC-05 The **/usr/lib/nls/loc/src** directory reside in **/usr/lib/nls/loc.**

	Discovery Questions	Look here:
OSS-POLICY	Who are the users responsible for maintaining global definitions?	Policy
USR-OSSOWN-05	Are the **locale** source files owned by SUPER.SUPER?	ls -al
USR-LOCALE-02	Are the **locale** source files secured correctly?	ls -al
LOC-DIROWN-05	Is the **/usr/lib/nls/loc/src** directory owned by SUPER.SUPER?	ls -al
LOC-DIRSEC-05	Is the **/usr/lib/nls/loc/src** directory secured correctly?	ls -al

Source Files for Supported Character Set Descriptions

The **/bin/localedef** program uses the source files for supported character set descriptions (charmap) located in the **/usr/lib/nls/loc/charmap** directory.

BP-LOCALE-CHARMAP-01 Only SUPER.SUPER should have WRITE and PURGE access to these files. Only users responsible for building new locale files require READ access to these files.

BP-USR-LOCALE-03 The **charmap** files should be secured 644 (rw- r-- r--).

BP-USR-OSSOWN-04 The **charmap** files should be owned by SUPER.SUPER.

BP-USR-OSSLOC-04 The **charmap** files reside in **/usr/lib/nls/loc/charmap.**

BP-CHARMAP-DIRSEC-05 The **/usr/lib/nls/loc/charmap** directory should be secured 644 (rw- r-- r--).

BP-CHARMAP-DIROWN-05 The **/usr/lib/nls/loc/charmap** directory should be owned by SUPER.SUPER.

BP-CHARMAP-DIRLOC-05 The **/usr/lib/nls/loc/charmap** directory
reside in **/usr/lib/nls/loc**

	Discovery Questions	Look here:
OSS-POLICY	Who are the users responsible for maintaining the system **locale** file?	Policy
USR-OSSOWN-04	Are the **charmap** files owned by SUPER.SUPER?	ls -al
USR-LOCALE-03	Are the **charmap** files secured correctly?	ls -al
CHARMAP-DIROWN-05	Is the **/usr/lib/nls/loc/charmap** directory owned by SUPER.SUPER?	ls -al
CHARMAP-DIRSEC-05	Is the **/usr/lib/nls/loc/charmap** directory secured correctly?	ls -al

Related Topics

kill

ksh

lex

locale configuration file

localedef

lp

lpstat

logger User Program

The **/bin/logger** program writes entries in the system log file. By default, it
writes to $0. What will be written depends on the current system log config-
uration. Refer to the *OSS Gazette* chapter on **syslog** for more information.

Securing /bin/logger

BP-BIN-LOGGER-01 **logger** should be secured 711 (rwx --x --x).

BP-BIN-OSSOWN-01 logger should be owned by SUPER.SUPER.

BP-BIN-OSSLOC-01   logger resides in **/bin.**

	Discovery Questions	Look here:
BIN-OSSOWN-01	Is **/bin/logger** owned by SUPER.SUPER?	ls -al
BIN-LOGGER-01	Is **/bin/logger** secured correctly?	ls -al

Related Topics

syslog

logname User Program

The **/bin/logname** program displays the current user's login name. It can be used to write the name to the standard output file, so the value can be retrieved by other programs.

Securing /bin/logname

BP-BIN-LOGNAME-01   **logname** should be secured 711 (rwx --x --x).

BP-BIN-OSSOWN-01   **logname** should be owned by SUPER.SUPER.

BP-BIN-OSSLOC-01   **logname** resides in **/bin.**

	Discovery Questions	Look here:
BIN-OSSOWN-01	Is **/bin/logname** owned by SUPER.SUPER?	ls -al
BIN-LOGNAME-01	Is **/bin/logname** secured correctly?	ls -al

Related Topics

env

lp User Program

The **/bin/lp** program sends files to a printer. Various conmmand options allow users to set print parameters. **/bin/lp** does not do any preprocessing, so some special characters may not be treated correctly.

Securing /bin/lp

BP-BIN-LP-01   **lp** should be secured 711 (rwx --x --x).

BP-BIN-OSSOWN-01 **lp** should be owned by SUPER.SUPER.

BP-BIN-OSSLOC-01   **lp** resides in **/bin**.

	Discovery Questions	Look here:
BIN-OSSOWN-01	Is **/bin/lp** owned by SUPER.SUPER?	ls -al
BIN-LP-01	Is **/bin/lp** secured correctly?	ls -al

Related Topics

cancel

lpstat

lpstat User Program

The **/bin/lpstat** program displays printer, print process, and print job statuses. Various command options enable the user to control the information displayed.

Jobs can be in one of four states: OPEN, READY, PRINT, or HOLD:

When a job request is in the process of being copied to the spooling area, it is in the OPEN state.

When the job reaches the spooler queue it is in the READY state.

When a printer accepts the job from the spooler queue, the job is in the PRINT state.

If errors prevent a job from being copied to the spooler, the job is in the HOLD state.

The Guardian spooler utilities PERUSE and SPOOLCOM display the same information as **/bin/lpstat** for any print job.

Securing /bin/lpstat

BP-BIN-LPSTAT-01   lpstat should be secured 711 (rwx --x --x).

BP-BIN-OSSOWN-01   lpstat should be owned by SUPER.SUPER.

BP-BIN-OSSLOC-01   lpstat resides in **/bin**.

	Discovery Questions	Look here:
OSS-POLICY	Who is allowed to control printers?	Policy
BIN-OSSOWN-01	Is **/bin/lpstat** owned by SUPER.SUPER?	ls -al
BIN-LPSTAT-01	Is **/bin/lpstat** secured correctly?	ls -al

Related Topics

lp

ls User Program

The **/bin/ls** program lists files and their characteristics. Various command flags allow users to control the information displayed and the format it is displayed in.

AP-ADVICE-ROOTDIR-01   Users should be careful about running **/bin/ls** on the **root** directory. If work must be done in the root directory, use the **–W NOG** and **–W NOE** flags

Securing /bin/ls

BP-BIN-LS-01   ls should be secured 711 (rwx --x --x).

BP-BIN-OSSOWN-01 ls should be owned by SUPER.SUPER.

BP-BIN-OSSLOC-01   ls resides in /bin.

	Discovery Questions	Look here:
BIN-OSSOWN-01	Is /bin/ls owned by SUPER.SUPER?	ls -al
BIN-LS-01	Is /bin/ls secured correctly?	ls -al

Related Topics

chmod

find

ln

locale

stty

UTILSGE

magic File

The /bin/files program uses the /etc/magic file to identify files that have a "magic" number; that is, that the file contains a string constant that indicates file type.

The following **magic** values are supported:

Byte Offset	Value Type	Magic Value	Printed String
0	string	070707	ASCII CRON archive
0	String	%!	PostScript document
0	String	<MakerFile>	FrameMaker document

(Continued)

Byte Offset	Value Type	Magic Value	Printed String
0	String	<MIFFile>	FrameMaker MIF document
0	String	<MML>	FrameMaker MML document
0	String	!<arch>	archive
257	String	Ustar	tar archive
40	String	SunBin	Sun binary

Other values can be added to the **/etc/magic** file to customize it to your system.

Securing /etc/magic

BP-BETC-MAGIC-01 **magic** should be secured 644 (rw- r-- r--).

BP-ETC-OSSOWN-01 **magic** should be owned by SUPER.SUPER.

BP-BETC-OSSLOC-01 **magic** resides in /etc.

	Discovery Questions	Look here:
ETC-OSSOWN-01	Who owns the **magic** file?	ls -al
ETC-MAGIC-01	Is the **magic** secured correctly?	ls -al

Related Topics

inetd.conf

rsh

services

make User Program

The **/bin/make** program is used to maintain program dependencies. It lets programmers define a set of rules about how application files should be compiled and linked together. The rules reside in files called **makefiles**. There can be more than one **makefile** on a system. Users must specify the appropriate file to process when they invoke **/bin/make**. By default, **/bin/make** first searches for the **./makefile** and then the **./Makefile**.

RISK   The dependencies and relationships established by the **makefile** can affect application and even systemwide processing.

BP-BIN-MAKE-01   **/bin/make** should be secured so that only those users responsible for managing application and system dependencies can execute it.

AP-ADVICE-COMPILER-01   To protect applications from inadvertent or malicious changes or outages, compilers and related utilities should be absent or very tightly locked down on secure systems.

Securing /bin/make

BP-BIN-MAKE-01   make should be secured 711 (rwx --x --x).

BP-BIN-OSSOWN-01 make should be owned by SUPER.SUPER.

BP-BIN-OSSLOC-01   make resides in **/bin**.

	Discovery Questions	Look here:
BIN-OSSOWN-01	Is **/bin/make** owned by SUPER.SUPER?	ls -al
BIN-MAKE-01	Is **/bin/make** secured correctly?	ls -al

Related Topics

sh

environment

makefile

makefile Configuration Files

makefile files consists of a series of commands listing files required by other files or programs. They are used by programmers to define a set of rules about how application files should be compiled and linked together. Various command flags determine the type and configuration of dependencies.

There can be more than one makefile on a system. Users must specify the appropriate file to process when they invoke **/bin/make**. By default, make first searches for the **./makefile** and then the **./Makefile**.

There are four types of dependencies:

1. **File dependencies** relationships where targets depend on sources and are usually created from them. There are two types of file dependencies:

   Target rules, which determine how the target should be built.

   Inference rules, which determine how a target should be kept up-to-date.

2. **Shell commands** a series of shell commands used to create a target.

3. **Variable assignments** variable values meant to be passed in as a target is created.

4. **Comments** explanatory comments to document the particular **makefile**.

RISK The dependencies and relationships established by a **makefile** can affect application and even system-wide processing.

AP-ADVICE-MAKEFILE-01 All **makefile** files on the system should be secured so that only those users responsible for managing application and system dependencies can alter them.

Securing makefile Files

BP-ANYDIR-MAKEFILE-01 **makefile** files should be secured 644 (rwx r—r--).

BP-ANYDIR-OSSOWN-07 **makefile** files should be owned by an appropriate user.

BP-ANYDIR-OSSLOC-07   **makefile** files can be placed in any appropriate location.

	Discovery Questions	Look here:
ANYDIR-OSSOWN-01	Is /?/**makefile** owned by the correct userid?	ls -al
ANYDIR-MAKEFILE-01	Is /?/**makefile** secured correctly?	ls -al

Related Topics

sh

environ

make

man User Program

The **/bin/man** program displays the requested pages of the online OSS reference manual. **/bin/man** determines the location of the reference material using the MANPATH environment variable.

/bin/man Components

The **/bin/man** reference pages, usually referred to as "man pages," are contained in subdirectories named cat# and man#:

cat1	Commands available to the general interactive user
cat2	Application program interface functions
cat3	Application program interface functions for C and C++programs
cat4	Application program interface header files and other file formats
cat5	Miscellaneous topics
cat6	Empty on the NonStop Server
cat7	Special file information
cat8	Commands intended for system administrators

If **man** doesn't find the requested information in the cat# subdirectories, it searches the man# subdirectories, if present.

The cat# subdirectories exist in the following directories:

HP products:

– **/usr/share/man,** which contains the basic OSS product set reference pages

– **/nonnative/usr/share/man,** which contains reference pages for the TNS C compiler

Other products:

– Independent products either create additional directories for reference pages or add their reference page files to one of these

AP-ADVICE-MAN-01 All users should have READ access to the system **man** pages. Only SUPER.SUPER should have WRITE and PURGE access.

AP-ADVICE-MAN-01 Only appropriate users should have WRITE and PURGE access to specialized or third party man pages.

Securing /bin/man

BP-BIN-MAN-01	**man** should be secured 711 (rwx --x --x).
BP-BIN-OSSOWN-01	**man** should be owned by SUPER.SUPER.
BP-BIN-OSSLOC-01	**man** resides in /bin.
BP-USR-MAN-01	**man** pages should be secured 744 (rwx r-- r--).
BP-USR-MAN-02	**man** pages* should be secured 744 (rwx r-- r--).
BP-USR-OSSOWN-03 SUPER.	**man** pages should be owned by SUPER.
BP-USR-OSSLOC-03	native **man** pages resides in **/usr/share/man.**
BP-USR-OSSLOC-04 share/man.	nonnative **man** pages reside in **/nonnative/usr/share/man.**

BP-MAN-DIRSEC-03   man page directories should be secured
744 (rwx r-- r--).

BP-MAN-DIROWN-03   man page directories should be owned
by SUPER.SUPER.

BP-MAN-DIRLOC-02   the native **man** page directory resides in
/usr/share/.

BP-NONNATIV-DIRSEC-03   man page directories should be secured
744 (rwx r-- r--).

BP-NONNATIV-DIROWN-03 man page directories should be owned
by SUPER.SUPER.

BP-MAN-DIRLOC-04   the nonnative **man** page directory resides
in **/nonnative/usr/share.**

	Discovery Questions	**Look here:**
OSS-POLICY	Does the security policy restrict who is allowed to add man pages?	Policy
BIN-MAN-01	Is **/bin/man** owned by SUPER.SUPER?	ls -al
USR-OSSOWN-03	Are the **/usr/share/man/*** man pages owned by SUPER.SUPER?	ls -al
MAN-DIROWN-03	Is the **/usr/share/man** directory owned by SUPER.SUPER?	ls -al
NONNATIV-DIROWN-03	Is the **/nonnative/share/man** directory owned by SUPER.SUPER?	ls -al
USR-MAN-01	Is **/usr/man** secured correctly?	ls -al
USR-MAN-02	Are the **/usr/share/man/*** man pages secured correctly?	ls -al
MAN-DIRSEC-03	Is the **/usr/share/man** directory secured correctly?	ls -al
NONNATIV-DIRSRC-03	Is the **/nonnative/usr/share** directory secured correctly?	ls -al

Related Topics

apropos

more

merge_whatis

merge_whatis System Utility

The **/bin/merge_whatis** program creates and updates the **whatis** database used by the **/bin/man**, **/bin/apropos** and **/bin/whatis** programs.

Message Text Files (.msg)

A message text source file is a text file created to hold messages meant to be displayed or printed by a program. Please refer to the *OSS Gazette* section on **gencat** or **mkcatdefs** user programs for more information.

migrate

The **/usr/tandem/sqlmx/bin/migrate** file is the OSS file for the migrate utility. Please refer to the *OSS Gazette* section on SQL/MX for more information.

mkcatdefs User Program

The **/bin/mkcatdefs** program preprocesses a message source file, changing symbolic identifiers to numbers. It produces a file called **<catalog name>.msg.h**, which shows both the numeric and source values (symbolic names).

A message text source file is a text file created to hold messages meant to be printed by a program.

Message source files usually have the .msg suffix. They are created and altered with a text editor. Messages can be grouped into sets for functional subsets of a program. Each message must have a unique numeric identifier. The message text source file can also contain commands recognized by **/bin /gencat** for manipulating sets and individual messages.

RISK   Because the intent of the **/bin/mkcatdefs** program is to create message catalogs, it does not alter existing catalogs, it deletes the old catalog and creates a new one.

AP-ADVICE-GENCAT-01   Only users responsible for creating and maintaining program messages should have WRITE and PURGE access to message text files.

AP-ADVICE-GENCAT-02   Only users responsible for creating and maintaining program messages should have EXECUTE access to the **/bin /gencat** program.

AP-ADVICE-MKCATDEF-01   Only users responsible for creating and maintaining program messages should have EXECUTE access to the **/bin /mkcatdefs** program.

The only difference between **/bin/gencat** and **/bin/mkcatdefs** is that **/bin /gencat** requires that each message have a numeric identifier. **/bin/mkcat-defs** accepts either the message number or the symbolic name.

Securing /bin/mkcatdefs

BP-BIN-MKCATDEF-01 (rwx --x --x).

mkcatdefs should be secured 711

BP-BIN-OSSOWN-01 SUPER.

mkcatdefs should be owned by SUPER.

BP-BIN-OSSLOC-01

mkcatdefs resides in /bin.

BP-ANYDIR-MKCATDEF-02 (rwx r-x r--).

*.msg source files should be secured 754

BP-ANYDIR-OSSOWN-00 appropriate application userid.

*.msg source files should be owned by

BP-ANYDIR-MSG-00   *.msg source files resides in any appropriate location.

	Discovery Questions	Look here:
BIN-OSSOWN-01	Is **/bin/mkcatdefs** owned by SUPER.SUPER?	ls -al
BIN-MKCATDEF-01	Is **/bin/mkcatdefs** secured correctly?	ls -al
ANYDIR-OSSOWN-01	Are any **.msg** files owned by an appropriate userid?	ls -al
ANYDIR-MSG-02	Are any **.msg** files secured correctly?	ls -al

Related Topics

gencat

runcat

mkdir User Program

The **/bin/mkdir** program creates a new directory. It also creates the hard links to the "." (dot) and ".." (dot dot) directories for itself and its parent. The -m flag lets the user set the permissions for the new directory.

In OSS, files are actually identified by their inode number. Directories are actually files containing link-to-inode pairs.

The user must have WRITE permission in the new directory's parent directory in order to create it. (Creating a subdirectory implies updating the parent directory's link-to-inode pairs.)

Securing /bin/mkdir

BP-BIN-MKDIR-01   **mkdir** should be secured 711 (rwx --x --x).

BP-BIN-OSSOWN-01   **mkdir** should be owned by SUPER.SUPER.

BP-BIN-OSSLOC-01   **mkdir** resides in **/bin**.

	Discovery Questions	**Look here:**
BIN-OSSOWN-01	Is **/bin/mkdir** owned by SUPER.SUPER?	ls -al
BIN-MKDIR-01	Is **/bin/mkdir** secured correctly?	ls -al

Related Topics

chmod

rm

rmdir

sh

mkfifo User Program

FIFOs are pipes with names. The **mkfifo** program creates FIFO special files or assigns pathnames to character special files.

The OSS pipe servers support the transfer of data between OSS processes that use pipes or FIFOs between processors.

The -m flag sets the file permissions on the new files. To set the permissions, a process must have WRITE and EXECUTE permission in the parent directory of the *path* parameter.

Securing /bin/mkfifo

BP-BIN-MKFIFO-01   **mkfifo** should be secured 711 (rwx --x --x).

BP-BIN-OSSOWN-01   **mkfifo** should be owned by SUPER.SUPER.

BP-BIN-OSSLOC-01   **mkfifo** resides in **/bin.**

	Discovery Questions	**Look here:**
BIN-OSSOWN-01	Is **/bin/mkfifo** owned by SUPER.SUPER?	ls -al
BIN-MKFIFO-01	Is **/bin/mkfifo** secured correctly?	ls -al

Related Topics

mknod

chmod

mkdir

umask

moduli Configuration File

The **/usr/local/etc/moduli** file contains Diffie-Hellman groups used for Diffie-Hellman Group Exchange. Please refer to the section on the SSH Subsystem in Part 4, *TCP/IP,* for more information or the *OSS Gazette* section on SSH for Best Practice recommendations.

more User Program

The **/bin/more** program displays the contents of a file, one screen at a time. The default is 23 lines per screen. Users can only display files they have READ access to.

Most systems contain many text files. Text files are used for configuration files, documents, and help files, among other things. They are resident in every directory. It is extremely hard to control the security of the numerous text files.

RISK   If critical text files, whether application or system configuration files, are not properly secured, **/bin/more** can be used to display their contents.

/bin/more is often required by most users for everyday work. Securing such programs to restrict access is often not reasonable, but the risks remain.

AP-ADVICE-CAT-01   Rather than securing the **/bin/more** object file, secure sensitive application data and scripts that are stored as text files so that they can only be viewed or copied by authorized personnel.

Securing /bin/more

BP-BIN-MORE-01   more should be secured 711 (rwx --x --x).

BP-BIN-OSSOWN-01   more should be owned by SUPER.SUPER.

BP-BIN-OSSLOC-01   more resides in /bin.

	Discovery Questions	Look here:
BIN-OSSOWN-01	Is /bin/more owned by SUPER.SUPER?	ls -al
BIN-MORE-01	Is /bin/more secured correctly?	ls -al

Related Topics

cat

grep

man

sh

named User Program

The /etc/dns<version>/named program is the HP implementation of BIND. Please refer to the *OSS Gazette* section on the Berkeley Internet Name Domain (BIND) Server.

named.conf Configuration File

The /etc/named.conf file is the main configuration file of the **named** Server. Please refer to the *OSS Gazette* section on the Berkeley Internet Name Domain (BIND) Server.

mv User Program

The **/bin/mv** program moves files and directories. It can also be used as a rename utility.

Users must have appropriate privileges in order to be able to move files:

Users must have WRITE access to the file being moved.

Users must have WRITE and EXECUTE permission to the both the file's current directory and the target directory to move a file because the directory files are being modified to reflect the change.

RISK Existing files can be overwritten unless the -i flag is specified to prompt the user before writing.

RISK OSS shell programs that perform recursive actions make no distinction between Guardian and OSS files or between local and remote files. And /G and /E both appear in users' local root directory, which puts both remote files and Guardian files at risk.

Securing /bin/mv

BP-BIN-MV-01   mv should be secured 711 (rwx --x --x).

BP-BIN-OSSOWN-01 mv should be owned by SUPER.SUPER.

BP-BIN-OSSLOC-01   mv resides in **/bin**.

	Discovery Questions	Look here:
BIN-OSSOWN-01	Is **/bin/mv** owned by SUPER.SUPER?	ls -al
BIN-MV-01	Is **/bin/mv** secured correctly?	ls -al

Related Topics

cp
ln

rm
rmdir
rename
UTILSGE

mxci

The **/usr/tandem/sqlmx/bin/mxci** program is the command interpreter for SQL/MX.

mxcierrors.cat

The **/usr/tandem/sqlmx/bin/mxcierrors.cat** file is the OSS-based file that contains the error message text for all SQL/MX errors and is used by all SQL/MX components that display SQL/MX error text.

mxcmp

The **mxcmp** file is the SQL/MX compiler. It is an OSS program installed in the Guardian $SYSTEM.SYSTEM subvolume (/G/system/system/ in the OSS environment). It must run in the OSS environment and does not run as a Guardian process. It is used to compile an SQL/MX module definition file and produce the query execution plan.

mxCompileUserModule

The **/usr/tandem/sqlmx/bin/mxCompileUserModule** file is the symbolic link to the Guardian MXCOMPILEUSERMODULE program. This utility is used to compile one or more SQL/MX module definitions embedded in an object file created by the C/C++ or COBOL compilers or produced by the linker.

mxexportddl

The **/usr/tandem/sqlmx/bin/mxexportddl** file is the OSS command-line utility to capture production SQL/MX meta data to diagnose problems.

mxsqlc

The **/usr/tandem/sqlmx/bin/mxsqlc** file is the OSS-based C preprocessor for embedded SQL statements in C/C++ programs.

mxsqlco

The **/usr/tandem/sqlmx/bin/mxsqlco** file is the OSS-based preprocessor for embedded SQL statements in COBOL programs. Please refer to the *OSS Gazette* section on SQL/MX for more information.

mxtool

/usr/tandem/sqlmx/bin/mxtool is the object file for the **mxtool** OSS command-line utility. Please refer to the *OSS Gazette* section on SQL/MX for more information.

nawk User Program

The **/bin/nawk** program provides text manipulation for report generation. It allows pattern matching and action statements more powerful than **grep** or **sed**.

Securing /bin/nawk

BP-BIN-NAWK-01   nawk should be secured 711 (rwx --x --x).

BP-BIN-OSSOWN-01 nawk should be owned by SUPER.SUPER.

BP-BIN-OSSLOC-01   nawk resides in /bin.

	Discovery Questions	Look here:
BIN-OSSOWN-01	Is /bin/nawk owned by SUPER.SUPER?	ls -al
BIN-NAWK-01	Is /bin/nawk secured correctly?	ls -al

Related Topics

awk

grep

printf

sed

networks Configuration File

The **networks** file contains information about the known networks that constitute the DARPA (Defense Advanced Research Projects Agency) Internet. Please refer to the *OSS Gazette* section on the **inetd** subsystem for more information.

newgrp User Program

The /bin/newgrp program changes the user's active group. It is useful when a user wants to create files for another group. The user gains all the privileges of the target group.

Only SUPER.SUPER can use the /bin/newgrp program to become a member of any defined group.

Correct behavior of the **/bin/newgrp** program depends on whether the user has a SHELL environment variable defined for his current session or has an INITIAL-PROGRAM defined in the Safeguard user record.

The user's INITIAL-PROGRAM is run unless the user enters the hyphen (-) command flag, which causes **/bin/newgrp** to load the target group's environment instead.

If no INITIAL-PROGRAM is defined, then the SHELL environment variable is used.

/bin/newgrp always replaces the current shell with a new shell. The user remains logged in and the current directory is unchanged. Both the user's real group ID and the effective group ID are changed.

Securing /bin/newgrp

BP-BIN-NEWGRP-01 **newgrp** should be secured 4711 (rws --x --x).

BP-BIN-SETUID-01 **newgrp** should have the **setuid** attribute.

BP-BIN-OSSOWN-01 **newgrp** should be owned by SUPER.SUPER.

BP-BIN-OSSLOC-01 **newgrp** resides in **/bin**.

	Discovery Questions	Look here:
BIN-OSSOWN-01	Is **/bin/newgrp** owned by SUPER.SUPER?	ls -al
BIN-NEWGRP-01	Is **/bin/newgrp** secured correctly?	ls -al

Related Topics

/etc/group

Safeguard user record INITIAL-PROGRAM parameter (Volume One)

sh

nice User Program

The **/bin/nice** program runs a command at a priority different than the priority of the current session. It adds or subtracts from the priority of the shell process that starts it.

Possible priorities:

-19	↑	highest
-1 to -18		
1 to 18		
10		default value
19		lowest

The default priority is 10. Unprivileged users can set values between 1 and 19. Privileged users can set priorities between –19 and +19.

Securing /bin/nice

BP-BIN-NICE-01   nice should be secured 711 (rwx --x --x).

BP-BIN-OSSOWN-01 nice should be owned by SUPER.SUPER.

BP-BIN-OSSLOC-01   nice resides in **/bin**.

	Discovery Questions	Look here:
BIN-OSSOWN-01	Is **/bin/nice** owned by SUPER.SUPER?	ls -al
BIN-NICE-01	Is **/bin/nice** secured correctly?	ls -al

Related Topics
nohup
sh

nl User Program

The **/bin/nl** program numbers lines in a file. Various flags allow the user to control what lines will be numbered and how the numbers will be incremented.

The user must have READ access to the file. Output is sent to the terminal.

Securing /bin/nl

BP-BIN-NL-01   nl should be secured 711 (rwx --x --x).

BP-BIN-OSSOWN-01 nl should be owned by SUPER.SUPER.

BP-BIN-OSSLOC-01   nl resides in **/bin**.

	Discovery Questions	**Look here:**
BIN-OSSOWN-01	Is **/bin/nl** owned by SUPER.SUPER?	ls -al
BIN-NL-01	Is **/bin/nl** secured correctly?	ls -al

Related Topics

cat

pr

locale

nld User Program

The **/bin/nld** program is the OSS version of the Guardian NLD program. It resolves references to the Shared Run-time Libraries that are specified when building an executable program in native languages:

Native C

Native C++

Native Cobol

PTAL

The NLD utility links one or more TNS/R object files to produce an executable or nonexecutable native object file. An executable native object file cannot be input to the NLD utility at a later time, but a nonexecutable native object file can:

Link one or more TNS/R native object files to produce a loadfile or linkfile

Modify existing loadfiles

In Guardian, NLD cannot be run interactively. It is run from the native compilers or from a batch obey file containing NLD commands. In OSS, NLD can be invoked directly or via the c89 utility.

The OSS version of NLD searches for SRLs and archive files in the following locations. Please refer to the *OSS Gazette* section on OSS Libraries for more information.

/G/system/sysnn

/lib

/usr/lib

/usr/local/lib

AP-ADVICE-COMPILER-01 To protect applications from inadvertent or malicious changes or outages, compilers and related utilities should be absent or very tightly locked down on secure systems.

Securing /bin/nld

BP-BIN-NLD-01   nld should be secured 711 (rwx --x --x).

BP-BIN-OSSOWN-01 nld should be owned by SUPER.SUPER.

BP-BIN-OSSLOC-01   nld resides in **/bin**.

	Discovery Questions	Look here:
OSS-POLICY	Are compilers allowed on the secure system?	Policy
BIN-OSSOWN-01	Is **/bin/nld** owned by SUPER.SUPER?	ls -al
BIN-NLD-01	Is **/bin/nld** secured correctly?	ls -al

Related Topics

c89

noft

nm User Program

The **/usr/bin/nm** program lists symbolic information appearing in an object file, executable file, or object-file library.

The user needs READ access to the object file.

Securing /usr/bin/nm

BP-USR-NM-01   nm should be secured 711 (rwx --x --x).

BP-USR-OSSOWN-02 nm should be owned by SUPER.SUPER.

BP-USR-OSSLOC-02 nm resides in **/usr/bin.**

	Discovery Questions	Look here:
OSS-POLICY	Are compilers allowed on the secure system?	Policy
USR-OSSOWN-02	Is **/usr/bin /nm** owned by SUPER.SUPER?	ls -al
USR-NM-01	Is **/usr/bin /nm** secured correctly?	ls -al

Related Topics

ar

make

strip

nmcobol User Program

The **/usr/bin/nmcobol** program compiles native COBOL85 programs.

The native COBOL85 compiler subsystem consists of **nmcobol, nld,** and some additional programs for SQL preprocessing: **sqlco, mxsqlco, sqlcomp,** and **mxcmp.**

AP-ADVICE-COMPILER-01   To protect applications from inadvertent or malicious changes or outages, compilers and related utilities should be absent or very tightly secured on secure systems.

Securing /usr/bin/nmcobol

BP-USR-NMCOBOL-01 nmcobol should be secured 711 (rwx --x --x).

BP-USR-OSSOWN-02   nmcobol should be owned by SUPER.SUPER.

BP-USR-OSSLOC-02   nmcobol resides in **/usr/bin.**

	Discovery Questions	Look here:
OSS-POLICY	Are compilers allowed on the secure system?	Policy
USR-OSSOWN-02	Is **/usr/bin/nmcobol** owned by SUPER.SUPER?	ls -al
USR-NMCOBOL-01	Is **/usr/bin/nmcobol** secured correctly?	ls -al

Related Topics
nld
noft
mxcmp
mxsqlco
sqlco
sqlcomp

noft User Program

/usr/bin/noft is the OSS version of the Guardian NOFT program, which reads and displays information from native object files. It is the native equivalent of BIND for native code programs written in Native C, Native C++, Native COBOL, and PTAL.

AP-ADVICE-COMPILER-01 To protect applications from inadvertent or malicious changes or outages, compilers and related utilities should be absent or very tightly locked down on secure systems.

Securing /bin/noft

BP-USR-NOFT-01	noft should be secured 711 (rwx --x --x).
BP-USR-OSSOWN-02	noft should be owned by SUPER.SUPER.
BP-USR-OSSLOC-03	noft resides in /usr/bin.

	Discovery Questions	Look here:
OSS-POLICY	Are users allowed to use background processing?	Policy
USR-OSSOWN-02	Is /usr/bin/noft owned by SUPER.SUPER?	ls -al
USR-NOFT-01	Is /usr/bin/noft secured correctly?	ls -al

nohup User Program

The /bin/nohup program runs a utility while ignoring hangup requests. It is used to run programs in the background after logging off. Utilities started with /bin/nohup cannot include shell compound commands, pipelines, or built-in shell programs.

RISK /bin/nohup should only be used if the user understands that the process no longer has a home terminal once the user logs off.

AP-ADVICE-NOHUP-01 Rather than securing the **/bin/nohup** program, which may be required for legitimate activity, secure any sensitive programs so that only authorized personnel have EXECUTE access to them.

Securing /bin/nohup

BP-BIN-NOHUP-01	**nohup** should be secured 711 (rwx --x --x).
BP-BIN-OSSOWN-01	**nohup** should be owned by SUPER.SUPER.
BP-BIN-OSSLOC-01	**nohup** resides in **/bin**.

	Discovery Questions	Look here:
OSS-POLICY	Are users allowed to use background processing?	Policy
BIN-OSSOWN-01	Is **/bin/nohup** owned by SUPER.SUPER?	ls -al
BIN-NOHUP-01	Is **/bin/nohup** secured correctly?	ls -al

Related Topics

sh

NSM/web Subsystem

NSM/web manages and configures MXCS service and provides Web browser–based functions and tools used by SQL/MX DBAs. It requires an installed Web server like iTP Webserver and runs as a small, independent, HP NonStop Pathway/iTS environment.

NSM/web can run under a traditional *TCP/IP* or parallel *TCP/IP* environment. It uses both HTTP and direct dynamic *TCP/IP* socket connections and cannot be accessed through a firewall but does work through a VPN tunnel. All session-specific NSM/web servers run under the user-specified ID and password. All security is standard NonStop Server system security.

NSM/web requires a Web browser such as Microsoft Internet Explorer. It also requires the Sun Java Plug-in 1.4.2_01 (or later), which may be found on the Sun Web site. For client systems that are not usually connected to the Internet,

HP recommends that the person installing NSM/web connect to the Internet during installation to find and install the most current version of the plug-in.

NSM/web uses CORBA for applet communication to the NonStop system. The Sun plug-in on the client machine includes CORBA and requires no configuration and no daemons to run. HP includes customized CORBA components that are a small subset of NonStop DOM and are not usable for any other purpose.

NSMweb Host Components

The host pieces of the NSMweb product are:

NSMweb.html

NSMwebMXCSServer

NSMwebNSKServer

NSMwebServerFactory

NSMwebSqlMXServer

NSMweb.html

The **/usr/tandem/webserver/root/NSMweb/NSMweb.html** file provides the initial browser access to logon and use NSM/web. It provides single-logon access across all NSM/web-supported products (currently SQL/MX and MXCS).

When a user logs on to NSM/web, the userid logon information is propagated to other products, as needed, with user access privileges to all objects based on SQL/MX and MXCS rules. Each connection can process only one userid at a time. If a users needs to log on with a different userid, they must either log off and then log on using a different userid or start another browser and make a connection using the different userid.

BP-USR-NSMWEB-01   NSMweb.html should be secured 711 (rwx --x --x).

BP-USR-OSSOWN-05   NSMweb.html should be owned by SUPER.
SUPER.

BP-USR-OSSLOC-05   NSMweb.html resides in **/usr/tandem/web-server/root/NSMweb.**

	Discovery Questions	Look here:
USR-OSSOWN-05	Is **/usr/tandem/webserver/root/NSMweb/ NSMweb.html** owned by SUPER.SUPER?	ls -al
USR-SQLMX-01	Is **/usr/tandem/webserver/root/NSMweb/ NSMweb.html** secured correctly?	ls -al

NSMwebMXCSServer

The **/usr/tandem/NSMweb/NSMwebMXCSServer** file performs MXCS management commands. One instance runs for each NSM/web client.

BP-USR-NSMWEB-02   NSMwebMXCSServer should be secured 711 (rwx --x --x).

BP-USR-OSSOWN-03   NSMwebMXCSServer should be owned by SUPER.SUPER.

BP-USR-OSSLOC-03   NSMwebMXCSServer resides in **/usr/tandem/ NSMweb.**

	Discovery Questions	Look here:
USR-OSSOWN-03	Is **/usr/tandem/NSMweb/NSMwebMXCSServer** owned by SUPER.SUPER?	ls -al
USR-SQLMX-01	Is **/usr/tandem/NSMweb/NSMwebMXCSServer** secured correctly?	ls -al

NSMwebNSKServer

The **/usr/tandem/NSMweb/NSMwebNSKServer** file performs utility commands. One instance runs for each NSM/web client.

BP-USR-NSMWEB-03   NSMwebNSKServer should be secured 711 (rwx --x --x).

BP-USR-OSSOWN-03 NSMwebNSKServer should be owned by SUPER.SUPER.

BP-USR-OSSLOC-03 NSMwebNSKServer resides in **/usr/tandem/ NSMweb.**

	Discovery Questions	Look here:
USR-OSSOWN-03	Is **/usr/tandem/NSMweb/NSMwebNSKServer** owned by SUPER.SUPER?	ls -al
USR-SQLMX- 03	Is **/usr/tandem/NSMweb/NSMwebNSKServer** secured correctly?	ls -al

NSMwebServerFactory

The **/usr/tandem/NSMweb/NSMwebServerFactory** file is the persistent process (runs under Pathway/iTS) that spawns the required NSM/web server.

BP-USR-NSMWEB-04 NSMwebServerFactory should be secured 711 (rwx --x --x).

BP-USR-OSSOWN-03 NSMwebServerFactory should be owned by SUPER.SUPER.

BP-USR-OSSLOC-03 NSMwebServerFactory resides in **/usr/tandem/ NSMweb.**

	Discovery Questions	Look here:
USR-OSSOWN-03	Is **/usr/tandem/NSMweb/NSMwebServerFactory** owned by SUPER.SUPER?	ls -al
USR-SQLMX- 04	Is **/usr/tandem/NSMweb/NSMwebServerFactory** secured correctly?	ls -al

NSMwebSqlMXServer

The **/usr/tandem/NSMweb/NSMwebSqlMXServer** file performs SQL DDL commands. One instance runs for each NSM/web client.

BP-USR-NSMWEB-05   NSMwebSqlMXServer should be secured 711 (rwx --x --x).

BP-USR-OSSOWN-03   NSMwebSqlMXServer should be owned by SUPER.SUPER.

BP-USR-OSSLOC-03   NSMwebSqlMXServer resides in **/usr/tandem/ NSMweb**.

	Discovery Questions	Look here:
USR-OSSOWN-03	Is **/usr/tandem/NSMweb/NSMwebSqlMXServer** owned by SUPER.SUPER?	ls -al
USR-SQLMX-05	Is **/usr/tandem/NSMweb/NSMwebSqlMXServer** secured correctly?	ls -al

nsupdate User Program

The **/etc/dns<version>/nsupdate** is used to submit Dynamic DNS update requests to a BIND 9 domain name server. Please refer to the *OSS Gazette* section on the Berkeley Internet Name Domain (BIND) Sever.

od User Program

The **/bin/od** program writes the contents of a file to the terminal or standard output file. Various flags allow the user to determine the nature of the output, such as octal, hexadecimal, or some other format. Settings in the **locale** file can affect the **/bin/od** display.

Users must have READ access to the source or "specified" file.

RISK   **/bin/od** exposes the contents of the files; therefore, files containing sensitive information must be secured so that only appropriate users have READ access.

Securing /bin/od

BP-BIN-OD-01   **od** should be secured 711 (rwx --x --x).

BP-BIN-OSSOWN-01 **od** should be owned by SUPER.SUPER.

BP-BIN-OSSLOC-01 **od** resides in **/bin**.

	Discovery Questions	**Look here:**
BIN-OSSOWN-01	Is **/bin/od** owned by SUPER.SUPER?	ls -al
BIN-OD-01	Is **/bin/od** secured correctly?	ls -al

Related Topics

locale

pack User Program

The **/bin/pack** program compresses files. The program preserves the permissions, modification dates, and owner of the original file if the user has the appropriate privileges; otherwise, the invoking user's userid and groupid are assigned to the file and his default permissions are used.

Each packed file is replaced by one with the filename extention of **.z** (lower case) as opposed to the file extension used by the **/bin/compress** program, **.Z** (upper case).

Users must have READ access to the files they wish to pack and WRITE access to the directory where the packed file will be placed.

RISK Packing production files makes them unusable until they are unpacked.

unpack User Program

The **/bin/unpack** program expands files compressed by the **/bin/pack** program. Unpack searches for the specified file with a **.z** suffix (it will add the suffix even if the user doesn't enter it) and, if found, expands it. The newly expanded file will have the same name but with the **.z** removed. The new file will be owned by the invoking userid.

The user must have READ access to the packed file and be able to create the unpacked output file.

The target file will not be unpacked if:

The target file is not a packed file

The target file cannot be opened for any reason, including file security

The new unpacked filename already exists

The new unpacked file cannot be created for any reason, including directory security

RISK /bin/unpack poses minimal risk as long as any packed files containing sensitive or confidential information are properly secured.

Securing /bin/pack and /bin/unpack

BP-BIN-PACK-01   pack should be secured 711 (rwx --x --x).

BP-BIN-OSSOWN-01 pack should be owned by SUPER.SUPER.

BP-BIN-OSSLOC-01 pack resides in /bin.

BP-BIN-PACK-02   unpack should be secured (711) rwx--x--x.

BP-BIN-OSSOWN-01 unpack should be owned by SUPER.SUPER.

BP-BIN-OSSLOC-01 unpack resides in /bin.

	Discovery Questions	Look here:
BIN-OSSOWN-01	Is /bin/pack owned by SUPER.SUPER?	ls -al
BIN-PACK-01	Is /bin/pack secured correctly?	ls -al

(Continued)

	Discovery Questions	Look here:
BIN-OSSOWN-01	Is **/bin/unpack** owned by SUPER.SUPER?	ls -al
BIN-PACK-02	Is **/bin/unpack** secured correctly?	ls -al

Related Topics

cat

compress

uncompress

unpack

zcat

passwd Configuration File

On systems other than the NonStop Server, user account information and passwords are stored in the **/etc/passwd** file. On the NonStop Server, Safeguard manages user records and passwords.

HP OSS security processing does not use the **/etc/group**, **/etc/passwd** or **/etc/shadow** files. Some third-party software, such as Samba, NFS, Tuxedo, and OSI, may, however, make use of the files. Please refer to HP's and/or the manufacturer's documentation on each of these products for information on the placement and use of these files, as well as the risks involved.

paste User Program

The **/bin/paste** program joins lines from one or more files. Various flags enable the user to configure how the lines will be joined. Entries in the **locale** file can affect the output.

Users must have READ access to the files being joined as well as the ability to create the output file.

RISK   /bin/paste poses minimal risk as long as critical or sensitive application and system files are properly secured.

Securing /bin/paste

BP-BIN-PASTE-01	paste should be secured 711 (rwx --x --x).
BP-BIN-OSSOWN-01	paste should be owned by SUPER.SUPER.
BP-BIN-OSSLOC-01	paste resides in /bin.

	Discovery Questions	Look here:
BIN-OSSOWN-01	Is /bin/paste owned by SUPER.SUPER?	ls -al
BIN-PASTE-01	Is /bin/paste secured correctly?	ls -al

Related Topics

cut

grep

pr

locale

patch User Program

The /bin/patch program applies changes to text files. When a patch to an application is released, it is often done as a **patch-diff**, a file that describes which lines should be added, changed, or removed in order to produce the new version. The /bin/diff program produces the comparison file, and the /bin/patch program is used to apply it. Then the new code is recompiled and installed.

/bin/patch provides flags to enable the user to control patches and to determine whether or not the patched file replaces the original file.

RISK **/bin/patch**'s default behavior is to replace the original file with the patched file.

AP-ADVICE-PATCH-01 Create procedures and scripts that preserve the original source code file, either with a version control package or with naming conventions such as <source file><version>.orig.

AP-ADVICE-PATCH-02 Because **/bin/patch** attempts to skip any leading text before applying the **diff**, it is possible to feed a message containing a **diff** listing to **/bin/patch** as a header.

AP-ADVICE-PATCH-03 HP recommends that you keep a patch log file, which would itself be patched to reflect each source code upgrade.

Your security policy should determine whether or not code may be modified and patched on production (secure) systems.

Securing /bin/patch

BP-BIN-PATCH-01   **patch** should be secured 711 (rwx --x --x).

BP-BIN-OSSOWN-01 **patch** should be owned by SUPER.SUPER.

BP-BIN-OSSLOC-01 **patch** resides in **/bin**.

	Discovery Questions	Look here:
OSS-POLICY	Does policy allow patch to be used on application code on the system?	Policy
BIN-OSSOWN-01	Is **/bin/patch** owned by SUPER.SUPER?	ls -al
BIN-PATCH-01	Is **/bin/patch** secured correctly?	ls -al

Related Topics

diff

pathchk User Program

The **/bin/pathchk** program validates that each component of the specified pathname(s) can be used to access or create a file without causing syntax errors. The program checks:

That the full pathname does not exceed the maximum (1023 bytes) allowed

That the name of any component of the pathname does not exceed the maximum (248 characters) allowed

That search (EXECUTE) permission is allowed for all components of the pathname

That the full pathname does not contain any invalid characters

It is not necessary that each component of the pathname actually exist as long a file matching the pathname could be created without violating any of the syntax rules above.

Securing /bin/pathchk

BP-BIN-PATHCHK-01   pathchk should be secured 711 (rwx --x --x).

BP-BIN-OSSOWN-01   **pathchk** should be owned by SUPER. SUPER.

BP-BIN-OSSLOC-01   **pathchk** resides in **/bin.**

	Discovery Questions	Look here:
BIN-OSSOWN-01	Is **/bin/pathchk** owned by SUPER.SUPER?	ls -al
BIN-PATHCHK-01	Is **/bin/pathchk** secured correctly?	ls -al

pax Utility

The **/bin/pax** utility creates archives. It is essentially a combination of the **/bin/cpio** and **/bin/tar** programs. It can also read, write, and list the files within an archive and copy directory hierarchies. **/bin/pax** uses Guardian tape devices, which are controlled by the Guardian tape processes executing in the Guardian Mediacom environment.

/bin/pax does not distinquish between Guardian and OSS files.

RISK   Guardian files will be restored as unstructured files, code 180. Only files that are supported by the OSS function calls open( ), read( ), and write( ) can be processed.

RISK   Guardian file names restored via **/bin/pax** may be invalid syntactically; such files cannot be reliably restored to a Guardian target.

RISK   Multiple files with similar names could potentially be converted to the same Guardian name. This could result in the newly restored file overwriting a previously restored file.

RISK   The USTAR data exchange format does not support filenames longer than 100 characters.

AP-ADVICE-PAX-01   To archive files with names greater than 100 characters long, use the **/bin/pax** command with the **-x cpio** flag to change the archive file format to **cpio**.

Users must have READ access to the files being archived.

Securing /bin/pax

BP-BIN-PAX-01	**pax** should be secured 711 (rwx --x --x).
BP-BIN-OSSOWN-01	**pax** should be owned by SUPER.SUPER.
BP-BIN-OSSLOC-01	**pax** resides in **/bin**.

	Discovery Questions	Look here:
BIN-OSSOWN-01	Is **/bin/pax** owned by SUPER.SUPER?	ls -al
BIN-PAX-01	Is **/bin/pax** secured correctly?	ls -al

Related Topics

cp

cpio

pinstall

tar

Pcleanup Utility

The **/bin/Pcleanup** utility moves or removes obsolete OSS files left behind by the **pinstall** utility after an IPM or an OSS release upgrade. **/bin/Pcleanup** uses a set of **remove_list** files provided in the PAX archive files for OSS products.

RISK Removing files created by DSM/SCM can invalidate the DSM/SCM database used for file maintenance.

AP-ADVICE-PCLEANUP-01 Do not use **/bin/Pcleanup** if you use DSM/SCM to install IPMs or operating system upgrades.

Users must be able to PURGE files from the directories where they reside.

AP-ADVICE-PCLEANUP-02 When uncertain of what can be deleted, save a copy of the files to tape so they can be restored if necessary.

Securing /bin/Pcleanup

BP-BIN-PCLEANUP-01 Pcleanup should be secured 710 (rwx --x ---).

BP-BIN-OSSOWN-01 Pcleanup should be owned by SUPER.SUPER.

BP-BIN-OSSLOC-01 Pcleanup resides in **/bin**.

	Discovery Questions	Look here:
BIN-OSSOWN-01	Is **/bin/Pcleanup** owned by SUPER.SUPER?	ls -al
BIN-PCLEANUP-01	Is **/bin/Pcleanup** secured correctly?	ls -al

Related Topics

pax

pinstall

pinstall User Program

The **/bin/pinstall** program extracts files from pax USTAR format archives. **/bin/pinstall** invokes a Guardian process that does the copying. **/bin/pinstall** cannot create archives.

The root directory must exist when **/bin/pinstall** is invoked. The **-s** flag is used to copy files to the OSS file system. Without the **-s**, copies will be put in the current file system, even if it is Guardian.

/bin/pinstall uses Guardian tape devices, which are controlled by the Guardian tape processes executing in the Guardian environment. Use Mediacom to manage the tape subsystem.

AP-ADVICE-PINSTALL-01   HP recommends that **/bin/pinstall** not be used to install HP product files from the ZOSSUTL subvolume if you have DSM/SCM installed on the system.

AP-ADVICE-PINSTALL-01   On systems where DSM/SCM is not used to maintain the OSS file system, do not use **/bin/pinstall** on files with Guardian filenames beginning with the characters ZFB or ZPG to avoid overwriting files maintained by DSM/SCM.

Securing /bin/pinstall

BP-BIN-PINSTALL-01   **pinstall** should be secured 711 (rwx --x --x).

BP-BIN-OSSOWN-01   **pinstall** should be owned by SUPER.SUPER.

BP-BIN-OSSLOC-01   pinstall resides in **/bin.**

	Discovery Questions	Look here:
OSS-POLICY	Is DSMSCM used on the system?	Policy
BIN-OSSOWN-01	Is **/bin/pinstall** owned by SUPER.SUPER?	ls -al
BIN-PINSTALL-01	Is **/bin/pinstall** secured correctly?	ls -al

Related Topics

copyoss

pax

pname User Program

The **/bin/pname** program displays the OSS pathname of a Guardian file. It will also display the full pathname of a file in an OSS fileset when given the Guardian filename.

Securing /bin/pname

BP-BIN-PNAME-01   pname should be secured 711 (rwx --x --x).

BP-BIN-OSSOWN-01 pname should be owned by SUPER.SUPER.

BP-BIN-OSSLOC-01   pname resides in **/bin.**

	Discovery Questions	Look here:
BIN-OSSOWN-01	Is **/bin/pname** owned by SUPER.SUPER?	ls -al
BIN-PNAME-01	Is **/bin/pname** secured correctly?	ls -al

Related Topics

gname
filename

pr User Program

The **/bin/pr** program displays the contents of a file, page by page, with a header at the top of each page that includes the filename, page number, and the date and time.

Users must have READ access to display the target file's contents.

RISK **/bin/pr** exposes the contents of files, therefore files containing sensitive information must be secured so that only appropriate users have READ access.

Securing /bin/pr

BP-BIN-PR-01   **pr** should be secured 711 (rwx --x --x).

BP-BIN-OSSOWN-01   **pr** should be owned by SUPER.SUPER.

BP-BIN-OSSLOC-01   **pr** resides in **/bin**.

	Discovery Questions	Look here:
BIN-OSSOWN-01	Is **/bin/pr** owned by SUPER.SUPER?	ls -al
BIN-PR-01	Is **/bin/pr** secured correctly?	ls -al

Related Topics

cat

printf User Program

The **/bin/printf** program converts, formats, and displays its arguments. Various command flags allow the user to customize the formatting. It is used for creating small formatted output files.

Securing /bin/printf

BP-BIN-PRINTF-01   printf should be secured 711 (rwx --x --x).

BP-BIN-OSSOWN-01 printf should be owned by SUPER.SUPER.

BP-BIN-OSSLOC-01   printf resides in /bin.

	Discovery Questions	Look here:
BIN-OSSOWN-01	Is /bin/printf owned by SUPER.SUPER?	ls -al
BIN-PRINTF-01	Is /bin/printf secured correctly?	ls -al

Related Topics

read

printcap Configuration File

Guardian tape drives and printers are not treated as devices in the OSS environment and do not appear in the /dev directory, so OSS users cannot access them directly. And, though printer processes are visible to OSS shell users through Guardian file system entries in the /G directory, they are not visible to OSS programs. Therefore, application programs cannot access printers directly in the OSS environment, but users can access them indirectly through the shell.

Printer management in the OSS environment consists of defining aliases for Guardian spooler-location names. The **printcap** file contains a list of OSS aliases for Guardian spooler LOCATION names. The aliases in the /etc/printcap file provide a systemwide set of definitions. A user can also define aliases in his or her own **printcap** file.

Many companies create a **printcap** file in each user's initial working directory. This practice allows you to assign a conveniently located printer to each user.

When a user invokes an OSS printing utility such as the OSS shell lp program, the OSS environment searches the following items, in the order listed, to determine the destination printer:

1. The program line (for example, in the lp -d <printer>)

2. The LPDEST environment variable value

3. The PRINTER environment variable value

4. The printer listed as the first entry in the **/etc/printcap** file

5. The printer listed in the first line of the **printcap** file in the user's initial working directory

The **/bin/lp** program, for example, checks the **printcap** file to resolve name mapping. If the destination name does not map to a physical printer device, the files to be printed are left in the spooling area for further disposition, but if the destination name maps to an invalid printer location, **/bin/lp** generates an error and closes.

RISK If no printer is specified in any of these items, an error is generated and the print job will not be completed.

RISK All the above listed locators can be omitted or accidentally removed by user actions except the **/etc/printcap** file, assuming that it is properly secured.

BP-OSS-PRINTCAP-01   The first line in the file must define the alias of the default printer (4 in the above list), because all the other items can be omitted or accidentally removed by user actions if the file isn't secured properly.

BP-OSS-PRINTCAP-02 The **/etc/printcap** file must be properly secured to prevent malicious or inadvertent changes.

The corporate security policy should state whether or not users should have individual **printcap** files.

printcap.sample Configuration File

The **/etc/printcap.sample** file contains a list of aliases and the corresponding Guardian spooler-location names for printers. It is installed as part of the OSS file system with a single, sample, entry: the Guardian spooler-location name associated with the alias "default."

Securing /etc/printcap

BP-ETC-PRINTCAP-01	**printcap** should be secured 644 (rw- r-- r--).
BP-ETC-OSSOWN-01 SUPER.	**printcap** should be owned by SUPER.
BP-ETC-OSSLOC-01	**printcap** resides in **/etc**.
BP-ETC-PRINTCAP-02 (rwx --- ---).	**printcap.sample** should be secured 600
BP-ETC-OSSOWN-01 SUPER.SUPER.	**printcap.sample** should be owned by
BP-ETC-OSSLOC-01	**printcap.sample** resides in **/etc**.
BP-HOME-PRINTCAP-03 700 (rwx --- ---).	Individual **printcap** files should be secured
BP-HOME-OSSOWN-00 by each user.	Individual **printcap** files should be owned
BP-HOME-OSSLOC-00 initial working directory.	Individual **printcap** files reside in each user's

	Discovery Questions	Look here:
FILE-POLICY	Does policy allow users to maintain their own **printcap** files?	ls -al
ETC-OSSOWN-01	Who owns **/etc/printcap**?	ls -al
ETC-OSSOWN-01	Who owns **/etc/printcap.sample**?	ls -al

(Continued)

	Discovery Questions	Look here:
HOME-OSSOWN-00	Who owns the individual **printcap** files?	ls -al
ETC-PRINTCAP-01	Is **/etc/printcap** secured correctly?	ls -al
ETC-PRINTCAP-02	Is **/etc/printcap.sample** secured correctly?	ls -al
HOME-PRINTCAP-03	Are the individual **printcap** files secured correctly?	ls -al

Related Topics

lp

services configuration file

/private Directory

The **/usr/local/private** directory contains very sensitive files that must be tighted secured. Only SUPER.SUPER should be able to browse or make changes to this directory. It is created by some open source software, such as Samba.

Securing /private

BP-PRIVATE-DIRSEC-03   /private should be secured 700 (rwx --- ---).

BP-PRIVATE-DIROWN-03 /private should be owned by SUPER. SUPER.

BP-PRIVATE-DIRLOC-03   /private resides in /usr/local/Private.

	Discovery Questions	Look here:
PRIVATE-DIROWN-03	Is **/private** owned by SUPER.SUPER?	ls -al
PRIVATE-DIRSEC-03	Is **/private** secured correctly?	ls -al

Related Topics

jobs

sh

prngd System Utility

/usr/local/bin/prngd is the object file for the Random Number Generator process used by the cryptographic algorithms for SSH. Please refer to the *OSS Gazette* section the SSH Subsystem for more information.

.profile Configuration Files

The **/etc/profile** file is the OSS equivalent of the Guardian $SYSTEM.SYSTEM.TACLLOCL file. It is a global startup file that is executed during the logon of every user. It is intended to to configure an environment that should be uniform for all users.

Some of the values can be overridden by entries in personal **.profile** files located in each user's home directory.

RISK   If the security of the **/etc/profile** file permits a user other than the owner WRITE or PURGE access, they could modify the file or PURGE it and replace it with a new one.

If a macro is executed within the **/etc/profile**, the macro file must be also secured so that only authorized users can WRITE or PURGE it, otherwise someone could rename it and then install another file with the same name or simply insert commands that execute a Trojan horse program by invoking the macro via the **/etc/profile** file.

BP-ETC-PROFILE-01   Only SUPER.SUPER should have WRITE or PURGE access to **/etc/profile**.

The profile.sample File

HP provides a **profile.sample** file, which resides in the same directory. It provides examples of common settings. Do not make your changes to the sample file since they will be overwritten when a new operating system version is installed.

BP-ETC-PROFILE-02   Only the SUPER.SUPER should have WRITE or PURGE access to **/etc/profile.sample**.

Personal .profile Files

Personal **.profile** files are the OSS equivalent of the Guardian TACLCSTM files, but unlike TACLCSTM files, the **.profile** is not created automatically.

RISK   If the security of the **.profile** file permits a user other than the owner WRITE or PURGE access, they could modify the file or PURGE it and replace it with a new one.

RISK   The **.profile** commands will override the similar commands in the global **/etc/profile** commands.

RISK   The **.profile** file is created using the user's default security. The default security may not adequately secure these files.

RISK   The **.profile** file can contain PATH commands to alter the location that the shell uses to find a program file when a RUN command is issued in which the file name is not fully qualified, which is the common practice.

RISK   SUPER group members should not be able to alter their **.profile** files. They could put destructive commands in the file that will execute prior to shell's first prompt.

If a script is executed within a **.profile**, the script file must be also secured so that only authorized users can WRITE or PURGE it, otherwise someone could rename it and then install another file with the same name or simply insert commands that execute a Trojan Horse program by invoking the macro via the **.profile** file.

AP-POLICY-PROFILE-01   The corporate security policy should determine whether or not users are allowed to modify their own **$HOME/.profile** file.

AP-ADVICE-PROFILE-01   Use a **/bin/cron** task to periodically:

Report the contents of all **.profile** files

Repair any unauthorized settings.

Securing /etc/profile

BP-ETC-PROFILE-01   **profile** should be secured 644 (rw- r-- r--).

BP-ETC-OSSOWN-01   **profile** should be owned by SUPER.SUPER.

BP-ETC-OSSLOC-01   **profile** resides in **/etc**.

BP-ETC-PROFILE-02   **profile.sample** should be secured 640 (r-- r-- ---).

BP-ETC-OSSOWN-01   **profile.sample** should be owned by SUPER. SUPER.

BP-ETC-OSSLOC-01   **profile.sample** resides in **/etc**.

BP-HOME-PROFILE-03 Personal **.profile** files should be secured 700 (rwx --- ---).

BP-HOME-OSSOWN-00 Personal **.profile** files should be owned by the individual user.

BP-HOME-OSSLOC-00   Personal **.profile** files reside in the user's home directory.

	Discovery Questions	**Look here:**
OSS-POLICY	Who maintains the **/etc/profile** file?	Policy
ETC-OSSOWN-01	Is **/etc/profile** owned by SUPER.SUPER?	ls -al
ETC-PROFILE-01	Is **/etc/profile** secured correctly?	ls -al
ETC-OSSOWN-01	Is **/etc/profile.sample** owned by SUPER.SUPER?	ls -al

(Continued)

	Discovery Questions	Look here:
ETC-PROFILE-02	Is /etc/profile.sample secured correctly?	ls -al
OSS-POLICY	Are users allowed to create personal .profile files?	Policy
HOME-OSSOWN-00	Is each .profile owned by the appropriate user?	ls -al
HOME-PROFILE-03	Is each .profile secured correctly?	ls -al

Related Topics

nfs

program User Program

The /bin/program program treats program arguments as a simple program. It allows users to run user-defined and system programs whose names correspond to shell built-in programs. For example, typing "/bin/program -p pwd" ensures that the pwd program is invoked rather than the shell built-in pwd program.

RISK /bin/program poses minimal risk as long as critical or sensitive application and system files are properly secured

Securing /bin/program

BP-BIN-PROGRAM-01 **program** should be secured 711 (rwx --x --x).

BP-BIN-OSSOWN-01 **program** should be owned by SUPER.SUPER.

BP-BIN-OSSLOC-01 **program** resides in /bin.

	Discovery Questions	Look here:
BIN-OSSOWN-01	Is /bin/program owned by SUPER.SUPER?	ls -al
BIN-PROGRAM-01	Is /bin/program secured correctly?	ls -al

Related Topics

sh

.proto Configuration File

The **/var/adm/cron/.proto** file contains shell commands required to provide the correct **cron** shell environment for **at** and **batch** jobs.

queuedefs Configuration File

The **/var/adm/cron/queuedefs** file configures the task queues to be used for the **/bin/at**, **/bin/batch**, and **/bin/crontab** programs.

protocols Configuration File

The **protocols** file contains a list protocol names supported by NonStop *TCP/IP.* Please refer to the *OSS Gazette* section on the **inetd** subsystem for more information.

ps User Program

The **/bin/ps** program provides a snapshot of process statuses. Various command flags allow the user to select processes to include in the display and the type and format of the information about them. Guardian processes can be included or excluded.

Securing /bin/ps

BP-BIN-PS-01   **ps** should be secured 711 (rwx --x --x).

BP-BIN-OSSOWN-01 **ps** should be owned by SUPER.SUPER.

BP-BIN-OSSLOC-01   ps resides in **/bin.**

	Discovery Questions	Look here:
BIN-OSSOWN-01	Is **/bin/ps** owned by SUPER.SUPER?	ls -al
BIN-PS-01	Is **/bin/ps** secured correctly?	ls -al

Related Topics

kill

nice

pwd User Program

The **/bin/pwd** program displays the user's current working directory's pathname.

There are two versions of the **pwd** command that are identical except for the following:

> The **/bin/pwd** program starts a new shell process to display the directory information.

> The built-in shell **pwd** command doesn't start a new shell process to display the directory information.

The built-in shell **pwd** command is the default. To invoke the program rather than the built-in command, you must use the full pathname to invoke **/bin/pwd.**

Securing /bin/pwd

BP-BIN-PWD-01   **pwd** should be secured 711 (rwx --x --x).

BP-BIN-OSSOWN-01 **pwd** should be owned by SUPER.SUPER.

BP-BIN-OSSLOC-01 **pwd** resides in **/bin.**

	Discovery Questions	Look here:
BIN-OSSOWN-01	Is **/bin/pwd** owned by SUPER.SUPER?	ls -al
BIN-PWD-01	Is **/bin/pwd** secured correctly?	ls -al

Related Topics

cd

sh

rc Configuration File

$HOME/.ssh/rc files are much like a shell startup file (a **.profile**, for example), but they execute only when a user's account is accessed by SSH. They are run for both interactive logins and remote commands. Please refer to the chapter on the SSH Subsystem in Part 4, *TCP/IP* for more information or the *OSS Gazette* section on SSH for Best Practice recommendations.

read User Program

The **/bin/read** program prompts the user for a single line from the display and assigns the values of each field to a shell variable. It is frequently used with the **/bin/printf** program.

There are two versions of the **read** command that are identical except for the following:

The **/bin/read** program starts a new shell process.

The built-in shell **read** command doesn't start a new shell process.

The built-in shell **read** command is the default. To invoke the program rather than the built-in command, you must use the full pathname to invoke **/bin/read**.

Securing /bin/read

BP-BIN-READ-01 **read** should be secured 711 (rwx --x --x).

BP-BIN-OSSOWN-01 **read** should be owned by SUPER.SUPER.

BP-BIN-OSSLOC-01 **read** resides in **/bin**.

	Discovery Questions	Look here:
BIN-OSSOWN-01	Is **/bin/read** owned by SUPER.SUPER?	ls -al
BIN-READ-01	Is **/bin/read** secured correctly?	ls -al

Related Topics

printf

Remote Name Daemon Control (rndc) User Program

The **/etc/dns<version>/rndc** program controls the operation of a BIND 9 domain name server either locally or remotely. Please refer to the *OSS Gazette* section on the Berkeley Internet Name Domain (BIND) Server.

resolv.conf Configuration File

The **resolv.conf** file is the *TCP/IP* domain name resolver configuration file. Please refer to the *OSS Gazette* section on **inetd** for more information.

rexecd

The **/bin/rexecd** (Remote Execution Daemon) is a server program that listens for service requests at the port indicated in the the **/etc/services** file and validates the remote user as if he was logging on. If the authentication is successful, **/bin/rexecd** changes to the user's home directory, and establishes the user and group protections of the user. The user's session inherits all the network connections established by **/bin/rexecd**.

A remote execution client process, such as **mxcmp**, opens up a connection to the remote **/bin/rexecd** process and transmits a message that specifies the username, password, and the name of the command to execute.

Each user of the **/bin/rexecd** server must have:

> An OSS initial directory defined in his Safeguard user record
>
> Remote access to the remote host's **/bin/rexecd** server

A **rexecd** session is equivalent to a context-free, one-line telnet session with enforced user validation and should be secured as such.

/bin/rexecd doesn't use the trusted host mechanism, and it can be executed from anywhere. The password is, however, transmitted across the network unencrypted.

RISK   Rexec/**rexecd** requires that the password be transmitted over the network without encryption, therefore it is vulnerable to password snooping.

RISK   Unlike LOGON and TELNET, **/bin/rexecd** error messages differ for invalid userids versus invalid password. This flaw allows an attacker to use **/bin/rexecd** to probe your system for valid accounts to target with password attacks.

AP-ADVICE-REXECD-01   All requests to **/bin/rexecd** should be filtered by the node's firewall.

BP-POLICY-REXECD-01   Do not use **/bin/rexecd** unless it is required on the system; use the more secure SSH Subsystem instead.

/bin/rexecd is used for the remote NonStop SQL/MX compiler (**mxcmp**) invoked from the TNS/R native C/C++ and NMCOBOL cross-compilers on a PC, running with or without the Enterprise Toolkit (ETK) NonStop Edition. **/bin/rexecd** is started by the **inetd** process, which must be running in order to do remote SQL/MX compiling.

Inetd.conf

Because the **rexecd** server is started by the **inetd** process, **/bin/rexecd** must be defined in the target node's **/etc/inetd.conf** file. Please refer to the *OSS Gazette* section on the **inetd** Subsystem for more information.

rhosts Configuration File

The **rhosts** file is one of the "remote authentication" databases for the **rsh** program. It specifies remote hosts and users that are considered trusted. Only trusted users logged on to a trusted remote host are allowed to access the local system. These users must have userids on the local system.

The **rhosts** files can also be used to specify a single, specific trusted user for each trusted host. This allows all users from that host to use a single local trusted userid.

RISK Specifying a trusted userid to be used by every user connecting from a particular trusted host results eliminates individual accountability.

The remote authentication procedure determines whether a user from a remote host should be allowed to access the local system using a local userid. This procedure first checks the **/etc/hosts.equiv** file and then checks for an rhosts file in the home directory of the local trusted userid. The **rsh** program fails if this remote authentication procedure fails.

RISK If any **rhost** file on the system is vulnerable, an attacker could add a username to it so that they could break in again more easily.

BP-POLICY-RHOSTS-01 Do not use a **/etc/rhosts** file unless it is required on the system; use the more secure SSH Subsystem instead.

BP-POLICY-RHOSTS-02 Never allow an **.rhosts** file owned by SUPER.SUPER in any system directory.

If /etc/rhosts file(s) must be used, take the following precautions:

AP-ADVICE-RHOSTS-01   *Never* put the symbols "−" or "+" as the first character in this file, as this may allow anyone access to the system.

AP-ADVICE-RHOSTS-02   Always use *fully qualified hostnames* (i.e. host.domain.com).

AP-ADVICE-RHOSTS-03   Specify individual users and hosts rather than netgroups to avoid unintended access to the system.

Individual rhosts Files

The **rsh** client (**/etc/rsh**) will read the user's **$HOME/.rhosts** file when it attempts to start a remote shell.

RISK   Individual users can create and maintain **rhosts** files in their own home directories but there are few genuine needs for them.

BP-HOME-RHOSTS-01   Do not allow personal copies of a **rhosts** file in users' home directories.

If personal **rhosts** file must be allowed, take the following precautions to mitigate the risks:

AP-ADVICE-RHOSTS-02   Any allowed personal **rhosts** files should be justified and documented.

AP-ADVICE-RHOSTS-02   Use **/bin/cron** to periodically to:

> Check for the existence of any unexpected **rhosts** files
>
> Report the contents of all **rhosts** files
>
> Delete (or clear) any unapproved copies, especially the **$HOME /.rhosts** files

Securing rhosts

BP-ETC-RHOSTS-01   /etc/**rhosts** should be secured 700 (rwx --- ---).

BP-ETC-OSSOWN-01   /etc/**rhosts** should be owned by SUPER.SUPER.

BP-ETC-OSSLOC-01   **/etc/rhosts** resides in /etc.

BP-HOME-RHOSTS-02   **.rhosts** should be secured 700 (r-- --- ---).

BP-HOME-OSSOWN-00 **.rhosts** should be owned by individual userids.

BP-HOME-OSSLOC-00   **.rhosts** resides in users' $HOME.

	Discovery Questions	**Look here:**
OSS-POLICY	Does the policy allow a **rhosts** file in /etc?	ls -al
ETC-OSSOWN-01	Who owns the **/etc/rhosts** file?	ls -al
ETC-RHOSTS-01	Is **/etc/rhosts** secured correctly?	ls -al
OSS-POLICY	Does the policy allow for the use of personal **rhosts** files?	Policy
HOME-OSSOWN-00	Is each individual's **$HOME.rhosts** file owned by the user?	ls -al
HOME-RHOSTS-02	Is each individual's **$HOME.rhosts** file secured correctly?	ls -al

Related Topics

inetd.conf

rsh

services

rm User Program

The **/bin/rm** program removes files from a directory, or, to be more exact, it unlinks or severs the connection between the filename in the directory and the inode number. If another link still exists to the inode number, the file continues to exist, but not in the directory it was removed from. When all links are severed and the file is closed, its space is reclaimed and it is no longer accessible.

To remove a file from a directory, a user doesn't have to have permissions to READ or WRITE the file, but he must have WRITE permission to its directory (because the directory file is being modified to remove the name/inode connection).

RISK   OSS shell programs that perform recursive actions make no distinction between Guardian and OSS files or between local and remote files. /G and /E both appear in the local root directory, which puts both remote files and Guardian files at risk.

Securing /bin/rm

BP-BIN-RM-01   rm should be secured 711 (rwx --x --x).

BP-BIN-OSSOWN-01   rm should be owned by SUPER.SUPER.

BP-BIN-OSSLOC-01   rm resides in /bin.

	Discovery Questions	Look here:
BIN-OSSOWN-01	Is /bin/rm owned by SUPER.SUPER?	ls -al
BIN-RM-01	Is /bin/rm secured correctly?	ls -al

Related Topics

ln

mv

rmdir

UTILSGE

rmdir User Program

The /bin/rmdir program removes a directory. A directory cannot be removed if it contains files or subdirectories.

The -p flag tells rmdir to remove all directories in a pathname.

Deleting a directory requires WRITE access to the directory's parent because the parent directory file is modified to remove the subdirectory.

Securing /bin/rmdir

BP-BIN-RMDIR-01   **rmdir** should be secured 711 (rwx --x --x).

BP-BIN-OSSOWN-01   **rmdir** should be owned by SUPER.SUPER.

BP-BIN-OSSLOC-01   **rmdir** resides in **/bin**.

	Discovery Questions	Look here:
BIN-OSSOWN-01	Is **/bin/rmdir** owned by SUPER.SUPER?	ls -al
BIN-RMDIR-01	Is **/bin/rmdir** secured correctly?	ls -al

Related Topics

gname

filename

rndc User Program

The **/etc/dns<version>/rndc** (Remote Name Daemon Control) program controls the operation of a BIND 9 domain name server either locally or remotely. Please refer to the *OSS Gazette* section on the Berkeley Internet Name Domain (BIND) Server.

rndc.conf Configuration File

The **rndc.conf** is the configuration file for **rndc**, the BIND 9 name server control utility. Please refer to the *OSS Gazette* section on the Berkeley Internet Name Domain (BIND) Server.

rsh/rshd Subsystem

The **rsh/rshd** subsystem allows a user to execute a single command on a remote node without logging on to the remote system. Any messages returned from the remote program are sent back to the local user's terminal.

The **rsh/rshd** subsystem requires that the local node be trusted by the remode node, that is, it must be named in the remote system's **/etc/hosts.equiv** file.

RISK   If the local host trusts a remote host, any user who has the same userid on both systems can log on to the local system from the trusted remote host without a password.

Please refer to the section on the **inetd** Subsystem for a discussion of all the risks related to the trusted host mechanism.

By default, the remote **/bin/rshd** server invoked via **/bin/rsh** will run as the invoking user, but the **-1** option allows a different userid to be specified. Either way, the remote host will only allow access if:

The local userid invoking **/bin/rsh** is not SUPER.SUPER or an alias to SUPER.SUPER

The name of the local node is included in the target node's **/etc/hosts.equiv** file

The target remote userid, whether it is the invoking user or specified via the -l flag:

Exists on the target node.

Has an INITIAL-DIRECTORY specified in the target node's Safeguard user record.

Has a **$HOME/.rhosts** file in its home directory that includes the fully qualified domain name and userid on the same line.

The remote authentication procedure determines whether a user from a remote host should be allowed to access the local system with the identity of a local user. This procedure first checks the **/etc/hosts.equiv** file and then checks the **/etc/rhosts** file in the home directory of the local user who is requesting access. The **/bin/rsh** program fails if the remote authentication procedure fails.

RISK   **/bin/rsh** allows access to the local node even if the remote user account does not have a password defined.

RISK   **/bin/rsh** sends passwords across the network in the clear, therefore it is vulnerable to password snooping. It should not be used.

BP-POLICY-INETD-07   Do not rely on the trusted host mechanism. Do not use **rsh/rshd**; use SSH instead.

rsh/rshd Components and Dependencies

The **rsh/rshd** subsystem requires the following components:

inetd.conf*

rsh

rshd

/etc/hosts.equiv*

rhosts

Those components marked with an asterisk are discussed in the *OSS Gazette* section on the **inetd** subsystem.

inetd.conf

To be usable, **/bin/rshd** must be configured in the target node's **inetd.conf** file.

rsh

/bin/rsh is the client program for the **rsh/rshd** subsystem. It starts the remote shell server process on the remote node.

rshd

The **/bin/rshd** program is the server process for the **rsh/rshd** subsystem. It executes the requested command on the remote node. It is started by the **/bin/inetd** process, which must be running for **rsh/rshd** to function.

/bin/rshd must be defined in the **inetd.conf** file.

/etc/hosts.equiv

/bin/rsh queries the **/etc/hosts.equiv** file, which specifies remote hosts from which users can execute programs on the local host (if these users have an account on the local host). This file can also specify a trusted user for each host.

rhosts

/bin/rsh queries the **$HOME/.rhosts** file which specifies the remote hosts from which users can execute programs on the local host (if they have userids on the local host). This file can also specify a trusted user for each host. Please refer to the *OSS Gazette* section on the **rhosts** file for more information.

Securing /bin/rsh

BP-BIN-RSH-01   rsh should be secured 711 (rwx --x --x).

BP-BIN-SETUID-01   rsh should have the **setuid** attribute.

BP-BIN-OSSOWN-01 rsh should be owned by SUPER.SUPER.

BP-BIN-OSSLOC-01   rsh resides in **/bin**.

BP-BIN-RSH-02   rshd should be secured 711 (rwx --x --x).

BP-BIN-OSSOWN-01 rshd should be owned by SUPER.SUPER.

BP-BIN-OSSLOC-01   rshd resides in **/bin**.

	Discovery Questions	Look here:
OSS-POLICY	Is the **rsh/rshd** subsystem authorized for use on the system?	Policy
OPSYS-OSSOWN-01	Who owns the **rsh** object file?	ls -al
FILE-RSH-01	Is the **rsh** secured correctly?	ls -al
OPSYS-OSSOWN-01	Who owns the **rshd** object file?	ls -al
BIN-RSH-02	Is the **rshd** secured correctly?	ls -al

Related Topics

hosts.equiv

rhosts

ssh

TELNET

runcat User Program

The **/bin/runcat** program invokes the **/bin/mkcatdefs** program and pipes the resulting message-catalog source data to the **/bin/gencat** program.

RISK Because the intent of the **/bin/mkcatdefs** program is to create message catalogs, it does not alter existing catalogs; it deletes the old catalog and creates a new one.

AP-ADVICE-GENCAT-01 Only users responsible for creating and maintaining program messages should have WRITE and PURGE access to message text files.

AP-ADVICE-GENCAT-01 Only users responsible for creating and maintaining program messages should have EXECUTE access to the **/bin/gencat** program.

AP-ADVICE-MKCATDEF-01 Only users responsible for creating and maintaining program messages should have EXECUTE access to the **/bin/ mkcatdefs** program.

AP-ADVICE-RUNCAT-01   Only users responsible for creating and maintaining program messages should have EXECUTE access to the /bin/runcat program.

Securing /bin/runcat

BP-BIN-RUNCAT-01   runcat should be secured 711 (rwx --x --x).

BP-BIN-OSSOWN-01   runcat should be owned by SUPER.SUPER.

BP-BIN-OSSLOC-01   runcat resides in /bin.

	Discovery Questions	Look here:
BIN-OSSOWN-01	Is /bin/runcat owned by SUPER.SUPER?	ls -al
BIN-RUNCAT-01	Is /bin/runcat secured correctly?	ls -al

Related Topics

gencat

mkcatdefs

runv User Program

The /bin/runv program starts an OSS program in Visual Inspect.

RISK   Visual Inspect provides a mechanism whereby running processes can be traced and modified by human interaction.

RISK   A user running Visual Inspect could capture sensitive data, userids, passwords, etc. as they are used internally in a program.

INSPECT is used extensively on a development system, but should rarely be used on a secure system. Therefore, the security requirements are vastly different. If INSPECT is not authorized for use on a system, /bin/runv should be secured so that it can't be used.

AP-ADVICE-RUNV-01 Depending on corporate security policy, on a secure system, no one or only users responsible for troubleshooting applications should have EXECUTE access to **/bin/runv**.

AP-ADVICE-RUNV-02 Critical or sensitive application and system object files and processes should tightly secured to prevent unauthorized access.

Securing /bin/runv

BP-BIN-RUNV-01   **runv** should be secured 711 (rwx --x --x).

BP-BIN-OSSOWN-01 **runv** should be owned by SUPER.SUPER.

BP-BIN-OSSLOC-01   **runv** resides in **/bin**.

	Discovery Questions	Look here:
BIN-OSSOWN-01	Is **/bin/runv** owned by SUPER.SUPER?	ls -al
BIN-RUNV-01	Is **/bin/runv** secured correctly?	ls -al

Samba Subsystem

Samba provides file and print services for Microsoft Windows clients. The services can be hosted on any *TCP/IP*-enabled platform. It enables users to print the contents of a NonStop file on a PC printer.

Samba can be maliciously exploited if not configured properly.

This section focuses on securing the components of the Samba Subsystem. Please refer to the chapter on the Samba section of Part 5, *File Sharing Protocols*, for more information about the Samba subsystem and its components.

Securing the Samba Subsystem Components

The Samba Subsystem is made up of the following components:

nmbd program

nmbd.pid file

passdb file

secrets file

smbclient program

smb.conf file

smbcontrol program

smbd program

smbd.pid file

smbpasswd program

smbpasswd file

smbrun program

smbstatus program

smbspool program

smbtar program

testparm program

nmbd

The **/usr/local/samba/bin/nmbd** (NetBIOS name server) is used to provide NetBIOS over IP naming service to clients. It listens for IP address requests from Samba clients, which broadcast the DNS name of the host the client user wishes to contact. When its NetBIOS name is specified, **/usr/local/samba/bin/nmbd** responds with the IP address of the host it is running on.

BP-USR-SAMBA-01   nmbd should be secured 700 (rwx --- ---).

BP-USR-OSSOWN-04 nmbd should be owned by SUPER.SUPER.

BP-USR-OSSLOC-04   nmbd resides in **/usr/local/samba/bin**.

	Discovery Questions	Look here:
OSS-POLICY	Is Samba authorized for use on the system?	Policy
USR-OSSOWN-04	Is **/usr/local/samba/bin/nmbd** owned by SUPER.SUPER?	ls -al
USR-SAMBA-01	Is **/usr/local/samba/bin/nmbd** secured correctly?	ls -al

nmblookup

The **/usr/local/bin/nmblookup** program is the **nmb** client used to lookup NetBIOS names. It can be used to query NetBIOS names and map them to IP addresses in a network using NetBIOS over *TCP/IP* queries. Queries can be directed at a particular IP broadcast area or to a particular machine. All queries are done over UDP.

BP-USR-SAMBA-02   nmblookup should be secured 700 (rwx --- ---).

BP-USR-OSSOWN-03 nmblookup should be owned by SUPER.SUPER.

BP-USR-OSSLOC-03   nmblookup resides in **/usr/local/bin**.

	Discovery Questions	Look here:
OSS-POLICY	Is Samba authorized for use on the system?	Policy
USR-OSSOWN-03	Is **/usr/local/bin/nmblookup** owned by SUPER.SUPER?	ls -al
USR-SAMBA-02	Is **/usr/local/bin/nmblookup** secured correctly?	ls -al

nmbd.pid

The **/usr/local/var/locks/nmbd.pid** contains the process ID of the **nmbd** process. This file is updated by the **nmbd** process.

BP-USR-SAMBA-03   nmbd.pid should be secured 600 (rw- --- ---).

BP-USR-OSSOWN-04 nmbd.pid should be owned by SUPER.SUPER.

BP-USR-OSSLOC-04   nmbd.pid resides in **/usr/local/var/locks**.

	Discovery Questions	Look here:
OSS-POLICY	Is Samba authorized for use on the system?	Policy
USR-OSSOWN-04	Is **/usr/local/var/locks/nmbd.pid** owned by SUPER.SUPER?	ls -al
USR-SAMBA-03	Is **/usr/local/var/locks/nmbd.pid** secured correctly?	ls -al

passdb Configuration File

The **passdb** file will exist only when the **tdbsam** password backend is used on the system. It stores the SambaSAMAccount information. This file requires that user POSIX account information be availble from either the **/etc/passwd** file or from an alternative system source.

This file contains very sensitive information that must be tightly secured.

BP-USR-SAMBA-04   **passdb** should be secured 600 (rw- --- ---).

BP-USR-OSSOWN-03   **passdb** should be owned by SUPER.SUPER.

BP-USR-OSSLOC-03   **passdb** resides in **/usr/local/private**.

	Discovery Questions	Look here:
USR-OSSOWN-03	Is **/usr/local/bin/passdb** owned by SUPER.SUPER?	ls -al
USR-SAMBA-04	Is **/usr/local/bin/passdb** secured correctly?	ls -al

secrets Configuration File

The **/usr/local/private/secrets.tdb** file contains Samba domain configuration information.

BP-USR-SECRETS-05   **secrets** should be secured 600 (rw- --- ---).

BP-USR-OSSOWN-03   **secrets** should be owned by SUPER.SUPER.

BP-USR-OSSLOC-03   **secrets** resides in **/usr/local/private**.

	Discovery Questions	Look here:
USR-OSSOWN-03	Is **/usr/local/bin/secrets** owned by SUPER.SUPER?	ls -al
USR-SAMBA-05	Is **/usr/local/bin/secrets** secured correctly?	ls -al

smbclient Program

The **/usr/local/bin/smbclient** program is used by NonStop Samba users to connect to a remote Samba server. It presents an interface similar to FTP. If the host to which the user wishes to connect requires a password, the user must supply a password.

All NonStop Server users allowed to run Samba from the host need EXECUTE permission for this program.

BP-USR-SAMBA-06   **smbclient** should be secured 700 (rwx --- ---).

BP-USR-OSSOWN-03   **smbclient** should be owned by SUPER.SUPER.

BP-USR-OSSLOC-03   **smbclient** resides in **/usr/local/bin**.

	Discovery Questions	Look here:
OSS-POLICY	Is Samba authorized for use on the system?	Policy
USR-OSSOWN-03	Is **/usr/local/bin/smbclient** owned by SUPER.SUPER?	ls -al
USR-SAMBA-06	Is **/usr/local/bin/smbclient** secured correctly?	ls -al

smb.conf Configuration File

The location of the **smb.conf** file is determined at compile-time. If you install the precompiled ITUG version of Samba, the file will be placed in the **/usr/local/lib** directory. This is the location used in this book.

The **/usr/local/lib/smb.conf** file is used to configure the Samba environment. Many of the parameters configured in this file directly affect the security of the NonStop host's files. Please refer to Part 8, File Sharing Protocols, for more information, including the Best Practice recommendations for the security-related parameters in this file.

BP-USR-SAMBA-07   smb.conf should be secured 644 (rw- r-- r--).

BP-USR-OSSOWN-03   smb.conf should be owned by SUPER.SUPER.

BP-USR-OSSLOC-03   smb.conf resides in **/usr/local/lib**.

	Discovery Questions	Look here:
OSS-POLICY	Is Samba authorized for use on the system?	Policy
USR-OSSOWN-03	Is **/usr/local/lib/smb.conf** owned by SUPER.SUPER?	ls -al
USR-SAMBA-07	Is **/usr/local/lib/smb.conf** secured correctly?	ls -al

smbcontrol Program

/usr/local/bin/smbcontrol is the object file for the **smb** command interpretor. It communicates with the **smbd** and **nmbd** servers. Any item that can be configured in the **smb.conf** file can be submitted to the running **smbd** server.

Only users responsible for managing the Samba subsystem should have EXECUTE access to this program.

3P-ACCESS-SAMBA-01   Use a third-party access control product to grant the users responsible for managing the Samba subsystem the ability to run **smbcontrol** as SUPER.SUPER.

BP-USR-SAMBA-08   smbcontrol should be secured 700 (rwx --- ---).

BP-USR-OSSOWN-03   smbcontrol should be owned by SUPER.SUPER.

BP-USR-OSSLOC-03   smbcontrol resides in **/usr/local/bin**.

	Discovery Questions	Look here:
OSS-POLICY	Is Samba authorized for use on the system?	Policy
USR-OSSOWN-03	Is **/usr/local/bin/smbcontrol** owned by SUPER.SUPER?	ls -al
USR-SAMBA-08	Is **/usr/local/bin/smbcontrol** secured correctly?	ls -al

smbd

/usr/local/bin/smbd is the object file for the Samba server daemon. It provides filespace and printer services to clients using the SMB protocol or LanManager clients.

BP-USR-SAMBA-09   smbd should be secured 700 (rwx --- ---).

BP-USR-OSSOWN-03   smbd should be owned by SUPER.SUPER.

BP-USR-OSSLOC-03   smbd resides in /usr/local/sbin.

	Discovery Questions	Look here:
OSS-POLICY	Is Samba authorized for use on the system?	Policy
USR-OSSOWN-03	Is /usr/local/sbin/smbd owned by SUPER.SUPER?	ls -al
USR-SAMBA-09	Is /usr/local/sbin/smbd secured correctly?	ls -al

smbd.pid

The /usr/local/var/locks/smbd.pid contains the process ID of the smbd process. This file is updated by the smbd process itself.

BP-USR-SAMBA-10   smbd.pid should be secured 600 (rw- --- ---).

BP-USR-OSSOWN-04   smbd.pid should be owned by SUPER.SUPER.

BP-USR-OSSLOC-04   smbd.pid resides in /usr/local/var/locks.

	Discovery Questions	Look here:
OSS-POLICY	Is Samba authorized for use on the system?	Policy
USR-OSSOWN-04	Is /usr/local/var/locks/ smbd.pid owned by SUPER.SUPER?	ls -al
USR-SAMBA-10	Is /usr/local/var/locks/ smbd.pid secured correctly?	ls -al

smbpasswd Program

The /usr/local/bin/smbpasswd program allows users to change their encrypted Samba password, which is stored in the smbpasswd file. It handles the encryption of the stored password.

BP-USR-SAMBA-11   The **smbpasswd** program should be secured 711 (rwx --x --x).

BP-USR-OSSOWN-03 The **smbpasswd** program should be owned by SUPER.SUPER.

BP-USR-OSSLOC-03   The **smbpasswd** program resides in **/usr/local/bin**.

	Discovery Questions	Look here:
OSS-POLICY	Is Samba authorized for use on the system?	Policy
USR-OSSOWN-03	Is the **/usr/local/bin/smbpasswd** program owned by SUPER.SUPER?	ls -al
USR-SAMBA-11	Is the **/usr/local/bin/smbpasswd** program secured correctly?	ls -al

smbpasswd File

The **/usr/local/private/smbpasswd** file contains users' encrypted Samba passwords.

This file is only used if the Samba server is configured for encrypted passwords.

BP-USR-SAMBA-12   The **smbpasswd** file should be secured 600 (rw- --- ---).

BP-USR-OSSOWN-03   The **smbpasswd** file should be owned by SUPER. SUPER.

BP-USR-OSSLOC-03   The **smbpasswd** program resides in **/etc/samba /private**.

	Discovery Questions	Look here:
OSS-POLICY	Is Samba authorized for use on the system?	Policy
USR-OSSOWN-03	Is the **/etc/samba/private/smbpasswd** file owned by SUPER.SUPER?	ls -al
USR-SAMBA-12	Is the **/etc/samba/private/smbpasswd** file secured correctly?	ls -al

smbrun System Program

The **/usr/local/bin/smbrun** program is an interface program that runs shell commands for the Samba server. The program can only be started by the Samba server (**smbd**).

BP-USR-SAMBA-13   **smbrun** should be secured 700 (rwx --- ---).

BP-USR-OSSOWN-03   **smbrun** should be owned by SUPER.SUPER.

BP-USR-OSSLOC-03   **smbrun** resides in **/usr/local/bin**.

	Discovery Questions	**Look here:**
OSS-POLICY	Is Samba authorized for use on the system?	Policy
USR-OSSOWN-03	Is **/usr/local/bin/smbrun** owned by SUPER.SUPER?	ls -al
USR-SAMBA-13	Is **/usr/local/bin/smbrun** secured correctly?	ls -al

smbstatus Program

The **/usr/local/bin/smbstatus** program returns a list of current Samba connections and locks and their statuses.

If **status = no**, in the **smb.conf file**, the **smbstatus** program won't be able to show what connections are active.

BP-USR-SAMBA-14   **smbstatus** should be secured 711 (rwx --x --x).

BP-USR-OSSOWN-03   **smbstatus** should be owned by SUPER.SUPER.

BP-USR-OSSLOC-03   **smbstatus** resides in **/usr/local/bin**.

	Discovery Questions	**Look here:**
OSS-POLICY	Is Samba authorized for use on the system?	Policy
USR-OSSOWN-03	Is **/usr/local/bin/smbstatus** owned by SUPER.SUPER?	ls -al
USR-SAMBA-14	Is **/usr/local/bin/smbstatus** secured correctly?	ls -al

smbspool Program

The **/usr/local/bin/smbspool** is a print-spooling program that sends a print file to a Samba printer. The **smbspool** can be used with any printing system or from a program or script.

BP-USR-SAMBA-15   smbspool should be secured 711 (rwx --x --x).

BP-USR-OSSOWN-03 smbspool should be owned by SUPER.SUPER.

BP-USR-OSSLOC-03   smbspool resides in **/usr/local/bin**.

	Discovery Questions	**Look here:**
OSS-POLICY	Is Samba authorized for use on the system?	Policy
USR-OSSOWN-03	Is **/usr/local/bin/smbspool** owned by SUPER.SUPER?	ls -al
USR-SAMBA-15	Is **/usr/local/bin/smbspool** secured correctly?	ls -al

smbtar Program

The **/usr/local/bin/smbtar** program is used to backup and restore files on remote shares to tape via the **smbclient** utility.

RISK   /usr/local/bin/smbtar requires only READ access to perform the file READ function. If the **/usr/local/bin/smbtar** program is accessible to general users, files containing sensitive data could be backed up and restored under their userid.

BP-USR-SAMBA-16   smbtar should be secured 711 (rwx --x --x).

BP-USR-OSSOWN-03 smbtar should be owned by SUPER.SUPER.

BP-USR-OSSLOC-03   smbtar resides in **/usr/local/bin**.

	Discovery Questions	**Look here:**
OSS-POLICY	Is Samba authorized for use on the system?	Policy
USR-OSSOWN-03	Is **/usr/local/bin/smbtar** owned by SUPER.SUPER?	ls -al
USR-SAMBA-16	Is **/usr/local/bin/smbtar** secured correctly?	ls -al

swat Program

/usr/local/bin/swat is a Web-based graphical interface used to edit the smb.conf file. It is part of the freeware Samba package. The program should only be moved to the PCs used by the people authorized to configure the smb.conf file.

Samba Directories

The following directories may be present on your system:

/usr/local/Floss/samba-<version>*
/usr/local/var/locks
/usr/local/private

/usr/local/Floss/samba-<version>* Directories

The /usr/local/Floss/samba-<version> directory and all the subdirectories under it contain the files required for installation, as well as supporting files such as the Samba man pages.

BP-USR-SAMBA-17 The samba-<version>* directories should be secured 700 (rwx --- ---).

BP-USR-DIROWN-04 The samba-<version>* directories should be owned by SUPER.SUPER.

BP-USR-DIRLOC-04 The samba-<version>*directories reside in /usr /local/var/Floss.

	Discovery Questions	**Look here:**
OSS-POLICY	Is Samba authorized for use on the system?	Policy
USR-DIROWN-04	Are the /usr/local/var/Floss/Samba-<version> * directories owned by SUPER.SUPER?	ls -al
USR-SAMBA-17	Are the /usr/local/var/Floss/Samba-<version> * directories secured correctly?	ls -al

/usr/local/var/locks Directory

The **/usr/local/var/locks** contains some configuration files and the temporary files that Samba creates during processing. Only SUPER. SUPER should have access to the files in this directory.

Temporary Files Created and Maintained by Samba	
Name	**Description**
brlock	Byte-range locking information.
connections	Cached current connection information used to enforce max connections.
login_cache	Cached login information, especially bad password attempts.
messages.tdb	Temporary storage of messages being processed by **smbd**.
nonetsamlogon_cache	Cached user **net_info_3** structure data from **net_samlogon** requests (as a domain member).
perfmon/*.tdb	Cached performance information.
printing.tdb	Caches output from **lpq** command created on a per-print-service basis.
schannel_store	A confidential file, stored in the PRIVATE_DIR, containing crytographic connection information so that clients who have temporarily disconnected can reconnect without needing to renegotiate the connection setup process.
sessionid	Temporary cache for miscellaneous session information and for **utmp** handling.
share_info.tdb	Stores per-share access information for Samba services (shares).
unexpected.tdb	Stores packets received for which no process is actively listening.

BP-USR-SAMBA-18
(rwx --- ---).

The **locks** directory should be secured 700

BP-USR-DIROWN-03 The **locks** directory should be owned by SUPER.SUPER.

BP-USR-DIRLOC-03 The **locks** directory resides in **/usr/local/var**.

	Discovery Questions	Look here:
OSS-POLICY	Is Samba authorized for use on the system?	Policy
USR-DIROWN-03	Is the **/usr/local/var/locks** owned by SUPER.SUPER?	ls -al
USR-SAMBA-18	Is the **/usr/local/var/locks** secured correctly?	ls -al

/usr/local/private Directory

The **/usr/local/private** contains some configuration files and the temporary files that Samba creates during processing. Only SUPER.SUPER should have access to the files in this directory.

BP-USR-SAMBA-19 The **private** directories should be secured 700 (rwx --- ---).

BP-USR-DIROWN-02 The **private** directories should be owned by SUPER.SUPER.

BP-USR-DIRLOC-02 The **private** directories reside in **/usr/local**.

	Discovery Questions	Look here:
OSS-POLICY	Is Samba authorized for use on the system?	Policy
USR-DIROWN-02	Is the **/usr/local/private** directory owned by SUPER.SUPER?	ls -al
USR-SAMBA-19	Is the **/usr/local/private** directory secured correctly?	ls -al

testparm Program

The **/usr/local/private/testparm** program is used to check syntax and display the currect parameters set in the **smb.conf** file.

This file contains very sensitive information that must be tightly secured.

BP-USR-SAMBA-20   **testparm** should be secured 711 (rwx --x --x).

BP-USR-OSSOWN-03   **testparm** should be owned by SUPER.SUPER.

BP-USR-OSSLOC-03   **testparm** resides in **/usr/local/private**.

Discovery Questions		Look here:
USR-OSSOWN-03	Is **/usr/local/bin/testparm** owned by SUPER.SUPER?	ls -al
USR-SAMBA-20	Is **/usr/local/bin/testparm** secured correctly?	ls -al

scp User Program

/usr/local/bin/scp (Secure Copy Client) copies files between hosts on a network. It uses SSH for data transfer and uses the same authentication and security as SSH. **/usr/local/bin/scp** prompts the user for a password or passphrase if they are required for authentication.

Any filename may contain a host name and user name to indicate that the file is to be copied to or from that host. Copies to two remote hosts are allowed.

BP-USR-SCP-01   **scp** should be secured 711 (rwx --x --x).

BP-USR-OSSOWN-03   **scp** should be owned by SUPER.SUPER.

BP-USR-OSSLOC-03   **scp** resides in **/usr/local/bin**.

Discovery Questions		Look here:
USR-OSSOWN-03	Is **/usr/local/bin/scp** owned by SUPER.SUPER?	ls -al
USR-SCP-01	Is **/usr/local/bin/scp** secured correctly?	ls -al

secrets Configuration File

The **/usr/local/private/secrets** file stores critical environmental data that is necessary for Samba to operate correctly.

sed User Program

The **/bin/sed** program is a stream line editor. It makes it possible to select only certain lines for changes. **/bin/sed** processes an input file, applying **sed** subcommands one by one and writing the changes.

RISK An attacker can embed commands in **sed** scripts.

AP-ADVICE-SED-01 Rather than securing the **/bin/sed** object file, secure sensitive application data and scripts that are stored as text files so that they can only be viewed or altered by authorized personnel.

Securing /bin/sed

BP-BIN-SED-01   sed should be secured 711 (rwx --x --x).

BP-BIN-OSSOWN-01   sed should be owned by SUPER.SUPER.

BP-BIN-OSSLOC-01   sed resides in **/bin**.

	Discovery Questions	Look here:
BIN-OSSOWN-01	Is **/bin/sed** owned by SUPER.SUPER?	ls -al
BIN-SED-01	Is **/bin/sed** secured correctly?	ls -al

Related Topics

awk

ed

grep

vi

services Configuration File

The **/etc/services** file contains Internet port-level services that might be available with NonStop *TCP/IP.*

setmxdb

The **/usr/tandem/sqlmx/bin/setmxdb** file is the OSS installation script for the SQL/MX sample database.

SFTP Subsystem

SFTP (Secure File Transfer Program) is a client server system. It is used to connect to a remote system. **/usr/local/bin/sftp-server** is the local server process. It responds to connection requests from remote systems.

sftp

usr/local/bin/sftp is the SSH secure file transfer client program. It is similar to FTP, but it moves the files via encrypted SSH. It may also use other features of SSH, such as public key authentication and compression.

If an interactive authentication method is used, **sftp** connects and logs into the specified host and then enters interactive command mode. It can also start an SFTP session on a remote host.

If a noninteractive authentication method is used, **sftp** can be used to automatically retrieve files from a remote host.

sftp-server

/usr/local/libexec/sftp-server is the SSH secure file transfer server. It is never accessed by users directly. It is started by the SSH server (**sshd**) when a file transfer request from a remote system arrives. The **sftp-server** must be entered as the argument for the **subsystem** parameter in the **sshd_config** file.

BP-USR-SFTP-01	**sftp** should be secured 711 (rwx --x --x).
BP-USR-OSSOWN-03	**sftp** should be owned by SUPER.SUPER.
BP-USR-OSSLOC-03	**sftp** resides in **/usr/local/bin**.

BP-USR-SFTP-02	**sftp-server** should be secured 711 (rwx --x --x).
BP-USR-OSSOWN-03	**sftp-server** should be owned by SUPER.SUPER.
BP-USR-OSSLOC-03	**sftp-server** resides in **/usr/local/libexec**.

	Discovery Questions	**Look here:**
OSS-POLICY	Is **sftp** in use on the system?	Policy
USR-OSSOWN-03	Is **/usr/local/bin/sftp** owned by SUPER.SUPER?	ls -al
USR-SFTP-01	Is **/usr/local/bin/sftp** secured correctly?	ls -al
USR-OSSOWN-03	Is **/usr/local/bin/sftp-server** owned by SUPER.SUPER?	ls -al
USR-SFTP-02	Is **/usr/local/bin/sftp-server** secured correctly?	ls -al

sh Command Interpreter

/bin/sh is the OSS shell. Like TACL, it is an interactive command interpreter and also a programming language for commands. **/bin/ksh** is an alias for **/bin/sh**.

The OSS shell carries out commands either interactively from a terminal keyboard or from scripts.

The following words are reserved. If they appear as the first word of a command or of a line in a shell script, they are interpreted as commands. Aliases cannot be used to redefine these words.

case	fi	time
do	for	intil
done	function	while
elif	if	{ }
else	select	[[ ]]
esac	then	

For a full discussion on the many features of the shell, refer the section on the **ksh** or **sh** commands in HP's *OSS Shell and Utilities Reference Manual.*

Securing /bin/sh

BP-BIN-SH-01	**sh** should be secured 711 (rwx --x --x).
BP-BIN-OSSOWN-01	**sh** should be owned by SUPER.SUPER.
BP-BIN-OSSLOC-01	**sh** resides in **/bin**.

	Discovery Questions	**Look here:**
BIN-OSSOWN-02	Is **/bin/sh** owned by SUPER.SUPER?	ls -al
BIN-SH-01	Is **/bin/sh** secured correctly?	ls -al

shadow Configuration File

On systems other than the NonStop Server, user account information and passwords are stored in the **/etc/shadow** file. On the NonStop Server, Safeguard manages user records and passwords.

HP OSS processing does not use the **/etc/group**, **/etc/password**, or **/etc/ shadow** files. Some third-party software, such as Samba, NFS, Tuxedo, and OSI, may, however. Please refer to HP and the manufacturer's documentation on each of these products for information on the placement and use of these files as well as the risks involved.

share_info File

The **share-info** file stores per-share access information for Samba services (shares). Please refer to the chapter on the SAMBA Subsystem in Part 5, File Sharing Protocols, for more information or to the *OSS Gazette* section on Samba for Best Practice recommendations.

shift User Program

The **/bin/shift** program shifts positional parameters to the left by the number of positions specified.

There are two versions of the shift command that are identical except for the following:

The **/bin/shift** program starts a new shell process.

The built-in shell **shift** command doesn't start a new shell process.

The built-in shell shift command is the default. To invoke the program rather than the built-in command, you must use the full pathname to invoke **/bin/shift**.

Securing /bin/shift

BP-BIN-SHIFT-01   **shift** should be secured 711 (rwx --x --x).

BP-BIN-OSSOWN-01   **shift** should be owned by SUPER.SUPER.

BP-BIN-OSSLOC-01   **shift** resides in **/bin**.

	Discovery Questions	Look here:
BIN-OSSOWN-01	Is **/bin/shift** owned by SUPER.SUPER?	ls -al
BIN-SHIFT-01	Is **/bin/shift** secured correctly?	ls -al

Related Topics

sh

shosts Configuration File

The **/usr/local/etc/shosts** is processed exactly the same as the **/etc/hosts.equiv** file. Please refer to the SSH section in Part 4, *TCP/IP*, and the *OSS Gazette* section on the SSH Subsystem for more information.

sleep User Program

The **/bin/sleep** program suspends execution of a process for the number of seconds specified. A SIGALARM signal can wake a sleeping process before the sleep interval has elapsed.

Users other than SUPER.SUPER can only manipulate processes they own.

3P-PROCESS-ADVICE-01   Third-party process control software can be used to delegate the ability to manage processes by users other than the process owner.

Securing /bin/sleep

BP-BIN-SLEEP-01   sleep should be secured 711 (rwx --x --x).

BP-BIN-OSSOWN-01   **sleep** should be owned by SUPER.SUPER.

BP-BIN-OSSLOC-01   **sleep** resides in **/bin**.

	Discovery Questions	Look here:
OSS-POLICY	Are individual userids allowed in the SUPER Group?	Policy
BIN-OSSOWN-01	Is **/bin/sleep** owned by SUPER.SUPER?	ls -al
BIN-SLEEP-01	Is **/bin/sleep** secured correctly?	ls -al

sort User Program

The **/bin/sort** program sorts or merges files. It will sort all lines of specified files or merge them. It can perform multilevel sorts. It can be affected by settings in the locale file.

Users must have READ access to the file being sorted.

RISK   SORT has a performance risk if not controlled.

AP-ADVICE-SORT-01   It may be desirable to limit interactive sorts, allowing sorts of application data files to be controlled via application processes.

Securing /bin/sort

BP-BIN-SORT-01   **sort** should be secured 711 (rwx --x --x).

BP-BIN-OSSOWN-01   **sort** should be owned by SUPER.SUPER.

BP-BIN-OSSLOC-01   **sort** resides in **/bin**.

	Discovery Questions	**Look here:**
BIN-OSSOWN-01	Is **/bin/sort** owned by SUPER.SUPER?	ls -al
BIN-SORT-01	Is **/bin/sort** secured correctly?	ls -al

Related Topics

joins

uniq

locale

split User Program

The **/bin/split** program splits a file into pieces based on the parameters specified.

Users must have READ access to the file being split apart and EXECUTE access to the directory where the new files ("pieces") are being created.

Securing /bin/split

BP-BIN-SPLIT-01   **split** should be secured 711 (rwx --x --x).

BP-BIN-OSSOWN-01   **split** should be owned by SUPER.SUPER.

BP-BIN-OSSLOC-01   split resides in **/bin**.

	Discovery Questions	Look here:
BIN-OSSOWN-01	Is **/bin/split** owned by SUPER.SUPER?	ls -al
BIN-SPLIT-01	Is **/bin/split** secured correctly?	ls -al

Related Topics

join

SQL/MX Subsystem

HP's NonStop SQL/MX is a relational database management system that allows applications to use the SQL/MX query compiler and executor to access both SQL/MX and SQL/MP database objects.

The SQL/MX query compiler and executor run in the HP NonStop Kernel Open System Services (OSS) environment. To allow ANSI-compliant applications to access SQL/MP database objects, the SQL/MX query compiler and executor provide basic logical name support.

Safeguard cannot secure individual SQL catalog or objects, even though the object's name is a diskfile name. SQL tables and other objects can only be secured at the VOLUME or SUBVOLUME level. Safeguard can secure the SQL component files and processes, except for the System Catalog. See the Securing Application chapter for more discussion on SQL objects.

Please refer to Part 6, NonStop SQL and Database Security, for more information.

The **/usr/bin/c89** utility provides a single command interface to build C or C++ programs containing embedded SQL/MX statements. Please refer to the Guardian Gazette section on Integrity NonStop Compilers for more information.

The **/usr/bin/nmcobol** utility provides a single command interface to build COBOL programs containing embedded SQL/MX statements. Please refer to the *Guardian Gazette* section on Integrity NonStop Compilers for more information.

SQL/MX Components

The OSS components of SQL/MX are:

import

InstallSqlmx

migrate

mxci

mxcierrors.cat

mxcmp

mxCompileUserModule

mxexportddl

mxsqlc

mxsqlco

mxtool

setmxdb

import

The **/usr/tandem/sqlmx/bin/import** file is the symbolic link to the Guardian IMPORT program. The file IMPORT utility program copies data from an input file containing ASCII or UCS2 formatted data into an SQL/MX table. DataLoader/MX can be used in conjunction with **import** to load and maintain SQL/MX databases. It can be used only if the SQL/MX tables feature is has been licensed for the system.

BP-USR-SQLMX-01   **import** should be secured 711 (rwx --x --x).

BP-USR-OSSOWN-04   **import** should be owned by SUPER.SUPER.

BP-USR-OSSLOC-04   **import** resides in **/usr/tandem/sqlmx/bin**.

	Discovery Questions	Look here:
USR-OSSOWN-04	Is **/usr/tandem/sqlmx/bin/import** owned by SUPER.SUPER?	ls -al
USR-SQLMX-01	Is **/usr/tandem/sqlmx/bin/import** secured correctly?	ls -al

InstallSqlmx

The **/usr/tandem/sqlmx/bin/InstallSqlmx** file is the SQL/MX install script. When first installing SQL/MX on a system, the installer runs this script from an OSS system prompt. It begins by verifying several prerequisites (such as required hardware support within CPUs), then creates a simple Guardian text file named $SYSTEM.ZSQLMX.MXANCHOR, an anchor file that contains the volume location of the SQL/MX system metadata tables. The anchor file is assigned a security of "N---."

BP-USR-SQLMX-02   **InstallSqlmx** should be secured 711 (rwx --x --x).

BP-USR-OSSOWN-04   **InstallSqlmx** should be owned by SUPER.SUPER.

BP-USR-OSSLOC-04   **InstallSqlmx** resides in **/usr/tandem/sqlmx/bin.**

	Discovery Questions	Look here:
USR-OSSOWN-04	Is **/usr/tandem/sqlmx/bin/InstallSqlmx** owned by SUPER.SUPER?	ls -al
USR-SQLMX-02	Is **/usr/tandem/sqlmx/bin/InstallSqlmx** secured correctly?	ls -al

migrate

The **/usr/tandem/sqlmx/bin/migrate** file is the OSS file for the migrate utility. The migrate utility preserves SQL/MX (and ODBC/MX) Release 1.8 settings stored within several SQL/MP tables, by copying the contents of these tables to their corresponding Release 2.0 or Release 2.1 metadata tables.

This utility is only used on systems that previously installed SQL/MX Release 1.8 and are migrating to SQL/MX Release 2.1 or Release 2.0. It does not apply to systems that are installing SQL/MX for the first time.

BP-USR-SQLMX-03   **migrate** should be secured 711 (rwx --x --x).

BP-USR-OSSOWN-04   **migrate** should be owned by SUPER.SUPER.

BP-USR-OSSLOC-04   **migrate** resides in **/usr/tandem/sqlmx/bin**.

	Discovery Questions	Look here:
USR-OSSOWN-04	Is **/usr/tandem/sqlmx/bin/migrate** owned by SUPER.SUPER?	ls -al
USR-SQLMX-03	Is **/usr/tandem/sqlmx/bin/migrate** secured correctly?	ls -al

mxci

The **/usr/tandem/sqlmx/bin/mxci** program is the command interpreter for SQL/MX.

RISK If a user has access to **mxci** and has been granted READ and/or WRITE access to a table, then the user can effectively add, alter, or delete one, many, or all rows within the table. If a user has READ access to a table, all data within the table is accessible, regardless of its sensitivity.

AP-FILE-MXCI-02   Application users should not have access to SQLCI **mxci**. They should use the application's programmatic interfaces to insert, update, and retrieve data from SQL databases.

Controlling mxci

The **mxci** program provides the interface for inquires for queries about SQL objects and for SQL management functions. There is no internal security within **mxci** to limit SQL commands on objects where a user has been granted access other than the ownership requirements.

RISK Without a third-party Access Control Product, there is no way to control a user's use of unauthorized commands within **mxci**.

With a third-party access control product:

3P-ACCESS-SQL-01 Use a third-party access control product to allow the users responsible for using sensitive commands the ability to run **mxci** commands as SUPER.SUPER.

3P-ACCESS-SQL-02 Use a third-party access control product to give the use of certain **mxci** commands to a limited group of users only.

BP-USR-SQLMX-04 mxci should be secured 711 (rwx --x --x).

BP-USR-OSSOWN-04 mxci should be owned by SUPER.SUPER.

BP-USR-OSSLOC-04 mxci resides in **/usr/tandem/sqlmx/bin**.

	Discovery Questions	Look here:
USR-OSSOWN-04	Is /usr/tandem/sqlmx/bin/mxci owned by SUPER.SUPER?	ls -al
USR-SQLMX -04	/usr/tandem/sqlmx/bin/mxci secured correctly?	ls -al

mxcierrors.cat

The **/usr/tandem/sqlmx/bin/mxcierrors.cat** file is the OSS-based file that contains the error message text for all SQL/MX errors and is used by all SQL/MX components that display SQL/MX error text, including the NT-hosted preprocessors, **mxci**, and **mxcmp**.

BP-USR-SQLMX-05 mxcierrors.cat should be secured 711 (rwx --x --x).

BP-USR-OSSOWN-04 mxcierrors.cat should be owned by SUPER. SUPER.

BP-USR-OSSLOC-04 mxcierrors.cat resides in **/usr/tandem/sqlmx/bin**.

	Discovery Questions	Look here:
USR-OSSOWN-04	Is /usr/tandem/sqlmx/bin/mxcierrors.cat owned by SUPER.SUPER?	ls -al
USR-SQLMX-05	Is /usr/tandem/sqlmx/bin/mxcierrors.cat secured correctly?	ls -al

mxcmp

The **mxcmp** file is the SQL/MX compiler. It is an OSS program installed in the Guardian $SYSTEM.SYSTEM subvolume (/G/system/system/ in the OSS environment). It must run in the OSS environment and does not run as a Guardian process. It is used to compile an SQL/MX module definition file and produce the query execution plan. The SQL/MX compiler (**mxcmp**) does not register the program or dependencies within the SQL/MX catalog. This is a major change from SQL/MP.

mxcmp must be explicitly invoked to compile static SQL statements. The SQL/MX executor will also invoke **mxcmp** at run time to compile dynamic SQL statements and to recompile any static SQL statements that refer to database objects that changed and that affect the SQL statement's execution plan.

AP-FILE-MXCMP-01   DBAs should statically recompile a program that accesses a table that has changed since the last static compilation to improve performance. Otherwise, SQL/MX will dynamically recompile the program before each execution.

AP-FILE-MXCMP-02   **mxcmp** should be available for execution by the SQL subsystem on any system to perform SQL recompilations.

BP-USR-SQLMX-06   **mxcmp** should be secured 711 (rwx --x --x).

BP-USR-OSSOWN-04   **mxcmp** should be owned by SUPER.SUPER.

BP-USR-OSSLOC-04   **mxcmp** resides in /usr/tandem/sqlmx/bin.

	Discovery Questions	Look here:
USR-OSSOWN-04	Is /usr/tandem/sqlmx/bin/mxcmp owned by SUPER.SUPER?	ls -al
USR-SQLMX-06	Is /usr/tandem/sqlmx/bin/mxcmp secured correctly?	ls -al

mxCompileUserModule

The **/usr/tandem/sqlmx/bin/mxCompileUserModule** file is the symbolic link to the Guardian MXCOMPILEUSERMODULE program. This utility is used to compile one or more SQL/MX module definitions embedded in an object file created by the C/C++ or COBOL compilers or produced by the linker.

BP-USR-SQLMX-07   mxCompileUserModule should be secured 711 (rwx --x --x).

BP-USR-OSSOWN-04   mxCompileUserModule should be owned by SUPER.SUPER.

BP-USR-OSSLOC-04   mxCompileUserModule resides in **/usr/tandem /sqlmx/bin.**

	Discovery Questions	Look here:
USR-OSSOWN-04	Is **/usr/tandem/sqlmx/bin/mxCompileUserModule** owned by SUPER.SUPER?	ls -al
USR-SQLMX-07	Is **/usr/tandem/sqlmx/bin/mxCompileUserModule** secured correctly?	ls -al

mxexportddl

The **/usr/tandem/sqlmx/bin/mxexportddl** file is an OSS command-line utility to capture production SQL/MX metadata to diagnose problems. **mxexportddl** saves the data on a NonStop Server in XML format. This allows developers to compile SQL queries and generate the same plans that were used in a production setting.

The **mxexportddl** program can only be executed by SUPER.SUPER.

BP-USR-SQLMX-08   mxexportdll should be secured 700 (rwx --- ---).

BP-USR-OSSOWN-04   mxexportdll should be owned by SUPER. SUPER.

BP-USR-OSSLOC-04   mxexportdll resides in /usr/tandem/sqlmx/bin.

	Discovery Questions	Look here:
USR-OSSOWN-04	Is **/usr/tandem/sqlmx/bin/mxexportdll** owned by SUPER.SUPER?	ls -al
USR-SQLMX-08	Is **/usr/tandem/sqlmx/bin/mxexportdll** secured correctly?	ls -al

mxsqlc

The **/usr/tandem/sqlmx/bin/mxsqlc** file is the OSS-based C preprocessor for embedded SQL statements in C/C++ programs. The program replaces SQL statements with C function calls to the call-level interface (CLI).

BP-USR-SQLMX-09   mxsqlc should be secured 711 (rwx --x --x).

BP-USR-OSSOWN-04 mxsqlc should be owned by SUPER.SUPER.

BP-USR-OSSLOC-04   mxsqlc resides in **/usr/tandem/sqlmx/bin**.

	Discovery Questions	Look here:
USR-OSSOWN-04	Is **/usr/tandem/sqlmx/bin/mxsqlc** owned by SUPER.SUPER?	ls -al
USR-SQLMX-09	Is **/usr/tandem/sqlmx/bin/mxsqlc** secured correctly?	ls -al

mxsqlco

The **/usr/tandem/sqlmx/bin/mxsqlco** file is the OSS-based preprocessor for embedded SQL statements in COBOL programs.

BP-USR-SQLMX-10   mxsqlco should be secured 711 (rwx --x --x).

BP-USR-OSSOWN-04 mxsqlco should be owned by SUPER.SUPER.

BP-USR-OSSLOC-04   mxsqlco resides in **/usr/tandem/sqlmx/bin**.

	Discovery Questions	Look here:
USR-OSSOWN-04	Is **/usr/tandem/sqlmx/bin/mxsqlco** owned by SUPER.SUPER?	ls -al
USR-SQLMX-10	Is **/usr/tandem/sqlmx/bin/mxsqlco** secured correctly?	ls -al

mxtool

/usr/tandem/sqlmx/bin/mxtool is the object file for the **mxtool** OSS command-line utility that performs various utility functions:

FIXUP repairs problems in the SQL/MX database that cannot be repaired by normal operations.

GOAWAY removes Guardian files (data fork and resource fork) associated with an SQL/MX object. It does not remove corresponding metadata entries and does not use ANSI names.

INFO displays the Guardian file name, the ANSI name, the ANSI namespace, and the object schema version.

VERIFY reports whether SQL/MX objects and programs are consistently described in file labels, resource forks, and metadata.

BP-USR-SQLMX-11   **mxtool** should be secured 711 (rwx --x --x).

BP-USR-OSSOWN-04   **mxtool** should be owned by SUPER.SUPER.

BP-USR-OSSLOC-04   **mxtool** resides in **/usr/tandem/sqlmx/bin**.

Discovery Questions	Look here:
USR-OSSOWN-04 Is **/usr/tandem/sqlmx/bin/mxtool** owned by SUPER.SUPER?	ls -al
USR-SQLMX-11 Is **/usr/tandem/sqlmx/bin/mxtool** secured correctly?	ls -al

setmxdb

The **/usr/tandem/sqlmx/bin/setmxdb** file is the OSS installation script for the SQL/MX sample database. The sample database provided with SQL/MX Release 2.x uses SQL/MX tables. If the system is migrating from SQL/MX Release 1.8 to Release 2.x, or users want to retain a sample database consisting of SQL/MP tables, then the installer must rename or make a copy of the **setmxdb** script that generates the Release 1.8 sample database before installing SQL/MX Release 2.

BP-USR-SQLMX-12   **setmxdb** should be secured 711 (rwx --x --x).

BP-USR-OSSOWN-04   **setmxdb** should be owned by SUPER.SUPER.

BP-USR-OSSLOC-04   **setmxdb** resides in **/usr/tandem/sqlmx/bin**.

Discovery Questions	Look here:
USR-OSSOWN-04 Is **/usr/tandem/sqlmx/bin/setmxdb** owned by SUPER.SUPER?	ls -al
USR-SQLMX-12 Is **/usr/tandem/sqlmx/bin/setmxdb** secured correctly?	ls -al

/usr/tandem/sqlmx/SYSTEMMODULES Directory

The **/usr/tandem/sqlmx/USERMODULES** directory contains SQL compiles code supplied with SQL. Only SUPER.SUPER should have WRITE access to the files in this directory.

BP-USR-SQLMX-14   The **USERMODULES** directory should be secured 774 (rwx r-- r--).

BP-USR-DIROWN-03   The **SYSTEMMODULES** directory should be owned by SUPER.SUPER.

BP-USR-DIRLOC-03   The **SYSTEMMODULES** directory resides in **/usr/tandem/sqlmx**.

	Discovery Questions	Look here:
USR-DIROWN-03	Is the **/usr/tandem/sqlmx/SYSTEMMODULES** directory owned by SUPER.SUPER?	ls -al
USR-SQLMX-13	Is the **/usr/tandem/sqlmx/SYSTEMMODULES** directory secured correctly?	ls -al

/usr/tandem/sqlmx/USERMODULES Directory

The **/usr/tandem/sqlmx/USERMODULES** directory contains global SQL/MX compiled modules.

Users who run SQL/MX programs need to READ files in this directory.

Users who run SQL/MX programs need READ access to files in this directory.

BP-USR-SQLMX-14   The **USERMODULES** directory should be secured 775 (rwx rwx r-t).

BP-USR-SQLMX-14   The **USERMODULES** directory should be secured 744 (rwx r-- r--).

BP-USR-DIROWN-03   The **USERMODULES** directory should be owned by SUPER.SUPER.

BP-USR-DIRLOC-03   The **USERMODULES** directory reside in **/usr /tandem/sqlmx.**

	Discovery Questions	Look here:
USR-DIROWN-03	Is the **/usr/tandem/sqlmx/USERMODULES** directory owned by SUPER.SUPER?	ls -al
USR-SQLMX-14	Is the **/usr/tandem/sqlmx/USERMODULES** directory secured correctly?	ls -al

/usr/tandem/sqlmx/udr Directory

The **/usr/tandem/sqlmx/udr** directory contains SPJ and SQLJ product files.

AP-ADVICE-UDRDIR-01   The **/usr/tandem/sqlmx/udr/mxlangman.jar** file should not be moved from this directory, or problems will occur when invoking SPJs.

BP-USR-SQLMX-15   The **udr** directory should be secured 744 (rwx r-- r--).

BP-USR-DIROWN-03   The **udr** directory should be owned by SUPER. SUPER.

BP-USR-DIRLOC-03   The **udr** directory reside in **/usr/tandem/sqlmx.**

	Discovery Questions	Look here:
USR-DIROWN-03	Is the **/usr/tandem/sqlmx/udr** directory owned by SUPER.SUPER?	ls -al
USR-SQLMX-15	Is the **/usr/tandem/sqlmx/udr** directory secured correctly?	ls -al

SSH Subsystem

SSH (Secure SHell) is a protocol for encrypted remote logins, file copying and TCP connection tunneling (port forwarding).

SSH is a client/server system.

/usr/local/bin/ssh is the HP client. It is used by local users to connect to remote systems.

/usr/local/bin/sshd is the local server process. It responds to connection requests from remote systems.

This section focuses on securing the components of the SSH Subsystem. Please refer to the SSH section in Part 4, *TCP/IP,* for a complete discussion of SSH and its configuration.

Securing the SSH Subsystem Components

The SSH subsystem consists of the following components:

SSH Client Program (ssh)

SSH Server Program (sshd)

SSH Configuration Files

SSH libraries

prngd

Encryption Key Related Programs

Private Key Files

Public Key Files

SSH-Related Programs

ssh

The object file for the SSH client is **/usr/local/bin/ssh**. The client is used to logon to a remote machine and to execute commands on a remote machine. It is intended as a more secure replacement for **/bin/rlogin** and

/bin/rsh by providing encrypted communications between two hosts over an insecure network without specifying either as trusted hosts.

BP-USR-SSH-01	/usr/local/bin/ssh should not be **setuid** to SUPER.
SUPER.	
BP-USR-SSH-02	ssh should be secured 711 (rwx --x --x).
BP-USR-OSSOWN-03	ssh should be owned by SUPER.SUPER.
BP-USR-OSSLOC-03	ssh resides in /usr/local/bin.

	Discovery Questions	Look here:
USR-OSSOWN-03	Is /usr/local/bin/ssh owned by SUPER.SUPER?	ls -al
USR-SSH-01	Is /usr/local/bin/ssh set to setuid?	ls -al
USR-SSH-02	Is /usr/local/bin/ssh secured correctly?	ls -al

sshd

The object file for the SSH server (daemon) is /usr/local/sbin/sshd. The server listens for connections from remote clients. For each connection made, the server forks a new process. These forked processes handle key exchange, encryption, authentication, command execution, and data exchange.

BP-PROCESS-SSHD-01	The sshd process should be running.
BP-USR-SSH-03	sshd should be secured 700 (rwx --- ---).
BP-USR-OSSOWN-03	sshd should be owned by SUPER.SUPER.
BP-USR-OSSLOC-03	sshd resides in /usr/local/sbin.

	Discovery Questions	Look here:
USR-OSSOWN-03	Is /usr/local/sbin/sshd owned by SUPER.SUPER?	ls -al
USR-SSH-03	Is /usr/local/sbin/sshd secured correctly?	ls -al

SSH Configuration Files

The SSH client is configured by settings in the **/usr/local/etc/ssh_config** file or the individual **$HOME/.ssh/config** files. The client configuration determines how it will respond to requests for authentication from remote SSH servers that it contacts.

The SSH server is configured by settings in the **/usr/local/etc/sshd_config** file. The server configuration determines the security on the local system because it controls how the server will respond to connection requests from remote SSH clients.

Please refer to the chapter on the SSH Subsystem in Part 4, *TCP/IP*, for more information or to the *OSS Gazette* section on SSH for Best Practice recommendations.

ssh_config Configuration File

Parameters established in this file determine how your local SSH client will interact with the remote SSH servers that it contacts. The values determine, among other things, the method of authentication that will be used when connecting to each remote host.

BP-USR-SSH-04   ssh_config should be secured 644 (rw- r-- r--).

BP-USR-OSSOWN-03 ssh_config should be owned by SUPER.SUPER.

BP-USR-OSSLOC-03 ssh_config resides in **/usr/local/etc**.

Discovery Questions		Look here:
USR-OSSOWN-03	Is /usr/local/etc/ssh_config owned by SUPER.SUPER?	ls -al
USR-SSH-04	Is /usr/local/etc/ssh_config secured correctly?	ls -al

Personal SSH Configuration Files

When a user initiates an SSH session, he or she supplies the remote host name on the command line. The client then obtains the host configuration data from the following sources in the following order:

1. Command-line options

2. Individual user's configuration files

3. System-wide configuration file

If users have personal **$HOME/.ssh/config** files, their configuration values will take precedence over the global values set by the local system administrator in the **/usr/local/etc/ssh_config** file. There are few genuine needs for personal SSH config files and their use opens up security holes.

BP-SSH-SSHCONF-01   Do not allow personal copies of SSH config (**$HOME/.ssh/config**) files.

BP-HOME-SSH-04   Each user's **ssh config** file should be secured 600 (rw- --- ---).

BP-HOME-OSSOWN-00   Each users's **ssh config** file should be owned by the user.

BP-HOME-OSSLOC-00   Each user's **ssh config** file resides in **$HOME/.ssh**.

	Discovery Questions	Look here:
OSS-POLICY	Does policy allow users to have personal **$HOME/.ssh/config** files?	ls -al
HOME-OSSOWN-00	Is each user's **$HOME/.ssh/config** file owned by the individual users?	ls -al
HOME-SSH-05	Is each user's **$HOME/.ssh/config** file secured correctly?	ls -al

sshd_config Configuration File

The behavior of the SSH server is determined by parameters in the **/usr/local/etc/sshd_config** file. The server configuration protects its local system.

BP-SSH-CONFIG-01   Because of the security ramifications of the file, there should be a single (global) copy of the **/usr/local/etc/sshd_config** file on a system. This ensures that important security-related changes are made to the correct file and tracked.

BP-USR-SSH-06   sshd_config should be secured 644 (rw- r-- r--).

BP-USR-OSSOWN-03 sshd_config should be owned by SUPER.SUPER.

BP-USR-OSSLOC-03   sshd_config resides in **/usr/local/etc**.

	Discovery Questions	**Look here:**
OSS-POLICY	Does policy allow users to have personel **$HOME/.ssh/environment** files.	
USR-OSSOWN-03	Is **/usr/local/etc/sshd_config** owned by SUPER.SUPER?	ls -al
USR-SSH-06	Is **/usr/local/etc/sshd_config** secured correctly?	ls -al

environment File

The SSH **environment** file contains parameters that configure the entire SSH environment. It is read at login.

The **/usr/local/bin/environment** file is global: It is read whenever any user logs on via SSH.

Individual users may have their own **environment** files. If so, they reside in each user's **$HOME/.ssh** directory. The values in these personal files override the global environment settings.

BP-USR-SSH-07   environment should be secured 644 (rw- r-- r---).

BP-USR-OSSOWN-03 environment should be owned by SUPER. SUPER.

BP-USR-OSSLOC-03   environment resides in **/usr/local/bin**.

	Discovery Questions	**Look here:**
OSS-POLICY	Does policy allow users to have personal **$HOME/.ssh/environment** files?	ls -al
USR-OSSOWN-03	Is **/usr/local/bin/environment** owned by SUPER.SUPER?	ls -al
USR-SSH-07	Is **/usr/local/bin/environment** secured correctly?	ls -al

Personal environment Files

SSH **environment** files contain parameters that configure an SSH environment. Individual **environment** files reside in each user's **$HOME/.ssh**. They are read at login, and the values override the global environment settings.

RISK   If personal environment files are allowed, users may bypass restrictions using mechanisms such as LD_RELOAD.

BP-SSH-ENVIRONM-01 Do not allow individual **$HOME/.ssh/re** files unless required in your environment. Use the global **/usr/local/bin/environment** file instead.

BP-HOME-SSH-08   Each user's **environment** file should be secured 600 (rw- --- ---).

BP-HOME-OSSOWN-00 Each user's **environment** file should be owned by the user.

BP-HOME-OSSLOC-00 Each user's **environment** file resides in **$HOME**.

	Discovery Questions	Look here:
OSS-POLICY	Does policy allow personal **environment** files on the system?	ls -al
HOME-OSSOWN-00	Is each user's **$HOME/.ssh/environment** file owned by the user?	ls -al
HOME-SSH-08	Is each user's **$HOME/.ssh/environment** file secured correctly?	ls -al

moduli File

/usr/local/etc/moduli contains Diffie-Hellman groups used for Diffie-Hellman Group Exchange.

BP-USR-SSH-09   **moduli** should be secured 744 (rwx r-- r--).

BP-USR-OSSOWN-03 **moduli** should be owned by SUPER.SUPER.

BP-USR-OSSLOC-03 **moduli** resides in **/usr/local/bin**.

	Discovery Questions	Look here:
USR-OSSOWN-03	Is **/usr/local/etc/moduli** owned by SUPER.SUPER?	ls -al
USR-SSH-09	Is **/usr/local/etc/moduli** secured correctly?	ls -al

rc File

$HOME/.ssh/rc files are much like a shell startup file (a **.profile**, for example), but the scripts execute only when a user's account is accessed by SSH. The file is used to run any initialization routines necessary before the user's home directory becomes usable. The file is processed for both interactive logins and remote commands.

Any commands that the user would like executed instead of the ordinary login when connecting via SSH can be placed in **$HOME/.ssh/rc** files. For example, users could load their **ssh-agent**.

AP-SSH-RC-07   Do not use individual **$HOME/.ssh/rc** files unless required in your environment. Use the global **/usr/local/bin/ssh/sshrc** file instead.

If no **$HOME/.ssh/rc** file exists, the **/usr/local/bin/ssh/sshrc** file is used. If neither file exists, **xauth** must be used to run initialization routines.

BP-HOME-SSH-09   **rc** files should be secured 700 (rwx --- ---).

BP-HOME-OSSOWN-00   **rc** files should be owned by the individual user.

BP-H0ME-OSSLOC-00   **rc** files resides in **$HOME/.ssh**.

	Discovery Questions	Look here:
OSS-POLICY	Does policy allow personal rc files on the system?	ls -al
HOME-OSSOWN-00	Is **$HOME/.ssh/rc** owned by SUPER.SUPER?	ls -al
HOME-SSH-10	Is **$HOME/.ssh/rc** secured correctly?	ls -al

sshrc File

/usr/local/bin/ssh/sshrc is used to specify machine-specific login initializations for all users. It is the global equivalent of the individual **$HOME/.ssh/rc** files.

If no **$HOME/.ssh/rc** file exists, the **/usr/local/bin/ssh/sshrc** file is used. If neither file exists, **xauth** must be used to run initialization routines.

AP-SSH-RC-07   Do not use individual **$HOME/.ssh/rc** files unless required in your environment. Use the global **/usr/local/bin/ssh/sshrc** file instead.

BP-USR-SSH-11   sshrc should be secured 644 (rw- r-- r---).

BP-USR-OSSOWN-03   sshrc should be owned by SUPER.SUPER.

BP-USR-OSSLOC-03   sshrc resides in **/usr/local/bin/ssh**.

	Discovery Questions	Look here:
USR-OSSOWN-03	Is **/usr/local/bin/ssh/sshrc** owned by SUPER.SUPER?	ls -al
USR-SSH-11	Is **/usr/local/bin/ssh/sshrc** secured correctly?	ls -al

shosts File

The **/usr/local/etc/shosts** is processed exactly the same as the **/etc/hosts.equiv** file. It should not be present on your system unless you must run both **rsh/rlogin** and SSH.

BP-USR-SSH-12   shosts should be secured 600 (rw- --- ---).

BP-USR-OSSOWN-03   shosts should be owned by SUPER.SUPER.

BP-USR-OSSLOC-03   shosts resides in **/usr/local/bin**.

	Discovery Questions	Look here:
USR-OSSOWN-03	Is **/usr/local/etc/shosts** owned by SUPER.SUPER?	ls -al
USR-SSH-12	Is **/usr/local/etc/shosts** secured correctly?	ls -al

prngd

/usr/local/bin/prngd is the object file for the Random Number Generator process used by the cryptographic algorithms for SSH.

BP-USR-SSH-13   **prngd** should be secured 711 (rwx --x --x).

BP-USR-OSSOWN-03   **prngd** should be owned by SUPER.SUPER.

BP-USR-OSSLOC-03   **prngd** resides in **/usr/local/bin**.

	Discovery Questions	Look here:
USR-OSSOWN-03	Is **/usr/local/bin/prngd** owned by SUPER.SUPER?	ls -al
USR-SSH-13	Is **/usr/local/bin/prngd** secured correctly?	ls -al

Encryption Key-Related Programs

There are several key-related programs:

ssh-add

ssh-agent

ssh-keygen

ssh-keyscan

ssh-keysign

ssh-add

The **/usr/local/bin/ssh-add** program inserts and removes keys from the **ssh-agent's** key cache. On the HP NonStop Server, it adds RSA or DSA identities.

ssh-add can also be used to display the keys currently being held by the **ssh-agent**.

BP-USR-SSH-14   **ssh-add** should be secured 711 (rwx --x --x).

BP-USR-OSSOWN-03   **ssh-add** should be owned by SUPER.SUPER.

BP-USR-OSSLOC-03   **ssh-add** resides in **/usr/local/bin**.

	Discovery Questions	Look here:
USR-OSSOWN-03	Is **/usr/local/bin/ssh-add** owned by SUPER.SUPER?	ls -al
USR-SSH-14	Is **/usr/local/bin/ssh-add** secured correctly?	ls -al

ssh-agent

ssh-agents perform two tasks:

Store the private keys in memory

Answer questions (from SSH clients) about those keys

BP-USR-SSH-15   ssh-agent should be secured 711 (rwx --x --x).

BP-USR-OSSOWN-03   ssh-agent should be owned by SUPER.SUPER.

BP-USR-OSSLOC-03   ssh-agent resides in **/usr/local/bin**.

	Discovery Questions	Look here:
USR-OSSOWN-03	Is **/usr/local/bin/ssh-keyagent** owned by SUPER.SUPER?	ls -al
USR-SSH-15	Is **/usr/local/bin/ssh-keyagent** secured correctly?	ls -al

ssh-keygen

/usr/local/bin/ssh-keygen generates authentication keys for SSH. It also manages and converts the keys. It will create RSA keys for use by the SSH protocol and for Diffie-Hellman group exchange (DH-GEX).

BP-USR-SSH-16   ssh-keygen should be secured 711 (rwx --x --x).

BP-USR-OSSOWN-03   ssh-keygen should be owned by SUPER.SUPER.

BP-USR-OSSLOC-03   ssh-keygen resides in **/usr/local/bin**.

	Discovery Questions	Look here:
USR-OSSOWN-03	Is **/usr/local/bin/ssh-keygen** owned by SUPER.SUPER?	ls -al
USR-SSH-16	Is **/usr/local/bin/ssh-keygen** secured correctly?	ls -al

ssh-keyscan

/usr/local/libexec/ssh-keyscan is a utility used to gather the public host keys of multiple hosts. It is used to build and verify **ssh_known_hosts** files.

BP-USR-SSH-17   **ssh-keyscan** should be secured 711 (rwx --x --x).

BP-USR-OSSOWN-03   **ssh-keyscan** should be owned by SUPER.SUPER.

BP-USR-OSSLOC-03   **ssh-keyscan** resides in **/usr/local/bin**.

	Discovery Questions	Look here:
USR-OSSOWN-03	Is **/usr/local/bin/ssh-keyscan** owned by SUPER.SUPER?	ls -al
USR-SSH-17	Is **/usr/local/bin/ssh-keyscan** secured correctly?	ls -al

ssh-keysign

/usr/local/libexec/ssh-keysign is a helper process used by SSH to access the local host keys and generate the digital signature required during host-based authentication with SSH protocol version 2.

ssh-keysign is not invoked by users directly, only via the SSH client (**ssh**) or the SSH server (**sshd**).

By default, this program is not enabled. It is enabled by setting the **EnableSSHKeySign** value to YES in the SSH client's global configuration file (**ssh_config**).

BP-USR-SSH-18   **ssh-keysign** should be secured 711 (rwx --x --x).

BP-USR-OSSOWN-03   **ssh-keysign** should be owned by SUPER. SUPER.

BP-USR-OSSLOC-03   **ssh-keysign** resides in **/usr/local/libexec**.

Discovery Questions		Look here:
USR-OSSOWN-03	Is **/usr/local/libexec/ssh-keysign** owned by SUPER.SUPER?	ls -al
USR-SSH-18	Is **/usr/local/libexec/ssh-keysign** secured correctly?	ls -al

Host Private Key Files

The host private key files are:

/usr/local/usr/etc/ssh_host_key

/usr/local/etc/ssh_host_dsa_key

/usr/local/etc/ssh_host_rsa_key

These file are updated by the **/usr/local/bin/ssh-keygen** program. It is possible to enter a passphrase when generating any of these keys. If entered, the passphrase will be used to encrypt the private part of the key using triple DES.

The contents of these files should be kept secret. They should not be readable by anyone but SUPER.SUPER.

RISK These files contain various keys used for SSH secure data exchanges. Improper security on these files can result in the compromise of communications to and from the NonStop server.

In addition to these files, the **/usr/local/ssh/ssh/known_hosts** file is of interest to security.

ssh_host_key File

The **/usr/local/etc/ssh_host_key** file contains the protocol version 1 RSA authentication **ssh_host_key** of the host. This file is not created automatically by **ssh-keygen**, but it is the default location used if no other filename is entered. The contents of this file should be kept secret.

The SSH client (**/usr/local/bin/ssh**) will read this file when the user attempts to logon to a remote system via SSH.

BP-USR-SSH-19   ssh_host_key file should be secured 600 (rw- --- ---).

BP-USR-OSSOWN-03   ssh_host_key file should be owned by SUPER.
SUPER.

BP-USR-OSSLOC-03   ssh_host_key file resides in **/usr/local/etc**.

	Discovery Questions	Look here:
USR-OSSOWN-03	Is **/usr/local/etc/ssh_host_key** owned by SUPER.SUPER?	ls -al
USR-SSH-19	Is **/usr/local/etc/ssh_host_key** secured correctly?	ls -al

ssh_host_dsa_key File

The **/usr/local/etc/ssh_host_dsa_key** file contains the protocol version 1 RSA authentication ID of the host. This file is not created automatically by **ssh-keygen**, but it is the default location used if no other filename is entered. The contents of this file should be kept secret.

The SSH client (**/usr/local/bin/ssh**) will read this file when the user attempts to logon to a remote system via SSH.

BP-USR-SSH-20   ssh_host_dsa_key file should be secured 600
(rw- --- ---).

BP-USR-OSSOWN-03 ssh_host_dsa_key file should be owned by SUPER.SUPER.

BP-USR-OSSLOC-03   ssh_host_dsa_key file resides in **/usr/local/etc**.

	Discovery Questions	Look here:
USR-OSSOWN-03	Is **/usr/local/etc/ssh_host_dsa_key** owned by SUPER.SUPER?	ls -al
USR-SSH-20	Is **/usr/local/etc/ssh_host_dsa_key** secured correctly?	ls -al

ssh_host_rsa_key File

The **/usr/local/etc/ssh_host_rsa_key** file contains the protocol version 2 RSA authentication ID of the host. This file is not created automatically by ssh-keygen, but it is the default location used if no other filename is entered. The contents of this file should be kept secret.

The SSH client (/usr/local/bin/ssh) will read this file when the user attempts to logon to a remote system via SSH.

BP-USR-SSH-21   ssh_host_rsa_key file should be secured 600 (rw- --- ---).

BP-USR-OSSOWN-03 ssh_host_rsa_key file should be owned by SUPER.SUPER.

BP-USR-OSSLOC-03   ssh_host_rsa_key file resides in **/usr/local/etc**.

	Discovery Questions	Look here:
USR-OSSOWN-03	Is /usr/local/etc/ssh_host_rsa_key owned by SUPER.SUPER?	ls -a
USR-SSH-21	Is /usr/local/etc/ssh_host_rsa_key secured correctly?	ls -al

ssh_known_hosts Files

The SSH client has a list that maps the host names and IP addresses of every remote host the host has connected to, along with its public key. This database is called the **ssh_known_hosts** file. It resides in **/usr/local/etc**.

The **/usr/local/etc/ssh_known_hosts** file contains host public keys for all known hosts. This global file should be maintained by the system administrator.

BP-USR-SSH-22   ssh_known_hosts should be secured 600 (rw- --- ---).

BP-USR-OSSOWN-03 ssh_known_hosts should be owned by SUPER. SUPER.

BP-USR-OSSLOC-03   ssh_known_hosts resides in **/usr/local/etc**.

	Discovery Questions	Look here:
USR-OSSOWN-03	Is **/usr/local/etc/ ssh_known_hosts** owned by SUPER.SUPER?	ls -al
USR-SSH-22	Is **/usr/local/etc/ ssh_known_hosts** secured correctly?	ls -al

Host Public Key Files

These file are updated by the **/usr/local/bin/ssh-keygen** program. The public key files are:

/usr/local/etc/ssh_host_key.pub

/usr/local/etc/ssh_host_dsa_key.pub

/usr/local/etc/ssh_host_rsa_key.pub

These files are updated by the **/usr/local/bin/ssh-keygen** program.

RISK   If these files can be modified, the ability to encrypt and decrypt communications could be disabled.

ssh_host_key.pub File

The **/usr/local/etc/ssh_host_key.pub** file contains the protocol version 1 DSA public key for authentication of each host. The contents of the file should be added to the **/usr/local/etc/authorized_keys** file on each system where users will log in using public key authentication.

The SSH client (**/usr/local/bin/ssh**) will read this file when the user attempts to logon to a remote system via SSH.

BP-USR-SSH-23   ssh_host_key.pub file should be secured 600 (rw- --- ---).

BP-USR-OSSOWN-03   ssh_host_key.pub file should be owned by SUPER.SUPER.

BP-USR-OSSLOC-03   ssh_host_key.pub file resides in **/usr/local/etc**.

	Discovery Questions	Look here:
USR-OSSOWN-03	Are **/usr/local/etc/ssh_host_key.pub** files owned by each individual user?	ls -al
USR-SSH-23	Are **/usr/local/etc/ssh_host_key.pub** files secured correctly?	ls -al

ssh_host_dsa_key.pub File

The **/usr/local/etc/ssh_host_dsa_key.pub** file contains the protocol version 1 DSA public key for authentication of each host. The contents of the file should be added to the **/usr/local/etc/authorized_keys** file on each system where users will log in using public key authentication.

The SSH client (**/usr/local/bin/ssh**) will read this file when the user attempts to logon to a remote system via SSH.

BP-USR-SSH-24   **ssh_host_dsa_key.pub** file should be secured 600 (rw- --- ---).

BP-USR-OSSOWN-03   **ssh_host_dsa_key.pub** file should be owned SUPER.SUPER.

BP-USR-OSSLOC-03   **ssh_host_dsa_key.pub** file resides in **/usr/local /etc**.

	Discovery Questions	Look here:
USR-OSSOWN-03	Is **/usr/local/etc/ssh_host_dsa_key.pub** owned by each individual user?	ls -al
USR-SSH-24	Is **/usr/local/etc/ssh_host_dsa_key.pub** secured correctly?	ls -al

ssh_host_rsa_key.pub File

The **/usr/local/usr/local/bin/ssh_host_rsa_key.pub** file contains the protocol version 2 RSA public key for authentication of each host. The contents of the file should be added to the **/usr/local/etc/authorized_keys** file on each system where users will log in using public key authentication.

The SSH client (**/usr/local/bin/ssh**) will read this file when the user attempts to logon to a remote system via SSH.

BP-USR-SSH-25   ssh_host_rsa_key.pub file should be secured 600 (rw- --- ---).

BP-USR-OSSOWN-03 ssh_host_rsa_key.pub file should be owned SUPER.SUPER.

BP-USR-OSSLOC-03   ssh_host_rsa_key.pub file resides in **/usr/local /etc/**.

	Discovery Questions	**Look here:**
USR-OSSOWN-03	Is **/usr/local/etc/ssh_host_rsa_key.pub** owned by each individual user?	ls -al
USR-SSH-25	Is **/usr/local/etc/ssh_host_rsa_key.pub** secured correctly?	ls -al

AP-SSH-RC-07   Do not use individual **$HOME/.ssh/rc** files unless required in your environment. Use the global **/usr/local/bin/ssh/sshrc** file instead.

Individual Private Key Files

Each user has his or her own set of private key files. These file are updated by the **/usr/local/bin/ssh-keygen** program. The individual private key files are:

$HOME/.ssh /identity

$HOME/.ssh /id_dsa

$HOME/.ssh /id_rsa

These file are updated by the **/usr/local/bin/ssh-keygen program**. It is possible to enter a passphrase when generating any of these keys; if entered, the passphrase will be used to encrypt the private part of the key using triple DES.

RISK   If these files can be read by anyone other than the owner, unauthorized data can be encrypted as if it originated from the owner.

The contents of these files should be kept secret. They should not be readable by anyone but the user.

BP-SSH-SSHDIR-01 All **$HOME/.ssh** directories should be owned and accessible only by the user. This directory contains SSH key files and other confidential information.

identity Files

Each user's **$HOME/.ssh/identity** file contains the protocol version 1 RSA authentication identity of the user. This file is not created automatically by **ssh-keygen**, but it is the default location used if no other filename is entered. The contents of this file should be kept secret.

The SSH client (**/usr/local/bin/ssh**) will read this file when the user attempts to logon to a remote system via SSH.

RISK If these files can be accessed by anyone other than the owner, it could allow an unauthorized party to spoof the owner's identity.

BP-HOME-.SSHDIR-01 All **$HOME/.ssh** directories should be owned and accessible only by the user. This directory contains SSH key files and other confidential information.

BP-HOME-SSH-26 Each user's **identity** file should be secured 600 (rw- --- ---).

BP-HOME-OSSOWN-00 Each user's **identity** file should be owned by the user.

BP-HOME-OSSLOC-00 Each user's **identity** file resides in **$HOME/.ssh**.

	Discovery Questions	Look here:
HOME-OSSOWN-00	Is each user's **$HOME/.ssh/identity** file owned by the user?	ls -al
HOME-SSH-26	Is each user's **$HOME/.ssh/identity** file secured correctly?	ls -al

id_dsa Files

Each user's **$HOME/.ssh/id_dsa** file contains the protocol version 1 DSA authentication ID of the user. This file is not created automatically by **ssh-keygen**, but it is the default location used if no other filename is entered. The contents of this file should be kept secret.

The SSH client (**/usr/local/bin/ssh**) will read this file when the user attempts to logon to a remote system via SSH.

RISK If these files can be accessed by anyone other than the owner, it could allow an unauthorized party to spoof the owner's indentity.

BP-HOME-SSH-27   Each **id_dsa** file should be secured 600 (rw- --- ---).

BP-HOME-OSSOWN-00   Each **id_dsa** file should be owned by the user.

BP-HOME-OSSLOC-00   Each **id_dsa** file resides in **$HOME/.ssh**.

	Discovery Questions	**Look here:**
HOME-OSSOWN-00	Is each individual's **$HOME/.ssh/id_dsa** file owned by the user?	ls -al
HOME-SSH-27	Is each individual's **$HOME/.ssh/id_dsa** file secured correctly?	ls -al

id_rsa Files

Each user's **$HOME/.ssh/id_rsa** file contains the protocol version 2 RSA authentication ID of the user. This file is not created automatically by **ssh-keygen**, but it is the default location used if no other filename is entered. The contents of this file should be kept secret.

The SSH client (**/usr/local/bin/ssh**) will read this file when the user attempts to logon to a remote system via SSH.

RISK If these files can be accessed by anyone other than the owner, it could allow an unauthorized party to spoof the owner's indentity.

BP-HOME-SSH-28   Each user's **id_rsa** file should be secured 600
(rw- --- ---).

BP-HOME-OSSOWN-00 Each user's **id_rsa** file should be owned by the user.

BP-HOME-OSSLOC-00   Each user's **id_rsa** file resides in **$HOME/.ssh.**

	Discovery Questions	Look here:
HOME-OSSOWN-00	Is each user's **$HOME/.ssh/id_rsa** file owned by the user?	ls -al
HOME-SSH-28	Is each user's **$HOME/.ssh/id_rsa** file secured correctly?	ls -al

Individual Public Key Files

Each user has his own set of public key files. These file are updated by the **/usr/local/bin/ssh-keygen** program. The individual public key files are:

>   **$HOME/.ssh/identity.pub**
>
>   **$HOME/.ssh/id_dsa.pub**
>
>   **$HOME/.ssh/id_rsa.pub**

These files are updated by the **/usr/local/bin/ssh-keygen** program.

RISK Unauthorized access to these files can disable cryptographic services and compromise communications to and from the NonStop server.

In addition, there are two related files of interest to security:

>   **$HOME/.ssh/authorized_keys**
>
>   **$HOME/.ssh/known_hosts**

BP-HOME-SSHDIR-01   All **$HOME/.ssh** directories should be owned and accessible only by the user. This directory contains SSH key files and other confidential information.

identity.pub Files

Each user's **$HOME/.ssh/identity.pub** file contains the protocol version 1 RSA public key for authentication of the user. The contents of the file, if it exists, should be added to the **$HOME/.ssh/authorized_keys** files on each system where the user will log in using RSA authentication.

BP-HOME-SSH-29 Each user's **identity.pub** file should be secured 600 (rw- --- ---).

BP-HOME-OSSOWN-00 ach user's **identity.pub** file should be owned by the user.

BP-HOME-OSSLOC-00 Each user's **identity.pub** file resides **$HOME/.ssh**.

	Discovery Questions	Look here:
OSS-POLICY	Does the policy allow individual **identity.pub** files?	Policy
HOME-OSSOWN-00	Is each user's **$HOME/.ssh/identity.pub** file owned by the user?	ls -al
HOME-SSH-29	Is each user's **$HOME/.ssh/identity.pub** file secured correctly?	ls -al

id_dsa.pub Files

Each user's **$HOME/.ssh /id_dsa.pub** file contains the protocol version 1 DSA public key for authentication of the user. The contents of the file, if it exists, should be added to the **$HOME/.ssh/authorized_keys** files on each system where the user will log in using public key authentication.

BP-HOME-SSH-30 Each user's **id_dsa.pub** file should be secured 600 (rw- --- ---).

BP-HOME-OSSOWN-00 Each user's **id_dsa.pub** file should be owned by the user.

BP-HOME-OSSLOC-00 Each user's **id_dsa.pub** file resides in **$HOME/ssh**.

	Discovery Questions	Look here:
OSS-POLICY	Does the policy allow individual **id_id_dsa.pub** files?	Policy
HOME-OSSOWN-00	Is each individual's **$HOME/ssh /id_id_dsa.pub** file owned by the user?	ls -al
HOME-SSH-30	Is each individual's **$HOME/ssh /id_id_dsa.pub** file secured correctly?	ls -al

id_rsa.pub Files

Each individual's **$HOME/.ssh /id_rsa.pub** file contains the protocol version 1 RSA public key for authentication of each user. The contents of the file, if it exists, should be added to the **$HOME/.ssh/authorized_keys** files on each system where the user will log in using public key authentication.

BP-HOME-SSH-31   Each user's **id_rsa.pub** file should be secured 600 (rw- --- ---).

BP-HOME-OSSOWN-00 Each user's **id_rsa.pub** file should be owned by the user.

BP-HOME-OSSLOC-00 Each user's **id_rsa.pub** file resides in **$HOME/.ssh**.

	Discovery Questions	Look here:
OSS-POLICY	Does the policy allow individual **id_id_rsa.pub** files?	Policy
HOME-OSSOWN-00	Is each individual's **$HOME/.ssh/ id_id_rsa.pub** file owned by the user?	ls -al
HOME-SSH-31	Is each individual's **$HOME/.ssh/ id_id_rsa.pub** file secured correctly?	ls -al

authorized_keys Files

The SSH client stores a file in each user's home directory. It maps the host names and IP addresses of every remote host to which the user has connected with each host's public key. This database is known as the **authorized_keys** file. It resides in each user's **$HOME/.ssh/**.

Getting the public keys from **authorized_keys** isn't particularly useful in itself; public keys are, after all, *public* keys. Much more dangerous is the exposure of the private key counterparts. If both the public and the private keys are exposed, there may be an easy path to another machine.

BP-HOME-SSH-32   Each **authorized_keys** file should be secured 600 (rw- --- ---).

BP-HOME-OSSOWN-00   Each **authorized_keys** file should be owned by the user.

BP-HOME-OSSLOC-00   Each **authorized_keys** file resides in **$HOME/.ssh**.

	Discovery Questions	Look here:
HOME-OSSOWN-00	Is each individual's **$HOME/.ssh /authorized_keys** file owned by the user?	ls -al
HOME-SSH-32	Is each individual's **$HOME/.ssh /authorized_keys** file secured correctly?	ls -al

known_hosts Files

The SSH client stores within each user's home directory a list that maps the host names and IP addresses of every remote host the user has connected to with each hosts public key. This database is known as the **known_hosts** file. It resides in **$HOME/.ssh/**.

These per-user files are maintained automatically: whenever the user connects from an unknown host, its key is added to his **$HOME/.ssh/ known_hosts** file.

RISK   If both the hosts' public keys and the user's private keys are known, the remote hosts are at risk.

Authorized_keys files should only be readable by the user.

BP-HOME-SSH-33   Each **known_hosts** file should be secured
600 (rw- --- ---).

BP-HOME-OSSOWN-00   Each **known_hosts** file should be owned by
the user.

BP-HOME-OSSLOC-00   Each **known_hosts** file resides in **$HOME**
/.ssh.

	Discovery Questions	Look here:
HOME-OSSOWN-00	Is each individual's **$HOME/.ssh** **/known_hosts** owned by the user?	ls -al
HOME-SSH-33	Is each individual's **$HOME/.ssh** **/known_hosts** file secured correctly?	ls -al

sshrc Configuration File

/usr/local/bin/ssh/sshrc is used to set machine-specific login initializations
that must be run by all users before their home directory becomes available.

There may also be individual **$HOME/.ssh/rc** files.

Please refer to the chapter on the SSH Subsystem in Part 4, *TCP/IP,* for
more information or the *OSS Gazette* section on SSH for Best Practice
recommendations.

strings User Program

The **/bin/strings** program looks for printable strings in ASCII or binary
files. A printable string is any sequence of four or more printable characters
terminated by a new line or NULL character. By default, the program scans
for strings in the code, data, and extended data areas of TNS and accelerated object files and in the **.data, .rodata** and **.sdata** areas of TNS/R native
object files.

Users must have READ access to the file being examined.

RISK **/bin/strings** poses minimal risk as long as critical or sensitive application and system files are properly secured.

Securing /bin/strings

BP-BIN-STRINGS-01 **strings** should be secured 711 (rwx --x --x).

BP-BIN-OSSOWN-01 **strings** should be owned by SUPER.SUPER.

BP-BIN-OSSLOC-01 **strings** resides in **/bin**.

	Discovery Questions	Look here:
BIN-OSSOWN-01	Is **/bin/strings** owned by SUPER.SUPER?	ls -al
BIN-STRINGS-01	Is **/bin/strings** secured correctly?	ls -al

Related Topics

od

strip User Program

The **/usr/bin/strip** program removes unnecessary information from executable files. For TNS/R object files, this includes the Binder and Inspect symbols regions. For accelerated objects, this includes the Binder, Inspect, and Accelerator regions.

Users must have READ and WRITE access to the file being stripped.

AP-ADVICE-STRIP-01 To protect applications from inadvertent or malicious changes or outages, compilers and related utilities should be absent or very tightly locked down on secure systems.

Securing /bin/strip

BP-BIN-STRIP-01 **strip** should be secured 711 (rwx --x --x).

BP-BIN-OSSOWN-02 strip should be owned by SUPER.SUPER.

BP-BIN-OSSLOC-02   strip resides in **/usr/bin.**

	Discovery Questions	Look here:
BIN-OSSOWN-02	Is **/bin/strip** owned by SUPER.SUPER?	ls -al
BIN-STRIP-01	Is **/bin/strip** secured correctly?	ls -al

Related Topics

ar

c89

nld

stty User Program

The **/bin/stty** program sets terminal characteristics. If the program is started without arguments, it instead displays the current settings.

Securing /bin/stty

BP-BIN-STTY-01   stty should be secured 711 (rwx --x --x).

BP-BIN-OSSOWN-01 stty should be owned by SUPER.SUPER.

BP-BIN-OSSLOC-01   stty resides in **/bin.**

	Discovery Questions	Look here:
BIN-OSSOWN-01	Is **/bin/stty** owned by SUPER.SUPER?	ls -al
BIN-STTY-01	Is **/bin/stty** secured correctly?	ls -al

Related Topics

tty

tcsetattr

tcgetattr

ttyname

termios

su User Program

The **/bin/su** (Substitute User) program allows a user to temporarily assume another userid. It is used primarily to assume the identity of SUPER.SUPER or another privileged userid such as an application owner or job function userid. It also allows a user to change someone else's password.

/bin/su starts a login shell and the user must complete a normal login dialog for the assumed target userid, which means that he must know the target user's password.

BP-POLICY-SU-01   Users should not share passwords, especially of privileged userids such as application owners and SUPER.SUPER.

RISK   If no target userid is included in the command, **/bin/su** assumes the target userid is SUPER.SUPER. It therefore prompts for SUPER.SUPER's password.

RISK   SUPER.SUPER can use **/bin/su** to logon as any other userid without a password if the Safeguard Global parameter PASSWORD_REQUIRED is OFF.

AP-USER-PRIVLEGE-10   All Privileged IDs, including SUPER.SUPER should be treated as "check out" or "firecall" IDs, their passwords should not be shared.

Once authenticated as the target userid, **/bin/su** starts a shell running as the target userid:

The CWD is set to the target user's home directory.

By default, the **ENV** and **HOME** environment variables are also set, however, if the-(hyphen) option is not specified, the **ENV** and **HOME** environment variables are not changed.

RISK   Once authenticated, the user is, for all practical purposes, the target user. Any file, job, or process available to the target userid is accessible.

RISK   **/bin/su** can be used to change the target user's password. The password can be changed either on the command line or during the login dialog by putting a comma immediately after the current password.

When the user exits the shell, he reverts back to his original shell.

When the **/bin/su** program is invoked, a record is sent to EMS and Safeguard. This is the only audit event generated when a user changes from one userid to another. The record includes who issued the command, when it was issued, the terminal where it was issued, and whether the attempt was successful or "refused."

RISK   When a user switches to another userid via **/bin/su**, none of his activity as the assumed userid is audited. There is no accountability.

BP-POLICY-SU-01   If a user is allowed to assume another user's identity, all of his actions as the assumed userid must be audited, especially if the assumed userid is a privileged ID such as an application owner or SUPER.SUPER.

3P-ACCESS-ADVICE-01   Third-party products are available that can start shell sesssions as a privileged ID, including SUPER.SUPER. Though a user's activities cannot currently be restricted, they can be audited and, therefore, monitored so that users can be held accountable for their actions while operating as the privileged ID.

If the use of **/bin/su** is required in your environment, take the following precautions:

RISK   To protect against Trojan Horses, it is important to be sure that it is **/bin/su** being invoked and not a different program that has been named **su**.

AP-ADVICE-SU-01   Users should always invoke **/bin/su** with a fully qualified pathname.

RISK   When changing to SUPER.SUPER, it is important to be sure that SUPER.SUPER's search path is used during the session.

AP-ADVICE-SU-01   Users should always invoke **/bin/su** with the – (dash) option, which causes **/bin/su** to invoke the new shell with the dash, which causes the shell to process all relevant startup files (including the **ENV** and **HOME** environment variables) and simulate a login. This is particularly important when SUPER.SUPER is the target userid. It guarantees that SUPER.SUPER's path is used, rather than that of the user who invoked **/bin/su**.

The **su** command can change:

> The login name, and therefore the userid used for a new shell

> The password used for the userid of a new shell

The new userid stays in force until the shell exits. The new password stays in force until it is changed again.

Securing /bin/su

BP-BIN-SU-01   su should be secured 711 (rwx --x --x).

BP-BIN-OSSOWN-01 su should be owned by SUPER.SUPER.

BP-BIN-OSSLOC-01   su resides in **/bin**.

	Discovery Questions	Look here:
OSS-POLICY	Are users allowed to use **/bin/su** to change to another userid?	Policy
OSS-POLICY	If **/bin/su** is in use, have precautions been taken to prevent users from invoking a spurious program or failing to assume the appropriate search path?	Policy
BIN-OSSOWN-01	Is **/bin/su** owned by SUPER.SUPER?	ls -al
BIN-SU-01	Is **/bin/su** secured correctly?	ls -al

Related Topics

sh

sum User Program

The **/bin/sum** program displays the checksum and block count of a file. Users must have READ access to checksum a file.

Securing /bin/sum

BP-BIN-SUM-01   **sum** should be secured 711 (rwx --x --x).

BP-BIN-OSSOWN-01   **sum** should be owned by SUPER.SUPER.

BP-BIN-OSSLOC-01   **sum** resides in **/bin**.

	Discovery Questions	Look here:
BIN-OSSOWN-01	Is **/bin/sum** owned by SUPER.SUPER?	ls -al
BIN-SUM-01	Is **/bin/sum** secured correctly?	ls -al

Related Topics

cksum

wc

syslog System Utility

UNIX provides a general-purpose logging facility called **syslog**, which consists of:

/etc/syslog.conf – specifies the events to be logged and where they are to be saved.

syslogd – a daemon that reads the configuration file, reads the log events and processes them accordingly.

Log files – a set of files created by the daemon, typically stored in /dev/var on UNIX systems.

UNIX domain socket – usually **/var/run/log** or **/dev/log**; it receives log events from any system program and sends them to the **syslogd** daemon.

UDP socket – usually port 514; it receives log events from remote hosts and sends them to the daemon.

Llibrary – programs use the library to create **syslog** events.

logger – a program that can be used by scripts to send log messages to **syslog**.

Individual programs send information to **syslog**. The messages are then logged to various files, devices or computers, depending on the sender of the message and its severity.

The syslog message consists of:

Time the message was generated
The syslog facility
The syslog priority
The name of the program that generated the message
The process ID that generated the message
The computer where the message was generated
The text of the message

RISK   The syslog facility allows any user to create log entries, therefore, it is possible to introduce false data into the logs.

NonStop Implementation of syslog

On the HP NonStop server, the OSS logging mechanism sends event messages to EMS rather than to a **syslogd** process. The EMS collector gathers EMS events and their associated tokens and sends them to destinations determined by the system manager.

Authorization, demon, kernel and mail facilities all reside in the Guardian environment and, therefore, do not generate OSS events or messages.

OSS file auditing mechanisms and policies are implemented through the Guardian environment Safeguard product instead of such UNIX commands or utilities as:

    /etc/reboot
    /etc/shutdown
    /etc/syslog
    passwd

OSS file auditing features are not available through third party Security Event Exit Process (SEEP) programs but can be reported on via third party Safeguard report products and Safeart.

tail User Program

The **/bin/tail** program opens the file, displays the first 10 lines, then waits for more lines to be written to the file. It then displays them as they arrive.

This is a very useful utility for watching open log files.

Users must have READ access to the file being examined.

Most systems contain many text files. Text files are used for configuration files, documents, and help files, among other things. They are resident in every directory. It is extremely hard to control the security of the numerous text files.

AP-ADVICE-TAIL-01   Rather than securing the **/bin/tail** object file, secure sensitive application data and scripts that are stored as text files so that they can only be viewed or altered by authorized personnel.

Securing /bin/tail

BP-BIN-TAIL-01   tail should be secured 711 (rwx --x --x).

BP-BIN-OSSOWN-01   tail should be owned by SUPER.SUPER.

BP-BIN-OSSLOC-01   tail resides in /bin.

	Discovery Questions	Look here:
BIN-OSSOWN-01	Is /bin/tail owned by SUPER.SUPER?	ls -al
BIN-TAIL-01	Is /bin/tail secured correctly?	ls -al

Related Topics

cat

more

tar Program

The /bin/tar utility is used to save and restore archive-tape-format (tar) files.

During execution, a temporary file called /tmp/tar is created.

The user needs EXECUTE access to /tmp.

RISK The USTAR data exchange format does not support filenames longer than 100 characters.

AP-ADVICE-TAR-01   To archive files with names greater than 100 characters long, use the /bin/pax program with the -x cpio flag to change the archive file format to cpio.

RISK Archives that contain data from the production files can be used to obtain sensitive information.

AP-ADVICE-TAR-01   Archives should be as well secured as the files being archived.

RISK   Archived files can be moved to a system with less security, leaving the information vulnerable to unauthorized access to the data.

RISK   Archived files can be restored, overwriting existing files.

RISK   Because archived files can contain sensitive data, protection of the utilities that can READ or copy the data must be considered.

AP-ADVICE-TAR-01   Archiving should be permitted for authorized personnel only.

Securing /bin/tar

BP-BIN-TAR-01   tar should be secured 711 (rwx --x --x).

BP-BIN-OSSOWN-01   tar should be owned by SUPER.SUPER.

BP-BIN-OSSLOC-01   tar resides in /bin.

	Discovery Questions	Look here:
BIN-OSSOWN-01	Is /bin/tar owned by SUPER.SUPER?	ls -al
BIN-TAR-01	Is /bin/tar secured correctly?	ls -al

Related Topics

cpio

pax

chdir

umask

tee User Program

The /bin/tee program displays the output from a program as it saves it to a file. The program is useful for troubleshooting programs.

Users need to be able to EXECUTE the program they're observing and to be able to create and WRITE to the target directory.

RISK   Program output may contain sensitive application data.

AP-ADVICE-TEE-01   Rather than securing the **/bin/tee** object file, secure the object files so that only appropriate users can **tee** them.

Securing /bin/tee

BP-BIN-TEE-01   **tee** should be secured 711 (rwx --x --x).

BP-BIN-OSSOWN-01   **tee** should be owned by SUPER.SUPER.

BP-BIN-OSSLOC-01   **tee** resides in **/bin**.

	Discovery Questions	Look here:
BIN-OSSOWN-01	Is **/bin/tee** owned by SUPER.SUPER?	ls -al
BIN-TEE-01	Is **/bin/tee** secured correctly?	ls -al

Related Topics

echo

termcap Configuration File

The **/etc/termcap** file is a database containing terminal capabilities for various types of terminals. It is used by the **libtermcat** library.

Only the VT100 terminal type is supported when using TELNET to connect to OSS.

The **termcap** file is provided only for compatibility. Lines and columns are now stored by the kernel, as well as in the **termcap** entry. According to HP, most applications now use the kernel information primarily; the information in **termcap** is used only if the kernel does not have any information.

Securing /etc/termcap

BP-ETC-TERMCAP-01   termcap should be secured 744 (rwx r-- r --).

BP-ETC-OSSOWN-01   termcap should be owned by SUPER.SUPER.

BP-ETC-OSSLOC-01   termcap resides in /etc.

	Discovery Questions	Look here:
ETC-OSSOWN-01	Is /etc/termcap owned by SUPER.SUPER?	ls -al
ETC-TERMCAP-01	Is /etc/termcap secured correctly?	ls -al

Related Topics

printf

test User Program

The /bin/test program evaluates conditional expressions. The expression is made up of operators and objects such as files names, directories, permission strings, named pipes, and sticky bits. It can be used, for example, to determine if a set of directories matching a designated pattern have the **sticky bit** set or an object file has the **setuid** attribute.

If the conditions being tested are for a file, the user needs READ access to the directory where the file resides.

Securing /bin/test

BP-BIN-TEST-01   test should be secured 711 (rwx --x --x).

BP-BIN-OSSOWN-01   test should be owned by SUPER.SUPER.

BP-BIN-OSSLOC-01   test resides in /bin.

	Discovery Questions	Look here:
BIN-OSSOWN-01	Is /bin/test owned by SUPER.SUPER?	ls -al
BIN-TEST-01	Is /bin/test secured correctly?	ls -al

Related Topics

find

sh

time User Program

The **/bin/time** program reports, in seconds, the time required to complete a command. It details the time elapsed, the processing time, and the execution time.

There are two versions of the time command that are identical except for the following:

The **/bin/time** command starts a new shell process to display the information.

The built-in shell **time** command doesn't start a new shell process to display the information.

The built-in shell time command is the default. To invoke the program rather than the built-in command, you must use the full pathname to invoke **/bin/time**.

Securing /bin/time

BP-BIN-TIME-01   time should be secured 711 (rwx --x --x).

BP-BIN-OSSOWN-01   time should be owned by SUPER.SUPER.

BP-BIN-OSSLOC-01   time resides in /bin.

	Discovery Questions	Look here:
BIN-OSSOWN-01	Is /bin/time owned by SUPER.SUPER?	ls -al
BIN-TIME-01	Is /bin/time secured correctly?	ls -al

Related Topics

sh

times User Program

The **/bin/times** program returns the total time used by the shell and any processes run by the shell.

There are two versions of the times command that are identical except for the following:

The **/bin/times** program starts a new shell process.

The built-in shell **times** command doesn't start a new shell process.

The built-in shell times command is the default. To invoke the program rather than the built-in command, you must use the full pathname to invoke **/bin/times**.

Securing /bin/times

BP-BIN-TIMES-01	times should be secured 711 (rwx --x --x).
BP-BIN-OSSOWN-01	times should be owned by SUPER.SUPER.
BP-BIN-OSSLOC-01	times resides in **/bin**.

	Discovery Questions	Look here:
BIN-OSSOWN-01	Is /bin/times owned by SUPER.SUPER?	ls -al
BIN-TIMES-01	Is /bin/times secured correctly?	ls -al

Related Topics

sh

/tmp Directory

The **/tmp** directory is intended for use by programs that create temporary files during processing. The programs will create the temporary files with the correct permissions, generally 700 (rwx --- ---).

BP-OSSDIR-TMP-01 All users need to be able to CREATE, WRITE, and PURGE their own files in **/tmp**.

Securing /tmp

BP-OSSDIR-TMP-01 /tmp should be secured 777 (rwx rwx rwx).

BP-TMP-OSSOWN-01 /tmp should be owned by SUPER.SUPER.

BP-TMP-OSSLOC-01 /tmp resides in / (root).

	Discovery Questions	Look here:
TMP-OSSOWN-01	Is /tmp owned by SUPER.SUPER?	ls -al
OSSDIR-TMP-01	Is /tmp secured correctly?	ls -al

Related Topics

ar

float

nld

strip

locale

touch User Program

The **/bin/touch** program updates the access time and modification time of a file to the time specified on the command line. If no time is specified, the current time is used.

If a user "touches" a file that does not exist, the file will be created unless the -c flag is used. The file will be owned by the user and secured based on his **umask**, if defined.

The time will be set to the current time unless specified by using -t or -r flags or by the *time* argument.

RISK   If neither the -a (access time) or -m (modified time) flags are specified, **touch** behaves as if both of these flags were specified and sets both the access and modified times.

RISK   The **LC_TIME** environment variable, if defined, specifies the order of month and day in the date specification and of hour and minute in the time specification. Otherwise, these orders default to *MMdd* and *hhmm*.

Users need WRITE and EXECUTE for the target directory.

Securing /bin/touch

BP-BIN-TOUCH-01   touch should be secured 711 (rwx --x --x).

BP-BIN-OSSOWN-01 touch should be owned by SUPER.SUPER.

BP-BIN-OSSLOC-01   touch resides in **/bin**.

	Discovery Questions	Look here:
BIN-OSSOWN-01	Is **/bin/touch** owned by SUPER.SUPER?	ls -al
BIN-TOUCH-01	Is **/bin/touch** secured correctly?	ls -al

Related Topics
date

locale

utime

tr User Program

The /bin/tr program translates characters; replacing the characters in one string with those in another. It is used to find and replace characters such as square brackets ([ ]) with curly brackets ({ }).

RISK /bin/tr poses minimal risk as long as critical or sensitive application and system files are properly secured.

Securing /bin/tr

BP-BIN-TR-01   tr should be secured 711 (rwx --x --x).

BP-BIN-OSSOWN-01   tr should be owned by SUPER.SUPER.

BP-BIN-OSSLOC-01   tr resides in /bin.

	Discovery Questions	Look here:
BIN-OSSOWN-01	Is /bin/tr owned by SUPER.SUPER?	ls -al
BIN-TR-01	Is /bin/tr secured correctly?	ls -al

Related Topics

sh

tty User Program

The /bin/tty program returns the pathname of the terminal device. It provides a mechanism for processes to make sure that they are talking to their controlling terminals. No matter how it is opened, the **tty** device will READ and WRITE data to the terminal to which the login session was originally attached. This allows a utility to verify that it is reading from the terminal from which it was invoked.

Securing /bin/tty

BP-BIN-TTY-01   tty should be secured 711 (rwx --x --x).

BP-BIN-OSSOWN-01   tty should be owned by SUPER.SUPER.

BP-BIN-OSSLOC-01   tty resides in /bin.

	Discovery Questions	Look here:
BIN-OSSOWN-01	Is /bin/tty owned by SUPER.SUPER?	ls -al
BIN-TTY-01	Is /bin/tty secured correctly?	ls -al

Related Topics

stty

tty

ttyname

tty File

/dev/tty is a generic name for a user's current shell's terminal. When invoked, it expands to the physical name of the device where the user is logged on, typically $<device>.#<subdevice> representing the user's current *TCP/IP* connection.

The **/dev/tty** is a pseudodevice representing the user's controlling terminal. It is a remnant of the days when users logged on to a hardwired async terminal that was defined in **/dev** during a SYSGEN.

BP-TTY-OSSFILE-01   **/dev/tty** is installed as 666 (rw- rw- rw-) and should not be modified because it is a virtual device.

To prevent writing undesirable output to an output file (for example, to write a prompt in a shell script to the screen, while writing the response to the prompt to an output file), standard output is redirected to **/dev/tty**.

Securing /dev/tty

BP-DEV-TTY-01   tty should be secured 666 (rw- rw- rw-).

BP-DEV-OSSOWN-01   tty should be owned by SUPER.SUPER.

BP-DEV-OSSLOC-01   tty resides in /dev.

	Discovery Questions	Look here:
DEV-OSSOWN-01	Is /dev/tty owned by SUPER.SUPER?	ls -al
DEV-TTY-01	Is /dev/tty secured correctly?	ls -al

Related Topics

stty

tty

ttyname

umask User Program

The /bin/umask program sets the default permissions for files created by users.

When a user creates a file or directory, the system automatically supplies predetermined permissions. The default permissions are set by the system administrator in the /etc/profile file. The defaults relieve users of the task of specifying permissions every time they create a file or directory. However, if a user wants to customize the defaults for his own files, he can change the permissions with the /bin/umask program.

/bin/umask specifies the access is to be *subtracted* from the default permissions. Umask requires that the desired permissions be entered in octal form. Please refer to Appendix D, Understanding OSS Permission Strings and Octal Values, for a full discussion of permission strings and calculating their binary and octal equivalents.

If the **/bin/umask** command is added to **the .profile** file in the user's home directory, the permissions will be applied to every file and directory that he creates. The **umask** command in individual **.profile** files overrides the system **umask** values.

There are two versions of the umask command that are identical except for the following:

The **/bin/umask** program starts a new shell process.

The built-in shell **umask** command doesn't start a new shell process.

The built-in shell **umask** command is the default. To invoke the program rather than the built-in command, you must use the full pathname to invoke **/bin/umask**.

RISK   Users may set their **umask** values to allow "the world" full access to any of their files. If any of the files contain confidential or sensitive information, that information is at risk.

Securing /bin/umask

BP-BIN-UMASK-01   umask should be secured 711 (rwx --x --x).

BP-BIN-OSSOWN-01 umask should be owned by SUPER.SUPER.

BP-BIN-OSSLOC-01   umask resides in **/bin**.

	Discovery Questions	Look here:
BIN-OSSOWN-01	Is **/bin/umask** owned by SUPER.SUPER?	ls -al
BIN-UMASK-01	Is **/bin/umask** secured correctly?	ls -al

Related Topics

chmod

sh

unalias User Program

The **/bin/unalias** program removes command alias definitions. Please refer to the *OSS Gazette* section on the **/bin/alias** program for more information.

uname User Program

The **/bin/uname** program displays the node name and the current OS version and release number. Use the **-a** command flag to display all three parameters.

Securing /bin/uname

BP-BIN-UNAME-01   **uname** should be secured 711 (rwx --x --x).

BP-BIN-OSSOWN-01   **uname** should be owned by SUPER.SUPER.

BP-BIN-OSSLOC-01   **uname** resides in **/bin**.

	Discovery Questions	Look here:
BIN-OSSOWN-01	Is **/bin/uname** owned by SUPER.SUPER?	ls -al
BIN-UNAME-01	Is **/bin/uname** secured correctly?	ls -al

uncompress User Program

The **/bin/uncompress** program expands compressed data. Please refer to the *OSS Gazette* section on the **compress** User Program for more information.

unexpand User Program

The **/bin/unexpand** program replaces tab characters that were previously removed via the **/bin/expand** program. Please refer to the *OSS Gazette* section on the **expand** User Program for more information.

unpack User Program

The **/bin/unpack** program expands files created by the **/bin/pack** program. Please refer to the *OSS Gazette* section on the **pack** User Program for more information.

uniq User Program

The **/bin/uniq** program removes repeated lines from a file. Only consecutive repeats are found.

Users must have READ and WRITE access to the target files.

RISK   /bin/unpack poses minimal risk as long as files containing sensitive or confidential information are properly secured.

Securing /bin/uniq

BP-BIN-UNIQ-01   **uniq** should be secured 711 (rwx --x --x).

BP-BIN-OSSOWN-01 **uniq** should be owned by SUPER.SUPER.

BP-BIN-OSSLOC-01   **uniq** resides in **/bin**.

	Discovery Questions	Look here:
BIN-OSSOWN-01	Is **/bin/uniq** owned by SUPER.SUPER?	ls -al
BIN-UNIQ-01	Is **/bin/uniq** secured correctly?	ls -al

Related Topics

comm

sort

/unsupported Directory

The **/bin/unsupported** directory is provided on the HP Site Update Tape (SUT). It primarily contains symbolic links to programs in **/bin**. Because these are symbolic links, the security of the programs in **/bin** determines user access to these programs. These links could potentially be deleted, since they serve no purpose.

The nonlinked programs in this directory are:

codesize

dot1test

getg

putg

testutil

versions

HP states that these programs are undocumented and unsupported.

RISK   Undocumented software has the potential to damage a system.

AP-UNSUPPOR-DIRSEC-01   Running undocumented and unsupported software is generally prohibited on secure systems. The **/bin/unsupported** directory should be secured so that the general user population cannot access it.

Securing /bin/unsupported

BP-UNSUPPOR-DIRSEC-01   **/unsupported** directory should be secured 700 (rwx --- ---).

BP-UNSUPPOR-DIROWN-01 /unsupported directory should be owned by SUPER.SUPER.

BP-UNSUPPOR-DIRLOC-01 /unsupported directory resides in **/bin**.

	Discovery Questions	**Look here:**
UNSUPPOR-DIROWN-01	Is the **/bin/unsupported** directory owned by SUPER.SUPER?	ls -al
UNSUPPOR-DIRSEC-01	Is the **/bin/unsupported** directory secured correctly?	ls -al

Related Topics

ar

float

nld

strip

locale

/usr/bin Directory

The **/usr/bin** directory primarily contains development tools. Many are links to programs in **/bin**.

Securing /usr/bin

BP-USRBIN-DIRSEC-01 /usr/bin should be secured 755 (rwx r-x r-x).

BP-USRBIN-DIROWN-02 /usr/bin should be owned by SUPER. SUPER.

BP-USRBIN-DIRLOC-02 /usr/bin resides in /usr/bin.

	Discovery Questions	Look here:
USRBIN-DIROWN-02	Is the **/usr/bin** directory owned by SUPER.SUPER?	ls -al
USRBIN-DIRSEC-02	Is the **/usr/bin** directory secured correctly?	ls -al

/usr/include Directory

OSS functions are defined in library header files in the **/usr/include** directory. Developers require READ access to these files because NLD (and ELD on Integrity servers) requires READ to these files.

These library files should not be modified.

BP-INCLUDE-DIRSEC-01   Only SUPER.SUPER should have WRITE or EXECUTE access to the **/usr/include directory.**

Securing /usr/include

BP-INCLUDE-DIRSEC-01   **/include** should be secured 744 (rwx r-- r--).

BP-INCLUDE-DIROWN-01   **/include** should be owned by SUPER. SUPER.

BP-INCLUDE-DIRLOC-01   **/include** resides in **/usr.**

	Discovery Questions	Look here:
INCLUDE-DIROWN-01	Is the **/usr/include** directory owned by SUPER.SUPER?	ls -al
INCLUDE-DIRSEC-01	Is the **/usr/include** directory secured correctly?	ls -al

Related Topics

getconf

/usr/local/bin Directory

The **/usr/local/bin** directory contains primarily third-party application programs installed on the system. Some examples would be the Samba and SSH subsystems.

The directory contains symbolic links to programs in **/bin**. These are primarily text editors and text.

BP-LOCAL-DIRSEC01   Many users may need EXECUTE access to programs in the bin directory, but only SUPER.SUPER or another appropriate application owner userid should have WRITE and PURGE access.

Securing /usr/local/bin

BP-LOCAL-DIRSEC-01   **/local/bin** should be secured 755 (rwx r-x r-x).

BP-LOCAL-DIROWN-02 **/local/bin** should be owned by SUPER.
SUPER.

BP-LOCAL-DIRLOC-02   **/local/bin** resides in **/usr**.

	Discovery Questions	Look here:
OSS-POLICY	Are third-party subsystems installed on the system?	Policy
LOCAL-DIROWN-02	Is the **/usr/local/bin** directory owned by SUPER.SUPER?	ls -al
LOCAL-DIRSEC-02	Is the **/usr/local/bin** directory secured correctly?	ls -al

/usr/local/Floss Directory

The **/usr/local/Floss** directory (Freeware Look for OSS) is where freeware ported to the NonStop Server OSS environment by HP is placed.

RISK   The **man pages** for freeware packages are in **nroff/troff** format, which is not supported by the **man** utility supplied with OSS.

AP-ADVICE-FLOSS-01   Install **groff** so you can view the **floss man pages**. A package called **man.db** can also be installed. It simplifies queries on the **floss man pages**.

General Notes on Securing Freeware Packages

Refer to the chapter on Samba in the Part 5, *File Transfer Protocols*, for more information.

AP-ADVICE-FLOSS-02   Freeware packages should be installed as a user other than SUPER.SUPER.

RISK   If the location of the freeware package is placed at the beginning of the **PATH**, the freeware commands will be used instead of the OSS commands.

BP-FLOSS-ADMIN-01   If freeware packages are in use on your system, place the **/usr/local/bin** at the end of the PATH.

BP-FLOSS-ADMIN-02   Only users responsible for installing and configuring freeware should have WRITE and EXECUTE access to the **/usr/local/Floss** directory.

BP-ADVICE-FLOSS-03   Only users authorized to run each freeware package should have access to the **/usr/local/bin/<package>** directory.

AP-ADVICE-FLOSS-04   Profiles and alias shell features should be used to limit access to freeware packages to appropriate users only.

Securing /usr/local/floss

BP-FLOSS-DIRSEC-01   **/Floss** should be secured 755 (rwx r-x r-x).
BP-FLOSS-DIROWN-02   **/Floss** should be owned by SUPER.SUPER.
BP-FLOSS-DIRLOC-02   **/Floss** resides in **/usr/local**.

	Discovery Questions	Look here:
FLOSS-DIROWN-02	Is the **/usr/Floss** directory owned by SUPER.SUPER?	ls -al
FLOSS-DIRSEC-01	Is the **/usr/Floss** directory secured correctly?	ls -al

Related Topics

jobs

sh

UTILSGE

The **UTILSGE** environment variable affects the execution of many programs. This keyword specifies that HP extensions to the root directory (/G and /E) should be omitted when the initial directory is root and a recursive operation occurs in an OSS shell program. The **UTILSGE** value can be any of the following:

NOE Omit the /E directory.

NOG Omit the /G directory.

NOG:NOE Omit both the /G and /E directories.

uudecode

The **/bin/uudecode** program reads a file, strips off any leading and trailing lines added by mailers, and recreates the original file with its original file access permissions and pathname.

The user must have READ access to the encoded file and be able to create the decoded output file.

RISK The target file is overwritten.

AP-ADVICE-UUDECODE-01 Application files on production systems should be tightly secured to prevent the accidental replacement of the file by **/bin/uudecode**.

AP-ADVICE-UUDECODE-02 **/bin/uudecode** should be secured against accidental use on production systems. Only appropriate users should have EXECUTE access.

Securing /bin/uudecode

BP-BIN-UUDECODE-01   **uudecode** should be secured 711 (rwx --x --x).

BP-BIN-OSSOWN-01   **uudecode** should be owned by SUPER.
SUPER.

BP-BIN-OSSLOC-01   **uudecode** resides in **/bin**.

	Discovery Questions	Look here:
OSSFILE-POLICY	Does policy allow the use of **/bin/uudecode** on this system?	Policy
OSSFILE-POLICY	Who is allowed to use **/bin/uudecode** on this system?	Policy
BIN-OSSOWN-01	Is **/bin/uudecode** owned by SUPER.SUPER?	ls -al
BIN-UUDECODE-01	Is **/bin/uudecode** secured correctly?	ls -al

Related Topics

uuencode

uuencode

The **/bin/uuencode** program reads the selected file and produces an encoded file containing only printable **ASCII** characters, the file permissions and the file's pathname.

The user must have READ access to the target object file and be able to create an encoded output file.

RISK   The target file is overwritten.

AP-ADVICE-UUENCODE-01   Application object files on production systems should be tightly secured to prevent the accidental replacement of the file by **/bin/uuencode**.

AP-ADVICE-UUENCODE-02   **/bin/uuencode**   should   be   secured
against accidental use on production systems. Only appropriate users
should have EXECUTE access.

Securing /bin/uuencode

BP-BIN-UUENCODE-01   **uuencode** should be secured 711 (rwx
--x --x).

BP-BIN-OSSOWN-01   **uuencode** should be owned by SUPER.
SUPER.

BP-BIN-OSSLOC-01   **uuencode** resides in **/bin**.

	Discovery Questions	Look here:
OSSFILE-POLICY	Does policy allow the use of **/bin /uuencode** on this system?	Policy
OSSFILE-POLICY	Who is allowed to use **/bin/uuencode** on this system?	Policy
BIN-OSSOWN-01	Is **/bin/uuencode** owned by SUPER.SUPER?	ls -al
BIN-UUENCODE-01	Is **/bin/uuencode** secured correctly?	ls -al

Related Topics
umask
uudecode

vi User Program

/bin/vi is a text editor. It is based on **/bin/ex**, so both **/bin/ex** and **/bin/vi**
commands can be used within the program.

RISK   Editors can be used to alter data or modify text data files.

Most systems contain many text files. Text files are used for configuration files, documents, and help files, among other things. They are resident in every directory. It is extremely hard to control the security of the numerous text files.

In addition, editors are often required by most users for everyday work. Securing editor programs to restrict access is often not reasonable, but the risks remain.

AP-ADVICE-VI-01   Rather than securing the edit program's object files, secure sensitive application data and scripts that are stored as text files so that they can only be viewed or altered by authorized personnel.

AP-ADVICE-VI--02   System text files, especially those in **/bin/etc**, **/usr/bin**, **/usr/include**, and **/usr/ucb**, should be secured properly to prevent changes by unauthorized personnel.

Securing /bin/vi

BP-BIN-VI-01	**vi** should be secured 711 (rwx --x --x).
BP-BIN-OSSOWN-01	**vi** should be owned by SUPER.SUPER.
BP-BIN-OSSLOC-01	**vi** resides in **/bin**.

	Discovery Questions	**Look here:**
BIN-OSSOWN-01	Is **/bin/vi** owned by SUPER.SUPER?	ls -al
BIN-VI-01	Is **/bin/vi** secured correctly?	ls -al

Related Topics

ed

ex

grep

vproc User Program

The **/bin/vproc** (Version Procedure) program displays the version number for program and files developed by HP or third-party vendors and a time-stamp that is either the time when the object file was compiled or the time when the object was processed by the NLD or ELD programs.

/bin/vproc calls the Guardian **VPROC** utility. It can be run in interactive mode, allowing the user to enter filenames, pathnames, or the path oper-and. Both Guardian and OSS files can be evaluated. To evaluate Guardian files, the Guardian **VPROC** is invoked via **GTACL**.

/bin/vproc creates a temporary file during processing. It is called **/tmp/ <invoking username>/vproc.tempfile.<OSS process ID>**.

Securing /bin/vproc

BP-BIN-VPROC-01	**vproc** should be secured 711 (rwx --x --x).
BP-BIN-OSSOWN-01	**vproc** should be owned by SUPER.SUPER.
BP-BIN-OSSLOC-01	**vproc** resides in /bin.
BP-FILE-BINDER-03	**VPROC** should be secured "UUNU".
BP-BIN-OSSOWN-02	**VPROC** should be owned by SUPER.SUPER.
BP-BIN-FILELOC-02	**VPROC** must reside in $SYSTEM.SYSTEM.

	Discovery Questions	**Look here:**
BIN-OSSOWN-01	Is **/bin/vproc** owned by SUPER.SUPER?	ls -al
BIN-VPROC-01	Is **/bin/vproc** secured correctly?	ls -al

Related Topics

BINDER

find

gtacl

osh

wait User Program

The **/bin/wait** program waits for the selected job and reports its termination status and, optionally, the status of all the job's child processes.

There are two versions of the **wait** command that are identical except for the following:

The **/bin/wait** program starts a new shell process.

The built-in shell **wait** command doesn't start a new shell process.

The built-in shell **wait** command is the default. To invoke the program rather than the built-in command, you must use the full pathname to invoke **/bin/wait**.

Securing /bin/wait

BP-BIN-WAIT-01   **wait** should be secured 711 (rwx --x --x).

BP-BIN-OSSOWN-01 **wait** should be owned by SUPER.SUPER.

BP-BIN-OSSLOC-01   **wait** resides in **/bin**.

	Discovery Questions	Look here:
BIN-OSSOWN-01	Is **/bin/wait** owned by SUPER.SUPER?	ls -al
BIN-WAIT-01	Is **/bin/wait** secured correctly?	ls -al

Related Topics

sh

wall User Program

The **/bin/wall** program broadcasts a message to all users. The message can be contained in a file or entered interactively. The invoking user must have the privileges necessary to override protections put in place by other users.

Securing /bin/wall

BP-BIN-WALL-01   wall should be secured 711 (rwx --x --x).

BP-BIN-OSSOWN-01 wall should be owned by SUPER.SUPER.

BP-BIN-OSSLOC-01   wall resides in /bin.

	Discovery Questions	Look here:
BIN-OSSOWN-01	Is /bin/wall owned by SUPER.SUPER?	ls -al
BIN-WALL-01	Is /bin/wall secured correctly?	ls -al

wc User Program

The /bin/wc program counts lines, words, characters, and bytes in the specified files.

Users must have READ access to the file being examined.

Securing /bin/wc

BP-BIN-WC-01   wc should be secured 711 (rwx --x --x).

BP-BIN-OSSOWN-01 wc should be owned by SUPER.SUPER.

BP-BIN-OSSLOC-01   wc resides in /bin.

	Discovery Questions	Look here:
BIN-OSSOWN-01	Is /bin/wc owned by SUPER.SUPER?	ls -al
BIN-WC-01	Is /bin/wc secured correctly?	ls -al

Related Topics

ls

whatis User Program

The **/bin/whatis** program displays the meaning or use of a command, system call, library function, filename, or POSIX regular expression. It is the equivalent of the **man -f** command.

whatis Databases

The **whatis** databases reside in the following directories:

/usr/share/man/whatis, which is the **whatis** keyword database for the reference pages in **/usr/share/man**

/nonnative/usr/share/man/whatis, which is the **whatis** keyword database for the reference pages in **/nonnative/usr/share/man**

The merge_whatis System Utility

The merge_whatis program creates and updates the **whatis** databases used by the **/bin/man**, **/bin/apropos**, and **/bin/whatis commands.**

Securing /bin/whatis

BP-USR-WHATIS-01   **whatis** should be secured 711 (rwx --x --x).

BP-USR-OSSOWN-03   **whatis** should be owned by SUPER.SUPER.

BP-USR-OSSLOC-03   **whatis** resides in **/usr/share/man**.

BP-USR-WHATIS-02   **merge_whatis** should be secured 711 (rwx --x --x).

BP-USR-OSSOWN-03   **merge_whatis** should be owned by SUPER. SUPER.

BP-USR-OSSLOC-03   **merge_whatis** resides in **/usr/share/man**.

BP-USR-DATABASE-03 The **whatis** databases should be secured 744 (rwx r-- r--).

BP-USR-OSSOWN-03   The **whatis** databases should be owned by
SUPER.SUPER.

BP-USR-OSSLOC-03   The **whatis** databases reside in **/usr/share/man**
and **/nonnative/usr/share/man/**.

	Discovery Questions	Look here:
USR-OSSOWN-03	Is the **whatis** owned by SUPER.SUPER?	ls -al
USR-OSSOWN-03	Is the **merge_whatis** owned by SUPER.SUPER?	ls -al
USR-WHATIS-01	Is the **whatis** secured correctly?	ls -al
USR-WHATIS-02	Is the **merge_whatis** secured correctly?	ls -al

Related Topics

apropos

man

who User Program

The **/bin/who** program displays a list of the users who are currently logged
on to the local node.

RISK   The **/bin/who** program make it easier to attack a system.

AP-ADVICE-WHO-01   The corporate security policy should determine
whether or not general users are allowed to EXECUTE the **/bin/who**
command.

Securing /bin/who

BP-BIN-WHO-01   who should be secured 711 (rwx --x --x).

BP-BIN-OSSOWN-01   who should be owned by SUPER.SUPER.

BP-BIN-OSSLOC-01   who resides in **/bin**.

	Discovery Questions	Look here:
BIN-OSSOWN-01	Is /bin/who owned by SUPER.SUPER?	ls -al
BIN-WHO-01	Is /bin/who secured correctly?	ls -al

Related Topics

date

wait

whoami User Program

The **/bin/whoami** program displays the user name and userid of the invoking user.

Securing /bin/whoami

BP-BIN-WHOAMI-01 whoami should be secured 711 (rwx --x --x).

BP-BIN-OSSOWN-01 whoami should be owned by SUPER.SUPER.

BP-BIN-OSSLOC-01   whoami resides in /bin.

	Discovery Questions	Look here:
BIN-OSSOWN-01	Is /bin/whoami owned by SUPER.SUPER?	ls -al
BIN-WHOAMI-01	Is /bin/whoami secured correctly?	ls -al

Related Topics

who

xargs User Program

The **/bin/xargs** program contructs argument lists and runs commands. It contructs a command line by combining a command string with additional arguments that can be entered interactively.

Securing /bin/xargs

BP-BIN-XARGS-01   xargs should be secured 711 (rwx --x --x).

BP-BIN-OSSOWN-01   xargs should be owned by SUPER.SUPER.

BP-BIN-OSSLOC-01   xargs resides in /bin.

	Discovery Questions	Look here:
BIN-OSSOWN-01	Is /bin/xargs owned by SUPER.SUPER?	ls -al
BIN-XARGS-01	Is /bin/xargs secured correctly?	ls -al

Related Topics

comm

sort

yacc User Program

The /bin/yacc ("Yet Another Compiler Compiler") program takes a grammar specification for a language (for example the command language that mxci uses) and converts it to C data structures to do the parsing in conjunction with supplied C code.

AP-ADVICE-COMPILER-01   To protect applications from inadvertent or malicious changes or outages, compilers and related utilities should be absent or very tightly locked down on secure systems.

Securing /bin/yacc

BP-BIN-YACC-01   yacc should be secured 711 (rwx --x --x).

BP-BIN-OSSOWN-01   yacc should be owned by SUPER.SUPER.

BP-BIN-OSSLOC-01   yacc resides in /bin.

	Discovery Questions	Look here:
BIN-OSSOWN-01	Is /bin/yacc owned by SUPER.SUPER?	ls -al
BIN-YACC-01	Is /bin/yacc secured correctly?	ls -al

Related Topics

comm

sort

zcat User Program

The /bin/zcat program expands compressed data. It is equivalent to the /bin/uncompress -c command. The compressed (.Z) file remains untouched.

Users must have READ access to the compressed files and EXECUTE access to the directory where the new files will be created.

Securing /bin/zcat

BP-BIN-ZCAT-01   zcat should be secured 711 (rwx --x --x).

BP-BIN-OSSOWN-01 zcat should be owned by SUPER.SUPER.

BP-BIN-OSSLOC-01   zcat resides in /bin.

	Discovery Questions	Look here:
BIN-OSSOWN-01	Is /bin/zcat owned by SUPER.SUPER?	ls -al
BIN-ZCAT-01	Is /bin/zcat secured correctly?	ls -al

Related Topics

compress

uncompress

A

Understanding OSS Permission Strings and Octal Values

This appendix explains how to interpret file permission strings and translate between the symbolic (letter) string, the binary value, and the octal value.

It also discusses overriding the default permission string with the **umask** command.

Permission Strings and Their Binary and Octal Equivalents

The symbolic (or letter) permission string can be viewed in two other ways, binary and octal.

Permissions String	Binary Equivalent	Octal Equivalent
---	000	0
--x	001	1
-w-	010	2
-wx	011	3

(Continued)

Permissions string	Binary Equivalent	Octal Equivalent
r--	100	4
r-x	101	5
rw-	110	6
rwx	111	7

Binary

A binary system is one where each digit can have only two values, on or off, 1 or 0, yes or no. Because the OSS file permission string is a binary system, any permission string can be described as a series of zeros and ones—a binary number. If a letter (r, w, or x) is present, it represents a 1. If no letter is present, the value is 0.

/bin/cp is owned by SUPER.SUPER and secured rwx r-x --x.

To calculate the binary value of this permission string, start by substituting a 1 (one) for each letter, then replace each – (dash or hyphen) with a 0 (zero):

111 101 001

Octal

The nine permissions in the string representing owner, group, and everyone else are represented by nine bits, each of which has an octal value as shown in the diagram below. To translate an entire permission string, treat the owner position as the 64s value of a 3-digit octal number. Treat the group position as the 8s value and the other position as the 1s value.

Or, to show the values another way:

User	Group	Other	Permission
400	40	4	Read
200	20	2	Write
100	10	1	Execute
700	70	7	rwx (777) = octal permission

Figure A.1
*Calculating octal
file permission
values.*

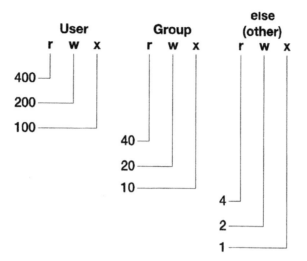

So if the file's owner has full access to the file, the owner position of the permission string is 700 (400+200+100). If he has only READ and WRITE, then the value is 600 (400+200). If he has EXECUTE only, the value is 100. READ and EXECUTE would be 500 (400+100).

If the files's group also has full access to the file, the group position of the permission string is 70 (40+20+10). If the group has READ and WRITE, the value is 60 (40+20). If the group has execute only, the value is 10. READ and EXECUTE would be 50 (40+10).

If other users also have full access to the file, the "other" or "everyone else" position of the permission string is 7 (4+2+1). If other has only READ and WRITE, the value is 6 (4+2). If other has EXECUTE only, the value is 1. READ and EXECUTE would be 5 (4+1).

Add the values of the owner, group, and other positions to find the value of the entire permission string. Thus:

rwx rwx rwx	= 777
rwx r-- r--	= 744
rw- rw- rw-	= 666

$$--x --x --x \qquad = 111$$
$$r-x \ r-x \ r-x \qquad = 555$$

setuid

The **setuid** bit adds a 4 in the leading position.

Or, to show the values another way:

User	Group	Other	Permission
400	40	4	Read
200	20	2	Write
100	10	1	Execute
4000	10	1	Execute as uid
4700	**70**	**7**	**rws rwx rwx** (4777) = octal permission

Thus:

$$rws --x --x \qquad = 4711$$

setgid

The **setgid** bit adds a 2 to the leading position.

Or, to show the values another way:

User	Group	Other	Permission
400	40	4	Read
200	20	2	Write
100	10	1	Execute
2000	10	1	Execute as gid
2700	**70**	**7**	**rwx rws rwx** (2777) = octal permission

Thus:

$$rwx --s --x \qquad = 2711$$

sticky bit

The **sticky bit** adds a 1 to the leading position. The octal version of the security of a **public** directory, for example, is 1777.

Or, to show the values another way:

User	Group	Other	Permission
400	40	4	Read
200	20	2	Write
100	10	1	Execute
1000	10	1	Sticky bit
1700	70	7	**rwx rwx rwt** (1777) = octal permission

Thus:

    rwx --s --t   = 2711

Umasks and Their Octal Equivalents

The **/bin/umask** program sets the default permissions for files created by users.

When a user creates a file or directory, the system automatically supplies predetermined permissions. The default permissions are set by the system administrator in the **/etc/profile** file. The defaults relieve users of the task of specifying permissions every time they create a file or directory. However, if a user wants his defaults to differ from the default, he can change the permissions with the **/bin/umask** command.

There is no **umask** for **setuid**, **setgid**, or the **sticky bit**.

Umask specifies what access is to be *subtracted* from the system default permissions. The permissions must be entered in the octal form:

Umask Octal Values

Octal	Maximum Access Allowed	Result
0	rwx	Read, write, and execute
1	rw-	Read and write
2	r-x	Read and execute
3	r--	Read
4	-wx	Write and execute
5	-w-	Write
6	--x	Execute
7	---	No permissions granted

The user must enter an octal value for each of the three positions: the owner, his group, and everyone else.

The easiest way to calculate the **umask** is to:

1. Convert the permission string to binary
2. Write the binary equivalent of the system default permission string
3. "Add" the two strings together, remembering that *any value greater than 1 = 0*
4. Translate the result back to binary
5. The binary value will be *subtracted* from the default permission string, yielding the desired permissions.

Please note that "Add the two strings together" actually means "Add with no carry," that is, the remainder will be ignored rather than carried to the next column.

<u>Example 1:</u>

```
The default permission string:              rwx rwx rwx (777)
The user's desired permission string:       rwx --- --- (700)

1) Convert the desired string to binary:    111 000 000
2) Convert default rwx rwx rwx to binary:   111 111 111
3) "Add" the two binary values together:
```

```
111 000 000 (700)
111 111 111 (777)
000 111 111 (077)
```

4) Convert the sum from step 3 (000 111 111), back to octal: 077

5) Because a umask of 077 (777 - 700) subtracts nothing from the owner's permissions, all permissions (7) from his group and all permissions (7) from other, the user's new default permission string is rwx --- --- (700).

Example 2:

The default permission string: rwx r-x r-- (754)
The user's desired permission string: rwx --- --- (700)

1) Convert the desired string to binary:

   111 000 000

2) Convert the default rwx r-x r-- to binary:

   111 101 100

3) "Add" the two binary values together:

```
111 000 000 (700)
111 101 100 (754)
000 101 100 (054)
```

4) Convert the sum from step 3 (000 101 100), back to octal: 054

5) Because a umask of 054 subtracts nothing from the owner's permissions, read and execute permissions (5) from his group, and read from everyone else, the user's new default permission string is rwx --- --- (700).

Table of File and Directory Permissions

Mask	Mask Octal	Mask Binary	Umask Binary	Umask Octal
--- --- ---	000	000 000 000	111 111 111	777
--- --- --x	001	000 000 001	111 111 110	776
--- --- -w-	002	000 000 010	111 111 101	775
--- --- -wx	003	000 000 011	111 111 100	774
--- --- r--	004	000 000 100	111 111 011	773
--- --- r-x	005	000 000 101	111 111 010	772
--- --- rw-	006	000 000 110	111 111 001	771
--- --- rwx	007	000 000 111	111 111 000	770
--- --x ---	010	000 001 000	111 110 111	767
--- --x --x	011	000 001 001	111 110 110	766
--- --x -w-	012	000 001 010	111 110 101	765
--- --x -wx	013	000 001 011	111 110 100	764
--- --x r--	014	000 001 100	111 110 011	763
--- --x r-x	015	000 001 101	111 110 010	762
--- --x rw-	016	000 001 110	111 110 001	761
--- --x rwx	017	000 001 111	111 110 000	760
--- -w- ---	020	000 010 000	111 101 111	757

Mask	Mask Octal	Mask Binary	Umask Binary	Umask Octal
--- -w- --x	021	000 010 001	111 101 110	756
--- -w- -w-	022	000 010 010	111 101 101	755
--- -w- -wx	023	000 010 011	111 101 100	754
--- -w- r--	024	000 010 100	111 101 011	753
--- -w- r-x	025	000 010 101	111 101 010	752
--- -w- rw-	026	000 010 110	111 101 001	751
--- -w- rwx	027	000 010 111	111 101 000	750
--- -wx ---	030	000 011 000	111 100 111	747
--- -wx --x	031	000 011 001	111 100 110	746
--- -wx -w-	032	000 011 010	111 100 101	745
--- -wx -wx	033	000 011 011	111 100 100	744
--- -wx r--	034	000 011 100	111 100 011	743
--- -wx r-x	035	000 011 101	111 100 010	742
--- -wx rw-	036	000 011 110	111 100 001	741
--- -wx rwx	037	000 011 111	111 100 000	740
--- r-- ---	040	000 100 000	111 011 111	737
--- r-- --x	041	000 100 001	111 011 110	736
--- r-- -w-	042	000 100 010	111 011 101	735
--- r-- -wx	043	000 100 011	111 011 100	734
--- r-- r--	044	000 100 100	111 011 011	733
--- r-- r-x	045	000 100 101	111 011 010	732
--- r-- rw-	046	000 100 110	111 011 001	731
--- r-- rwx	047	000 100 111	111 011 000	730
--- r-x ---	050	000 101 000	111 010 111	727
--- r-x --x	051	000 101 001	111 010 110	726
--- r-x -w-	052	000 101 010	111 010 101	725
--- r-x -wx	053	000 101 011	111 010 100	724
--- r-x r--	054	000 101 100	111 010 011	723
--- r-x r-x	055	000 101 101	111 010 010	722
--- r-x rw-	056	000 101 110	111 010 001	721
--- r-x rwx	057	000 101 111	111 010 000	720
--- rw- ---	060	000 110 000	111 001 111	717
--- rw- --x	061	000 110 001	111 001 110	716

(*Continued*)

Mask	Mask Octal	Mask Binary	Umask Binary	Umask Octal
--- rw- -w-	062	000 110 010	111 001 101	715
--- rw- -wx	063	000 110 011	111 001 100	714
--- rw- r--	064	000 110 100	111 001 011	713
--- rw- r-x	065	000 110 101	111 001 010	712
--- rw- rw-	066	000 110 110	111 001 001	711
--- rw- rwx	067	000 110 111	111 001 000	710
--- rwx ---	070	000 111 000	111 000 111	707
--- rwx --x	071	000 111 001	111 000 110	706
--- rwx -w-	072	000 111 010	111 000 101	705
--- rwx -wx	073	000 111 011	111 000 100	704
--- rwx r--	074	000 111 100	111 000 011	703
--- rwx r-x	075	000 111 101	111 000 010	702
--- rwx rw-	076	000 111 110	111 000 001	701
--- rwx rwx	077	000 111 111	111 000 000	700
--x --- ---	100	001 000 000	110 111 111	677
--x --- --x	101	001 000 001	110 111 110	676
--x --- -w-	102	001 000 010	110 111 101	675
--x --- -wx	103	001 000 011	110 111 100	674
--x --- r--	104	001 000 100	110 111 011	673
--x --- r-x	105	001 000 101	110 111 010	672
--x --- rw-	106	001 000 110	110 111 001	671
--x --- rwx	107	001 000 111	110 111 000	670
--x --x ---	110	001 001 000	110 110 111	667
--x --x --x	111	001 001 001	110 110 110	666
--x --x -w-	112	001 001 010	110 110 101	665
--x --x -wx	113	001 001 011	110 110 100	664
--x --x r--	114	001 001 100	110 110 011	663
--x --x r-x	115	001 001 101	110 110 010	662
--x --x rw-	116	001 001 110	110 110 001	661
--x --x rwx	117	001 001 111	110 110 000	660
--x -w- ---	120	001 010 000	110 101 111	657
--x -w- --x	121	001 010 001	110 101 110	656
--x -w- -w-	122	001 010 010	110 101 101	655

Mask	Mask Octal	Mask Binary	Umask Binary	Umask Octal
--x -w- -wx	123	001 010 011	110 101 100	654
--x -w- r--	124	001 010 100	110 101 011	653
--x -w- r-x	125	001 010 101	110 101 010	652
--x -w- rw-	126	001 010 110	110 101 001	651
--x -w- rwx	127	001 010 111	110 101 000	650
--x -wx ---	130	001 011 000	110 100 111	647
--x -wx --x	131	001 011 001	110 100 110	646
--x -wx -w-	132	001 011 010	110 100 101	645
--x -wx -wx	133	001 011 011	110 100 100	644
--x -wx r--	134	001 011 100	110 100 011	643
--x -wx r-x	135	001 011 101	110 100 010	642
--x -wx rw-	136	001 011 110	110 100 001	641
--x -wx rwx	137	001 011 111	110 100 000	640
--x r-- ---	140	001 100 000	110 011 111	637
--x r-- --x	141	001 100 001	110 011 110	636
--x r-- -w-	142	001 100 010	110 011 101	635
--x r-- -wx	143	001 100 011	110 011 100	634
--x r-- r--	144	001 100 100	110 011 011	633
--x r-- r-x	145	001 100 101	110 011 010	632
--x r-- rw-	146	001 100 110	110 011 001	631
--x r-- rwx	147	001 100 111	110 011 000	630
--x r-x ---	150	001 101 000	110 010 111	627
--x r-x --x	151	001 101 001	110 010 110	626
--x r-x -w-	152	001 101 010	110 010 101	625
--x r-x -wx	153	001 101 011	110 010 100	624
--x r-x r--	154	001 101 100	110 010 011	623
--x r-x r-x	155	001 101 101	110 010 010	622
--x r-x rw-	156	001 101 110	110 010 001	621
--x r-x rwx	157	001 101 111	110 010 000	620
--x rw- ---	160	001 110 000	110 001 111	617
--x rw- --x	161	001 110 001	110 001 110	616
--x rw- -w-	162	001 110 010	110 001 101	615
--x rw- -wx	163	001 110 011	110 001 100	614

(Continued)

Mask	Mask Octal	Mask Binary	Umask Binary	Umask Octal
--x rw- r--	164	001 110 100	110 001 011	613
--x rw- r-x	165	001 110 101	110 001 010	612
--x rw- rw-	166	001 110 110	110 001 001	611
--x rw- rwx	167	001 110 111	110 001 000	610
--x rwx ---	170	001 111 000	110 000 111	607
--x rwx --x	171	001 111 001	110 000 110	606
--x rwx -w-	172	001 111 010	110 000 101	605
--x rwx -wx	173	001 111 011	110 000 100	604
--x rwx r--	174	001 111 100	110 000 011	603
--x rwx r-x	175	001 111 101	110 000 010	602
--x rwx rw-	176	001 111 110	110 000 001	601
--x rwx rwx	177	001 111 111	110 000 000	600
-w- --- ---	200	010 000 000	101 111 111	577
-w- --- --x	201	010 000 001	101 111 110	576
-w- --- -w-	202	010 000 010	101 111 101	575
-w- --- -wx	203	010 000 011	101 111 100	574
-w- --- r--	204	010 000 100	101 111 011	573
-w- --- r-x	205	010 000 101	101 111 010	572
-w- --- rw-	206	010 000 110	101 111 001	571
-w- --- rwx	207	010 000 111	101 111 000	570
-w- --x ---	210	010 001 000	101 110 111	567
-w- --x --x	211	010 001 001	101 110 110	566
-w- --x -w-	212	010 001 010	101 110 101	565
-w- --x -wx	213	010 001 011	101 110 100	564
-w- --x r--	214	010 001 100	101 110 011	563
-w- --x r-x	215	010 001 101	101 110 010	562
-w- --x rw-	216	010 001 110	101 110 001	561
-w- --x rwx	217	010 001 111	101 101 000	550
-w- -w- ---	220	010 010 000	101 101 111	557
-w- -w- --x	221	010 010 001	101 101 110	556
-w- -w- -w-	222	010 010 010	101 101 101	555
-w- -w- -wx	223	010 010 011	101 101 100	554
-w- -w- r--	224	010 010 100	101 101 011	553

Mask	Mask Octal	Mask Binary	Umask Binary	Umask Octal
-w- -w- r-x	225	010 010 101	101 101 010	552
-w- -w- rw-	226	010 010 110	101 101 001	551
-w- -w- rwx	227	010 010 111	101 101 000	550
-w- -wx ---	230	010 011 000	101 100 111	547
-w- -wx --x	231	010 011 001	101 100 110	546
-w- -wx -w-	232	010 011 010	101 100 101	545
-w- -wx -wx	233	010 011 011	101 100 100	544
-w- -wx r--	234	010 011 100	101 100 011	543
-w- -wx r-x	235	010 011 101	101 100 010	542
-w- -wx rw-	236	010 011 110	101 100 001	541
-w- -wx rwx	237	010 011 111	101 100 000	540
-w- r-- ---	240	010 100 000	101 011 111	537
-w- r-- --x	241	010 100 001	101 011 110	536
-w- r-- -w-	242	010 100 010	101 011 101	535
-w- r-- -wx	243	010 100 011	101 011 100	534
-w- r-- r--	244	010 100 100	101 011 011	533
-w- r-- r-x	245	010 100 101	101 011 010	232
-w- r-- rw-	246	010 100 110	101 011 001	531
-w- r-- rwx	247	010 100 111	101 011 000	530
-w- r-x ---	250	010 101 000	010 010 111	527
-w- r-x --x	251	010 101 001	010 010 110	526
-w- r-x -w-	252	010 101 010	010 010 101	525
-w- r-x -wx	253	010 101 011	010 010 100	524
-w- r-x r--	254	010 101 100	010 010 011	523
-w- r-x r-x	255	010 101 101	010 010 010	522
-w- r-x rw-	256	010 101 110	010 010 001	521
-w- r-x rwx	257	010 101 111	010 010 000	520
-w- rw- ---	260	010 110 000	101 001 111	517
-w- rw- --x	261	010 110 001	101 001 110	516
-w- rw- -w-	262	010 110 010	101 001 101	515
-w- rw- -wx	263	010 110 011	101 001 100	514
-w- rw- r--	264	010 110 100	101 001 011	513
-w- rw- r-x	265	010 110 101	101 001 010	512

(*Continued*)

Mask	Mask Octal	Mask Binary	Umask Binary	Umask Octal
-w- rw- rw-	266	010 110 110	101 001 001	511
-w- rw- rwx	267	010 110 111	101 001 000	510
-w- rwx ---	270	010 111 000	101 000 111	507
-w- rwx --x	271	010 111 001	101 000 110	506
-w- rwx -w-	272	010 111 010	101 000 101	505
-w- rwx -wx	273	010 111 011	101 000 100	504
-w- rwx r--	274	010 111 100	101 000 011	503
-w- rwx r-x	275	010 111 101	101 000 010	502
-w- rwx rw-	276	010 111 110	101 000 001	501
-w- rwx rwx	277	010 111 111	101 000 000	500
-wx --- ---	300	011 000 000	110 111 111	677
-wx --- --x	301	011 000 001	110 111 110	676
-wx --- -w-	302	011 000 010	110 111 101	675
-wx --- -wx	303	011 000 011	110 111 100	674
-wx --- r--	304	011 000 100	110 111 011	673
-wx --- r-x	305	011 000 101	110 111 010	672
-wx --- rw-	306	011 000 110	110 111 001	671
-wx --- rwx	307	011 000 111	110 111 000	670
-wx --x ---	310	011 001 000	110 110 111	667
-wx --x --x	311	011 001 001	110 110 110	666
-wx --x -w-	312	011 001 010	110 110 101	665
-wx --x -wx	313	011 001 011	110 110 100	664
-wx --x r--	314	011 001 100	110 110 011	663
-wx --x r-x	315	011 001 101	110 110 010	662
-wx --x rw-	316	011 001 110	110 110 001	661
-wx --x rwx	317	011 001 111	110 110 000	660
-wx -w- ---	320	011 010 000	110 101 111	657
-wx -w- --x	321	011 010 001	110 101 110	656
-wx -w- -w-	322	011 010 010	110 101 101	655
-wx -w- -wx	323	011 010 011	110 101 100	654
-wx -w- r--	324	011 010 100	110 101 011	653
-wx -w- r-x	325	011 010 101	110 101 010	652
-wx -w- rw-	326	011 010 110	110 101 001	651

Mask	Mask Octal	Mask Binary	Umask Binary	Umask Octal
-wx -w- rwx	327	011 010 111	110 101 000	650
-wx -wx ---	330	011 011 000	110 100 111	647
-wx -wx --x	331	011 011 001	110 100 110	646
-wx -wx -w-	332	011 011 010	110 100 101	645
-wx -wx -wx	333	011 011 011	110 100 100	644
-wx -wx r--	334	011 011 100	110 100 011	643
-wx -wx r-x	335	011 011 101	110 100 010	642
-wx -wx rw-	336	011 011 110	110 100 001	641
-wx -wx rwx	337	011 011 111	110 100 000	640
-wx r-- ---	340	011 100 000	110 011 111	637
-wx r-- --x	341	011 100 001	110 011 110	636
-wx r-- -w-	342	011 100 010	110 011 101	635
-wx r-- -wx	343	011 100 011	110 011 100	634
-wx r-- r--	344	011 100 100	110 011 011	633
-wx r-- r-x	345	011 100 101	110 011 010	632
-wx r-- rw-	346	011 100 110	110 011 001	631
-wx r-- rwx	347	011 100 111	110 011 000	630
-wx r-x ---	350	011 101 000	110 010 111	627
-wx r-x --x	351	011 101 001	110 010 110	626
-wx r-x -w-	352	011 101 010	110 010 101	625
-wx r-x -wx	353	011 101 011	110 010 100	624
-wx r-x r--	354	011 101 100	110 010 011	623
-wx r-x r-x	355	011 101 101	110 010 010	622
-wx r-x rw-	356	011 101 110	110 010 001	621
-wx r-x rwx	357	011 101 111	110 010 000	620
-wx rw- ---	360	011 110 000	110 001 111	617
-wx rw- --x	361	011 110 001	110 001 110	616
-wx rw- -w-	362	011 110 010	110 001 101	615
-wx rw- -wx	363	011 110 011	110 001 100	614
-wx rw- r--	364	011 110 100	110 001 011	613
-wx rw- r-x	365	011 110 101	110 001 010	612
-wx rw- rw-	366	011 110 110	110 001 001	611
-wx rw- rwx	367	011 110 111	110 001 000	610

(*Continued*)

Mask	Mask Octal	Mask Binary	Umask Binary	Umask Octal
-wx rwx ---	370	011 111 000	110 000 111	600
-wx rwx --x	371	011 111 001	110 000 110	606
-wx rwx -w-	372	011 111 010	110 000 101	605
-wx rwx -wx	373	011 111 011	110 000 100	604
-wx rwx r--	374	011 111 100	110 000 011	603
-wx rwx r-x	375	011 111 101	110 000 010	602
-wx rwx rw-	376	011 111 110	110 000 001	601
-wx rwx rwx	377	011 111 111	110 000 000	600
r-- --- ---	400	100 000 000	011 111 111	377
r-- --- --x	401	100 000 001	011 111 110	376
r-- --- -w-	402	100 000 010	011 111 101	375
r-- --- -wx	403	100 000 011	011 111 100	374
r-- --- r--	404	100 000 100	011 111 011	373
r-- --- r-x	405	100 000 101	011 111 010	372
r-- --- rw-	406	100 000 110	011 111 001	371
r-- --- rwx	407	100 000 111	011 111 000	370
r-- --x ---	410	100 001 000	011 110 111	367
r-- --x --x	411	100 001 001	011 110 110	366
r-- --x -w-	412	100 001 010	011 110 101	365
r-- --x -wx	413	100 001 011	011 110 100	364
r-- --x r--	414	100 001 100	011 110 011	363
r-- --x r-x	415	100 001 101	011 110 010	362
r-- --x rw-	416	100 001 110	011 110 001	361
r-- --x rwx	417	100 001 111	011 110 000	360
r-- -w- ---	420	100 010 000	011 101 111	357
r-- -w- --x	421	100 010 001	011 101 110	356
r-- -w- -w-	422	100 010 010	011 101 101	355
r-- -w- -wx	423	100 010 011	011 101 100	354
r-- -w- r--	424	100 010 100	011 101 011	353
r-- -w- r-x	425	100 010 101	011 101 010	352
r-- -w- rw-	426	100 010 110	011 101 001	351
r-- -w- rwx	427	100 010 111	011 101 000	350
r-- -wx ---	430	100 011 000	011 100 111	347

Mask	Mask Octal	Mask Binary	Umask Binary	Umask Octal
r-- -wx --x	431	100 011 001	011 100 110	346
r-- -wx -w-	432	100 011 010	011 100 101	345
r-- -wx -wx	433	100 011 011	011 100 100	344
r-- -wx r--	434	100 011 100	011 100 011	343
r-- -wx r-x	435	100 011 101	011 100 010	342
r-- -wx rw-	436	100 011 110	011 100 001	341
r-- -wx rwx	437	100 011 111	011 100 000	340
r-- r-- ---	440	100 100 000	011 011 111	337
r-- r-- --x	441	100 100 001	011 011 110	336
r-- r-- -w-	442	100 100 010	011 011 101	335
r-- r-- -wx	443	100 100 011	011 011 100	334
r-- r-- r--	444	100 100 100	011 011 011	333
r-- r-- r-x	445	100 100 101	011 011 010	332
r-- r-- rw-	446	100 100 110	011 011 001	331
r-- r-- rwx	447	100 100 111	011 011 000	330
r-- r-x ---	450	100 101 000	011 010 111	327
r-- r-x --x	451	100 101 001	011 010 110	326
r-- r-x -w-	452	100 101 010	011 010 101	325
r-- r-x -wx	453	100 101 011	011 010 100	324
r-- r-x r--	454	100 101 100	011 010 011	323
r-- r-x r-x	455	100 101 101	011 010 010	322
r-- r-x rw-	456	100 101 110	011 010 001	321
r-- r-x rwx	457	100 101 111	011 010 000	320
r-- rw- ---	460	100 110 000	011 001 111	317
r-- rw- --x	461	100 110 001	011 001 110	316
r-- rw- -w-	462	100 110 010	011 001 101	315
r-- rw- -wx	463	100 110 011	011 001 100	314
r-- rw- r--	464	100 110 100	011 001 011	313
r-- rw- r-x	465	100 110 101	011 001 010	312
r-- rw- rw-	466	100 110 110	011 001 001	311
r-- rw- rwx	467	100 110 111	011 001 000	310
r-- rwx ---	470	100 111 000	011 000 111	307
r-- rwx --x	471	100 111 001	011 000 110	306

(*Continued*)

Mask	Mask Octal	Mask Binary	Umask Binary	Umask Octal
r-- rwx -w-	472	100 111 010	011 000 101	305
r-- rwx -wx	473	100 111 011	011 000 100	304
r-- rwx r--	474	100 111 100	011 000 011	303
r-- rwx r-x	475	100 111 101	011 000 010	302
r-- rwx rw-	476	100 111 110	011 000 001	301
r-- rwx rwx	477	100 111 111	011 000 000	300
r-x --- ---	500	101 000 000	010 111 111	277
r-x --- --x	501	101 000 001	010 111 110	276
r-x --- -w-	502	101 000 010	010 111 101	275
r-x --- -wx	503	101 000 011	010 111 100	274
r-x --- r--	504	101 000 100	010 111 011	273
r-x --- r-x	505	101 000 101	010 111 010	272
r-x --- rw-	506	101 000 110	010 111 001	271
r-x --- rwx	507	101 000 111	010 111 000	270
r-x --x ---	510	101 001 000	010 110 111	267
r-x --x --x	511	101 001 001	010 110 110	266
r-x --x -w-	512	101 001 010	010 110 101	265
r-x --x -wx	513	101 001 011	010 110 100	264
r-x --x r--	514	101 001 100	010 110 011	263
r-x --x r-x	515	101 001 101	010 110 010	262
r-x --x rw-	516	101 001 110	010 110 001	261
r-x --x rwx	517	101 001 111	010 110 000	260
r-x -w- ---	520	101 010 000	010 101 111	257
r-x -w- --x	521	101 010 001	010 101 110	256
r-x -w- -w-	522	101 010 010	010 101 101	255
r-x -w- -wx	523	101 010 011	010 101 100	254
r-x -w- r--	524	101 010 100	010 101 011	253
r-x -w- r-x	525	101 010 101	010 101 010	252
r-x -w- rw-	526	101 010 110	010 101 001	251
r-x -w- rwx	527	101 010 111	010 101 000	250
r-x -wx ---	530	101 011 000	010 100 111	247
r-x -wx --x	531	101 011 001	010 100 110	246
r-x -wx -w-	532	101 011 010	010 100 101	245

Mask	Mask Octal	Mask Binary	Umask Binary	Umask Octal
r-x -wx -wx	533	101 011 011	010 100 100	244
r-x -wx r--	534	101 011 100	010 100 011	243
r-x -wx r-x	535	101 011 101	010 100 010	242
r-x -wx rw-	536	101 011 110	010 100 001	241
r-x -wx rwx	537	101 011 111	010 100 000	240
r-x r-- ---	540	101 100 000	010 011 111	237
r-x r-- --x	541	101 100 001	010 011 110	236
r-x r-- -w-	542	101 100 010	010 011 101	235
r-x r-- -wx	543	101 100 011	010 011 100	234
r-x r-- r--	544	101 100 100	010 011 011	233
r-x r-- r-x	545	101 100 101	010 011 010	232
r-x r-- rw-	546	101 100 110	010 011 001	231
r-x r-- rwx	547	101 100 111	010 011 000	230
r-x r-x ---	550	101 101 000	010 010 111	227
r-x r-x --x	551	101 101 001	010 010 110	226
r-x r-x -w-	552	101 101 010	010 010 101	225
r-x r-x -wx	553	101 101 011	010 010 100	224
r-x r-x r--	554	101 101 100	010 010 011	223
r-x r-x r-x	555	101 101 101	010 010 010	222
r-x r-x rw-	556	101 101 110	010 010 001	221
r-x r-x rwx	557	101 101 111	010 010 000	220
r-x r-x ---	560	101 110 000	010 001 111	217
r-x r-x --x	561	101 110 001	010 001 110	216
r-x r-x -w-	562	101 110 010	010 001 101	215
r-x r-x -wx	563	101 110 011	010 001 100	214
r-x r-x r--	564	101 110 100	010 001 011	213
r-x r-x r-x	565	101 110 101	010 001 010	212
r-x r-x rw-	566	101 110 110	010 001 001	211
r-x r-x rwx	567	101 110 111	010 001 000	210
r-x rwx ---	570	101 111 000	010 000 111	207
r-x rwx --x	571	101 111 001	010 000 110	206
r-x rwx -w-	572	101 111 010	010 000 101	205
r-x rwx -wx	573	101 111 011	010 000 100	204

(*Continued*)

Mask	Mask Octal	Mask Binary	Umask Binary	Umask Octal
r-x rwx r--	574	101 111 100	010 000 011	203
r-x rwx r-x	575	101 111 101	010 000 010	202
r-x rwx rw-	576	101 111 110	010 000 001	201
r-x rwx rwx	577	101 111 111	010 000 000	200
rw- --- ---	600	110 000 000	001 111 111	177
rw- --- --x	601	110 000 001	001 111 110	176
rw- --- -w-	602	110 000 010	001 111 101	175
rw- --- -wx	603	110 000 011	001 111 100	174
rw- --- r--	604	110 000 100	001 111 011	173
rw- --- r-x	605	110 000 101	001 111 010	172
rw- --- rw-	606	110 000 110	001 111 001	171
rw- --- rwx	607	110 000 111	001 111 000	100
rw- --x ---	610	110 001 000	001 110 111	167
rw- --x --x	611	110 001 001	001 110 110	166
rw- --x -w-	612	110 001 010	001 110 101	165
rw- --x -wx	613	110 001 011	001 110 100	164
rw- --x r--	614	110 001 100	001 110 011	163
rw- --x r-x	615	110 001 101	001 110 010	162
rw- --x rw-	616	110 001 110	001 110 001	161
rw- --x rwx	617	110 001 111	001 110 000	160
rw- -w- ---	620	110 010 000	001 101 111	157
rw- -w- --x	621	110 010 001	001 101 110	156
rw- -w- -w-	622	110 010 010	001 101 101	155
rw- -w- -wx	623	110 010 011	001 101 100	154
rw- -w- r--	624	110 010 100	001 101 011	153
rw- -w- r-x	625	110 010 101	001 101 010	152
rw- -w- rw-	626	110 010 110	001 101 001	151
rw- -w- rwx	627	110 010 111	001 101 000	150
rw- -wx ---	630	110 011 000	001 100 111	147
rw- -wx --x	631	110 011 001	001 100 110	146
rw- -wx -w-	632	110 011 010	001 100 101	145
rw- -wx -wx	633	110 011 011	001 100 100	144
rw- -wx r--	634	110 011 100	001 100 011	143

Mask	Mask Octal	Mask Binary	Umask Binary	Umask Octal
rw- -wx r-x	635	110 011 101	001 100 010	142
rw- -wx rw-	636	110 011 110	001 100 001	141
rw- -wx rwx	637	110 011 111	001 100 000	140
rw- r-- ---	640	110 100 000	001 011 111	137
rw- r-- --x	641	110 100 001	001 011 110	136
rw- r-- -w-	642	110 100 010	001 011 101	135
rw- r-- -wx	643	110 100 011	001 011 100	134
rw- r-- r--	644	110 100 100	001 011 011	133
rw- r-- r-x	645	110 100 101	001 011 010	132
rw- r-- rw-	646	110 100 110	001 011 001	131
rw- r-- rwx	647	110 100 111	001 011 000	130
rw- r-x ---	650	110 101 000	001 010 111	127
rw- r-x --x	651	110 101 001	001 010 110	126
rw- r-x -w-	652	110 101 010	001 010 101	125
rw- r-x -wx	653	110 101 011	001 010 100	124
rw- r-x r--	654	110 101 100	001 010 011	123
rw- r-x r-x	655	110 101 101	001 010 010	122
rw- r-x rw-	656	110 101 110	001 010 001	121
rw- r-x rwx	657	110 101 111	001 010 000	120
rw- rw- ---	660	110 110 000	001 001 111	117
rw- rw- --x	661	110 110 001	001 001 110	116
rw- rw- -w-	662	110 110 010	001 001 101	115
rw- rw- -wx	663	110 110 011	001 001 100	114
rw- rw- r--	664	110 110 100	001 001 011	113
rw- rw- r-x	665	110 110 101	001 001 010	112
rw- rw- rw-	666	110 110 110	001 001 001	111
rw- rw- rwx	667	110 110 111	001 001 000	110
rw- rwx ---	670	110 111 000	001 000 111	107
rw- rwx --x	671	110 111 001	001 000 110	106
rw- rwx -w-	672	110 111 010	001 000 101	105
rw- rwx -wx	673	110 111 011	001 000 100	104
rw- rwx r--	674	110 111 100	001 000 011	103
rw- rwx r-x	675	110 111 101	001 000 010	102

(*Continued*)

Mask	Mask Octal	Mask Binary	Umask Binary	Umask Octal
rw- rwx rw-	676	110 111 110	001 000 001	101
rw- rwx rwx	677	110 111 111	001 000 000	100
rwx --- ---	700	111 000 000	000 111 111	077
rwx --- --x	701	111 000 001	000 111 110	076
rwx --- -w-	702	111 000 010	000 111 101	075
rwx --- -wx	703	111 000 011	000 111 100	074
rwx --- r--	704	111 000 100	000 111 011	073
rwx --- r-x	705	111 000 101	000 111 010	072
rwx --- rw-	706	111 000 110	000 111 001	071
rwx --- rwx	707	111 000 111	000 111 000	070
rwx --x ---	710	111 001 000	000 110 111	067
rwx --x --x	711	111 001 001	000 110 110	066
rwx --x -w-	712	111 001 010	000 110 101	065
rwx --x -wx	713	111 001 011	000 110 100	064
rwx --x r--	714	111 001 100	000 110 011	063
rwx --x r-x	715	111 001 101	000 110 010	062
rwx --x rw-	716	111 001 110	000 110 001	061
rwx --x rwx	717	111 001 111	000 110 000	060
rwx -w- ---	720	111 010 000	000 101 111	057
rwx -w- --x	721	111 010 001	000 101 110	056
rwx -w- -w-	722	111 010 010	000 101 101	055
rwx -w- -wx	723	111 010 011	000 101 100	054
rwx -w- r--	724	111 010 100	000 101 011	053
rwx -w- r-x	725	111 010 101	000 101 010	052
rwx -w- rw-	726	111 010 110	000 101 001	051
rwx -w- rwx	727	111 010 111	000 101 000	050
rwx -wx ---	730	111 011 000	000 100 111	047
rwx -wx --x	731	111 011 001	000 100 110	046
rwx -wx -w-	732	111 011 010	000 100 101	045
rwx -wx -wx	733	111 011 011	000 100 100	044
rwx -wx r--	734	111 011 100	000 100 011	043
rwx -wx r-x	735	111 011 101	000 100 010	042
rwx -wx rw-	736	111 011 110	000 100 001	041

Mask	Mask Octal	Mask Binary	Umask Binary	Umask Octal
rwx -wx rwx	737	111 011 111	000 100 000	040
rwx r-- ---	740	111 100 000	000 011 111	037
rwx r-- --x	741	111 100 001	000 011 110	036
rwx r-- -w-	742	111 100 010	000 011 101	035
rwx r-- -wx	743	111 100 011	000 011 100	034
rwx r-- r--	744	111 100 100	000 011 011	033
rwx r-- r-x	745	111 100 101	000 011 010	032
rwx r-- rw-	746	111 100 110	000 011 001	031
rwx r-- rwx	747	111 100 111	000 011 000	030
rwx r-x ---	750	111 101 000	000 010 111	027
rwx r-x --x	751	111 101 001	000 010 110	026
rwx r-x -w-	752	111 101 010	000 010 101	025
rwx r-x -wx	753	111 101 011	000 010 100	024
rwx r-x r--	754	111 101 100	000 010 011	023
rwx r-x r-x	755	111 101 101	000 010 010	022
rwx r-x rw-	756	111 101 110	000 010 001	021
rwx r-x rwx	757	111 101 111	000 010 000	020
rwx rw- ---	760	111 110 000	000 001 111	017
rwx rw- --x	761	111 110 001	000 001 110	016
rwx rw- -w-	762	111 110 010	000 001 101	015
rwx rw- -wx	763	111 110 011	000 001 100	014
rwx rw- r--	764	111 110 100	000 001 011	013
rwx rw- r-x	765	111 110 101	000 001 010	012
rwx rw- rw-	766	111 110 110	000 001 001	011
rwx rw- rwx	767	111 110 111	000 001 000	010
rwx rwx ---	770	111 111 000	000 000 111	007
rwx rwx --x	771	111 111 001	000 000 110	006
rwx rwx -w-	772	111 111 010	000 000 101	005
rwx rwx -wx	773	111 111 011	000 000 100	004
rwx rwx r--	774	111 111 100	000 000 011	003
rwx rwx r-x	775	111 111 101	000 000 010	002
rwx rwx rw-	776	111 111 110	000 000 001	001
rwx rwx rwx	777	111 111 111	000 000 000	000

C

Gathering the Audit Information

The following series of commands and examples demonstrate how to gather information to complete the discovery of information from an HP NonStop Server.

3P-POLICY-QUERY-01   Use a third-party tool to gather and query information about the HP NonStop Server Security.

Legend

Syntax:
Command syntax.

Examples:
Examples will generally follow a Syntax heading.

Output:
Output generated from the examples will be displayed in a shaded outlined box. "←" denotes items of interest.

```
SYSINFO - T9268D37 - (27 Nov 97) SYSTEM \SYDNEY Date 23 Apr 2003, 16:46:21
COPYRIGHT TANDEM COMPUTERS INCORPORATED 1985, 1987-1997
System name            \SYDNEY
EXPAND node number     111
Current SYSnn          SYS01
System number          44301                              ←
Software release ID    G06.18
```

Guardian Wildcarding

These wildcard characters can be used to match characters anywhere in a process name, filename, subvolume, or volume name (but not a node name):

* The asterisk matches zero to eight characters.

? The question mark matches a single character.

More than one wildcard can be used in the same command. *If a wildcard is used in the volume name, a dollar sign must be included.*

Wildcards cannot be used to match the dots (.) that separate the elements of a filename string (system.volume.subvolume.file name).

Example 1:

`FILES $SYSTEM.SYS*`

Example 1 lists all the files in every subvolume on the $SYSTEM disk whose subvolume name begins with the letters SYS.

Example 2:

`FILEINFO $DATA*.MN?.*`

Example 2 lists all files that reside in the subvolume that has a three-character name beginning with MN on volumes beginning with $DATA.

Example 3:

`FILEINFO $DATA*.MN?.CASH*`

Example 3 lists all files with names beginning with CASH that reside in the subvolume that has a three-character name beginning with MN on volumes beginning with $DATA.

Example 4:

`FILEINFO $DA??01.SAFE*.A00*`

Example 4 lists all files with names beginning with A00 that reside in the sub-volume with a name beginning with SAFE on all volumes with six-character names starting with DA and ending with 01.

OSS Wildcarding and Metacharacters

If you have spent any time on NonStop Servers, you are already familiar with the metacharacters asterisk (*) and question mark (?). When used in PURGE, FILEINFO, FUP, SAFECOM, and many others, these characters have special meaning as wildcards:

    * = zero or more characters

    ? = a single character

The use of metacharacters such as this are much more prevalent in UNIX, hence OSS, than in the Guardian world. While a complete explanation of all the metacharacters and their uses is beyond the scope of this book, the following tables list of some of the more common.

Figure C.1
Filename and path wildcard characters.

Character	Description
/	Separates the parts of a file's pathname
?	Matches any single character except a dot
*	Matches 0 or any number of repetitions of the previous pattern
.	Matches any character
[ ]	Matches any *single character* within the brackets
( )	Matches any of the *strings* enclosed within the parentheses
		Separates the strings within the parentheses
~	Specifies the home directory when used at the beginning of a filename

Figure C.2
Quotation or "escape characters."

\	Specifies that the following character should be interpreted literally rather than as a metacharacter
'...'	Characters within the quote marks, except single quotes, including $, and /, are treated as a literal string
"..."	Any characters within the quote marks, except $, and \, are treated as a literal string

Figure C.3	<	Redirects input
Directing input/	>	Redirects output to a specified file
output.	<<	Redirects input and specifies that the shell should read input up to a specified line
	>>	Redirects output to the end of a specified file

Figure C.4	|	Separates commands that are part of a pipeline
Metacharacters	&&	Runs the next command if the current one succeeds
used in commands.	||	Runs the next command if the current command fails
	;	Separates commands that should be executed sequentially
	::	Separates elements of a case context
	&	Runs commands in the background
	( )	Groups commands to run as a separate process in a subshell
	{ }	Groups commands without creating a subshell

OSS Commands

Commands generally take the form of:

```
<cmd name> <options> < file list>
```

Example 5:

```
ls -l *
```

In Example 5, the **ls** command list files, the -l option specifies the long format, and the asterisk includes all files in the current subdirectory (except the hidden files that begin with a dot (.).

Figure C.5	Guardian Command	Description	OSS Command Equivalent
Cross reference	ALTPRI	Changes priority of process	
of Guardian	ASSIGN	Assigns physical filename to logical name	
commands to OSS	COMPUTE	Displays value of expression	bc
commands.	CREATE	Creates unstructured file	cat > filename
	DEFAULT	Changes logon default settings	[env, umask]

(Continued)

Figure C.5 (*Continued*)

Guardian Command	Description	OSS Command Equivalent
DSAP	Displays use of space on disk volume	du
EDIT TEDIT	Editor	vi ed
ENV	Displays environmental params	env
EXIT	Stops current shell	exit
FC	Processes command history list	fc
FILEINFO	Displays file information	[file, ls -al]
FILENAMES	Displays filenames using template	ls, find
FILES	Displays names in a subvolume	ls, find
FUP COPY	Record-by-record copy jes of a file (or append)	cp
FUP DUP	Creates file and copies block-by-block	cp
FUP GIVE	Changes owner of file	chown
FUP PURGE	Deletes a file	rm
RENAME FUP RENAME	Renames a file	mv
FUP SECURE	Changes the file access security	chmod
HELP	Provides information about command interpreter	man
HISTORY	Displays previously issued commands	fc
HOME	Specifies where command interpreter looks for VARs	env
INFO DEFINE	Displays attributes of current command interpreter process	info_define *
LOGOFF	Log off system	exit
PARAM	Parameter to process	set,export
PAUSE	Causes command interpreter to wait for prompting	
PERUSE SPOOLCOM	Monitors and changes spooler jobs	lpstat
PMSEARCH	Defines program/macro search path	env, .profile
PPD	Displays names, IDs, and ancestors of processes	ps

Figure C.5 (*Continued*)

Guardian Command	Description	OSS Command Equivalent
PURGE	Deletes a disk file	`rm`
RUN	Executes a program	`run`
SETPROMPT	Changes command interpreter prompt	`env, .profile`
SHOW	Displays attribute values set with SET command	`set`
SHOW DEFINE	Displays working attribute set	`show_define *`
STATUS	Displays status of running processes	`ps`
STOP	Stops and deletes a process	`kill`
SUSPEND	Prevents process from running until reactivated	`^Z, kill`
SYSTEM	Sets the default system	`cd`
TACL	Starts command interpreter process	`sh`
TIME	Displays date and time	`date`
USERS	Displays attributes of users and groups	`logname, who, id, env, umask`
VOLUME	Temporarily changes the default volume, subvol, security	`cd, chmod`
VPROC	Displays product version information	`vproc *`
WHO	Displays information about the current TACL process	`id, tty, env`
!	Reexecutes previous command line	`r, fc`
?	Displays previous command line	`fc, history`

The **man** command in OSS is short for "manual." It is an online help system. To display syntax and other information about a command, type:

Syntax

```
man <command or topic>
```

Example 6:

```
man su
```

Example 6 would display the **man** pages on the **su** command.

The output from **man** can be printed out by piping it to a printer.

Syntax:
```
man <command or topic> | lp -d <printer name>
```
Example 7:
```
man sshd_config | lp -d hp1
```
Example 7 would send the **man** pages on the **sshd_config** file to printer hp1.

Anyone new to OSS and/or the UNIX environment should familiarize themselves with the **man** pages about the **sh** (shell) command.

Pipes and Filters

A pipe directs the output of one command to another command rather than to a file. The | symbol is used for piping.

Example 8:
```
ls -l * | sort
```
Example 8 lists the contents of the present subdirectory and **pipes** the output to the **sort** command.

Redirection

Redirection directs the input or output to or from files, unlike a pipe, which directs the output of one command to another command. The >, < and >> symbols are used for redirection:

< filename	Accepts the specified file as input
> filename	Sends the output to the specified file
>> filename	Uses filename as output; it appends to the file if it already exists

Examining Text Files

This section provides examples for viewing the contents of text files.

Guardian FUP COPY Command

You must have READ access to the file you wish to view.

Syntax:
```
FUP COPY $<volume>.<subvolume>.<filename>
```

Example 9:

FUP COPY $VABC.BRADY.TACLCSTM

```
?TACL MACRO
== TACL created this file for your protection.
setprompt both
ATTACHSEG SHARED $system.sjutacl.TACLSEG :sjuSEG
#set #uselist :sjuseg [#uselist]
#set #pmsearchlist [#pmsearchlist] $system.sjuobj
#set #pmsearchlist [#pmsearchlist] $system.p05probj
[#if [#fileinfo/existence/ $system.p05prop.taclcstm] |then|
   run $system.p05prop.taclcstm
]
```

Example 9 displays the contents of the user's TACLCSTM file.

OSS cat Command

The **cat** command can be used to display the contents of a text file without any risk of altering the file. You must have READ access to the file you wish to view.

Syntax:

cat <filename>

Example 10:

cat /etc/profile

```
# /bin/unsupported removed from PATH
# Note: /usr/ucb contains the OSS ftp client
alias status="gtacl -c 'status ' "
alias peruse="gtacl -p peruse "
alias spoolcom="gtacl -p spoolcom "
alias files="ls -al "
alias purge="rm -i "
alias info="ls -al "
alias whoson="ps -oruser -otty * "
alias fup="gtacl -p fup "
alias safecom="gtacl -p safecom "
alias scf="gtacl -p scf "
alias opencmon="gtacl -p opencmon "
alias tacl="gtacl "
export PATH=/bin:/usr/bin:/usr/local/bin:/usr/ucb
# Note: /usr/ucb contains the OSS ftp client
alias status="gtacl -c 'status ' "
alias peruse="gtacl -p peruse "
alias spoolcom="gtacl -p spoolcom "
alias files="ls -al "
alias purge="rm -i "
alias info="ls -al "
alias whoson="ps -oruser -otty * "
alias fup="gtacl -p fup "
```

```
alias safecom="gtacl -p safecom "
alias scf="gtacl -p scf "
alias opencmon="gtacl -p opencmon "
alias tacl="gtacl "
export PATH=/bin:/usr/bin:/usr/local/bin:/usr/ucb
export JREHOME=/usr/tandem/nssjava/jdk142_v20/jre
export JAVA_HOME=/usr/tandem/nssjava/jdk142_v20
export CLASSPATH=/usr/tandem/jdbcMx/current/lib/jdbcMx.jar
export TERM=vt100
export HOME=$HOME
cd $HOME
```

Example 10 displays the contents of the **/etc/profile** file.

CTOEDIT and EDITTOC Programs

Those not familiar with the **vi** or other UNIX-like editors can use the CTO-EDIT and EDITTOC commands to edit files for the OSS environment.

To use EDITTOC, you must first:

1. Copy (**mv**) the file to a Guardian subvolume.
2. Use the CTOEDIT program to convert the file to the Guardian format.

If you want to return the edited file to the OSS environment, you must first:

1. Use the CTOEDIT program to convert the file back to the OSS format.
2. Move the file to an OSS directory.

This is cumbersome, but can be temporarily useful while administrators are becoming familiar with the **vi** editor.

<u>Syntax:</u>
CTOEDIT fromfile, tofile

<u>Example 11:</u>
CTOEDIT $dataa.oss.info, $dataa.oss.infoedit

AP–ADVICE–EDITTOC–01 Great care should be taken not to alter the contents of the various OSS configuration files. Because the security or audit staff are generally not responsible for maintaining the files in question, they should probably not return the file to the OSS environment.

Gathering File Information

This section provides examples for viewing information about files.

Guardian FILEINFO Command

The FILEINFO command lists information about one or more files. Use this command to discover the location of files, their owners, and their Guardian security string.

<u>Syntax:</u>

```
FILEINFO <filename>
```

<u>Example 12:</u>

```
FILEINFO $SYSTEM.SYS*.OSMON
```

```
$SYSTEM.SYS00
                CODE     EOF    LAST  MODIFIED  OWNER      RWEP      PExt   SExt
OSMON      O     700  477512 16 APR2001 10:16  255,255    NUNU        32     32
$SYSTEM.SYS06
                CODE     EOF    LAST  MODIFIED  OWNER      RWEP      PExt   SExt
OSMON            700  477512  16APR2001  10:16  255,255    NUNU        32     32
```

Example 12 displays all the OSMON object files in any $SYSTEM.SYSnn subvolume.

<u>Example 13:</u>

```
FILEINFO $*.*.APPDEV
```

```
$SYSTEM.APPDEV
                CODE      EOF    LAST    MODIFIED    OWNER    RWEP    PExt    SExt
APPDEV  O        100  4763648  24JUN2001  21:51    255,255   UUUU     278      64
```

Example 13 displays the APPDEV object file found on any volume or subvolume.

The file listing can be sent to a file or the spooler.

<u>Example 14:</u>

```
FILEINFO /OUT $USER.BRIAN.SAFELIST/ $*.DATA*.A*
```

Example 14 sends the listing to a file called SAFELIST in the $USER.BRIAN subvolume. If the file already exists, the listing will be appended to the file.

Example 15:
`FILEINFO /OUT $S.#WIRELST/ $AUDIT*.WIRE.*`
Example 15 sends the listing to the SPOOLER location $S.#WIRELST.

OSS ls Commands

The examples shown are executed from the Guardian environment and, therefore, use the OSH command. The same **ls** commands can be issued in the OSS environment. Just leave off the "osh" and the quote marks shown in the examples.

The **ls** command without any options creates a "short list" of the files in a directory. It is the equivalent of the Guardian FILES command.

Syntax:
`ls`

Example 16:
`osh -c " ls /$HOME "`

```
1> osh -c "ls /$HOME"
afile               file2           nhac            nxpc
dirlist             myfile          nhaccopy        tlh
```

Example 16 displays the "short" list of files in the user's $HOME directory.

Adding the -l option to the ls command displays the "long" listing. **ls -l** is the equivalent of the Guardian FILEINFO command. The listing shows:

the security or permission string

the owner and group

the date the file was created

the type of file

if the file is symbolically linked, the underlying file

The file types are:

"d" = directory
"l" = link
"-" = Regular file

Example 17:

`osh -c " ls -l /usr/bin "`

```
-r-xr-xr-x 1  SUPER.SUPER  SUPER   249408 Jul 12  2004  ar
-r-xr-xr-x 1  SUPER.SUPER  SUPER   254328 Feb 9   2005  c89
lrwxrwxrwx 1  SUPER.SUPER  SUPER        8 Nov 14  2003  cut -> /bin/cut
lrwxrwxrwx 1  SUPER.SUPER  SUPER        8 Nov 14  2003  env -> /bin/env
lrwxrwxrwx 1  SUPER.SUPER  SUPER       11 Nov 14  2003  expand-> /bin/exd
lrwxrwxrwx 1  SUPER.SUPER  SUPER        9 Nov 14  2003  grep -> /bin/grep
lrwxrwxrwx 1  SUPER.SUPER  SUPER        7 Nov 14  2003  id -> /bin/id
-r-xr-xr-x 1  SUPER.SUPER  SUPER  5872912 Jan 23  2005  ld
```

In Example 17, there are five linked files: **cut**, **env**, **expand**, **grep**, and **id**. Their underlying files are displayed. **ar, c89**, and **ld** are regular files.

Adding the option **–a** to the **ls** command displays any hidden files. Hidden files are generally referred to as "dot files" because they are preceded by a dot (.).

Example 18:

`osh -c " ls -a /$HOME "`

```
.                    .sh_history      myfile          nxpc
..                   afile            nhac            tlh
.profile             file2            nhaccopy
```

Example 18 displays the short listing with the "dot files," **.sh.history** and **.profile**.

Use both the -a and -l options to display information about all the files in the directory, including the dot files.

Example 19:

`osh -c " ls -al "`

```
drwxrwxrwx 1  SUPER.SUPER    SUPER   4096 Nov 29  11:58  .
drwxr-xr-x 1  SUPER.SUPER    SUPER   4096 Feb 16  09:22  ..
-rwxrwxrwx 1  SEC.BRYAN      BANKX    490 Nov 29  13:44  .profile
-rw------- 1  BANK.OSSBRYAN  BANKX   3406 Mar 29  15:54  .sh_history
-rw-rw-rw- 1  BANK.OSSBRYAN  BANKX     56 Oct 28  14:19  afile
-rw-r--r-- 1  BANK.OSSBRYAN  BANKX     26 Oct 28  14:20  file2
-rw-rw-rw- 1  BANK.OSSBRYAN  BANKX     22 Jun 20  2005   myfile
-rwxrwxrwx 1  BANK.OSSBRYAN  BANKX    372 Jun 21  2005   nhac
-rwxrwxrwx 1  BANK.OSSBRYAN  BANKX    376 Jun 21  2005   nhaccopy
-rwxrwxrwx 1  BANK.OSSBRYAN  BANKX    379 Jun 22  2005   nxpc
drwxrwx--- 1  BANK.OSSBRYAN  BANKX   4096 Aug 16  2004   tlh
```

Example 19 displays the long listing, including the "dot files" and the . (dot) and .. (dot dot) directories.

Adding the option **-F** (upper case) to the **ls** command changes the display to indicate file type:

/ = directory

* = executable

Example 20:
```
OSH -C " ls -aF /$HOME "
```

```
afile           myfile          nhaccopy*       abc/
file2           nhac*           nxpc*
```

Example 20 displays the short listing. **nhac**, **nhaccopy**, and **nxpc** are all executable files. **abc/** is a directory.

Example 21:
```
osh -c " ls -alF /$HOME "
```

```
drwxrwxrwx 1 SUPER.SUPER     SUPER    4096    Nov 29 11:58 ./
drwxr-xr-x 1 SUPER.SUPER     SUPER    4096    Feb 16 09:22 ../
-rwxrwxrwx 1 XYPRO.TERRI     BANKX     490    Nov 29 13:44 .profile*
-rw------- 1 BANK.OSSBRYAN   BANKX    3432    Mar 29 16:00 .sh_history
-rw-rw-rw- 1 BANK.OSSBRYAN   BANKX      56    Oct 28 14:19 afile
-rw-r--r-- 1 BANK.OSSBRYAN   BANKX      26    Oct 28 14:20 file2
-rw-rw-rw- 1 BANK.OSSBRYAN   BANKX      22    Jun 20  2005 myfile
-rwxrwxrwx 1 BANK.OSSBRYAN   BANKX     372    Jun 21  2005 nhac*
-rwxrwxrwx 1 BANK.OSSBRYAN   BANKX     376    Jun 21  2005 nhaccopy*
-rwxrwxrwx 1 BANK.OSSBRYAN   BANKX     379    Jun 22  2005 nxpc*
drwxrwx--- 1 BANK.OSSBRYAN   BANKX    4096    Aug 16  2004 abc/
```

Example 21 displays the long list with both the -a and -F options.

Redirection

Save the **ls** results to a file and then view the file with the editor of choice. Example 22 is performed within the OSS environment. Example 8 is performed in the Guardian environment via OSH.

Syntax:
```
ls -al > <filename>
```
Example 22:
```
ls -al > dirlist
```

```
total 35
drwxrwxrwx 1 SUPER.SUPER      SUPER  4096   Mar 29 16:16 .
drwxr-xr-x 1 SUPER.SUPER      SUPER  4096   Feb 16 09:22 ..
-rwxrwxrwx 1 BANKX.TERRI      BANKX   490   Nov 29 13:44 .profile
-rw------- 1 BANKX.OSSTERRI   BANKX  3482   Mar 29 16:16 .sh_history
-rw-rw-rw- 1 BANKX.OSSTERRI   BANKX    56   Oct 28 14:19 afile
-rw-rw-rw- 1 BANKX.OSSTERRI   BANKX     0   Mar 29 16:16 dirlist
-rw-r--r-- 1 BANKX.OSSTERRI   BANKX    26   Oct 28 14:20 file2
-rw-rw-rw- 1 BANKX.OSSTERRI   BANKX    22   Jun 20  2005 myfile
-rwxrwxrwx 1 BANKX.OSSTERRI   BANKX   372   Jun 21  2005 nhac
-rwxrwxrwx 1 BANKX.OSSTERRI   BANKX   376   Jun 21  2005 nhaccopy
-rwxrwxrwx 1 BANKX.OSSTERRI   BANKX   379   Jun 22  2005 nxpc
drwxrwx--- 1 BANKX.OSSTERRI   BANKX  4096   Aug 16  2004 tlh
```

Example 22 sends the long listing of the current directory to a file called **dirlist**. The **dirlist** file can then be displayed using the **cat** command.

Append new information to an existing file by using the **>>** option.

Example 23:
osh -c " ls -l /usr/local/etc >/G/data/oss/info "

```
> fileinfo $dataa.oss.info

$DATAA.OSS

            CODE      EOF      LAST    MODIFIED  OWNER    RWEP   PExt SExt
INFO         180     1455   24MAR2006   10:40   222,205   CCCC      2  112
```

Example 23 puts the file containing the listing into the Guardian space. Use CTOEDIT to convert the file to Guardian format.

The listing can be sent to a printer.

Guardian FUP (File Utility Program) Commands

FUP is designed to manage disk files on the HP NonStop system. Use FUP to create, display, and duplicate files, load data into files, alter file characteristics, and purge files.

The FUP INFO command displays the basic file attributes.

The listing shows:

> the file code
> the file size
> the date the file was last altered

the owner

the security string

<u>**Syntax:**</u>

FUP INFO

<u>**Example 25:**</u>

FUP INFO $DATA01.TEMP.CATDEL

```
                CODE    EOF    LAST     MODIF    OWNER   RWEP   TYPE  REC  BL
$DATA01.TEMP
  CATDEL        101     8312   4Feb2002 09:11    222,11  CCCC
```

Example 25 displays the basic file attributes of $DATA01.TEMP.CATDEL.

Use the INFO DETAIL command to display more attributes of a file.

<u>**Example 26:**</u>

FUP INFO $DATA01.TEMP.CATDEL, DETAIL

```
$DATA01.TEMP.CATDEL                  30 Jun 2003, 8:49
 ENSCRIBE
 TYPE U
 FORMAT 1
 CODE 101
 EXT ( 4 PAGES, 28 PAGES )
 MAXEXTENTS 978
 BUFFERSIZE 4096
 OWNER 222,11
 SECURITY (RWEP): CCCC
 DATA MODIF: 4 Feb 2002, 9:11
 CREATION DATE: 9 Apr 2003, 11:13
 LAST OPEN: 9 May 2003, 11:24
 FILE LABEL: 158 (3.8% USED)
 EOF: 8312 (0.0% USED)
 EXTENTS ALLOCATED: 2
```

Example 26 shows all the attributes of the $DATA01.TEMP.CATDEL file.

Gathering ODBC/MP Information

This section provides examples for viewing information about the ODBC configuration.

NOSCOM is the command interpreter for ODBC. It is used to configure the subsystem and manage Alias-names.

Examining What Ports ODBC Is Using

Use NOSCOM to examine the ODBC configuration:

1. Start NOSCOM
2. Perform queries

Use the INFO NET_SERVICE command to obtain a list of all the network definitions.

Note that it is possible to assign a SERVICES file other than the default file located in $SYSTEM.ZTCPIP. If you don't find an entry for ODBC, you may need to do a FILENAME or FILEINFO command to locate all the SERVICES files present on the system.

Use the FUP COPY command to view the contents of the SERVICES file.

Syntax:

NOSCOM

Example 27:

NOSCOM> INFO NET_SERVICE *

```
SCS_NAME:                \PROD1.$NSOAD
NET_PROTOCOL:            TCP/IP
NET_NAME:                NSOADMIN ← The name used in the SERVICES file
SERVICES_FILENAME:
IOP PROCESSNAME:         \PROD1.$ZTCP2
SO_KEEPALIVE:            1
SO_OOBINLINE:            1
SO_LINGER:
SO_REUSEADDR:            1
LAST_UPDATED:            2005-02-02:09:31:33.341413
```

Example 27 shows the SCS name (\PROD1.$NSOAD) and the associated SERVERCLASS name (NET_NAME NSOAMIN). A corresponding NET_NAME entry will exist in the SERVICES file.

Mapping Logical-usernames to ODBC Alias-names

Use the INFO USERS command to see the map of Logical-usernames to Guardian userids.

Example 28:

NOSCOM> INFO USER *

```
NOSCOM>info user *
NSODBC_USERNAME:      KELLY

NSODBC_UID:           56841
G_USERNAME:           BANK.KELLY
LAST_UPDATED:         2005-08-25:10:13:49.115272

NSODBC_USERNAME:      ANONYMOUS
NSODBC_UID:           0
G_USERNAME:           NULL.NULL
LAST_UPDATED:         2005-02-01:11:13:30.540381

NSODBC_USERNAME:      NSODBC_USERBNAME
NSODBC_UID:           57031
G_USERNAME:           BANK.RON
LAST_UPDATED:         2006-02-07:09:27:16.284933

NSODBC_USERNAME:      JORDAN
NSODBC_UID:           57082
G_USERNAME:           BANK.JORDAN
LAST_UPDATED:         2005-08-12:10:56:32.400600
```

Example 28 shows four Alias-names and their respective Guardian User Names.

Use the INFO ALIAS command to see the map of ODBC Alias-names to Logical-usernames and Profiles.

Example 29:

NOSCOM> INFO ALIAS *

```
NOS_ALIASNAME:                KELLY
NOS_USERNAME:                 KELLY

PROFILE:                      LICPROF                    ←

CHANGE_PASSWORD_OPTION: 0
LAST_UPDATED:        2006-03-02:14:41:04.372634

NOS_ALIASNAME:                ANONYMOUS
NOS_USERNAME:                 ANONYMOUS
PROFILE:                      ANONYMOUSPROF
CHANGE_PASSWORD_OPTION: 0
LAST_UPDATED:        2005-02-01:11:13:30.724335

NOS_ALIASNAME:                NSOADMIN
NOS_USERNAME:                 DBO
PROFILE:                      NSOADMINPROF
CHANGE_PASSWORD_OPTION: 0
LAST_UPDATED:        2005-02-01:11:12:59.837693

NOS_ALIASNAME:                NSODBC_USERBNAME
NOS_USERNAME:                 NSODBC_USERBNAME

PROFILE:                      LICPROF                    ←
CHANGE_PASSWORD_OPTION: 0
LAST_UPDATED:                 2006-02-07:09:27:16.489429
```

```
NOS_ALIASNAME:              JORDAN
NOS_USERNAME:               JORDAN
PROFILE:                    LICPROF                        ←
CHANGE_PASSWORD_OPTION: 0
LAST_UPDATED:               2005-08-12:10:56:32.654635
```

Example 29 shows five ODBC Alias-names, their Logical-usernames, and their profiles. Note that KELLY, NSODBC_USERNAME, and JORDAN all share the LICPROF profile.

Examining the Trace Configuration

Use NOSCOM to verify the record exists in the TRACE Table. Then examine each TRA_NAME record for the following values:

LOG_TO_HOMETERM

INPUT_STREAM

OUTPUT_STREAM

NSSQL

TRA_ERROR

CACHE_STATISTICS

SP_WRITE

SP_READ

SYNTAX:
NOSCOM> INFO TRACE <TRA_NAME>

Example 30:
NOSCOM> INFO TRACE trace1

```
TRACE_NAME: TRACE1
TRACE_LOGTABLE: DSMSCM_SQL.SUPER_SUPER.TRACE1
LEVEL:
LOG_TO_HOMETERM: N
INPUT_STREAM: N
OUTPUT_STREAM: N
NSSQL: N
TRA_ERROR: N
CACHE_STATISTICS: Y
SP_WRITE: Y          ←
SP_READ: N           ←
LAST_UPDATED: 2006-05-17:14:43:29.712001
```

Example 30 shows the settings in the Trace Table for TRA_NAME trace1. Note that WRITE messages sent between the NonStop ODBC Server and the Pathway server via a stored procedure will be traced but READ statements will not.

Use the INFO PROFILE command to display the parameters of each profile.

Examining ODBC Profiles

Use the INFO PROFILE command to display the parameters of each profile.

Example 31:

NOSCOM> INFO PROFILE NSOADMINPROF

```
PROFILE_NAME:                    LICPROF
DEFAULT_DATABASE:                XYS7000_DATAA_XPLPRDAT          ←
DEFAULT_SCHEMA:
DEFAULT_LOCATION:                $DATA1.LICAPP                   ←
DEFAULT_SECURITY:                NCCU                            ←
TRA_MODE_ON:                     Y                               ←
TRA_NAME:                        TRACE1                          ←
ACC_MODE_ON:                     Y                               ←
ACC_LOGTABLE_NAME:               MASTER.DBO.MASTER               ←
ACC_LEVEL:                       SQL_STATEMENT
GOV_MODE_ON:                     N
GOV_NAME:
QST_MODE_ON:                     N
SQL_ACCESS_MODE:                 RW                              ←
SQL_CURSOR_MODE:                 RW                              ←
SQL_DIALECT:                     TDM_CORE
SQL_MAX_STATEMENT_CACHE:         0
SQL_TXN_ISOLATION:               1
SQL_UNSUPPORTED:                 E
OBJ_NAME_CACHE:                  Y
STMT_CACHE_LEVEL:                1
CON_MODE_ON:                     N
CON_NAME:
CLOSE_TABLES_PER_SESSION:        N
LAST_UPDATED:                    2005-03-22:11:24:07.150292
```

Example 31 shows the configuration of the LICPROF profile. Resource accounting is the audit method assigned to this profile. Because is set to SQL_STATEMENT, each SQL statement issued will be written to the MASTER.DBO.MASTER log table.

Note that because TRA_MOD_ON is set to Y(es), tracing will also be performed. What will be traced is determined by the information in the Trace Table as show in Example 30.

Gathering OSS Fileset Information

Use the SCF INFO command to verify that the OSSMON process is named $ZPMON:

1. Start SCF

2. Perform queries

SCF Syntax:

`SCF`

Example 32:

`->INFO PROCESS $ZPMON`

```
MgrName      *IOTimeout   *FsckCPU      *ZOSSVol   *Report    *AutoStart
$ZPMON           60          -1         $SYSTEM               MANUAL
```

Example 31 displays information about the $ZPMON process.

To see all the filesets on the system, do INFO FILESET on $ZPMON.*

Example 33:

`->INFO FILESET $ZPMON.*`

```
OSS Info FILESET \XYS7000.$ZPMON.*

FilesetName                        *MntPoint
ROOT                               /
TEST                               /test
```

Example 33's output shows that this system has two filesets, **/** (**root**) and **/test**.

To examine individual filesets on the system, do INFO FILESET:

SCF Syntax:

`INFO FILESET $<fileset name>`

Example 34:

`->info fileset $ZPMON.ROOT, detail`

```
OSS Detailed Info FILESET \XYS7000.ROOT

 DeviceLabel............           000000
*Catalog...............           $DATAA          *NameServer........#ZPNS    ←
*Buffered..............           LOG             *NFSPool...........16
*ReadOnly..............           FALSE           *NFSTimeout........120
*Pool..................           STORPOOL
 CreateBy..............           $ZPMON
 CreateTime............           11 Aug 1999, 13:17:40.338
 AlterBy...............           SUPER.SUPER
 AlterTime.............           13 Nov 2003, 9:07:46.184
*MntPoint-FilesetName...
*MntPoint-NameServer....
*MntPoint..............           /
*AuditEnabled..........           ON      ←
*DesiredState..........           STOPPED
*FsckCPU...............           0
*Report................
*MaxDirtyInodeTime......           30
*MaxInodes.............           500000
*ftIOmode..............           UNBUFFEREDCP
*normalIOmode..........           OSSBUFFEREDCP
```

Example 34 displays the details about the root fileset. Notice the **AuditEn-abled** value and that the **NameServer** for the root fileset is **#ZPNS**.

Use the STATUS FILESET command to display more detailed information about the fileset, including the disks in the fileset's storage pool.

Example 35:

->STATUS FILESET $ZPMON.ROOT, DETAIL

```
OSS Detailed Status FILESET \XYS7000.ROOT
 State..................  STARTED
 MountTime..............  12 Dec 2003, 9:18:34.150
 LastError..............  0
 ErrorDetail............  0
 ErrorTime..............  05 Jan 2006, 10:46:53.187
 FsckName...............
 LastControlSyncTime....
 AlterAfterSyncOrMount..  FALSE
*AuditEnabled...........  OFF
*Buffered...............  LOG
*ReadOnly...............  FALSE
*NFSTimeout.............  120
*NFSPool................  16
*Pool...................  STORPOOL
*MaxDirtyInodeTime......  30
*MaxInodes.............  500000
 InodesInuse............  45823 (9% of MaxInodes)
 MaxInodesUsed..........  46003 (9% of MaxInodes)
 TimeMaxInodesUsed......  05 Jan 2006, 10:46:00.176
 TimeMaxInodesReset.....  05 Jan 2006, 10:46:00.176
```

```
*ftIOmode...............  UNBUFFEREDCP
*normalIOmode..........  OSSBUFFEREDCP
 NumVols...............  2
 Volumes:
 $DATAG    $DATAH
*VolumesEligibleForFileCreation:
 $DATAG    $DATAH
 VolumesNotEligibleForFileCreation:

 VolumesWithZeroFiles:
 $DATAG    $DATAH
 VolumesWithFiles:

 VolumeInformation:
              -- Capacity (Mb) --     %        -- Free Extents --
 Volume (M)     Total      Free     Free    Count         Biggest
 $DATAG        4238.96   2063.80   48.68    12           1525.67
 $DATAH        4238.96   1098.94   25.92    9             357.06
```

Example 35 displays the details about the root fileset. Notice that $DATAG and $DATAH are the disks assigned to the root fileset.

Examining a Fileset's Catalog

To examine the catalog, you must first locate it:

Step 1, in SCF, do an INFO FILESET, DETAIL command for the desired fileset and make a note of the fileset's DeviceLabel and Catalog location.

Step 1:

->INFO FILESET $ZPMON.TEST, DETAIL

```
 DeviceLabel............ 000000
*Catalog............... $DATAA
```

In the output from Step 1, make a note of the device label and volume name. The device label value becomes the characters following the ZX in the subvolume name used in step 2.

Because all OSS files reside in the ZX* subvolumes on the disks in the storage pool, do a fileinfo on $DATAA.ZX000000.*

Step 2, at TACL, do a fileinfo on the catalog subvolume:

Step 2:
```
> FI $DATAA.ZX000000.*
```

```
$DATAA.ZX000000

               CODE        EOF    LAST  MODIFIED   OWNER    RWEP   PExt  SExt
PXIN0000       444      233472  25SEP1999  16:06  255,255   ----    20   100
PXIN0001       444      339968  17NOV2000  12:10  255,255   ----    20   100
PXINODE   O    444     5636096  28MAR2006  15:40  255,255   ----    20   100
PXLI0000       444       77824  27AUG1999  16:20  255,255   ----    20   100
PXLI0001       444      102400  06NOV2000  13:41  255,255   ----    20   100
PXLINK    O    444     1957888  28MAR2006  15:34  255,255   ----    20   100
PXLO0000       444           0  11AUG1999  13:21  255,255   ----    20   100
PXLO0001       444           0  25SEP1999  16:06  255,255   ----    20   100
```

The output of Step 2 shows the tables that make up the fileset's catalog.

Step 3, at TACL, do a FUP INFO, DETAIL to sample the characteristics of each catalog file:

Step 3:
```
> FUP INFO $DATAA.ZX000000.PXINODE, DETAIL
```

```
$DATAA.ZX000000.PXINODE            28 Mar 2006, 15:51
 ENSCRIBE
 TYPE K
 FORMAT 1
 CODE 444
 EXT ( 20 PAGES, 100 PAGES )
 REC 4024
 BLOCK 4096
 KEYLEN 4
 KEYOFF 0
 REFRESH
 MAXEXTENTS 978
 OWNER -1                              ←
SECURITY (RWEP): ----                  ←
DATA MODIF: 28 Mar 2006, 15:51, OPEN
CREATION DATE: 17 Nov 2000, 12:10
LAST OPEN: 6 Jan 2006, 9:14
FILE LABEL: 266 (6.5% USED)
EOF: 5636096 (2.8% USED)
EXTENTS ALLOCATED: 29
INDEX LEVELS: 2
```

The output from Step 3 shows the characteristics of the PXINODE catalog file, including its owner and file security string. In this case, the owner is SUPER.SUPER (-1) and the file security string allows only SUPER.SUPER access (----).

Step 4, at TACL, do a FUP LISTOPENS to see what processes have the catalog open:

<u>Step 4:</u>

> **FUP LISTOPENS PXINODE**

```
$DATAA.ZX000000.PXINODE
      PID      MODE   USERID   SD   MYTERM      PROGRAM FILE NAME
   253,00,0331   R/W-S  255,255  01   $ZHOME      $SYSTEM.SYS15.NS
   253,00,0331   R/W-S  255,255  01   $ZHOME      $SYSTEM.SYS15.NS
   253,00,0331   R/W-S  255,255  01   $ZHOME      $SYSTEM.SYS15.NS
   253,00,0331   R/W-S  255,255  01   $ZHOME      $SYSTEM.SYS15.NS
```

The output from Step 4 shows that the Name Server has the catalog open.

Examine all the filesets on the system in this same manner.

Gathering Pathway Information

This section provides examples for viewing information about pathways.

Locating the Existing Pathways

Use the TACL STATUS command to determine whether there are any PATHWAY applications running and to identify their owners. Other system information, such as HOMETERM and PRIORITY, is also shown.

<u>Syntax:</u>

STATUS *,PROG \$*.*.PATHMON
<u>Example 36:</u>

STATUS *,PROG \$*.*.PATHMON

```
Process          Pri  PFR  %WT  Userid   Program file              Hometerm
$BEN    0,100    145       001  222,9    $SYSTEM.SYSTEM.PATHMON    $VHS
$YPHI   0,144    100       005  255,255  $SYSTEM.SYSTEM.PATHMON    $ZHOME
$BMA1   0,146    145       001  222,210  $SYSTEM.SYSTEM.PATHMON    $VHS
$ABOP   0,183    160       005  255,255  $SYSTEM.SYSTEM.PATHMON    $VHS
$QAPQ   0,187    145       001  222,212  $SYSTEM.SYSTEM.PATHMON    $VHS
$DVMA   0,192    145       001  222,9    $SYSTEM.SYSTEM.PATHMON    $VHS
$BFMA B 0,212    145       001  222,11   $SYSTEM.SYSTEM.PATHMON    $VHS
$AMA    0,222    145       001  222,9    $SYSTEM.SYSTEM.PATHMON    $VHS
$ABOP B 1,22     160       001  255,255  $SYSTEM.SYSTEM.PATHMON    $YMIOP.#CLCI
$ZVHS B 1,31     148       001  255,255  $SYSTEM.SYSTEM.PATHMON    $YMIOP.#CLCI
$XPLP   0,97     145       005  255,255  $SYSTEM.SYSTEM.PATHMON    $VHS
```

Example 36 displays the list of pathways running on the system. The "B" in column 10 denotes the backup for processes defined as NONSTOP.

Examining Individual Pathways

Use PATHCOM to view the internal configuration information for each Pathway system. To start PATHCOM, you must provide the process name of the pathway application you wish to research:

1. Start PATHCOM
2. Perform queries

Syntax:

PATHCOM $<process>

Example 37:

PATHCOM $XPLP

```
$Y7D7: PATHCOM - T8344D44 - (02MAY01)
COPYRIGHT HP COMPUTER CORPORATION 1980 - 1985, 1987 - 2001
=
```

Example 37 starts PATHCOM using the $XPLP pathway process name.

Use the INFO command to display information about the pathway:

Example 38:

INFO PATHWAY

```
PATHWAY
  MAXASSIGNS 50                          [CURRENTLY 0]
  MAXDEFINES 20                          [CURRENTLY 0]
  MAXEXTERNALTCPS 0                      [CURRENTLY 0]
  MAXLINKMONS 5                          [CURRENTLY 0]
  MAXPARAMS 20                           [CURRENTLY 0]
  MAXPATHCOMS 5                          [CURRENTLY 2]
  MAXPROGRAMS 10                         [CURRENTLY 2]
  MAXSERVERCLASSES 50                    [CURRENTLY 23]
  MAXSERVERPROCESSES 70                  [CURRENTLY 23]
  MAXSPI 1                               [CURRENTLY 0]
  MAXSTARTUPS 20                         [CURRENTLY 0]
  MAXTCPS 5                              [CURRENTLY 1]
  MAXTELLQUEUE 4
  MAXTELLS 32                            [CURRENTLY 0]
  MAXTERMS 5                             [CURRENTLY 1]
  MAXTMFRESTARTS 5
  OWNER \LA.255,255              ←

  SECURITY "U"                   ←

=
```

Example 38 displays information about the $XPLP pathway, including the SECURITY and OWNER.

Use the INFO TCP command to view the details about TCPs:

Example 39:

`INFO TCP *`

```
SERVER TCP-1
  CPUS (1:0)
  PRI 140
  MAXTERMS 5
  PROCESS $XTCP
  PROGRAM $SYSTEM.SYSTEM.PATHTCP2
  TCLPROG $DATA1.APP1.POBJ
```

Example 39 displays information about the TCP-1 server.

Use the INFO TERM command to view the details about TERMs:

Example 40:

`INFO TERM *`

```
TERM T1
  FILE $TERM01
  TCP TCP-1
  INITIAL STARTER
  TMF OFF
```

Example 40 displays information about the $TERM01 terminal in the pathway.

Use the INFO PROGRAM command to view the details about programs:

Example 41:

`INFO PROGRAM *`

```
PROGRAM MYPROG
  TYPE T16-6520 INITIAL STARTER
  ERROR-ABORT ON
  TCP TCP-1
  TMF OFF
```

Example 41 displays information about the MYPROG program.

Use the INFO SERVER command to view the details about the servers in the pathway:

Example 42:

INFO SERVER *

Example 42 displays information about the XPLS000 server.

```
SERVER XPLS000
  PROCESSTYPE GUARDIAN
  AUTORESTART 0
  CPUS (1:0)
  CREATEDELAY 1 MINS
  DEBUG OFF
  DELETEDELAY 10 MINS
  HIGHPIN OFF
  HOMETERM \LA.$VHS
  LINKDEPTH 1
  MAXSERVERS 1
  NUMSTATIC 1
  OWNER \LA.255,255
  PRI 120
  PROGRAM \LA.$DATAA.XPLPROBJ.XPLS000
  SECURITY "N"
  TMF OFF
  VOLUME \LA.$DATAA.XPLPRDAT
```

Example 43:

INFO SERVER * (for an OSS Server)

```
SERVER XPLS002
 PROCESSTYPE OSS
 ARGLIST "102", 29, 10545, "California"
 AUTORESTART 0
 CPUS (1:0)
 CWD /users/boba/osscode
 CREATEDELAY 1 MINS
 DEBUG OFF
 ENV env3=henv3
 DELETEDELAY 10 MINS
 HIGHPIN OFF
 HOMETERM \LA.$VHS
 LINKDEPTH 1
 MAXSERVERS 1
 NUMSTATIC 1
 OWNER \LA.255,255
 PRI 120
 PROGRAM ossserver4
 STDERR serrorfile
 STDIN stdinfile
 STDOUT stdoutfile
 SECURITY "N"
 TMF OFF
 VOLUME \LA.$DATAA.XPLPRDAT
```

Example 43 displays the SERVER information for an OSS server.

Use the STATUS command to view the Pathway's PATHMON:

Example 44:

Status PATHMON

```
PATHMON \XYS7000.$PWOSS - STATE=RUNNING CPUS 1
PATHCTL (OPEN) $DATAA.BOB.PATHCTL
LOG1 S  (OPEN) $DATAA.BOB.PWLOG
LOG2    (CLOSED)


REQNUM   FILE    PID   PAID   WAIT
1      PATHCOM  $Y287     222,230
```

Example 44 displays the status of of the $PWOSS pathway.

Gathering Process Information

This section provides examples for viewing information about processes.

Examining a Process's Status

The STATUS command is used to list information about processes running on a system.

Syntax:

STATUS $<PROCESS NAME>

Example 45:

STATUS $CMON

```
System \LA
Process             Pri  PFR  %WT  Userid   Program file              Hometerm
$CMON    1,171     180        001 255,255  $SYSTEM.APPCM.APPCM         $VHS
                       Swap File Name: $AUDIT.#0
         Current Extended Swap File Name: $AUDIT.#0483691
$CMON    B 0,226   180        001 255,255  $SYSTEM.APPCM.APPCM         $VHS
                       Swap File Name: $AUDIT.#0
         Current Extended Swap File Name: $AUDIT.#0483692
```

Examining a Process's Object File

Use the FILEINFO $<volume>.<subvolume>.<filename> to list the owner and RWEP string for the CMON process's object and source files. The STATUS command shown above displays the CMON process's object file, $SYSTEM.APPCM.APPCM.

Syntax:

FILEINFO $<volume>.<subvolume>.<filename>

Example 46:

FILEINFO $SYSTEM.APPCM.APPCM

```
$SYSTEM.APPCM

          CODE   EOF        LAST   MODIFIED    OWNER    RWEP    PExt      SExt
APPCM  O   100   4763648    24JUN2001 21:51    255,255  0000    278         64
```

Examining OSS Subsystem Processes

Use PPD commands to see the NS (NameServer) process pairs, if any:

```
> ppd $zpns
> status $zpns,detail
```

```
Name    Primary   Backup    Ancestor
$ZPNS   0,331     1,291     $ZPMON
```

Use TACL status commands to examine the NameServer process:

```
> status $zpns,detail
```

```
System: \XYS7000                              March 28, 2006 16:18
Pid: 1,291    ($ZPNS) Backup
PRIV
Priority: 199
Wait State: %015    (LCAN, LDONE, LREQ)
Userid: 255,255    (SUPER.SUPER)
Myterm: $ZHOME
Program File Name: $SYSTEM.SYS15.NS
Swap File Name: $SYSTEM.#0
Process Time: 0:11:12.704
Process Creation Time: January 5, 2006 10:46:51.213742
Process States: RUNNABLE
GMOMJOBID
```

Examine all of the OSS processes:

OSS message queue server (ZMSGQ; $ZMSGQ)

OSS name server(s) (NS; $ZPNS)

OSS sockets local server (OSSLS; $ZPLS)

OSS transport agent server (OSSTA; $ZTAnn)

OSS file manager (OSSFM; $ZFMnn)

OSS pipe server (OSSPS; $ZPPnn)

Gathering Safeguard Information

The Safeguard commands necessary to gather audit information are provided in the following table; some examples follow.

Information Needed	Safeguard Command
Diskfile access rules	INFO DISKFILE { $<vol name>.<subvol name>.<filename> }, DETAIL
Diskfile-pattern access rules	INFO DISKFILE-PATTERN { $<vol name>,<subvol name>,<filename> }, ALL
Subvolume access rules	INFO SUBVOL { $<vol name>.<subvol name> },DETAIL
Volume access rules	INFO VOL { $<volume name > }, DETAIL
Process access rules	INFO PROCESS { $<process name> }, DETAIL
Subprocess access rules	INFO SUBPROCESS {$<subprocess name> },DETAIL
Device access rules	INFO DEVICE { $<device name> }, DETAIL
Subdevice access rules	INFO SUBDEVICE {$<subdevice name> },DETAIL
Safeguard global settings	INFO SAFEGUARD,DETAIL
Audit Pool	INFO AUDIT-POOL
Audit Service	INFO AUDIT-SERVICE
Groups—Security	INFO SECURITY-GROUP SECURITY-ADMINISTRATOR INFO SECURITY-GROUP SYSTEM-OPERATOR INFO SECURITY-OSS-ADMINISTRATOR
Groups—File-sharing	INFO GROUP NAME <group name>,DETAIL INFO GROUP NUMBER <group number>,DETAIL
Audit Configuration	INFO AUDIT SERVICE INFO AUDIT POOL <audit pool>
User—Audit parameters	INFO USER {user name | user number},AUDIT
User—Remote passwords	INFO USER {user name | user number},REMOTEPASS-WORD
User—OSS parameters	INFO USER {user name | user number},OSS
User—CI parameters	INFO USER {user name | user number},CI
User—Aliases	INFO USER {user name | user number},ALIAS
User—STATUS	INFO USER {user name | user number},GENERAL
User—File Sharing Groups	INFO USER {user name | user number},GROUP
User—all parameters	INFO USER {user name | user number},DETAIL

(Continued)

Information Needed	Safeguard Command
Alias—Audit parameters	INFO ALIAS {alias },AUDIT
Alias—Remote passwords	INFO ALIAS {alias},REMOTEPASSWORD
Alias—OSS parameters	INFO ALIAS {alias},OSS
Alias—CI parameters	INFO ALIAS {alias},CI
Alias—STATUS	INFO ALIAS {alias},GENERAL
Alias—File Sharing Groups	INFO ALIAS {user name | user number},GROUP
Alias—All fields	INFO ALIAS {alias},DETAIL
Objecttype settings	INFO OBJECTTYPE {objecttype},DETAIL

Many Safeguard OBJECTs, such as User Group Name or Number, Volume, Subvolume or Diskfile names can be wildcarded with an asterisk (*).

Examining Safeguard Globals

Use the INFO SAFEGUARD DETAIL command to display all the Global Security attributes of Safeguard. To start SAFECOM:

1. Start SAFECOM
2. Perform queries

Syntax:

SAFECOM
Example 47:

= info safeguard, detail

```
SAFEGUARD IS CONFIGURED WITH SUPER.SUPER UNDENIABLE
 AUTHENTICATE-MAXIMUM-ATTEMPTS =    3
 AUTHENTICATE-FAIL-TIMEOUT      =    60 SECONDS
 AUTHENTICATE-FAIL-FREEZE       =    OFF

 PASSWORD-REQUIRED = OFF PASSWORD-HISTORY = 0
 PASSWORD-ENCRYPT  = ON  PASSWORD-MINIMUM-LENGTH = 5
 PASSWORD-MAY-CHANGE   = 364 DAYS BEFORE-EXPIRATION
 PASSWORD-EXPIRY-GRACE = 31 DAYS AFTER-EXPIRATION

 SYSTEM-WARNING-MODE = OFF WARNING-FALLBACK-SECURITY = GUARDIAN
 OBJECT-WARNING-MODE = ON

 ALLOW-NODE-ID-ACL    = ON

 DIRECTION-DEVICE      = SUBDEVICE-FIRST CHECK-DEVICE = ON
 COMBINATION-DEVICE    = FIRST-ACL CHECK-SUBDEVICE = ON
 ACL-REQUIRED-DEVICE   = OFF
```

```
DIRECTION-PROCESS       = SUBPROCESS-FIRST CHECK-PROCESS = ON
COMBINATION-PROCESS     = FIRST-ACL CHECK-SUBDEVICE = ON
ACL-REQUIRED-PROCESS    = OFF

DIRECTION-DISKFILE      = FILENAME-FIRST CHECK-VOLUME = OFF
COMBINATION-DISKFILE    = FIRST-ACL CHECK-SUBVOLUME = ON
ACL-REQUIRED-DISKFILE   = OFF CHECK-FILENAME = ON
CLEARONPURGE-DISKFILE   = OFF CHECK-DISKFILE-PATTERN = LAST

ALLOW-DISKFILE-PERSISTENT = NORMAL

AUDIT-OBJECT-ACCESS-PASS = NONE AUDIT-AUTHENTICATE-PASS = ALL
AUDIT-OBJECT-ACCESS-FAIL = NONE AUDIT-AUTHENTICATE-FAIL = ALL
AUDIT-OBJECT-MANAGE-PASS = ALL AUDIT-SUBJECT-MANAGE-PASS = ALL
AUDIT-OBJECT-MANAGE-FAIL = ALL AUDIT-SUBJECT-MANAGE-FAIL = ALL

AUDIT-DEVICE-ACCESS-PASS = NONE AUDIT-PROCESS-ACCESS-PASS = NONE
AUDIT-DEVICE-ACCESS-FAIL = ALL AUDIT-PROCESS-ACCESS-FAIL = ALL
AUDIT-DEVICE-MANAGE-PASS = ALL AUDIT-PROCESS-MANAGE-PASS = ALL
AUDIT-DEVICE-MANAGE-FAIL = ALL AUDIT-PROCESS-MANAGE-FAIL = ALL

               AUDIT-DISKFILE-ACCESS-PASS = NONE
               AUDIT-DISKFILE-ACCESS-FAIL = ALL
               AUDIT-DISKFILE-MANAGE-PASS = ALL
               AUDIT-DISKFILE-MANAGE-FAIL = ALL

               AUDIT-CLIENT-SERVICE = OFF

CI-PROG = $SYSTEM.SYSTEM.TACL        CMON         = ON
CI-LIB  = * NONE *                   CMONERROR    = ACCEPT
CI-SWAP = * NONE *                   CMONTIMEOUT  = 30 SECONDS
CI-CPU  = ANY                        BLINDLOGON   = ON
CI-PRI  = 150                        NAMELOGON    = ON
CI-PARAM-TEXT =
TERMINAL-EXCLUSIVE-ACCESS = OFF
(255,255)-2
```

Example 47 displays the Safeguard Globals. Note the first line, which shows that SUPER.SUPER is undeniable.

Example 48:

INFO OBJECTTYPE VOLUME

```
            LAST-MODIFIED          OWNER           STATUS
VOLUME
            30SEP02, 15:10        \*.255,255      THAWED
    253,001                       C,O
    \*.253,001                    C,O

AUDIT-ACCESS-PASS = ALL             AUDIT-MANAGE-PASS = ALL
AUDIT-ACCESS-FAIL = ALL             AUDIT-MANAGE-FAIL = ALL
```

Example 48 shows an OBJECTTYPE VOLUME record.

Examining User/Alias Records

Example 49:

INFO USER 222,77,DETAIL

```
GROUP.USER       USER-ID    OWNER   LAST-MODIFIED  LAST-LOGON   STATUS
ABCO.PAM         222,77  \*.253,1   12APR06, 11:00 23DEC06, 7:45 THAWED

 UID                           = 56909
 USER-EXPIRES                  = 23DEC02, 7:45
 PASSWORD-EXPIRES              = 23DEC02, 7:45
 PASSWORD-MAY-CHANGE           = * NONE *
 PASSWORD-MUST-CHANGE EVERY    = 30 DAYS
 PASSWORD-EXPIRY-GRACE         = 29 DAYS

 LAST-LOGON                    = 23DEC02, 7:45
 LAST-UNSUCCESSFUL-ATTEMPT     = 4DEC02, 13:11

 LAST-MODIFIED                 = 12APR02, 11:00
 FROZEN/THAWED                 = THAWED
 STATIC FAILED LOGON COUNT     = 4
 GUARDIAN DEFAULT SECURITY     = NCCC
 GUARDIAN DEFAULT VOLUME       = $DATAA.PAM

 AUDIT-AUTHENTICATE-PASS = ALL      AUDIT-MANAGE-PASS = ALL
 AUDIT-AUTHENTICATE-FAIL = ALL      AUDIT-MANAGE-FAIL = ALL
 AUDIT-USER-ACTION-PASS  = NONE
 AUDIT-USER-ACTION-FAIL  = ALL

TEXT-DESCRIPTION = "Emp#: AB12345678 Supervisor: Sandy Kofax"    ←

BINARY-DESCRIPTION LENGTH = 0          ←

 CI-PROG = * NONE *
 CI-LIB  = * NONE *
 CI-NAME = * NONE *
 CI-SWAP = * NONE *
 CI-CPU  = * NONE *
 CI-PRI  = * NONE *
 CI-PARAM-TEXT =

 INITIAL-PROGTYPE = PROGRAM
 INITIAL-PROGRAM =
 INITIAL-DIRECTORY =

 PRIMARY-GROUP = ABCO
 GROUP = ABCO

 REMOTEPASSWORD = \LA la
 REMOTEPASSWORD = \SYDNEY sydney
 REMOTEPASSWORD = \LONDON london

 ALIAS = pamela
 ALIAS = pam1
 ALIAS = pam-noseg
 ALIAS = plh1a

 SUBJECT DEFAULT-PROTECTION SECTION UNDEFINED!

SUBJECT OWNER-LIST SECTION                      ←
 \*.020,001
 \*.222,077
```

Example 49 shows a user record, including the new text fields and multiple record owners introduced in G06.27.

Example 50:

`INFO USER 222,77,REMOTEPASSWORD`

```
GROUP.USER   USER-ID  OWNER     LAST-MODIFIED  LAST-LOGON   STATUS
ABCO.PAM     222,77  \*.253,1 12APR02, 11:00  23DEC02, 7:45 THAWED

 REMOTEPASSWORD = \LA      xxxx
 REMOTEPASSWORD = \SYDNEY xxxx
 REMOTEPASSWORD  = \LONDON xxxx
```

Example 50 shows only the remote passwords in a user record.

Examining Safeguard File Security

Example 51:

`INFO DISKFILE $DATAA.PAM.*,WARNINGS OFF`

```
              LAST-MODIFIED     OWNER     STATUS
$DATAA.PAM
 MYFILE        13AUG01, 10:08     20,245    THAWED
        \*.020,245   R,W,E,P,C,O
        \*.222,077   R
        \*.222,210   R,W

 AUDIT-ACCESS-PASS = ALL       AUDIT-MANAGE-PASS = ALL
 AUDIT-ACCESS-FAIL = ALL       AUDIT-MANAGE-FAIL = ALL

 LICENSE = OFF PROGID = OFF CLEARONPURGE = OFF PERSISTENT = ON
```

Example 51 displays the single DISKFILE record in the $DATAA.PAM subvolume.

Example 52:

`INFO DISKFILE $DATA1.BRYAN.*`

```
* WARNING * RECORD FOR DISKFILE $DATA1.BRYAN.LOGUA27: NOT FOUND
* WARNING * RECORD FOR DISKFILE $DATA1.BRYAN.LOGVOL: NOT FOUND
* WARNING * RECORD FOR DISKFILE $DATA1.BRYAN.MEASON: NOT FOUND
* WARNING * RECORD FOR DISKFILE $DATA1.BRYAN.NAMEUSER: NOT FOUND
* WARNING * RECORD FOR DISKFILE $DATA1.BRYAN.NEWSOFT: NOT FOUND
 LAST-MODIFIED   OWNER    STATUS     WARNING-MODE
$DATA1.BRYAN
  MEASON      5APR06, 1:04  \*.253,1  THAWED        OFF

          \*.255,255 R,W,E,P, O
* WARNING * RECORD FOR DISKFILE $DATAD.P23HHTSS.OBJNAME1: NOT FOUND
```

Example 52 shows an INFO DISKFILE query without the WARNINGS OFF option.

To omit files, subvolumes, or volumes that match a wildcarded query but don't have Protection Records, use the WARNINGS OFF modifier for the INFO command.

Example 53:

`INFO DISKFILE $DATAD.BRYAN.*, WARNINGS OFF`

```
LAST-MODIFIED      OWNER     STATUS    WARNING-MODE
$DATAD. BRYAN
   MEASON           5APR06,  1:04 \*.253,1  THAWED  OFF

              \*.255,255 R,W,E,P, O
```

Example 53 shows an INFO DISKFILE query with the WARNINGS OFF option.

Example 54:

`INFO DISKFILE-PATTERN $VABC*.ABC???.*, ALL`

```
                  LAST-MODIFIED  OWNER  STATUS    WARNING-MODE
$VABC.ABC???
  *               11JUL05, 17:16 253,1 THAWED OFF

              242,077 R,W,E,P,C,O
              242,078 R, E
          \*.*,*   R

  AUDIT-ACCESS-PASS = NONE        AUDIT-MANAGE-PASS = NONE
  AUDIT-ACCESS-FAIL = NONE        AUDIT-MANAGE-FAIL = NONE

             CREATION                    LAST-MODIFIED

  USER NAME SUPER.SUPER                  SUPER.SUPER
  USER TYPE USER (ID 255,255)            USER (ID 255,255)
  USER NODE LOCAL                        LOCAL
  TIMESTAMP 11JUL2005, 16:56:32.927      11JUL2005, 17:16:53.065
```

Example 54 shows a DISKFILE-PATTERN record. Note the extra fields that show the user who created the record and made the most recent change to the record.

Examining Safeguard SECURITY-GROUPs

Example 55:

`INFO SECURITY-GROUP SECURITY-ADMINISTRATOR`

```
                LAST-MODIFIED     OWNER     STATUS
SECURITY-ADMINISTRATOR
            7JAN03,  11:12    255,255    THAWED

        222,233    E,        O
        222,250    E,        O
        253,001    E,        O
```

Example 55 shows a the SECURITY-ADMINISTRATOR SECURITY-GROUP record.

Example 56:

`INFO GROUP NAME TEST,DETAIL`

```
GROUP NAME                 NUMBER       OWNER        LAST-MODIFIED
TEST                         300       255,255      8DEC00, 17:53
    AUTO-DELETE = OFF
    DESCRIPTION = "aaa;bbb"
    MEMBER      = Manuel
    MEMBER      = sec-bryan
    MEMBER      = daryll
```

Example 56 shows a FILE-SHARING Group record.

If the INFO AUDIT POOL command is entered without a specific Audit Pool name, the Current Audit Pool is assumed.

Example 57:

`INFO AUDIT POOL`

```
AUDIT POOL $SECURE.SAFEAUD      CONFIGURATION
    MAXFILES                        5
    MAXEXTENTS                      16
    EXTENTSIZE                     128,      128
```

Example 57 displays the configuration of the Current Audit Pool, $SECURE.SAFEAUD.

Example 58:

`INFO AUDIT POOL $DATAA.TEMPPOOL`

```
AUDIT POOL $DATAA.TEMPPOOL      CONFIGURATION
    MAXFILES                        15
    MAXEXTENTS                      32
    EXTENTSIZE                      256, 256
```

Example 58 displays the configuration of a secondary Audit Pool, $DATAA.TEMPPOOL.

The INFO AUDIT SERVICE command displays parameters that determine Safeguard's RECOVERY OPTIONS and the manner in which audit records are written to the Audit Trail.

Example 59:

INFO AUDIT SERVICE

```
CURRENT AUDIT POOL $SECURE.SAFE
  CURRENT AUDIT FILE      $SECURE.SAFE.A0007739
  NEXT AUDIT POOL         $WORK.SFGAUDIT
  RECOVERY                RECYCLE FILES
  CURRENT STATE           RECYCLING FILES
  WRITE-THROUGH CACHE     OFF
  EOF REFRESH             OFF
```

Example 59 displays the AUDIT SERVICE parameters. The current Audit Pool is $SECURE.SAFE. The next Audit Pool is $WORK.SFGAUDIT. Audit files are being RECYCLED. Audit records are held in memory before being written to disk, and the End of File point is not updated until the records are actually written to disk.

Gathering Samba Information

Samba is configured by setting parameters in the **smb.conf** file. Use the **/usr /local/bin/testparm** program to view the current **smb.conf** parameters.

Syntax.

testparm

Example 60:

testparm

```
Load smb config files from /usr/local/lib/smb.conf
Processing section "[home]"
No path in service home - using /tmp
Processing section "[printers]"
Processing section "[using_samba]"
Processing section "[files]"
Loaded services file OK.
WARNING: You have some share names that are longer than 8 chars
These may give errors while browsing or may not be accessible
to some older clients
Press enter to see a dump of your service definitions

# Global parameters
  [global]
      admin users =
      browseable = Yes
      config file =
      create mask = 0744
    default service =
      dont descend =
      encrypt passwords = No
```

```
        force group =
        force user =
        guest account = nobody
      guest ok = No
        guest only = No
        hide dot files = Yes
        hosts allow = 10.1.1. localhost
        hosts deny =
        hosts equiv =
        include =
        invalid users =
        keepalive = 300
        log file = /var/log/samba.log.%m
        log level = 3
        magic script =
        map hidden = No
        map to guest = Never
        null passwords = No
        only user = No
        password level = 0
        password server = XYSERVD
        postexec =
        preexec =
        printable = No
        read list =
        read only = No
        root directory =
        root postexec =
        root preexec =
        security = SERVER
        security mask = 0777
        status = Yes
        username =
        username level = 0
        username map = /usr/local/samba/etc/usermap.txt
        valid users =
        wide links = Yes
        workgroup = XYPRO-23
        write list =
[home]
        comment = Home Directories
        path = /tmp
        read only = No
        browseable = No

[printers]
        comment = All Printers
        path = /var/spool/samba
        printable = Yes
        browseable = No

[using_samba]
        comment = using samba docs
        path = /usr/local/swat/using_samba
        valid users = @XYPRO

[files]
      comment = /abc share
      path = /
      read only = No
```

Example 60 displays the contents of the **smb.conf** file. To save space, the output has been edited to show only the security-related parameters.

Gathering SSH Configuration Information

SSH is configured by setting parameters in the two configuration files:

The SSH client's **/usr/local/usr/local/bin/ssh_config** file

The SSH server's **/usr/local/usr/local/bin/sshd_config** file

Both files are text files and can be viewed via **/bin/cat**. Because the files may be fairly long, it is easiest to pipe the output to a printer or a file for review. Example 6 sends the output to a printer (hp1), while Example 62 sends the output to a file **sshdconf_review**.

<u>Syntax.</u>
```
cat <configuration filename> | lp <printer>
```

<u>Example 61:</u>
```
Cat ssh_config | lp hp1
```

```
# This is the ssh client system-wide configuration file.
# Configuration data is parsed as follows:
#  1. command line options
#  2. user-specific file
#  3. system-wide file

# Any configuration value is only changed the first time it is set.
# Thus, host-specific definitions should be at the beginning of the
# configuration file, and defaults at the end.

# Site-wide defaults for various options:
# Host *
#    AddressFamily any
     BatchMode no
     CheckHostIP yes
     ConnectTimeout 0
     Cipher 3des
#    Ciphers aes128-cbc,3des-cbc,blowfish-cbc,cast128-cbc,arcfour,aes192-
cbc,aes256-cbc
#    EscapeChar ~
#    ForwardAgent no
#    ForwardX11 no
     HostbasedAuthentication no
#    IdentityFile ~/.ssh/identity
#    IdentityFile ~/.ssh/id_rsa
#    IdentityFile ~/.ssh/id_dsa
#    PasswordAuthentication no
     Port 22
#    Protocol 2,1
     PubkeyAuthentication yes
#    RhostsRSAAuthentication no
#    RSAAuthentication yes
     StrictHostKeyChecking ask
```

Example 61 shows the contents of the **ssh_config** file.

Syntax.
`cat <configuration filename> > <target filename>`

Example 62:
`Cat sshd_config > sshdconf_review`

```
# This is the sshd server system-wide configuration file.  See
# sshd_config(5) for more information.
# This sshd was compiled with PATH=/usr/bin:/bin:/usr/sbin:/sbin:/usr/
local/bin

# The strategy used for options in the default sshd_config shipped with
# OpenSSH is to specify options with their default value where
# possible, but leave them commented.  Uncommented options change a
# default value.

#Port 22
#Protocol 2,1
#ListenAddress 0.0.0.0
#ListenAddress ::

# HostKey for protocol version 1
# HostKey /usr/local/etc/ssh_host_key
# HostKeys for protocol version 2
# HostKey /usr/local/etc/ssh_host_rsa_key
# HostKey /usr/local/etc/ssh_host_dsa_key

# Lifetime and size of ephemeral version 1 server key
# KeyRegenerationInterval 3600
# ServerKeyBits 768

#Logging:
#obsoletes QuietMode and FascistLogging:
# SyslogFacility AUTH
# LogLevel INFO

#Authentication:
PubkeyAuthentication yes
# LoginGraceTime 600
# PermitRootLogin no
#To disable tunneled clear text passwords, change to no here!
PasswordAuthentication no
# PermitEmptyPasswords no
# PermitUserEnvironment no
# StrictModes yes
# RSAAuthentication yes
# AuthorizedKeysFile .ssh/authorized_keys
#rhosts authentication should not be used:
# RhostsAuthentication yes
#Don't read the user's ~/.rhosts and ~/.shosts files
# IgnoreRhosts yes
#For this to work, also need host keys in /usr/local/etc/ssh_known_hosts:
# RhostsRSAAuthentication no
#similar for protocol version 2:
# HostbasedAuthentication no
#Change to yes if you don't trust ~/.ssh/known_hosts for
#RhostsRSAAuthentication and HostbasedAuthentication:
# IgnoreUserKnownHosts no
 #Change to no to disable s/key passwords
# ChallengeResponseAuthentication yes

#Kerberos options
# KerberosAuthentication no
```

```
# KerberosOrLocalPasswd yes
# KerberosTicketCleanup yes
# AFSTokenPassing no
# Kerberos TGT Passing only works with the AFS kaserver
# KerberosTgtPassing no

#Set this to 'yes' to enable PAM keyboard-interactive authentication
#Warning: enabling this may bypass the setting of 'PasswordAuthentication'
# PAMAuthenticationViaKbdInt yes

# X11Forwarding no
# X11DisplayOffset 10
# X11UseLocalhost yes
# PrintMotd yes
# PrintLastLog yes
KeepAlive no
# UseLogin no
AllowTcpForwarding yes
UsePrivilegeSeparation no
# Compression yes
# MaxStartups 10
#no default banner path
# Banner /some/path
# VerifyReverseMapping no
#override default of no subsystems:
Subsystem                    sftp      /usr/local/libexec/sftp-server
```

Example 62 shows the contents of the **sshd_config** file.

Gathering SQL/MP Information

This section provides examples for viewing information about SQL/MP catalogs.

Examining the SQL/MP System Catalog

The SQLCI program is used to interact with the SQL database system. To find the SQL system catalog and version, start SQLCI:

1. Start SQLCI

2. Perform queries

<u>**Syntax:**</u>

SQLCI

SQLCI has two prompt levels. A prompt of two right carets (>>) is displayed when SQLCI is ready to start processing a command. A prompt of a plus sign and a right caret is displayed when SQLCI is in the middle of processing an extended line command. All commands in SQLCI are terminated with a semicolon; otherwise, SQLCI assumes extended line commands and continues processing for input.

Example 63:

`GET CATALOG OF SYSTEM;`

```
CATALOG: \LA.$DSMSCM.SQL
--- SQL operation complete.
```

Use the GET VERSION command to display the SQL/MP version number.

Example 64:

`GET VERSION OF CATALOG $DSMSCM.SQL;`

```
VERSION: 345
--- SQL operation complete.
```

Now that you know the location of the system catalog, use FUP INFO or FILEINFO to view the file information for SQL objects.

Example 65:

`FILEINFO $DSMSCM.SQL.*;`

```
$DSMSCM.SQL

            CODE   EOF    LAST       MODIFIED  OWNER     RWEP  PExt  SExt
BASETABS O  572A   20480  08AUG2005   9:24     255,255   NNNN   16   128
CATALOGS O  571A   20480  04APR2006  14:23     255,255   NNUU   16   128
CATDEFS  O  900A   12288  05FEB2004  14:23     255,255   AA-A   16    64
COLUMNS  O  573A  221184  08AUG2005   9:24     255,255   NNNN   16   128
COMMENTS    574A       0  04DEC1998   7:02     255,255   NNNN   16   128
CONSTRNT    575A       0  04DEC1998   7:02     255,255   NNNN   16   128
CPRLSRCE    587A       0  04DEC1998   7:02     255,255   NNNN   16   128
CPRULES     586A       0  04DEC1998   7:02     255,255   NNNN   16   128
FILES    O  576A   24576  08AUG2005   9:24     255,255   NNNN   16   128
INDEXES  O  577A   28672  08AUG2005   9:24     255,255   NNNN   16   128
IXINDE01 O  577A   24576  08AUG2005   9:24     255,255   NNNN   16    64
IXPART01    579A       0  22MAY2000   8:27     255,255   NNNN   16    64
IXPROG01    580A   12288  15NOV2005   9:50     255,255   NNNN   16    64
IXTABL01 O  581A   12288  08AUG2005   9:24     255,255   NNNN   16    64
IXUSAG01 O  583A   36864  14MAR2006  11:07     255,255   NNNN   16    64
KEYS     O  578A   32768  08AUG2005   9:24     255,255   NNNN   16   128
PARTNS      579A       0  22MAY2000   8:27     255,255   NNNN   16   128
PROGRAMS    580A   12288  15NOV2005   9:50     255,255   NNNN   16   128
TABLES   O  581A   20480  08AUG2005   9:24     255,255   NNNN   16   128
TRANSIDS    582A       0  14MAR2006  11:07     255,255   NNNN    1     1
USAGES   O  583A   45056  14MAR2006  11:07     255,255   NNNN   16   128
VERSIONS    584A    1536  04DEC1998   7:02     255,255   NNNN    1     1
VIEWS       585A   20480  01FEB2005  11:10     255,255   NNNN   16   128
```

Example 65 displays the tables that make up the system catalog, their file codes, sizes, and security strings.

Examining Other SQL/MP Catalogs

Researching SQL catalog information is performed using the SQL query language to execute queries against the SQL catalogs. Generally, research of this type requires extensive knowledge of SQL and SQL query format. An infinite number of queries can be performed against the SQL catalogs. Some examples are:

To display a list of catalog names from the System Catalog:

Example 66:

```
select * from $dsmscm.sql.catalogs for browse access;
```

CATALOGNAME	SUBSYSTEMNAME		VERSION
VERSIONUPGRADETIME	CATALOGCLASS	CATALOGVERSION	
\LA.$DATA1.AMACATL	SQL		A350
0 U		350	
\LA.$DATA1.AMATEST	SQL		A350
0 U		350	
\LA.$DATA1.P05AACAT	SQL		A350
0 U		350	
\LA.$DATA1.TAPECAT	SQL		A350

Example 66 displays four application catalogs.

To display a list of tables from a specified catalog:

Example 67:

```
select * from $dsmscm.tapecat.tables for browse access;
```

TABLENAME	TABLETYPE	TABLECODE	COLCOUNT	GROUPID
USERID CREATETIME	REDEFTIME	SECURITYVECTOR	SECURITYMODE	
OBJECTVERSION SIMILARITYCHECK				
\LA.$DSMSCM.TAPECAT.BASETABS	TA	572	9	255
255 211793825082668460	211793824964685790	NNCC	G	
1 DISABLED				
\LA.$DSMSCM.TAPECAT.COLUMNS	TA	573	26	255
255 211793825082824170	211793824964685790	NNCC	G	
1 DISABLED				

To discover the security and owner of catalog tables, query the TABLES table as shown:

Syntax:
```
LOG <log-file> CLEAR;
SELECT TABLENAME, SECURITYVECTOR, GROUPID, USERID
FROM <catalog-name>.TABLES
WHERE TABLENAME = "\SYSTEM.$<VOLUME>.<CATALOG-NAME>.TABLES";
```

Examining the USAGES, TRANSIDS, and PROGRAMS Tables

To find out the security and owner of the USAGES, TRANSIDS, and PROGRAMS tables:

Syntax:
```
SELECT TABLENAME, SECURITYVECTOR, GROUPID, USERID
FROM <catalog-name>.TABLES
WHERE TABLENAME = "\SYSTEM.$<VOLUME>.<CATALOG-
NAME>.USAGES"
OR TABLENAME = "\SYSTEM.$<VOLUME>.<CATALOG-
NAME>.TRANSIDS"
OR TABLENAME = "\SYSTEM.$VOLUME.<CATALOG-
NAME>.PROGRAMS";
```

Examining SQL/MP Object and Program Dependencies

Database security relies on controlling access to an object. This includes knowing the dependencies between database objects and the SQL programs that can access those objects. Each user catalog contains a USAGES table that stores relationships between objects and the other objects on which they depend. Since these two types of objects can be registered in different user catalogs, the USAGES tables in both user catalogs will contain an entry about the dependency. This table lists initial and dependent objects:

Initial Object	Dependent Objects
Table	Index
	Protection view
	Shorthand view
	SQL object program

(Continued)

Initial Object	Dependent Objects
Protection view	Shorthand view
	SQL object program
Shorthand view	Shorthand view
	SQL object program
Index	SQL object program
Collation	Table
	Index
	Protection view
	Shorthand view
	SQL object program

To create a list of the dependencies between objects registered within a single user catalog (found on its own $<VOLUME>.<SUBVOL>), query its USAGES table as shown:

Syntax:
```
VOLUME \<system>.$<volume>.<subvol>;
SELECT * FROM USAGES;
```

To display a specific SQL/MP object's dependencies and their security across all catalogs in a database, use the DISPLAY USE OF command. If specific AT nodes are not listed, this command will search user catalogs for dependent objects and programs on all nodes in the network:

Syntax:
```
DISPLAY USE OF \<system>.$<volume>.<subvol>.<object-name>
  [ AT \node [, \node ] ... ) ];
```

Gathering SQL/MX Information

This section provides examples for viewing information in SQL/MX catalogs. Please refer to the latest *HP NonStop SQL/MX Installation and Management Guide* for the most recent **mxci** command syntax.

Locating the SQL/MX System Catalog

First use the FUP COPY command from a TACL prompt to display the SQL/MX anchor file named $SYSTEM.ZSQLMX.MXANCHOR.

Example 68:

FUP COPY $SYSTEM.ZSQLMX.MXANCHOR

```
SQLMX_MetaData_Loc=$data00
```

Next, go to the ZSD0 subvolume on the referenced Guardian volume and use the FILES command from a TACL prompt to list the physical (Guardian) names of the system schema tables (except the SQL/MX System Defaults table):

VOLUME $data00.ZSD0

FILES

```
$DATA00.ZSD0

ALLUID00 ALLUID01 CATREF00 CATREF01 CATSYS00 CATSYS01
SCHEMA00 SCHEMA01 SCHREP00 SCHREP01
```

Finally, use the FUP INFO, DETAIL command to display the ANSI table name for each file name ending in 00. This example only lists the first metadata table and only the first few lines that contain the fields of importance, which are ANSI NAME and VERSION.

FUP INFO alluid00, DETAIL

```
$DATA08.ZSD0.ALLUID00       4 Dec 2006, 8:10
 SQL METADATA TABLE
 ANSI NAME NONSTOP_SQLMX_FIGARO.SYSTEM_SCHEMA.ALL_UIDS
 RESOURCE FORK \FIGARO.$DATA08.ZSD0.ALLUID01
 SYSTEM METADATA \FIGARO.$DATA08.ZSD0
 VERSION 1200
```

The OSS **mxci** program is used to interact with the SQL/MX database system.

    1.   Start **mxci**

    2.   Perform queries

Syntax:

mxci

When the system catalog is created, the SQL/MX System Defaults table is created using a Guardian physical location with a system-generated

subvolume name. Use the SHOWLABEL command from the **mxci**
prompt to locate the SYSTEM_DEFAULTS table:

<u>Syntax:</u>
```
SHOWLABEL NONSTOP_SQLMX_<node-name>
.SYSTEM_DEFAULTS_SCHEMA.SYSTEM_DEFAULTS;
```

Examining Other SQL/MX Catalogs

To list the ANSI names for all catalogs found in the System Catalog on a
node, use an SQL SELECT from the **mxci** prompt:

<u>Syntax:</u>
```
SET SCHEMA NONSTOP_SQLMX_<node-name>.SYSTEM_SCHEMA;
SELECT CAT_NAME
 FROM CATSYS C, CAT_REFERENCES CR
 WHERE C.CAT_UID=CR.CAT_UID
    AND CR.NODE_NAME = '<node-name>'
    AND CR.REPLICATION_RULE = 'A';
```

To list ANSI names for all schemas found in a catalog on a node, use an
SQL SELECT from the **mxci** prompt:

<u>Syntax:</u>
```
SET SCHEMA NONSTOP_SQLMX_<node-name>.SYSTEM_SCHEMA;
SELECT SCHEMA_NAME,
    FROM SCHEMATA S, CATSYS C
    WHERE CAT_NAME = '<catalog-name>'
      AND S.CAT_UID = C.CAT_UID
    ORDER BY SCHEMA_NAME
    FOR READ UNCOMMITTED ACCESS;
```

To list all schema tables, base tables, views, and stored procedures for a specific schema with their associated owners, use an SQL SELECT from the
mxci prompt:

<u>Syntax:</u>
```
SET SCHEMA <catalog-name>.DEFINITION_SCHEMA_VERSION_1200;
SELECT SUBSTRING (OBJECT_NAME, 1, 25) AS OBJECT_NAME,
    CASE OBJECT_TYPE
        WHEN 'BT' THEN 'MX Base table'
        WHEN 'MP' THEN 'MP alias'
        WHEN 'PV' THEN 'MP Prot View'
        WHEN 'SV' THEN 'MP Shrthnd Vw'
        WHEN 'VW' THEN 'MX View'
```

```
                    WHEN 'UR' THEN 'Stored Proc'
                    ELSE 'OTHER'
                  END AS OBJECT_TYPE,
                  CASE OBJECT_SECURITY_CLASS
                    WHEN 'UT' THEN 'User Table'
                    WHEN 'SM' THEN 'System Metadata'
                    ELSE 'OTHER'
                  END AS SEC_CLASS
                  OBJECT_OWNER AS OWNED_BY
            FROM NONSTOP_SQLMX_<node-
                  name>.SYSTEM_SCHEMA.CATSYS C,
          NONSTOP_SQLMX_<node-name>.SYSTEM_SCHEMA.SCHEMATA S,
            OBJECTS O
            WHERE C.CAT_UID = S.CAT_UID
        AND C.CAT_NAME = '<catalog-name>'
            AND S.SCHEMA_UID = O.SCHEMA_UID
              AND S.SCHEMA_NAME = '<schema-name>'
              AND O.OBJECT_NAME_SPACE = 'TA'
          ORDER BY OBJECT_NAME
          FOR READ UNCOMMITTED ACCESS;
```

Examining the Security of SQL/MX Tables

To generate a list of who has been granted access to which SQL tables and views within a schema, use an SQL SELECT from the **mxci** prompt:

<u>Syntax:</u>

```
SET SCHEMA <catalog-name>.DEFINITION_SCHEMA_VERSION_1200;
SELECT SUBSTRING (O.OBJECT_NAME, 1, 25) AS OBJECT_NAME,
      O.OBJECT_TYPE AS TYP
      GRANTOR AS GRNT_BY,
      CASE (GRANTOR_TYPE)
        WHEN 'S' THEN 'System'
        WHEN 'U' THEN 'User'
        ELSE 'Unknown'
      END AS GRANTR,
      GRANTEE AS GRNT_TO,
      CASE (GRANTEE_TYPE)
        WHEN 'P' THEN 'Public'
        WHEN 'U' THEN 'User'
        ELSE 'Unknown'
      END AS GRNTEE,
      CASE (PRIVILEGE_TYPE)
        WHEN 'S' THEN 'Sel'
        WHEN 'I' THEN 'Ins'
      WHEN 'D' THEN 'Del'
```

```
        WHEN 'U' THEN 'Upd'
        WHEN 'R' THEN 'Ref'
        Else 'Unknown'
   END AS PRIV,
   IS_GRANTABLE AS GRANTABLE
 FROM TBL_PRIVILEGES T, OBJECTS O
WHERE T.TABLE_UID = O.OBJECT_UID
  AND O.OBJECT_NAME_SPACE = 'TA'
  AND O.SCHEMA_UID =
        (SELECT SCHEMA_UID
        FROM NONSTOP_SQLMX_<node-
name>.SYSTEM_SCHEMA.SCHEMATA

    WHERE
    SCHEMA_NAME = '<schema-name>' AND
        CAT_UID =
            (SELECT CAT_UID
            FROM NONSTOP_SQLMX_<node-
name>.SYSTEM_SCHEMA.CATSYS
            WHERE CAT_NAME = '<catalog-name>'
            )
        )
 ORDER BY O.OBJECT_NAME
 FOR READ UNCOMMITTED ACCESS;
```

Examining SQL/MX Usage Relationships

To list usage relationships between SQL/MX objects and SQL/MX-compiled modules, use the DISPLAY USE OF utility from the **mxci** prompt. (Note: because this command uses EXPLAIN output, we must first set the control query default GENERATE_EXPLAIN to ON before using the DISPLAY USE OF command.):

To display all SQL/MX modules (in default path /usr/tandem/sqlmx/ USERMODULES) and their dependent objects:

Syntax:

```
DISPLAY USE OF;
```

To display all SQL/MX-compiled modules located in an alternative directory path, along with their dependent objects:

Syntax:

```
DISPLAY USE OF MODULE_DIR '<module-directory-path>';
```

To display all SQL/MX-compiled modules that depend on a certain object (where the *object-name* may be either an SQL/MX table, index or SQL/MP alias (using a fully qualified SQL/MX catalog.schema.object name) or else an SQL/MP table or index (using a fully qualified Guardian name, including node name)):

Syntax:

```
DISPLAY USE OF OBJECT '<object-name>';
```
Example 69:
```
DISPLAY USE OF OBJECT '\NODE1.$DATA08.ORDERS.T1';
```

```
Object: \NODE1.$DATA08.ORDERS.T1
 Object: \NODE1.$DATA08.ORDERS.T1 Module:
TANDEM_SYSTEM_NSK.SCH.INS1M
Object: \NODE1.$DATA08.ORDERS.T1 Module:
TANDEM_SYSTEM_NSK.SCH.MULTCURM
Object: \NODE1.$DATA08.ORDERS.T1 Module:
TANDEM_SYSTEM_NSK.SCH.MULTIM
Object: \NODE1.$DATA08.ORDERS.T1 Module:
TANDEM_SYSTEM_NSK.SCH.STRUCTM Table: \NODE1.$DATA08.ORDERS.T1
Module: TANDEM_SYSTEM_NSK.SCH.T1INDM
Object: \NODE1.$DATA08.ORDERS.T1 Module:
TANDEM_SYSTEM_NSK.SCH.T1ROWSM
```

Gathering Information with SCF

SCF (Subsystem Control Facility) is used to gather information about devices, the network configuration, system processes, and OSS filesets.

Examining Devices

Use the LISTDEV command to display all processes that have a device type and are known to SCF. To start SCF:

1. Start SCF

2. Perform queries

SCF Syntax:
```
SCF
```
Example 70:
```
->LISTDEV
```

```
LDev    Name     PPID    BPID    Type      RSize  Pri  Program
   0    $0       0,5     1,5     ( 1,0 )    102   201  \LA.$SYSTEM.SYS01.OSIMAGE
   1    $NCP     0,16    1,13    (62,6 )      1   199  \LA.$SYSTEM.SYS01.NCPOBJ
   3    $YMIOP   0,256   1,256   ( 6,4 )     80   205  \LA.$SYSTEM.SYS01.OSIMAGE
   5    $Z0      0,7     1,7     ( 1,2 )    102   200  \LA.$SYSTEM.SYS01.OSIMAGE
   6    $SYSTEM  0,257   1,257   ( 3,41)   4096   104  \LA.$SYSTEM.SYS01.OSIMAGE
   7    $ZOPR    0,8     1,8     ( 1,0 )    102   201  \LA.$SYSTEM.SYS01.OSIMAGE
  63    $MPATH   0,284   1,284   (63,1 )      0   199  \LA.$SYSTEM.SYS01.LHOBJ
  64    $ZZKRN   0,15    1,23    (66,0 )    132   180  \LA.$SYSTEM.SYS01.OZKRN
  65    $ZZWAN   0,277   1,289   (50,3 )    132   180  \LA.$SYSTEM.SYS01.WANMGR
  66    $ZZW01   1,266   0,0     (50,0 )      0   199  \LA.$SYSTEM.SYS01.CONMGR
. . 246 $QA0     1,357   0,363   ( 1,0 )   4024   130  \LA.$SYSTEM.SYS01.EMSACOLL
 247    $DV0     1,358   0,369   ( 1,0 )   4024   130  \LA.$SYSTEM.SYS01.EMSACOLL
 253    $ZPHI    0,375   1,356   ( 1,0 )   4024   130  \LA.$SYSTEM.SYS01.EMSACOLL
 264    $Z03H    0,104   0,0     ( 1,30)    132   150  \LA.$SYSTEM.SYS01.EMSDIST
 270    $NMTRM   1,380   0,0     (46,0 )   6144   150  \LA.$SYSTEM.SYSOPR.ENFORM
 280    $Z6ND    1,390   0,0     (46,0 )   6144   150  \LA.$SYSTEM.SYSOPR.ENFORM
 282    $Z0WY    0,216   0,0     ( 1,30)    132   100  \LA.$SYSTEM.SYS01.EMSDIST
 284    $Z6NJ    1,378   0,0     (46,0 )   6144   150  \LA.$SYSTEM.SYSOPR.ENFORM
 338    $X7MX    1,392   0,0     ( 1,30)    132   130  \LA.$SYSTEM.SYS01.EMSDIST

Total Errors = 0   Total Warnings = 0
```

Example 70 displays the devices and their types.

Examining the TCP/IP Configuration

Use the LISTDEV TCP/IP command to display all TCP/IP processes.

Example 71:

->LISTDEV TCPIP

```
LDev    Name     PPID    BPID    Type   RSize Pri  Program
 145    $ZTC0    0,329   1,308   (48,0 )32000 200  \LA.$SYSTEM.SYS01.TCPIP
 161    $ZTC2    1,54    0,75    (48,0 )32000 200  \LA.$SYSTEM.SYS01.TCPIP
 164    $ZTC1    1,318   0,334   (48,0 )32000 200  \LA.$SYSTEM.SYS01.TCPIP
 175    $ZB018   0,345   1,328   (48,0 )32000 200  \LA.$SYSTEM.SYS01.TCPIP
 176    $ZB01B   0,340   1,322   (48,0 )32000 200  \LA.$SYSTEM.SYS01.TCPIP
 182    $ZTC3    0,351   1,333   (48,0 )32000 200  \LA.$SYSTEM.SYS01.TCPIP
Total Errors = 0   Total Warnings = 0
```

Example 71 displays the TCP/IP processes.

Use the INFO SUBNET command to display TCP/IP SUBNET information. This information is particularly useful to determine what TCP/IP addresses are configured for access to the system.

Example 72:

->INFO SUBNET $ZTC0.*

```
TCPIP Info SUBNET \LA.$ZTCP0.*

Name      Devicename      *IPADDRESS    TYPE        *SUBNETMASK  SuName QIO *R

#LOOP0    \NOSYS.$NOIOP   127.0.0.1     LOOP-BACK %HFF000000          OFF  N
#SN1      \LA.LANX        192.168.55.32 ETHERNET  %HFFFFFF00          ON   N
2->
```

Example 72 displays the information about the $ZTC0 subnet.

Use the LISTDEV TELSERV command to display all TELSERV processes.

Example 73:

->LISTDEV TELSERV

```
LDev  Name    PPID   BPID    Type      RSize Pri Program
147   $ZTN0   0,324  1,293   (46,0 )   6144  170 \LA.$SYSTEM.SYS01.TELSERV
165   $ZTN1   1,319  0,336   (46,0 )   6144  170 \LA.$SYSTEM.SYS01.TELSERV
179   $ZN018  0,339  1,330   (46,0 )   6144  150 \LA.$SYSTEM.SYS01.TELSERV
210   $ZTN2   1,341  0,361   (46,0 )   6144  170 \LA.$SYSTEM.SYS01.TELSERV
211   $ZTNPX  1,337  0,352   (46,0 )   6144  170 \LA.$SYSTEM.SYS01.TELSERV
```

Example 73 displays the TELSERV processes.

Use the ASSUME and INFO commands to display a list of services associated with a TELSERV process.

Example 74:

->ASSUME PROCESS $ZTN1
->INFO SERVICE *

```
TELSERV Info SERVICE \LA.$ZTN1.*
Name      *Type           *Subtype   *Access  *Display *Program
TACL      CONVERSATION    DYNAMIC    ALL      ON       $SYSTEM.SYSTEM.TACL
ZVTL      VTL             STATIC     N/A      OFF      N/A
ZTELNET   CONVERSATION    DYNAMIC    N/A      OFF      N/A
ZBLOCK    BLOCK           STATIC     N/A      OFF      N/A
ZCONV     CONVERSATION    STATIC     N/A      OFF      N/A
ZPRINT    PRINT           STATIC     N/A      OFF      N/A
ZSPI      SPI             STATIC     N/A      OFF      N/A
```

Example 74 displays the services associated with the $ZTN1.TELSERV process.

Use the INFO SERVICE command to display details of a TELSERV service.

Example 75:

```
->INFO SERVICE TACL,DETAIL
```

```
TELSERV Detailed Info SERVICE \LA.$ZTN1.tacl

*Type................... CONVERSATION  *Subtype................ DYNAMIC
*Display................ ON            *Autodelete............. OFF
*Owner.................. N/A           *Access................. ALL
*CPU.................... N/A           *Pri.................... N/A
*Swap.................. N/A
*Program............... $SYSTEM.SYSTEM.TACL
*Lib................... N/A
*Resilient............. OFF
*Param................. N/A
*Assigned Window........ OFF
*Default Service....... OFF
```

Example 75 displays the processes associated with the $ZTN1 service.

Examining the Network Configuration

Use the INFO command to list details about the current nodes and the EXPAND network.

Example 76:

```
INFO PROCESS $NCP,DETAIL
```

```
EXPAND    Detailed  Info  PROCESS  $NCP      AT \LA (253)

 Max System Number..          254  *Aborttimer.........0:02:30.00
 Algorithm.........  SPLITHORIZON   AutomaticMaptimer..         ON
*Connecttime........   0:00:00.00   Framesize..........        132
*Maxtimeouts........            3  *Maxconnects........         10
*NetworkDiameter....           15   Type...............     (62,0)
*Message 43.........          OFF   Message 44.........         ON
 Message 45.........           ON  *Message 46.........        OFF
 Message 47.........           ON  *Message 48.........        OFF
*Message 49.........          OFF  *AutoRebal..........        OFF
 Next Rebalance Time   0/00:00:00  *AutoRebalTime......1/00:00:00
 Trace File Name....         none
```

Example 76 displays the information about the $NCP process.

Use the NETMAP command to list all nodes on the EXPAND network. Compare this list to a network diagram provided by operations.

Example 77:

->INFO PROCESS $NCP,NETMAP

```
EXPAND Info PROCESS $NCP, NETMAP

    NETMAP AT \LA (253) #LINESETS=2 TIME: DEC 13,2002 15:38:01

SYSTEM          TIME      (DISTANCE)  BY   PATH             INDEX
252 \Chicago 190K(01)*  inf(--)                            [  2]
254 \ABCO       inf(--)  380K(01)*                         [  2]
     ------------------------------------------------------------

          LINESETS AT \LA (253) #LINESETS=2

LINESET    NEIGHBOR    LDEV    TF    PID    LINE    LDEV   STATUS  FileErr#
   1       \Chicago   (252)   117  190K ( 0, 330)
                                                     1     117    READY
   2       \ABCO      (254)    63  380K ( 0, 285)
                                                     1     119    READY
                                                     2     118    READY
```

Example 77 displays the nodes on the EXPAND network.

Use the SCF PROFILE command to check the PASSTHRU setting.

SCF Syntax:

INFO PROFILE $ZZWAN.#< profile-name >

Example 78:

->INFO PROFILE $ZZWAN.#EXPIP

```
WAN MANAGER Info profile \LA.$ZZWAN.#EXPIP
Devices using this profile
Device.......... 1   : $EXPIP
DEVICE SPECIFIC MODIFIERS:
NEXTSYS 253
L4CONGCTRL_ON
L4RETRIES 3
L4TIMEOUT 2000
COMPRESS_ON
PASSTHRU_ON                         ←
L4EXTPACKETS_ON
SUPERPATH_OFF
L4SENDWINDOW 254
PATHBLOCKBYTES 0
PATHPACKETBYTES 1024
RXWINDOW 7
TXWINDOW 7
```

```
AUTOMATICMAPTIMER 1
CONNECTTIME 0
FRAMESIZE 132
MAXTIMEOUTS 3
MAXCONNECTS 5
NETWORKDIAMETER 15
ABORTTIMER 15000
```

Example 76 displays information about the $EXPIP profile, including the PASSTHRU value.

Gathering NFS Information

Use SCF to examine the NFS configuration.

1. Start SCF

2. ASSUME the NFS subsystem

3. Perform queries

SCF Syntax:
```
SCF
ASSUME SUBSYS <$process name>
INFO USER <user name>
```

Example 79:
```
> SCF
-> assume subsys $znfs
-> info user *
```

```
 NFS Info USER \ABC.$ZNFS.*

Objname      *UID       *GID    *Alias Name        Type *Comment
antonio       248        222    BANKA.ANTONIO      OSS
jamb          215        222    BANKA.JAMB         OSS
nobody      65534        222    BANKA.HAILEY       OSS
marko         250        222    BANKA.MARKO        OSS
bryan         555          0    BANKA.BRYAN         OSS
```

Example 79 shows all the NFS users on node \ABC. Note that the **nobody** userid is NFS userid 65534.

Use the INFO EXPORT command to examine the file systems that can be EXPORTed.

SCF Syntax:
`INFO EXPORT <$process>.<mount point>`

Example 80:
`-> info export $znfs./`

```
NFS Info EXPORT \ABC.$ZNFS./

Objname                    *Access
/                           everyone
```

Example 80 shows that any client can access the / (**root**) file system.

Use the INFO LAN command to examine the security settings for the NFS LAN objects.

SCF Syntax:
`INFO LAN <$process.lan>`

Example 81:
`-> info LAN $znfs.lan0`

```
  NFS Detailed Info LAN \ABC.$ZNFS.LAN
*Process.......... $ZZLAN
*Program.......... $SYSTEM.ZOSSNFS.NFSLAN
*Swap............. $WORK1
*TCP/IP Process... $ZTCP2
*TCP/IP Host File. $SYSTEM.ZTCPIP.HOSTS
*TCP/IP Resolver.. $SYSTEM.ZTCPIP.RESCONF
*Primary.......... 1 *Backup ......... -1
*Priority......... 148 (DEFAULT)
*Histogram........ 128, 256, 512, 1024, 2048, 4096
*Addr Check....... ON
*Domain Name...... BANKA.com
```

Example 81 shows information about the $ZZLAN process. Note that the **Addr Check** parameter is ON.

Use the INFO SERVER command to examine security settings for the NFS server.

SCF Syntax:
INFO SERVER <server>

Example 82:
-> info server *,detail

```
  NFS Detailed Info SERVER \ABC.ROOT

*Mount Point...... /
*Program.......... $SYSTEM.ZOSSNFS.NFSSVRHP
*Process.......... $ROOT                *Server Type...... OSS
 Primary.......... 1                    *Backup........... -1
*Read Only........ FALSE                *Priority......... 190
*Root User OK..... FALSE                *Max File Size.... 2147483647
*Write Thru....... TRUE                 *Null Alias OK.... FALSE
```

Example 82 shows information about the NFS server process, NFSSVRHP.
Note the following parameters:

The **Read Only** parameter is FALSE.

The **Root User OK** parameter is FALSE.

The **WRITE Thru** parameter is TRUE.

The **Null Alias OK** parameter is FALSE.

D

Tandem File Codes

When viewing files in the FILEINFO utility or FUP utility, each file has a file code of up to five digits displayed. HP has certain designated file codes that it uses for purposes of identifying subsystem files.

File Code	Definition or Subsystem
0-99	Reserved for users
OSS	OSS file
100	TNS executable file
101	EDIT text format
110-111	Edit recovery and VS dump files
115	TEDIT profile files
120-128	Spooler control files
129	Spooler job file
130	Inspect save files
134	TMF audit trail files
144	CPU dump files
175	Measure data files
176	NonStop SQL/MP surveyor files
180	C data files

(Continued)

File Code	Definition or Subsystem
210	Pathmaker Installs file
223	Enable log file
230-232	ADA data files
250-299	Transfer subsystem files
300-399	TPS (Pathway) subsystem files
400-401	Tape simulator files
405	KMSF subsystem file
410-430	Exercise subsystem
440	TACL saved variable segment file
450	Viewpoint configuration file
451	Event configuration file
500-525	Microcode files
530-539	NFS configuration files
540-549	Safeguard subsystem files
550-599	NonStop SQL subsystem files
600-620	Mumps subsystem files
660-669	Encore subsystem files
700	TNS/R executable object files
800	Integrity NonStop Native code executable object files
830-835	Data Communications files
832	Expand Profile template files
839	EMS template
840	Snax utility output file
841-842	Coup files
843-845	EMS subsystem files
846	Cover file
847-848	Netbatch file
849-850	DNS subsystem files
851	Snax5 configuration files
852	NonStop CLX shutdown file
853-854	Optical disk file
855	FUP restart file
858	ORSERV status file

File Code	Definition or Subsystem
863	SysHealth event key file
888	Enform compiled query
904	Exchange trace files
1000-65535	Reserved for users

E

Third-Party HP NonStop Server Security Vendors

ACI

http://www.aciworldwide.com/

Baker Street

http://www.bakerstreetsoftware.com/

Bowden Systems

http://www.bsi2.com/

Cail

http://www.cail.com/

ComForte

http://www.comforte.com/

Cross-El

http://www.crossel.com/

Crystal Point

http://www.crystalpoint.com/

CSP

http://www.compsec.com/

Greenhouse

http://www.greenhouse.de/

Gresham

http://www.greshamsoftwarelabs.com.au/

Hewlett-Packard

http://www.hp.com/

K2Defender

http://www.K2defender.com/

Nexsion

http://www.nexsion.com/

Unlimited Software Associates

http://www.usahero.com/

XYPRO Technology

http://www.xypro.com/

Index

A

ACC_LEVEL parameter, 273–74
ACC_LOGTABLE_NAME parameter, 274
ACC_MODE_ON parameter, 274
ACI, 890
ACLs, node-specific, 27
Add_define command, 455, 514
ADDTCPIP script, 288–89, 295–96, 316, 360–62, 419–21
ADDTOSCF script, 289, 296–98, 316, 362–68, 421–22
Ad hoc reporting, 16
Agents
    authentication, 121
    SNMP, 114, 116, 398, 401
Alarm, snapshot, scan files
    OSM, 301, 374–75
    TSM, 292, 429–30
Alerting, real-time, 16
Alias command, 453, 514, 521

Aliases
    BINARY-DESCRIPTION field for, 36
    command, 455–56, 557–58
    definition, 521
    OWNER-LIST for, 34–35
    permanent, 456
    temporary, 456
    TEXT-DESCRIPTION field for, 35–36
    uses, 455–56
Alias user program, 521
    defined, 521
    securing, 522–23
    versions, 521
ALLOW-DISKFILE-PERSISTENT para-meter, 21–22
ALLOW-NODE-ID-ACL parameter, 25–26
ALTERIP script, 316
American National Standards Institute. *See* ANSI SQL

Printed and bound by CPI Group (UK) Ltd, Croydon, CR0 4YY

03/10/2024

01040342-0008